THE
OFFICIAL HISTORY
OF THE
NEW ZEALAND RIFLE BRIGADE
(The Earl of Liverpool's Own)

Covering the period of service with the New Zealand Expeditionary Force in the Great War from 1915 to 1919.

Compiled by
LIEUT.-COL. W. S. AUSTIN, D.S.O.

The Naval & Military Press Ltd

Published by
The Naval & Military Press Ltd
Unit 10, Ridgewood Industrial Park,
Uckfield, East Sussex,
TN22 5QE England
Tel: +44 (0) 1825 749494
Fax: +44 (0) 1825 765701
www.naval-military-press.com
www.military-genealogy.com

© The Naval & Military Press Ltd 2007

In reprinting in facsimile from the original, any imperfections are inevitably reproduced and the quality may fall short of modern type and cartographic standards.

Printed and bound by Lightning Source

To the Memory of Fallen Comrades

PREFACE.

In the pages of this work is set forth the story of a Brigade which served as part of the New Zealand Expeditionary Force in the Great War. As a regimental history it is not as exhaustive as could be wished, the official records, from which for the most part it has been compiled, being astonishingly meagre as to material of moment. That a general call for personal accounts of specially-interesting incidents with which to supplement the recorded information met with a less ready response than could be desired, must be ascribed to a diffidence that shrinks from the recounting of any deed, the full story of which must unavoidably contain reference to a writer's own share therein.

Mention is made from time to time of bold leading and collective and individual acts of daring. Instances of this kind, it must be borne in mind, are such as have been placed on definite record in the field from the accounts of witnesses, these last being for the most part officers and non-commissioned officers commanding larger or smaller bodies of men. A little reflection will show how probable it is that these observers have themselves been worthy of special honour, but that such notice has been impossible because their own actions had not been similarly witnessed. In this connection, too, one could wish to speak definitely of the many who, unmarked, perished in the very act of heroism; but the individual is lost in the great host who sealed their devotion with their lives, and whose sacrifice has earned for them an enduring place in the grateful hearts of their countrymen.

One is constrained to mention here, also, what might not be apparent to the ordinary reader, but what all who have seen service will gladly enough acknowledge, namely, that often the exceptionally meritorious work of a body of men has been recognized by special mention of the leader only, and many an officer is proud to wear a decoration conferred in appreciation of some achievement of his command.

Again, the compiler of a regimental history feels that scant justice can be done to those officers and men whose work was largely unspectacular, but none the less important. Some attempt has been made to indicate the difficulties constantly encountered and gallantly overcome by signallers, runners, stretcher-bearers and transport drivers; but practically nothing has been said of the devotion of the medical officers and the chaplains, or of the labours of the quartermasters, cooks, sockmen, pioneers, shoemakers, tailors and men of the sanitary sections, upon whose faithfulness the well-being of their comrades so intimately depended.

As to the general plan of the account, it may be explained that though the work of the individual soldier of whatever rank has been so inadequately treated, an effort has been made to set out as completely as possible the story of the Brigade as a whole. It may, perhaps, be thought that much unnecessary detail has been introduced, both in the body of the work and in the various appendices. It must be remembered, however, that unlike the territorial units of the New Zealand Expeditionary Force which were in existence long before the outbreak of the Great War, and which continue in being now that peace is again with us, the whole life of the New Zealand Rifle Brigade was compressed within the period from 1st May, 1915, to 1st February, 1919; and in these circumstances the historian may be pardoned if he is unable to refrain from retailing much that might otherwise have been passed over without mention.

The bare story of the Brigade would have been lacking in perspective, and therefore shorn of much of its interest, if it had been told without a proper setting. For this reason connective passages have been inserted in such a way as to show how our movements and actions fitted in with the general scheme of things, and to give a clear view of the moving scenes over comparatively wide sections of the battlefront. In accordance with this plan many of the chapters have been arranged in the order of the subdivisions of the official despatches, each of which is devoted to the account of some particular phase of the general operations, or of a series of actions grouped as one major battle. It is hoped that to the general reader the passages introduced, and in particular that which tells in the briefest manner the story of the war on the British Front up to the time of our first going into the line at Armentieres, will not be without value in this respect. To our own men some of these will serve as reminders that many of the spots with which they became all too familiar had already been hallowed by the glorious deeds of the old British regiments that had stemmed the tide of advancing hordes at the price of virtual extermination. Compilation of passages of this kind has in the main been based upon the official despatches of the General Officers Commanding in Chief of the British Forces in Egypt and on the Western Front, though various other sources have been drawn upon where more localized detail has appeared to be necessary. Of these, Nelson's "History of the War," by John Buchan, has been of special value for this purpose, and I am indebted to the author and publishers for permission to incorporate certain extracts that seemed to me to be particularly apt and illuminating. In developing the setting of some of the actions in which the New Zealand Rifle Brigade participated, but which of necessity were told in few words in the official despatches, I have sometimes found our own records either deficient or conflicting as regards the formations operating beyond the flanks of the Division. Where such has been the case I have taken advantage of the labours of Colonel H. Stewart, C.M.G., D.S.O., M.C., who, in collecting information for his volume "The New Zealanders in France," diligently searched the records of the War Office in London.

There is one aspect of the story of the Brigade that has been passed over with not more than an occasional word. I refer to routine life in training-camps and elsewhere, life, that is, apart from the grim duties, the weary toiling, and the stark bloodshed. The lighter side is of no mean importance, and one could wish that space could be found for the telling. It is impossible to estimate, for instance, the uplifting power of humour in the midst of most trying conditions, but there can be little doubt that as a contributing factor to ultimate success it ranked with that characteristic feature of the New Zealanders, a never-failing belief in the righteousness of the Empire's cause and a steady confidence in our ability to win through. But one British soldier is very much like another, and while for the moment this seemingly insignificant part of our story remains untold, the reader may gain some slight idea of it by referring to Ian Hay's " The First Hundred Thousand," and to Captain Bairnsfather's succession of "Fragments from France." Hay's description of soldiering in camp, in billets and in the line, might in almost all respects be adopted as fitting our own case. This is so even down to the references to those odd fellows, known in soldiers' language as the "bad hats," who, when not actually in the trenches, displayed a special genius for getting into mischief, but who, in almost every instance, acquitted themselves magnificently under fire. In one respect, however, there was a most marked difference. While the English soldier sang more or less heartily on the march, our own men were invariably silent. During the earliest days in camp this method of shortening the route usually found a place, but as training progressed, singing on the march as steadily diminished, and at the front it was absolutely unknown. Like the reluctance attached to the formality of saluting, the New Zealanders' silence on the march appears to be still an unsolved mystery.

As to Bairnsfather's "Fragments," these are by no means the pure absurdities they might to the uninitiated appear to be. They are in fact but very slightly overdrawn, and of all the episodes and situations so delightfully recorded, there is scarcely one that might not have been taken from an actual occurrence within our own experience. Two characteristics in particular are well brought out—the grumbling or "grousing" in which it is the soldier's special privilege to indulge, and cheerfulness and humour triumphant when the misery of the conditions had reached its utmost limit. In common with others, our men had their complaints to make, but it is to their credit that these were seldom voiced when the Brigade was in the line. The least satisfied, indeed, were to be found in the base camps rather than in the trenches, and of these the greatest grumblers were the men who had never been within sound of the guns.

As esprit de corps, a matter of vital importance in military life, is too intangible a thing to make itself apparent in a mere formal chronicle, one may be pardoned for mentioning here that this feature was nowhere more fully developed than in the New Zealand Rifle Brigade. The number of reinforcements received approximated 10,000, replacing a wastage averaging 60 per week; yet the excellent spirit, strongly evident from the commencement of our activities, was maintained unabated until the end. It was, indeed, a matter of astonishment even to ourselves, that in every case a man joining up with the Brigade in the trenches but yesterday was an out-and-out Rifleman to-day; and it is told of a certain officer coming over from another Brigade to take command of one of our battalions, that almost before his first action was concluded he issued instructions to the effect that the regimental tailor was to come up to headquarters immediately for the purpose of altering his buttons and badges without delay. Mention might also be made of the fact that the remarkable esprit de corps was able to stand the test of the appointment to positions in their own battalions of non-commissioned officers promoted in the field to commissioned rank; and how faithfully and well these same junior officers continued to strive to uphold the good name of the Brigade may be seen from the casualty lists of the latter part of the war, when so many of the erstwhile sergeants with brilliant records fell while leading their respective commands in the thick of the fight.

It is hoped that the appendices to the history will be found of some value. In most cases they have been inserted with the object of making the work in a measure self-contained. In this class are the Diary of the War, taken from " The Times;" an account of the 3rd Field Ambulance, for which I am indebted to Lieut.-Col. J. Hardie Neil, D.S.O., telling of that part of our military experiences of which the ordinary records take little cognizance; a note on the Reserve Battalion; and a somewhat bare outline of the doings of the "Hush Hush Brigade," to which detachments of our officers and men so mysteriously departed at the beginning of 1918, this sketch being compiled in the main from a report furnished for the purposes of our History by Captain S. T. Seddon, M.C., of the Auckland Regiment. The notes on the Imperial Rifle Brigade consist of adapted extracts from the handbook written during the war by Captain H. G. Parkyn for the use of officers of the parent Brigade in preparing lecturettes for their companies. The list of recipients of honours and awards, and the roll of officers, non-commissioned officers and men who made the extreme sacrifice, were specially compiled, from official documents, under the supervision of the officer in charge of the War Records Branch of the New Zealand Military Headquarters. An abridgment of the first draft of the chapter on the Senussi Campaign was supplied for inclusion in Vol. IV of the Official History of New Zealand's Effort in the Great War.

Throughout the work every effort has been made to ensure accuracy, but the possibility of error in details is recognized, and it is requested that where such should be discovered a note of correction may be forwarded to the Secretary, New Zealand Rifle Brigade Trustees, care of Military Headquarters, Wellington, so that the copy kept for record purposes may be amended. It may be explained here that in the case of officers holding acting or temporary rank, the substantive rank is used where their names are mentioned. To be strictly official, both, of course, should be stated, but for the sake of convenience and uniformity the simpler method has been adopted. Convenience must be pleaded also as the reason for the omission of reference to decorations, except in special cases, such, for example, as the first or last mention of a name.

For the general illustrations various sources have been drawn upon in addition to the incomplete New Zealand collection of official war-photographs; and as the object in view was simply the provision of an informative series, no thought has been given to artistic considerations. The Revd. A. G. Parham, M.C., formerly chaplain in the composite formation of Berks, Bucks and Dorset Yeomanry serving with the Western Frontier Force, readily granted permission to use certain of his copyright photographs; and to him, as to all others who have placed the Brigade under an obligation for favours of this kind, thanks are here returned. The page-charts giving the order of battle in some of the more important engagements are, it need hardly be explained, purely diagrammatic. Of the maps, all of which were prepared by Rifleman W. G. Harding from adaptations of war-maps in use at the front, some are drawn to a large scale to display the main features of certain battlefields, while the others cover all the sections of Egypt, France and Flanders in which the Brigade was stationed at any time, whether resting, training, digging or fighting.

To all who have in any way assisted in the compilation of this History, I tender my sincere thanks.

W. S. A.

Wellington, New Zealand.

FOREWORDS

1.
BY THE COMMANDER OF THE NEW ZEALAND DIVISION, MAJOR-GENERAL SIR A. H. RUSSELL, K.C.B., K.C.M.G.

To the fact that Lord Liverpool, Governor-General of New Zealand during the period of the Great War, was himself a Rifleman, the 3rd Brigade of the New Zealand Division, formed early in 1915, owes its distinguishing title. Many of our territorial units were already affiliated with regiments of the British Army: and in like manner, recognized and accepted by the Regular Rifle Brigade as a family connection, somewhat distant it may be, our own Brigade formed yet another link between the New Zealand Expeditionary Force and that Army by whose side it was already fighting.

Reaching Egypt before the close of the year, the Brigade, after an interesting experience with the Western Frontier Force engaged in the campaign against the Senussi, was joined by the war-seasoned veterans from Gallipoli, whose laurels gained at the historic landing and in the attack on Chunuk Bair were at once an object of envy to the newcomers and a spur to their ambition. Differences in drill, in dress, in title, had, even before they left New Zealand, given rise to that indefinable feeling that they were something apart, in a measure distinguished from the territorial regiments. The older soldiers, with whom they were now in contact, were quick to mark peculiarities, and henceforth they were even more than Riflemen—they were the Dinks!

They were to prove the value of their esprit de corps in France. The almost uniform success of their raids on the Armentieres front must be ascribed to something more than mere luck, large though the element of chance may be in these risky enterprises. But it was on the Somme in 1916 that the Brigade was to win its spurs. To it was entrusted what appeared to the Staff to be the most important share in the operations of September 15th. Doubts were expressed by the

Higher Command as to the wisdom of using comparatively inexperienced troops for so difficult a task. The contention that their eagerness to win a solid reputation would carry the Riflemen far was justified by the result. A brilliantly-executed attack was crowned with success. Henceforth the mana of the Brigade was assured, and its distinction was to rest on surer grounds than differences in drill and title.

Throughout the ensuing two long years of fighting on various parts of the Western Front the prestige of the Brigade was maintained undimmed. Whether patiently holding on through the miseries of stationary trench-warfare, the monotony of which was relieved only by dashing patrolling and raiding excursions; whether participating in set actions such as Messines, and even ill-fated Passchendaele; or whether detailed for long-drawn-out tasks with pick and shovel, the troops of the Brigade could ever be relied upon to accomplish all that it was in the power of men to achieve. They were the first into the breach caused by the German spring offensive on the Somme in March, 1918, and bore with conspicuous success the brunt of the counter-attack a week later. They took a no mean share in turning the tide when our offensive opened later in the year, and finally, by the capture of Le Quesnoy, more spectacular if not more solid than its previous exploits, completed the fighting record of a Brigade which had worthily upheld the traditions of its namesake of the Regulars.

The name of General Harry Fulton is inseparably linked with that of the New Zealand Rifle Brigade. Largely responsible for its early training, he was associated with it till he fell in action at Colincamps in 1918. In a sense the Brigade was his child, and indeed he cared for it as a father. His youthful Brigade Major, Robert Purdy, will likewise long be remembered: keen, able and fearless, he was killed by the same shell which mortally wounded his chief. The double loss was a severe blow.

The distinguishing marks of the New Zealand Rifle Brigade, though somewhat superficial, were important enough in their place, and the tradition established, confined though it was to the period of the Great War, is of no small value. In an age of standardization the importance of uniformity is not to be gainsaid; but it is to be hoped that in our search for it we shall not fail to give due consideration to the encouragement of individuality of regiments, and that in the future organization of the Defence Force of New Zealand a place may be found for a Rifle Brigade.

2.
BY THE HONORARY COLONEL OF THE REGIMENT, HIS EXCELLENCY THE EARL OF LIVERPOOL, P.C., G.C.M.G., G.B.E., M.V.O.

As an old Rifleman, I am very glad to have the opportunity of writing a few prefatory lines regarding the New Zealand Rifle Brigade.

The initiation of the New Zealand Rifle Brigade amongst the Forces of the Crown was in some respects not dissimilar to that of the Imperial regiment. The latter was raised in 1800 from drafts found from other regiments, and was known successively as The Rifle Corps, The Rifle Regiment, and The Rifle Brigade. Raised in 1915, the New Zealand regiment was formed of officers and men drawn from all parts of the country rather than from any particular territorial district, and absorbed the greater portion of the Samoan Expeditionary Force as well as some of the officers and non-commissioned officers transferred from the 3rd and 4th Reinforcements. It first saw the light as The Trentham Regiment, but was afterwards renamed The New Zealand Rifle Brigade. Both the Imperial regiment and that formed in New Zealand are, if we exclude those regiments incorporated with the British Army on the disbandment of the East India Company's Forces, the youngest amongst the infantry units of their own lands.

The record of the Imperial regiment shows that wherever there was something required of the Army during the nineteenth and twentieth centuries, there the regiment was to be found; that of the New Zealand Rifle Brigade, short though it be, speaks of general efficiency and the performance of a succession of gallant deeds in whatever quarter of the globe it was called upon to serve during the Great War.

It would be futile in this short note to attempt any detailed reference to the many officers and men of the New Zealand Rifle Brigade who contributed so splendidly to the annals of the regiment. Alas, the senior officer died on the field of battle! The regiment was indeed fortunate in its sponsor, for Colonel Fulton, a New Zealander of conspicuous ability, was a Gurkha Rifleman of long experience and imbued with all the best traditions of the Rifle Brigade. He served his country well.

I earnestly trust that this young regiment may have a long and useful career, and that it will become even more closely associated with the sister regiment of Great Britain. In that both have the same Colonel-in-Chief, who watches closely over their interests, they are thus far linked together by a common bond; and I know that should occasion arise both will again be found winning fresh laurels as they fight side by side in the Empire's cause.

Liverpool

INTRODUCTORY NOTE

THE OUTBREAK OF THE GREAT WAR, AND NEW ZEALAND'S OFFER.

On the 28th June, 1914, the Austrian Archduke Francis Ferdinand was assassinated at Serajevo by a Serbian. Subsequent events showed that Germany had long been preparing for a war that should give her predominance in Europe and pre-eminence as a world-power; and the shooting of the Archduke, an event which took place while the British fleet was still in Kiel Harbour on its friendly visit to Germany, was eagerly seized upon as a pretext for the commencement of hostilities. Within a week the Kaiser held his famous War Council at Potsdam, and on the 23rd of July, Austria, Germany's "brilliant second," handed to Serbia an impossible Note, followed five days later by a declaration of war. Russia, the champion of her smaller ally, was drawn in; Belgium, whose only offence was that she stood in the way of the march on Paris, had her articles of neutrality contemptuously treated as "a scrap of paper;" France entered the lists, and Great Britain, despite the mightiest efforts of diplomacy to avoid conflict, was compelled by the claims of right as against might to take her due share in the struggle, and, on the 4th of August, 1914, declared war against Germany.

New Zealand in the meantime had not been idle. As early as July 31st, while the statesmen of Great Britain were still striving for peace, yet fearing that all their endeavours might prove to be fruitless, the Prime Minister of New Zealand, in Parliament assembled, voiced the determination of the people of this country to support the Empire to the uttermost, and if such necessity should arise, to take upon themselves a full share of the burden of the war. This was no empty statement. Preliminary arrangements were at once made for the preparation of an expeditionary force for service in Europe or elsewhere, if such assistance were required by the Imperial Government, and immediately after Great Britain's declaration of war the definite offer of a suitable contingent was made.* Advice was sought regarding the composition of this body, and on August 7th notification was sent to the effect that New Zealand was prepared to supply at once an expeditionary force exceeding in strength that suggested by the Home authorities; and this was followed by the intimation that New Zealand proposed to assume all financial responsibility for that force, including the cost of its transportation to the theatre of war.

As originally constituted, the New Zealand Expeditionary Force thus placed at the disposal of the Imperial Government consisted of the Headquarters Staff of a Division, a Mounted Rifles Brigade, a Battery of Field Artillery, a section of a Field Artillery Brigade Ammunition Column, a section of a Divisional Ammuntion Column, headquarters and two sections of a Signalling Company, an Infantry Brigade, a Company of a Divisional Train, a Field Ambulance, and an Independent Mounted Rifles Regiment.

For various reasons, mainly because of the presence of powerful enemy cruisers in the South Pacific, the departure of the force was postponed from time to time. This delay enabled

*The first occasion on which the Colonies contributed military aid for an Imperial enterprise was in Cromwell's Expedition to Jamaica, in 1653-4. On that occasion the Barbadoes furnished 4000 men from its militia of white apprentices on the plantations. The next instance came in the Carthagena Expedition of 1740, when the American Colonies supplied a force of 4000 men. After that the American Colonies helped consistently in the conquest of Canada, until the final victory of Amherst in 1760. During that period the first two American regiments were placed on the British establishment, and in 1758 were created the ''Royal Americans,'' which are still with us as the King's Royal Rifle Corps. Then the American Colonies were lost, and everyone thought that the British Empire had come to an end. Immediately afterwards followed the war in which our losses in the West Indies compelled us to raise a regiment of African negroes, still with us as the West Indian Regiment. During the 19th century the Empire was consolidated. The Canadians helped gallantly to defend their country from American invasion from 1812 to 1814. The Cape Colonists joined in the fights against the Kaffirs, and the New Zealand Colonists in the wars against the Maoris.

Then came the war in Egypt, and for the first time Australia offered a battalion for that service. In the South African War practically all the Colonies sent contingents. And finally, in the present war, not only has every part of the Empire given us freely of its men, but the descendants of the Peninsula veterans in South America have sent their sons, whose native tongue was Spanish and who knew not a word of English, to fight for the Old Country.—(Hon. J. W. Fortescue at the Royal Institution, London, 21/2/'19.)

the New Zealand military authorities to augment its quota of artillery, which was now brought up to a complete Field Artillery Brigade and a whole Field Artillery Brigade Ammunition Column, and, in addition, a Howitzer Battery of four guns, which was to follow with the Second Reinforcements. The Expeditionary Force, with its First Reinforcements, finally got away on the 16th October. These troops disembarked at Egyptian ports and went into camp near Cairo for a period of special training.

No sooner had the mobilization of volunteers for the Main Body commenced than New Zealand was called upon to face an additional task. This was the immediate despatch of a special force for the capture of the German possessions in Samoa. The response was so prompt and the preparations so rapidly conducted that the Samoan Expeditionary Force, a self-contained organization of all arms, including three companies of infantry, and numbering in all 55 officers and 1358 other ranks, was able to set out on its mission on August 15th,* and a fortnight later Samoa was in our hands. Towards the end of March, 1915, these troops were replaced by a relief force of men over the ordinary age limit, and on their return to New Zealand they were in the main held for absorption into either the reinforcements then in camp or those special battalions the formation of which was at that time under consideration, and which were destined to become the first two units of the New Zealand Rifle Brigade.

Reinforcements for the New Zealand Expeditionary Force were sent to Egypt at intervals of about two months, and in order of despatch the New Zealand Rifle Brigade ranks with the Seventh, in company with which it sailed almost exactly twelve months after the departure of the Main Body.

*The British Expeditionary Force commenced to land in France on August 7th, and the disembarkation of the first four Divisions was completed on the 16th.

CONTENTS

Chapter		Page
I.	FROM NEW ZEALAND TO EGYPT.	
	Part 1. Preparation	1
	Part 2. Departure for Egypt	16
II.	THE SENUSSI CAMPAIGN.	
	Part 1. General	24
	Part 2. The 2nd Battalion on the Line of Communications	27
	Part 3. The 1st Battalion at Mersa Matruh	30
III.	ON THE SUEZ CANAL.	
	Part 1. Brigade Headquarters and the 1st and 2nd Battalions	55
	Part 2. The 3rd and 4th Battalions	59
	Part 3. The Brigade Complete	63
IV.	IN THE BATTLE ZONE OF THE FLANDERS FRONT.	
	Part 1. Movements	69
	Part 2. The Fighting on the Flanders Front from the Outbreak of War till May, 1916	77
V.	ARMENTIERES.	
	Part 1. In the Trenches	87
	Part 2. Training for the Somme	110
VI.	THE BATTLE OF THE SOMME, 1916.	
	Part 1. The Earlier Fighting	113
	Part 2. The Third Phase: New Zealanders Engaged.	
	Section 1—General	117
	Section 2—The Advance Beyond Flers, September 15th	122
	Section 3—General Attack Renewed, September 25th	137
	Section 4—Further Progress of the Battle	146
VII.	FROM FLEURBAIX TO PLOEGSTEERT.	
	Part 1. The Boutillerie Sector	148
	Part 2. The Cordonnerie Sector	168
	Part 3. The Ploegsteert Sector	174
VIII.	THE BATTLE OF MESSINES.	
	Part 1. Before the Battle	184
	Part 2. The Place of the Battle of Messines in the General Scheme of Operations	190
	Part 3. The Battle	193
IX.	AFTER MESSINES.	
	Part 1. The Advance in the Ploegsteert Sector	214
	Part 2. With the French First Army in Northern Belgium	220
	Part 3. The Warneton Sector	223

Chapter			Page
X.	THE THIRD BATTLE OF YPRES.		
	Part 1.	Digging in the Ypres Salient	227
	Part 2.	Progress of the British Offensive Operations	230
	Part 3.	Passchendaele, October 12th	235
	Part 4.	Concluding Stage of the Third Battle of Ypres	248
XI.	THE YPRES SALIENT.		
	Part 1.	After Passchendaele	250
	Part 2.	Stationary Trench Warfare	251
	Part 3.	In Corps Reserve	268
XII.	THE ANCRE, 1918.		
	Part 1.	The German Thrust at Amiens	271
	Part 2.	The New Zealand Rifle Brigade into the Gap	275
	Part 3.	Straightening the Line	288
	Part 4.	The German Attack, April 5th	300
	Part 5.	Stationary Trench Warfare	310
XIII.	THE BEGINNING OF THE ADVANCE TO VICTORY		327
XIV.	THE BATTLE OF BAPAUME.		
	Part 1.	The General Situation	342
	Part 2.	Puisieux-au-Mont, August 21st	345
	Part 3.	Miraumont, August 23rd	352
	Part 4.	Bapaume, August 26th to 29th	355
	Part 5.	Fremicourt, August 30th to September 1st	366
XV.	THE BATTLE OF THE SCARPE		374
XVI.	THE BATTLE OF HAVRINCOURT AND EPEHY.		
	Part 1.	Trescault Spur, September 9th	377
	Part 2.	Trescault Spur, September 12th	384
XVII.	THE BATTLE OF CAMBRAI AND THE HINDENBURG LINE.		
	Part 1.	The General Attack	396
	Part 2.	Crevecoeur, October 5th	399
XVIII.	FROM CREVECOEUR TO LE QUESNOY (THE BATTLE OF LE CATEAU AND THE BATTLE OF THE SELLE RIVER).		
	Part 1.	Lesdain and Beyond, October 8th	404
	Part 2.	The Advance to the Selle River	415
	Part 3.	The Battle of the Selle River	417
XIX.	LE QUESNOY AND THE ARMISTICE (THE BATTLE OF THE SAMBRE).		
	Part 1.	Minor Operations	421
	Part 2.	The Capture of Le Quesnoy, November 4th, 1918	435
	Part 3.	Concluding Stage	465
XX.	TO THE RHINE.		
	Part 1.	After Le Quesnoy	468
	Part 2.	The March to Germany	472
	Part 3.	The End	478

APPENDICES

Appendix		Page
I.	Honours and Awards	481
II.	The Honoured Dead	490
III.	The New Zealand Rifle Brigade Training Battalion	525
IV.	Dress Regulations of the New Zealand Rifle Brigade, 1918	533
V.	The Dunsterforce Expedition	536
VI.	The Third Field Ambulance	542
VII.	"Digger" and "Dink"	568
VIII.	Cheerfulness at Warneton	570
IX.	Notes on Marlborough's Campaigns, 1708–1710	572
X.	The Rifle Brigade (Prince Consort's Own)	575
XI.	Diary of the War	581

LIST OF MAPS, ETC.

Map No. 1. Northern Egypt .. End of Volume.
„ „ 2. Matruh .. „ „ „
„ „ 3. Flanders .. „ „ „
„ „ 4. The Somme .. „ „ „
„ „ 5. Flers .. „ „ „
„ „ 6. Messines .. „ „ „
„ „ 7. Passchendaele .. „ „ „
„ „ 8. Hebuterne to Puisieux-au-Mont .. „ „ „
„ „ 9. Trescault Spur .. „ „ „
„ „ 10. Le Quesnoy .. „ „ „
„ „ 11. The Advance to Victory .. „ „ „

MISCELLANEOUS:— Page
Sketch Map of a Battalion Sector, L'Epinette, Armentieres .. 96
Aeroplane Photograph of British and German Trench Systems, Pont Ballot, Armentieres .. 97
Aeroplane Photograph of Le Quesnoy and neighbourhood .. 432

ORDER OF BATTLE:—
Somme, September 15, 1916 .. 123
Messines, June 7, 1917 .. 199
Passchendaele, October 12, 1917 .. 239
Colincamps, March, 1918 .. 297
Colincamps, April 5, 1918 .. 303
Puisieux-au-Mont, August 21, 1918 .. 346
Bapaume, August 26, 1918 .. 356
Trescault Spur, September 9, 1918 .. 380
Trescault Spur, September 12, 1918 .. 386
Lesdain and Beyond, October 8, 1918 .. 408
Le Quesnoy, November 4, 1918 .. 446

LIST OF ILLUSTRATIONS

	Following page
Brigadier-General H. T. Fulton, C.M.G., D.S.O.	*Frontispiece*
Trentham Camp, 1915	
Rangiotu Camp, 1915	
The Officers of a Battalion	
The Non-Commissioned Officers of a Battalion	16
Major-General Sir A. H. Russell, K.C.B., K.C.M.G.	
Field Marshal H.R.H. the Duke of Connaught, K.G., K.T.	
Colonel the Earl of Liverpool, P.C., G.C.M.G.	
El Dabaa	
Bedouin Prisoners	
Disembarking at Mersa Matruh	32
The Compound at Force Headquarters, Matruh	
Representative South Africans, Sikhs and New Zealanders, Matruh	
Camel Transport	
A Field Dressing Station at Halazin	
A Mobile Column Returning to Matruh	48
The First Graves	
Gafaar Pasha a Prisoner	
Colonel (Maj.-Gen. Sir) E. W. C. Chaytor, K.C.M.G., K.C.V.O., C.B.	
Brigadier-General W. G. Braithwaite, C.B., C.M.G., D.S.O.	
Lieut.-Col. W. S. Austin, D.S.O.	64
Lieut.-Col. J. A. Cowles	
Major W. Kay, O.B.E.	
A Trench on the Somme	
Night, 14th/15th September, 1916	
A Relic of the Somme—One of the First Tanks	
A Lewis Gun in the Front Line	128
A Trench Mortar Shoot	
An 18-pounder	
Howitzers	
A 9·2-inch Gun	
Battalion Transport	
Field-Kitchens (Cookers)	
The Water Cart	160
A Y.M.C.A. Canteen	
The Veteran Sergeant-Major	
Winter on the Western Front	
In Ploegsteert Wood	
Anti-Aircraft Guns	
General Fulton Studies Messines	192
Ruins of Messines	
The Plank Road Follows the Advance	
The Colonel-in-Chief Inspects a Detachment at Bailleul	
Lieut.-Col. J. G. Roache, D.S.O.	
Lieut.-Col. R. St. J. Beere, D.S.O.	208
Lieut.-Col. A. Winter-Evans, D.S.O.	
Lieut.-Col. (Maj.-Gen.) C. W. Melvill, C.B., C.M.G., D.S.O.	
Sergeant (Lieut.) Samuel Frickleton, V.C.	
A Trench in the Warneton Sector	
A Company Headquarters in the Front Line	224
Brigadier-General F. Earl Johnston, C.B.	
Colonel (Brig.-Gen.) R. Young, C.B., C.M.G., D.S.O.	

Bogged in the Passchendaele Mud	
A Passchendaele "Pill-Box"	
Lieut.-Col. E. Puttick, D.S.O.	
Lieut.-Col. P. H. Bell, D.S.O.	
Major W. G. Bishop	240
German Prisoners Carrying Wounded	
The Runner Sets Out	
Signallers Laying Telephone Wire	
A Plank Road in the Ypres Salient	
Dead Mule Gully	
An Anti-Tank Gun near the Menin Road	
The Menin Road Under Snow	
The Ancient Cloth Hall of Ypres	256
And Its Ruins	
Band and "Bivvies" near Ypres	
"The Counter-Attack"	
Brigadier-General A. E. Stewart, C.M.G., D.S.O.	
Lieut.-Col. J. Pow, D.S.O.	
Lieut.-Col. L. H. Jardine, D.S.O., M.C.	
A Captured German Machine-Gun in Use near La Signy Farm	288
Another Part of the Front Line near the Farm	
A "Whippet"	
A Derelict Tank	
Digging the Purple Line	
Trophies from the German Trenches East of Hebuterne	
The Padre's Free Canteen in a Forward Trench	320
A Burial Party	
Brigadier-General H. Hart, C.B., C.M.G., D.S.O.	
Prisoners from Puisieux	352
A German Observation-Post, Bapaume	
Lieut.-Col. N. F. Shepherd, D.S.O.	
Major J. Murphy	384
Sergeant (2nd-Lieut.) Harry John Laurent, V.C.	
Lieut.-Col. R. C. Allen, D.S.O.	
Major G. W. Cockroft	
Towing a Captured Tank	416
A Ruined Factory—smashed, not bombarded	
The Front Line Before Le Quesnoy	
A Reserve Company on the Railway, November 4th	
The Inner Ramparts of Le Quesnoy	
The Ramparts at Another Point	448
Major H. E. Barrowclough, D.S.O., M.C.	
The 4th Battalion in the Square of Le Quesnoy	
Prisoners from About Le Quesnoy	
The New Zealand Flag Presented to Le Quesnoy	
The First Stage of the March to Germany	
The Hohenzollern Bridge over the Rhine	
H.R.H. the Prince of Wales at Brigade Headquarters	480
The Longueval Memorial on the Flers Battlefield	
The Memorial at Le Quesnoy	
The Cross of Sacrifice	524
The Stone of Remembrance	
A Regimental Medical Officer Attending to the Wounded	
A Field Ambulance	
The Interior of a Dressing Station (1) and (2)	560
A Stationary Hospital	

The Illustrations "A Trench on the Somme," "Night, 14th/15th September, 1916," "A Relic of the Somme—One of the First Tanks" (following page 128), and "Winter on the Western Front" (facing page 161), reproduced from "Sir Douglas Haig's Great Push," are wrongly attributed to Hutchinson. The originals are the property of the Trustees of the Imperial War Museum; Crown copyright reserved. The views have been inserted by permission.

BRIGADIER-GENERAL H. T. FULTON, C.M.G., D.S.O.

Frontispiece.

THE NEW ZEALAND RIFLE BRIGADE.

CHAPTER I.
FROM NEW ZEALAND TO EGYPT.

PART 1.—PREPARATION.

Formation—Preliminary training of officers and non-commissioned officers—Men march in—Posting—Training—Fatigues—Complete establishment—The first move—Rangiotu Camp—Advance parties—Musketry, leave, manœuvres, inspections—Hospitality—Changes in title.

The regiment afterwards known as the New Zealand Rifle Brigade came into being officially on May 1st, 1915, nine months after the outbreak of the Great War. February had seen the fruitless attempts of the Allied fleet to force the Dardanelles, and it was recognized that to ensure success there must be preparatory or coincident land operations. Plans were therefore laid for a landing on Gallipoli on April 25th by a military force the material for which, in the shape of the Imperial and Colonial troops then in Egypt, lay ready to hand, for it was clear that after the defeat of the Turks on the Canal at the beginning of the month there was little fear of any serious attack from this quarter for some time to come. Now, the casualties suffered by the New Zealand regiments in the Canal fighting had been practically negligible, while three bodies of reinforcements were already in Egypt, a fourth was almost ready to sail, and a fifth was in active training.

In the circumstances it was considered by the Imperial Government that the Dominion could best satisfy its desire further to assist in the great effort by sending out an entirely new regiment of infantry, quite apart from the original main body, supplying this, as well as the older force, with the required stream of reinforcements. The intention was to begin the mobilization and training of two battalions at once, and when these should be well established, to follow with a further two units at a convenient interval. The offer was accepted by the War Office on April 16th, the eve of the departure of the Fourth Reinforcements.

Thus began the evolution of a body of citizen-soldiers known first as the Trentham Infantry Regiment and later as the New Zealand Rifle Brigade, and destined to participate in the achievements and share in the glories of the invincible New Zealand Division.

Lieut.-Col. H. T. Fulton, D.S.O. (Major in the 2nd King Edward's Own Gurkha Rifles), who in the South African War had served with the New Zealand contingents, had recently returned with troops from Samoa, and on April 8th assumed command of the Fourth Reinforcements. On April 16th he embarked with them, but on the following day was withdrawn to take charge of the new regiment. Certain other selected officers and non-commissioned officers of the Fourths were also held back to carry on under his command.

Following the plan first adopted in connection with the training of the Fifth Reinforcements, officers and non-commissioned officers for the new regiment were brought in for special preliminary instruction some time before the arrival of the rank and file, and all but a few of the former marched into Trentham Camp, Wellington, on April 28th. The training, which included the most elementary parts of infantry drill, supplemented by a course of special lectures, commenced at once under the general direction of Lieut.-Col. Fulton and the immediate supervision of Lieut. A. Cheater, of the Permanent Staff. Presently experienced officers, notably Lieuts. Burn, Purdy and Wilkes, all of the N.Z.S.C., but now on the strength of the regiment, took over the instruction of the non-commissioned officers, the remainder continuing under Lieut. Cheater. At the commencement of the period of training the weather conditions were fairly good, but towards the end fog and rain somewhat interfered with the work.

On May 29th and 30th, 2,207 men reported in camp. Of these, 540 came from the Auckland military district, 631 from

Wellington, 534 from Canterbury, and 502 from Otago. The weather was now miserably wet and cold, and the general conditions were most discouraging for civilians just entering upon a period of military life. However, they were speedily allotted to companies, provided with "knife, fork, spoon, plate, mug," and marched off for their first meal in camp. Arms and equipment were issued, the men sworn in, and the long and tedious process of making up the rolls and filling in the many forms commenced.

Hitherto the method of posting in the Main Body and its reinforcements had been to keep officers and men together according to the territorial district from which they came. Thus in the Main Body there were four regiments—Auckland, Wellington, Canterbury and Otago; and within these regiments the companies comprised as far as possible the men from the various territorial regiments. Similarly each infantry reinforcement consisted of four companies, A, B, C, D, made up of men from Auckland, Wellington, Canterbury, and Otago, respectively. In the new regiment this system was not adopted, but every opportunity was given for friends, at the first posting, to keep together; and later, by means of transfers, this privilege was extended.

It had been decided that there should be two battalions, the 1st to be commanded by Lieut.-Col. Fulton, and the 2nd by Lieut.-Col. A. E. Stewart, late Commanding Officer of the 14th (South Otago) Regiment. Lieut.-Col. Fulton, however, still retained command of the regiment as a whole, and the immediate control of the 1st Battalion presently devolved upon Major W. S. Austin, late Second-in-Command of the 13th (North Canterbury and Westland) Regiment, who reported on transfer from the 5th Reinforcements of the Canterbury Regiment on 9th June.

In the regimental numbers assigned to officers and men the prefixes 23/ and 24/ distinguished members of the 1st and 2nd Battalions, respectively. Similarly, when the 3rd and 4th Battalions were established, the prefix-numbers 25/ and 26/ were used. This exceedingly satisfactory arrangement was continued for a considerable time in connection with reinforcements for the Brigade, but finally, owing to the difficulty experienced at the front in ensuring that men so numbered in

New Zealand should be posted to their corresponding units, especially after heavy engagements, the system of using the distinguishing bar-numbers was dropped altogether in the reinforcement camps.

For the accommodation of officers and men of the new battalions, the erection of a number of large huts, the first group of those buildings that were to transform Trentham from a tented field into a small town of houses and streets, had been commenced, but these were far from finished by the time they were required. To make matters worse, the workmen engaged in their construction were themselves occupying a goodly proportion of the accommodation, so that when the men arrived and settled down the quarters available were unduly crowded. These hutments were the first erected in the camp, and though they were more weatherproof than tents, they were not as comfortable as men accustomed to the latter might think. The shell was of corrugated iron, unlined, and unpleasant down-draughts gave the impression that they were as open as sieves.

Owing to the bad weather and the amount of movement about the huts, the surroundings began to assume the appearance of a sea of mud; and during the first five or six days practically the whole force was employed in making temporary drains, carrying stones for paths, and generally rendering more habitable the vicinity of their new homes. The officers worked hard in their endeavour to complete the uninteresting task of checking the rolls and filling up the many necessary forms.

By this time those concerned were beginning to realize the fact, which later experience confirmed, that the work of the unskilled labourer bulked surprisingly large in military life, and that to possess the pen of a ready writer sometimes appeared to be more important than to know and to apply all the rules and teachings of the military manuals. The man in the ranks was unconsciously being prepared to accept without surprise or comment the title of "Digger," while the officer was learning the significance of the term "a paper war."

King's Birthday was devoted to physical exercises and camp sports, and general training commenced in earnest on the 4th June, with a break on the 7th for anti-typhoid inoculation.

It may be said at once that, under the watchful eye of Lieut.-Col. Fulton, the training throughout was efficient and thorough to a degree, and eventually reached an unusually high standard of excellence. To this result there were many contributory factors. Amongst the foremost of these was the fact that the commander was an Imperial officer who had had considerable experience in the management and direction of Colonial as well as of British and Indian regular troops in actual warfare. He was able, therefore, to exercise the finest discrimination, and while enforcing the strictest discipline, and exacting from all ranks under his command the fullest measure of thought and work and care, he was able to modify his methods in accordance with his knowledge of the possibilities and limitations of the civilian who had just thrown down his tools to take up arms in the service of his country. Added to this, we had amongst the officers and non-commissioned officers several members of the New Zealand Permanent Staff, not merely as instructors, but as integral parts of the unit, and the benefit we derived from their special training was enhanced by the particular zeal arising from their intimate connection with the regiment. We had a further advantage in the presence of a number of officers and non-commissioned officers transferred from the Fourth and Fifth Reinforcements and from the force lately returned from Samoa; for these, having been through the mill in camp and abroad, not only possessed a definite knowledge of the work required but were already experienced in the handling of recruits. Lastly, there was esprit de corps, by no means the least important factor. The spirit of the regiment rapidly developed, was maintained throughout the period of training, and reached its highest pitch under fire. There was no cleavage between men of different districts. We were many companies but one regiment, whose honour as a whole was, and still remains, very precious to us. There may be some who, after the fact, hold that New Zealand was too small to supply and maintain a regiment entirely separate and distinct from those already in existence. Be that as it may, it cannot be denied that the distinction led to a very honest spirit of emulation which was in no inconsiderable degree beneficial to the Expeditionary Force in general. As in the case of old-established British regiments, this commendable rivalry occasionally engendered a feeling of antagonism; but, happily, all signs of animosity disappeared when we rubbed shoulders with our comrades of the other regiments in the trenches of Flanders; and perhaps the least that can be said of us is embodied in the word of praise from the Corps Commander after the Somme engagements of 1916: "You have justified your existence."

At the end of May the officers of the regiment established a mess, a building for that purpose having been specially erected. There was nothing pretentious about the outfit, the gear being purchased with an eye to its use on active service, and there was no useless expenditure upon ornamental or luxurious accessories. The regiment gained not a little through its officers being thus brought into close contact with one another off the parade-ground. On the 18th June the comfort and well-being of the officers was still further improved through their being able to move from damp tents to the more cheerful living-quarters in the cubicles of the hutments that had been for some time under construction for their use.

In the earlier stages of training our two greatest drawbacks were the unfavourable nature of the weather and the ever-recurring demands for large fatigue parties for work on the camp as a whole. The first of these was, of course, unavoidable; but to the harassed platoon, company and battalion officers, whose interests were centred on the welfare and progress of their own commands, the matter of working-parties did not always appear to be well-regulated. Indeed, right through our career, at home and at the front, this was a never-ending source of "grouse," and the opinion is generally held that for work of a non-military character more use might have been made of volunteers found physically unfit for ordinary military service.

From the moment the men first marched into camp steps were taken to ensure that the regimental and battalion headquarters should be as complete as possible. Captain P. H. Bell, who had been acting as Adjutant to the Regiment from the beginning, now continued in that capacity in the 1st Battalion. Captain R. St. J. Beere was appointed Second-in-Command and Lieut. A. H. Burn Adjutant of the 2nd, and each battalion had its own orderly-room and necessary clerks. Captains G. E. Simeon and W. E. Christie, Quartermasters respectively of the 1st and 2nd, were given adequate staffs, and all clothing, equipment, rations, etc., were issued through them instead of being drawn direct from the Camp Quartermaster.

The detail, on the regulation scale, of butchers, cooks, tailors, shoemakers, and so forth, was provided for, and military police, signal, transport, sanitary and pioneer sections were told off permanently. The stretcher-bearer sections were organized into a regimental brass band, and the buglers combined into a drum and bugle band; and in each case part of the training time was devoted to music practice and part to drill and the more immediate work for which the personnel had been detailed. Both bands, the former under the leadership of Sergeant (afterwards Hon. Lieut.) P. E. Cole, and the latter under the instruction of Sergeant J. Lee, made rapid progress in their training and soon became the pride of the regiment. Later, each battalion had its own brass band, and it is impossible fully to gauge the beneficial influence of these upon the morale of the men. Many a weary mile in our innumerable marches from billet to billet in France was shortened by their cheering strains; and after a relief from the trenches for a brief rest in camp or bivouac, the daily programmes played by the battalion bands were of inestimable value in helping to remove that "fed-up" feeling, and in driving away the unpleasant memories of experiences in the line.

During our first six months in the trenches at Armentieres the bandsmen in their capacity of stretcher-bearers suffered many casualties, and as this entailed a double loss it was decided, before the Brigade went to the Somme in 1916, to keep the bandsmen out of action and appoint special company and battalion stretcher-bearers.

The first uniform dress was the unsightly but useful suit of denims, which from an economical point of view served its purpose well. With this was worn the well-known felt hat technically known as the "smasher." The head of the hat was creased longitudinally in accordance with the custom then in vogue in the New Zealand camps. On the 19th June the ordinary issue of khaki uniforms and forage caps was made, but these were for use only on ceremonial occasions and when going on leave. The distinguishing badge was a patch or "blaze" of black melton cloth on the puggaree of the hat, one on each side, and in the centre of the cap-band. In each case the blaze was a square of one and a half inch side, that of the 1st Battalion being placed diamond-wise, and that of the 2nd Battalion lying horizontally; while the personnel of regimental headquarters wore a blaze in the form of an eight-pointed star, representing the diamond and the square superimposed. Rifle Brigade buttons and "Liverpool" badges were first worn on August 31st.

Throughout June and the earlier part of July the training continued with vigour. Owing to the bad state of the camp grounds the battalions did a good deal of work further afield, and in the frequent and carefully-supervised route marches they began to excel. The somewhat congested state of the camp area, added to the long-continued bad weather, was, however, telling on the health of the men. Roads and drains were being improved as rapidly as possible, but evil-smelling mud still abounded, and although baths and drying-rooms were being pushed to completion, their commencement had been unduly late. So rapidly had sickness increased that the grandstand of the adjoining racecourse was pressed into service as a temporary hospital. At last came the decision to evacuate the camp of all troops except the Sixth Reinforcements, several cases of illness having been diagnosed as cerebro-spinal meningitis. Orders came for our move at only six hours' notice, and the regiment had its first experience of shifting quarters with practically no preliminary preparation. Operations had to be pushed on with speed, and were looked upon as a very serious business. In later days, when changing billets and relieving in the trenches were so oft-repeated as to work almost automatically, we were to look back with some amusement on this our first move. However, in the circumstances, all went extremely well. At an early hour on the morning of the 10th of July the regiment had entrained in pouring rain, and by 7 a.m. had started from Trentham for Rangiotu, near Palmerston North. Instructions were received en route to detrain at Palmerston North, the 1st Battalion to occupy the buildings in the Show Grounds and the 2nd Battalion those at Awapuni Racecourse, until the bad weather abated. We found our new quarters fairly comfortable, and by degrees succeeded in drying our clothes. On the first morning in the Show Grounds, in place of the distressing "Rouse" by the bugles, we had the band on duty at reveille with more inspiring airs. So heavy had been the rain that no training was possible except on the roads, but not an hour was lost that could profitably be employed, however elementary the nature of the work.

On the 12th of July, Capt. E. Puttick. O.C. "B" Company, 1st Battalion, was appointed temporary Camp-Quartermaster, and on the same day went with Lieut.-Col. Fulton to Rangiotu, a farming settlement on the Foxton road, some nine miles from Palmerston North, to make arrangements for establishing the camp there. It was decided to pitch a temporary camp about a mile and a half from the site of the permanent one. On the following day an advance party of 600 men commenced work and had everything ready for occupation on the 15th July, on which date the two battalions moved out from Palmerston to their new quarters. Situated close beside the road and the railway line, the camp was quite convenient as a temporary home, and the decision to occupy it for the time being proved to be very wise, as it gave ample time for the drawing up of plans for the establishment of a permanent camp so laid out as to ensure the maximum of health and comfort for the troops. The training-grounds were almost unlimited in area; the grassy sandhills and dry river-flats remained practically unaffected by the rains, and left nothing to be desired in the way of diversity; and taken altogether the conditions were almost ideal. In these new circumstances, and aided by an improvement in the weather, all ranks rapidly regained their health and vigour. As a precautionary measure, "gargle parades" were ordered for four days. These parades were held by whole battalions on the roadside at some distance from the camp, and though the proceedings seemed odd enough the treatment must have been of value, for cases of meningitis were practically unknown at Rangiotu.

By the end of July the lines of the permanent camp had been completely pegged and everything was ready for the move, which took place on August 14th, heavy rain having delayed the transfer. Marquees, tents, floors, indeed everything in the camp, even to a cookhouse intact, were conveyed by hand a distance of over a mile, and in a very little time our new canvas town was completely erected. The site had been inspected by the military and medical authorities and had met with general approval. The camping-ground was extensive, and Lieut.-Col. Fulton's plan was to occupy the whole area at once, providing for two large spaces, each for one battalion, and allowing for very wide roadways separating the various company blocks. This was supported by the medical officers as preferable to camping in a small space and shifting camp periodically. In order to avoid cutting up the ground, no wheeled vehicle was allowed in the camp; all stores, etc., had to be brought in by hand until tramways were constructed from the special railway siding to the cookhouses and quartermasters' stores.

In the meantime, Lieut.-Col. Fulton having gone on sick leave, owing to trouble from an old wound, Lieut.-Col. R. W. Tate, commanding the Wellington District, assumed command on July 24th and continued in charge until August 23rd, when Lieut.-Col. Fulton returned.

At the beginning of September a supply of transport horses and harness arrived in camp, and the special training of drivers and grooms was taken in hand by Lieut. Wilson, R.N.Z.A., who reported for this duty on the 6th. We had had the vehicles for some time, and it was not long before the transport section of each battalion was able to carry out the practical tests with a considerable degree of efficiency. As in the subsequent history of the regiment, little reference is made to these sections, it may be stated that in later days we learned to look with pride on our men of the transport. Their turn-out did not always compare most favourably in appearance with that of their brothers-in-arms of some English regiments, but in the greatest of all their duties—the supply of rations—they never once failed. No matter what the state of the weather, the condition of the roads, the length or number of the journeys, or the intensity of the shell-fire, they always "got there," never counting the cost in the faithful service of their comrades. To mention here only one instance of such devotion to duty, it is recorded that on April 5th, 1918, when the Germans made their big attack on our newly-established line in front of Colincamps, the water-carts of one battalion actually passed through the enemy barrage and took supplies practically to the front line itself.

The Advance Party of the Brigade, consisting of 50 other ranks of the 1st Battalion under Lieut. R. O. Brydon, and a like number of the 2nd under Lieut. T. M. Wilkes, left for Egypt on September 18th.

Practically the only disadvantage connected with the Rangiotu Camp as compared with Trentham was the lack of facilities for carrying out the regulation musketry course. The only existing rifle-ranges within fairly easy reach were those at Palmerston North and Wanganui, on both of which accommodation was limited. For this reason it was decided to send off the 2nd Battalion on the seven days' final leave on August 20th and place both ranges at the disposal of the 1st Battalion, the companies of which left for final leave as they completed the course. The preliminary grouping practices were carried out on a very useful temporary range we constructed for the purpose in the vicinity of the camp, and the first company marched out to the range at Palmerston North on August 17th. On the return of the companies of the 2nd Battalion from their final leave they were put through their musketry in a similar manner. Notwithstanding the drawbacks, the standard attained by both units in this branch of training was very high.

Shortly after the completion of the musketry course and the final leave, the two battalions went out in turn to the sandhills in the neighbourhood of Bainesse, near the West Coast, for continuous training in attack and defence, outpost work and field firing, and in the short period at their disposal gained considerable practical experience in working over unknown country, patrolling, bivouacking, field-cooking, supplying rations and ammunition, writing orders and reports, etc. On return to Rangiotu, more intensive training was carried out with the object of emphasizing the lessons learned in this general work, and the rapid setting-out of the various forms of bivouac-camps was practised.

It should be mentioned that the facilities for entrenching work at Rangiotu were utilized to the full. The use of the entrenching-tool in throwing up temporary cover was constantly practised; the varied nature of the country gave excellent opportunities for instruction in the proper siting of trenches; and laying out and digging, both by night and by day, formed a very important part in the general scheme of training.

On September 28th the regiment was inspected by the Honorary Colonel, His Excellency the Earl of Liverpool, who, after complimenting all ranks on the smartness of their appearance and their steadiness on parade, referred to the traditions of the Imperial Rifle Brigade, and exhorted the officers and men to emulate the deeds of that famous regiment and strive to excel in every respect, both in camp and on the field. He was pleased to say he felt confident that when the time came for this young Brigade to participate in active operations alongside British regiments, their conduct would be such as to redound to their own honour and add lustre to the fair name of their country.

The final official inspection was held on October 5th, a few days before embarkation, when Colonel Gibbon, Chief of the General Staff, took the parade.

Throughout the stay of the regiment at Rangiotu, much kindness was received at the hands of the citizens of Palmerston North, Wanganui and Foxton, and of the people of the district generally. Their patriotic societies sent regularly gifts of fruit, puddings and other dainties, to relieve the monotony of the regulation rations, and the concerts given in camp by parties from town were as heartily appreciated as they were excellent in quality.

We were glad to know that the efforts of the Regimental Band to give some pleasure in return, by playing programmes and taking part in concerts in several of the neighbouring towns, met with marked signs of approval. Grants from patriotic societies, together with the receipts from five special concerts and a subsidy from the Trentham Camp Commandant, were sufficient to enable the band to leave New Zealand free of debt. When the instruments were destroyed by shell-fire just two years later, the riddled remains were forwarded to the Mayor of Palmerston North as mementoes.

The band's final concert in New Zealand was given, at the invitation of the Wellington Patriotic Society, on the eve of departure overseas. This was held in the Town Hall, and Lieut. Cole conducted with the baton presented by His Excellency the Honorary Colonel at the afternoon parade and subsequently carried safely through the whole of the campaign.

This may be a fitting place in which to set out in detail the changes made in the designation of the regiment from time to time.* They were many. In the earliest days, while preparations were being made for its mobilization, it was spoken of vaguely as "The New Battalions," On May 27th, 1915, it received the title "The Trentham Regiment" (Earl of Liverpool's Own) as from May 1st, and at the same time His Excellency the Governor became its Honorary Colonel.

*Nicknames are referred to in Appendix VII.

Extract from New Zealand Gazette, 27th May, 1915 :—

Wellington, 19th May, 1915.

His Excellency the Governor has been pleased to approve that the special infantry battalions now mobilised at Trentham Camp be designated "The Trentham Regiment" (The Earl of Liverpool's Own), and with effect from May 1st, 1915.

(Signed) J. ALLEN,
Minister of Defence.

Department of Defence,
Wellington, 19th May, 1915.

His Excellency the Governor has been pleased to approve of The Right Honourable Arthur William de Brito Savile, Earl of Liverpool, G.C.M.G., M.V.O., Lieut.-Colonel 8th (City of London) Battalion, the London Regiment (Post Office Rifles), Reserve of Officers, the Rifle Brigade (The Prince Consort's Own), Honorary Colonel, 11th Regiment (Taranaki Rifles), as Colonel of "The Trentham Regiment" (The Earl of Liverpool's Own), New Zealand Expeditionary Force, and with effect from 1st May, 1915.

(Signed) J. ALLEN,
Minister of Defence.

Both the Commanding Officer and the Honorary Colonel of the Regiment were Rifle Brigade officers, and it soon became evident that it was their desire to have it transformed into a Rifle Regiment with the dress and drill modified accordingly. Samples of Rifle Brigade buttons were procured from India about the middle of May, and negotiations were entered into with the object of obtaining sanction to use as a regimental badge the crest and motto of the Earl of Liverpool—a lion rampant supporting a man-of-war's pennant proper; motto "Soyes Ferme."

From August 18th till 30th, the title was given in Regimental orders as "The Trentham Infantry Brigade" (Earl of Liverpool's Own), and in Brigade orders of the latter date it was laid down that in future the correct nomenclature would be "The Trentham Rifle Brigade" (Earl of Liverpool's Own). On the following day the wearing of Rifle Brigade buttons and the "Liverpool" badge was ordered.

In the middle of September, 1915, the mobilization of the 3rd and 4th Battalions commenced, and in Brigade orders of the 28th the following correspondence was published for general information:—

From His Excellency the Governor,

To Field Marshal His Royal Highness the Duke of Connaught, Colonel-in-Chief of the Rifle Brigade (The Prince Consort's Own).

Wellington, N.Z., September 23rd, 1915.

The newly-raised Regiment, the New Zealand Rifle Brigade, shortly proceeding to the Dardanelles, consisting of four battalions, tender to your Royal Highness, as Colonel-in-Chief of the Rifle Brigade, their resolution to do their utmost to emulate the glorious record of the Imperial Regiment with whom they hope they may be associated on service.

(Signed) LIVERPOOL, Honorary Colonel,
New Zealand Rifle Brigade.

From Field-Marshal His Royal Highness the Duke of Connaught, Colonel-in-Chief of the Rifle Brigade (The Prince Consort's Own).

To Colonel His Excellency the Earl of Liverpool,
New Zealand Rifle Brigade.

September 24th, 1915.

As Colonel-in-Chief of the Rifle Brigade, I warmly appreciate your message from New Zealand comrades, and wish them all luck and success.

(Signed) ARTHUR.

The change of title from "Trentham Rifle Brigade" to "New Zealand Rifle Brigade" will be noted. The alteration in name, however, did not appear in the New Zealand Gazette till October 7th, 1915, when the following announcement was made:—

New Zealand Gazette No. 115, of 7th October, 1915.

Abolition of the Designation of "Trentham Regiment" (Earl of Liverpool's Own), and its formation into a Rifle Brigade.

Department of Defence,
Wellington, 5th October, 1915.

His Excellency the Governor has been pleased to abolish the designation of the "Trentham Regiment" (Earl of Liverpool's Own), as published in the New Zealand Gazette of 27th May, 1915, and to approve of its formation into a Brigade to be designated as under:—

"The New Zealand Rifle Brigade—Earl of Liverpool's Own."

Dated 1st October, 1915.

(Signed) J. ALLEN,
Minister of Defence.

On the organization of the New Zealand Division in Egypt at the end of February, 1916, the New Zealand Rifle Brigade became the 3rd Brigade of the Division, and New Zealand Expeditionary Force Orders, dated April 22nd, laid down that in accordance with War Office instructions, it would in future be known as the "3rd New Zealand (Rifles) Brigade." Later the word "Rifle" was substituted for "Rifles." Thus, as a regiment it remained "The New Zealand Rifle Brigade," but as part of the Division "The 3rd New Zealand (Rifle) Brigade."

The following appeared in N.Z.E.F. Orders of 15th January, 1917:—

"241.—COLONEL-IN-CHIEF, NEW ZEALAND RIFLE BRIGADE.

"His Majesty the King has been graciously pleased to appoint Field Marshal His Royal Highness the Duke of Connaught and Strathearn, K.G., K.T., K.P., G.C.B., G.C.S.I., G.C.M.G., G.C.I.E., G.C.V.O., Col. G. Gds. and A.S.C., and Col.-in-Chief 6th Dns., High. L.I., R. Dub. Fus., and Rifle Brigade, Personal A.D.C. to the King, to be Colonel-in-Chief to the New Zealand Rifle Brigade."

Slight modifications in dress were made from time to time; indeed, so frequently were changes ordered that they became a source of no little irritation. The Dress Regulations as they finally stood are set out in Appendix IV.

As to drill, every effort was made to attain perfection by hard training along the lines in vogue in the different Imperial Rifle Regiments, but owing to the fact that "regimental quiffs" varied so greatly, and that there was no official Rifle Brigade drill manual extant, some difficulty was experienced in securing rigid uniformity.

PART 2.—DEPARTURE FOR EGYPT.

Embarkation—At sea—Albany—The convoy divides—1st Battalion via Fremantle to Suez—Aerodrome Camp, Heliopolis—2nd Battalion, via Colombo, arrives, and is warned for service in the field—2nd Battalion to Dabaa—Command, Col. Chaytor—Command, Lieut.-Col. Fulton—Unrest in Cairo—1st Battalion to Mersa Matruh.

On the morning of 8th October, 1915, the two battalions entrained for Wellington, and on arival at the port at mid-day marched with kit-bags and sea-kits to the troopships. After the men had been told off to their quarters and kits stowed away, they were granted leave till 10.30 p.m. This being their last evening ashore before departure, it might have been expected that there would be some trouble in the city; but the men were put on their honour, and all reports agreed that the behaviour was excellent.

Troops were taken off their ships at six o'clock next morning, and at 7 a.m. the official embarkation with checking of the rolls took place. At 1 p.m. they were marched off the ships and paraded for a farewell march through the town at 2.30 p.m. The parade comprised the two battalions of the Rifle Brigade, with the Honorary Colonel, His Excellency the Earl of Liverpool, Governor of New Zealand, at the head, and also the 7th Reinforcements under Major R. St. J. Beere. The quick swinging march of the Rifle Battalions with their arms at the trail was new to the great crowds that had assembled to watch the parade. The troops, having returned to the docks, re-embarked, and the troopships moved into the stream and anchored at 5 p.m.

At 6 a.m. on the 10th of October, 1915, the transports sailed from Wellington, the convoy consisting of:—

1. "Maunganui" (Transport No. 30), with Brigade Headquarters; 1st Battalion; 2nd Field Artillery Brigade; Divisional Ammunition Column, and Ambulance and other details.
2. "Tahiti" (Transport No. 31), with 2nd Battalion, and A.S.C. and Divisional Signalling Coy. details.
3. "Aparima" (Transport No. 32), with 7th Reinforcement Mounted Rifles, and Divisional Train and Ambulance details.

Trentham Camp, 1915.

Rangiotu Camp, 1915.

THE OFFICERS OF A BATTALION.

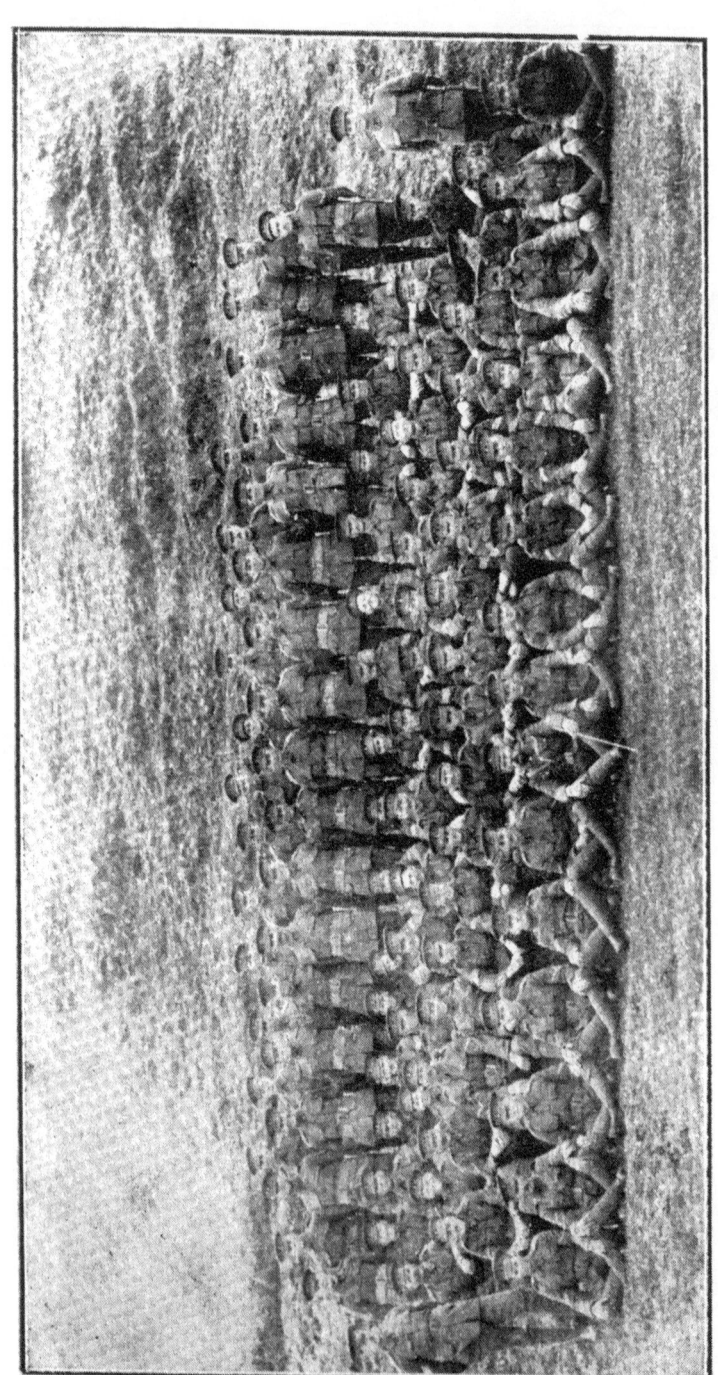

The Non-Commissioned Officers of a Battalion.

Colonel the Earl of Liverpool,
P.C., G.C.M.G.,
Honorary Colonel of the N.Z.R.B.

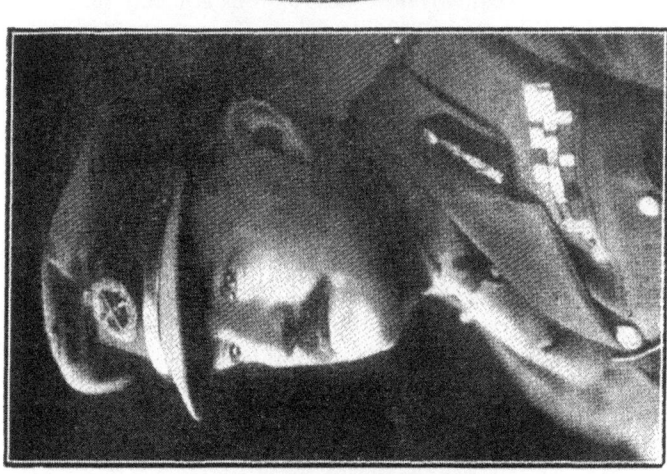

Major-General Sir A. H. Russell,
K.C.B., K.C.M.G.
Commander of the N.Z. Division.

Field Marshal H.R.H.
The Duke of Connaught, K.G., K.T.
Colonel-in-Chief of the N.Z.R.B.

4. "Navua" (Transport No. 33), with 7th Reinforcement Mounted Rifles, and Artillery, Infantry and Ambulance details.

5. "Warrimoo" (Transport No. 34), with 7th Reinforcement Infantry and Ambulance details.

There was no escort of warships.

The sea journey on the whole was interesting but uneventful. Food and quarters were good, and the daily inspections by the Master, accompanied by the O.C. Ship, revealed a state of order and cleanliness very creditable indeed to all ranks. All available deck-space was made use of for such drill as could be carried out, this training being supplemented by lecturettes given at frequent intervals by officers and non-commissioned officers. Signallers had excellent practical work sending and receiving messages from ship to ship. Boxing tournaments were frequent, and impromptu concerts beguiled many a tedious evening, and revealed much talent that was carefully noted for future use in arranging company and battalion concerts in camp and billets in the more strenuous days to come. On the "Maunganui," the ship's disused printing-press was commandeered, and a weird and wonderful magazine, called "The Periscope," was produced. It was an eight-paged paper, printed with decrepit type and faded ink, on such sheets of absorbent paper as could be spared from the battalion orderly-room; a poor thing, doubtless, but nevertheless prized as being entirely our own. At Fremantle, by means of judicious purchases, the type-founts were augmented and a supply of paper and ink laid in, and as a result there blossomed forth, before we reached our destination, a second number of the magazine, somewhat thin in bulk, yet resplendent in its crimson binding and gold lettering. An endeavour had been made to secure a green cover, as more fitting for a Rifle Brigade paper, but the resources of Fremantle proved to be limited.

At 5 p.m. on the 19th October we reached Albany, our first port of call, the weather on the way across having been, with the exception of two rather rough days in the Australian Bight, decidedly good. We were greatly interested in the picturesque appearance of King George's Sound and the harbour of Albany. Naturally enough, disappointment was felt on learning that owing to some irregularities on the part of troops (not from our own country) that had been ashore some time previously, the military authorities could not grant permission for general leave, and we had to content ourselves with a route march to town next day, from 8.30 to 10 a.m. The march proved to be a pleasant break to the monotony of life on board ship. The "Willochra," with sick and wounded for New Zealand, being in port, an interchange of visits was carried out, and old acquaintanceships renewed.

At Albany the convoy divided, the "Tahiti," with the 2nd Battalion, sailing in company with the "Navua" and "Aparima," for Suez via Colombo. The "Maunganui" and the "Warrimoo," on the other hand, called at Fremantle, where the 1st Battalion and troops of the 7th Reinforcements went ashore for a route march and three hours' general leave. These two transports sailed from Fremantle at 8 p.m. on 23rd October, and by the 25th the weather had become sufficiently hot for awnings to be spread. The Line was crossed on November 4th, and four days later Cape Gardafui, the north-eastern point of Africa, was sighted. The passage of the dreaded Red Sea, much less distressing, however, than was anticipated, was completed by 7.15 a.m. on the 14th, at which hour the "Maunganui" dropped anchor at Suez. Reveille had been sounded at 4 a.m., and by 7 a.m. the troops were drawn up ready to disembark. However, orders were received to the effect that we were not to go ashore until the following day, and we were able to contemplate at leisure our strange and interesting surroundings. Away to the north-east was enemy country, the fawn-coloured desert sloping to the bare hills on the horizon. Nearer at hand were the weird sights and sounds of an Eastern port, with its gangs of noisy and gesticulating coolies, whose tendency to adopt "go-slow" tactics was met by prompt and energetic application of the big stick. The activities and cries of the vendors of fruit in the boats alongside, the calls for "Backsheesh! Backsheesh!" and the exploits of the native divers, all excited our interest and curiosity; but we were brought back to the realities of our mission when a number of New Zealanders came aboard to look up friends and acquaintances, and recounted some of their experiences on Gallipoli.

On November 15th the 1st Battalion disembarked from the "Maunganui" and entrained for Aerodrome Camp, near Cairo. The operation of transferring the troops, waggons, gear and stores from the ship to the trains was by no means simple. We had our plans worked out down to the smallest detail, but these, it appeared, did not coincide with those of the local entraining officer, and considerable friction resulted until Captain Purdy, who had been detailed for the special duty, prevailed upon the regular official to leave us to own our devices. Thereafter the entraining proceeded with precision and expedition, and the feats of our carrying and loading parties were quite evidently a source of wonderment to both the English soldiers and the native labourers.

The open trucks of the troop-trains were altogether comfortless, and the jolting stops and starts astonishingly disconcerting; but the novelty of the experience and the interest attaching to the mysterious land through which we moved served to divert the mind from the contemplation of troubles that in other circumstances might have been sufficiently annoying. From Suez northwards the line ran close to the Canal, along which were numerous posts garrisoned mainly by Indian troops, the first we had seen on definite active service. At Ismailia we turned westward, and presently passed from the barren and monotonous desert to the fertile delta land, intersected by its innumerable irrigation ditches, the broad fields of growing crops and clumps of waving palms affording a veritable feast for the eye. At every stop, whether by day or by night, crowds of natives, carrying baskets of oranges and hard-boiled eggs, besieged the train and hawked their wares with strange new cries. " Eggs-a-cook! Eggs-a-cook!" was fairly easily interpreted, but the meaning of " Orranghees! Orranghees! Verra nice! Verra sweet! Verra clean! Orranghees! Orranghees! Two forra half!" was more difficult of comprehension. Experience, however, is the best of teachers, and we soon learned that the mysterious "half" was half a piastre, the equivalent of a penny farthing. Our education advanced a further step during the following day, when the newspaper boys overran the camp bawling " 'Mbaberr! 'Mbaberr! 'Mbaberr tomorra! Egyptian 'mbaberr! Timees! Verra good news!" and we discovered that this country was so up-to-date as to publish the morning paper on the previous afternoon.

After a journey of seven hours, the last of the three trains by which the battalion moved reached Helmieh Siding, some two miles from camp, half-an-hour before midnight. The

Regimental Band had accompanied the 1st Battalion from New Zealand, and now marched a detachment across the desert to the camp, playing, in the darkness, "Left, Right," a tune repeated by one of our bands just three years later as it led the march of its battalion across the Rhine, again during the night.

Aerodrome Camp was part of a large base camp situated quite close to the modern portion of the town of Heliopolis, which is practically a suburb of Cairo, though distant some six miles from the centre of that city. Our area was close to that of the Australian Light Horse, whose officers kindly extended hospitality to those of the 1st Battalion until the latter were able to complete arrangements for their own mess. The pushful native caterers and refuse contractors were early on the scene on business intent, and Battalion Headquarters were pestered by guides and hawkers bent on securing passes to enable them to ply their nefarious trades and callings within the lines.

On the first day in camp the companies drilled from 10 a.m. till noon, and in the afternoon the battalion had an interesting route march through Heliopolis and Zeitoun. Lieut.-Col. Fulton and Brigade Headquarters arrived from Suez late in the evening.

On the 17th the 1st Battalion officers opened their own mess. The native caterer was anxious to please, but the curious French-Egyptian dishes did not meet with an enthusiastic reception. By degrees we instructed him in the peculiarities of our requirements and brought to his notice certain joints cooked in the British fashion in a company kitchen. With due thought for his finer feelings, we hinted delicately that his chickens were really pigeons and his eggs the product of the same bird. Proceeding diplomatically, yet firmly and with patience, we at last secured a very passable mess; but we were grieved to notice that as the table improved, the snowy robes of the great six-foot native waiters as surely changed from their pristine whiteness to an indescribable dun-colour, and patchy withal. It is interesting to record that the caterer's name was Morgan, that one of his ancestors was a Welshman, and that he claimed to have been guide to sundry crowned heads of Europe in the palmier tourist days. He also dealt in scarabs and other interesting curios, as did countless other natives. We knew that these baubles were genuine, for had we not the vendors' solemn declaration to that effect, and, in addition, full particulars of the tomb or temple or ruin from which each was obtained? In view of such affirmation, could the sceptic have the hardihood to suggest that the cunning craftsmen of Birmingham had been more intimately concerned in the production than had the long-vanished subjects of the Pharaohs?

It will be remembered that the 2nd Battalion in the "Tahiti" left the convoy at Albany. They reached Colombo on November 1st, and after a pleasant break ashore sailed again for Suez, at which port they disembarked on the 18th, and moved by rail to Aerodrome Camp. On the following evening this battalion was warned to be ready to go forward at a moment's notice for active service with the Western Frontier Force. The 1st Battalion was to have been vaccinated on the way from New Zealand, but apparently through some oversight the necessary supplies of vaccine had not been put on board. On the morning of the 19th vaccination had been carried out, and all ranks of the 1st Battalion were disgusted to find that but for this it would have been their good fortune to move instead of the 2nd, who had been through the ordeal of vaccination on the troopship.

Both battalions had brought from New Zealand full equipment for their transport sections,—waggons, harness, tools and spare parts, but no animals. Horses and chargers for the Brigade were drawn at the Aerodrome Camp on the 21st November.

On the evening of the 22nd, the 2nd Battalion left by rail for Alexandria, to join the Western Frontier Force on the line of communications in the direction of Dabaa.

Colonel E. W. C. Chaytor, C.B., assumed command of the Brigade on the 23rd, and Major M. M. Gard'ner, R.N.Z.A., took over the duties of Brigade Major from Capt. P. H. Bell. On the 26th, Lieut.-Col. Fulton returned from Alexandria, where he had been attending to the despatch of the 2nd Battalion, and resumed command of the 1st Battalion. Capt. Purdy, Acting-Adjutant, returned to his company, and Capt. P. H. Bell returned to the battalion as Adjutant.

On December 3rd, a New Zealand and Australian Reserve Brigade was formed of details from the camp at Gizeh, the command to be taken over by the Brigadier of the New Zealand Rifle Brigade in addition to his ordinary duties. The units of which it was composed were the New Zealand and the 4th, 6th and 7th Australian Training Battalions, and its special duty was the defence of Cairo in case of emergency.

On the 5th of December, Colonel Chaytor returned to A.N.Z.A.C. to command the Mounted Rifle Brigade. Lieut.-Col. Fulton assumed command of the N.Z.R.B., and of the N.Z. and A. Reserve Brigade, and Major Austin resumed command of the 1st Battalion, N.Z.R.B.

At about this time there were fears of a possible native rising, and on the 10th Brigade Headquarters received the revised scheme for the defence of Cairo if this trouble should eventuate. Orders in accordance with the plan were issued to the 1st Battalion and to the units of the Reserve Brigade, and their commanding officers instructed to reconnoitre their areas in preparation for any possible development.

The 1st Battalion received warning on the evening of December 15th that it would replace the 2/5th Devons at the Citadel of Cairo, and all preparations for the relief were well forward when, at 8 p.m. on the 16th, the orders were cancelled and replaced by fresh instructions to be ready to leave at short notice for service with the Western Frontier Force at Mersa Matruh. Orders for the move were received at mid-day on the 18th, and by 6 p.m. the complete battalion, strength 30 officers and 968 other ranks, had left for Alexandria.

During the 1st Battalion's five weeks' stay at the Aerodrome Camp much useful training was done. As it was the winter season, the heat was not unduly oppressive. The midday hours were hot, but as a rule the parades were held in the morning and evening, with a long interval in the middle of the day and early afternoon. Trench-digging by day and by night formed an important part of the work, and night advances and attacks were frequently practised. Even the process of entraining with order and speed was rehearsed on the desert, car and truck spaces being marked out on the sand.

Here we had our first experience, so often repeated in later days, of sending men for training for a short period at an Army School of Instruction, 2 officers and 40 other ranks for a course in bombing, and 2 officers and 20 other ranks for signalling being detailed on November 22nd. The Machine Gun Section also was detached for special training at the school, returning to battalion on 4th December.

Route marches, gradually increasing in length, had a fine effect in hardening the men after their long sea voyage. These, too, were made interesting as far as possible. Often they were planned so that halts should take place near a New Zealand or an Australian hospital. The band would play outside the building, and the men were given an opportunity to meet friends and acquaintances within. Amongst the interesting points visited in this way were the finer portions of Heliopolis and Zeitoun, Napoleon's Towers on the Suez Road, Old Heliopolis, the Virgin's Well, and the companion obelisk to Cleopatra's Needle, still standing at Matarieh. As often as the Regimental Band could be spared it was sent to the various hospitals, and to the Esbekieh Gardens and the New Zealand Y.M.C.A. establishment in Cairo; and the many expressions of thanks received indicated a keen appreciation of services gladly rendered. The temporary effects of vaccination somewhat interfered with the work, but eventually when the battalion marched out of camp for their first taste of active service all ranks were in a better state of fitness than they had ever been.

CHAPTER II.
THE SENUSSI CAMPAIGN.

PART 1.—GENERAL.

The Senussi sect—Senussi unrest—Enemy influence—Commencement of hostilities—Enemy strength—Western Frontier Force.

The Senussi sect may be described as the Puritans of the Moslems. The doctrine of its founder, Sidi Mohammed ben Ali es Senussi, who was born in Algeria in 1787 and completed his education at Mecca, was the Koranic Law in its original simplicity as delivered by the Prophet. He rapidly gained a religious following throughout the north of Africa from Tunis to Egypt, and even in Arabia, and from one end to the other of this great stretch of country he established zawias or monasteries for the propagation of the pure principles of the faith. He eventually settled in the Benghazi district, or Cyrenaica, the area just beyond Egypt's western frontier. Sidi Mohammed died in 1859 and was succeeded by his son Mohammed el Mahdi, whose reputation for sanctity and power extended throughout the whole of northern Africa, the Soudan and Arabia, and was not unknown in Europe. On the death of Mohammed el Mahdi in 1902, his nephew, Ahmed el Sherif, a grandson of the founder, was elected to the headship of the sect, his own eldest son, Sidi Mohammed Idris, being then a minor. The new ruler was known as Sayed Ahmed, or more commonly as The Senussi.

Though begun as an ascetic religious confraternity, the Senussi brotherhood has expanded and developed from a loose association of tribes to a dynastic entity with a mercantile and political influence not less important than that of any other people in Northern Africa. The rise of The Senussi to temporal power came with the war waged between Italy and Turkey in Tripoli, which lies just to the west of Cyrenaica. Through the influence of Enver Pasha, Commander-in-Chief of the Turkish forces in Tripoli, The Senussi was induced to cooperate with the Turks against the Italians. On the withdrawal of the Turkish forces from Tripoli and Cyrenaica he considered himself the virtual ruler of these districts, and, as such, continued the struggle with Italy. In his efforts he had the assistance of several Turkish officers who remained behind after the declaration of peace.

Sayed Ahmed was not personally anti-British. He had established friendly relations with Egypt, and his cousin and agent, who lived at Alexandria, was held in high regard by Europeans and Egyptians alike. The Senussi's disapproval of the Mahdist movement in Eastern Soudan won for him the approval of the Sirdar, Sir Reginald Wingate. General surprise, therefore, not unmixed with some consternation, was felt when it was announced in November, 1915, that it had been necessary to withdraw the Egyptian garrisons from western frontier posts, and when it was learned that shortly afterwards Western Egypt was invaded by a considerable force of Arabs, Turks and Berbers, under Sayed Ahmed, augmented by some thousands of Egyptian Bedouin. The danger of an invasion of Egypt from Syria had been foreseen, but the menace from the Senussi movement was much more serious than the Turkish attempt from the Sinai Peninsula to cross the Canal, for trouble on the Western Frontier might easily lead to serious religious and internal disorders.

The invasion is directly traceable to Turco-German influence. Signs that pressure on The Senussi to move against Egypt was begininng to take effect were first apparent in May, 1915. During the previous month Gaafar Pasha, described as "a Germanized Turk of considerable ability," had arrived in Cyrenaica with large supplies of arms and ammunition. There he joined Nury Bey, the half-brother of Enver Pasha, leader of the Turkish party in Cyrenaica. Later, a number of Turks and Germans gained access to the country by means of disguise. In June the French captured in the Eastern Mediterranean a sailing-boat flying the Greek flag, provided with false papers, and carrying a party of Turks whose luggage consisted of valuable presents for Sayed Ahmed. From the German Kaiser was sent, in a handsome embossed casket, a letter to The Senussi couched in the usual bombastic terms, extolling his own virtues as the protector of Islam and inciting to war against "the infidels." This was followed by another from the same source, asking Sayed Ahmed to declare a Holy War in Egypt.

On November 5th, 1915, H.M. auxiliary cruiser "Tara" was torpedoed off Sollum by the German submarine U35. On the following day an enemy submarine shelled the Egyptian post at Sollum, and of the two small coastguard cruisers in the harbour, one, the "Abbas," was sunk at her moorings, and the other, the "Noor el Bahr," badly damaged. On November 7th the British horse-transport "Moorina" was sunk off the Cyrenaican coast. The camp at Sollum was sniped on November 15th; on the 17th the zawia at Barrani, fifty miles within the frontier, was occupied by the Senussi regulars; and next day the coatstguard barracks at the same station were attacked.

The garrisons of Sollum were withdrawn to Matruh, but not without the loss of 12 native officers, two cadets, and 120 of other ranks, all of the Egyptian Coastguard Camel Corps. These treacherously seceded to the enemy, taking with them 176 camels.

The available enemy force at the commencement of hostilities was probably not less than 20,000. It had a nucleus of Turkish troops and a number of Turkish, German and Arab officers. The main formation consisted of the Senussi Regulars, or muhafzia, thirteen companies of well-disciplined men, numbering in all 3,370. These wore a uniform of khaki faced with red or green, and puttees, while the irregulars, who varied in number from time to time, were attired in the characteristic native dress. In the event of a successful advance into Egypt the total strength would have rapidly increased. The Senussi were known to possess nine mountain-guns, ten mitrailleuses, and six field-guns, all captured from the Italians; but they were reported to have had other field pieces as well as machine-guns landed from German submarines. Of guns of an older pattern, they had the two Egyptian Army 9 cm. Krupp guns abandoned at Sollum, and two Turkish Mantelli 8.7 cm. movable fortress guns. They were well supplied with Turkish, German and Italian rifles, and had abundance of ammunition. The force contained a considerable number of mounted troops, and the supply of camels for transport was practically unlimited. The Commander-in-Chief was Nury Pasha, but Gaafar Pasha was usually in immediate command of any operating column.

Orders for the formation of a Western Frontier Force

were issued on November 20th, 1915, and Major-General A. Wallace, C.B., was appointed to the command.

The original composition of the force was as under:—

MOUNTED BRIGADE.
> Brigadier-General Tyndale Biscoe, Commanding.
> 3 Composite Yeomanry Regiments from the 2nd Mounted Division, and comprising details from more than twenty different regiments.
> 1 Composite Regiment of Australian Light Horse, made up of details from Australian Light Horse Brigades.
> Notts. Battery of Royal Horse Artillery (Territorial Force) and Ammunition Column.

INFANTRY BRIGADE.
> Brigadier-General Lord Lucan, Commanding.
> 1 Battalion 1/6th Royal Scots (Territorials).
> 1 Battalion 2/7th Middlesex Regiment (Territorials).
> 1 Battalion 2/8th Middlesex Regiment (Territorials).
> 1 Battalion 15th Sikhs.
> 1 Squadron Royal Flying Corps.
> Divisional Train from the 1st Australian Division.

A detachment from the Egyptian Army Military Works Department took the place of the Royal Engineers, none of the latter being available.

The composition of the force was constantly changing, and it was not till the middle of February, 1916, that it became really fixed.

PART 2.—THE 2ND BATTALION ON THE LINE OF COMMUNICATIONS.

> Lieut.-Col. A. E. Stewart in command—Troops—Dispositions—A monotonous service—Return to Alexandria—Move to Moascar.

The 2nd Battalion arrived at Quamaria Camp, Alexandria, on the night of 22/23rd November. On the following day Lieut.-Col. A. E. Stewart was appointed to command the Line of Communications from Alexandria westward towards Mersa Matruh.

In addition to the 2/N.Z.R.B., Lieut.-Col. Stewart had under his command the following details:—A squadron of the Royal Naval Armoured Car Division (afterwards sent to Matruh); 150 men of the Bikaner Camel Corps, with an Egyptian

Army Machine Gun Section; an armoured train, manned by a detachment of the 1/10th Gurkha Rifles, with two 12½ pounders of the Egyptian Army Artillery and two searchlights; and, for a time, a company of the 15th Sikhs.

The Mariut Railway, a broad-gauge line approximately 100 miles in length, runs westward along the Mediterranean coast. A narrow-gauge line had been partially constructed from rail-head at El Dabaa to Bir Fuka, some 30 miles further on, but at this time the rails had been removed. A motorable road, the remains of an ancient Roman highway, runs from El Dabaa right on to Sollum on the western frontier, and passes through Matruh, which is about 90 miles west of El Dabaa.

Lieut.-Col. Stewart established his headquarters at El Dabaa, and by the 25th November the 2nd Battalion, now under the immediate command of Major R. St. J. Beere, was disposed along the line from Alexandria to the rail-head.

Posts were established at the following points:—Sidi Mergheb (near Alexandria), Amria, Hawaria, El Ghirbaniat. El Roweisat, El Alamein, El Gazel, Jemeima, Abd El Kader, Ikingi Mariut, Bahig, El Hammam, El Omeiyid, Sidi Abd El Rahman, and El Dabaa.* These were either at railway stations or in the vicinity of the larger native villages, and the garrisons varied in strength from one officer and 24 other ranks at less important points, to 12 officers and 300 other ranks at rail-head.

The garrisons immediately set to work to put their posts into a state of defence, and to lay in supplies of food, water and ammunition. The materials used for walls and breastworks consisted either of loose and quarried rock or of sandbags, according to the nature of the country. An admirable rivalry sprang up amongst the various garrisons, which stimulated the men to extraordinary exertions, and in a few days each post became a veritable stronghold.

As time wore on, however, the men's enthusiasm waned. They had come out west full of hopes of an early conflict with the invaders, but they were disappointed to find nothing more exciting to relieve the monotony than the ordinary patrolling

*The spelling of place-names varies. "G" and "J," for instance, are practically interchangeable, and the "Q" of the ordinary Egyptian survey maps is on the War Office maps written either "G" or "K," according to the local pronunciation. Thus we have Gemaima or Jemeima, Baqqush or Baggush, Majid or Merjid, or even Mergid.

into the desert, the capture of an occasional suspected spy, the stopping and bringing in of suspicious-looking caravans, and the passing of mounted troops, artillery and transport bound for Matruh. Even the novelty of the conditions and the natural curiosity regarding the country and its inhabitants began to pall, and especially so when sand-colic became prevalent. Perhaps the most exciting incident was that experienced by the garrison of a newly-established post at the village of Hammam. In the dusk of the evening of the first day on duty, streams of men and beasts of burden appeared to be converging on the post from all points of the horizon. Later on, camp-fires gleamed on every side, and the officer in command of the post came to the conclusion that the end of all things was at hand. After standing to arms all night, the men of the little garrison were somewhat relieved in the morning to find that the sudden growth of population in the neighbourhood was merely the accompaniment to the holding of the periodic and peaceful market, warning of which had not reached the post.

At the beginning of December the company of 15th Sikhs was sent westward to establish posts at the wells of Gerab, Baggush and Jerawala, on the road to Matruh. The garrisons of these, however, were withdrawn by the middle of the month, and later on the Sikhs rejoined their regiment, which had gone to Matruh by sea.

Definite reports were received from time to time of concentrations of Bedouin in the vicinity of the Line of Communications, but no attacks thereon eventuated. The most important of these camps was that of Sayed Harun, located near Baggush, but this, as will be seen, was dealt with by a column from Matruh at the end of December.

There was much satisfaction when, on December 19th, the battalion was warned that it would probably be relieved within the next few days. On that date, Lieut.-Col. Ferguson-Davie, of the 54th Sikhs, took over command of the Line of Communications, and on the 28th the various posts were relieved by troops of the 54th Division. The 2/N.Z.R.B., on relief, went by rail to Quamaria Camp, Alexandria, to rest and refit. Having now returned to Brigade, the battalion was inspected by the Brigadier on 1st January, 1916, and again on the 14th The battalion took over from the 2nd Composite Regiment of

Infantry the defence of the Mariut Canal from the 12th to the 17th January, "D" Company, under Capt. A. Digby-Smith, being despatched to hold all railway and traffic bridges over the Canal. The battalion was relieved of this duty by the 1st Battalion of the South African Brigade, and on the 18th January moved from Alexandria to Ismailia, and was quartered at Moascar Camp.

PART 3.—THE 1ST BATTALION AT MERSA MATRUH.

From Alexandria to Mersa Matruh by sea—Mersa Matruh—Earlier engagements of the Western Frontier Force—1st Battalion's baptism of fire, the fight at Wadi Majid, Christmas Day, 1915—On column to Bir Zarka—Church parade—Command, Lieut.-Col. Fulton — Duties, rest, training — Halazin fight — Arrivals and departures—Inspection by General Maxwell—On column towards Sollum—Um Rakham—Return to Matruh—Note on completion of campaign—Return to Alexandria—Move to Moascar.

On the arrival of the 1st Battalion at Gabarri Camp siding, Alexandria, on the night of 18th/19th December, it was found that no transport had been detailed to move the baggage, and that at the camp only a few tents had been pitched for us. These difficulties were eventually surmounted, however, but the men were not settled down before 4 a.m. Again, on going to Western Frontier Force Headquarters to report during the forenoon, as instructed, the commanding officer found the rooms empty, and no information appeared to be available, except that apparently the whole of the staff had moved to Mersa Matruh. The Embarkation Officer, who had been sufficiently busy elsewhere, came at about noon with instructions to the effect that part of the Battalion was to be sent away by sea in the evening, and by 4.30 p.m. "B" and "C" Companies had left for Matruh in H.M.S. "Clematis" and two or three trawlers. At 5 p.m. on the following day, "A" Company embarked on the "Missir," and about the same time on the 21st, "D" Company (less one platoon) and Battalion Headquarters (less Machine Gun, Transport, Signal and Stretcher-bearer Sections) departed on the "Noor El Bahr."

The gunboat and the tiny traders and trawlers were packed to their full capacity, and there was barely room to turn. As in each case the journey was made at night, it had few interesting features beyond those attaching to the sights of the harbour of Alexandria as we passed out in the early evening, and to the unusual nature of the country that came into view with the dawn of the following day as we approached Mersa Matruh. There was, of course, the ever-present possibility of an encounter with a submarine. The "Clematis," indeed, received en route a wireless message that a U-boat had been sighted off Matruh, but no untoward incident marred the voyage.

Mersa Matruh* is a village lying near the shore of a little bay about a mile and a half long from east to west, and half a mile broad. The harbour and anchorage are good, completely sheltered from seawards by rocks which extend from each side of the bay, and may be used by steamers up to 1,000 tons. It is the first landing-place west of Alexandria, from which city it is distant about 200 miles. There is no wharf, but for military purposes an anchored barge was made use of as an improvised landing-stage. A fort stands on a rocky ridge and overlooks both the harbour and the open water of the Mediterranean. The shores of the harbour are of snow-white sand. The village lies beyond an outcrop of limestone and in the neighbourhood of a tiny oasis. Its population in pre-war days numbered about 200, mainly Greeks and Italians. The camps of the various units of the Frontier Force located here were spread out between the shore and a low, sandy, limestone ridge, some 1500 yards inland, along the crest of which ran part of the outpost line. To the east of the bay, on the hard sand between the harbour and a lagoon, stood canvas aeroplane hangars.

Owing to the precarious state of the lines of communication, all frontier and desert posts must to a great extent be self-contained and self-supporting. Mersa Matruh, which was selected as the British advanced base for the operations against the Senussi Moslems and their supporters, was no exception, for though it had two lines of communication, neither of these was secure. El Dabaa, at the head of the railway from Alexandria, was nearly 90 miles away, and the connecting road was too long and too exposed for use as a means of supply. Dur-

*Strictly speaking, Mersa Matruh is the name of the harbour, Mersa meaning "anchorage."

ing our stay at Matruh, the road was used only by motor vehicles and mounted troops, and that only occasionally. The main line of communication was by sea, but Alexandria, the nearest port to the eastward, was very far away, and interruption through storms or submarine attacks was an ever-present possibility.

To meet the contingencies due to its isolation, and to ensure efficient all-round defence, a chain of outposts numbering 13 in all was constructed to cover the harbour, village and encampments. From the western entrance of the harbour, where No. 1 outpost was situated, this line ran southwards to the limestone ridge, and then eastwards along its crest to the El Dabaa road, where it turned again towards the coast, ending at No. 13 outpost, some 400 yards from the Coastguard Station at the entrance. The whole system was further protected by barbed wire entanglements. Each outpost consisted of a sangar of rough rock walls enclosing an area of some 200 square yards, in which place were shelters improvised from the very scanty material obtainable. The complete outer system was admirably sited, and formed a typical example of fortification capable of withstanding attacks by an enemy who depends mainly on the rifle. Surrounding the Force Headquarters, the ordnance and supply depots, and the main encampment, was an inner line of defence consisting of smaller rock and sandbag posts. This line also was heavily wired. The necessary patrolling beyond the outposts was carried out mainly by the mounted troops, while an aeroplane made periodical reconnoitring flights far out across the desert. A gunboat was usually present in the harbour, the equipment of the fort on the headland was augmented, and a Krupp gun was placed in the outpost line itself.

The supply of water for a large force was a difficult matter. In the village there were some six wells, and at Bir Farag*, on the eastern outskirts, a group of two or three others, but the yield was limited, and the greater part of our drinking water was canal-water brought from Alexandria by sea. Occasionally, owing to shipping interruptions, the daily

*A bir, or ber, is an underground cistern cut in the rock and filled by rainfall. A well fed by an underground spring, such as those at Matruh, is called a "sania," but the use of the word "bir" as part of a place-name is an indication of the presence of a water-source of any kind.

EL DABAA.

Copyright, Rev. A. G. Parham, M.C.

BEDOUIN PRISONERS.

Copyright, Rev. A. G. Parham, M.C.   *Face p. 32.*

DISEMBARKING AT MERSA MATRUH.
Copyright, Rev. A. G. Parham, M.C.

THE COMPOUND AT FORCE HEADQUARTERS, MATRUH.
N.Z.R.B. Camp in the distance.

ration, already sufficiently meagre, was cut down, but the installation of a condenser subsequently effected a general improvement. For animals, brackish water was obtained from hessis, which were holes dug in the sands of the beach.

The country inland is rocky, but interspersed with patches of a peculiar hard, brown, clayey soil, said to produce the finest barley in the world. Such roads as exist in the neighbourhood have been made by simply removing the loose stones from the surface of the ground. The coastal strip is subject to occasional heavy rainstorms, as we learned from bitter experience. The camp of the 1st Battalion was twice flooded out, and on one expedition in particular we found that, after rain, marching was exceedingly difficult, and the strength and patience of the men were tried almost to breaking point by the repeated calls to extricate cars and transport waggons from the mud. Wild vegetation is scarce, and beyond a few dry flower-stems and roots of scrubby thorns sufficient to boil a mess-tin of water, the country produces no fuel.

Scattered over the countryside are many evidences of past occupation by a considerable population. One finds here and there fragments of sculptured pillars, dating back to Græco-Roman times; while large mounds of red pottery refuse mark the sites of kilns belonging to a still more ancient period. Antiquarians had quite recently been at work at various points in the district, and they were reported to have made many valuable finds, including some beautiful statues and vases discovered in the caves of a neighbouring wadi. Matruh is the ancient Parætonium, and was one of Cleopatra's favourite pleasure resorts; and during the stay of the 1st Battalion at the station the remains of her villa were found and partially uncovered. If legend is to be believed, it was at Mersa Matruh that Alexander the Great landed on his way to the Oasis of Siwa to consult the oracle there before founding the town of Alexandria.

General Wallace transferred his headquarters from Alexandria to Matruh on December 7th, 1915, and four days later had his first encounter with Senussi forces. From five to six miles south of Matruh is a tableland some 300 feet high, dropping to the coastal strip in a steep escarpment. The outline of the plateau is irregular, and ten miles to the west of the station it is only two miles from the sea. Intersecting the escarpment at right angles are numerous dry, rocky watercourses, miles in length, and having extremely steep sides. In one or other of these deep, gullies, known as "wadis," the enemy would establish his temporary stronghold. He had been located at Wadi Senaab, eight miles to the westward, and on December 11th a column moved out to attack him. The Yeomanry, aided by a squadron of Australian Light Horse, inflicted over a hundred casualties and cleared the wadi, the British losses being slight. The force, which included the Sikhs, camped on the ground won, and spent the following day rounding up prisoners.

Being reinforced by the Royal Scots, the column started again on the 13th for a spot twelve miles further west, to engage the enemy, but in crossing Wadi Shaifa was itself attacked by a force of 1,200. The enemy was defeated, leaving 180 dead. He was pursued till dark, when the column returned to Matruh.

The Senussi forces began to concentrate again, this time in the vicinity of Jebel Medwa, a prominent hill some eight miles to the south-west of Matruh. From air reconnaissance and other sources the enemy strength here was estimated to have reached in the course of a week the number of about 5,000 men, of whom more than half were muhafzia, or regular soldiers, with four guns and some machine-guns, the whole being under the command of Gaafar Pasha. It had become evident that the force at the disposal of General Wallace was not sufficiently strong in numbers both to hold Matruh and at the same time to bring the enemy to a decisive engagement, and it was in response to a request for reinforcements that the 1st Battalion of the New Zealand Rifle Brigade had been despatched from Cairo, together with a battery of the Honourable Artillery Company and two four-inch naval guns.

We were warned on December 23rd of an impending operation in which we were to take part. The adjutant, quartermaster, machine-gun officer, transport officer, and signalling officer were still at Alexandria, and upon the shoulders of Capt. Purdy, the acting-adjutant, there now fell a very great deal of extra work. Having no transport with us, we were instructed to make the best arrangements possible with the 1/6th Royal Scots and the 2/7th Middlesex for the loan of horses and vehicles. These arrangements proved somewhat vexatious and unsatisfactory, but we were finally helped out of our difficulty through the kind offices of Major Francis, commanding the Australian Train. The only chargers obtainable were those for the commanding officer and the adjutant. These were neither ornamental nor useful, Capt. Purdy's horse being particularly impossible, and both were, without regret, abandoned to the grooms long before the engagement was over. Fortunately the machine-gun officer with the personnel of his section arrived at Matruh on the eve of the battle, but his work next day was greatly hampered by the many defects that became apparent in the borrowed limber-teams as they negotiated the steep slopes of the rough wadi-country.

Definite orders for the morrow's operations were not received until about noon on Christmas Eve, and the companies being engaged at construction work on the outpost line, these orders were not communicated to the men until evening. All ranks were very fit and keen, and the prospect of a fight aroused the utmost enthusiasm.

As this was to be our baptism of fire, it will be of interest to record in detail the operation orders for the action in which we were to participate.

OPERATION ORDERS

By

MAJOR-GENERAL A. WALLACE, C.B.,

Commanding Western Frontier Force.

Reference Map: Mersa Matruh,
Africa 1/250,000.   24th December, 1915.
Matruh Sheet.

1. The following troops will move to-morrow to operate against the enemy force now occupying WADI MAJID and neighbourhood.

2. The left column, under Brigadier-General Tyndale Biscoe, will move via the WADI TOWEIWIA and thence westward.

TROOPS.
        Australian Light Horse, 3 squadrons.
        D.L.O. Yeomanry, 3 squadrons.
        Yeomanry Machine Gun Section.
        Notts R.H.A. (less one section).

PER MACHINE GUN:

	With M.G. Section.	In Section Reserve.	In Bde. Amm. Col.	Total per gun.
Yeomanry	3,500	16,000	—	⎫
Infantry, T.F.,				⎬ 19,500
N.Z.R.B. ...	3,500	8,000	8,000	⎭
Indian Infantry	6,000	4,000	8,000	18,000

AMMUNITION.

2. Infantry will complete to 200 rounds per man before moving into action.

AMMUNITION.

3. A Brigade S.A.A. Column will be formed under command of Lieut. Chaplin, Australian A.S.C., consisting of Infantry Regimental Reserve S.A.A. carried in vehicles.

	Vehicles.		Rounds
	G.S. Limbered Wagons.	G.S. Wagons.	carried.
5 G.S. Limbered Wagons per Brit. & N.Z. Regt. ..	10	—	160,000
3 G.S. Wagons per Indian Regt. ..	—	3	75,000

With this unit will move 9 rank and file per regiment.

AMMUNITION.

4. All other regimental infantry ammunition wagons will join this column after troops move into action. Empty wagons will not be sent back to camp without orders from the O.C. Brigade Ammunition Column.

AMMUNITION.

5. The Notts R.H.A. Ammunition Column will remain a separate formation and will carry:
   50 rounds per gun and
   180 rounds per rifle
in 2 ammunition wagons and 8 G.S. limbered wagons respectively.

RATIONS.

6. The remainder of the current day's rations will be carried on the person, and one day's ration per man will be carried in the train.

WATER.

7. A total of half a gallon per man will be carried in the train. None will be carried for horses.

EQUIPMENT: INFANTRY.

8. Packs must be made as light as possible. Only the greatcoat is to be carried therein.

WATER AND EXPLOSIVES UNITS.

9. Special water and explosives units have been organized and will accompany the column. They will be commanded by Capt. Eaton and Lieut. Wilson respectively.

SCALE OF AMMUNITION FOR R.N.A.C.D.

10. Per Machine Gun, 3000 rounds.
Per Rifle, 100 rounds.

(Signed) H. W. TOBIN,
Captain, General Staff.

Copies to, etc.

General Wallace's force moved out before daylight on Christmas morning.

The plan of attack was for the right column to advance directly on Jebel Medwa, the left column to make a wide detour southward round the right flank of the enemy to deny his retreat to the west. H.M.S. "Clematis" stood off-shore to assist with gunfire as occasion offered.

By 5 a.m. the right column was on the move south-west along the Khedival Motor Road. The Bucks Hussars formed the screen, and were followed by the 15th Sikhs, who provided the advance guard. The 1/N.Z.R.B. was next in order, and supplied right and left flank guards to the infantry.

At about 6 a.m. the enemy gave warning of our approach by means of a flare on one of the sandhills, and half an hour later the advance guard came under artillery fire from the south-west. The Sikhs immediately shook out into artillery formation, and the 1/N.Z.R.B. was ordered to conform to their movements, bring in the flank guards, and detail one platoon as escort to the guns. Advanced elements of the Senussi were pushed back by the leading sections of the Sikhs, and by 7.15 a.m. our main body had crossed the Wadi Ramleh.

The enemy was now discovered occupying in strength an escarpment about a mile south of Jebel Medwa, and at 7.30 a.m. the Sikhs were ordered to attack the enemy on his right flank, the Bucks Hussars and 2/8th Middlesex to co-operate by a containing attack along his front. West of the road the Sikhs came under rifle and machine-gun fire, but their advance was not checked. They moved steadily forward in extended order, the 1/N.Z.R.B. following in artillery formation for a distance of about a mile. The Middlesex men were soon able to occupy Jebel Medwa, and the right flank was thus secured. The section of the Notts Battery came into action on the high ground near the road 2000 yards east of Jebel Medwa and silenced the enemy's artillery, and at 7.45 a.m. H.M.S. "Clematis" opened an accurate and useful fire, her shooting being "spotted" by our aeroplane.

In the nullahs of the Wadi Medwa the Sikhs met with considerable opposition, and our "A" Company (Major W. Kay) was sent forward to prolong the firing-line on the left flank. At 9.30 a.m. "B" Company (Capt. E. Puttick) also reinforced the line, going in on the right of the Sikhs, and by ten o'clock the Wadi Medwa was cleared.

The advance now continued across the rock-strewn ground beyond, and the guns were soon afterwards brought forward to the western side of the wadi, with "C" and "D" Companies (Captains J. Pow and J. R. Cowles), in reserve under cover behind the guns.

At 11 a.m., the left column could be seen operating about two miles to the south-west, and being communicated with by signal, it changed direction northwards along the Wadi Majid.

At the second gun position some casualties to the personnel of the artillery and Col. Gordon's staff details were caused by the fire of a party of the enemy that had crept round to a position on a ridge beyond the nullah on our left. A platoon of "D" Company, under Lieut. H. Holderness, was despatched to clear up this locality, an operation attended by no little difficulty, and one exceedingly interesting to watch by those in the vicinity of the guns, for they were able to follow the movements of both parties while each was frequently invisible to the other. The platoon, admirably handled, successfully accomplished its mission and left no one to cause further annoyance from this quarter.

By noon "C" and "D" Companies and the four machine-guns were sent into the firing-line, extending it to the right, and the work of clearing out the many branching nullahs at the head of Wadi Majid was carried on, the whole line moving forward slowly but surely. Much delay in getting the Vickers guns up was caused by the unsatisfactory nature of the borrowed teams for the limbers, and Lieut. J. A. D. Hopkirk, who was in command of the section, found it necessary to employ all his men at the exhausting work of assisting the teams in order to get the limbers sufficiently far forward over the rock-strewn country to enable him to bring the guns into action.

Our battalion was held up for some time by hot rifle and machine-gun fire from a donga running forward at right angles from the main enemy position, two companies, with the Sikhs, being on one side of this, and two companies on the other. The line was somewhat long and thin, and at 2.30 p.m. Col. Gordon gave instructions for part of the left to be withdrawn and pushed into the centre. For this purpose "A" Company was brought round through a donga from the left of the Sikhs to their right, thus joining up with "B" Company, which was then engaged in driving the forward parties of the enemy from the branch donga referred to above. The enemy's position here was held with great tenacity, and "B" Company's task was not accomplished without considerable difficulty.

It now became evident that the enemy's stronghold was the edge of the main wadi towards our right front, along which he occupied an entrenched position, and at this stage the Sikhs were withdrawn, apparently so as not to hamper the movements of the mounted troops, who had now come into action on the high ground beyond that section of the wadi immediately opposite the Sikhs. The situation being clear and definite, all four companies advanced by steady rushes across the intermediate stretch of plateau, a platoon of "B" Company making sure of the awkward branch donga, and soon after 4 p.m. the final position was taken. A company of the Middlesex Battalion had come up in the rear of our right company, but their aid was not required.

The mopping-up of the wadi was done with thoroughness, and by the time it was completed fully 100 enemy dead were left in the trenches, caves and hollows. Disorganized groups of the Senussi, forestalling the action of our mounted troops, made good their escape through the seaward end of the wadi or over the ridge to the west. Some 34 prisoners were taken, however, while 80 camels and a number of asses, sheep and goats found in the stronghold were destroyed, and about 30.000 rounds of small-arms ammunition, with three cases of nine-pounder shells, were brought away and buried.

While the clearing of the wadi was in progress we received orders to return to Jebel Medwa as soon as this duty was completed, and accompanying these instructions was the intimation that the remainder of the force had already left the field. It was after 5 p.m. before the battalion was reformed, and the return march, which had to be carried out in the dark over strange country intersected by a maze of nullahs, and with no guide or suitable map, proved a difficult and trying task. We had several of our own and enemy wounded to bring in, and as we were now short of stretchers, a whole platoon had to be detailed to attend to this problem alone. Thanks largely to the good management and untiring efforts of the medical officer, Capt. G. V. Bogle, and Lieut. N. L. Macky and Corporal W. McNab, all difficulties in this connection were finally overcome. In addition, we were hampered by the slow movement of the machine-gun limbers whose teams had made such a poor showing during the hours of daylight. However, the bivouac camp at Jebel Medwa was reached at last, and here we rested under the stars until four o'clock next morning, when the column moved off again for Matruh.

The total casualties during the day were 14 rank and file killed, and 3 officers and 47 other ranks wounded. The enemy lost 370 dead and 82 prisoners. Amongst the booty were the office and personal effects of Gaafar Pasha, abandoned by him in his flight. The casualties of our battalion numbered 6 killed* and 14 wounded. The dead were brought in and buried in the little military cemetery at Matruh, the officers of the battalion acting as bearers, and before we left the station permanent memorials were erected over their graves.

In his despatch regarding this action, General Maxwell, Commanding the Forces in Egypt, specially mentions Lieut.-Col. Gordon, commanding the right column; and the 15th Sikhs and the 1st Battalion, with their respective temporary commanding officers, Major Evans and Major Austin. Mention is also made of Quartermaster-Sergeant A. L. McCormick, Corpl. R. Lepper and Rifleman T. Nimmo, for distinguished conduct

*These, the first of our Glorious Dead, were: Sergeant-Major R. C. Purkis, Sergeant S. F. Weir, Corporal A. Woollatt, Corporal E. C. Beresford-Wilkinson, Rifleman T. F. York, and Rifleman J. M. Todd. Of the wounded, Rifleman E. N. Davis died before the year had ended.

under fire. Of the New Zealanders, it was said: "This was the first time the men of the 1st Battalion had been in action, but they fought with the steadiness of seasoned troops." All ranks were pleased to have from Colonel Gordon personally his expressions of praise of the battalion's work, and from His Excellency the Honorary Colonel the following message: "Best congratulations to the New Zealand Rifle Brigade on their first action. Trust wounded are doing well."

The immediate result of the action was the retirement of The Senussi with his staff and the remains of his force to Unjeila and Halazin, some twenty-five miles to the west, and subsequent events show that the Christmas Day fight was the turning-point in the campaign that ultimately brought about his downfall.

Monday, 27th December, was a day of rest, but towards evening there were rumours that the battalion was to go out on column again. On the 28th orders were received for a march, at 2 p.m. of the same day, to Bir Jerawala (Gerowle), twelve miles to the south-east, to operate against a hostile force under Sayed Harun, then threatening the Line of Communications between Matruh and Dabaa.

The mobile column consisted of a detachment of the Royal Naval Armoured Car Division, 6 squadrons of Royal Bucks Hussars, a section each of the Notts R.H.A. and "A" Battery of the H.A.C., the 1/N.Z.R.B., 15th Sikhs, 2/7th Middlesex (less two companies), Force Signalling Section, Ammunition Column, 1st South Midland and 137th Indian Field Ambulances, a Water Section and the Australian Train, and was commanded by Brigadier-General the Earl of Lucan.

The force arrived at Bir Jerawala at 7 p.m. and bivouacked there. At midnight orders were issued for a continuance of the march on the 29th, and at 5 a.m. the column was on the move for Bir Zarka, some nine miles farther to the south, where we expected to meet the enemy. Failing to get touch with him here, we went on five miles beyond Bir Zarka and halted. It became evident that the hostile force had taken alarm and had cleared away in haste; and as it was impossible to pursue farther, we were compelled to commence the return march, taking with us as booty one month's supplies, 400 sheep, 90 camels and 200 tents abandoned by Harun. We bivouacked at Bir Zarka on the night of 29th/30th, reached

Jerawala at 10 a.m. on the 30th, where we rested till 2 p.m., and then marched in to Matruh, reaching camp at 7.30 p.m.

This expedition was an extremely arduous one. The country was exceedingly trying, low-lying stretches of loose sand alternating with rock-strewn tablelands, and in the anxiety to get on to the heels of Sayed Harun's force the customary halts were frequently dispensed with. There were several march casualties, even the hardy, seasoned Sikhs finding the strain almost unbearable.

On New Year's Day, Capt. Purdy, with his old platoon of "C" Company, together with the adjutant and medical officer, and an escort of Australian Light Horse and two armoured cars, went out at 6 a.m. to Wadi Majid to bring in the body of Corporal Beresford-Wilkinson, who had been killed in the Christmas Day fight while endeavouring to get a wounded comrade under cover. All our casualties of that day had been safely brought in with this exception. On going forward from the position Beresford-Wilkinson's companions had hastily covered the body, but later, in the darkness of evening, had not been able to locate the spot. Owing to the risks entailed, permission to send out our party was granted by Force Headquarters with some misgivings, but the mission was accomplished without mishap. The party returned at 5 p.m., and the body was buried in the military cemetery beside those of his comrades.

On Sunday, 2nd January, the battalion attended the Force Church Parade in the coastguard barrack square, Force Headquarters being present. Rain fell on the 3rd, 4th and 5th, gradually increasing in quantity until finally part of the camp was inundated and had to be shifted to higher ground.

The hospital-ship "Rasheed" arrived on January 8th, and two days later sailed again for Alexandria with sick and wounded.

The instruments having come to hand from Alexandria, the band played a programme in camp on the 8th, to the great delight of everyone, and on the following day, Sunday, headed the battalion in its march to church parade, where it accompanied the singing of the hymns.

In accordance with Brigade Orders, Lieut.-Col. Fulton arrived on the evening of January 9th, and resumed command of the battalion. Capt. Bell had already reported on December

26th and taken up the duties of adjutant again, Capt. Purdy returning to "C" Company.

From 2nd January until the 21st the battalion was employed on outpost duty, supplied parties for construction work on the outpost line or at the landing-stage, or was engaged in training and route-marching. During this period a column, of which we did not form a part, went out in the direction of Baggush. It failed to gain touch with the enemy, but brought in a very large number of camels. We opened our first regimental canteen on the 11th of January, and did a brisk trade in goods brought from Alexandria; and on the 15th held our first camp concert, the performers being our own men, volunteers from the neighbouring Middlesex camp, and the battalion band. Many similar entertainments were given in the various camps, but perhaps the one best remembered was that held at Force Headquarters, by a combined party of New Zealanders and Australians, at which the "star" items were the Earl of Denbigh's French-Canadian song and his story of Waterloo.

On January 19th, 1916, aerial reconnaissance disclosed a concentration of a considerable enemy force, estimated at about 5,000, at Halazin,* 25 miles south-west of Matruh. In the encampment the tent of the Grand Senussi was recognized by the observer.

The infantry at Matruh was augmented by the arrival, on January 20th and 21st, of the 2nd Battalion, South African Brigade, and on the 22nd an attacking force moved out at 3.30 p.m. under the personal command of General Wallace. The 1/N.Z.R.B. was the leading battalion of the main body, which reached Bir Shola (16 miles) at 8.30 p.m. Here the force bivouacked for the night in a perimeter camp, our battalion forming the west face.† On account of the fact that a perimeter bivouac is usually established at dusk, or later, after a long day's march with possibly a fight thrown in, it seldom comes up to the ideal as set forth in the training-manuals, though the principle is carried out in effect. The infantry are extended along the four sides and are told to dig in. Outposts

*This name is incorrectly given in some maps as Hazalin.

†Here we saw for the first time the recently-invented Lewis gun, which in the days to come was to prove so effective in both attack and defence. Our new comrades, the South Africans, had four of these.

are placed from 400 to 500 yards out in front of the sides of the square, and these also dig in. They are lucky, however, if these defensive arrangements are carried out only once, for readjustments are sometimes necessary, in which case the lines may be pushed forward or drawn back, and, to the annoyance of all concerned, the digging has to be done all over again. Inside the square, the artillery, cavalry, ambulances, transport and so forth, are allotted spaces; and in sure reliance on the watchfulness of the outpost sentries the camp settles down to rest, till dawn heralds another day's trek and perchance a fight.

At 6 a.m. on the 23rd, after a night's heavy rain, the force moved out from Bir Shola on a compass bearing of 270 deg. in the direction of the enemy camp. It was disposed as under:—

RIGHT COLUMN (Lieut.-Col. J. L. R. Gordon, 15th Sikhs):
1 Squadron D.L.O. Yeomanry.
Notts Battery, R.H.A.
15th Sikhs.
2nd Battalion South African Brigade.
1st Battalion N.Z.R.B.

LEFT COLUMN (Brig.-General J. D. T. Tyndale Biscoe):
1 Squadron Australian Light Horse.
3 Squadrons Royal Bucks Hussars.
1 Squadron Dorset Yeomanry.
1 Squadron Herts Yeomanry.
Mounted Brigade Machine Gun Section.
"A" Battery H.A.C. (less one section).

RESERVE:
2 Troops Surrey Yeomanry.
1/6th Battalion Royal Scots (less two companies).
S.A.A. Column.
Detachment of Royal Naval Armoured Car Division, intended for action against the enemy's left flank.

The 1/N.Z.R.B. was the rear battalion of the right column, and found the right flank guard of a half-company and the rear guard of one company. The left column was echelonned to the left front of the right column, moving parallel to and in close touch with it. The reserve moved half a mile in rear of the right column. The train, with a half-battalion of the 2/8th Middlesex Regiment, remained parked at Bir Shola.

At 9 a.m. the right column halted for breakfast, and presently reports came in from the advanced mounted troops on the left that the enemy had been sighted about two miles ahead. At 9.40 a.m., after the march had been resumed, distant firing was heard, the covering screen having become engaged. To support these leading troops, the Bucks Hussars and the battery of the H.A.C. were now sent forward, and the advance continued steadily for some time.

At 10.30 a.m. the infantry filled up to 200 rounds, closed up its column, and the Sikhs, followed by the remaining infantry, advanced to the attack as the mounted troops uncovered the front.

By 11 a.m. the infantry column began to suffer casualties from long-range fire, and the 1st Battalion opened out into artillery formation in rear of the South Africans. A few minutes later the enemy were observed working round our right and driving in the mounted troops. To check this, our flank guard, under Capt. A. I. Walker, was pushed out to about 1,500 yards. The main attack was pressed on, and by 12 noon our battalion, coming under heavy long-range rifle and machine-gun fire, was shaken out into extended lines behind the South Africans, to whose movements we conformed. Half-an-hour later it was found necessary to reinforce the right flank guard with two more platoons and two machine-guns, and this whole company, under Captain Puttick, succeeded in driving off from that quarter an attack by some 400 of the enemy, and silencing his two machine guns. At 1 p.m. "C" Company (Capt. Pow) was sent to the left in support of the left company of the Sikhs, and was eventually brought into the firing-line there. At the same time half of "A" Company was brought forward from the rear guard to the reserve.

By 2.45 p.m. the Sikhs, South Africans and part of the New Zealand Battalion were approaching the enemy's main line of resistance, but the mounted troops on the left had not been so successful. Indeed, they had been pushed back to such an extent that by 2.30 p.m. they were occupying, with the guns of the H.A.C., a position nearly 1,000 yards in rear of the Field Ambulance. To restore the situation here, a composite company (half of "A" and half of "D"), under Major Kay, was hurried off to Force Headquarters, where it received orders from General Wallace to attack that section of the enemy, estimated to be some 250 strong, which had almost succeeded in completing its enveloping movement. A sharp fight ensued, and the enemy was at once brought to a standstill. Our men now advanced by successive rushes; the tide was turned; and by 3.30 p.m. the enemy in this quarter was driven off in disorder. The arrival of "B" Company under Capt. Puttick, which had been withdrawn for the purpose from its position on our right flank, completed the security of this point. The position for the time had been very critical, and Major Kay was personally complimented by General Wallace on his quick grasp of the situation and his prompt and thorough action in dealing with it.

In the meantime, the main attack by Colonel Gordon had progressed satisfactorily. His firing-line extended over a mile in length and had moved across ground absolutely destitute of cover, while mirage in the early stages made it impossible to locate the enemy's positions with any degree of certainty. Casualties caused by artillery and machine-guns had been somewhat severe, the enemy's fire being both rapid and accurate. Nevertheless the enemy was slowly but surely pressed back, though his retirement of nearly three miles to his main line of resistance was conducted with such great skill as to deny all efforts to come to close quarters with him.

At about 3.30 p.m., under steady pressure from our infantry, the enemy began to fall back from his main position. Soon his retirement developed into a complete rout, and by 4 p.m. he had finally fled from the field. Pursuit was out of the question. The heavy rain of the previous night had converted the whole country into a quagmire, with the result that the cavalry horses were exhausted, the armoured cars could not operate, and the supply train had not been able to advance more than three miles from Bir Shola. Orders were therefore issued that the advance was to proceed no further than the enemy's camp, which in his flight he had left standing.

Sayed Ahmed himself had left the field early. It appears that, unaware of our movements, he had decided to move south on the night of the 23rd to Siwa, where he was establishing a base for an early direct attack on Egypt. News of our advance did not reach him till after sunrise on that day, and as soon as the first shot was fired he fled westward with a small escort, leaving his main force to cover his retreat. The whole equipment of tents, rugs, camel-packs, arms, ammunition, cooking utensils, medical and general stores, was now burned or otherwise destroyed, and the force moved back some two miles

Representative South Africans, Sikhs and New Zealanders at Matruh, Lieut.-Col. Gordon in the centre, and Lieut.-Col. Fulton on the right of middle row.

Camel Transport.

A Field Dressing Station at Halazin.

Head of a Mobile Column Returning to Matruh.
Copyright, Rev. A. G. Parham, M.C.

Sergt.-Major Robert Charles Purkis, Sergeant Stanley Francis Weir, Corpora Ernest Charles Beresford-Wilkinson, Corporal Archibald Woollat, Rifleman John Mathew Todd.

Riflemen Edgar Norman Davis, Robert Greenlees Blaikie, Leslie Garnet Hookings.

THE FIRST GRAVES.

GAFAAR PASHA A PRISONER.
Copyright, Rev. A. G. Parham, M.C

to the position taken up by the field ambulance. Here the situation was somewhat serious, for the number of wounded was considerable. Under ordinary conditions most of the cases would have been despatched in the motor wagons to Matruh without delay, but owing to the deep mud it was impossible to move the vehicles. A perimeter camp was formed and sentries posted, and the troops spent a miserable night without coats, blankets, food or water, the weather being wet and bitterly cold.

On the 24th there was no sign of the enemy, and at 8 a.m. the force started on the return march to Bir Shola. Owing to the state of the ground this proved an arduous undertaking, as all wheeled vehicles had to be assisted by hand. To the New Zealanders, the rear battalion of the main body, fell the greater part of this exhausting labour. The transport of the wounded presented the greatest difficulty. They could not be taken in the ambulances, and those unable to ride had to be carried on stretchers, a severe strain upon the troops already tired out by their own exertions and a sleepless night, and still without food or water. At 2 p.m. we reached the point where the train had been parked, filled our water-bottles, and in somewhat better spirits continued the trudge to Bir Shola. Here, at 5 p.m., we bivouacked, but as it rained again during the night, and the coats and blankets were already wet, very little sleep was obtained.

On the 25th the weather cleared, and the troops marched back to Mersa Matruh, the last of the column getting in by 4.30 p.m.

The total British casualties in this action were:—1 officer killed and 13 wounded; other ranks, 30 killed and 278 wounded. Our battalion had 1 other rank killed and 2 officers and 30 other ranks wounded. The enemy's casualties were estimated from observation and prisoners' reports to be not less than 200 killed and 500 wounded. The British dead were buried at Halazin, but on the discovery later that the enemy had interfered with the graves for the sake of loot, a special expedition went out and brought in the bodies for interment at Matruh.*

*In accordance with the principles guiding the activities of the Imperial War Graves Commission, the bodies of our dead comrades were, at the conclusion of the war, removed from Matruh to the Chatby Military Cemetery at Alexandria.

The enemy had received a very severe blow, and it afterwards transpired, from the reports of deserters, that the effect of this reverse, following upon that at Wadi Majid on Christmas Day, had not only gone far to discourage the Grand Senussi himself, but had shaken the faith of his followers, many of whom, especially those from the eastern Bedouin tribes, deserted his cause and cleared away to their own country.

Referring to the success attained on the 23rd, General Maxwell states in his despatches: " Especial praise is due to the leading of Colonel Gordon, who commanded the main attack, and to the gallantry of the Sikhs, South Africans and New Zealanders, who fought with invincible dash and resolution throughout the day."

At about this time many changes were being made in the compositon of the Western Frontier Force at Matruh. The monitor "Humber" arrived in port on 30th January and commenced a survey of the harbour. She had been one of the ships employed in bombarding the German right at Nieuport on 18th October, 1914, and doubtless she was now intended for service in co-operation with contemplated land operations in connection with the retaking of Sollum. The Royal Naval Armoured Car Detachment left on 28th January, and was replaced by the Duke of Westminster's Armoured Car Batteries, which were destined to perform some brilliant feats at Sollum and beyond. The Australian Light Horse departed for Alexandria via Dabaa on the 30th. We hoped that the rumour to the effect that the relieving units would come from the New Zealand Mounted Brigade would prove to be correct, but in this we were disappointed, for troops of a Home cavalry regiment came through from Dabaa on 2nd February.

The 2nd Battalion of the South African Brigade, which had arrived at Matruh on 20th January, was joined by another battalion from the same brigade at the end of the month.

On January 26th we ourselves received warning orders that we were to leave Matruh for Ismailia, beginning with one company on the following day,* but the weather proved to be

*The following General Order was issued on January 27th:—
" On the departure of the New Zealand Rifle Brigade, the General Officer Commanding the Western Frontier Force desires to place on record the universal regret of the Force at losing the comradeship of a reliable body of men of whom England may well be proud."

too unfavourable for a move, and on the 28th these warning orders were cancelled, the departure being postponed to permit of the 15th Sikhs going first. In the afternoon the first party of the Sikhs left by sea, our band playing them off. We were sorry to see them go. They and our men had fraternized most intimately on the field and in camp, and throughout displayed feelings of sincere mutual regard. We strove to emulate them in battle, and they for their part applauded the dash of our big fellows, whom they spoke of as " all the same Guards."

General Sir John Maxwell, K.C.B., commanding the Force in Egypt, arrived at Matruh on the 1st February, and on the following day inspected the battalion. He left the station again in the evening, accompanied by General Wallace, whose health had broken down. Major-General W. E. Peyton, C.B., D.S.O., succeeded General Wallace, taking over the command of the Western Frontier Force on February 9th, 1916.

The departure of the battalion was postponed from time to time, and general training and route-marching were continued. A camel-transport detachment having arrived at the station, all ranks were instructed and practised in the art of adjusting camel-packs and making up loads.

The power of the Senussi having been so broken in the engagements of Christmas Day and January 23rd that any danger to Matruh was practically at an end, it was now decided to clear the enemy from the coast westward and retake Sollum.

In connection with this scheme the 1st Battalion, with attached troops, was despatched on a three days' march to the west with the object of establishing an advanced base at Unjeila. Included in the column, which was under the command of Lieut.-Col. Fulton, were a troop of Yeomanry from the 2nd Mounted Brigade, a section of the Notts Royal Horse Artillery, a detachment of the Egyptian Royal Engineers and Labour Corps, and a detachment of the Notts and Derby Field Ambulance. There was practically no wheeled transport, the kits, ammunition, tools and general supplies being conveyed by some 900 camels in charge of about 500 native drivers of the Camel Transport Corps. On the line of march the camels were arranged in four parallel columns and moved on the left flank of the combatant units. Starting from the mosque on the west of the harbour at 9.30 a.m. on 13th February, and proceeding along the coast road, the column reached the end of the first stage and bivouacked at Zawia Um Rakham, after an interesting march of fifteen miles. About half-way from Matruh we came to the break that the enemy had made in the telephone line from Sollum. The line had been dismantled for a long distance and diverted southwards to the camp in the Wadi Majid that we had attacked and broken up on Christmas Day. Repairs were made by a party from headquarters signal corps and connection restored between Um Rakham and Matruh. Repairs to the road were carried out by the men of the Egyptian Engineers, and we were struck with the skill and rapidity with which the work was accomplished, particularly the difficult section at the ascent from Wadi Shaifa, just to the west of Um Rakham.

Along the line of march we passed numerous deserted plantations forming tiny oases about the wells, at which, by means of the quaint shadufs, we watered our animals. Reconnaissances inland towards the south, amongst the sandhills on our right, and for a considerable distance westward of our final halting-place revealed no sign of either men or animals.

The bivouac camp at Um Rakham had an extremely picturesque appearance. Within the regular faces of the perimeter formed by companies of infantry were the little groups of guns, the picket lines of the mounted troops, and the well-ordered sections of kneeling camels with their loads neatly arranged in rows before them and their attendants squatted in the sand nearby, the whole picture being set off by the white sand of the hills towards the shore and the scattered palms and quaint stone huts and tombs of the deserted village. Column headquarters were established outside a group of low buildings which had formed a sort of monastery or college in which the preachers and teachers of the Senussi sect were trained.

Instructions for the following day's march were issued, the outposts, especially those on the plateau to the south-west, were strengthened, and the camp settled down for the night. At 10 p.m., however, orders came through by wire that we were to be relieved next day by a battalion of the South African Brigade, and were to return to Matruh. This alteration in the general plans, as we rightly conjectured, was to mark the conclusion of our service with the Western Frontier Force. During the following morning preparations were made for the transfer of our own ammunition and stores from the camel transport to the wheeled vehicles of the South Africans, which were to be taken over by us. Further reconnaissances were made in all directions, but no signs of the enemy were seen; and the only positive result of these was the finding on the seashore of a large number of cases of pure rubber that had been washed ashore from a torpedoed trading-ship. These we salved and brought in, and by their subsequent sale our regimental funds were considerably augmented.

The South Africans arrived during the afternoon, and we commenced our return march at 4.30 p.m. We had a delightfully cool moonlight night, and reached Matruh comfortably by 9.30 p.m. Our recall was a great disappointment to all ranks, as we had been looking forward to taking part in the recapture of Sollum, which would have been a fitting climax to our service in this interesting theatre of war.*

The return to Alexandria commenced forthwith. Battalion headquarters and "D" Company left by sea at 3 p.m. on February 15th, followed by "A" Company on the 16th, and the remainder of the battalion on the 17th. Our new quarters were at the Matras Rest Camp, where the battalion remained for some ten days resting, refitting and training. In consequence of some local disturbance in connection with a

---

*An advanced depot was duly established at Unjeila on 16th February, and on the 20th a force, the infantry of which consisted mainly of the 1st and 3rd South Africans, moved out to establish itself at Barrani, thus securing the second stepping-stone on the way to Sollum. This force ascertained on the 26th that the enemy was in strength near Agagia (fourteen miles to the south-east of Barrani), and they moved out at once to attack him. The ensuing action resulted in a severe defeat to the Senussi forces and the capture of the commander, Gaafar Pasha, who, it is reported, afterwards did valuable service on the side of the Allies as Staff Officer to the King of the Hedjaz in Arabia.

The enemy retreated westward towards Sollum, the Egyptian Bedouin deserting him in large numbers; and the bulk of the Western Frontier Force, including the remaining two battalions of the South African Brigade, was brought forward to Barrani. Two columns operating from this station attacked and took Sollum on March 14th, and by a dash of some twenty miles beyond that village the armoured cars under Major the Duke of Westminster succeeded in capturing all the enemy's guns and machine-guns, besides a number of prisoners, including three Turkish officers.

The campaign came to an end with the rescue, by the Armoured Car

threatened attack from the west, for the moment considered imminent, leave was stopped on the night of the 26th, and all ranks were held in readiness to move at a moment's notice. Fortunately the danger passed, and on the night of February 28th the battalion moved from Alexandria and rejoined the Brigade at Moascar on the 29th, pitching its camp next to that of the 2nd Battalion.

Detachment, of the survivors of the crews of the "Tara" and "Moorina" from an enemy camp some sixty miles west of Sollum.

General Maxwell, in his despatch, says:—" I think it may fairly be claimed that seldom has a small campaign been so completely successful or had such far-reaching results. The effect of this success has been to remove the anxiety which was at one time felt as to the possibility of hostile outbreaks in Egypt itself, where agitation was known to be rife. The attitude of the people in Alexandria, and more especially of the very large Bedouin population of the Behera province, has completely changed; and any prestige which we may have lost through the evacuation of Sollum has been more than recovered. Moreover, through his failure as a temporal leader, Sayed Ahmed has lost much of the influence which was attached to him as a spiritual head."

Sayed Ahmed afterwards fled to Turkey and was succeeded by Sidi Mohammed Idris, who was the eldest son of Ahmed's predecessor, and who had strongly opposed the entry of the Senussi into the war against the British.

CHAPTER III.
ON THE SUEZ CANAL.

PART 1: BRIGADE HEADQUARTERS AND THE 1ST AND 2ND BATTALIONS.

Brigade Headquarters at Heliopolis — Command, Brig.-Gen. Braithwaite—Reinforcements—Move to Ismailia—Formation of the New Zealand Division—Command, Col. Fulton—To the forward zone, Ferry Post.

This account must now go back to the date of the 1st Battalion's departure for Matruh, namely, 18th December, and deal with the Brigade less the two detached units. The headquarters' personnel were still at Aerodrome Camp, Heliopolis, with Lieut.-Col. Fulton in command of the Rifles and also of the New Zealand and Australian Reserve Brigade.

The day after the 1st Battalion left, the 2nd Reinforcements for the Rifle Brigade arrived in camp. This draft consisted of 10 officers and 394 other ranks. The 1st Reinforcements had, of course, come with the first two battalions of the Brigade.

Lieut.-Col. (Temp. Col,) W. G. Braithwaite, D.S.O., assumed command of the Brigade on December 27th.* Lieut.-Col. Fulton retained command of the N.Z. & A. Reserve Brigade, with Major Gibson, Northumberland Fusiliers, as Brigade Major.

A change was effected in Brigade headquarters on January 11th, 1916, Capt. C. W. Melvill, N.Z.S.C., taking over the duties of Brigade Major from Major Gard'ner, transferred. The appointment was, however, ante-dated to December 7th,

---

*The temporary rank of Brigadier-General was granted to Col Braithwaite while commanding the New Zealand Rifle Brigade.

1915, and Capt. Melvill was granted the temporary rank of Major.

The reinforcements were temporarily organized as a battalion, and at once commenced intensive training of a comprehensive nature, and this was carried on steadily throughout the remainder of December and the whole of January and February. Brigade Headquarters, together with this unit and other details, moved on February 6th to Moascar Camp, Ismailia, whither the 2nd Battalion had gone direct from Alexandria on the 18th of the previous month. Here, in addition to its own company and battalion training, the latter unit had been taking part in manœuvres on a large scale in conjunction with the troops lately returned from Gallipoli. General Birdwood, commanding the Anzac Corps, inspected the Brigade troops at Heliopolis on January 26th, and the 2nd Battalion alone at Ismailia on February 18th. At the end of the month, as we have seen, the 1st Battalion joined up with the Brigade.

After its glorious service on Gallipoli, from the famous landing in April, 1915, to the brilliant withdrawal at the end of the year, the New Zealand and Australian Division, which formed part of the Australian and New Zealand Army Corps, concentrated at Moascar during the first week of January, 1916. Here, in common with the other formations of the Mediterranean Expeditionary Force, it entered upon a period of intensive training to fit it for action in the defence of the Canal, to take the field against the Germans, or to meet any other emergency that might arise. In the course of the process of reorganization, however, it soon became patent that the Australian and New Zealand reinforcements and convalescents had accumulated to such an extent that they could not be absorbed under normal conditions, and that the training formations into which they were being drafted were becoming unwieldy. Reinforcements alone were coming forward every month at the rate of twenty per cent. in excess of ordinary requirements, and in addition there was a large number of surplus men intended for mounted units, who, because of their desire to get early into the firing-line, were willing and eager to transfer either to artillery or to infantry units. Moreover, half the New Zealand Rifle Brigade was already in Egypt, and the remaining two battalions were expected early in March. Careful investigation made it clear that it would be quite feasible, as well as eminently desirable, to form additional Australian Brigades, detach the Australian formations from the New Zealand and Australian Division, and reconstitute the latter as a Division composed entirely of New Zealand troops. Negotiations to this end were immediately entered into, and by the middle of February the establishment of an additional Anzac Corps and of a purely New Zealand Division within the Ist Anzac Corps was commenced.

By the end of the month the various adjustments had been completed, and on March 1st the change of name from "The New Zealand and Australian Division" to "The New Zealand Division" was announced. Major-General Sir A. H. Russell, who in the previous November had succeeded General Godley, continued in command.

In the New Zealand Rifle Brigade very few alterations were entailed, for though the 3rd and 4th Battalions had not arrived, they were expected in the course of a few days, and the organization was already practically complete. Indeed, beyond the transfer of reinforcements and some of our officers to the 1st and 2nd Brigades, which had been formed of the old New Zealand Infantry Brigade, we were scarcely affected by the change.

On this date our Brigade Commander, Brig.-Gen. W. G. Braithwaite, D.S.O., with Major C. W. Melvill, N.Z.S.C., his Brigade Major, went over to similar appointments in the newly-formed 2nd Brigade, and Lieut.-Col. Fulton was again appointed to the temporary command of the Rifle Brigade, with Capt. H. M. W. Richardson, N.Z.S.C., as Brigade Major. Capt. E. Puttick, one of the original 1st Battalion company commanders, was on the same date seconded for duty with the 2nd Brigade as Staff Captain.

Inter-brigade operations were carried out on March 3rd. The 1st Brigade represented a British force coming from Tel-el-Kebir, and was attacked by our two battalions, representing a Turkish force. It is noteworthy that to the total of 131 march casualties sustained during this trying day on the desert we contributed only five.

The 1st Battalion was inspected by G.O.C. Ist Anzac Corps on March 6th, and on the following day the Brigade moved out to the camp at Ferry Post, about half a mile east of the Suez Canal, where the New Zealand Division took over the defensive sector from the 2nd Australian Division, which was being withdrawn for despatch to France.

Ferry Post covered one of the most important bridgeheads established during the recent rapid development of the Canal defences. When the Turks attacked in February, 1915, the fighting had taken place on the very banks of the Canal itself, the British forces being for the most part on the western side. Now, however, the defensive works extended far to the eastward, the first line being from six to seven miles distant. Some two and a half miles behind this ran the second line of defence, while the third was close to the Canal. Metalled roads, railways and water-pipe lines had been carried well up towards the front and were being rapidly extended. The trench systems in the forward lines of defence consisted mainly of self-contained "localities," each prepared for a strong garrison of from a battalion to a brigade, and were very strongly wired. They were temporarily held by troops of the Mounted Brigade, but were reconnoitred by representatives of the various infantry units told off for their occupation in case of enemy attack. Beyond the foremost line, patrols of Mounted Rifles scoured the desert, while air-men prosecuted their investigations still farther afield, for though the Turkish Military Railway was still far from the Canal, nothing was left to chance.

Even in the third line, which was practically on the Canal, the utmost watchfulness was maintained. No traffic was allowed after dark except through the examining post, and then only if the outpost commander was satisfied on the points of identity and business. Natives without armlets or passes were not permitted to pass through in either direction, and as an additional precaution, a strip along the front of the line was smoothly swept each day before nightfall, so that any possible eluding of the sentries might be discovered.

To the men of our Brigade, who had had little experience in duties of trench-construction beyond that gained in the moist soils of the New Zealand training-grounds, the defensive works were a striking example of skill and perseverance. The dry sand appeared to be more or less continually flowing; the sides of the trenches could be maintained in position only by the use of framing and matting, while the frequent high winds were accompanied by a drift which here and there almost obliterated the works. It appeared to us that when we came to occupy the trenches we should find it more difficult to fight against the forces of Nature than against those of the enemy.

On the 11th the 2nd Battalion replaced the 1st Brigade troops in the defensive line from Bastion "A" on the right to the Beacon Light on the Suez Canal on the left, the strength employed being two companies. The 2nd Battalion was relieved of this duty on the 15th by the 1st Battalion, which in turn handed over to the 1st Brigade on the 17th.

PART 2.—THE 3RD AND 4TH BATTALIONS.

Inauguration and training—Dress—Maymorn and Rangiotu Camps—Departure for Egypt—Arrival at Ferry Post.

While the Brigade was at Ferry Post, the 3rd and 4th Battalions arrived from New Zealand, and this may be a fitting place for a record of their early history; but as the organization and training of the "left half" of the Brigade followed so closely on the lines adopted by the older portion, a mere outline will be found sufficient for our purpose.

Colonel V. S. Smyth, N.Z.S.C. (Reserve of Officers, Royal Warwickshire Regiment), was appointed to the temporary command, with Capt. John Bishop, N.Z.S.C., as Camp Adjutant. Having served in a similar capacity with Lieut.-Col. Fulton during a considerable portion of the training period of the "right half," Capt. Bishop, who had been retained for this purpose, was specially qualified for the position of staff officer; while Col. Smyth had had, in addition to his service in the Imperial Army, several years' experience in command of military districts in New Zealand.

The special preparatory training of officers and non-commissioned officers commenced at Trentham on September 7th, 1915, and the men marched in on the 11th and 12th of the following month. On the 15th a move was made to Maymorn, some six miles to the north of Trentham, where a tented camp was occupied, and general training commenced at once.

Major J. A. Cowles, of the 17th (Ruahine) Regiment, took over the command of the 3rd Battalion, with Captain H. S. N. Robinson, N.Z.S.C., as Adjutant. The 4th was commanded by Major A. E. Wolstenholme, of the 4th (Otago) Regiment, his Adjutant being Lieut. J. L. Turnbull, of the 1st (Canterbury) Regiment. All appointments were, of course, provisional, being subject to alteration when the battalions should join up with Brigade on active service.

As in the case of the earlier battalions, each unit had its orderly-room with complete staff, and the establishment of headquarters' sections and details received early attention, so that, if called upon, it could move out at a moment's notice completely organized. Efficiency in all respects was the one aim, and this, in spite of adverse conditions, was, as the event proved, amply attained. The ill-luck that attended the career of the band was felt as a great drawback. It suffered repeated casualties owing to sickness, and was often practically defunct.

In the matter of dress, the 3rd and 4th Battalions were in some respects more fortunate than their predecessors, for by this time some slight degree of finality had been reached. The blaze of the 3rd was a black cloth triangle of 1½ inch side, standing on its base, while that of the 4th was a similar patch placed with its base uppermost. These were worn on the hats and caps as in the other two battalions. The puggarees issued, however, were plain khaki without the central strip of scarlet, a defect that was remedied in due time after the units joined up with the Brigade. Unfortunately the men could not be issued with khaki uniforms for some six weeks after their enlistment, and, as a consequence, could not be given leave to town for that period—a deprivation which they bore with admirable patience and resignation. In the case of officers of all grades, boots, puttee-tapes, belts, frogs, scabbards, ties, etc., were black, in which respect they differed somewhat from the officers of the 1st and 2nd, and consternation reigned when it was found on arrival in Egypt that certain modifications had to be carried out for the sake of uniformity.

Owing to long-continued bad weather, Maymorn at last became untenable, and at the beginning of December the battalions moved to the site of the old Rifle Brigade camp at Rangiotu, where, as in those former days, much better conditions obtained, and where both the general health and the work of the units rapidly improved. From the people of the neighbouring towns they received the same kindly treatment as was bestowed upon their predecessors. They were hospitably entertained by various clubs and patriotic societies, and the indefatigable concert parties from Palmerston North continued their good work as of old.

Final leave commenced on December 19th, and continued for fourteen days, and on its conclusion work was resumed with renewed vigour. The usual short period of special continuous training in attack and defence, outpost work and bivouacking, was carried out on the sandhills about Himatangi; and this was followed by the musketry course, taken by the 3rd at Palmerston North and by the 4th at Wanganui. During the period of general training, Colonel C. R. Macdonald, of the General Staff, delivered a series of lectures on trench warfare and machine-gun tactics.

Towards the end of January, when the time for departure was at hand, a general inspection parade was held by the Honorary Colonel, His Excellency the Earl of Liverpool, who complimented the new units on their fine appearance and smart work, and referred in graceful terms to the good reports of the older battalions already on active service.

The 4th Battalion left for Auckland on February 3rd, and after a march through the city in pouring rain, embarked on the 4th. The battalion (less "C" Company) was accommodated on the "Mokoia" (Transport No. 43), and "C" Company went aboard the "Navua" (Transport No. 44), in company with the 3rd Field Ambulance and the Maori Reinforcements. These transports sailed from Auckland at 1 a.m. on February 5th. The 3rd Battalion left camp on the 4th, marched through Wellington, embarked on the "Ulimaroa" (Transport No. 42), and sailed at midnight on the same date.

Unlike the 1st and 2nd Battalions, these two units embarked without equipment or rifles. There was little space on board ship for training, but the work done was carried out regularly and efficiently. Lectures were given daily, and every effort was made by means of physical drill and sports to keep all ranks fit. The monotony of the long voyage was relieved by frequent concerts, mock trials, and the time-honoured ceremonial of Neptune's Court, well and truly carried out, on passing from the Southern to the Northern Hemisphere. Each unit produced its ship's magazine, that of the 3rd being known as "The Blast," and that of the 4th as "The Mokoian." There was considerable excellence in both, and probably "The Blast," printed at Colombo, could hold its own with any similar publication. Its printed matter was well selected and written in fine style, while the illustrations by Lance-Corporals Thompson and Bell were produced with that clever and humorous touch which afterwards became famous throughout the Division.

The transports called at Albany on 15th February, leaving on the 17th, and were at Colombo on the 28th and 29th. At each of these places route marches were held and general leave given, and at Albany the officers were invited to a ball given by the citizens. The behaviour of the men at both ports of call was the subject of favourable comment on the part of shore officials and the people generally, the only "regrettable incident" being the stranding of two or three of the personnel at Colombo owing to a misunderstanding as to the hour of departure. As the last of the troopships left the latter port and was making good headway westwards, a small tug came racing out and signalled her to stop. There was much speculation as to the reason for this action, and the usual wild explanations multiplied as the tug was seen to lower a boat which pulled smartly over to the trooper. The gangway was put down, and up this majestically stepped a solitary Rifleman. This was the famous New Zealand footballer, "Wing" David, afterwards killed in action in France—a man much beloved by his comrades and something of a trial to, though secretly admired by, his officers. Arrived on deck, he waved a haughty dismissal to the tug and a condescending signal to the bridge that the troopship might now proceed. The usual cold formalities regarding the matter of absence without leave engaged the attention of the delinquent and his commanding officer at orderly-room next morning.

The troops disembarked at Suez, moved by rail to Ismailia, and marched to the Brigade camp across the Canal at Ferry Post, the 3rd Battalion reporting on March 13th and the 4th Battalion two days later.

PART 3.—THE BRIGADE COMPLETE.

Command, Brig.-Gen. Fulton—Promotions and adjustments—No. 3 Machine-gun Company—Lewis Gun Sections—Training Battalion—Return to Moascar—Training—Preparations for departure—Inspections—Embarkation—Arrival at Marseilles.

On the arrival of the 3rd and 4th Battalions the rearrangement of the officers of the Brigade, already commenced in connection with the formation of the Division, was proceeded with. The adjustment involved transfers and promotions which necessitated reference to the Expeditionary Force Headquarters, and were not completed until the last week of March, when the undesirable suspense and uncertainty which had been felt as a drawback right from the inception of the Brigade gave place to the feeling of satisfaction that approximate finality had at last been reached. In this matter the settlement of the command of the Brigade was not the least gratifying feature. The principal details of the adjustment were as under:—

BRIGADE HEADQUARTERS:

Lieut.-Col. (Temp. Col.) H. T. Fulton to command the New Zealand Rifle Brigade, with the temporary rank of Brigadier-General.

Capt. T. R. Eastwood (The Rifle Brigade) to be Brigade Major, with the rank of Major.

Capt. R. G. Purdy, N.Z.S.C., to be Staff Captain.

1ST BATTALION:

Major W. S. Austin to be Lieut.-Colonel, and to command the Battalion.

Capt. J. G. Roache to be Major, and to be Second-in-Command.

Lieut. H. Holderness to be Captain, and to be Adjutant.

Capt. G. E. Simeon, Quartermaster, to be Major.

2ND BATTALION:

Major R. St. J. Beere to be Second-in-Command.

Lieut. E. J. Brammall to be Quartermaster.

3RD BATTALION:

Major J. A. Cowles to be Lieut.-Colonel, and to command the Battalion.

Major A. Winter-Evans to be Second-in-Command.

2nd Lieut. J. S. D'H. Birkby to be Lieutenant, and to be Adjutant.

Capt. J. McD. Johnston to be Major, and to be Quartermaster.

4TH BATTALION:

Major C. W. Melvill, N.Z.S.C., to be Lieut.-Colonel, and to command the Battalion.

Major A. E. Wolstenholme to be Second-in-Command.

2nd Lieut. D. Kennedy to be Adjutant.

Captains P. H. Bell, J. Pow and E. Puttick, of the 1st Battalion, and A. Digby-Smith, of the 2nd, were promoted to be Majors. Major Puttick was for the time being with the 2nd Brigade as Staff Captain, and did not return to us until the middle of July, when he took over the position of Second-in-Command of the 4th Battalion on the death of Major Wolstenholme. Majors Bell, Pow and Digby-Smith became senior Company Commanders of the 1st, 4th and 3rd Battalions, respectively. Capt. A. J. Powley had been appointed Adjutant of the 2nd Battalion in January, and Lieut. H. Eastgate Quartermaster of the 4th in the previous October.

Immediately after his arrival with the 3rd and 4th Battalions, Col. Smyth left us to take over the control of the New Zealand Base at Kasr-el-nil Barracks, Cairo. When the Base was moved to England, he brought the training units from Egypt, and for some time commanded Sling Camp, Salisbury Plain.

Coincident with the organization of the Division, the Machine Gun Sections were withdrawn from their battalions and combined into Machine Gun Companies, one of which was attached to each Brigade. That formed of Rifle Brigade sections was known as No. 3 Company, and came into being officially on March 1st. As the establishment of a Machine Gun Company was headquarters and four sections of four guns each the organization was a simple matter, for the sections were ready-made, and it was only necessary to draft in the personnel for the Company Headquarters and the extra officer now required for each section. The following were the officers as finally arranged:—

Officer Commanding: Capt. J. Luxford (3rd Battalion).

No. 1 Section: Lieut. R. G. Gallien (1st Battalion), Lieut. L. S. Cimino (1st Battalion).

No. 2 Section: Lieut. A. C. Finlayson (Otago Mounted Rifles), 2/Lt. K. D. Ambrose (1st Battalion).

Colonel (Major-General Sir)
E. W. C. Chaytor,
K.C.M.G., K.C.V.O., C.B.

Brigadier-General
W. G. Braithwaite,
C.B., C.M.G., D.S.O.

Major W. Kay, O.B.E.

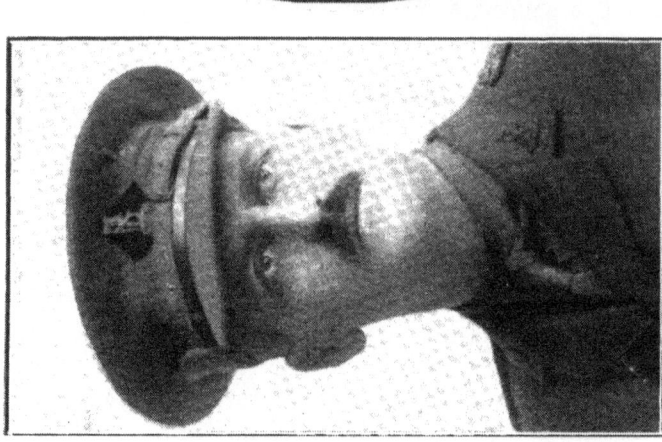

Lieut.-Col. W. S. Austin, D.S.O.

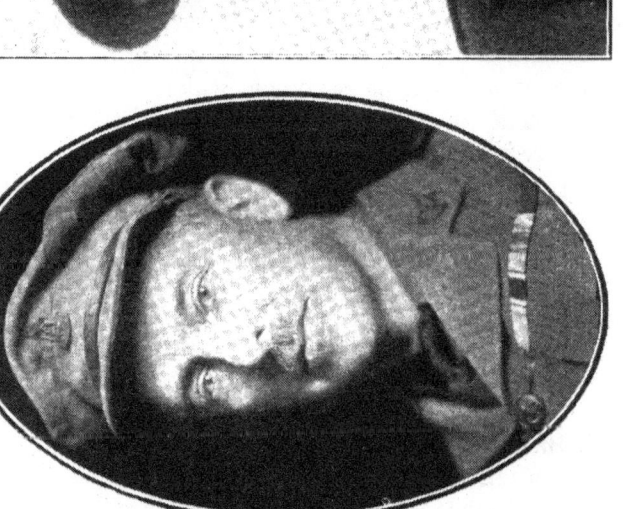

Lieut.-Col. J. A. Cowles.

Face p. 65.

No. 3 Section: Lieut. C. G. Hayter (Canterbury Mounted Rifles), 2/Lt. P. D. Russell (Otago Mounted Rifles).

No. 4 Section: Lieut. C. S. Geddis (Otago Mounted Rifles), Lieut. J. A. D. Hopkirk (1st Battalion).

The Company served with the Brigade until January, 1918, when all the machine-gun sections of the Division were organized into the New Zealand Machine Gun Battalion of four Companies (Auckland, Wellington, Canterbury, Otago), and so passed from the control of Brigade commanders.

To take the place of the Machine Gun Sections, preparations were made for the establishment of Lewis Gun Sections in each battalion, and the following officers were appointed as specialists to supervise the training of the personnel and to superintend the general work:—1st Battalion, 2nd Lieut. N. H. Arden; 2nd, 2nd Lieut. H. M. Keesing; 3rd, 2nd Lieut. C. E. Bridge; 4th, Lieut. J. W. Snaddon. Lewis guns, however, were a new and practically untried arm, and were not available for issue at a greater rate than two per battalion, though the regulation scale of four per unit, as laid down by the Army Council at the beginning of the year, was made up before we entered the trenches on the Flanders front. As the usefulness of the guns, both in attack and in defence, became more and more clearly demonstrated, the rate of issue steadily increased until it stood, towards the close of the war, at 36 per battalion, 32 for ordinary use and four for anti-aircraft purposes.

To complete the adjustment there now only remained the formation of a Training Battalion, which would absorb the reinforcements for the Brigade, and from which would be drawn as required drafts of officers and men whose training would be completed under conditions more nearly approaching in general character those of active service than could be expected to obtain in the home training camps. This unit, known as the New Zealand Rifle Brigade Training Battalion, was established at Moascar on March 21st, the details being taken in the main from the second and third reinforcements for the first two, and the officers from all four battalions. Major W. Kay, from the 1st Battalion, was placed in command, with Captains J. Bishop and W. E. Christie as Adjutant and Quartermaster, respectively. Following were the first company officers:—No. 1 Company, Capt. W. G. Bishop and Lieut. A. Hoggans; No. 2 Company, Capt. O. W. Williams and 2nd Lieut. W. G. Ivil; No. 3 Company, Capt. C. Horsnell and Lieut. F. E. Greenish; No. 4 Company, Capt. P. V. Hackworth and 2nd Lieuts. E. A. Winchester and N. W. Shackleford.

When the Division left Egypt for France the Training Battalion remained at Moascar. A brief outline of its subsequent history is given in Appendix III.

The Brigade moved on March 20th from Ferry Post to Moascar Camp, where it remained until it left for France early in the following month. During the stay at these camps, training was continued with unabated energy. Company, battalion and brigade parades, route marches and staff rides, night operations and trench-digging, specialist training and transport work, each had its place, till at last all ranks, the newer arrivals as well as the "old hands," felt that they were fit for any emergency. Yet, with all our labours, there was time and opportunity for much pleasure. The hot season was not far advanced, and the general surroundings had a special interest. There was a liberal allowance of leave to Cairo. Ismailia and its beautiful plantations and gardens, Lake Timsah and the Suez Canal with their naval and mercantile shipping, even the open desert itself with its scattered remains of bygone civilizations, all had a charm that was irresistible. Bathing parades to the lake or the Canal were a special joy, and often practically the whole personnel of the Brigade would be in the water at one time; and, though reminders of the great world-strife were never absent, there was a refreshing restfulness in a quiet evening stroll to the Canal after a crowded day of toil on the sands of the desert.

Then, too, we had, what so seldom occurred in after-days, the whole of the Division assembled in one place. There was consequently an opportunity for our fellows to mix with the stalwarts from Gallipoli and hear from them at first hand what it meant to be in close contact with the enemy under conditions which would probably prevail in that theatre of war whither we were destined soon to go. We saw much of the other Anzacs also, and in this connection a spontaneous display of goodwill is worthy of note. A brigade of Australians marching across the desert from Tel-el-Kebir was overtaken by a heat-wave, with the result that the men were suffering march casualties to an appalling extent. Word of their plight reached the camp of the New Zealanders near by, and at a hint, rather than an order, every available water-cart, every spare dixie, and every water-bottle within reach was taken out by our men, who streamed over the sands hastening to bring relief to their neighbours in distress.

The time for the departure of the Division was now near at hand, and the final preparations were pushed to completion with all speed. Para-typhoid inoculation had been carried out twice towards the end of March. Kits were reduced by sending away all private belongings, forage caps were finally handed in,* and on April 1st the new charger-loading, short M.L.E. rifles were drawn in exchange for the old M.L.E. long rifles that had hitherto been in use.

We had been inspected by General Godley and seen at training by H.R.H. the Prince of Wales, and now, on April 3rd, the whole Division paraded before General Sir A. J. Murray, commanding the Forces in Egypt. To us this was a very imposing parade, the first occasion on which we had seen ceremonial work on such a scale; but we left the ground at the conclusion of the march past with the consciousness that our hard training had not been in vain so far as it affected our physique, smartness, steadiness, and general appearance. With due thoughtfulness the quicker step of the Rifle Brigade had been provided for, the band accommodated its time accordingly, and, notwithstanding the drawback of loose sand, the several battalions in close column of platoons swung by at the trail in fine form.

On the same evening orders were received for moving out and embarking for France. The Advance Party of the Brigade under Capt. Purdy entrained for Port Said on the evening of the 5th April, and embarked there on the "Franconia."

---

*The felt hats, officially known as "smasher" hats, were still worn with the longitudinal crease in the top, and the distinguishing black patch was retained on the puggaree until May 23rd, when it was transferred to the sleeve of the tunic. It was not until the 7th September following that the now familiar peaked arrangement of the crown was ordered. The resemblance between our hats and those of the Americans was afterwards freely commented upon. This likeness, however, was only general; for whereas we had a puggaree the Americans had a cord, and while our creasing brought the ridges one running from front to rear and the other across on the line of the shoulders, the ridges of the American hats crossed diagonally.

On the same day the 1st Battalion left Moascar for Alexandria and embarked on the "Arcadian." The 2nd, 3rd, and 4th Battalions and the 3rd M.G. Company departed from Moascar on the 6th at different times, commencing at 3 a.m., and embarked at Alexandria, the 2nd (less a small party which went on the "Minnewaska") on the "Arcadian," and the 3rd and 4th and the M.G. Company on the "Alaunia," a fine transport which, unfortunately, was torpedoed on her return journey from Marseilles, a fate which also subsequently befell both the "Franconia" and the "Arcadian." Brigade and Battalion Transport Sections, with their horses and mules, were quartered on the "Elele" and the "Menominee." The complete outfit of vehicles, which we had brought with us from New Zealand, was left behind in Egypt.

The departure from Alexandria commenced on April 7th. Little space was available on the ships for training exercises, but much time was devoted to lectures on trench warfare and preventive measures against gas attacks. In addition to the usual precautions taken against attack from submarines, all ranks wore lifebelts constantly both by day and by night, and each ship supplemented quick-firer, Lewis gun and Vickers gun sentries with sections of men with loaded rifles specially posted on either side.

No untoward event occurred, however, though there appeared to be frequent scares, and the course taken sometimes seemed to be a very roundabout one. Off the coast of Sardinia, for instance, the "Alaunia" was compelled to "about ship" for half a day and then zigzag to her destination. Except in the Gulf of Lions, the weather was fine and the sea smooth, and the transports arrived at Marseilles all well on the 12th, 13th and 14th.

CHAPTER IV.

IN THE BATTLE ZONE OF THE FLANDERS FRONT.

PART 1.—MOVEMENTS.

Marseilles to Steenbecque—First billets—Training—Detachments—Tunnellers—Trench mortars—Inspection by General Plumer—To Estaires—First visit to trenches—To Morbecque—To Armentieres.

The journey from Marseilles across France to the battle zone occupied the greater part of three days. Battalions moved at different times, each in a single train composed for the most part of fairly comfortable coaches. We had not the omnipresent Y.M.C.A. of later days to supply us with tea and biscuits, and, as halts for any length of time were very few and far between, we had to be content with the ordinary fare as provided for on the army scale of rations. From our observations we concluded that there was one long line of ration-tins, in various stages of decay, from the Mediterranean to the Channel; for wherever the train paused for a time, and these stops seldom took place at a station, the permanent way was lined on both sides with the familiar square cans lying in the open in defiance of the strict rule that "What you cannot burn you must bury." Indeed, sanitary matters of any kind seemed to have entered not at all into the calculations of the authorities concerned.

Long railway journeys are always more or less wearisome, and this was no exception to the general rule; but the novelty of the scenes which succeeded each other as we moved northward served to relieve the tedium. The monotony of the desert here gave place to green fields, early flowers, trees putting forth their first buds, extensive and orderly vineyards, quaint villages, ancient towns and thriving cities, and, in the south at least, bright sunshine bathing all. It seemed like a special privilege to see white folk again, and the smiles and cries of the cheering children were particularly touching to men so far from home. In the bleak north the line approached the coast, and before turning inland again we caught a glimpse of the waters of the English Channel, and one is safe to say that few of us failed to be stirred by the thought that not far beyond stood the white cliffs of the Motherland whose welfare lay so close to our hearts.

From Marseilles our route ran through Arles, Avignon, Orange, Vienne, Lyons, Macon, Dijon, Montereau, Corbeil, Juvisy (on the outskirts of Paris), Creil, Clermoine, Longneau, Amiens, St. Roche, Longpre, Abbeville, Etaples, Bifur d'Boulogne, St. Omer, Bifur Wallon Capelle, Hazebrouck, Steenbecque. With many of these points to the north of Paris we were destined to become more familiar during the years that lay before us.

The first unit to move left Marseilles at 4.24 p.m. on April 13th, and, travelling day and night, reached Hazebrouck, the official destination, at about midnight on the 15th/16th. Here the commanding officer was verbally informed by a full corporal that the battalion was to go on to Steenbecque. After some trouble these instructions were verified and the train proceeded accordingly. The remaining battalions arrived at Steenbecque station at short intervals. Each battalion on detraining was met by the French billeting officer, and officers and men were immediately told off into groups and marched to their quarters under the guidance of members of the advance party, who had come on ahead with Brigade Headquarters.

Brigade Headquarters and the 2nd Battalion were quartered at Steenbecque, an interesting village with a quaint old church the gate-posts of which were unusually curious. The 1st Battalion was billeted in neighbouring farmhouses, and the 3rd and 4th in the adjoining villages of Tannay and Thiennes. On a readjustment of the area, which now came under the command of General Fulton, the 1st Battalion a few days later moved to the village of Boeseghem.

The various Transport Sections of the Brigade detrained with their horses at Abbeville, and having drawn at that base the vehicles to replace those we had left in Egypt, commenced the long three days' trek of sixty miles to the Steenbecque area, where they arrived on April 22nd.

This was our first experience of billets, and it will readily be understood that there was no little difficulty in getting comfortably settled down, especially on the part of those units that arrived in the middle of the night. Hitherto we had lived for the most part in orderly-arranged hutments or tented camps, or had bivouacked in the open; but here we had to fit ourselves into such accommodation as was afforded by barns, lofts and sheds, none too liberally supplied with straw, but paid for by the British authorities at a fixed rate per head. For the officers, rooms were usually found wherein they slept and messed and carried out with moderate convenience their administrative duties. The peculiarities of the French farmhouse were in many respects a source of wonderment. In the darkness, one unfortunate company commander made an involuntary personal reconnaissance of the ancestral midden which formed the most striking feature of the courtyard of his quarters, and received his commanding officer, on the latter's round of inspection during the morning, in an ill-fitting suit of velveteen provided by his obliging host. The notices in English posted up at all the house-pumps—"Not to be used for drinking purposes"—at first appeared odd, but careful consideration of the position of the well led to a most respectful obedience of the instruction.

We found the inhabitants of the district kindly and obliging to a degree, and such good people as those of La Belle Hotesse and the other hamlets and villages will long be remembered for their solicitude on our behalf. Cupidity, an unfortunate trait displayed by the country people in some billeting areas occupied in later days, was not a characteristic here. Usually the greatest kindness was displayed by those who had suffered most. The war, it will be remembered, was already drawing to the close of its second year, and signs of its effects were not wanting. There was a marked absence of able-bodied men; in the fields women and old men followed the plough or executed other forms of manual labour from daylight till dark; and as the people wended their way to church on Sundays and Saints' days, one noticed that the majority of the women and children wore mourning.

On arrival in the battle zone the New Zealand Division became reserve to the 1st Anzac Corps under Lieut.-General Birdwood, the 1st and 2nd Australian Divisions being already in the line.

General training, specialist work and route-marching commenced at once. Every possible square foot of land being under cultivation, our exercises had perforce to be carried out on the roads. Flannelette gas-helmets were issued, and training in their use formed an important part of our daily exercises. Before the end of the month the whole Brigade attended a special demonstration, every man being subjected to the ordeal of the gas-cloud and passing through trenches charged with both lethal and lachrymatory gas.

As early as April 20th, battalion commanders received the first of a long series of orders couched in such terms as these: " Please detail (so many) other ranks to report at (such-and-such) School of Instruction for a course in (subject) . . . . . ." Orders of this kind came to hand with more or less frequency right through our career in France, as often as not while the unit was moving up to take over a new sector in the line, or even in the thick of a fight.* The system itself was an excellent one, providing as it did for the special training of officers and other ranks in various branches of military work, and ensuring that the unit as a whole was kept up-to-date in all developments in the art of fighting; but to the fretting commanding officer, chronically under establishment in officers and non-commissioned officers, it seemed to be carried out with a merciless unconcern as to the fitness of things. The order on this occasion was for the despatch of eight non-commissioned officers per battalion for gas-helmet instruction at the Gas School at Oxelaere.

" Please detail an officer of the rank of Captain for duty as Town Major at Estaires." This was a class of order that was always received with dismay, for it was a point of honour that officers so detached should be in the highest degree efficient. For this particular post Capt. R. O. Brydon was detailed on the day after our arrival at Steenbecque, and the services of a very able officer were lost to the 1st Battalion for a period extending over many months. It is still an unsolved mystery why such a position was not filled by an ex-service officer from England, too old for active service but still willing and able to carry out non-combatant duties of this nature. At

---

*When the Brigade was in the line during the Battle of the Somme, in September, 1916, one officer and fifteen other ranks were detached for a course of instruction at the Lewis Gun School, Le Touquet.

that time, it must be remembered, battalions had to find their "specialist" officers from amongst their platoon commanders, and companies were correspondingly short. In this case Capt. Brydon was the second-in-command of a company.

Two officers and 100 other ranks were detached for duty with the 172nd Tunnelling Company on April 30th. As practically all of these men were thus, as the event proved, finally separated from the Brigade, brief mention may here be made of their subsequent career. They were in every case experienced either in mining or in some allied occupation that would specially fit them for the particular service for which they were now detailed. The men drawn from the 1st and 2nd Battalions were commanded by 2nd Lieut. G. Lewis, and those from the 3rd and 4th by 2nd Lieut. S. J. E. Closey. They were privileged to be the first New Zealand troops to serve in the trenches of the battle-front in France, for on the day after leaving us they entered the line in the Bois Grenier Sector, then held by the 19th and 21st Australian Battalions. Three days later they were called upon to man the trenches when the sector was raided by the Germans, but fortunately, though the bombardment was especially severe, they escaped without casualties. They were thanked by the Australian brigadier for their assistance in the fighting as well as for their service as stretcher-bearers. When the New Zealand Division went into the line on May 10th, our detachment relieved part of the 1st Canadian Tunnelling Company in the New Zealand sector, and later, on the arrival in France of the 2nd Australian Tunnelling Company, the New Zealanders were transferred from their old company, the 172nd, and were attached to the Australians, remaining on duty, however, on the New Zealand front. While here, the New Zealand miners were specially detailed for the sinking of the "Anzac Shaft," with its series of galleries, in trench 74 of the Armentieres sector. This was the first satisfactory steel-lined water-tight shaft ever sunk in the Second Army area; and as the whole of the work was executed by New Zealanders, the achievement is one of which we have no small reason to be proud. The detachment experienced a second raid on the evening of July 3rd, the enemy's main objective being, on that occasion, the underground works in course of execution at another point. As soon as it became clear, during the artillery preparation, that the enemy would probably attempt the destruction of the shaft, the sappers were withdrawn from the galleries where they were at work, and 2nd Lieut. Closey remained behind with two or three of their number to mask and protect, by means of sandbagging, the entrance to the shaft-head. When shells began to fall thickly about the spot, the officer sent the men back to the shelter of a dug-out in rear and completed the work alone, just managing to escape when the raiders entered the trench in search of the shaft-head. This, however, had by then been so effectively covered and disguised that the enemy failed to locate it, and the number of unexploded mobile charges left behind at this spot testified to the raiders' disappointment. The Australian officer reporting upon the matter states in conclusion: "There is not a question of doubt in my mind that 2nd Lieut. Closey, by sticking to his duty under heavy shell-fire, saved our mining system from possible destruction." From time to time our men were drafted in small parties from the Australian to the New Zealand Tunnelling Company, with which unit the majority continued to serve in various sectors, for the most part far removed from those held by the New Zealand Division, until the end of the war.

On April 22nd the Brigadier and the Battalion Commanders attended an interesting demonstration, held at Berthen, in the use of light, medium and heavy trench mortars. Important improvements had recently been made in this comparatively new arm, and the display was distinctly heartening. Visions of the period of tragic stress were called up by the fact that the journey to the trench mortar school was made in a London motor-'bus.

In addition to inspections at various dates by the Brigadier and the Divisional Commander, the battalions were seen at work on April 25th by General Sir H. Plumer, the Commander of the Second Army, of which we now formed a part.

The Brigade marched fifteen miles, from Steenbecque to billets in Estaires, on May 1st, and the same evening we had our first experience of a gas-alarm, which, however, eventually proved to be false. We were now well within the battle zone. On our first morning in Steenbecque we heard the rumble of distant artillery fire, and at night the flashes of the guns could be distinctly seen. At Estaires, bursts of machine-gun fire were frequently heard, sometimes in great intensity.

On May 6th, the Brigadier, Brigade Major, the Commanding Officers and Company Commanders of the 1st and 2nd Battalions went to Armentieres and were attached to the 51st Brigade, 17th Division, for a twenty-four hours' tour of duty in the trenches. By this means valuable information was obtained as to the new conditions under which we were presently to work, but, as frequently happens, the sector which was so closely studied did not prove to be the one the Brigade eventually took over.

Three days later the Brigade marched back to Morbecque for a special course in musketry and practical Lewis and Vickers gun training. Here our first Brigade School was established, bombing being the principal subject taken up.

The New Zealand Division commenced to take over from the 17th Division east of Armentieres on 10th May, the 1st Brigade going into the right sector of the front line on the 13th, and the 2nd Brigade into the left sector on the 14th. The length of the front occupied was 6,000 yards. On the right were the 2nd Australians. The Division was on the left of the Corps sector, and on the left again, north of the River Lys, was the 9th Division, afterwards relieved by the 41st.

On May 13th the Brigade moved forward again, the 1st and 2nd Battalions marching to Doulieu and the 3rd and 4th to Estaires. A further move towards the front was made on the 15th, when the Brigade marched in to the town of Armentieres as part of the Divisional reserve. The 1st Battalion, with two companies in Armentieres and two in Houplines, relieved the 9th West Riding Battalion as reserve to the left Brigade sector, the Brigade there having all four battalions in the line. A readjustment was made on June 8th, after which date each Brigade found its own reserve.

Before the war Armentieres was a town of some importance, and had a population of over 25,000. It is situated close to the Belgian frontier, some ten miles west of Lille. The canalized Lys, on the banks of which it stands, was one of those inland waterways so greatly valued in this part of the country, and Armentieres was a small but busy river port. It was particularly famous, however, as one of the more important manufacturing centres. Its many factories were engaged mainly in the spinning of flax, hemp and cotton yarn, and in the production of woollens, cottons and linens. In addition there were several large distilleries, soap works and tanneries; the minor manufactures were various; and there were extensive brick-making works.

When we first came to Armentieres a considerable proportion of the inhabitants was still in the town, for only certain quarters had as yet suffered from shell-fire. During our short stay we were to witness some remarkably accurate shooting on the part of the German gunners, such churches of the town as were then intact coming in for special attention; and more than once we were to suffer casualties through sudden bursts of concentrated "hate" upon the neighbourhood of our billets. It was not till the following year, however, that the place was systematically shelled, and in connection with the temporary German advance in this area in 1918, the destruction of the town was completed. While we were quartered at Armentieres we had excellent billets situated mainly in abandoned factories, while certain of the more pretentious dwellings, now deserted, formed convenient homes for the various Brigade and Battalion Headquarters. One of our battalions was, during a spell out of the line, billeted in a large building that had been a Girls' College, and the lady-principal was still in residence. It is worthy of note that this lady was able to tell us of our next move into the line some time before official warning or definite orders reached the headquarters of the battalion, and she complained most bitterly that, apparently through the soldiers' unguarded talk, such information frequently filtered out till it reached the civilian residents, amongst whom it became the common topic of conversation.

The transport lines of the various units of the Brigade were established at Pont de Nieppe, just west of the town; and here also were situated the Divisional Baths for the men's use, and the laundry establishments through which clean underclothing was issued.

PART 2.—THE FIGHTING ON THE FLANDERS FRONT FROM THE OUTBREAK OF WAR TILL MAY, 1916.

First German advance—Liege—General German advance—Brussels — Mons — Namur — Lille — The Aisne — The Marne — The British to the left of the line—West Flanders campaign—New Corps come in—Armentieres—Nieuport—La Bassee—Arras—Ypres—Messines—Positions—Neuve Chapelle—Second Battle of Ypres—Minor offensives—Trench fighting—Line readjusted—Loos—Winter trench-work.

It may not be out of place to give here a brief outline of the progress of the fighting on or about the Flanders front from the outbreak of war up till the beginning of 1916. This account will of necessity be somewhat disconnected and sketchy; but it may serve to get the situation from time to time into proper perspective, and clear away erroneous ideas formed from the reading of contemporary newspaper accounts, which, as we now know, were not always strictly impartial.

The German advance towards France was first attempted mainly through Liege, the gateway to the Belgian plains. By the evening of August 3rd, 1914, German columns were on Belgian territory, and on the following day were closing in on Liege from the north-east, east and south. At this time the Belgian army was still in process of mobilization and was being placed in position to resist a German advance on Brussels and Antwerp. It was realized that Liege must eventually fall, but the city was nevertheless held in order to gain time, for as long as its forts could withstand the enemy's attacks he could make no progress by rail towards the plain beyond. The bombardment of the Liege forts commenced on August 4th, and three days later the city was entered; but Liege did not become an open gateway until the 15th, when the last of the forts was taken.

In the meantime the general advance of the German forces had begun. The enemy had got six armies in position, the First in the north and the Sixth in Alsace in the south. The general plan was to carry out a great sweeping movement, pivoting on the Sixth Army opposite Belfort, the First and Second Armies passing through Belgium, and forming the right of the German front descending upon Paris and the Marne Valley. This movement commenced on August 7th. By August 15th the First and Second Armies passed through Liege for Namur and

France, and four Army Corps were sent against Brussels and Antwerp. Five days later Brussels surrendered.

The British Army was in position before Mons, west of Namur, by August 21st, on a front of about 25 miles. This "contemptible" force, commanded by Sir John French, consisted of the Ist Army Corps (Haig), the IInd Army Corps (Smith-Dorrien), and one Cavalry Division (Allenby). On the right of the British was the French Fifth Army, while away to the westward beyond the British left was a force of French Territorials. The task of the British was to protect the left of the general advance to the north. The Allies' plan was, first to meet the shock of the German advance on the defensive, and then to take the offensive against the German right by a turning movement with Namur as the pivot. This was expected to raise the siege of Namur, and thus open the way to re-occupy Brussels and form a junction of the British left with the Belgian Army advancing from Antwerp.

On August 22nd the Germans attacked the front and right flank and rear of the French Fifth Army, which gave way. Information as to the situation did not reach Sir John French, and the result was that the attack on the British next day was doubly severe. Under pressure from the front and on the right flank the British were slowly but surely forced back, and the famous retirement from Mons began.

The worst of the retreat from Mons was over by the evening of August 28th, by which date our IInd Army Corps was on the Somme. Thenceforward the pursuit was slack, and the British were in position on the Aisne on the 30th.

Notwithstanding the lesson of Liege, the fortress of Namur was held to be invincible; yet, attacked on August 20th, it was entered by the Germans three days later.

In the vicinity of Lille was the extreme right of the German force advancing upon Northern France. This force consisted mostly of cavalry and horse artillery, with the IInd Corps of Infantry, the last being rushed forward by motor transport. It operated beyond the right of the German First Army (von Kluck) and formed a huge raiding-party, which had for its object the cutting of the communications of the British force with its principal bases at Boulogne and Havre. Moving southwards with its right on the River Lys, it created panic amongst the civilians in the district, and took Lille. That city, with its obsolete fortresses, the Allies made no attempt to hold. British Marines were hurried across the Channel to save Ostend, but the Germans had no intention of occupying that port, their main line of advance being by Arras towards Amiens. The raiding force for the time being met with no opposition. The Allies, relying on their anticipated victorious advance into Belgium, had made no preparation to meet this contingency. Amiens was evacuated forthwith. British Headquarters sent orders to abandon Boulogne as the main supply base, and a new base was established at St. Nazaire at the mouth of the Loire.

We return now to the British Army which, on August 30th, had reached the Aisne, and had on its left a new French Army, the Tenth, which had come into position on August 28th. The line now held by the left of the Allies was an ideal position: indeed, it was the one actually selected forty years before by the French Staff for a final stand against an invading force that might overcome the frontier defences and be marching on Paris. The enemy's pressure on the centre, with the object of dividing the force and then mopping up the western portion, including, of course, the British, proved, however, to be too great, and a general retirement to the Marne was ordered. The great retreat from Mons, in which 100,000 British were opposed to a quarter of a million Germans, came to an end on September 5th.

Von Kluck's First Army, instead of continuing its sweep towards Paris, now changed direction to the south-east and attempted to drive a wedge between the left of the French Fifth Army and the right of the British force, which he was pleased to consider demoralized. As a result of this change, the raiding force of cavalry off on von Kluck's right was drawn in to conform, and Lille was evacuated by the Germans. Advantage was immediately taken of von Kluck's mistake in moving across our front. His right was attacked on September 6th, by the British and French on the left of the Allied line; pressure was continued on the 7th; and on the following day the German right was in retreat. On the 9th the German centre was badly beaten, and on the 10th the Battle of the Marne became a drive. The enemy, however, was too strong in numbers for us to convert his retreat into a rout, and on September 12th he had got back in good order to the Aisne.

The position taken up was as nearly perfect as could be imagined, situated as it was on the crest of a plateau some two miles north of the Aisne stream. In passing over this ground a few days before, the enemy had left behind working parties to prepare defensive trenches in case of a retirement.

On the supposition that the enemy was merely holding a delaying position, the British opened the Battle of the Aisne with a frontal attack. We succeeded in crossing the stream on September 14th, but, after a five days' struggle, realized that this was no rearguard matter, and a weary war of entrenchments began.

To turn the enemy's right, the two new French Armies on our left, the Seventh and the Tenth, extended our line at right angles from the Aisne beyond Albert to Arras and Lens, and almost to the Belgian frontier, a distance of nearly seventy miles. Then the Germans took the offensive, stretching out their right in the endeavour to outstrip our movement. In this new effort, by which he hoped to secure the Channel ports and the Seine Valley for an advance on Paris, the enemy had the advantage of the better railway systems.

By the end of September, Sir John French had come to the conclusion that in consequence of the extension of the line the British Army was in the wrong place. At Mons it had been on the extreme left. Now it was almost in the centre of the Allied line, and consequently there were difficulties in the matter of communications and supplies, which crossed those of the French Armies. If the British were transferred to the left of the line, we should then be within easy reach of the Channel ports. There was also another aspect to be considered, namely, the imminence of a great offensive against Britain herself, with the possession of the Channel ports as the immediate objective. Antwerp was at its last gasp, and when that city should fall to the Germans a fresh army would be available for a dash at the gap between Lille and the sea. Even now the finest of the German troops were under orders for the north, and in the first week of October large masses of German cavalry appeared again in the neighbourhood of Lille and Armentieres. General Joffre concurred in the views of Sir John French, and the transfer was accordingly arranged.

Now commenced the West Flanders campaign, which proved to be harder and more intricate than any the Allies had yet fought. It was a self-contained campaign, in which only three out of the eleven Allied Armies, namely, the French Eighth, the British, and the French Tenth, took part. When it was seen that Antwerp must fall the following plan was adopted by the Allies. The Belgian Army, covered by Sir Henry Rawlinson's British force, consisting of the 7th Division and the 3rd Cavalry Division, recently landed at Ostend and Zeebrugge for the purpose of assisting in the defence of Antwerp, would retire by Bruges and Ghent to the line of the Yser to protect the Allied left, and, together with the new French reinforcements, meet any attack along the coast by German troops released after the fall of Antwerp; Lille and La Bassee to be held by the Allies; and the British, pivoting on La Bassee, to swing south-east, isolate the northern wing of the Germans, and threaten the communications to the south.

By September 30th the French Tenth Army had got into position, with its right on the River Ancre near Albert and its left extending beyond Arras to the vicinity of Lens. Several French Territorial Divisions occupied Lille and Douai opposite the German right. On October 8th the Germans, who still held Lens, took Douai and shelled Arras and Lille. Their cavalry were still scouring this region as far west as Hazebrouck, Bailleul and Cassel, and were therefore within twenty miles of Dunkirk.

On October 11th, the IInd Corps (Smith-Dorrien), on the way to the new position in the line, had marched from Abbeville and was placed on the left of the French, between Bethune and Aire. On the same day the Corps wheeled round till its left rested on Merville, and during the next four days pushed the Germans back to the La Bassee-Lille Road. Further advance was checked by strong counter-attacks. Indian troops first came into the line on 19th October, the Lahore Division being placed near Bethune in support of the IInd Corps.

The IIIrd Corps (Pulteney) arrived at St. Omer on October 11th and marched to Hazebrouck. On the 13th it moved towards the line Armentieres–Wytschaete, linking up the Ypres and the La Bassee sections of the front. This Corps came into conflict with the enemy in strength at Meteren, and, after a sharp fight, drove him out of Meteren and Bailleul and occupied the line Bailleul–St. Jans Cappelle. By October 17th the IIIrd Corps had taken Sailly, Nieppe and Armentieres, and pushed forward to a position with its right at Bois Grenier, three miles south of the Lys, and its left at Le Gheer, a mile north of the river. Here we were against the main German line, and it was found impossible to recover Lille, from which the enemy had driven the French Territorials on the 14th, or, indeed, to make any further advance from the position taken up here on October 19th. "This, the British right centre [about the Armentieres sector] was destined to have one of the most awkward places in all the coming battle. It was not itself the object of any great massed attack, as on the Yser, at Ypres, and at La Bassee, but it suffered from being on the fringe of the two latter zones, ... and was gravely endangered in the German enveloping movements."*

The nucleus of the IVth Corps (Rawlinson) was the 7th Division and the 3rd Cavalry Division (Byng), which, as we have seen, had gone from Ostend and Zeebrugge to help the Belgians at Antwerp. When that city fell on October 9th, the Belgians and the British, in accordance with the general plan, fell back towards the Yser Canal. The Belgians took up the line of the Yser from Houthulst Forest (north-east of Ypres) through Dixmude to Nieuport, with French Territorials in support. Our 7th Division took up a position east of Ypres on the line Zandvoorde–Gheluvelt–Zonnebeke, with the 3rd Cavalry Division as advanced guard on a line roughly from Bixschoote to Poelcapelle, French Cavalry holding Passchendaele. On October 18th, two days after the Allies had secured these positions, four reserve corps, rushed up from Germany, were put into the line from Roulers to Menin. Our IVth Corps, in the endeavour to secure the latter place as a pivot for a turning movement, came into contact with this overwhelming force, and being unable to make headway, entrenched itself on an eight-mile line just east of Gheluvelt cross-roads.

The Ist Corps (Haig) having detrained at St. Omer and marched to Hazebrouck on October 19th, was ordered to move through Ypres to Thourout, and to march thence against Bruges and Ghent. The presence of the four new German corps was not fully known to our Headquarters; and the Ist Corps, soon meeting with determined opposition at their hands, had to settle down east of Ypres as the left wing in the great struggle.

*John Buchan: "Nelson's History of the War."

Opposed to the Allied line of nearly 100 miles from Albert to the sea at Nieuport were one and a half million German troops, outnumbering us by five to one. The four principal points in the line, at any one of which an advantageous breach might be made for a German advance against the Channel ports and our lines of communications, were, in descending order of importance, Arras, La Bassee, Ypres, and Nieuport. Strangely enough, the Germans, in the great series of battles which now commenced, struck at all four points simultaneously.

The struggle for the shortest route to Calais, via Nieuport, came to an end on October 31st through the deliberate flooding of the countryside by the Belgians, who blocked the mouth of the Yser Canal for that purpose.

The fighting about La Bassee, where the Germans attacked in great strength on October 22nd, resulted in the pushing back of the left of the British line in that region, till, by the middle of November, the front ran from Givenchy (west of La Bassee) northwards past the west of Neuve Chapelle to near Laventie, thence bending back towards Estaires. Indian troops were employed with the British in these engagements, but the climatic conditions proved unsuitable.*

The heavy stroke at Arras by the Germans from October 20th to 26th was considered by them to be one of the main battles of the war, but by the beginning of November this attack had definitely failed.

The First Battle of Ypres commenced on October 21st, when Haig, in accordance with instructions, endeavoured to advance with the Ist Corps to Thourout and thence to Bruges and Ghent. In the course of the fighting the French Territorials were driven out of Houthulst Forest. The 7th Division and the 2nd Cavalry Division, then in the vicinity of Becelaere, were strongly attacked and the IInd Corps was compelled to halt on the line Zonnebeke–St. Julien–Langemarck–Bixschoote. The German attack was heavy all along the line; in the region of Armentieres, the posts on the left of the IIIrd Corps were driven in, Le Gheer being occupied by the Germans, though recovered later. Day after day the fighting continued. On October 29th a cumulative attack was made on the whole line,

---

*The Indian Divisions were transferred to eastern theatres of war towards the end of the following year.

marking the beginning of the sternest struggle of the campaign in the West. The critical point of the whole battle, the crisis of the Flanders campaign and perhaps of the whole Western war, came on the 31st, but still the Allies held out. We lost Messines on November 1st. On November 11th the Germans made their supreme effort, the Prussian Guards being put in against Gheluvelt. They failed, however, and by November 20th both sides fell back generally upon the ordinary routine of trench warfare. So ended one of the most remarkable contests of the war, a great German army of a million being checked and bewildered by one only a fifth of its size. We had yielded some ground, but our line remained unbroken.*

From this time onward till early March of 1915, both sides devoted themselves to trench construction, with occasional raids, small attacks and counter-attacks. Of the raids the most important were those made by and upon the Indian troops about Givenchy, and of the minor attacks the heaviest were those at La Bassee.

In March, 1915, a new British Corps, the Vth, under Sir Herbert Plumer, came into the line north of Wytschaete; to the south of the Vth was the IInd Corps, behind Wytschaete and Messines; the IIIrd Corps (Pulteney) was east of Armentieres; the IVth Corps (Rawlinson) lay southwards from Estaires to west of Neuve Chapelle; thence the Indian Corps extended towards Givenchy; and finally came the Ist Corps linking up with the French. North of Ypres the French, with British cavalry at intervals, held from the salient to Dixmude, whence the Belgians continued the line to the sea at Nieuport. The Canadian Division came in in February.

We now had two armies in the field, the First Army (Haig), consisting of the Ist, the IVth, and the Indian Corps, and the Second Army (Smith-Dorrien), comprising the IInd, the IIIrd and the Vth Corps. The total strength of all arms was approximately half a million.†

*For the three weeks' Battle of Ypres the German losses are estimated at not less than 250,000; those of the Allies from Albert to Nieuport were over 100,000; in the Ypres fight alone the British lost 40,000.

†"It is instructive to remember that the British under Marlborough were rarely more than a division strong; that at Waterloo we had a division and a half; that at our strongest in the Peninsula we had no more than one modern army corps; that in the Crimea we had under two divisions; and that at the full tide of the South African War we

A new British offensive opened on March 10th, when troops of the First Army attacked at Neuve Chapelle, south of Armentieres, with the object of straightening the line and securing the ridge commanding Lille, Roubaix and Turcoing. To distract attention the Ist Corps attacked from Givenchy, and the IIIrd Corps advanced just south of Armentieres. They succeeded in capturing the village of Neuve Chapelle, but not the ridge. The hamlet of l'Epinette was taken on March 12th by troops of the IIIrd Corps, who advanced their line 300 yards on a front of half a mile.

The Second Battle of Ypres raged from April 22nd to May 13th, 1915, the Germans directing their attack mainly against the northern part of the salient between Ypres Canal and the Menin Road. Owing to operations elsewhere, the enemy found our line thinly held. On this occasion the Germans first used gas* in large quantities against our lines, the Canadians, who had put up a magnificent fight, suffering heavily from this barbarous weapon. As a result of the succession of attacks the salient was considerably reduced in size, but our line still remained unbroken.

Our minor offensives, such as that at Festubert, near La Bassee, in the middle of May, showed the necessity for greater artillery strength, and also that under our attacks the enemy's front did not bend but would break up into a series of field fortresses. The net result proved to be a condition of stalemate.

Midsummer activities in the West were a succession of small things, the one outstanding exception being the German attack on the French in the Argonne; and trench fighting now rose to the rank of a special science.

During the late summer of 1915 the British took over some thirty miles of additional line, and the front line from the North Sea southwards to the Somme was held thus:—Belgians and French on the Yser; British Second Army (Plumer) from

had less than a quarter of a million men. March, 1915, saw a British army assembled on the Flemish borders twelve times as large as that which had triumphed under Wellington in the Peninsula, and fifty-five times greater than the force which charged with King Harry at Agincourt."—John Buchan: "Nelson's History of the War."

*Liquid fire was first used by the Germans in their attack on the British trenches at Hooge Crater two months later.

Boesinghe, round Ypres, to a point south-west of Armentieres; the First Army (Haig) to a point due west of Lens; the French Tenth Army to the south of Arras; the new British Third Army (Monro) thence to the Somme.

The enemy held his front in varying degrees of strength, his troops being most heavily massed round Ypres, Armentieres, La Bassee, Lens, and all the avenues to Lille. For the present it was the task of the British to hold these forces in position, not necessarily to win ground.

In September the French advanced in Champagne, and as a subsidiary action to that operation we attacked at Loos on the 25th, our object being to isolate the railway junctions of Lens and open the way into the plain of the Scheldt. Loos was taken, but the greater objective was not secured. Four other but smaller attacks made at this time included one by troops of the IIIrd Corps from Bois Grenier, south-west of Armentieres, against the German trenches at le Bridoux.

This fighting died away by the beginning of November, and both sides settled down to trench work during the winter.* For several months there was little of importance to chronicle. There were endless local attacks and counter-attacks, mining and counter-mining, and an incessant struggle with nature, but no extensive operations. At this time, initiated, apparently, by the Canadians, the small raids were evolved, a novel form of minor operation by which damage was inflicted, prisoners taken for identification purposes, and the enemy kept in a constant state of tension, but in which the raiding parties always returned to their own lines without making any attempt to gain territory.

Such was the general position in Flanders when the New Zealand Division came to France in the spring of 1916.

---

*Sir Douglas Haig became Commander-in-Chief of the British Forces on December 15th, 1915.

CHAPTER V.

ARMENTIERES.

PART 1.—IN THE TRENCHES.

First tour in the line—A battalion sector—To reserve—First raid, 2nd Battalion—Australians relieved in the Rue Marle sector—Armentieres bombarded—Inter-battalion relief—4th Battalion raid—Germans raid 2nd Battalion—Enemy bombardments—Fighting patrols—Relieved by 18th Division.

On the night of 22nd/23rd of May the New Zealand Rifle Brigade commenced its first tour of duty in the trenches in France, taking over from the 2nd Brigade part of the sector due east of Armentieres. During the previous day or two a careful reconnaissance had been carried out by officers and non-commissioned officers, who made themselves as thoroughly acquainted as possible with the whole area, and more particularly with the front-line trenches and No Man's Land. Specialists, such as Lewis gunners and observers, went in on the 21st, thus ensuring that there should be no break in their particular work. The 1st Battalion relieved 2nd Auckland in the Epinette sub-sector—the point of the salient—while 2nd Otago was relieved by the 3rd Battalion. The 2nd and 4th Battalions came in on the night of 23rd/24th, the former relieving 2nd Canterbury in the Pont Ballot sub-sector on the left of the 1st Battalion, and the latter taking over from 2nd Wellington the remainder of the Brigade sector from Hobbs' Farm to the River Lys. The battalions were now in their normal order from right to left, and the area occupied by the Brigade formed the left sector of the Divisional front. The 1st Brigade was on our right, and across the River Lys on our left were troops of the 9th Division.

All ranks were fairly familiar with the sector generally, for, in addition to the preliminary visits paid by officers and non-commissioned officers, the battalions had, since the 19th, been supplying working parties for the trenches up to sixty per cent. of their total strength. It was, nevertheless, a strange experience, this first taking-over of a sector of the line, with all that it meant in the matter of responsibility, to say nothing of the possibilities before us. Yet, to many, these serious aspects bulked less largely than such immediate difficulties as the passage of the narrow communication trenches, in the darkness, and encumbered by the loads of impedimenta of various kinds, for in those days we took a good issue of blankets into the trenches, and the cooking was done even in the front line itself. The finding of dug-out quarters, the exchange of sentries in the fire-bays, the relief of trench-officers, the checking of stores and equipment, and a hundred other duties and formalities, were to us by no means an easy task; but all was successfully accomplished, and in good time we had returned the "Cheerio!" of the last of the outgoing troops, and had sent off in code the message "Relief complete."

The sketch-map opposite page 96 shows the more important details of a battalion sector of the front-line trench system. It is that occupied by the 1st Battalion when the Brigade first went into the line. The heavy lines represent the trenches, and those of the Germans opposite the sector are also shown, but in lesser detail. As an indication of the low-lying nature of the ground, it may be pointed out that what appear to be narrow roads are really drains as they originally existed, the water from most of these finding its way into a larger drain, the Becque de la Blue, and thence into the River Lys at Armentieres. With this word of explanation in mind, the two or three roads leading forward, as well as that along which the front trench had been constructed, will easily be distinguished. The roads, of course, even if they had not been broken up by shell-fire, were useless as ordinary means of access to the various parts of the sector, for, as the ground rose behind the German line, the enemy had our area well under observation. The actual front-line trench, some 1300 yards in length, extended from Auckland Avenue on the right to Hepburn Avenue on the left, where the 2nd Battalion sector began. As will be seen, it followed the line of scattered houses, or rather their remains, that once formed the hamlet of l'Epinette. It was not held continuously throughout its whole length, but was divided into four "localities" separated by "gaps," with the object of breaking up any attack the enemy might make. The localities were sited and constructed in such a way that not only were they practically self-contained, and so expected to hold out for a considerable time unaided, but they were also able to bring crossfire to bear in support of one another. The gaps were so placed that the enemy breaking through, which he would more easily do at these points, would be dealt with conveniently by the garrison of the covering trenches in rear, while at the same time he would be subjected to flanking fire from the localities. The gaps were not occupied, but were systematically patrolled under arrangements made by the officers in charge of the neighbouring garrisons; and every precaution was taken, by means of construction work and camouflage, to ensure that any difference between the occupied and the unoccupied trenches should be imperceptible from aeroplane or other observation.

As the soil-water level practically corresponded with the surface of the ground, all the trenches, whether in forward or rear lines, were formed of earthworks. The fighting trenches were broken up into fire-bays, the spaces between being solid and thick enough to minimize the lateral effect of shell-fire as well as to afford protection from flanking fire. Where the construction was well advanced, a travel-trench was added to and connected with the fire-trench, so that it was possible to walk along the trench either by winding in and out of the fire-bays, or by moving along the travel-trench without disturbing the men in the bays.

The earthworks were supported to a certain height on the inner side by means of wooden frames lined with boards or corrugated iron or "expanded-iron" netting. The most effective frame was made somewhat in the form of an inverted capital A; the "duck-board" flooring rested on the cross-bar, which at the same time acted as a strut, and the drainage collected and flowed beneath. Above the framing the required height of cover was secured by resorting to sandbagging. Owing to repeated bombardments and reconstructions the most advanced earthworks developed into an intricate maze of abandoned masses of tumbled timber and clay, with new fire-bays pushed into the most unexpected places. In the parados, the bank of earth forming the rear part of the trench, were little "dug-outs" where the men not on duty snatched their brief periods of fitful sleep. In general they were large enough to hold four men. The walls, formed of bags of clay, were sometimes lined with timber, while the discomfort was in some degree lessened by covering the earthen floor with sections of duck-board. The roofs were formed of corrugated iron resting on iron or wooden rails, with earth piled on top in sufficient thickness to afford protection from shrapnel. They were usually entered from the passages connecting the fire-bays with the travel-trench. Occasionally, where the parapet was unusually thick, these so-called dug-outs were constructed in that bank. In similar structures stores of water, rations and ammunition were kept. In the front line of the battalion sector there were two Vickers machine-guns in concrete emplacements which were sited to sweep the two sides of the angle forming the salient. As they were intended for defensive purposes only, they were normally silent. The positions of these and also of the Lewis guns are indicated in the diagram.

For the sake of clearness the belt of wire entanglement that ran along the forward side of the advanced trench is not shown; lines of crosses mark the position of barbed wire in other parts.

Behind the front line ran a close-support system, and in rear of this again a second support line. Much farther back was a reserve or subsidiary system. Owing to the peculiar shape of the front trench-line, the rear trenches had to be sited so as to cope with an attack on either or both sides of the salient.

Between the support and the reserve systems we had in this sector two strong-points known as S.P.X. and S.P.Y., and in the sector held by the 2nd Battalion there was a third, called S.P.Z. These were little all-round systems constructed on slightly-rising ground, and designed to break up the enemy's attack if that should succeed in breaking through the forward lines. The garrison of each was one platoon, strengthened by a Vickers gun and crew.

Access to this part of the Brigade sector was had mainly through the communication trench known as Buterne Lane, which, from the main road of Houplines, a suburb of Armentieres, led to the subsidiary line. Byrne's Boulevard led forward from this, and branched off to Plank Avenue, connecting up with the right of the forward system, and to Willow Walk and Japan Road, by means of which the other face of the salient was most conveniently reached. Each of these was well constructed, and was provided at intervals with fire-steps so that the communication trench could be used to form an effective flank if the need should arise.

The battalion sector was garrisoned as follows: "A" Company held the locality on the right, and found its own supports. "B" Company was responsible for the three smaller localities, namely, one consisting of the Retrenchment, with its advanced posts at 5th and 6th Houses, a second locality at 2nd House, and a third forming the miniature salient east of Japan Farm. Two platoons of "D" Company were in support to "B." These were located in the support and second support lines, supplied posts in the Pioneers' Retrenchment then under construction, and were to be prepared to reinforce the garrison of either face of the main salient. The remaining platoons of this company occupied S.P.Y. and S.P.X., which they were to hold at all costs. "C" Company, in reserve, had two platoons in the trenches of the subsidiary line and two in Quality Street. Battalion Headquarters and the Regimental Aid Post were in Willow Walk.

Rations and general supplies came up from Houplines by way of the tramway constructed along the road marked "Australia Avenue;" but as the forward portions of the tram-line were frequently out of repair owing to shell-fire, supplies were usually dumped near the junction of Willow Walk and Japan Road, and from this point distributed by carrying parties.

A word might be added as to the mode of indicating exactly positions on the map, and thus on the ground. A sheet to the scale of 1 in 20,000 would represent an area of, roughly, ten miles by six. This itself would be one-fourth of a larger rectangle, the four parts of which were distinguished by the terms N.W., N.E., S.W., and S.E., respectively. This greater division was numbered, and the particular sheet used by us for general purposes was known as 36 N.W. This sheet was divided into a number of large squares, bearing the letters A, B, C, etc., in capitals. Each of these was again divided, by what were known as the "grid-lines" of the map, into thirty or perhaps thirty-six squares, numbered accordingly. Finally, each of these was subdivided into four squares, the two upper being a and b, and the two lower c and d, but there was, of course, no necessity to show these letters on the map. The side of the quarter-square always represented a length of 500 yards. By judgment, or by means of a cardboard scale, the sides were again subdivided into ten, or where greater accuracy was required, into one hundred imaginary parts; but in maps drawn to a large scale the tenths were shown on the gridlines. Now, to state the position of a given point within the square, the eye runs along the bottom of the square from left to right until it reaches the part of the line immediately below the point, and the subdivision here is noted; similarly, the eye runs up the left side until opposite the point, and this subdivision is noted also. Thus, on the accompanying sketch, which is based on a small portion of Sheet 36 N.W., and covers part of the C and I rectangles, Chicken Farm is at point I. 5.c. 35.70. So, also, the map reference for Strong-Point Y would be given as I. 4.b. 95.65, and that for Strong-Point Z as C. 28.d. 80.25. The point of the salient would be stated as being at I. 5. central.*

Our men quickly adapted themselves to the new conditions and soon became proficient in all branches of stationary trench-warfare, as well as in the various forms of labour entailed in the upkeep and improvement of an extensive trench-system. The New Zealanders found that what had been sufficient cover for their predecessors was not nearly high enough for them.

*The printed trench-maps usually gave no details in the area occupied by the British, beyond what could be obtained from any ordnance map drawn to the same scale. On the other hand, they showed the German trench-system in great detail, information regarding which was obtained from aeroplane photographs, and, in the preparation of the plates, superimposed upon the ordinary French ordnance maps. The use of an ingenious prismatic instrument enabled this to be done by hand with great ease and exactitude.

The reproduction of an aeroplane photograph, facing page 97, to show the locality of the 2nd Battalion's raid, covers also a portion of the ground referred to in the description given above. It was taken about a fortnight before we went into the line. In this the bright, even lines of the roads are clearly contrasted with the dark lines of the drains. The abandoned fields in our own territory as well as in No Man's Land are plainly marked, and the practised eye may distinguish the shadows cast by orchard and hedge trees. The embankments forming the communication and fighting trenches show, as usual, with great clearness. Buterne Farm and the three strong-points, X, Y, and Z, may readily be picked up, as also may the patch of trampled ground between the tramway on Australia Avenue and Willow Walk, over which innumerable carrying parties had passed by night as they took supplies to the front-line trenches. The effects of artillery bombardment appear to be more striking on the German side of No Man's Land than on our own; Box Farm, for instance, had been so battered as to be almost indistinguishable, but it will be seen, also, that Buterne Farm had not escaped attention of this kind.

and they had to set to work at once to raise all breastworks by two or three additional layers of sandbags. It was soon discovered, also, that the entanglements in front of the line were far from perfect, and night wiring-parties found constant employment filling up breaks caused by shell-fire, and adding to the depth of the existing wire. Our snipers immediately began to gain ascendancy over those of our neighbours across the way, and very soon all old "windy" notice-boards in our line, bearing such warnings as "Keep low," "Beware of Sniper," were torn down. Above all, our patrols reached a high pitch of efficiency, moved about No Man's Land with great boldness and cunning, and frequently brought in trophies such as snipers' plates and samples of the enemy's wire. In the work of patrolling, all had to take their share, and the experience so gained was of inestimable value as one of the factors making for the maintenance of high morale.

Our casualties for the month of May were:—

	Killed.	Wounded.
Officers	—	1
Other Ranks	5	54

The first officer to become a casualty was 2nd Lieut. J. H. Cock, 3rd Battalion, who was wounded on May 31st.

Included in this list were three men of the 3rd Battalion killed and two wounded through the small dug-out they were occupying being struck by a high-explosive shell during a concentrated enemy bombardment of the trenches. The occupants were buried in the debris, and the company commander (Capt. Drummond), who happened to be in the vicinity on his round of inspection, proceeded, with the assistance of Sergeant S. F. Breach and Riflemen W. B. Thomson, J. H. Cannon and T. Barrow, to dig out the buried men—a task which, in spite of the continued heavy shell-fire and of the fact that they were in full view of the enemy owing to the breaching of the parapet, the fearless little party succeeded in accomplishing, fortunately without further casualties. Actions such as this were common enough in later days. Mention of the incident is made merely to indicate not only the fine spirit with which our men, as yet inexperienced and unseasoned, were imbued, but also that adaptability to strange circumstances which was to stand them in such good stead in the varied experiences that lay before them.

At the beginning of June we were relieved by the 2nd Brigade, 2nd Auckland and 2nd Otago taking over from the 1st and 3rd Battalions on the night of 1st/2nd, and the 2nd and 4th Battalions being relieved by 2nd Canterbury and 2nd Wellington on the following night. We were again billeted in Armentieres. The Brigade became Divisional reserve, and the 3rd Battalion was detailed as Brigade reserve to the left sector, the 1st Battalion as garrison of the Armentieres lines of defence.

The period spent out of the line was by no means one of slothful ease. Large parties were regularly supplied for construction and repair work in the forward lines, these duties being carried out under the general supervision of Engineer officers, and having for their object the rapid improvement of the defences of the sector. Thus our men, while having the advantage of better living-quarters, still had to face the same difficulties and dangers that formed part of their lot while holding the trenches. Certainly the strain was not so constant, but the opinion was often expressed—for it is the soldier's privilege to grumble—that they were better off in than out of the line. Training was carried on whenever possible, but this was perforce usually confined to practice in rapid wiring and the further instruction of specialists in their important work. In addition the 1st Battalion was employed in preparing to occupy the inner defences of the town in case of emergency, while a party of the 2nd Battalion was busily engaged perfecting its arrangements and training for a raid.

Our first raid on enemy trenches was carried out by the 2nd Battalion on June 25th.* The Somme offensive was about to open, and it was necessary to endeavour to compel the enemy to maintain his strength outside the region that the Allied forces were to assault. To this end a period of special artillery activity commenced on June 24th, and continued for eighteen days, and from Ypres southward to the Somme a great series of raids was carried out against the German trenches. The sector selected for our particular enterprise was opposite that which the battalion had recently held to the

*The Division's earliest raid was that undertaken by a party from the 2nd Otago Battalion under Capt. Alley and Lieut. Espiner, on June 16.

left of l'Epinette; and full knowledge of No Man's Land and of the enemy's wire had been gained by repeated patrolling during the period spent in holding the line, and also while the unit was out in reserve.

The orders for the raid, which are given below, indicate the extent to which every point was thought out and every emergency provided for. The various blanks in the orders were kept open till the very last convenient moment. Lieut.- Col. Stewart's temporary headquarters were in the front-line trench. All subsequent raids were executed along similar lines, though later on, as units became accustomed to this class of work, the written instructions gave less and less attention to minute detail.

How successful this operation proved to be will be seen from the report of the raid, which is also given in full.

3RD NEW ZEALAND (RIFLE) BRIGADE. Order No. 8.

Headquarters, 18th June, 1916.

Reference Map: Armentieres, Sheet 36, N.W.2, 1/10,000 and attached sketch 1/2,500.

1. On the night of......June, 1916, the 2nd Battalion, N.Z.(R.)Bde., will carry out a raid on the enemy's trenches opposite PONT BALLOT, from C.29.a.4.1½ to C.29.a.5.4. (where ditch enters trench), with the following objects:—
   (a) To take prisoners and secure identifications.
   (b) To capture or destroy any machine-guns or trench mortars found.
   (c) To report on enemy's trenches and dug-outs.
   (d) To decrease enemy's morale.
   (e) To obtain all information possible.

2. The following information has been obtained by reconnaissance:—
   (a) The stream running from C.29.a.1½.2¾. in N.E. direction to C.29.a.3.4½. is about 3 ft. wide and shallow, with a hedge on the eastern bank.
   (b) The ground rises slightly in a S.E. direction from the stream to mid-way to the "Four Daisies" Road (C.29.a.2½.2.), and then falls to the road.
   (c) The "Four Daisies" Road (C.29.a.2½.1½. to C.29.a.4.¾.) is a flat turf road, wired along its length except for a passage way on western side. The wire is composed of

knife rests covered with thick barbed wire. These rests could easily be lifted aside by hand or destroyed by T.M. bombs. From C.29.a.2½.1½. there is a shallow ditch 6 to 8 feet wide, filled with two-strand galvanized barbed wire, which runs for 50 yards along eastern face of road where the ditch ends. This wire is continued to within 20 ft. of C.29.a.4.3½.
- (d) The ditch running from C.29.a.3¾.4¼. in a S.E. direction through the enemy's trenches is dry throughout its length, but blocked with earth where "Four Daisies" Road crosses it.
- (e) From S.E. of "Four Daisies" patch to the PONT BALLOT—BRUNE RUE Road the ground is a mass of barbed wire.
- (f) There are two saps running out from the enemy's trenches, one on either end of the portion to be attacked. The northern end is known to be occupied as a listening post, and is guarded at its head by knife rests.
- (g) The grass is long between ASSEMBLY POINT, C.29.a. 3.4¼. and "Four Daisies" Road, but is shorter on the German side of the road.
- (h) There are not thought to be enemy machine-guns in the portion of the trench to be raided, and the trenches are reported to be lightly held.

3. The reasons why this portion of the enemy's line was chosen are as follow:—
- (a) Impossible for enemy to bring enfilade fire from the Southern trenches on our right, or near enfilade fire on our left flank.
- (b) Our artillery can establish a barrage on flanks and support line.
- (c) Only one communication trench (C.29.a.5¼.3.) into firetrench.
- (d) Nearest point of support trench is 120 yards in rear.
- (e) Ground in No Man's Land is suitable for an ASSEMBLY POINT in at least two places.
- (f) Roads and hedge on flank to keep direction.

4. The following troops, under Capt. A. J. Powley, 2nd Battalion, N.Z.(R.) Bde., will take part in the advance and attack:—
- (a) PATROL—1 N.C.O. and 4 men.
- (b) LEFT BOMBING PARTY—Lt. Castle, 2 N.C.O.'s and 10 men.
- (c) ASSAULT PARTY—Lt. Davidson, 2 N.C.O.'s, 10 men and 2 Engineers.

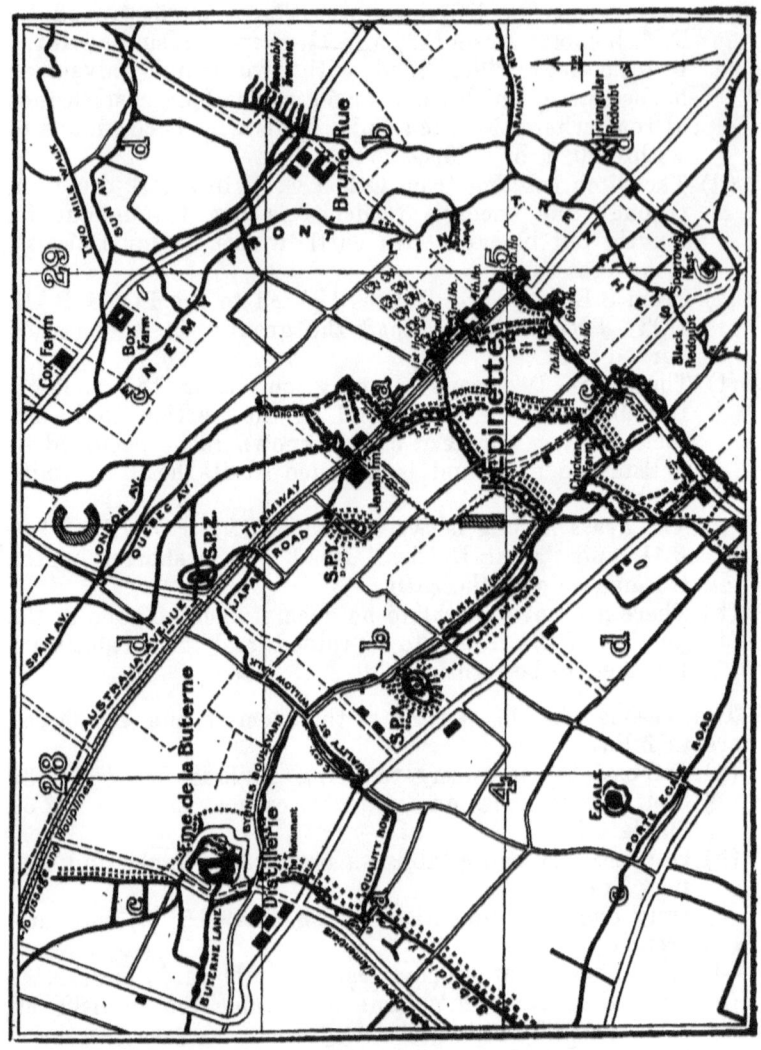

Sketch-Map of a Battalion Sector, L'Epinette, Armentieres.

Face p. 96.

AEROPLANE PHOTOGRAPH OF THE TRENCHES ABOUT PONT BALLOT, east of Armentieres, the scene of the raid by the 2nd Battalion on June 25th, 1916.

References:—
    E : the point of exit from our trench;
    B : the assembly-ditch;
    A and C : the flank point of the section raided ;
    D : the group of shell-holes known as the Four Daisies.

(d) INTELLIGENCE—2 men.
(e) RIGHT BOMBING PARTY—2 N.C.O.'s and 10 men.
(f) LEFT FLANK PARTY—1 N.C.O. and 2 men, with Lewis gun.
(g) O.C. RAID AND SIGNALLERS—Capt. A. J. Powley, 1 N.C.O. and 3 men.
(h) STRETCHER-BEARERS—1 N.C.O. and 8 men (4 stretchers).
(i) RIGHT FLANK PARTY—1 N.C.O. and 2 men, with Lewis gun.
(j) MESSENGERS—6 men.

TOTAL: 3 Officers, 11 N.C.O.'s, 59 men.

5. PATROL will leave our trenches (T.80 and 81) at C.29.a.$\frac{1}{2}.\frac{3}{4}$., and wait at Assembly Point until rest of party arrive; and after bombardment has lifted, they will move forward and will cut the wire at point selected. When wire is cut, they will inform O.C. Assault and guide the Assaulting Party through the gap. When Assaulting Party has entered the trenches, the Patrol will collect under the parapet and prepare an exit for Assault Party; they will take charge of any prisoners.

ASSAULT PARTY will leave our trenches at C.29.a.$\frac{1}{4}.\frac{1}{4}$., and will move to the point of assembly, C.29.a.3.4$\frac{1}{2}$, eastern bank of stream. When the Patrol moves forward, the Assault Party will follow in rear to within 30 yards of "FOUR DAISIES" ROAD, where they will wait until Patrol has reported wire to be cut. The O.C. Assault Party will give the order to move through the wire and enter the enemy's trenches.

The Assault Party will move through the gap in single file, extend on a frontage of one man per yard, and enter the trench to their front. They will take one prisoner at once, and then kill any other enemy met with there. When this has been done, half the party will move to either flank and get in touch with the bombing parties on our flanks, forming connecting links down the trench. The prisoners will be passed along the trench to O.C. Assault Party at the point of exit from the trench. The Assault Party will not take more than 3 prisoners in all.

As soon as the enemy's trenches are entered, the O.C. Assault Party will send back a runner to report to O.C. Raid. O.C. Raid will send back the word "entered" by telephone and lamp to O.C. Attack. As soon as the parties have returned to the Assembly Point after the raid, the O.C. Raid will send "returned" by telephone and lamp to O.C. Attack.

RIGHT BOMBING PARTY will follow the Assault Party and, on reaching the wire, will move up on their right in single file and enter the trench. Half the party, with senior N.C.O., will at once move along the trench to C.29.a.4.1½, killing any enemy met with. On their point being reached they will block the trench, and prevent anyone giving assistance to portion of trench raided. The remainder of the party will work up the trench from point of entry to the blocking party, clearing dug-outs and taking prisoners. Not more than 3 prisoners to be taken.

LEFT BOMBING PARTY will follow Assault Party and, on reaching the wire, will move up on their left, in single file, and enter the trench. Lt. Castle, 1 N.C.O., 2 bayonet men, and 6 bombers will move along trench, killing any enemy met with, to C.29.a.5.4. (ditch), where they will block the communication trench just SOUTH of the ditch, and also the main fire-trench. The remainder of the party will act in a similar manner to the remainder of the right bombing party.

INTELLIGENCE MEN will move in rear of ASSAULT PARTY in the trench and search enemy dead and dug-outs, and will remove and bring back pay-books, identity discs, shoulder-straps, letters, pocket-books, specimen of flares, revolvers, gas helmets, etc. They will pay particular attention to the construction and design of trenches and dug-outs.

MESSENGERS. One each with O.C. Assault Party, Right and Left Bombing Parties, and 2 to remain with O.C. Raid. The messenger with O.C. Assault Party will carry with him a luminous tape, which he will pay out from a point 30 yards in front of enemy's wire up to enemy's parapet and into trench.

LEFT FLANK PARTY will move out from our trenches in rear of Right Bombing Party to the Assembly Point C.29.a.3.4½., and will take up a position at junction of road and stream. They will be prepared to deal with any enemy who move out NORTH of the raiding area.

RIGHT FLANK PARTY will move out in rear of stretcher-bearers from our trenches, keeping to the NORTH side of PONT BALLOT—BRUNE RUE ROAD to junction of that road with the "FOUR DAISIES" ROAD, where they will take up a position to deal with any enemy who move out SOUTH of the raiding area.

SIGNALLERS will move out in rear of Left Flank Party and lay out two lines along stream bank to Assembly Point. They will take with them three telephone sets and two electric signal lamps.

6. Parties will move out from our trenches at C.29.a.½.¾. in the following order:—
>   Patrol.
>   Left Bombing Party.
>   Assault Party.
>   Intelligence Party.
>   Right Bombing Party.
>   Left Flank Party.
>   O.C. Raid and Signallers.
>   Stretcher-bearers.
>   Right Flank Party.

7. O.C. RAID will remain at Assembly Point C.29.a.3.4½. with signallers, 2 messengers and stretcher-bearers.

8. O.C. ATTACK, Lt.-Col. A. E. Stewart, 2nd Bn., will be at ....with signallers and messengers. With him will be the Divisional Trench Mortar Officer (Capt. White) and Artillery Liaison Officer.

9. DRESS. All ranks will wear general service uniform with boots and puttees. Steel helmets will be worn. Faces and hands will be blackened. Every man will have a piece of white material 3 inches broad on each arm. These will be covered with a piece of dark cloth, which will be removed on entering the hostile trenches. Gas helmets will be carried by all ranks.

10. THE RAIDING PARTY will assemble at ....p.m. at the head of FIJI AVENUE at junction of "stop" in LOCALITY 6a. Six spare men will also parade. O.C. Attack will carefully inspect all ranks to see that they are carrying nothing likely to be of value to the enemy.

11. ACTION. Parties will move out to the ASSEMBLY POINT from C.29.a.½.¾. at the following times:—
>   0 (Zero)*—Patrol.
>   0.15—The remainder of the Raiding Party in the order given in Para. 6. They will collect at the Assembly Point and there remain.
>   0.45—The artillery will open fire on the portion of the trench to be raided, and also on the flanks and supporting trenches in rear. At the same time the Trench Mortar Batteries will cut the wire as nearly as possible at C.29.a.4½.3.
>   1.00—The barrage will be lifted and concentrated on enemy's flank and support trenches. The raiding

*Zero hour was 10.30 p.m. The remaining times are given in hours and minutes after zero.

party, preceded by the patrol, will advance to within 30 yards of the enemy's wire, in 3 columns in single file from right to left: Right Bombing Party, Assault Party, Left Bombing Party. They will then carry on as in Para. 5.

NO ONE is on any account to move forward from the Assembly Point until 1.00.

The right flank party will not move from our trenches up to its position until 1.00, and, on the signal for withdrawal being received, will remain another 5 minutes in their position and then withdraw to our trenches.

12. Should the N.C.O. in charge of the Patrol find that all the wire has not been cut, he will send back to O.C. Assault and at once start cutting the wire. The O.C. Assault is responsible for keeping touch with the Patrol.

13. Wounded men will either walk or be carried back at once.

14. Prisoners will be handed out at once from the point of exit, and will be taken over by the Patrol, who will escort them to O.C. Raid.

15. WITHDRAWAL. The raiding party will not remain in the enemy's trenches more than 10 minutes, but may be withdrawn earlier on a signal given by the O.C. Assault. The signal for withdrawal will be two long and two short blasts on the whistle, which will be passed along the trench by the Assault Party, and repeated by Officers and N.C.O.'s in charge of parties. All parties must return to the point of exit within one minute of signal, and Officers or N.C.O.'s in charge must ensure that no man is left unwarned. There must be no delay in returning to exit after signal for withdrawal has been made; should any party be actively engaged they should hold on for a short time longer, but must send a man to report at once to O.C. Assault Party.

The LEFT BOMBING PARTY will be the last to leave, and will cover the retirement of the party. After passing through the wire, parties will move back to the Assembly Point as rapidly as possible, and report at once to O.C. Raid.

16. The O.C. Raid will decide whether parties are to remain at Assembly Point until retaliation has ceased, or return to our trenches. Should he adopt the former course, he will inform the O.C. Attack as to his action and the situation, so that our barrage can be discontinued. He must make similar arrangements for wounded and prisoners.

17. The O.C. Attack will arrange to evacuate prisoners and wounded to the rear, and to provide the escort for prisoners, who should be taken to Advanced Brigade Headquarters, together with any captured documents. Prisoners should not

be allowed to converse with each other, and should be kept apart. As soon as possible after return to the trenches, the O.C. Attack and all officers engaged in the raid, together with Intelligence men, will report to Advanced Brigade Headquarters.

18. The Raiding Party, on returning to our trenches, will give their names to O.C. Attack and move off to their billets. The names will also be checked again at exits from Spain and Gloucester Avenues.

19. The following special telephone wires will be laid:—
   (a) 1 line from Advanced Brigade Headquarters to O.C. Attack.
   (b) 1 line from artillery group to Liaison Officer.
   (c) 1 line from O.C. 2nd Auckland Bn. to O.C. Attack.

If these lines fail runners will have to be employed where possible.

20. All watches will be synchronized at 9 a.m., 3 p.m., and 8.30 p.m. on the day of the raid, by telephone with Brigade Headquarters.

21. In order to warn all units concerned, and also neighbouring units, of the night selected for the raid, the following message will be sent: "............," the hour named being the approximate time the patrol will leave our trenches. Should the operations be postponed, the following message will be sent: "............"

22. The O.C. Attack may at any time decide not to proceed with the operations, and if he so decides, must inform Advanced Brigade Headquarters at once.

23. The Brigade Grenade Officer will provide all the bombs necessary for the Raiding Party, and will carefully inspect these both before and after being fused.

24. O.C. 2nd Battalion will arrange with his Medical Officer for spare stretchers to be at hand.

25. A countersign will be arranged for all parties going over the parapets.

26. Major R. St. J. Beere, 2nd Bn., will remain in the vicinity of O.C. Attack during operations, and will take over the duties should the latter become a casualty. He should, however, not be in the same dug-out.

27. O.C. Artillery Group and O.C. Machine Gun Company will report to Advanced Brigade Headquarters at .... p.m.

28. Reports to Advanced Brigade Headquarters at 2nd N.Z. Infantry Brigade Headquarters, 5 Rue Jesuit.

REPORT ON RAID ON ENEMY'S TRENCHES BY PARTY OF 2ND BATTALION, 3RD NEW ZEALAND (RIFLE) BRIGADE.

NARRATIVE.

The raid was carried out in accordance with Brigade Order No. 8, dated 18th June, 1916.

The scouts went out at 10.30 p.m., cut a way through our wire, reconnoitred the ground to front and flanks, and heard a wiring party working on the wire at the point to be raided.

At 10.45 p.m. the Raiding Party commenced to leave the trenches for the Assembly Point. All ranks were in position at 11.9 p.m., and bombardment commenced at the appointed time, 11.15 p.m.

Both telephone wires to the Assembly Point were broken immediately bombardment commenced—it is thought by "blow-backs" from our own trench mortars, as the enemy's retaliation had not commenced. Enemy's retaliation commenced at 11.25 p.m., and fell on support trenches S 80 and 81.

At 11.30 p.m. our bombardment on front line trenches lifted.

The Assaulting Party, preceded by scouts, advanced, and found all enemy's entanglements broken up with the exception of three strands on a width of 20 yards at the nearest point and 20 feet at the parapet. The ditch in front of the enemy's trench was found to be about 8 feet wide and 5 feet deep, and was difficult to cross.

11.36 p.m. The party assaulted the trenches and carried out the programme arranged.

11.51 p.m. They remained in the trenches for fifteen minutes and then withdrew.

Up to this time there had been no casualties. While withdrawing, an enemy's bomb, carried by one of the men, Rifleman McPhee, exploded, killing him and wounding three others. These men were amongst the last seven or eight to leave, and there was some difficulty in getting them away. A large quantity of papers, equipment, etc., was left in No Man's Land in consequence. An attempt will be made to recover some of this to-night. During the withdrawal five other men were wounded.

The party came into our trenches between 12.5 and 12.30 a.m.

At 12.33 a.m. the artillery bombardment was stopped. The artillery should have stopped at about midnight, but, owing to telephonic communication breaking down, information could not be sent that all men were in.

From a careful estimate, 29 Germans were killed by the Assaulting Party, and 9 prisoners were brought in; 7 were handed to the A.P.M., and 2 Germans (wounded) are in the hospital.

ARTILLERY.—Support was excellent. No damage, however, was done by the howitzers to the portion of the trenches assaulted. Just beyond the northern end, the enemy's trench was well broken up by the howitzers.

The medium trench mortar fire was very good and effective.

The enemy was completely cowed, and put up practically no resistance.

TRENCHES. The enemy's trench is dug out of the ground—in fact is a trench with a parapet of about one foot, and a glacis to the ditch in front. It is revetted with hurdles, and is very narrow. The ditch was 8 feet wide and 5 feet deep, and, though quite dry, was found a difficult obstacle to negotiate. The width of his parapet was about 20 feet. The parados is solid earth. Fire-steps were similar to our own. Under the parapet was a good dug-out, with table and electric light; also a number of "funk-holes," lined with timber, and large enough to hold two or three men. The duck-boards were of the same kind as ours.

Two sappers were taken with the party, and were instrumental in doing considerable damage to the enemy's works. They located a gas-engine, similar to a Lister engine, used for pumping purposes, and absolutely wrecked it with five slabs of gun-cotton. The dug-out was also wrecked, and two bomb-stores blown up.

No machine-gun emplacement was found, nor any machine-guns. There was a wire from the trench to the support trenches, with a "pull," probably for a bell. In the trench was a big bell, probably for a gas alarm. No sign of mine-shafts could be found.

A large quantity of papers, bombs, five gas helmets, and five rifles were collected.

The attack was carried out under the orders of Lt.-Col. A. E. Stewart, O.C. 2nd Battalion, 3rd New Zealand (Rifle) Brigade.

The raiding party was commanded by Capt. A. J. Powley, and the assaulting party was under Lieuts. A. P. Castle and C. J. H. Davidson.

The raiding party consisted of 3 officers and 70 other ranks, 2nd Battalion, 3rd N.Z. (R.) Bde., and 2 other ranks N.Z. Engineers.

I desire to express my appreciation of the excellent work done by all ranks and the cool manner in which all the details were carried through.

(Signed) H. T. FULTON, Brigadier-General,
Commanding 3rd N.Z. (R). Bde.

In connection with this achievement, undoubtedly brilliant, and all the more noteworthy for the fact that it was a first attempt, only one modest recommendation was made for immediate recognition of meritorious service, and Capt. A. J. Powley was in due course awarded the Military Cross. Later, however, the special services of Lance-Corporals H. G. Le Comte and W. W. C. Bedggood, upon whose excellent work as scouts and patrols much of the success of the enterprise depended, were recognized by the award of the Military Medal.

Of the many commendatory messages received by the Brigade, probably the most highly prized was that sent through Divisional Headquarters by General Birdwood, commanding the Ist Anzac Corps, who telegraphed as follows:—

"Well done, New Zealand! Congratulations on success of your raid. Please convey congratulations to Rifle Brigade."

For the month of June the casualties in the Brigade were:

	Killed.	Wounded.
Officers	2	1
Other Ranks	21	90

It will be noted that although we were engaged in stationary trench warfare, the casualties were somewhat heavy. They were caused almost entirely by shell-fire, which was intermittently active both on the trenches and on the town.

The New Zealand Rifle Brigade relieved the 6th Australian Brigade in the Rue Marle sector, south of Armentieres, at the beginning of July. The 2nd Battalion took over from the 23rd Australian Battalion in the front line on the right, or Bois Grenier, sub-sector on the night of 2nd/3rd July, the 1st Battalion at the same time going into the subsidiary line at Bois Grenier, relieving the 22nd Australians. A very heavy bombardment of Armentieres rendered relief difficult, one company of the 1st Battalion being cut off in the town for an hour.

This was a lurid night. The artillery activity on both sides was more intense than anything we had yet experienced; and to make matters worse, the enemy's incendiary shells ignited buildings in various parts of Armentieres. The 4th Battalion Headquarters were repeatedly struck, and Major A. E. Wolstenholme, and the medical officer, Capt. F. E.

Guthrie, were killed by the explosion of an 8-inch shell. On the following night the 4th Battalion relieved the 24th Australians in the front line on the left, or Lille Road, sub-sector, and the 3rd Battalion went into Brigade reserve in Rue Marle, in which village Brigade Headquarters were established. The 4th Australian Brigade was in the line on our right, and the 1st New Zealand Infantry Brigade on our left. All three Brigades of the New Zealand Division were now in the line, and there was practically no reserve. During the night of 8th/9th July the Germans raided the "Mushroom," in the 1st Brigade's line, a good deal of the enemy's bombardment falling on our trenches.

At this time, in the deserted fields within the trench-system, poppies began to bloom, and the whole countryside, including even some parts of No Man's Land, was soon a blaze of scarlet. Here and there these gay flowers showed themselves in masses on the edges and down the sides of the otherwise prosaic communication-trenches; while in places whole stretches of barbed-wire belts behind our front line were transformed into delightful banks of brilliant silky bloom.

An inter-battalion relief was effected on the night of 11th/12th July, the 3rd Battalion* from Rue Marle changing places with the 1st in the Subsidiary Line at Bois Grenier.

General Plumer, commanding the Second Army, in company with G.O.C. Division, visited the Brigade on the 13th and expressed his appreciation of the successful efforts made in carrying out his general instructions as to holding the opposing force in position.

On July 14th orders were received for a readjustment of the line, our Brigade being instructed to side-step to the right, taking over from the 8th Australian Brigade, then under orders to move to the Somme battlefield, as far south as the Bridoux Salient, but retaining also half of the old sector. In accordance with these orders, the 1st Battalion moved up from Rue Marle on the same evening and relieved the 30th Australian Battalion on our right, and on the following night 1st Wellington took over our left sub-sector from the 4th Battalion. The adjustment was completed on the night of

---

*The 3rd Battalion was now under the command of Major A. Winter-Evans. Lieut.-Col. J. A. Cowles, who had been evacuated sick a few days previously, did not return to the unit.

16th/17th, when the 4th Battalion relieved the 31st Australians in the Subsidiary Line, and the 3rd Battalion took over from the 32nd Australians in reserve. The New Zealand Division now held a front normally occupied by two Divisions.

Before moving out, the 4th Battalion launched a successful raid on the enemy trenches opposite the Lille Road Salient on the night of 14th/15th July. The party consisted of three officers and 118 other ranks, Major J. Pow being in command, with Capt. H. C. Meikle and 2nd Lieut. A. J. Price in charge of the assaulting parties.

The plan of attack was generally on the lines of the raid by the 2nd Battalion, but in three respects it was somewhat unique. In the first place the artillery bombardment was divided into two phases, separated by an hour's interval, the first of these constituting what was known as a dummy raid, and the second, immediately preceding the real attack, being designed to catch the enemy at work while effecting repairs to his trenches. Then a machine-gun barrage, the idea of which originated with Lieut. L. S. Cimino, of the 3rd Machine Gun Company, was used for the first time, and this proved so satisfactory as to become a recognized feature in most subsequent operations, major as well as minor. In the third place, the troops participating in the raid had had no special training whatever, and the admirable smoothness with which the operation was carried out is sufficient indication of skilful planning, fine leadership, and excellent discipline. Our men, however, were somewhat disappointed at the results of their endeavours, for the double bombardment had been so intense and accurate that both the trenches and their garrison were found to be completely obliterated. Not a little of the success of the undertaking was due to the excellent work of the scouts and patrols, conspicuous among whom were Sergeant J. A. Martin and Rifleman D. P. Geaney. On the night prior to the raid, the patrol of which Geaney was a member was fired upon and an officer and a sergeant wounded. These, after almost superhuman effort, he succeeded in bringing into our lines. Again, on the night of the raid, Geaney was scouting on the left of the party, when he observed a number of Germans leave their trench and endeavour to work round our flank, but he attacked these single-handed and bombed them back. Unfortunately, on the return of our raiders Geaney was seriously wounded. Sergeant Martin, who saw him fall, bound up his wounds under heavy fire and brought him safely into our lines.

Our third raid was carried out on the night of 19th/20th July, when two officers and 60 other ranks of the 1st Battalion, operating from the sector held by the 2nd Battalion, entered the German trenches opposite a point just south of the Rue du Bois Salient. Capt. J. R. Cowles was in charge of the raid, and Lieut. N. J. Reed and 2nd Lieut. N. L. Macky commanded the two assaulting parties. The artillery fire was not so accurate as usual, the batteries operating having moved in only the night before, but it had the effect of shaking the Germans, most of whom retired to their dug-outs and refused to come out. As a result no prisoners could be brought in, but 33 of the enemy were killed by our men. Identifications and other valuable information were obtained. Owing to the skilful handling of his men by Capt. Cowles, who took full advantage of cover in No Man's Land, both before entry into and after withdrawal from the enemy's trenches, the casualties were very slight, only six of our men being wounded, most of these cases occurring as the party was leaving our parapet.

Sergeant J. R. Miller had a peculiarly exasperating experience. In charge of a section of bombers, he was rather seriously wounded on entering the German trench. Notwithstanding this, he led one group of his men to their appointed place, bombing the enemy along the trench as they went, and established a block as planned. This accomplished, he moved to where another group was carrying out a similar task in a branch of the trench and assisted them to complete this work also, thus rendering the flank secure. Presently the signal for the recall was sounded, and Sergeant Miller, though in great pain, struggled back with an inanimate form in his arms. On closer inspection at the first rest, he discovered that the object of his solicitude was not a wounded comrade, but a dead German. Lieut.-Col. W. S. Austin, who was in charge of the attack and had taken up his position in the front line, was wounded during the progress of the raid, and upon his evacuation the following day Major J. G. Roache assumed command of the 1st Battalion.

In connection with this operation some very fine preparatory reconnaissance work in No Man's Land had been carried out by the intelligence officer, 2nd Lieut. A. Hudson, who, unfortunately, was killed on patrol on the 14th July.

The 1st Battalion was also much indebted to Lance-Corporal H. E. Le Comte, a 2nd Battalion scout of conspicuous ability. This non-commissioned officer having thoroughly explored No Man's Land both by day and by night, was able to supply much valuable information. He had already located during daylight the bodies of two men killed on patrol, and was instrumental in bringing these in. On four different occasions he accompanied patrols of the 1st Battalion reconnoitring the area over which the raiding party was to operate, and by his intimate knowledge of the ground the work of these patrols was greatly simplified. In the raid itself he commanded the little group of scouts, consisting of Riflemen W. S. Howell, E. Erickson, W. Dean and F. C. O. Griffiths, who covered the assembly and moved up to the enemy's wire after the preliminary bombardment. The entanglements being found insufficiently broken, the party proceeded to complete the opening with wire-cutters. Though under heavy rifle fire, they succeeded in their task and returned to the assembly position to report, carrying back with them Rifleman Howell, who had been wounded. This done, they guided the attacking parties forward to the breach, and so on to their objective.

Before the whole of the raiding-party had returned, the trenches of the 2nd Battalion were subjected to intense artillery and minenwerfer fire, and an enemy raid developed on the Rue du Bois salient just to the left of the sally-port. Some twenty Germans effected an entrance into part of the forward trench known as the Dead End, but were immediately ejected, leaving prisoners in our hands. That the enemy penetration was not more extensive was largely due to the heroic work of Corporal H. Ashton, who, the only unwounded man of the sentry group at the block in the Dead End, kept the Germans at bay and thus facilitated their expulsion by parties under Lieutenants A. P. Castle and G. K. Dee. The effect of the bombardment by the German heavy trench mortars was so great that it was thought at first the enemy had sprung a mine. One of our light trench mortars was destroyed, and the officer in charge, together with nine men of his section, was killed. Other casualties numbered 38, including three missing. The redoubtable Le Comte, in company with Lance-Corporal W.

W. C. Bedggood and Rifleman Muff, followed the Germans across No Man's Land, and brought in mobile charges, bombs and equipment dropped in their flight.

It was during the enemy bombardment in connection with this raid on the 2nd Battalion's trenches that Capt. Cowles displayed such fine judgment in extricating his men from a difficult position. The assembly line for Cowles' parties, both before and after the assault, was a few short lengths of old trench in the middle of No Man's Land. From this position Cowles had sent back some small groups of his men, when the German barrage covering the enemy raiders came down and involved that part of the line to which our men had to return. Sizing up the situation with that readiness and certitude for which he was already noted, he held the remainder of his men with him until the bombardment slackened and then quickly withdrew them, thus escaping both the shelling on our lines and that which the Germans put down in No Man's Land to cover the retirement of their own men.

On this night also the 1st Brigade sent over a raiding party which met with considerable success.

These operations by the New Zealand Division, which included the liberation of smoke and gas at various points, were intended to distract attention from an attack made by the Australians against Fromelles from Fleurbaix and Laventie, just to the right of the New Zealand sector.*

An inter-battalion relief took place on the night of 24th/25th July, the 3rd Battalion relieving the 1st in the Bois Grenier sector on the right, and the 4th taking over from the 2nd in the Rue du Bois salient on the left.

From this date onwards the enemy continued his spiteful bombardment of our trenches by heavy minenwerfer, Rue du Bois salient coming in for more than its fair share. For our part there was much shooting by heavy artillery, the principal targets being the known and suspected minenwerfer positions. The period was marked also by reconnoitring and fighting patrol work by all battalions, and as the Germans displayed a like activity there were many interesting encounters in No Man's Land. In one of these exploits, on the night of 27th/28th July, a 3rd Battalion patrol came in contact with

*See p. 116.

a party of the enemy and suffered as well as inflicted casualties. In the darkness Rifleman Wood, known to have been wounded, was missed, and on the following night a fighting-patrol under Sergeant R. Simmers went out to endeavour to locate and bring him in. Evidently the patrol was expected, for the Germans, carefully concealed, surprised our men, one of whom was killed and four wounded. This seemed like a disaster for our party, but the position was immediately retrieved through the energy and fine leading of Sergeant Simmers. Pushing on at once with his four remaining men, Lance-Corporals Lind and Bassett, and Riflemen Hooper and Gibson, he bombed the Germans back, found the wounded man Wood, and brought him in to our lines. Lance-Corporal Bassett had performed a little exploit on his own account that afternoon, having gone out at four o'clock to investigate what appeared to be signals from Rifleman Wood, but to his disappointment finding only a white rag fluttering in the long grass.

Our casualties during the month of July were:—

	Killed.	Wounded.	Missing.
Officers	5	6	—
Other Ranks	22	187	3

PART 2.—TRAINING FOR THE SOMME.

Training at Armentieres—Second Army Training Area—Fourth Army Training Area—To the Somme Battlefield.

At the end of July and the beginning of August the Brigade received frequent visits from officers of the 18th Division, which was under orders to take over the section of the line held by the New Zealand Division.

The 55th Brigade commenced relieving on August 4th, when the 8th East Surreys took over from the 1st Battalion. On the following day the 2nd and 3rd Battalions were relieved respectively by the 7th Royal West Surreys and the Royal West Kents. The 4th Battalion was relieved by the 11th Royal Fusiliers on the 7th. Our battalions went into billets in Armentieres, and the Brigade became Divisional reserve. The 1st Battalion formed the garrison for the inner defences of the town. During the quiet days of the first week of

August we had no fewer than 20 casualties, including one killed.

Intensive training now began, and it became evident to all ranks that the Brigade was destined to participate in active operations at an early date, especially as contact aeroplane work formed an important part of the exercises. General Sir A. Godley, now commanding the IInd Anzac Corps, together with the G.O.C. Division, watched the battalions at work, and on August 12th inspected the Brigade.

On August 14th the New Zealand Rifle Brigade was relieved in Divisional Reserve by the 154th Brigade, and entrained at Steenwerck for the Second Army Training Area. Brigade Headquarters and the 1st and 2nd Battalions were quartered at Wallon Cappel, and the 3rd and 4th Battalions at Ebblinghem. While the various units were marching to the entraining station from their billeting-areas at Armentieres, the King passed in his car. His Majesty was greeted with the cheers peculiar to the New Zealanders—never vociferous, but none the less hearty and genuine. In the Second Army Training Area the Brigade, in the intervals of training, assisted the inhabitants in their harvesting work.

Having been farewelled by the Second Army Commander, General Plumer, the Brigade, on August 20th, marched to St. Omer, and there entrained for Abbeville. By the following day we had joined the Xth Corps of the Fourth Army and were settled down in the new training area, with Brigade Headquarters at Velma Chateau, Limercourt; the 1st Battalion in Doudelaineville; the 2nd Battalion in Fresne Tilloloy, and the 3rd and 4th in Huppy. Here training was continued at high pressure until the end of the month, the battalions specializing in the trench-to-trench attack and embodying in their work every possible lesson that could be learned from the fighting that had been for some time in progress on the Somme. In particular, the new attack formation was carefully rehearsed, and special training given in contact-plane work. Of the many specially-instructive lectures with which the period of intensive training were interspersed, our own Somme veterans will not readily forget that delivered in the fields of Doudelaineville by Col. Campbell, a British officer familiarly known as the "G.H.Q. Bayonet Agitator." The possibilities of the bayonet were so vividly portrayed by this fire-eater that every officer and man amongst his hearers "saw red" and positively ached to get to work with the cold steel.

We commenced the move from this area to the Somme Battlefield on September 2nd, the various units marching by road and reaching Dernancourt, two miles south of Albert, on the 8th. The 1st Battalion moved by stages through Le Quesnoy-sur-Airaines, Vaux and St. Gratien; the 2nd Battalion through Le Quesnoy-sur-Airaines, St. Sauveur and Alonville; the 3rd through Longpre, Fremont and St. Gratien; and the 4th through Longpre, St. Vast and Alonville. On September 4th, 5th and 6th, the units for the time being at rest continued their training, contact-plane work again receiving special attention.

The Brigade made the final march on September 9th, when Fricourt Camp, east of Albert, was reached.

CHAPTER VI.
THE BATTLE OF THE SOMME, 1916.

PART 1.—THE EARLIER FIGHTING.

Preparations for the summer campaign—Plan—Position—Preliminary bombardment—Opening of the attack—Progress—The French—Attack resumed—Results of second phase.

Before proceeding to deal with the part taken by the New Zealand Rifle Brigade in the battle of the Somme of 1916, it will be well to take a brief survey of the progress of events in that field from the commencement of the great series of engagements on July 1st up till the middle of September.

Preparations for a summer campaign had been long in progress, but the actual date of the opening of the offensive had not been fixed. The British armies had been rapidly growing in numbers, and the supply of munitions was increasing to a highly satisfactory degree; and, in order that the reinforcements should have the fullest opportunities for intensive training, and that the accumulations of munitions on the ground should in every way satisfy all requirements, the Commander-in-Chief was desirous of postponing the attack as long as possible, subject only to the necessity of commencing operations before the season was too far advanced. The Germans, however, were continuing their pressure on Verdun, and the Austrian offensive on the Italian front was gaining ground. Relief in the latter theatre, where by the end of May the pressure of the enemy was becoming alarming, was secured by the opening of the Russian campaign early in June. The enemy, however, did not in any way lessen the fury of his attacks on Verdun, where, though the heroic defence of our Allies had gained many weeks of inestimable value to us and to them, the strain was now becoming intolerable. In view of the general situation here and elsewhere, it was agreed that a combined French and British offensive should open not later than the end of June.

The right flank of the British joined up with the left of the French in the vicinity of Maricourt, about a mile north of the Somme river, and the plan agreed upon provided for a French advance along both sides of the river, while the British pushed from Maricourt to the Ancre in front of St. Pierre Divion.

The British faced a dominating ridge rising more than 500 feet high, and forming the main watershed between the Somme and its tributaries on one side, and the rivers of South-western Belgium on the other, and having a general direction from east-south-east to west-north-west. The southern face is steeper than the northern, and is broken up into a series of long irregular spurs and deep depressions. Well down the forward face, the enemy's first system of defence ran from the Somme northwards for two miles, then westwards for four miles to near Fricourt, where it turned nearly due north, forming a great salient. Six miles north of Fricourt the trenches crossed the River Ancre, a tributary of the Somme, and running northward still, passed over the summit of the watershed near Hebuterne and Gommecourt, and so on down its western spurs to Arras. Behind this twelve-mile front from the Somme to the Ancre the enemy had a strong second system of defence, sited near the crest of the watershed and from 3,000 to 5,000 yards in rear of the first system. Nature and art and infinite cunning had combined to make his position formidably strong; and, after his two years' labour at his defences, he not unnaturally looked upon them as impregnable.

During the last week in June artillery bombardments, gas and smoke discharges, and more than seventy raids, were carried out against the enemy trenches opposite the whole British front, which since April, 1915, had increased in length from thirty miles to ninety. The air force, too, was particularly active, on one occasion destroying every observation balloon visible.

At 7.30 a.m. on July 1st the British infantry assault was launched, and "the greatest one-day battle ever known in the world's history" commenced. The British main attack extended from Maricourt to St. Pierre Divion. Simultaneously a holding attack was directed against the enemy from the Ancre as far as Serre, with the object of containing his reserves and occupying his artillery; while further north a demonstration was made against both sides of the Gommecourt salient. The attack on the front from Maricourt to Serre was entrusted to the Fourth Army, under General Rawlinson, and the subsidiary attack at Gommecourt to troops from the Army commanded by General Allenby.

On the right our troops met with immediate success, and rapid progress was made. Montauban was carried, and the Briqueterie on the east and the ridge on the west of the village of Mametz were stormed and taken, as was a large section of trenches to the north of Fricourt, with the result that this village was threatened from three sides. Striking progress was made at numerous points from Fricourt to Gommecourt, but many of these gains had to be given up owing to the enemy's continued resistance at such points as Thiepval and Beaumont Hamel.

The French attack on a five-mile front on the banks of the Somme had also gone well. They penetrated to a depth of 1¾ miles, and on the following day pushed on and took Flaucourt, driving the Germans back towards Peronne. Their toll of prisoners for the two days was over 6,000.

The operations of July 1st had tested the German line, and, in view of the results, it was decided to press forward on a front from our junction with the French to a point midway between La Boisselle and Contalmaison; to maintain a steady pressure from La Boisselle to the Serre Road, this portion to form a pivot on which our line could swing as attacks to its right made progress to the north; and on the remainder of the front—from the Ancre to Gommecourt—to hold the enemy to his positions and prepare for a resumption of the subsidiary attack there later should this be found desirable. In order to give General Rawlinson a free hand for his operations from the south, General Gough was given command of the pivotal sector from La Boisselle to Serre.

On these lines the attack was continued, and by the middle of July the British had taken Bernafay Wood, Trones Wood, Longueval, Mametz Wood, the two Bazentin Woods and the two Bazentin villages, Contalmaison and La Boisselle; and from the French left at Maltz Horn Farm the line ran east of Trones Wood, west edge of Delville Wood, north of Longueval, Bazentin-le-Grand, Bazentin-le-Petit, Contalmaison Villa, Contalmaison, Contalmaison Wood, Ovillers.

The second phase of the great battle lasted from the middle of July till the middle of September, a contest during which "the enemy, having found his strongest defences unavailing, and now fully alive to his danger, put forth his utmost efforts to keep his hold on the main ridge. This stage of the battle constituted a prolonged and severe struggle for mastery between the contending armies, in which, although progress was slow and difficult, the confidence of our troops in their ability to win was never shaken. Their tenacity and determination proved more than equal to their task, and by the first week in September they had established a fighting superiority that has left its mark on the enemy, of which the possession of the ridge was merely the visible proof."*

During this period the policy of vigorous raiding all along other parts of the front was continued. The largest of these enterprises was that carried out on July 19th by an Australian Division, south of Armentieres.† The 1st Anzac Corps, under General Birdwood, moved down to the Somme front immediately after this exploit.

The main events of this second phase were the taking of Pozieres by the Australians, July 22nd to 26th; the capture, two days later, of the whole of Delville Wood, in which the good work of the South Africans was conspicuous; of Guillemont, Sept. 3rd; of Leuze Wood, Sept. 5th; and of Guinchy and the greater part of High Wood, Sept. 9th. In addition, slow but steady progress had been made in the advance against the stupendous defence works of Thiepval, and the concentrated efforts of the French had also been eminently successful. On 13th September the British line ran from midway between Maurepas and Combles, where it joined up with that of the French, east and north of Leuze Wood, east of Guillemont, north of Guinchy, north of Delville Wood, through High Wood, midway between Pozieres and Martinpuich, just south of Mouquet Farm, and thence to a point about 600 yards south of Thiepval. The remainder of the line northward was practically unaltered. The enemy had lost all observation posts

*Sir Douglas Haig's Despatches.
†See p. 109.

on the main ridge with the exception of those in High Wood and N.N.E. of Guinchy. The British, on the other hand, had now a clear view of Courcelette, Martinpuich, Flers, Lesboeufs, Morval and Combles. Combles itself was threatened, and the French advance towards Sailly-Saillisel along both sides of the Bapaume-Peronne road was thereby materially assisted. Gradually the enemy was being pushed into the low-lying ground in the apex of the triangle Albert–Bapaume–Peronne. That he recognized the desperate nature of his position is shown by an Order of the Day issued as early as July 30th, which contained the statement: "........The decisive battle of the war is now being fought on the fields of the Somme.... Attacks must break against a wall of German breasts...."

Such was the position at the end of the second phase of this great struggle, and it was the privilege of the New Zealand Rifle Brigade to participate in the opening events of the third and final phase, in which the British advance was pushed down the forward slopes of the ridge, extended on both flanks, and the whole of the plateau from Morval to Thiepval, with a good deal of the lower ground beyond, captured and firmly

PART 2.—THE THIRD PHASE: NEW ZEALANDERS ENGAGED.

SECTION 1—GENERAL.

The New Zealand Rifle Brigade in the line—Plans for the forthcoming attack—Tanks—"B Teams"—Objectives for the New Zealand Division—Method of attack—Artillery preparation—Conditions.

The Brigade having reached Fricourt on the 9th of September, proceeded on the following day and night to take over the sector held by troops of the 165th Brigade, 55th Division, and of the 2nd Brigade, 1st Division. The 1/N.Z.R.B. relieved the 1/5 King's in the front line from the junction of Peach and Tea Trenches inclusive, to Sap "A" exclusive. The 4/N.Z.R.B. relieved both the 2nd Bn., K.R.R., and the 2nd Bn., Royal Sussex, in the front line from Sap "A" inclusive to Cork Alley exclusive. Thus the front line ran south-east to north-west from a point 500 yards N.W. of the northern apex of Delville Wood, to within about a hundred yards of the eastern corner of High Wood. The 2/N.Z.R.B. went into Savoy and Carlton Trenches in support of 1/N.Z.R.B., relieving 1/7 King's, and the 3/N.Z.R.B. went into Carlton and Check Trenches, behind the 4/N.Z.R.B. The 3rd Machine Gun Company and the 3rd Light Trench Mortar Battery went into the sector at the same time. Brigade Headquarters were established at Bazentin-le-Grand. The Divisional front was covered by the 14th Division Artillery and half the N.Z. Division Artillery, all under command of C.R.A., N.Z. Division. On the night 11th/12th the greater part of the Brigade front line was swung forward, the right being advanced some 300 yards. Each front line battalion constructed three forward posts 20 yards long, with flank trenches of five yards, connected these up, and dug a communication-trench to complete the system.

On the evening of the 12th the four battalions were relieved respectively by the Auckland, Canterbury, Wellington and Otago Battalions of the 2nd Brigade, and went back for a short period of comparative rest, the 1st and 4th to Mametz Wood, and the 2nd and 3rd to Fricourt Wood. Brigade Headquarters moved to Pommiers Redoubt.

At 3 a.m. on September 14th, Brigade orders were issued for an attack on Flers in connection with a general advance of the line on the following day. It was at once evident, not only that plans for the forthcoming attack were exceedingly thorough as to minute detail, but that they were characterized by unusual features in at least two respects. Contrary to the usual practice, on the 15th September the whole force of the Allies was to move forward at the same time, from the line Vermandovillers to Thiepval, in a combined endeavour to thrust the enemy back over the whole front of attack. In the second place the new armoured cars known as "tanks" were to be employed for the first time. Light armoured cars had been used with great success in the flying-column work on the Egyptian deserts against the Senussi, but they would be useless in the trench country of Europe. A tank is well-nigh invulnerable except from a direct hit by a shell; can surmount any kind of obstacle except deep water or an excavation approximating its own length; can flatten out any barbed wire entanglement, however complicated; is practically a moving fortress, and even when its motive power fails can be turned into a ready-made strong-point. The event proved that, all things considered, the tanks, at this their first appearance in battle, came well up to expectations, the most serious drawback proving to be the slowness of their movements when compared with the impetuous dash of the infantry.

It may be mentioned here also that instructions were issued to the effect that a percentage of the officers, non-commissioned officers and specialists of each unit were to be left out of the line. Experience in the earlier stage of the Somme battle had shown the wisdom of such a precaution, for these officers and men, being experienced and well-trained, would, in case very heavy casualties were sustained, form a substantial nucleus round which the unit could be reconstituted without an undue break in its continuity or in its traditions. The second-in-command of each battalion was quartered at the transport lines, at which position he would be able most efficiently to carry out the duty of sending forward supplies of water, rations and ammunition. The personnel thus excluded from participation in a major action were styled the "B. Teams," and were for the time being included in what were known as the "Brigade Details."

The New Zealand Division had joined the XVth Corps, Fourth Army, and in the operations on the 15th September was to have the 41st Division on its right and the 47th Division, IIIrd Corps, on its left, and had four tanks allotted to it. The task set the New Zealand Division was an advance of from 2,500 to 3,000 yards on a front something over 800 yards wide, and the attack was planned to cut through Switch Trench, Flers Trench, Flers Support, the north-western corner of Flers Village, Grove Alley, beyond the village, and to terminate with the most advanced troops in position roughly in the form of a spear-head with its point on Factory Corner, 1,500 yards west of Gueudecourt.

The New Zealand Rifle Brigade and portion of the 2nd Brigade were detailed to carry out the attack, which was divided into four distinct phases, as under:—

First Objective, or Green Line: The Switch Trench from the junction of Coffee Lane therewith. This objective, roughly 600 yards from our front line, was allotted to the 2nd Brigade, and the troops employed were the 2nd

Auckland and the 2nd Otago Battalions, which were then occupying the front line.

Second Objective, or Brown Line: A zigzag line from the junction of Fat Trench with Flers Trench, about 600 yards almost due west of Flers Church, along Fat Trench, up Fish Alley, along Flag Lane and across to the Flers-High Wood Road at a point about 300 yards west of its crossing with the Longueval-Factory Corner Road. The Brown Line was roughly 1,000 yards in advance of the Green Line, and its capture was allotted to our 4th Battalion (Lieut.-Col. C. W. Melvill).

Third Objective, or Blue Line: A line running northwest from the extreme northern point of Flers to Abbey Road, and thence bending back as a flank line to the point where Flers Support crosses the Longueval-Factory Corner Road. The taking of this objective, which was from 900 to 1,000 yards in advance of the Brown Line, involved the capture in succession of sections of Flers Trench, Flers Support, Fort Trench, Grove Alley, Abbey Road, and a strong-point where Fort Trench joined Abbey Road. The task was allotted to the 2nd Battalion (Lieut.-Col. A. E. Stewart) and the 3rd Battalion (Lieut.-Col. A. Winter-Evans).

Fourth Objective, or Red Line: A line facing northwest, with its left on the forward point in the Blue Line at Abbey Road, and its right at the road-junction 300 yards south of Factory Corner, and also a defensive flank on the right, facing Gueudecourt. The capture of the Red Line, which, without reckoning the defensive flank towards the east, was over 1,100 yards in length and nearly at right angles to the preceding objectives, was entrusted to the 1st Battalion (Major J. G. Roache).

The final objective of the Division on our immediate right, the 41st, was to include Flers; while the 14th, on the right of the 41st, was expected to pass beyond Gueudecourt. The advance of the 47th Division on our left was not to go beyond Flers Support, their final objective being in the form of a right angle, one arm being about 500 yards of Flers Support, and the other a line about twice that length facing the High Wood-Ligny Thilloy Road. The Brigades on our right and left flanks were the 122nd and the 140th, respectively.

Two Vickers guns of the 3rd Machine Gun Company, and two Stokes mortars of the 3rd Light Trench Mortar Battery, were attached to each of the four battalions of the Brigade, and came under the orders of the respective commanding officers during the operations. The remainder of the machine-guns were held in Brigade reserve, and were detailed to give covering fire to the advance.

Two contact aeroplanes were detailed for duty over the sector operated on by the Division, and were to be in the air, weather permitting, from zero till dark on the 15th, and on the following day one was to be up from 6.30 a.m. till 8.30 a.m.

"Battle order" for every man consisted of rifle, bayonet and equipment less pack; 220 rounds of ammunition and two bombs; haversack, worn in place of the pack, with waterproof sheet, jersey, two empty sandbags, 24 hours' rations, iron rations, water-bottle filled; two gas helmets,* one worn on the chest at the alert position; and a steel helmet. Every alternate man carried a pick or a shovel strapped to his back.

For the units of the Brigade, positions of assembly were selected within 500 yards of the new front line held by the Auckland and Otago troops, and the battalions were instructed to complete their dispositions by 9.30 p.m. on the 14th.

The "leap-frog" method of attack was adopted; that is, as each objective was taken it became the jumping-off place for fresh troops in their attack on the next succeeding objective. The main drawback in this system is that the new assaulting troops assembling in the successive starting-places become intermingled with the men consolidating there, and unavoidable delay may be caused thereby. Besides this, the bodies advancing towards the more distant objectives are subject to the enemy fire directed on the successive captured positions as well as on themselves as they pass across the open.

The most intense artillery bombardment ever known in the previous history of the war had opened on the German lines on September 12th,† and continued unabated to the zero hour for the great infantry advance, which was fixed for 6.20 a.m., September 15th. The successive attacks were timed to fit in with the lifts of the more terrific barrages, and the hours set were as follow:—Infantry capture Green Line, 6.40 a.m.; capture Brown Line, 7.50 a.m.; capture Flers and establish Blue Line, 8.20 a.m.; advance from Blue Line and establish Red Line, 10.50 a.m.

*These were the old pattern, a saturated flannelette bag fitted with air outlet and eyepieces.
†The New Zealand Artillery alone fired approximately half-a-million rounds at the Somme.

Friday, September 15th, broke fine, but with a morning mist. The enemy artillery fire on our front was much below normal and no casualties had been suffered by our men overnight; everything, indeed, with the exception of our own artillery, was unusually quiet. A Royal Flying Corps report of an air reconnaissance, carried out shortly before zero, stated that Crest Trench, lying between our front line and the first objective, appeared to be in good order; that Switch Trench, the first objective, had been practically obliterated; that Fish Alley, running north from the right of our first objective and through our second to Flers Trench, had been to a great extent re-dug; and that Flers Trench and Flers Support appeared to be badly damaged in many places. Reports from battalions showed that all minor hitches incidental to the completion of preparations in the adverse conditions that prevailed had been overcome; and General Fulton awaited with confidence the opening of the attack. News received from Division at 6.15 a.m., to the effect that of the four tanks allotted to the sector one was out of action and the remaining three late, was somewhat disconcerting; but as the several advances had been arranged to coincide with the lifts of the barrage, and were not to be dependent on the movement of the tanks, it was realized that the delay on the part of the latter would not interfere with the infantry programme.

SECTION 2.—THE ADVANCE BEYOND FLERS, SEPTEMBER 15TH.

Second Brigade to Switch Trench—4th Battalion to Brown Line —3rd and 2nd Battalions to Flers Trench and Flers Support— Flers taken—1st Battalion to Grove Alley—Consolidation—2nd Wellington reinforce — Relief — Non-combatants — General progress—Results.

At zero hour, 6.20 a.m., the intense barrage opened, and six minutes later began creeping forward by lifts of 50 yards per minute until it joined the stationary barrage on Switch Trench, the first objective. Simultaneously with the commencement of the barrage, 2nd Auckland and 2nd Otago swarmed over the parapet, moved swiftly forward to the line

ORDER OF BATTLE—SOMME, SEPTEMBER 15, 1916.

N.N.E.

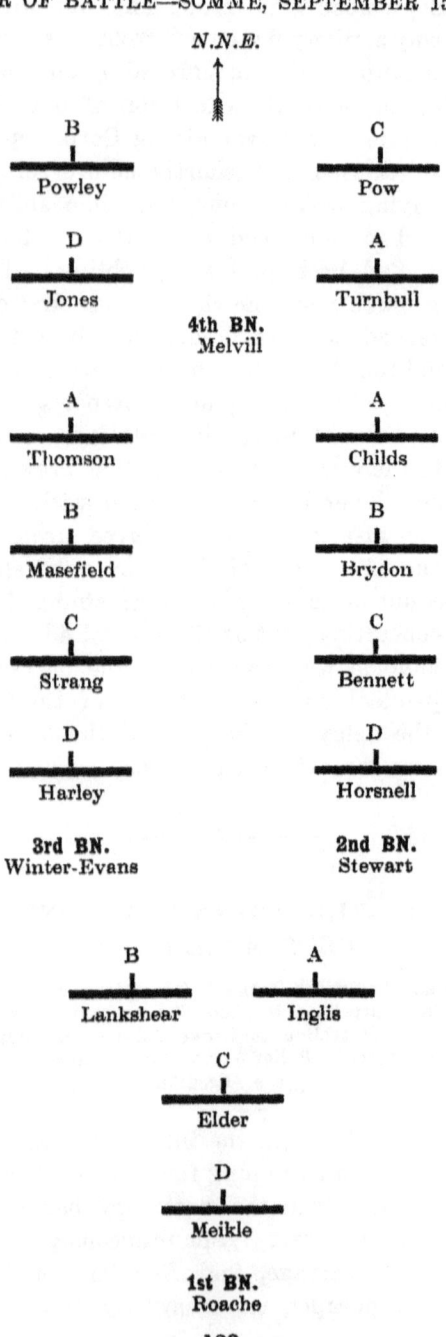

B	C
Powley	Pow

D	A
Jones	Turnbull

4th BN.
Melvill

A	A
Thomson	Childs

B	B
Masefield	Brydon

C	C
Strang	Bennett

D	D
Harley	Horsnell

3rd BN.   **2nd BN.**
Winter-Evans   Stewart

B	A
Lankshear	Inglis

C
Elder

D
Meikle

1st BN.
Roache

of shell-bursts, the regularity of which was beyond praise, and followed it forward step by step, until, at 6.40, it lifted from the section of Switch Trench which formed their goal. With a final rush the trench was carried, all resistance here as well as in Crest Trench, which they had taken in their stride, being overcome in a few minutes.

Ten minutes after zero the leading companies of the 4th Battalion, "C" (Major J. Pow) on the right and "B" (Capt. A. J. Powley) on the left, moved forward, following at a suitable distance the rear wave of 2nd Otago. All four companies had been arranged in the assembly-trench in such a manner that upon emerging they would fall at once into the new attack formation, which had been so assiduously practised during the period of training. Thus the platoons of "A" Company (Capt. J. L. Turnbull) were assembled alternately with those of "C," and the platoons of "D" Company (Capt. M. H. R. Jones) with those of "B," and by the time all had left the trench the battalion was moving in eight waves, each 60 paces behind the other, and each wave consisting of eight sections marching in single file. Between the sections an interval of 100 yards was preserved, so that the front covered was roughly 800 yards. Approaching Switch Trench the battalion halted and the men lay down to await the moving forward of the barrage. When this lifted the battalion advanced again, and presently wave after wave dashed in upon the trenches of the Brown Line. All ranks displayed magnificent spirit, and by 7.50 a.m. the enemy's stubborn resistance had been overcome, and the men were hard at work putting the captured trenches into fighting trim and constructing additional strong-points in preparation for withstanding more effectively a possible counter-attack. Of the two Vickers guns attached to the battalion, one was placed on either flank. That on the left had excellent targets in the shape of parties of retreating Germans, while the other, commanding both the road from Flers and also Flers Trench to the north, did some useful work against a counter-attack launched during the afternoon. The left was further strengthened by the posting there of a light trench mortar section with two guns. The tanks were not an unmixed blessing. One became disabled at 8 a.m., on reaching the centre of Brown Line, and drew heavy artillery fire, which was sufficiently inaccurate to leave the tank unscathed while inflicting casualties upon the troops in the vicinity.

Lieut.-Col. Melvill had come forward with his battalion to a position slightly in rear of the objective, but here his headquarters came under rifle and machine-gun fire, and the liaison officer and others of the personnel were struck. A move was therefore made to the Brown Line itself. Inspection of the position revealed the fact that the right company, in keeping touch with the troops of the flanking Division, had extended to a considerable distance beyond the boundary line, but no adjustment was made till later in the day.

Though the successful achievement of the 4th Battalion has been told in few words, it must not be supposed that the task was either simple or easy. The capture of the objective, together with the 1,000 yards' advance from the assembly position, had taken over an hour, and during that time the attacking troops had been subjected to heavy artillery and machine-gun fire. Casualties had been heavy right from the commencement. Lieut. K. R. J. Saxon and 2nd Lieut. W. W. McClelland each completed the advance in charge of a company, all other officers of the two companies having fallen. In a third company 2nd Lieut. H. G. Carter led in the final assault in the place of his company commander, who had been wounded in the earlier stages. Saxon and Carter had themselves been wounded but were able to carry on, and the work of all three officers was reported upon as being conspicuously good. Similar fine leadership was displayed by Sergt. J. A. Martin and Rifleman T. Wilson, who reached the objective as temporary platoon-commanders. Sergt. Martin was killed just as his work was accomplished. The trying duties of the stretcher-bearers commenced at once, and many stirring tales are told of the deeds of those patient and self-sacrificing workers. The names of Riflemen W. T. Douglas, W. C. Campbell and A. Dunthorn are recalled in this connection, these men having performed some remarkable feats in conveying wounded men to places of safety single-handed. Their work was supplemented by that of Corporal S. R. McDonald, a combatant non-commissioned officer, who, immediately after the capture of the objective, went forward from the trench, bound up the wounds of two men under fire, and brought them safely in, though he himself was severely wounded; and by that of Rifleman H. Youle, who similarly rescued no fewer than five men.

In the meantime, following closely behind the 4th Battalion's rear companies as they advanced to the attack, the 2nd and 3rd Battalions had been coming forward to gain a position in the Brown Line. This was to be their jumping-off line for an advance involving the capture of a large area intersected by such formidable works as Flers Trench, Flers Support, parts of Grove Alley and Flers Village, and the sunken Abbey Road with its strong-points and deep dug-outs. Each moved on a single company frontage, the platoons being in artillery formation with the sections arranged chequerwise. The companies were in the normal order, the commanders on this day being Major A. J. Childs and Captains R. O. Brydon, J. B. Bennett and C. Horsnell, in the 2nd Battalion; and Capt. A. Thomson, Lieut. W. N. Masefield, Capt. J. D. K. Strang and Capt. W. C. Harley in the 3rd. While crossing Switch Trench the troops came under severe fire from machine-gun nests in Crest Trench, the mopping-up of which had not at that moment been completed. The advance was not checked, however; indeed, the forward movement appears to have been carried on too impetuously, for a number of the men of these units had already mingled with the leading waves of the 4th Battalion when the latter made the assault on the Brown Line. There was ample time for such reorganization as was required, and punctually at 8.20 a.m., the 2nd and 3rd Battalions left the Brown Line and advanced towards the third objective. At this stage the 3rd Battalion lost three company leaders, Capt. Strang being killed and Capt. Thomson and Lieut. Masefield wounded.

On the right, the 2nd Battalion companies experienced little difficulty in dealing with their section of Flers Trench; but they came under heavy machine-gun fire from Flers Support as they moved forward from the former, and this caused a few minutes' check.

On the left, the 3rd Battalion found trouble at once. The wire in front of Flers Trench was practically intact, and, while held up by this obstacle, the leading companies suffered heavily at the hands of the German machine-gunners and snipers. Repeated efforts were made to break through the barrier, among these being a particularly daring bombing attack led by 2nd Lieut. R. A. Bennett, but all attempts proved utterly unavailing. The men thereupon took cover in shell-holes and awaited the arrival of the tanks, then momentarily expected. Lance-Corporal E. Bassett, becoming impatient, moved out into the open and repeatedly picked off enemy snipers as they showed their heads to fire. He put up an excellent score, and came through the ordeal without a scratch. Equally commendable was the work of a runner, Rifleman J. R. B. Harwood, who moved about the scattered parties in the shell-holes, establishing touch and aiding organization.

Two tanks came up at 10.30 a.m. One of them took up a position on the extreme left flank, while the second proceeded to deal with the wire and machine-guns holding up our men. Realizing the difficulties confronting the leading waves of the 3rd Battalion, Major J. Pow, of the 4th Battalion, together with 2nd Lieut. A. C. Fulton and a party of riflemen and bombers, moved forward to their assistance. Bombing along Flers Trench he met with wonderful success, capturing no fewer than 145 prisoners, including two officers. Bombing parties of the 3rd Battalion had also been active, and presently, this section of Flers Trench being taken, the rear waves of the battalion advanced. Sending parties up the saps and inwards from the left flank, they secured Flers Support and pressed on to capture their allotted portion of Abbey Road. Here a fine action was performed by Rifleman J. R. Walters. Going forward under fire, he dressed the wounds of eight men who had fallen in advance of the position, and brought them in unaided. Not content with this, he carried two of the worst cases overland to a more protected spot 200 yards in rear.

Meanwhile the 2nd Battalion was engaged in dealing with its section of Flers village. Progress in this locality was at first slow owing to machine-gun fire from the north-west corner of Flers and from Abbey Road. Here Major Childs, the senior company commander of the battalion, was killed while pressing forward with his men. Noting the delay, the commanding officer of the 4th Battalion sent up his reserve platoon to assist. Skilfully handled by 2nd Lieut. W. W. Dove, these additional men proved sufficient to turn the scale. Both the Abbey Road and the village positions were now smartly cleared, and when consolidation was well under way the platoon of reinforcements was withdrawn. Our men were by this time well beyond the right boundary of the Divisional sector, but this was rendered necessary through the Division on the right failing to cover the whole of its allotted front.

The capture of the Blue Line was now complete, and the two battalions got to work constructing strong-points and establishing blocks.

During the advance of the 3rd Battalion from the Brown Line and in the work of consolidating the captured objectives, 2nd Lieutenants A. L. Martin, S. J. E. Closey and W. A. Gray, who, owing to casualties amongst the officers, had had to assume the duties of company commanders, did conspicuously good work under most difficult conditions. Closey and Gray, indeed, found themselves the only officers left in their respective companies. Sergeants J. E. Day, S. F. Breach and R. Simmers took over the duties of their fallen platoon commanders with no less satisfactory results. To the north of Flers brilliant work was done by that fine officer, Capt. R. O. Brydon, of the 2nd Battalion, who reorganized the remains of two companies, established two strong-points, and beat off repeated enemy counter-attacks. Wounded early in the morning, he carried on with great tenacity and cheerfulness throughout the 15th, but was killed on the following day. Sergt. N. E. Fitzgerald, also of the 2nd Battalion, had all the officers of his company killed or wounded; he rallied forty men, and with them established a post north of Flers, and this he held with his garrison, now reduced to twenty-five, until the evening of the 16th.

The two Stokes mortars attached to each of the 2nd and 3rd Battalions got well forward and came into action, but their usefulness was curtailed owing to the insuperable difficulty experienced in bringing forward additional ammunition supplies. The four Vickers guns were of the greatest assistance. They covered the advance of these two units, and, later, that of the 1st Battalion, besides aiding materially in beating off a counter-attack on the left of the 3rd Battalion's position in the Blue Line. Ill-luck attended the gun sent forward to help on the men of this battalion held up at Flers Trench, for it was

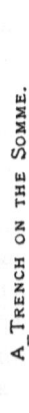

A Trench on the Somme.

"*Great Push,*" *Hutchinson's.*

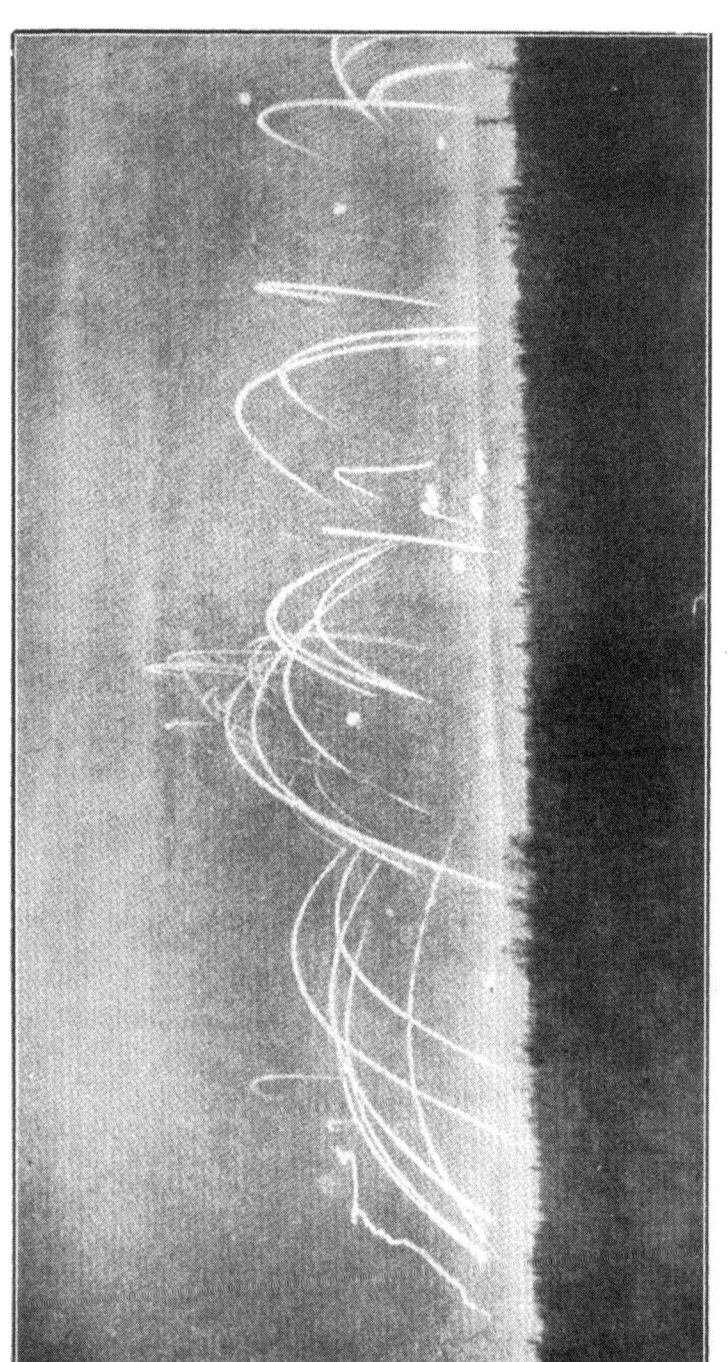

Night, 14th/15th September, 1916.

"*Great Push*," *Hutchinson's*.

A Relic of the Somme—One of the First Tanks.

A Lewis Gun in the Front Line.

A Trench Mortar Shoot.

An 18-Pounder.
(Gunners wearing Gas Masks.)

disabled by shell-fire before it could come into action. The work of Sergeants C. V. Ciochetto and P. J. Clark, Corporal G. R. Booth, and Private L. V. Gibson, all old Rifle Brigade men, in handling the guns during these stages, was specially praiseworthy. At 10 a.m., on a call from the 3rd Battalion for reinforcements, two guns from the Brigade reserve were sent up. They were so placed as to give good covering fire to the left flank, but they were not called upon to operate.

The 1st Battalion, detailed for the task of securing the final objective, consisting roughly of Grove Alley, moved forward immediately behind the 2nd and 3rd. The advance was made on a two-company frontage, "A" Company (Capt. L. M. Inglis) on the right and "B" (Capt. B. R. Lankshear) on the left, leading, with "C" (Capt. P. A. Elder) and "D" (Capt. H. C. Meikle) following in support. Part of "D" Company had been detailed as battalion reserve. Approaching the Blue Line the battalion began to suffer heavy casualties from machine-gun fire coming from the left. Lance-Corporal F. N. Fletcher, with a bombing-party of six men from one of the rear companies, swung out beyond the left flank, located the enemy machine-gun, and attacking it from flank and rear succeeded in bombing out the crew and destroying the gun, thus removing a serious obstacle to the advance. The check aggravated the slight confusion that had already arisen from the intermingling of the men of the 1st with those of the 2nd and 3rd Battalions. Indeed, the necessary orderly arrangement of sections of the 1st Battalion was repeatedly upset through yielding to the irresistible temptation to join in any local fighting that might be going on, and hence it was found imperative, when the Abbey Road was reached, to make a brief halt in order that proper organization might be restored before making the final swinging advance on Grove Alley.

The general situation at about 11 a.m. was as follows:—The Green Line occupied by 2nd Auckland and 2nd Otago; the Brown Line held by the 4th Battalion; Flers Trench, Flers Support and Blue Line generally being consolidated by the 2nd and 3rd Battalions; Flers village occupied by a mixture of New Zealand Rifle Brigade and English troops; and the 1st Battalion reorganizing in Abbey Road. Beyond the right the position was uncertain, although it was known that a small party from the Brigade on that flank was digging in north of Flers near the German strong-points known as Box and Cox.

At 11.30 a.m. the 1st Battalion continued the advance from the vicinity of Abbey Road, both leading companies coming under severe machine-gun fire from a number of guns on the high ground away to the left in the neighbourhood of Goose Alley, besides suffering many casualties from shell-fire in the general bombardment. They even had to face two field guns firing at point-blank range, though this difficulty was finally removed by the daring action of 2nd Lieut. J. R. Bongard, who with a party of seven men dashed forward in the face of the fire, bayoneted the teams and captured the guns. Section by section, however, these companies gained a footing in Grove Alley, and under a hail of bullets commenced the work of consolidation.

As time went on it became increasingly evident that the position occupied by the battalion was extremely precarious. The effective strength had been sadly reduced by casualties throughout the long advance of nearly two miles under fire and without a barrage, and now that the greater part of the objective was secured it was found that no touch could be got with the troops of the Division on our right, either to the north or to the north-east of Flers. It was concluded, rightly, as the event proved, that our neighbours were not on their objective, and even the small party about Cox had by this time disappeared. Thus the right flank was entirely "in the air," and the whole position, besides being under fire from both west and east, was enfiladed by machine-guns from about Factory Corner to the north-east. At about 2 p.m., therefore, when the awkwardness of the situation was fully realized, the captured guns were disabled and the right company was withdrawn slightly till it faced the north. The digging of a series of posts covering Flers, from Cox to the left of the Blue Line, was now begun, the position thus taken up being some 400 yards short of the extreme point of the final objective. The new line at once came under concentrated shell-fire and had to bear the brunt of repeated counter-attacks, and the situation called for prompt and energetic action on the part of the few junior officers and non-commissioned officers left. 2nd Lieut. N. L. Macky, who was in charge of the reserve of two platoons, on ascertaining that the right was still uncovered and that the enemy was advancing in that quarter, sent information back and immediately took his men forward to establish a defensive flank, a task which he succeeded in accomplishing only after much severe fighting. 2nd Lieut. W. G. Harrison, who had led two platoons to the final objective, now found his command reduced to twenty men. With these he commenced the establishment of a strong-point near Cox, and though for a long time completely isolated, he succeeded in beating off all attacks until troops eventually came up on either side. 2nd Lieut. N. Angus, who had been placed in charge of a burial party and had followed up the advancing lines in connection with his special duty, now found the work of defence more urgent and necessary, and having collected some scattered men he constructed a separate strong-point, which he handed over only when conditions had become more settled. This done, he realized the need for augmenting the ration parties, and he at once pressed his burial men into this new service, making four successive trips from the dump to the advanced posts before relinquishing his self-imposed task at daylight on the 16th. Company-Sergt.-Major G. H. Boles early in the afternoon found himself in command of his company, now without an officer, and both in Grove Alley as well as later in the line of posts north-east of Flers, displayed remarkable powers of leadership and organization. Here also Sergeants A. R. Blackmore, R. T. Caldwell and C. Gair proved their ability in grappling with unusual situations, and their independent work was of the utmost value during the establishment and final consolidation of the line covering Flers. Sergt. Caldwell's work in particular was noted by Major Gwyn Thomas, Brigade Major of the 122nd Brigade, who wrote in glowing terms of his display of intitiative, and referred especially to the support afforded to the troops on the right.

Machine-guns were promptly brought forward and placed in position under the personal supervision of 2nd Lieut. A. H. Preston, who proved to be of invaluable assistance both in establishing and in holding the advanced line. Particularly good work was performed by the two gun crews under the control of Sergt. W. Paine. The line, which now extended over 400 yards beyond the right of the Divisional boundary, was further materially strengthened by the arrival of a tank, which took up a position on the Flers-Ligny Thilloy Road.

At 3.20 p.m. the Brigade received orders from Division that the advance was to proceed no further than Blue Line, which, with Flers, was to be consolidated and held at all costs. This was welcome news to the much-tried men of the 1st Battalion, to whom the necessity of withdrawal from Grove Alley an hour before had proved a bitter experience. At this time the troops on our right advanced to Flea Trench, on the right of Cox, and linked up with us. They, however, withdrew again at 7.30 p.m., making it necessary for us to refuse our right still further. This extension was brilliantly carried out and, against a series of attacks, maintained by a composite party of men from the 1st and 2nd Battalions under Capt. L. M. Inglis. Later in the night a platoon from the 2nd Wellington Battalion reinforced the sparsely-held line on this flank.

No connection had been made with the troops of the 140th Brigade on our left, and it was ascertained later that they had not been successful in gaining that part of Flers Support which formed their objective, having advanced only as far as the Flers-Martinpuich Road in continuation of our Brown Line. The left flank was thus quite open, and to overcome this difficulty the 3rd and 4th Battalions were ordered to dig a trench forming a defensive flank back towards Flag Lane, and the 1st, 2nd and 4th were instructed to dig a support line to this. The night of 15th/16th September proved comparatively quiet, and this defensive work was successfully accomplished without serious interference.

During the night the 2nd Wellington Battalion, which had come up earlier to reinforce, took over the section of Abbey Road held by companies of our 2nd Battalion, the latter rejoining the remainder of the battalion in Flers Trench and Flers Support. In view of the very high percentage of casualties suffered by the New Zealand Rifle Brigade, the arrival of the 2nd Wellington companies was very welcome. They entered heartily into the struggle, and, in particular, the presence of the party with our refused right flank added greatly to our sense of security.

In addition to the close inspection of the lines, and of the position generally, made towards the end of the day by General Fulton, and by Major Hastings of the Divisional Staff, a notable reconnaissance was carried out by Capt. R. G. Purdy, Staff Captain, from 11 a.m. till 5.30 p.m. Incessant machine-gun and artillery fire, together with the truly awful state of the ground, had rendered communication almost impossible, and the general obscurity of the situation towards the end of the forenoon called for a personal investigation covering the whole sector. This was undertaken with eminent success by Capt. Purdy, and his report, together with those sent in from time to time by battalion commanders, showed that the work of the different units had been entirely satisfactory, and that, all things considered, the situation generally was even better than could have been expected.

The day of the 16th September was spent in consolidating the lines. At 9 a.m. the enemy made a more determined counter-attack than those that had developed during the previous afternoon. This came from the north-west, but was eventually beaten off, the Vickers guns attached to battalions putting in some excellent work. At 9.30 a.m., to facilitate the continuation of the advance of the Divisions on both flanks, the 1st Wellington Battalion passed through our line and retook Grove Alley.

On the night of 16th/17th September we were relieved by the 2nd Brigade, and went into Divisional Reserve in Savoy and Carlton Trenches and Check Line, Brigade Headquarters remaining at Carlton Trench.

The work of the various subsidiary sections on the 15th and 16th, such as the medical, transport and signal sections, and the carrying, ration, stretcher and burial parties, cannot be recounted at length. Under conditions that beggar description they carried on without pause in the face of the most fearful obstacles and with absolute contempt of danger. The recorded and unrecorded instances of heroism and persistence displayed by these men, many of whom had not the excitement of personal combat to spur them on, are beyond all praise.

In performing the duties in connection with the establishment and maintenance of communications, so vital an element in the successful conduct of operations, only the signaller knows the trials and dangers that have to be faced. It is shellfire that cuts his wire, and it is under shell-fire that he must go out and find and mend the break, and that without a moment's unnecessary delay. Conspicuous amongst those who laboured so faithfully and well in this important work were Lieutenants G. A. Avey and E. Burrows, Sergt. J. N. Beattie, and Riflemen N. L. Ingpen and A. Beattie. But wires cannot be taken far forward at once, nor can they serve all parts of the field. The bulk of the work of communication in a moving engagement must be performed by battalion and company runners, and many were the astonishing feats, not only of bravery but of endurance, that were placed to the credit of these indefatigable men. Of those who devotedly served in this capacity mention may be made of Corporal E. D. Duthie, Riflemen A. C. Elliott, W. G. Franklin, H. P. Parsons, C. C. Palmer, D. G. Irvine, A. W. Forsyth, H. Gowers, E. H. Campbell, A. Bridgeman, and A. E. White, the last being the sole survivor of six company runners.

The wounded can speak most feelingly of the medical officers and their orderlies and of the stretcher-bearers, but there were few with the Brigade at the Somme who did not see something of their self-sacrificing labours. Such will call to memory Capt. G. V. Bogle, who in the forward area worked at his dressing-station in the open unceasingly for thirty-six hours at a stretch, and was killed by a shell as he paused to take a first brief respite from his labours; his orderly, Lance-Corporal C. J. Henty, who had served with like devotion and now carried on alone, ceasing his labours twelve hours later, when the last wounded man of his battalion had been evacuated from the dressing-station; and Lance-Corporal H. Rosanowski and Rifleman Myers, two of the few stretcher-bearers who came through the ordeal unscathed. No less devoted was the action of the Revd. Clement Houchen, Chaplain to the 1st Battalion. He accompanied his unit throughout its long advance, rendered invaluable assistance to the medical officer, aided the stretcher-bearers, soothed the last moments of many a passing hero, and, when no further help could be given to the living, accompanied the burial parties to lighten their labours and perform the last sad offices to the dead. Removed from the stirring scenes of the forward area, yet still under fire, the seconds-in-command and quartermasters of battalions worked without ceasing at the dumps, sending forward supplies of water, food and ammunition, their duties being as trying, though perhaps not as arduous, as those of the carrying parties, some of whom had to trudge more than two miles each way. Finally, there were the men of the transport sections, equally faithful, and making good their boast that nothing should cause them to fail their comrades in the hour of need.

The advance of the Allied forces elsewhere had on the whole gone well. The scheme of operations is thus stated in Sir Douglas Haig's Despatches of 23rd December, 1916: "The general plan of the combined Allied attack which was opened on 15th September was to pivot on the high ground south of the Ancre and north of the Albert-Bapaume Road, while the French Army devoted its whole effort to the rearmost of the enemy's original systems of defence between Morval and Le Sars. Should our success in this direction warrant it, I made arrangements to enable me to extend the left of the attack to embrace the villages of Martinpuich and Courcelette. As soon as our advance on this front should reach the Morval line, the time would have arrived to bring forward my left across the Thiepval Ridge. Meanwhile on my right our Allies arranged to continue the line of advance in close co-operation with me from the Somme to the slopes above Combles, but directing their main effort northwards against the villages of Rancourt and Fregicourt, so as to complete the isolation of Combles and open the way for their attack upon Sailly-Saillisel."

The success of the morning's operations, resulting as they did in the capture of Flers, in the advancement of the English troops on the right to within striking distance of the strong line of defence running before Morval, Les Boeufs and Gueudecourt, and in the complete clearing of High Wood on our left, made it possible to carry out during the afternoon that part of the plan which provided for the capture of Martinpuich and Courcelette, and by the end of the day both these villages were in British hands. By the 18th September the advantages gained on the 15th were enhanced by further progress between Flers and Martinpuich, and by the capture of the Quadrilateral, an enemy stronghold just to the east of Ginchy, which had hitherto held up the advance of the right towards Morval.

The result of the fighting from the 15th to the 18th was, to quote from General Haig's Despatches, "a gain more considerable than any which had attended our arms in the course of a single operation since the commencement of the offensive. In the course of one day's fighting we had broken through two of the enemy's main defensive systems and had advanced on a front of over six miles to an average depth of a mile. In the course of this advance we had taken three large villages, each powerfully organized for prolonged resistance. Two of these villages had been carried by assault with short preparation in the course of a few hours' fighting. All this had been accomplished with a small number of casualties in comparison with the troops employed, and in spite of the fact that, as was afterwards discovered, the attack did not come as a complete surprise to the enemy."

Between the 15th and 18th of September, the French on our right had gone forward north of Priez Farm and were threatening Combles, while south of the Somme they had taken Berny, Deniecourt and Vermandovillers, and were before Bovent and Ablaincourt.

From this date forward the New Zealand Rifle Brigade as a whole was not engaged in any large attack on the Somme, though, in addition to the ordinary trench tours, it supplied individual battalions to one or other of the 1st and 2nd Brigades to assist in carrying on the advance, such units becoming temporarily attached for this purpose.

The Brigade remained in Divisional reserve until the night of 18th/19th September, when it moved forward into the intermediate area, with the 4th Battalion in Switch Trench and the remaining battalions in rear. Heavy rain had come on during the 18th, and the shattered surface of the country rapidly deteriorated into a sea of mud. During the following week the Brigades relieved one another in succession. The weather was too unfavourable for operations beyond small affairs of outposts, but no adverse conditions were permitted to interfere with work devoted to extending and improving the saps, strengthening the posts, and preparing generally for either continuing the advance or withstanding counter-developments.

SECTION 3.—GENERAL ATTACK RENEWED, SEPTEMBER 25TH.

General Objectives—1st Brigade to Factory Corner—N.Z.R.B. in reserve—1st Brigade to Gird Support—4th and 2nd Battalions attached—General success about Thiepval—2nd Brigade relieves the 1st—N.Z.R.B. in reserve—2nd and 3rd Battalions attached to 2nd Brigade—2nd Battalion bombing exploit—2nd Brigade and a 3rd Battalion company attack about Eaucourt l'Abbaye—Conditions—N.Z.R.B. relieves 2nd Brigade—Departure from the Somme—Congratulations—Casualties.

The weather having improved somewhat, the attack along the whole front was renewed on the 25th. The task for the New Zealand Division, the capture of the high ground from Factory Corner to Goose Alley, was allotted to the 1st Brigade, in support to which the New Zealand Rifle Brigade was held in readiness. The objectives on the British front included the villages of Morval, Les Boeufs and Gueudecourt, and a belt of country about 1,000 yards deep curving round the north of Flers to a point midway between that village and Martinpuich. The attack was successful everywhere except at Gueudecourt; but on the following day this village was captured, as also was Combles, in which the French and the British joined hands in the early morning.

On the 27th a further attack was made. In this the 1st Brigade again successfully participated, taking a section of Gird Trench and Gird Support west of the Ligny Thilloy Road. Our Brigade, less the 4th Battalion, which had been handed over to the G.O.C. 1st Brigade on the previous evening, continued in support. Two companies of the 4th Battalion were moved to the North Road and were for the time being attached to the 1st Wellington Battalion. At 2 a.m. on the 28th, one of these companies was sent forward to reinforce 1st Auckland and capture that portion of Gird Support still occupied by the Germans between the left of 1st Auckland and Goose Alley. This operation was successfully carried out during the early hours of the same day. At 9 a.m. the 2nd Battalion also passed to the command of the G.O.C. 1st Brigade, two companies being sent to Flers Trench and two to Flers Support. In the evening the 3rd Battalion took over the Brown Line from the 4th.

Following on the success of the push on the right on September 25th, the Fifth Army, at about noon on the 26th, launched a general attack against Thiepval and Thiepval Ridge on a front of 3,000 yards. The attack was a brilliant success. By the early morning of the 27th the famous enemy strongholds, Moquet Farm, and Zollern, Stuff and Schwaben Redoubts, besides the village of Thiepval, were taken. On the 27th, also, the enemy east of Thiepval was pushed back until he came to a stand in his strong defences running in front of Le Sars and Eaucourt l'Abbaye.

During the night of 28th/29th the 2nd Brigade relieved the 1st Brigade in the line, the New Zealand Rifle Brigade remaining in the intermediate area from Flers Support to the Longueval–Bazentin-le-Grand Road, with the 2nd Battalion, now under the command of the G.O.C. 2nd Brigade, in Flers Trench and Flers Support. The 4th Battalion returned to Brigade.

On 29th September the 3rd Battalion passed to the command of the G.O.C. of the 2nd Brigade, and the following night relieved 2nd Wellington in the front line, Gird Support, from Ligny Thilloy Road westward. Early in the morning of the 30th, 2nd Lieut. H. M. Preston, of the 2nd Machine Gun Company, who was with the 2nd Battalion, opened out on an enemy working-party of two officers and 20 other ranks and practically annihilated it, only two Germans escaping.

During the afternoon of the 30th, the 2nd Battalion, under orders from the G.O.C. 2nd Brigade, took part with the 19th London Regiment on our left in a bombing attack on Flers Trench and Flers Support beyond the High Wood–Ligny Thilloy Road. The attack, vainly attempted by the Londoners alone on the previous evening, was this time completely successful, excellent work being done by Capt. H. E. Barrowclough, Lieut. G. A. Avey, and Sergeant A. McLeod. At one point in this attack the advance was brought to a standstill through the skill and tenacity with which an enemy post was held, till finally Lance-Corporal J. W. Voyle, taking a few bombers, moved round its flank in the open and kept the garrison inactive, thus enabling the post to be rushed from the front.

The 2nd Brigade launched a further attack on 1st October, working in conjunction with the 47th Division on the left, the objective of the latter being Eaucourt l'Abbaye. It was not intended that our 3rd Battalion, still holding the right of the 2nd Brigade's line in Gird Support, should take part in this advance, and its commanding officer received definite instructions to this effect. Shortly after noon, however, he was ordered to make a local attack at zero hour (3.15 p.m.) in concert with troops of the 21st Division on our right, who were also pushing forward. The task was to be accomplished by "C" Company (Capt. W. Drummond), with a second company in support, and consisted of an advance of about 500 yards and the establishment of a forward line of strong-posts. This order was countermanded at 2 p.m., two platoons now being substituted for the whole company, the remaining half-company to be held in support. The operation was gallantly and successfully carried out, but it proved to be a very costly one. Heavy casualties were caused by machine-gun fire coming in from the high ground on the right, and it was found necessary on this flank to send forward not only the supporting platoon but also an additional platoon from "B" Company, then held in reserve. Much of the success in capturing and holding the position was due to the fine leadership displayed by 2nd Lieuts. A. L. Martin and S. J. E. Closey, and to the excellent work done by Sergeant A. Shearer, who, when his platoon commander was killed, carried on in control and completed the consolidation of two of the strong-points. When darkness fell, Sergeant Shearer made a thorough reconnaissance of No Man's Land and marked down with accuracy the position of the enemy's posts in the vicinity. Worthy of note, too, is the prompt action of one of the platoon-sergeants, Sergeant S. F. Breach. During the first advance the Lewis gun team giving covering fire was put out of action, with the result that the forward movement was brought to a standstill; but realizing the position, Sergeant Breach seized the gun himself, continued the covering fire, and so enabled his platoon to renew the advance.

The following extracts from the account of the officer in charge of one of the attacking parties will give some slight indication of the difficulties faced by our men in this and many similar tasks, of the awful conditions under which they worked, and of the dogged nature of their determination to carry on and win through in face of it all :—

"The troops on our immediate right dissolved under the German fire, and our attack was carried out after the fashion of a solo raid. We had had little time to prepare—only about two hours......... However, when the barrage lifted we gained our objective, an old German strong-point in and about the sunken part of the road from Flers to Ligny Thilloy, but our casualties had been exceedingly heavy. No sooner had we commenced consolidating than hurried orders came for a further advance. In executing this second attack we had to pass over dreadfully-exposed ground and under concentrated fire from all enemy weapons within reach. As a demonstration the advance had great value, for the Boche began to leave his trenches, and the forward party did enormous execution, so much so that the whole system was undoubtedly emptied of the enemy. The position lay well over the crest, some 150 yards away, and commanded a long-distance view in many directions. The rear party were pinned down on the crest, only one man getting through to those in the front position. The collection of wounded was impossible until dark came on, and so proved to be an extremely difficult task.

"I was in command of the strong-point established here; and when, at 4 a.m. on October 2nd, I received orders to evacuate, I went back overland to Battalion Headquarters to verify what seemed to me an extraordinary instruction. There I ascertained that the withdrawal had been ordered by the G.O.C. of the Brigade to which we were attached, because of the fact that the 21st Division on our right had no troops beyond Gird Support, and that consequently we were quite 'in the air.' By the time I had returned to my post, day was breaking. The dead were left where they were, and after a final scour for wounded, we withdrew, weary and sick at heart.

"At about 9 a.m. I received an order cancelling the withdrawal and instructing me to re-occupy the position. Could anything be more desperately hard? On the previous day my company had lost an officer and 15 other ranks killed, and 55 other ranks wounded. All my non-commissioned officers and all my specialists were casualties, and my company strength was down to 41. Could I ask these few remaining men to face again the ordeal they had already gone through at such a cost? They had had no real sleep and no hot food since the great battle opened on September 15th, and they were living now mainly because their high spirit had risen superior to physical exhaustion and the strain of the hellish fire of the previous day. If I should find them reluctant I could not blame them, but they rose splendidly to the occasion.

"I had settled on twenty men as sufficient for the effort, twelve riflemen and a Lewis gun team of eight, and instructed 2nd Lieut. Clark to send them after me in pairs, rushing from hole to hole, and I hoped he would stop the advance if the losses should prove to be too great. And so we started off on the task, in broad daylight and without a barrage. We had 700 yards to go, and I decided quite finally, as also, I think, did my men, that no one would reach the position alive. Of the twenty, only six got forward to the battered post. The others we never saw again. . . . .

"When we handed over on relief that night the strong-point was an advanced and isolated post, and the unit on our right was far in rear. I recall the expression on the relieving officer's face as I detailed frankly the plans I had for improving the parapets and traverses. It will be remembered that we had had heavy rain, and this, combined with the incessant shelling, had made the soil so yeasty that nowhere would it stand. I had therefore been compelled to resort to the only expedient left, and of the bodies that lay thickly about the remains of the trenches the few survivors of my party had already built two traverses and a parapet as a shield from the steady fire coming from the flanks as well as from the front."

The 2nd Brigade, having successfully carried out its task of advancing the line, was relieved by the New Zealand Rifle Brigade during the night of 2nd/3rd October, and 1st Canterbury and 1st Wellington came under command of our Brigadier. Our men cannot be said to have come into the line fresh and vigorous, for both the 2nd and 3rd Battalions had been attached to the 2nd Brigade since the 29th September, and as has been stated above, both battalions, especially the 3rd, had been engaged in severe fighting. In addition, the 1st Battalion had gone over to the G.O.C. of the 2nd Brigade on the night of 1st/2nd October, being placed in Flers Trench and Flers Support, with two platoons attached to 1st Canterbury, two platoons detailed as carrying party to our 2nd Battalion, and two told off for similar duties with the 3rd. Hence, for the time being, our Brigade had consisted merely of Headquarters and the 4th Battalion.

When we took over the sector the average strength of our own battalions was down to 380; and the front line, some 2,500 yards in length, extended from beyond the Flers–Ligny Thilloy Road on the right, to the road junction about 300 yards north-east of the Eaucourt Abbey ruins on the left.

Three battalions occupied the front line, the 3rd remaining in its old position on the right, the 4th taking over the centre, and the 1st the left. The 2nd Battalion was in support, with three companies in Goose Alley and one in Grove Alley; and the attached 1st Wellington and 1st Canterbury troops were held in reserve in Flers Trench, Flers Support, and Brown Line. Brigade Headquarters were at Ferret Trench. The weather was atrociously bad, and the trenches waist-deep in mud.

On the following night, 3rd/4th October, we were relieved by the 122nd Brigade of the 41st Division, and went into bivouac at Pommiers Redoubt.* Here we spent two days resting, cleansing and refitting—in so far as these could be accomplished in the circumstances—and General du Cane, Commanding the XVth Corps, having in felicitous terms farewelled the Division, we departed on October 6th on our return to the Armentieres region.

So ended our work on the Somme at this time. That the Division had done well may be gathered from the following messages of congratulation:—

From Sir Douglas Haig, Commander-in-Chief of the British Forces:

"The New Zealand Division has fought with the greatest gallantry in the Somme battle for 23 consecutive days, carrying out with complete success every task set, and always doing more than was asked of it. The Division has won universal confidence and admiration. No praise can be too high for such troops."

From General Rawlinson, Commanding the Fourth Army:
"I desire to express to all ranks of the New Zealand Divi-

---

*The command of the sector passed from the New Zealand Division to the 41st on the morning of October 4th, but, as was customary, the 3rd Machine Gun Company remained in position for some time after relief. At 5 a.m. on the 4th, some two hours after the infantry had changed over, the Germans counter-attacked, and in the action that followed our machine-guns put in some very useful work. Of the section in charge of Lance-Corporal C. O. Samson, one of the original 2nd Battalion machine-gunners, the General Officer Commanding the 122nd Brigade reports as follows:—

"The New Zealand machine-gun team was of particular assistance. All except one man of the team were hit, and the machine-gun was at length put out of action. This man, Lance-Corporal Samson, behaved with the greatest gallantry, working his gun to the end."

sion my hearty congratulations on the excellent work done during the Battle of the Somme.

"On three successive occasions (15th and 25th September and 1st October) they attacked the hostile positions with the greatest gallantry and vigour, capturing in each attack every objective that had been allotted to them. More than this, they gained possession of, and held, several strong-points in advance of and beyond the furthest objectives that had been allotted to them.

"The endurance and fine fighting spirit of the Division have been beyond praise, and their successes in the Flers neighbourhood will rank high amongst the best achievements of the British Army.

"The control and direction of the Division during the operations have been conducted with skill and precision, whilst the artillery support in establishing the barrage and defeating counter-attacks has been in every way most effective.

"It is a matter of regret to me that this fine Division is leaving the Fourth Army, and I trust that on some future occasion it may again be my good fortune to find them under my command."

The achievement had been glorious, but the price of victory was high, for the total casualties of the Division numbered nearly 7,000. Those of our own Brigade were as under:

	Killed.	Wounded.	Missing.	Total.
Officers ...	12	47	—	59
Other ranks	270	1171	233	1674

Grand total: 1733

The number "missing," it should be explained, is that given in the immediate returns, for which purpose it is ascertained by subtracting from the number going into action the total made up of those answering the roll-call at its conclusion, plus those actually known, by name, to have been killed or wounded. As the result of subsequent courts of enquiry it was reduced almost to vanishing-point. In the case of one battalion, for instance, a large parcel of identification discs collected by the burial-party was destroyed by shell-fire, and thus formal investigation as to the disappearance of an unusually large number of men had to be made.

It is interesting to note in this connection that of the whole Division not more than a score of prisoners were taken by the enemy.

It was with mingled feelings that we turned our backs upon the scene of our first participation, as a complete Brigade, in a prolonged engagement with the enemy on a grand scale. There was sadness in the thought of the gaps that had been made in our ranks, and grief that so many friendships cemented by common experiences in camp and billet and trench —friendships so exquisitely sincere that it is impossible to convey by mere words more than a faint suggestion of their nature—were now severed, never again to be renewed on this side of eternity. For we had left on the field of battle more than a full company-strength of officers and men who had paid the extreme price and yielded their all in the cause of Honour; and of those broken comrades, exceeding in number the strength of a whole battalion, there were many who, we knew full well, had fought their last fight.

But the soldier must steel himself. To yield to sadness would tend to unfit him for his task, and we knew that we had but touched the fringe of what lay before us. And so we cheered ourselves with the reflection that though we had suffered greatly we had served not indifferently. We had "done our bit" with a Division that had within the comparatively brief period of three weeks covered itself with glory and had earned definite distinction in an army that had accomplished what the enemy had confidently considered to be impossible. In the actions on the Somme the Division was always in a salient of its own making, and in the thrusting out and the holding of the first of these, when Flers was covered on the north on September 15th. the New Zealand Rifle Brigade by its successive bounds had carried forward the longest single advance made throughout the period of the Division's fighting in the great battle.

The sights and sounds of struggle and carnage burnt in upon our memories could never be entirely obliterated; fragments of the all-pervading mud and filth of the battered area over which we had fought and struggled still clung to arms, equipment, clothing, even to the very pores of the skin, and conspired with the weariness of mind and body to recall and again recall the horrors of our recent experiences. But our faces at last were turned towards the peaceful open country, and we were out for rest. Soon enough we should resume the tiresome stationary trench warfare further north, but in the meantime here were smiling fields, unbroken woods and villages, dry billets, and, above all, hard solid ground to walk erect upon. The past was gone; to dwell upon it would be unnerving. The future was in the lap of the gods, and our present duty was to prepare ourselves to meet whatever was in store for us with that spirit of confidence which had sustained us hitherto, and this end would best be served by enjoying to the full the blessings that now lay to our hands.

New Zealand has erected in France and Belgium four memorials to her soldiers. The first, at Longueval, commemorates their earliest exploits as assaulting troops in a great battle on the Western Front; the second, at Messines, serves as a reminder of the brilliant part they played in one of the most perfectly planned and executed actions of the war; the third, at Gravenstafel, is placed within view of the scenes of our activities in the various parts of the Ypres Salient, but perpetuates more particularly the memory of those who fought so victoriously about the village of Gravenstafel itself, as well as of those who struggled no less gallantly at ill-fated Passchendaele; while the fourth, at Le Quesnoy, stands as a monument to the achievements of the Division in the final advance to victory. The Longueval memorial, like those at Messines and Gravenstafel, takes the form of an obelisk. It has been placed where the road leading due north from that village crosses Switch Trench, and occupies a fine position at the highest point of the trench-site, a thousand yards east of High Wood. On the shaft is the inscription in English and in French: "In honour of the men of the New Zealand Division. First Battle of the Somme, 1916." On two of the panels of the massive base are engraved the sentence: "The New Zealand Division, after gaining this position as their first objective, launched from it the successful attack on Flers, September 15, 1916." This is sufficiently comprehensive, but the inscription on the rear panel, "New Zealand Division, Auckland, Wellington, Canterbury, Otago," would at first sight appear to be somewhat slighting to the troops of the 3rd Brigade, who carried the advance forward from Switch Trench to a position beyond Flers and who were not drawn from any particular province of New Zealand. The front panel has an exquisite design, with a suggestion of Maori carving, showing in the centre the words "New Zealand" enclosed within a laurel-wreath supported by crossed taiaha. The base bears in addition the phrase: "From the uttermost ends of the earth."

In the temporary church at Longueval, which is simply one of our Nissen huts with a bell-tower constructed of parts of a broken windmill, a small brass tablet has been placed bearing the simple inscription: "To the glory of God and in memory of those of the New Zealand Division who fell in the battles of the Somme, 1916, 1918."

SECTION 4.—FURTHER PROGRESS OF THE BATTLE.

October advances—Broken weather—Renewed offensive on the Ancre—End of the Battle of the Somme—Results achieved.

The account of the progress of the great battle from about the time of the departure of the New Zealand Division early in October up till the middle of November, when, owing to the continued bad weather, active operations of importance practically ceased, may be briefly summarized.

Eaucourt l'Abbaye on our immediate left, which had been captured early on October 2nd, was counter-attacked and retaken by the enemy on the same date, but it came finally into the possession of the British on the 3rd. In order to assist the French in their advance on Sailly Saillisel, Morval had been handed over to them. On October 7th another Allied advance began and by the afternoon Le Sars was taken, the line advanced close to Le Barque and Ligny Thilloy, and on to the crest before Le Transloy. The French advance brought them close to Sailly, and their right, farther south, had also gone forward. The general success could not be further exploited owing to heavy rain.

Operations re-opened on October 12th, the line being slowly pushed forward everywhere on the right. The French took Sailly on the 15th and Sailly Saillisel on the 19th. There is little doubt that only the abominable nature of the weather prevented the taking of Bapaume. Unfortunately "the moment for decisive action was rapidly passing away, while the weather showed no signs of improvement. By this time the ground had become so bad that nothing less than a prolonged period of drying weather, which at that season of the year was most unlikely to occur, would suit our purpose."*

On November 9th the weather moderated, being now dry and cold, with frosty nights and misty mornings, and final preparations for a renewed offensive on the Ancre were pushed on. The attack by the Canadians on the 11th brought the British close to the strong German positions immediately in front of Pys and Warlencourt, and on the 13th the attack on the Ancre front commenced. St. Pierre Divion, the famous Y-Ravine and the strong redoubts in rear, and the enemy's

*Sir Douglas Haig's Despatches.

front line system half a mile beyond Beaumont Hamel, fell to the British troops on that day, and on the 14th the gains in this neighbourhood were still further improved. Then the weather broke again and continued to be so unfavourable that the Battle of the Somme of 1916 came practically to an end.

The three main objectives of the offensive had, however, been achieved. Verdun had been relieved; the main German forces had been held on the western front; and the enemy's strength had been considerably worn down. "Any one of these three results is in itself sufficient to justify the Somme Battle. The attainment of all three of them affords ample compensation for the splendid efforts of our troops and for the sacrifices made by ourselves and by our Allies. They have brought us a long step forward towards the final victory of the Allied cause."*

The captures made by the British from July 1st to November 18th included: 38,000 officers and men, 29 heavy guns, 96 field-pieces and howitzers, 136 trench mortars, 514 machine-guns.

*Sir Douglas Haig's Despatches.

CHAPTER VII.

FROM FLEURBAIX TO PLOEGSTEERT.

PART 1.—THE BOUTILLERIE SECTOR.

From the Somme back to the Lys—Into the line, Boutillerie Sector—Small-box Respirators—Command—Inspections—1st Battalion raid on Turk's Point—The Colonel-in-Chief at Bailleul—2nd Battalion raid on the Angle—Raid by the Germans—4th Battalion raid on Corner Fort—3rd Battalion raid—Inspection by Sir Douglas Haig—Christmas Day "dummy raid"—Command and staff—Enemy's "dummy raid" on New Year's Day—2nd Battalion raid on the Lozenge—Out to Divisional reserve—General: trenches; artillery; patrolling; billets; schools; working-parties; aerial activity; regimental band; railway-construction party; a bitter winter.

After its participation in the Somme operations the New Zealand Rifle Brigade on October 6th marched to Albert, and there entrained for Longpre-les-Corps-Saints. From the detraining station the various units again took the road for their billeting areas, and by 6 a.m. on the 7th had settled down for a few days' rest in their new quarters, the 1st and 2nd Battalions at Mareuil, the 3rd at Villers-sur-Mareuil, and the 4th at Bray-les-Mareuil.

General Fulton departed on leave on October 9th, and Lieut.-Col. A. E. Stewart assumed temporary command of the Brigade.

On the evening of the 10th the Brigade proceeded by road to Abbeville, where train was taken for Bailleul, whence battalions, on their arrival, marched to and billeted at Outtersteene. Here General Godley, commanding the IInd Anzac Corps, to which we had now returned, held a conference with the Brigadier and battalion commanders on the 12th.

In accordance with orders for the Brigade to relieve the 14th Australian Brigade in the Boutillerie Sector, the 1st and 2nd Battalions marched on the 13th October to Vieux Berquin, and were transported thence by motor-bus to Bac St. Maur and Fleurbaix. During the night of 13th/14th these units relieved the 55th and 56th Australian Battalions, respectively, in the line. The remainder of the Brigade arrived at Fleurbaix and Bac St. Maur on the 14th, Brigade Headquarters being located at the former village.

The sector taken over had a front line exceeding 2,500 yards in length. It was immediately south of the Bois Grenier Sector, which, it will be remembered, was handed over by our Brigade when we moved out for the Somme. The 1st New Zealand Brigade came in on our immediate right. Beyond the 1st Brigade was the 61st Division, and the 34th Division joined up with us on the left.*

The new small-box respirators, which afterwards proved so effective against any form of gas projected against us by the enemy, were now being introduced, and on October 18th the Brigadier, commanding officers and company commanders attended at the Gas School at Nouveau Monde for instruction in their use.

Lieut.-Col. Austin, from hospital, and Lieut.-Col. Melvill, from leave, reported on October 15th and resumed command of the 1st and 4th Battalions respectively. General Fulton returned from leave on the 19th. Lieut.-Col. Winter-Evans, commanding the 3rd Battalion, and Lieut.-Col. A. E. Stewart, commanding the 2nd Battalion, proceeded to England on leave on the following day.

General Plumer, commanding the Second Army, accompanied by the G.O.C. Division, visited the Brigade and inspected the 4th Battalion on October 23rd.

On October 25th the 1st and 2nd Battalions were relieved in the line by the 3rd and 4th, and went to billets at Fleurbaix and Bac St. Maur. As the visibility was poor and the sector comparatively quiet, the interchange was carried out before nightfall, this being the first of many daylight reliefs.

On the morning of the 31st the Army Commander presented the ribands of a number of decorations awarded to officers and other ranks in connection with raids and the engagements in Egypt and on the Somme, and after this ceremony inspected the 2nd Battalion at Bac St. Maur. The Hon. W. F.

---

*The 2nd Brigade was detached to "Franks' Force," and remained with it until December 3rd. Franks' Force was a temporary organization formed of reserve Brigades from the two remaining Divisions of the IInd Anzac Corps after the 51st Division had been sent to the Somme. It was holding the Houplines Sector at Armentieres.

Massey, Prime Minister, and Sir Joseph Ward, who had been attending an Imperial Conference in London, were present at both these parades.

Our casualties for the month of October were:—

	Killed.	Wounded.
Officers	2	4
Other ranks	49	155

A daylight relief was effected on November 6th, the 1st and 2nd Battalions taking over the line from the 3rd and 4th.

At 6 p.m. on the 16th a party of two officers and 50 other ranks from the 1st Battalion, under the general direction of Capt. C. K. Gasquoine, carried out a raiding-assault on a section of the enemy's trench known as "Turk's Point," but under stress of our artillery preparation the Germans had temporarily evacuated that part of their line, and no prisoners were taken.

The raid was so well executed as to deserve some tangible results. The position selected for attack was a small salient adjoining a re-entrant in the enemy line, and while it was expected that at least one machine-gun position would be found there, the configuration of the German trench was such as to preclude any possibility of enfilade fire being brought to bear on the assaulting troops. Corporal O. A. Gillespie, a patrol leader of exceptional ability, had frequently traversed the ground to be passed over, and knew almost every inch of it, and under his guidance all the leaders and many of the men had been taken over it in order to gain personal knowledge of its features. A ditch ran directly across from our own to the enemy's parapet, and other ditches at right angles to this provided suitable cover and convenient assembly positions. On the night of the adventure Gillespie and his patrol preceded the raiders across No Man's Land, and ascertaining that the artillery and trench mortars had cut a perfect opening thirty yards in width through the strong belt of wire protecting the position, sent back word to this effect to Capt. E. H. Buckeridge, who had by this time filed his men into position at the point of assembly in No Man's Land and disposed his flanking parties with Lewis guns at their appointed places. 2nd Lieut. A. D. Smith and the twenty men told off for the actual entry were guided forward to the gap, and passing through this, they took up their stations under the parapet on a frontage of forty yards and awaited the signal for the final dash. This given, the entry was made simultaneously and bombing parties worked right and left for a hundred yards. All had gone exactly as on the practising-ground, even to the absence of an enemy to deal with, for the closest search failed to reveal any Germans, dead or alive, and nothing in the way of identification of any kind could be found. There was much water in the trench, and the ground behind as far as could be seen was more or less completely submerged. Mental notes were taken of the nature of the defences, one or two concrete dug-outs were blown up by the sappers accompanying the party, and the stated time having expired, the disappointed men were withdrawn to our lines. If Lieut. Smith's cup of irritation was not quite full as he beat the air in the German trench, it surely overflowed when he sprained his ankle during his return.

On the 18th the 3rd and 4th Battalions relieved the 1st and 2nd in the line, the interchange being completed by 4.50 p.m.

Representative officers of the Brigade went to Bailleul on November 4th to meet H.R.H. the Duke of Connaught, Colonel-in-Chief.

Our casualties for November were comparatively light, the numbers being:—

	Killed.	Wounded.
Officers	1	2
Other ranks	14	58

On December 1st the 1st and 2nd Battalions relieved the 3rd and 4th in the line, the latter units going into billets in Fleurbaix.

A week later a party from the 2nd Battalion, under Lieuts. G. A. Avey and H. H. Daniell, silently raided "The Angle," but found that the enemy garrison had beaten a retreat when they discovered our men approaching. We were not able to secure prisoners, but succeeded in blowing up bomb-stores and parts of the parapet with gun-cotton. Valuable information of a general kind was obtained.

The enemy attempted a raid on December 10th, directing his attack on part of the trenches held by "A" Company of the 1st Battalion. At dusk, and during the usual period of evening stand-to, very heavy machine-gun fire swept the parapet, the fire being continued for a considerable time. Presently it diminished on the right flank and was concentrated on the central portion of the battalion sector. Nothing unusual was apprehended, however, and the night sentries having been posted, the men stood down to draw their tea. At this moment an intense bombardment opened, trench-mortar fire being directed with considerable accuracy on the front trench and sap-heads, and an artillery barrage placed in rear and well down the communication-trenches. The significance of this was at once apparent and the garrison stood-to again, every man being at his post within three mintues of the opening of the bombardment.

The expected development was not long in coming. A German trench-mortar bomb landed in the bay where a Lewis gun post had been established to command a gap in our wire and also a line of trees that ran across No Man's Land from the enemy's trench to our own. This bomb wounded three men in the post, but the fourth, Rifleman W. H. Butler, as yet uninjured though somewhat shaken, continued his guard single-handed. By the light of a flare he now distinguished a party of the enemy making their way through the wire, and upon these he immediately opened fire. Unfortunately, his gun jammed before half a drum had been fired off, and while feverishly struggling with the mechanism he was struck by a stick-bomb and severely wounded. Another man in the post, Rifleman P. H. Gifford, though mortally wounded, now struggled once again to his place on the fire-step to protect his fallen comrades with rifle and bayonet, and continued with what little strength remained to him to fire on the attackers.

Fire had, of course, been taken up by the posts on the right and left, and this was supplemented by Sergeant P. Clark of the 3rd Machine Gun Company, who, when our Lewis gun ceased firing, mounted his Vickers gun on the parapet to take up the work. The attempted raid was thus brought to an abrupt conclusion. An interesting feature of the affair was the smooth manner in which Major Bell's plans for meeting eventualities of this kind worked out. No sooner had the point of attack been determined that the bombing parties told off for the purpose had taken up their appointed positions ready to bomb through; information was sent back, artillery support called for, touch with the flank companies secured, and the reserve platoon brought up, all without a hitch of any kind. When the artillery fire on both sides had died down sufficiently, patrols were sent out. These found two dead Germans, one on our parapet and one in the wire, both riddled with bullets; and, strung out along the line of approach by the trees, German bombs and steel helmets, eloquent indication of a hasty retreat.

The 3rd and 4th Battalions came into the line on December 12th, relieving the 1st and 2nd Battalions by 2.30 p.m.

At midnight on December 17th/18th a strong party of four officers (2nd Lieuts. G. E. F. Kingscote, F. T. Bennington, B. Mollison and A. Bongard) and 170 other ranks of the 4th Battalion, together with 12 sappers, the whole under the command of Capt. W. W. Dove, carried out a very successful raid. Profiting by the experience gained in our recent minor operations, the plans for this raiding force were laid on a more ambitious scale, and had for their primary object the close examination of the enemy's support line as well as his forward trench at a salient known as "Corner Fort." This point had been visited by our patrols on various occasions during the previous two or three weeks. Lance-Corporal H. S. Eastgate entered it without difficulty on 27th November, and on the following night took a patrol of seven men over to gain additional information, but this time he got into difficulties. He was met by a superior force and his party suffered casualties. Though himself wounded he carried back to a place of safety one of his men in worse case than himself, and then conducted a stretcher-party from our lines and brought the wounded man in. Rifleman N. A. Nicholson, one of the patrol, after leaving the enemy's trench, lay up for a time outside, and on hearing groans, went through the wire again and discovered a wounded comrade. He dressed his wounds, but these being too serious to permit of his being carried in single-handed, Nicholson came back to his own lines, reported the case, guided a bearer-party across, and so completed the rescue.

Corner Fort was inspected again by one of the six officers' patrols sent out at the end of the month, when the gap in the wire was found to be closed, and the position apparently strongly held. Sergeant W. McConachy also had carried out special investigations during the week previous to the raid, as had Capt. Dove and several of his section leaders.

Capt. Dove's raiding force consisted in the main of four platoons, one from each of the companies of the battalion. It was divided into three parties, besides the usual covering and flanking groups. Each had its own assembly position in No Man's Land, and each its separate point of entry. The party under Lieut. Bennington entered at the point of the salient, made good their hold on the 600 yards of front trench allotted to them, wiped out a sentry group of four men, and proceeded to investigate the maze of trenches comprising Corner Fort itself. These proved to be little more than dummies constructed of wood and canvas to deceive aeroplane observers. Such trenches as existed were so full of water that the men found it more satisfactory to move across the open. A group of trenches in rear of the so-called fort was found to be the real strong-point, and some difficulty was experienced in silencing the two machine-guns that were firing from it. A long-range bombing attack failed to do this, but more success eventually attended the action of Riflemen J. Keys and E. M. Phelan, who wormed their way up to the position from a flank and bombed the garrison from close range. Heavy wire and deep water unfortunately precluded the possibility of securing the guns.

2nd Lieut. Kingscote's party got into the front line some 200 yards to the right of the point with little opposition, and worked back towards the support line, but owing to the flooded state of the trenches and the intricate nature of the many saps that had to be searched, no further progress was made before the time for withdrawal. Only one dug-out was discovered and only one party of Germans met with by this section of the raiders.

The party under 2nd Lieut. Mollison entered at a point about 400 yards to the left of the apex of the salient, and, according to plan, split up into two groups, each of about 20 men. One of these, under the direction of 2nd Lieut. Bongard, secured the flank covering the main communication trench. A section was sent along the front-line trench to search those parts that were not obliterated. These found a strongly-wired post, the garrison of which succeeded in keeping their assailants at bay with egg-bombs, the ranging of which so greatly exceeded that of our own. Another section searched the main communication-trench. In a small cutting leading from this a bombing party under Sergeant H. C. Welch came across ten Germans, who at first showed fight, but on being beaten back, took refuge in a dug-out. This was at once attacked, five prisoners dragged out, and the remainder bombed. Further on, a second dug-out was discovered, but this contained nothing of greater interest than important papers.

In the meantime 2nd Lieut. Mollison with the second group pushed on down the communication trench to the support line, the redoubtable Sergeant McConachy leading. On the way two occupied dug-outs were located and bombed. The support line was found to be in splendid order, well revetted, and floored with wide duck-boards. Well sunk into the parapet at intervals of twenty yards were comfortable dug-outs, each provided with a porch fitted with rifle-racks, the main compartment being large enough for the accommodation of ten men. These were searched, but from all but one the occupants had fled. From this three prisoners were taken. The other inmates refused to come out and were promptly despatched with bombs.

The time allowed for the enterprise had now expired, and the engineers having completed the demolition of the tramline, pumping-plant and dug-outs, the raiders withdrew. Nine prisoners were captured, all but one being taken from the support line. Important documents were found in an officer's dug-out. During the progress of the raid there had been bursts of machine-gun and rifle fire from various points, and much bombing activity on both sides, yet our casualties had been surprisingly light. One man was killed just as the party left our lines, and four were wounded later. From time to time the Germans fired signal rockets, mainly from the support line, but the only artillery response was from a light gun, which threw six shells into our lines. Five of these were "blind" and fell on the support line as our men were crossing No Man's Land on their way back.

Congratulations on the successful issue of this minor operation were received from the Commanders of the Army, the Corps, and the Division.

A raid by two officers and 67 men of the 3rd Battalion on the 23rd proved less successful. The enemy was no doubt smarting under the treatment meted out to him by the 4th Battalion five days previously, and was determined not to be caught again so soon, for though the section now raided was opposite the other flank of our sector it was found to be held by a very strong garrison who were evidently expecting an attack. As planned and practised, the raid was to have been a "silent" one, in other words an assault without special artillery support in the form of either preliminary bombardment or accompanying barrage. At the last minute, however, and contrary to the expressed wish of the raiders themselves, a short bombardment by our medium trench-mortars on two suspected machine-gun posts was ordered. In accordance with these instructions the trench mortars fired while the assaulting party waited in their assembly position out in No Man's Land; and although only twelve mortar-bombs in all were thrown, it was considered that this brief bombardment served to put the garrison immediately on the alert. In any case the essential element of surprise was now non-existent.

The enemy allowed our men to make their way through the wire and form up by the parapet, and then opened up such an intense machine-gun, rifle and bomb fire upon them that further progress was impossible. Many gallant attempts were made still to push on in the face of this fire. 2nd Lieut. M. F. Walsh, who commanded the assaulting party, persisted till he fell mortally wounded. Sergeant H. Anderson, the first to reach the parapet, alone attacked one of the flanking machine-guns and bombed it out of action. But all was without avail, and withdrawal had reluctantly to be ordered. Rifleman J. Hansen, a stretcher-bearer, with extreme self-sacrifice remained behind, searching for wounded and tending them under fire in shell-holes, on the enemy parapet, and in the German wire, eventually guiding bearer-parties who brought them in. One of our wounded, known to have been lying near the enemy parapet, still remained unaccounted for. To accomplish his rescue, Rifleman W. D. H. Milne set out from our lines, found his man and brought him in, though in accomplishing this achievement Milne himself was mortally wounded.

Capt. W. A. G. Penlington, who was in general control of the operation, handled the awkward situation with promptitude and discretion; while the covering-party commanded by 2nd Lieut. W. A. Gray skilfully fulfilled its mission in the face of the enemy artillery fire which became intense in No Man's Land, and when this service was completed remained out for further voluntary duty with the stretcher-bearers.

Sir Douglas Haig, Commander-in-Chief, inspected the 2nd Battalion at Sailly on the 22nd.

During the afternoon of December 23rd the 1st and 2nd Battalions relieved the 3rd and 4th in the front line.

Throughout Christmas Day, to disabuse the mind of the enemy as to the possibility of any fraternization, our artillery carried out an intermittent but very heavy bombardment of the German lines, culminating in a "dummy raid" at 8.35 p.m. The enemy's retaliation was only slight.

General Fulton departed for England on December 28th for a month's leave, and on the 31st Lieut.-Col. H. Hart, D.S.O., 1st Wellington Regiment, assumed command of the Brigade. On the 13th Major W. H. Hastings reported for duty as Brigade Major, vice Major T. R. Eastwood, evacuated to England, sick. Lieut.-Col. C. W. Melvill, 4th Battalion, went over to the temporary command of the 2nd Brigade on the 20th.

The casualties for December were:—

	Killed.	Wounded.
Officers	—	2
Other ranks	10	55

On 1st January, 1917, the Germans returned the compliment of Christmas Day by bombarding our sector heavily from noon till 3 p.m. On the same day the 3rd and 4th Battalions relieved the 1st and 2nd in the front line, but fortunately our interchange had commenced unusually early, and consequently the casualties were not so numerous as they might otherwise have been.

A party from the 2nd Battalion, consisting of two officers (2nd Lieuts. L. I. Manning and D. C. Bowler) and 78 other ranks, the whole under the command of Capt. J. B. Bennett, executed an extremely successful raid on January 7th.

The objective was the "Lozenge," a rectangular set of trench works just behind the enemy front line opposite the left of the Brigade sector, and the enterprise involved not only the attack on this suspected strong-point, but also the taking and the temporary holding of three communication-trenches leading back from the front line. The preliminary scouting had been minute and thorough, and before five o'clock in the evening the raiders moved out from the lines full of confidence, crossed on portable bridges the stream running athwart the line of advance, and settled down in their appointed assembly positions to await the report of the scouts as to the state of the wire. This being favourable, they moved forward again, and in three columns, each in single file, penetrated the wire, silently waded through the four feet of icy water in the wide borrow-ditch, simultaneously rushed the parapet, and got to work on their respective tasks. The areas about the three sap-heads were immediately secured, and steps were taken to establish the necessary blocks on the flanks.

The right blocking party encountered the enemy some thirty yards along the trench, and a hot bombing fight ensued. The corporal in charge of our men was killed and another wounded. Sergeant G. Bates was meanwhile pressing forward through the communication-trench with a section bent on dealing with the Lozenge itself, but, hearing a cry for help from the blocking party, withdrew his men and went to the assistance of the former. Even against this additional strength the Germans held out for a time, but they were finally overcome, three being killed and three taken prisoner, the remainder making good their escape. Our party here had now to devote their attention to a machine-gun firing upon them from the front line still further along, and though by the time the gun was silenced with bombs it was too late to prosecute their attack on the strong-point in rear, this troublesome flank at least was made secure.

The party on the left flank established their block without difficulty beyond that of movement, for owing to the smashed and water-logged condition of the fire-trench they had to move along the parapet. They found four concrete dug-outs, two of which, as well as a machine-gun emplacement, had been reduced to ruins by our artillery fire. They encountered ten Germans, seven of whom they shot, and three who endeavoured to take cover in the ruins of the dug-outs were followed up and bombed. Proceeding down the sap they met three of the enemy running towards them. These also were promptly shot. The time limit having almost been exceeded, nothing further could be done on this side.

The centre party experienced some difficulty in finding the head of their particular communication-trench. In their search for this they discovered in the front line a domed concrete sentry-post containing two sentries, who were taken prisoner. The sap-head found, 2nd Lieut. Bowler took his men along towards the strong-point. They had not gone far when, near a tramline-opening, they found two concrete dug-outs, one of which had a circular stairway and was occupied. Three Germans, attempting to run off, were effectually dealt with, three near the doorway were taken prisoner, and as the remainder refused to come out and our men had other pressing work to do, two detonated Stokes mortar bombs were rolled in and the place demolished. In the meantime the section under Corporal E. E. Islip had discovered another deep dug-out near by, and had already gathered in ten prisoners. On Islip's call for assistance, Sergeant H. W. Harvey with a few men from the main party returned, took four more prisoners, and the remaining inmates proving recalcitrant, were all shot.

By this time, counter-attacking troops were observed on their way up from the support line, and as our men already had their hands full the signal for withdrawal was sounded. Of the 22 prisoners taken, three gave trouble while crossing No Man's Land and had to be shot.

Our casualties were one killed and five slightly wounded.

On January 8th, 1917, the Brigade was relieved in this sector by the 1st Brigade*, the relief being completed by

*A rearrangement of the 1st and 2nd New Zealand Infantry Brigades was made on 1st January, 1917, the 2nd Auckland and 2nd Wellington Battalions being transferred to the former, and the 1st Canterbury and 1st Otago to the latter. Thus, from this date, the 1st Brigade consisted only of North Island units, and the 2nd Brigade only of battalions from the South Island.

2.15 p.m., and we went into Divisional reserve with the 1st Battalion at Estaires, the 2nd at Bac St. Maur, the 4th at Sailly-sur-la-Lys, and Brigade Headquarters and the 3rd Battalion at Nouveau Monde.

Our three months' stay in the Boutillerie Sector passed pleasantly enough. The lines were fairly good, though the breastworks required constant attention. The ground, being very low, was subject to flooding, but the Engineers had been hard at work for over a year under a Drainage Officer who had made a special study of the problem. The main drain, dignified by the name of the River Laies, which traversed the area, had been widened and deepened and provided with several supplementary outlets at its confluence with the Lys immediately west of Armentieres, and the whole system was now in an extremely satisfactory state, only requiring such attention as was necessary after damage from shell-fire. The roads were good, and could be used by transport on dull days as far forward as the subsidiary system, some 2,000 yards from the front line, and at night to within 700 yards. Cooking could be carried on satisfactorily in the support line. Enemy activity was confined almost entirely to artillery and minenwerfer fire, and though the German guns did comparatively little damage, his heavy mortars kept us busy at night-work on repairs to our parapets. The New Zealand Divisional Artillery, having arrived from the Somme, came into the sector on November 8th and lost no time in returning the enemy's fire with interest. Our Stokes guns and medium trench mortars, the latter throwing the bombs familiarly known as "plum puddings," were exceedingly active throughout the period, wrecking long stretches of the enemy's wire, parapets, and communication-trenches. As most of the bombs that fell beyond the German parapet sent up columns of mud and water, we surmised that the enemy was living in very uncomfortable quarters—a conclusion that was confirmed by the subsequent reports of our patrols. Our snipers claimed a great harvest, the many breaches in the enemy's trenches causing him to expose himself with considerable frequency. The one heavy trench mortar in the sector, firing from our side, threw a bomb that wrought much greater execution than anything of the kind that the enemy could project, but its value was discounted by

HOWITZERS.

A 9.2-INCH GUN.

Face p. 160.

BATTALION TRANSPORT.

FIELD-KITCHENS (COOKERS).

THE WATER CART.

THE Y.M.C.A. CANTEEN.

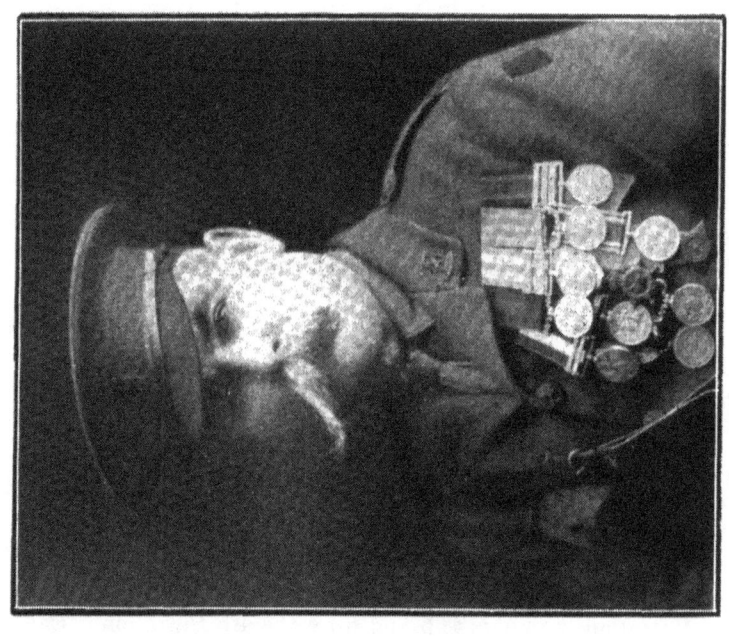

The Veteran Sergeant-Major,
R.S.M. C. Livesey, D.C.M.

Winter on the Western Front.
"Great Push," Hutchinson's.

the erratic nature of its shooting. It was carefully explained to the infantry that it was always problematical where the first round would fall, because the gun required warming up; but when, at the end of a certain mild "shoot" of six rounds, the last "flying pig" (as these bombs were nicknamed) just succeeded in escaping from the muzzle of the gun, our men naturally became somewhat sceptical; and they glady obeyed the orders to evacuate part of the trenches when this mortar was about to fire.

Patrols from our garrisons were unusually daring, and after one or two encounters with enemy reconnoitring parties they had No Man's Land completely controlled. Not content with this, they went farther afield and carried on their investigations actually inside the enemy's defences. The following extracts from the reports of six patrols of an average strength of twenty, operating on the night of 30th Nov./1st Dec., will serve to indicate the class of work done on these special reconnaissances. Numbers 1, 2 and 3 Patrols were furnished by the 3rd Battalion, numbers 4, 5 and 6 by the 4th Battalion. Each was in charge of an officer and all moved out at midnight:—

No. 1 Patrol: Left the trench on the extreme right of our sector (the portion which the enemy attempted to raid on December 10th) and arrived at the enemy's wire at 12.25 a.m. The entanglements were very badly damaged, but at no point could they be found to be broken completely through. A thorough survey of the wire on this portion of the front was made, and these defences were ascertained to be from fifty to sixty yards in depth. No Germans were seen or heard, and no flares were fired from this locality.

No. 2 Patrol: Proceeded across No Man's Land towards "Turk's Point" (the section raided by the 1st Battalion party on November 16th). Here the enemy's wire was found to be much blown about, the entanglements still remaining being nowhere more than fifteen feet through. The patrol leader, with three other ranks, entered the trench, and patrolled 200 yards to the right and 100 yards to the left without finding any sign of the enemy. The trench had been greatly damaged by our bombardments. A deep dug-out was seen, but this was full of water, and no wire was discovered in rear of the trench. The support lines, from which machine-guns and flares were being fired, lay from 300 to 400 yards behind the front trench, and in the intervening area there was very much water.

No. 3 Patrol: Left the trench at about the centre of our line, and moved across to the locality in the enemy's trenches known as "Clapham Junction," crossing two streams four feet wide on the way. At about eighty yards from the enemy's parapet progress was barred by a wire screen about six feet deep, almost intact, and extending right and left as far as could be seen. A gap was found, through which the patrol passed, but within a few feet of the parapet an impassable barrier was encountered, consisting of a moat from fourteen to sixteen feet wide, filled with a wire system, and containing water to a depth of six feet. This extended to the left as far as examined, and to the right it entered a stream running perpendicular to the trench. The patrol moved back 150 yards, crossed this stream, and approached the enemy's trench farther to the right. The wire here was not greatly damaged, but the patrol succeeded in getting through by gaps and low places. As, in spite of considerable noise, the party was not fired on, it was concluded that the trench was unoccupied. This proving to be correct, the officer commanding divided his patrol into three parties, one of which was sent forward towards the support line, and the others right and left along the trench. In the saps the forward party found several dug-outs like our own, but for the most part these were being dismantled and the timber stacked. The ground was very waterlogged and rough. An apparently new belt of wire had been erected about midway between the front and support lines, the latter being about 200 yards in rear of the main trench. The party discovered and destroyed a double-cable telephone wire.

The right party went some 250 yards along the trench, which was found to contain from one to three feet of water, with the parapet badly wrecked. "Clapham Junction" was not identified, but several wrecked communication-trenches connecting with the front line were seen and examined. Scouts moved forward towards the support line, and the information secured corresponded with that obtained by the forward party. An enemy wiring-party was heard at work about 350 yards to the right of the first point of entry.

The left party found the trench to be well constructed for a length of seventy yards. It was eight feet deep, with a parapet eighteen feet wide, well traversed, revetted with brushwood hurdles supported by 4 in. x 4 in. uprights, and provided with fire-step and elbow-rests, with piles of bombs at frequent intervals. In places the parapet was prepared for men to fire in the prone position, and for the whole distance was carefully levelled and trimmed. This section was protected in front by the moat already referred to. Still farther to the left the trench appeared to be permanently disused, and there seemed to have been no attempt at repairing the damage from shell-fire. No enemy were seen, but machine-guns were firing from a strong-point 350 yards behind the line. The time spent in their investigations by the parties of this patrol was over four hours.

No. 4 Patrol: Crossed No Man's Land towards a point where a previous patrol had reported a gap in the enemy's wire about 300 yards east of "Clapham Junction." On the way they observed a hostile patrol, which immediately withdrew through the wire near "Corner Fort." Arrived at the entanglements, our patrol discovered that the gap had been re-wired. The leader, with one non-commissioned officer, cut through twenty strands and, leaving a covering-party, took the bulk of the patrol forward and surmounted the parapet. Here the trench formed a bay about 35 feet long, revetted with planks. Both parapet and parados were found to be much damaged, there was approximately four feet of water in the trench, and no signs of recent occupation were visible. A sentry-group was seen about fifty yards to the right, and another some forty yards to the left, both apparently posted at communication-trenches, and strongly protected by wire nearly two chains deep. During the two hours the leader of our party spent on the parapet these sentry-groups were visited three times by patrols working up the communication-trenches from the support line. Immediately in rear of the parados ran a partially-submerged tramway, with a large dump of old timber near the line. Sheets of water prevented exploration towards the support line, in which there appeared to be a large number of ordinary dug-outs, the glare from which could be clearly seen.

No. 5 Patrol: Moved across towards "Corner Fort" (raided later by the 4th Battalion). The hostile patrol reported by No. 4 was also seen by this party. A gap previously discovered in the enemy wire, and through which our patrol expected to enter the trench, was found to have been re-wired, and the parapet strongly held, there being no fewer than three sentry-groups in a space of forty yards. From the volume of talking and coughing heard, it was concluded that a considerable number of men were on the alert and ready to man the parapet. It was therefore decided not to force an entry, but to lie up close to the wire and watch. The wire observed was very thick. The patrol leader formed the opinion that the head of each communication-trench was strongly held by sentry-groups.

No. 6 Patrol: Made for a known gap in the enemy's wire round "The Angle," a position raided a week later by the 2nd Battalion. The patrol passed through the gap and lay down on the parapet. The trench was found to be eight or nine feet deep and filled with a tangle of wire. A sentry being heard coughing at a point thirty yards to the right of the point of entry, the leader, taking two men, proceeded to stalk and capture him. It was discovered, however, that thick wire ran up the parapet on each side of the sentry's post. He was therefore bombed and rushed, but was found to have been killed. Shoulder-straps and cap were taken from the body for identification, but no documents were found upon him. A second man, wounded, seen crawling down a communication-trench, was chased by two of our men. He, however, succeeded in escaping into a dug-out provided with a steel door, but, before he could close this behind him, two bombs were thrown inside. It is considered that he and three unwounded men seen within must have been killed by the bombs.

Billets in the villages of Fleurbaix and Bac St. Maur occupied by battalions when not in the line were, on the whole, very satisfactory. In the latter place the 1st Battalion was fortunate enough to be able to establish a mess for all its officers, and the regular informal gatherings thus rendered possible were a delightful change from the comparative isolation forced upon the groups of officers within the unit by the exigencies of life in the trenches and in the ordinary scattered billets. At Fleurbaix the Engineers converted a battered and deserted school-building into a very fine Y.M.C.A. hall, in which we held several concerts, and at Bac St. Maur we were within easy reach of the Divisional Cinema Hall that had been constructed at Sailly. The 2nd and 4th Battalions enjoyed elaborate Christmas dinners by companies in their respective billeting areas. The 1st and 3rd, being in the line at the time, were less fortunately placed, but they "kept their Christmas merry still" at a later date.

Battalion schools for the instruction of additional specialists, such as signallers, Lewis-gunners, bombers, etc., were established while we were holding this sector, the training being carried on both in the line and while in support or reserve. One of the lessons of the Somme had been that the ordinary supply of specialists from Base, and the augmentation secured by sending men for training at Army, Corps and Divisional schools of instruction, proved insufficient for the replacement of casualties to the extent required in order to keep units up to the full state of efficiency. The ideal aimed at was not only to ensure an ample reserve of well-trained observers and signallers, but also to make every rifleman proficient in the use of the bomb and able to handle the Lewis gun; and although this result was not fully attained, yet we succeeded in taking a long step forward towards that end.

It must be borne in mind that when units were in support or reserve their time was not their own. It was a point of honour with the New Zealand Division that it should leave its defensive works of every nature in a far better state than that in which it found them. Hence the working-parties that had to be supplied daily by battalions nominally resting were required to be as strong as possible; and commanding officers had the greatest difficulty in meeting the demands of the Engineers for men, and at the same time to carry on the interior economy of their units, get all ranks to the baths, and provide for instructional work.

Aerial activity at this time was not very intense. Perhaps the most exciting incident was the visit of an enemy observer, who flew his 'plane at an extremely low altitude over the streets and neighbouring fields of Fleurbaix. The German airman must have had a charmed life, for, though fired on at close range by hundreds of Riflemen, he made good his escape apparently uninjured.

Some little space may conveniently be devoted here to a brief account of the vicissitudes of the Regimental Band, a matter of seemingly slight importance, but, as has already been indicated, one of very considerable interest to our men throughout the whole of their period on service.

It will be remembered that the band, as originally constituted, consisted of men whose main duty was that of stretcher-bearing. During the early stages of our service in France it was found that casualties amongst the stretcher-bearers were so heavy that the very existence of the band was threatened, and it was therefore decided to establish separate stretcher-bearer sections, and reserve the bandsmen for special duties out of the line, usually with the quartermaster's branch and in the transport lines. From the musicians still remaining in the four battalions a Brigade Band was formed consisting of thirty members, under Lieut. Cole; and as the band was, for rations and other purposes, formally attached to the 1st Battalion, it came about that this unit unavoidably received more than a fair share of its good influences. On starting off for the Somme battle area, efforts were made to retain the spare instruments; but at the last moment, owing to an unusually stringent inspection of the transport, these were put off the wagons, and with them, unfortunately, a case containing the bulk of the sheet music and a number of mouth-pieces and other spare parts.

So keenly was the lack of bands felt on the long marches to the Somme that, on arrival in that area, steps were at once taken to organize a band for each unit. In the first place the Brigade Band was divided into two portions and the moieties augmented to form bands for the 1st and 2nd Battalions, and much patient search at various bases enabled Lieut. Cole to locate and secure sufficient of our old instruments to equip these. The drums of the Bugle Band could not be found, but this was immaterial, as the maintenance of that little organization had long since become impossible.

At Fleurbaix, after the Somme battle, the task of establishing the remaining two battalion bands was proceeded with, but the difficulties encountered were so great that it was not until the Brigade came out of the line to train for the Battle of Messines that all four units were each in possession of its own band. Not the least of the obstacles in the way of success were the reluctance of the base depots to part with their trained musicians, the fact that the 4th Brigade was coming into existence, and the scarcity and cost of good instruments. Of two sets of band instruments obtained from Paris, one was of Continental pitch and had to be rectified by mechanical means at the front, while the other was of such inferior quality that the whole outfit was purchased for £60. At a later period the four bands were placed on an equal footing with complete sets of silver instruments. These are now in use with various territorial units in New Zealand.

A party numbering 300, made up of drafts from the four battalions, was despatched on January 8th for railway construction duty with the Vth Corps. Capt. P. F. McRae, of the

2nd Battalion, went in command of the detachment, and with him were Lieut. P. E. Salmon and 2nd Lieuts. H. J. Trevethick and J. G. Greenwood, in charge of the parties from the 1st, 3rd and 4th Battalions, respectively. The whole of the personnel were picked men who had had experience of railway construction or similar work in civil life.

The scene of operations was on a new railway line from Dunkirk to Poperinghe and Ypres, then being built in connection with preparations for the spring offensive. The main line ran south-east from Dunkirk to Bergues, thence south and south-east to Hazebrouck; and Poperinghe was reached by means of a branch line running fourteen miles north-easterly from Hazebrouck. To shorten this long roundabout journey, a new line was being constructed direct from Bergues across the frontier to Poperinghe, and passing through Proven. Our party was detailed for work on the stretch between Bergues and Proven, and the men were to be billeted at Vyfweg, a village at a railway-junction near the former town.

The forty-mile journey by motor lorries over the snow-covered country was an interesting yet comfortless experience, but the hearty welcome received by our men at the hands of the Maire and the people of Vyfweg, who turned out en masse to witness their arrival, served in no small measure to dispel their present misery. As no British troops had hitherto been quartered in this district, the novelty of the situation appealed strongly to the inhabitants, who proved themselves remarkably kind and hospitable.

Work commenced at once and proceeded as steadily as the weather conditions permitted. While the ground remained frozen to a considerable depth progress was necessarily slow, but rapid strides were made whenever a thaw set in; and altogether our men acquitted themselves so well as to earn high praise from the officers of the Railway Operating Department, under whose general direction they were working.

Notwithstanding the severity of the weather, the party's two months' stay at Vyfweg was more enjoyable than otherwise. There were few of the intimate realities of war beyond an occasional bombing of Bergues or Dunkirk; the quarters were good, rations arrived regularly, and the extra provisions dearly loved by the soldier were plentiful and cheap. Week-end leave was granted to a third of the men at a time, and the railway officers provided transport to Dunkirk and, for bathing parties, to Proven. The discipline was excellent, and there were no complaints whatever from the military authorities as to the behaviour of the men while on leave. Matron O'Gorman and the nurses on a Red Cross barge that was ice-bound in the Canal outside Bergues are gratefully remembered by our men for their kindness in giving several concerts for their entertainment. The only unusual occurrence was the arrest of a bogus interpreter who claimed to represent the French Mission. It was reported that he proved to be a spy, and that he was summarily dealt with accordingly.

The party set off by motor lorries on March 8th on their return to Brigade, the mutual expressions of regret at departure serving to indicate how deeply friendships had been established. A note of appreciation from the Vth Corps Commander was published in Divisional Orders.

PART 2.—THE CORDONNERIE SECTOR.

Into the line—Trench mortars and patrols—Command—Enemy raid—Relief by the 170th Brigade, 57th Division—General: arctic conditions; enemy activity; the veteran Sergeant-Major departs.

The Brigade remained in Divisional reserve from the 8th to the 24th of January, 1917. It was now the depth of the severest winter known in this region for thirty years. Snowstorms were frequent and the cold intense. The most popular pastime was skating, a novel form of amusement for the majority of our men, many of whom had never before seen ponds and ditches covered with ice of such thickness as to make skating possible. Life during this period, however, was not all fun. The 2nd, 3rd and 4th Battalions, notwithstanding the distance of their quarters from the trenches, had to supply large parties daily for wiring the subsidiary line in the old sector. The 1st Battalion was more fortunate. Estaires was so far from the line that the march to and from the site where the entanglements were being erected would in itself have constituted a day's work. This unit was therefore left in peace; and the opportunity was taken to carry out general training, which all ranks appreciated to the full. The ceremonial guard-mounting, performed daily with full band accompaniment, was a spectacle that excited a vast amount of interest in the good people of the town.

On January 24th we relieved the 2nd Brigade in the line in the Cordonnerie Sector, east of Laventie, all being reported complete by 2.30 p.m. The 1st and 2nd Battalions went into the front line, the 3rd being in support at Rouge de Bout, and the 4th in reserve at Bac St. Maur.

Units in the line immediately commenced a vigorous bombardment of the enemy's trenches with light and medium trench mortars, destroying and rendering untenable long stretches of his front line. The results of this work were investigated by patrols. Five of these entered the German lines at different points on January 25th, and again on the 26th and 28th, without in any case encountering the enemy. On the 30th one enemy post was located, and this was "scuppered" on the following night by a patrol of fifteen other ranks from the 2nd Battalion, under Lance-Corporal S. F. Hanson, two prisoners being taken and ten Germans killed. Patrols entering at other points on the same night met with no opposition.

The casualties in the Brigade during the month of January were:—

	Killed.	Wounded.
Officers	—	2
Other ranks	5	26

On February 1st, the 3rd and 4th Battalions relieved the 1st and 2nd in the front line, and the trench-mortar and patrolling activities were continued with unabated vigour. It soon became evident that, for a time at least, the enemy had practically abandoned his forward trench opposite our sector, and was holding his old support trench as his main line of resistance. Notwithstanding the fact that the usual illumination displays continued with a fair degree of regularity, our patrols exploring the enemy's front line and the saps in rear of it seldom caught sight of any Germans, and the common belief was that the garrison was represented by a solitary individual, popularly dubbed "the flare-boy" or "the caretaker," who wandered about from point to point discharging his flare-pistol with the idea of deceiving us regarding the enemy's strength. A patrol from the 3rd Battalion, however, discovered to their cost that this was not so. Some three hours before dawn on February 2nd this little party of a corporal and five men had penetrated some seventy yards within the enemy's territory, and, in scattered formation, were making a second entry into his line at another point, when they fell into an ambush. Challenged indistinctly, they paused to ascertain whether they had met friend or foe, when the enemy, either a strong patrol or the garrison of a post, opened fire at fifteen yards' range and wounded two of their number. One of these, who could not be found, was, it was afterwards ascertained, taken prisoner. Probably the least perturbed member of the patrol was Rifleman W. B. Thomson. Finding himself held fast by the leg in the barbed wire, he proceeded calmly to cut away the sandbag which had been doing duty as a combined puttee and sound muffler, picked up the other wounded man, carried him to safety, and then coolly returned to retrieve his rifle, which he secured without further mishap.

General Fulton returned from leave on February 4th and resumed command of the Brigade, Colonel Hart returning to the 1st Wellington Battalion. On the same date a number of officers of the 57th Division, recently arrived from England, were attached to our battalions for instruction in trench duties.

At 9 p.m. on February 8th, under cover of an intense minenwerfer bombardment, a party of the enemy, estimated at about thirty strong, made a fruitless attempt to raid the salient in the sub-sector held by the 4th Battalion. This attack, judging from the amount of wire-cutting by trench-mortar fire that had continued steadily during the two previous days, and by the tornado-like nature of the preliminary bombardment, promised to be an affair well worth while, but it dwindled off to a very insignificant business; for, though one or two of the enemy reached our parapet, where a bag containing bombs and wire-cutters was afterwards found, the raiders hesitated before our rifle fire and then hastily retreated when our artillery fire commenced. As a test of the efficiency of the garrison of the battalion sector it was useful enough. With the utmost precision and smoothness, every detail of the plans laid for the purpose of dealing with such an eventuality was, as it were, automatically followed out, as it had been when a similar attempt was made on the trenches held by the 1st Battalion two months previously. Our only casualties were two men slightly wounded during the bombardment.

The 1st and 2nd Battalions relieved the 3rd and 4th on February 9th, relief being reported complete soon after noon. The ensuing period proved very quiet in all respects.

Two battalions of the 170th Brigade, 57th Division, the 2/5th King's Own Royal Lancaster Regiment and the 2/4th Loyal North Lancashire Regiment, arrived at Sailly and came under the orders of the General Officer Commanding the New Zealand Rifle Brigade on February 13th. On the 15th these battalions commenced relieving our 1st and 2nd, one company in each daily. The relief was completed by 3 p.m. on the 18th, our Brigade then marching to billets at Outtersteene.

The extreme cold had continued throughout the whole of our tour in the Cordonnerie Sector. The frequent snowfalls caused general discomfort, but the most distressing effect was the solidifying of the snow on the duck-boards. This rendered movement exceedingly difficult and dangerous, and our men were forced to bind sand-bags upon their boots in order to get about with due speed and safety. Patrolling under these arctic conditions was unusually risky. White patrol-suits were made use of as far as possible, but there was no means of avoiding the noise of crashing ice as the men stumbled upon concealed shell-holes in No Man's Land.

Special instructions were issued regarding regular observation and treatment of the rubber valve of the box-respirator. Through this the breath was exhaled, and unless it was carefully attended to it was liable to become frozen and so render the apparatus useless in a sudden emergency. Out of the line, the bandsmen, who, while in Egypt, had been frequently inconvenienced by wind-blown sand which stopped the action of the valves, now had to come on parade with their instruments wrapped in blankets or articles of clothing to prevent a similar stoppage by freezing.

On February 17th the order "Impose thaw restrictions" was received by telephone. This was the prearranged signal for putting into operation the most elaborate restrictions on the movement of transport along the roads everywhere, regulations designed to prevent undue damage to the ice-bound highways that would ensue if, immediately after a thaw, traffic were permitted to go on at the normal rate.

In this sector the support company of one of the frontline battalions was accommodated in a deep dug-out with branching tunnels in which tiers of bunks were placed. The arrangement was not at all favoured by the commanding officer, for though the men were comfortable enough and practically safe from shelling, these advantages could not compensate for the unsatisfactory features. Water oozed into the exit-shafts and froze as it dripped upon the steps of the narrow winding stairs, and even ordinary movement thereon was dangerous as well as difficult. In any case the dug-out was too near the front line; and though getting the men above ground and at their posts was frequently practised, there was an ever-present uneasiness lest during a determined enemy attack it should prove to be a veritable death-trap.

The enemy's activity was confined mainly to minenwerfer fire, which in response to our trench-mortar bombardments, at times became intense. Most of his artillery shooting appeared to be the work of what we called his "travelling circus," an organization of special batteries that visited various parts of the front for the purpose of conveying the impression that he was strong in this arm.

In several of these spasmodic bombardments the enemy mixed gas-shells with the ordinary projectiles, and, as this was a new experience for us, the softer explosions of the former were not distinguished in the general din. A second shelling in one night caught the 4th Battalion unawares, and 31 men were gassed owing to their respirator valves having become frozen after use in the previous bombardment. The ammonia solution carried by every man as a precautionary measure gave partial relief in many cases, but in others the frightful agony ended only in death. This unfortunate occurrence led to immediate investigations by the gas-experts with the object of devising some simple means of preventing the freezing of the rubber valve, and within a few days an Army Order was issued directing the frequent application of glycerine, a treatment which was found to be entirely efficacious.

While we were in this sector there passed from the Brigade a very notable figure, in the person of Regimental Sergeant-Major Charles Livesey, D.C.M., of the 1st Battalion, who, on account of ill-health, but much against his own wish, was detached for depot duty in England early in February.

Born in 1853, he enlisted in the Scots Guards at the age of twenty, and up to the time of his departure from France had fought in no fewer than eight campaigns. His first active service was in the Egyptian campaign of 1882, and he was with his regiment in the famous battle of Tel-el-Kebir. In the Soudan campaign, three years later, he fought at Suakin and again at Hasheen, in the latter battle gaining the Distinguished Conduct Medal. He had the honour of being invested with this decoration by Queen Victoria in 1886, and the same year saw his promotion to Warrant Officer, 1st Class. He completed his service in the Regulars in the year 1893, and, joining the British South African Police, he was again on active service through the Matabele War of 1896, and the Mashona Rebellion operations of the following year. In the same force he fought through the whole of the Boer War of 1899-1902; and four years later, while serving in Royston's Horse, he took part in the operations that resulted in the quelling of the Zulu Rebellion.

At the outbreak of the Great War he was in New Zealand. He offered his services, was accepted, and left with the Main Body as a member of the 1st Otago Battalion. Returning to this country on troopship duty, he obtained a transfer to the New Zealand Rifle Brigade, which was just about to leave on active service. Here he received the appointment of Regimental Sergeant-Major of the 1st Battalion in the place of R.S.M. W. Catto, who had been attached to us hitherto, but was now required for further instructional duty in the training-camps.

Because of his knowledge of interior economy, drill, and active service conditions, derived from long years of experience, R.S.M. Livesey proved to be an acquisition of great value to the 1st Battalion. He was a strict disciplinarian, but by no means a martinet, and the influence of his example was felt throughout the whole of the unit. Notwithstanding his comparatively advanced age, for he was sixty-two when he joined the battalion, he "footed it" and carried his pack with the best of us; and at the close of each of the long treks over the desert at Mersa Matruh and the wearying marches on the pavé roads of France and Belgium, one knew that he would never fail to accomplish the performance of the many duties that fell to the lot of the sergeant-major long after most of the personnel were at rest. Though the unusual severity of the worst part of the winter of 1916-17 had left its mark, he still considered that he could weather the remainder of the season, but he was not permitted to continue to face the ordeal. After a brief stay in England, he was invalided to New Zealand on April 6, 1917.

At the close of the war Sergeant-Major Livesey was entitled to wear the following decorations and medals: The Distinguished Conduct Medal; the Egyptian Medal and Khedive's Star; the Soudan Bar on the Egyptian ribbon; the Matabele-Mashonaland Medal; the Queen's and the King's South African Medals; the Zulu Rebellion Medal; the 1914-15 Star, the General Service Medal, and the Victory Medal.

PART 3.—THE PLOEGSTEERT SECTOR.

Into the line—Enemy raids—Side-step towards Hill 63—Enemy raid—Out for special training—General: the trenches; Ploegsteert Wood; general activities; cable-burying for the Messines Battle.

From Outtersteene the Brigade marched to a new area on February 20th, the 1st and 3rd Battalions going to billets in Nieppe, the 2nd to quarters at De Seul Camp, Steenwerck, and the 4th to le Romarin Camp. The 3rd and 4th Battalions were temporarily under the command of Majors P. H. Bell and J. Pow, respectively.

On February 22nd the Brigade relieved the 7th (British) Brigade in the Ploegsteert Sector in Belgium, about four miles north of Armentieres. The 3rd and 4th Battalions went into the front line from the Warnave River to St. Yves, taking over from the 8th Loyal North Lancashires and the 3rd Worcesters, respectively; the 2nd Battalion relieved the 1st Wiltshires in the "Fort" Line in support; while the 1st Battalion, in reserve, took over the Regina Camp quarters from the 10th Cheshires. Brigade Headquarters were located at Rue de Sac.

The relief was completed by 11 p.m., but during its progress the enemy opened fire with minenwerfer on part of the trenches being taken over by the 4th Battalion. This continued intermittently on the same point throughout the night, and at 5.45 on the morning of the 23rd developed into an intense artillery and trench-mortar bombardment. At 6.10 a.m. the fire lifted and formed a "box-barrage," and at the same moment the enemy in strong force effected an entry into our line at the part where it had been blown in on the previous evening, and worked southward along the trench. As far as could be judged the raiders numbered 200, and they remained in our lines about five minutes, when they were driven out with rifle-fire and bombs.

Conspicuous amongst those who so promptly ejected the enemy from our line was Sergeant E. J. Hawke. Though three times buried owing to trench-mortar fire, his skill and judgment remained unimpaired, and he led his men with great gallantry and determination.

Our casualties were six men killed, Lieut. R. G. Ridling and twenty other ranks wounded, and three missing. It was afterwards ascertained that these three were taken prisoner. Two of them were stretcher-bearers attending to the wounds of the third, Rifleman J. W. B. Watson, who later succumbed to his injuries while in captivity. A fourth man, Rifleman J. Emerson, was wounded and taken prisoner. He succeeded in escaping, but was recaptured and forced to accompany a returning party of raiders estimated by him to have been eighty strong. When nearing the enemy's wire he seized a favourable opportunity and once again wrenched himself free and made off toward his own lines. Though his boots had been removed, he succeeded in eluding his captors, who, however, fired upon him, and he returned to his company suffering from two fresh wounds, and fainting from pain and exhaustion. At the time of the raid the country was enveloped in dense fog, and little could be seen of the enemy's movements. Moreover, the poor visibility prevented the artillery from picking up our "S.O.S." rocket signal, and all telephone wires from the front line to battalion headquarters had been cut during the final stages of the bombardment.

The casualties throughout the Brigade during the month of February were:—

	Killed.	Wounded.	Missing.
Officers	—	3	—
Other ranks	11	52	3

A daylight relief was effected on March 2nd, the 1st and 2nd Battalions taking over the position in the front line from the 3rd and 4th.

At 11 p.m. on March 9th the enemy made an abortive attempt to raid the part of the line held by the 2nd Battalion, the Germans being dispersed by rifle, machine-gun and artillery fire they could reach our trenches.

On March 10th the 2nd Battalion was relieved in the front line by the 4th Battalion, and two days later a readjustment of the sector was commenced. The 3rd Battalion, from support, took over the Douve sub-sector on the left from the 8th R.I.R., 107th Brigade, with headquarters at Limavady Lodge on the southern slopes of Hill 63; and the 44th Australian Battalion took over the right sub-sector from the 1st Battalion. The adjustment was completed on the 14th, when the 2nd Battalion, as battalion in reserve, moved north from Regina Camp to the Catacombs, a large tunnelled dug-out recently excavated in the side of Hill 63, above Hyde Park Corner. This side-step to the north gave the Brigade a position immediately facing Messines from the south-west, with its left opposite the German salient round La Petite Douve Farm. Brigade Headquarters moved to English Farm.

On March 18th the 2nd Battalion relieved the 4th in the front line, the latter going into support with its headquarters at Creslow Farm. A further relief followed on the 20th, when the 1st Battalion, which had replaced the 2nd in the Catacombs, relieved the 3rd in the line on the left.

Early in the morning of March 23rd the enemy attempted a raid which, by a sort of poetic justice, was directed upon the trenches of the 2nd Battalion, for the Germans had probably received more attentions of this kind from the 2nd than from any other unit in the Brigade. Just before 4 a.m. heavy and medium trench-mortar bombs began to land in regular flights of ten in quick succession upon the support line behind the broad salient north-east of St. Yves, and at the same time shrapnel and "pineapple" bombs were burst freely along the front line. The minenwerfer fire was maintained for more than half an hour, but the bombardment on the front line lifted after some ten minutes, and formed a box barrage so well defined that its outline showed up clearly in the snow. At this moment three parties of Germans came into view, one at the point where a communication-trench joined the front line, a second outside the wire at a small salient 300 yards to the right, and a third further out in No Man's Land 100 yards to the left. Beyond doubt the enemy's plans had been well laid. Evidently his main point of attack was the sap-head; two roads gave good direction for his two flank parties, while the ruins of Broken Tree House at the cross-roads gave sufficient cover for a forming-up position.

His plans miscarried, however. The avenue which formed the enemy's main objective, and upon which he had expended a vast amount of ammunition, had long been disused, and its head was counted of so little importance that not even a sentry-post had been placed there. This point was reached by some twenty Germans, but as their leading men commenced to enter they were noticed by Sergeant W. J. Murray, who was in charge of a working-party near by. He and another man at once opened fire on the raiders and checked their advance. Bombs were thrown at the sergeant and his comrade, but without effect, and presently the Germans withdrew. The two flanking parties had been dispersed by Lewis gun fire and bombs as soon as they were discovered. It is considered that many casualties had been inflicted on the enemy party as they assembled in the vicinity of Broken Tree House, a locality that was heavily bombarded by a section of the 3rd Light Trench Mortar Battery under Corporal J. McQuillan, one of the original 2nd Battalion men. The section itself suffered casualties during the enemy bombardment, but the corporal kept the gun working until the situation quietened, firing altogether a hundred rounds in forty-five minutes.

The 4th Battalion relieved the 2nd in the front line on March 26th, the 1st was relieved by the 3rd two days later, and at the end of the month the Brigade was withdrawn from the line for special training, the 1st Brigade taking over the sector from us.

During March we had 21 men killed, and 5 officers and 64 men wounded.

Major W. H. Hastings, D.S.O., Brigade Major, was recalled on March 16th to rejoin his unit, the 92nd Punjabis, in India, and Major N. W. Thoms, N.Z.S.C., was appointed in his stead on the 29th. Lieut.-Col. Austin was evacuated wounded on the 21st, the command of the 1st Battalion devolving upon Major J. G. Roache. On the 27th General Fulton left for the Officers' Rest House, and Lieut.-Col. A. E. Stewart assumed command of the Brigade in his absence.

When we first came into the Ploegsteert Sector we found the trenches in very bad condition, the breastworks in the forward lines being extremely dilapidated and the drainage entirely out of order. A vast amount of work had to be done to render the conditions at all bearable, and this was the more difficult of accomplishment owing to the intensity of the enemy's artillery and minenwerfer fire, especially on the left about St. Yves. Parts of the trenches, which in the main lay along the forward edge of Ploegsteert Wood, were curious in outline. At about our centre the front line formed a rectangular re-entrant, into which projected a similar-shaped enemy salient known as "Umbo Nose" or the "Birdcage." The "Birdcage" appeared to be tremendously strong, but when this apparently formidable place subsequently fell into our hands, it was seen to be strong only in the quantity of wire it contained. South of the salient our line ran out to a blind end, this portion, known as the "Hampshire T.," having No Man's Land on both sides of it. North of the salient the line lay very near the angle in the enemy's trench; between the two were mine-craters practically lip to lip, a double one held by us and a single one by the enemy. A little to the north of St. Yves, near Anton's Farm, was the bit of No Man's Land where, as told by Captain Bairnsfather, the British and Germans fraternized on a certain Christmas Day, exchanging mutual services in the matter of haircutting and photography.

A curious observation-post stood just behind the front line. This took the form of a standing tree from which the branches had been shot away. It was constructed of steel, carefully modelled and painted to represent the real tree whose place it took one dark night, and up the steps in its hollow interior the observer climbed to his peep-hole near the top.

At the time of our occupation of the sector, Ploegsteert Wood itself was a very pleasant area. It was fairly extensive, and, though subjected to frequent bursts of shelling, was, like the plantations on the rear slopes of Hill 63, strangely lacking in that blasted appearance one expected to find in such a locality so near the front line. About the feet of the elms and beeches, at first bare, but presently signalizing the onward march of spring by the swelling and bursting of their buds, snowdrops bloomed luxuriantly. The rear trenches and living-quarters in the Wood were well-constructed and comparatively comfortable. A log hut which served as a company headquarters, and which was dignified by the appellation of "Plugstreet Hall," was remarkable for the number of regimental crests and badges carved or painted by previous occupants on the ends of the timbers of which it was constructed. Doubtless the "Hall" went the way of many other good things in the course of the enemy operations of the following year. It would have made a fine "souvenir" if only we could have brought it away. The numerous duck-board tracks, named after well-known London streets, were for the most part open, the density of the forest growth ensuring freedom from observation; but as they approached the forward saps they assumed the nature of the communication-trenches with which in other sectors we had become so familiar, having revetted protective embankments on either side.

Towards the end of our tour of duty here the Brigade erected several miles of very strong wire in belts across the Wood, and within and beyond its perimeter. This supplementary work, we considered, should have gone far towards making the Wood impregnable, but it seems that the enemy, in his advance in 1918, passed round it and took the position by envelopment.

Throughout the whole of the period there had been intense activity of every sort on both sides. The enemy made increasing use of gas-shells on the Wood and of heavy trench mortars on our trenches and saps, and his airmen were very enterprising. For our part we cleared No Man's Land of enemy patrols, and by a combination of bold scouting and prompt

Lewis gun and artillery fire put an end to the enemy's endeavours to improve his wire. German snipers, at first troublesome, were quietened by the vigorous use of light trench mortars and rifle grenades. The Machine Gun Company attached to us continued the policy, found so valuable in former sectors, of subjecting back areas to fire at night, and, in concert with the artillery, kept the enemy in a constant state of tension by means of frequent "practice" barrages.

On the 12th of March a Working Battalion was formed of details from the three Brigades of the Division, each of which supplied some 300 officers and men for the purpose. Major J. Pow, of our 4th Battalion, was detached to command this temporary formation, which was organized into three companies, each representing the Brigade from which it had been drawn.

When it was observed that the Working Battalion was engaged in laying cable for a forward telephone system on an extensive scale, the old soldiers and other wiseacres predicted a big offensive at an early date. To those not in the secret—and, judging by the curiosity displayed by the enemy's airmen, and the attentions received at the hands of his artillerymen, the Germans may probably be included in that category—the activities of the new unit were indeed the first indication of the forthcoming battle of Messines.

The work was carried out under the supervision of the Director of Signals, IInd Anzac Corps, who issued general instructions and wisely left the details to the commander of the battalion. Major Pow was his own engineer, and personally selected and laid out the lines radiating from the main cablehead at Red Lodge, behind Hill 63, to the many future advanced battalion headquarters close up to the front trench. The whole scheme was carefully worked out in detail, and plans and instructions prepared, so that, in case a relief were ordered, the incoming unit could proceed with the work without interruption to its smooth progress.

Companies were told off to different lines, and at the outset company commanders employed all their men at the same time; but it was at once found that the digging progressed faster than the cable-laying could be done, and in addition to the disadvantage of having long stretches of open trench exposed to view there was the exasperation caused by the necessity of re-digging where, in the shell-shocked ground, the sides collapsed soon after the trench was dug. Better success followed the adoption of the method now devised. Only one platoon of each company was put on the job at one time, and as this finished its task it was succeeded by the next, so that three or four "shifts" were worked in one day. On the whole, the day's work for each man was comparatively easy. The trench was dug six feet deep and four feet wide at the top; and as a length of one yard and a half constituted a day's task for a man in an English labour unit, two yards was thought a fair quantity for each of our own men.. Casualties, of course, were inevitable, but most of these were suffered during the night-digging down the forward slopes of Hill 63.

Here and there, as, for instance, in the low-lying section in the vicinity of the trench known as Mud Lane, the ground was swampy, and the full depth of six feet could not be secured. To compensate for this, extra earth was piled on top when the cable had been buried, and over all a quantity of bricks or stone blocks to serve as "bursters" to minimize the danger of damage to the cable under shell-fire. The bursters were obtained from the ruins of the chateau on the hill. This, by the way, was reported to have been the property of Hennessy, the well-known distiller of brandy. At any rate, our men engaged at the work of carrying down the material had a merry time, but only by way of dodging the enemy shelling, for they were in full view and formed excellent targets for the German field-gun "snipers."

How thoroughly the whole task set the Working Battalion was performed may be judged from the fact that throughout the battle of Messines only one break occurred in the entire network, this solitary instance having been caused by a 5.9 shell striking the bury in soft ground. The importance of the work will, of course, be readily understood. Twice during its progress it was inspected by the Corps Commander, who on each occasion expressed his entire satisfaction with the manner in which it was being executed and with the expedition with which it was being pushed ahead. His appreciation was emphasized in the following communication to the New Zealand Division at the end of March:—

"The Corps Commander desires me to say he is pleased to have received from A.D.A.S., IInd Anzac, a very favourable report on the work done by the New Zealand Working Battalion engaged in burying telephone cable. 9,000 yards of line have been buried since the 15th instant, in spite of unfavourable conditions.

"He hopes you will convey to the battalion his appreciation of the manner in which they are carrying out a very important piece of work.

"(Signed) C. W. GWYNN,
"Brig.-General, G.S., IInd Anzac Corps."

Soon after the middle of April the Working Battalion was reinforced by the Cyclist Battalion, its commander, Lieut.-Col. C. H. Evans, taking over the command of the combined units; and, as the preparations for the "Magnum Opus" neared completion, parties of the infantry were from time to time released from this work and returned to their original units, the execution of the final stages of the cable-burying being left to the Cyclists alone.

Amongst the officers who did exceptionally good work with the Working Battalion were Capt. E. C. Parry and Lieuts. J. N. Rauch, H. E. McGowan, T. M. Sim, W. E. Anderson, T. Collins, R. J. Grant, and J. G. Greenwood.

While the men of the battalion were engaged in this special duty they were quartered in Regina Camp, near Romarin. Orders for the formation of the unit must have been sudden and unexpected, for it was found that little preparation had been made for the provision of transport and camp equipment. As an example, it may be mentioned that the first supply of fresh meat was cut up for issue by the commanding officer and his adjutant-quartermaster, Lieut. J. D. Swan, the only implements available being pocket-knives. Just why it was found necessary for Major Pow to carry out this operation personally is not known, unless it be that it was merely another manifestation of that extreme solicitude for the comfort of his men for which he had been noted throughout the Brigade from its earliest days.

It was not long, however, before Regina Camp, through the strenuous efforts of the commanding officer, became one of the best-run camps in France. The battalion secured a special transport of its own, consisting of two motor-lorries; a set of hot-water tanks for the men's bathing and washing; and a well-equipped drying-room. Even a battalion estaminet, or "wet" canteen, was established in the camp. This last innovation was the result of a desire to reduce the number of orderly-room cases arising from the men's visits to the open estaminets in Romarin during the evenings, and that laudable object was instantly and fully attained.

In connection with the Working Battalion's stay at Regina Camp, an amusing instance of attempted extortion by a downtrodden native of the country is recalled. When the Brigade first moved up to this area the 1st Battalion occupied Regina Camp, and on going into the line for its tour of duty it was at the last moment presented by the owner of the farm on which the camp stood with a bill for the value of a tree alleged to have been cut down by some of the men. The account was paid. The 4th Battalion, of which Major Pow was second-in-command, had a similar experience over the same tree a few days later. Now the enterprising landowner presents a claim to the Working Battalion, the well-known tree once more figuring in the bill. The dénouement may easily be imagined.

CHAPTER VIII.

THE BATTLE OF MESSINES.

PART 1.—BEFORE THE BATTLE.

To the Tilques Training Area—Return march—Into the Douve Sector—Staff—Aerial and artillery activity—Enemy raid—Assembly trenches—2nd Battalion raids on La Petite Douve Farm—Out to reserve.

On being relieved in the Ploegsteert sector by units of the 1st Brigade at the end of March, our four battalions went respectively to Aldershot, Romarin, De Seule and Bulford Camps.

The Brigade rested here till April 3rd, on which date the troops started on their three-days' march to the Tilques Training Area, some forty miles distant. Battalions moved by different routes for convenience in billeting at the end of each day's stage. The march commenced in wretched weather, a strong wind blowing, with sleet and snow at intervals. It was nevertheless capitally executed, the men, though just out of the trenches, standing the test well and arriving in the training area in fine spirits. The battalions went into billets in a number of scattered villages round about Wisques, some distance west of St. Omer.

The greater part of the Brigade rested on April 6th. One company from the 1st Battalion marched to the Second Army School at Wisques for the purpose of practising the latest attack formation, the majority of the officers of the Brigade being present to witness this introductory demonstration.

General Fulton now returned from the Rest House and resumed command.

The ensuing period of ten days was devoted almost entirely to strenuous training in the trench-to-trench attack and in open warfare fighting. The configuration of the country in the training area closely resembled that over which the projected advance at Messines was to be conducted, and as the outlines of the enemy defences were accurately reproduced here, the details of the various stages of the forthcoming action could be worked out with much precision and thoroughness. The more important rehearsals were witnessed by the General Officers commanding the Army, the Corps, and the Division.

The return march commenced on April 18th, in heavy rain, but notwithstanding the adverse conditions it was exceedingly well done. The Divisional Commander inspected each unit en route. On the 20th we were back in the vicinity of Messines, the 1st Battalion at Neuve Eglise, the 2nd at Kortepyp, the 3rd at De Seule, the 4th at Romarin, and Brigade Headquarters at Rue de Sac.

During the next six days the Brigade supplied working-parties of an average strength of 2,600 for cable-burying, road-making, and the construction of trenches and gun-pits.

On April 27th we relieved the 1st Brigade in the Douve Sector, the 1st and 2nd Battalions going into the front line, the 3rd to support at Stafford House, and the 4th to reserve at Red Lodge, the quarters of the last being hehind the shoulder of Hill 63. Brigade Headquarters were opened at English Farm. The 3rd Australian Division was on our right, and the 74th Brigade on our left, but the latter was relieved by the 1st N.Z. Brigade on April 30th.

Capt. R. G. Purdy, N.Z.S.C., was appointed Brigade Major on April 10th, vice Major Thoms, N.Z.S.C., recalled to Divisional Headquarters. On the same date Capt. G. C. Dailey was appointed Staff Captain in the place of Capt. Purdy.

During the month of April we had two men killed and eighteen wounded.

The period from April 27th to May 5th was characterized by great aerial and artillery activity. There were very many fights in the air, and it was noted with considerable satisfaction that in the majority of contests our airmen got the better of their opponents. The shelling of forward and back areas, camps, headquarters and transport lines was frequent and intense. On May 5th the quarters of the 1st Battalion Band were struck by a shell, four of the oldest players being killed and practically the whole of the instruments destroyed.

The heaviest shelling of back areas known since the fall of 1915 occurred during the afternoon of the 6th, Brigade

Headquarters coming in for an unusual share of the bombardment. This was repeated on the 7th. By way of retaliation, every heavy gun on our Army front opened up for five minutes twice during the evening of the 7th, thus effecting considerable amelioration of our discomfort.

On the night of 4th/5th May the 1st and 2nd Battalions were relieved by the 3rd and 4th. This interchange was completed by 1 a.m., and two hours later the enemy attempted a raid on the 4th Battalion front. Little damage was done, and the solitary German who succeeded in entering the trench was promptly captured.

The 2nd Battalion came up from reserve on the night of 11th/12th, and dug a new assembly-trench from 70 to 100 yards behind the front line. This well-constructed piece of work was provided throughout with a travel-trench and was over 700 yards in length, extending across the whole Brigade frontage. No casualties were sustained during the digging, but while inspecting the trench Lieut.-Col. Stewart met with a severe accident which prevented his taking any part in the subsequent battle beyond acting as the Division's liaison officer with the 3rd Australians. Two nights later 1st Otago dug a similar trench across the left Brigade's frontage, but on the far side of the Steenebeek well out in No Man's Land, a very notable feat.

In the ordinary front line and in these new trenches, the latter of course for the time being remaining unoccupied, the assaulting troops could be assembled in the order of their advance, and it was hoped that from them they would be able to move forward with such speed as to escape the enemy's S.O.S. barrage. The Otago trench provided for the leading troops of the left Brigade a good jumping-off line approximately at right angles to the direction of advance, and, in addition, the special advantage of position on the enemy's side of the bogs of the Steenebeek, which here were both wide and deep. Strangely enough, the construction of this trench was completed without serious interference, though the enemy later attempted to investigate it by means of fighting-patrols.

The battalions changed over again during the night of 13th/14th May. With curious perversity, one of our forward batteries, coming into the line on the same evening, established a gun-position immediately above the dug-out which was occupied by the headquarters of the 1st Battalion. Discretion being the better part of valour, and artillery the superior arm, battalion headquarters promptly found another home.

Opposite the sector held by the 2nd Battalion, the German line formed a very pronounced salient passing round the ruins of La Petite Douve Farm.* This, like the "Birdcage" in the Ploegsteert Sector farther south, had the general appearance of being a formidable strong-point, and in the plans for the battle of Messines the importance of the locality was stressed. The patrols of the 2nd Battalion therefore gave it special attention, but as they found no direct evidence of anything abnormal it was decided to prosecute a closer investigation. For this purpose a fighting-patrol of fifteen men under 2nd Lieut. R. P. Vaughan went out on the night of 18th/19th May. The officer, with two scouts, led the way, the remainder keeping some twelve yards in rear, and creeping cautiously forward, the head of the patrol finally reached a shell-hole just outside the enemy's trench. Here they found themselves close to a concrete dug-out with two loop-holes. They were not unobserved, however, for almost immediately a bomb was dropped from one of the openings, and this, landing in the shell-hole, wounded one of the scouts. Far from being a deterrent, this mishap served but as a spur to action, and Vaughan at once brought his main party forward and rushed the position. Two men moved along the trench to the right to form a block, while others dealt with the Germans about the dug-out. The latter retreated smartly underground, but were followed up closely. Lance-Corporal E. E. Islip, a scout of outstanding ability, was in the lead and called to the Germans inside the dug-out to surrender; but as there was no reply, another of the party threw in a bomb. This was followed by a second, which apparently was picked up by a wounded German, who staggered out of the doorway with it. Here he fell at the feet of our men, and the bomb exploding

---

*The Farm position was the objective of the first organized trench-raid launched by British troops. The methods adopted by the Canadians, who carried out that enterprise on 18th November, 1915, formed the basis upon which plans for subsequent attacks of this nature were laid. (See page 86.)

killed the German and Lance-Corporal Islip, and wounded 2nd Lieut. Vaughan and three of his men. The difficult task of bringing back the wounded from the enemy's trench now claimed attention, but this was accomplished with admirable skill, the Germans being held up until the injured men were well on their way across No Man's Land. As the little rearguard retired, however, fire was opened on them, and a sixth man was wounded.

Three nights later another investigation was made by a patrol working under cover of artillery support. Except half a dozen men hurriedly making off to the rear and two or three groups working their machine-guns in the support line, no Germans were seen, and a close inspection was made of the locality without direct molestation. The dug-out found by the previous patrol was seen to have been damaged by our trench-mortar fire, and the trenches in the vicinity were in ruins.

The results of these activities pointed to the fact that too much importance had been attached to the Farm as an enemy stronghold, and to verify these conclusions a daylight raid was carried out by a party from the 2nd Battalion at 3 p.m. on June 5th, two days before the Battle of Messines. The attack was led by Lieut. L. I. Manning and 2nd Lieut. H. B. Pattrick, and was carried out under an Army practice barrage. It was entirely successful, and the information gained proved that no greater resistance might be expected at this point than at any ordinary portion of the German line. Our artillery and trench-mortar fire had obliterated the trenches, and the sappers attached to Manning's party practically completed the work of destruction by demolishing with charges of ammonal two of the three remaining concrete pill-boxes. Upon withdrawal it was found that three men had not returned. Lieut. Manning thereupon doubled over to the Farm and sent these men across to our line. He himself, being out of breath from the exertion of his double journey, dropped into a shell-hole for a momentary rest on his way back. Capt. S. A. Atkinson, commanding the company that had supplied the raiding-party, thought that Lieut. Manning must have been wounded, and he immediately rushed out to his assistance; but before reaching his officer, Capt. Atkinson was killed by an enemy sniper. Our only other casualties were 2nd Lieut. Pattrick and two men wounded.

Amidst all the preparatory work for the Messines offensive, time was found for the holding of a very successful Divisional Horse Show in the rear area on May 13th.

The Corps Commander inspected the Brigade Demonstration Platoon on the 20th. This had been formed at the beginning of May, Lieut. D. C. Bowler being platoon commander, and Major J. R. Cowles, M.C., in charge of the training. The idea was to train one platoon to a state of perfection, and to have twelve subalterns attending for a ten days' course with it. By this means very good results were obtained, the general effect on the efficiency of the Brigade being most marked. At this time, to facilitate the passage of troops along the narrow and congested roads, marching in "threes" was introduced, but no instructions as to a uniform method of procedure in forming "threes" from "two-deep" were issued. Apparently each Brigade adopted its own system, ours being based on that devised at the platoon-school.

On May 22nd the Brigade was relieved in the line by the 2nd Brigade, the battalions going back to De Seule, Romarin, Canteen Corner and Kortepyp Camps, with Brigade Headquarters at Rue de Sac. From this date till the 31st strong parties were supplied daily for preparing the Divisional front for the approaching battle, a work that was greatly hampered by enemy shelling.

A Divisional Conference, at which the Commander-in-Chief was present, was held on the 24th, and on the 29th General Birdwood visited the Brigade.

On May 31st the Brigade moved to De Seule Concentration Area, where units remained resting until the eve of the Battle of Messines.

Our casualties for May were:—

	Killed.	Wounded.
Officers	1	4
Other ranks	18	120

PART 2.—THE PLACE OF THE BATTLE OF MESSINES IN THE GENERAL SCHEME OF OPERATIONS.

Situation after the Somme Battle—General plan of action for 1917—Modifications—Vimy Ridge and the Hindenburg Line—Ypres Salient—Messines-Wytschaete Ridge to be captured as a preliminary operation to the commencement of the summer offensive in Flanders—Second Army detailed for the task.

In our brief general account of the Battle of the Somme we saw that the operations, extending from July 1st, 1916, to about the middle of November, resulted in the capture of the dominating ridge extending from Peronne to the Ancre. In the enemy's line there now existed a sharp salient from the Ancre to the Scarpe in the neighbourhood of Arras.

Immediately following the close of the battle in November, a conference of representatives of all the Allied Powers was held at the French General Headquarters, at which the plan of campaign to be pursued by the Allied Armies during the following year was unanimously agreed upon. This provided for a series of offensives on all fronts, and so arranged as to secure the pinning down of the enemy's reserves evenly along his whole line.

Sir Douglas Haig's plan of action in connection with this scheme was to attack simultaneously both sides of the Ancre-Scarpe salient, with the Fifth Army operating on the Ancre front, and the Third attacking from Arras. To secure the left flank in these operations it was decided that the First Army should co-operate by taking the Vimy Ridge running north from Arras towards Lens. Possession of this high ground would give observation over the plains extending eastward from the foot of the ridge to Douai and beyond, and the fight for it was expected to result in a severe blow for the enemy, compelling him to use up his reserves.

Following these operations, which were to be carried out in the spring, a second blow was to be delivered, this time in Flanders, where, owing to the great proportion of low-lying country, the drier weather of summer was necessary to ensure the maximum degree of success.

In the early weeks of 1917 certain modifications were made in the original scheme. The new plans provided that the operations of the British Armies were to be more or less subsidiary to those of the French, but the alteration made little difference to us, except that the greater importance now attributed to the advance of the British right restricted the amount of attention to be given to preparations needed for the Flanders attack.

Later it was found that Italy could not be ready to co-operate in the general offensive by the time fixed in the modified plans, and on March 12th the revolution in Russia began. The latter event not only removed all hopes of support by action on the Eastern front, but enabled the enemy to transfer to the west as many as forty new Divisions.

Notwithstanding these drawbacks it was decided to proceed with the spring offensive. The enemy, by his voluntary retirement on the Arras–Soissons front to the Hindenburg Line, had removed the salient that was to be the first objective of our Fifth Army, the role of which now was to follow him up and hold his reserves to his new positions.

On the morning of April 9th the First and Third Armies attacked on a front of nearly fifteen miles, including Vimy Ridge and some five miles of the Hindenburg Line. The immediate success was followed up, and at the end of six days' fighting the British line had been pushed forward four miles. Ten days after the opening of the battle on April 9th the number of German infantry engaged against the British front had been nearly doubled, a highly important result in view of the approaching French offensive. Operations were continued on 23rd April, and by the middle of May Bullecourt was taken, rendering secure our footing in the Hindenburg Line.

Thus the first half of Sir Douglas Haig's plan had been successfully carried out, and now attention could be devoted to pushing on preparations for the summer campaign in Flanders. In this connection it was first necessary to render the position at Ypres more secure.

The Ypres Salient was very pronounced. It had been greatly reduced in extent in the Second Battle of Ypres of April–May, 1915, when the Germans with the aid of poisonous gas had strained the British line. Near Hollebeke we had been driven from Hill 60; we had had to abandon the woods, so celebrated in battle, on both sides of the Ypres–Menin Road; and had been compelled to evacuate Broodseinde and Zonnebeke. In the First Battle of Ypres the enemy had captured the woods north and west of Wytschaete, and also the end of the range from Wytschaete to Messines.

The Messines-Wytschaete Ridge, a group of hills lying about midway between Armentieres and Ypres, commanded the latter town, the whole of the British positions in the Ypres Salient, the valley of the Lys, and the British lines to the south. The capture of this dominating ground was a necessary preliminary to the projected offensive farther north. The natural advantages of the position were exceptional, and during more than two years of occupation the enemy had devoted the greatest skill and industry to developing them to the utmost. The German front line skirted the western foot of the ridge in a deep curve from the Lys opposite Frelinghien to the Menin Road. The second line system formed an inner curve following the crest of the ridge. Across the salient were two chord lines, one, the Oosttaverne Line, running north and south just east of Oosttaverne, the second, the Warneton Line, roughly parallel to and about a mile to the eastward of the first. The villages of Messines and Wytschaete had been organized as main centres of resistance, and numerous woods, farms and hamlets transformed into strong-points and fortresses.

Operations against the ridge were entrusted to the Second Army, under General Plumer, who for two years had successfully held the Ypres Salient against all enemy attacks. The Second Army, which side-stepped to the south to cover all objectives, consisted of the following Corps in order from the right: the 2nd Australian and New Zealand Corps, the IXth and the Xth. The first of these (the IInd Anzac) under General Godley, comprised the 3rd Australian, the 4th Australian, the New Zealand, and the 25th and 57th Divisions.

IN PLOEGSTEERT WOOD.

ANTI-AIRCRAFT GUNS.

GENERAL FULTON STUDIES MESSINES.

RUINS OF MESSINES.

PART 3.—THE BATTLE.

Local preparations—Plan of attack—Frontage and objectives—Two phases—Troops—Tasks for the New Zealand Division—Tasks of the 2nd Brigade and of the New Zealand Rifle Brigade—Machine-guns, trench mortars, tanks, artillery—Assembly—Attack opens—1st and 3rd Battalions capture the German front and support lines—Lance-Corporal Samuel Frickleton, V.C.—4th Battalion companies capture Messines and the trenches to the east—2nd Battalion in reserve position—Success of 2nd Brigade—1st Brigade troops pass through and capture the Black Line—Australians pass through to the Oosttaverne Line—General consolidation—German estimate of the importance of Messines and the Ridge.

The preparations for the forthcoming attack were unusually thorough. For many months companies of Tunnellers had been constantly at work day and night preparing under the German defence system a score of mines with an aggregate of five miles of galleries, until at last more than a million pounds of explosives were in position and ready for the fateful pressing of the button.* Positions and ammunition dumps had been made ready for the greatest accumulation of guns hitherto known in warfare. The special system of cables, buried to a depth of seven feet and reticulated throughout the area, was most extensive and complete, and no difficulty was anticipated as to effective communication between Divisions, Brigades, battalions and batteries, even though the enemy should rain upon us his fiercest and heaviest storms of shells. The supply of water to the troops who would take and hold

*The mines of the Messines sector have been a popular subject for picture and story. That underground fighting of this kind was no new thing may be seen from the following extract from an account of operations at the siege of Tournai during Marlborough's campaign in Flanders. The extract, quoted by Hon. J. W. Fortescue in his "History of the British Army," is from the newspaper "The Daily Courant" of August 20th, 1709:—

"Now, as to our fighting underground, blowing up like kites in the air, not being sure of a foot of ground we stand on while in the trenches. Our miners and the enemy very often meet each other, when they have sharp combats till one side gives way. We have got into three or four of the enemy's great galleries, which are thirty or forty feet underground and lead to several of their chambers; and in these we fight in armour and lanthorn and candle, they disputing every inch of the gallery with us to hinder our finding out their great mines. Yesternight we found one which was placed just under our bomb batteries, in which were eighteen hundredweight of powder besides many bombs; and if we had not been so lucky as to find it, in a very few hours our batteries and some hundreds of men had taken a flight into the air."

the coveted region was a vital question, but, like all other details great or small, this was amply provided for. As is well known, most of our water was drawn from the canals, and this, after being sterilized by the addition of bleaching-powder, was pumped to elevated tanks, from which it was led by means of pipes to water-points some considerable distance in rear of the front line. From these points the water was transported still farther forward in the water-carts of the various units, and the final stage to the front line was made in petrol-tins carried by hand. In anticipation of the advance, the pipe-lines from the sterilizing barges on the Lys, supplemented by those from the small catchment-reservoirs on Kemmel and other hills in the back area, were pushed so far forward that a week's labour would suffice to extend them right on to Wytschaete and Messines when those villages should at last come into our hands. To bridge the gap between the capture of the new territory and the construction of good roads across it, pack-trains made up of the horses and mules of the transport sections of battalions were organized and were practised in the work of bringing forward supplies of water, food, and ammunition.

For our part, we had been in the Ploegsteert and Messines sectors since the last week of February, with a break of a fortnight spent in intensive training in the Tilques area during the earlier part of April. At Tilques the general plans for the attack had become fairly well known, and the special rehearsals there had been facilitated and rendered all the more intelligible from the knowledge we had already unconsciously gained of the country upon which the real drama was to be staged. Then, on our return, while the normal tours in and out of the line were worked in the usual regular manner, repeated Divisional, Brigade and battalion conferences were held with the object of securing the utmost possible perfection in every detail of the scheme. Constant patrolling beyond our lines gave us complete knowledge of all parts of No Man's Land; whilst information regarding the country and systems of defence well in rear of the forward lines of the enemy, obtained from the close study of maps and aeroplane photographs, and supplemented by the excellent observation from Hill 63 facing Messines from the south-west, was enhanced in value by the frequent inspection of a fine large-scale model of Messines and its surroundings. This model, which, with its approaches, covered about a quarter of an acre of ground, had been constructed by the enterprising Australians near Romarin.

From the middle of April right on to the zero day aerial and artillery activity on both sides was intense. It was evident that an impending attack was suspected by the enemy, and trenches, roads, tracks, concentration areas and transport lines were almost constantly subjected to shell-fire and aeroplane bombing. In addition he made many attempts to raid various points along our whole line for the purpose of obtaining identifications, but these were all without result.

The frontage of the attack by the Second Army was planned to be some nine miles in length, gradually diminishing to six miles as the final objective, the chord of the salient, was approached, and the depth of penetration at the deepest part would be about three miles. To the IInd Anzac Corps, which was on the right, was allotted the three-mile sector from St. Yves to the Wulverghem–Wytschaete Road. The scheme of attack for this Corps was a swinging movement with the right flank as pivot, enveloping in its course the hill and village of Messines. It was arranged to be carried out in two phases, first the attack and capture of the Black Line, secondly the attack and capture of the Green or Oosttaverne Line. The Black Line ran, from the right flank at St. Yves, slightly west of north, but took a more westerly direction as it passed Messines, from which it lay from 600 to 700 yards to the east. Abreast of the village the Black Line was about a mile from our front trenches. The Green Line branched off from the Black Line where the latter crossed the Douve River, north of Grey Farm, swung out north-north-east for a distance of a mile, and then turned nearly due north to the west of Delporte Farm. This bend in the Green Line was about a mile east-north-east of Messines Church. The task thus allotted to the Corps was to be accomplished in one day's operations, and was to include the capture of the enemy's guns to the north-east of Messines and towards Oosttaverne.

The first phase, the capture of the Black Line, was to be carried out by three Divisions disposed side by side, namely, the 3rd Australians on the right, the New Zealanders in the centre, and the 25th on the left; and then the 3rd and 4th

Australian Divisions, passing through the captors of the Black Line, would carry on with the second phase and take the Green Line.

The taking of Messines thus fell to the New Zealand Division, with an attack frontage of from 1,500 to 1,600 yards. Within the Division it was arranged that Messines and its all-round defences should be taken by the 3rd and 2nd Brigades attacking side by side, the former on the right, the latter on the left, the 1st Brigade then passing through the 3rd and 2nd, capturing and consolidating the Black Line, establishing a line of posts still further eastward on what was known as the Black Dotted Line, and taking all enemy guns within reach. Again, in the task allotted to the 2nd and 3rd Brigades, there were three phases: first, over-running the enemy's front line and capturing and consolidating the Blue Line, which ran along his supports; secondly, the taking of the Brown Line, a reserve system running through the western edge of the village; and thirdly, the capture of the village together with the trenches running round its eastern outskirts and to the north and south, these latter forming a Yellow Line. Within our own Brigade area the tasks allotted to the several units were as follows: 1st Battalion and 3rd Battalion (plus two platoons from the 2nd) working abreast, to take the Blue and Brown Lines; the 4th Battalion (plus one company from the 2nd) to take the greater part of Messines and the Yellow Line beyond; the 2nd Battalion (less one company and two platoons, detached) to dig in behind the Brown Line as Brigade reserve. Brigade Headquarters were established in Regina Cut-off, just behind our front line.

The 3rd N.Z. Machine Gun Company detailed one gun to accompany each battalion, and one section was held in Brigade reserve; two sections came under orders of Division and were employed in laying down the barrage. Of light trench-mortars one gun accompanied each of the 1st and 3rd Battalions, two went with the 4th Battalion, and four were held in Brigade reserve. Tanks to the number of twelve were told off to co-operate with the Division, and the contact aeroplane programme was exceedingly complete as to detail.

A very fine artillery barrage scheme had been prepared, and this was supplemented by an intense machine-gun barrage covering the successive bounds of the infantry. The advance of the New Zealand Division was supported by one hundred and fourteen 18-pounders, forty-two 4.5-inch howitzers, and a large number of heavy pieces of artillery; and by seventy-two Vickers guns, including sixteen guns of the 3rd Australian Division. When the Army barrage for the offensive was practised on the afternoon of June 2nd the display was on a scale of magnificence not hitherto approached in any theatre of war. It was watched with great interest, and its effectiveness added in no small measure to the morale of the infantry who were presently to go over the top under its cover.

Zero-hour had been fixed for 3.10 a.m. on the 7th of June. At 6 p.m. on the previous evening, one company of the 3rd Battalion, then on Hill 63, took over the whole Brigade defensive front from a portion of the 2nd Auckland Battalion, and three hours later the remainder of the Brigade, from the bivouac area at De Seule, started off on their long silent march to the front trenches, moving by the specially-marked overland routes W and X, which, to reduce the liability to casualties from shelling, avoided the roads for practically their whole length. As a further precaution platoons moved at intervals of 200 yards. Shortly after midnight the last of our men had entered the communication-trenches, and by 2 a.m. the assembly was complete.

A short portion of the right of our Brigade front had been left clear for the use of the 40th Battalion of the 3rd Australian Division, which was to advance just north of the Douve, but as we had ample room otherwise, this caused no inconvenience. Our men were now in readiness with battalions, companies, platoons, sections and attached machine-guns and trench mortars all in order for the advance. Fortunately, there had been very few casualties during the march and assembly, though gas-shelling rendered the final stages extremely difficult and wearisome.

Now ensued the long, anxious wait, only a little more than an hour by the clock, but how slowly in such circumstances do the minutes pass! In his sorriest plight the soldier will generally maintain his own good spirits and the cheerfulness of his companions by banter and joke, but this resort was denied him, for strict silence was enjoined; and there was not even the solace of a pipe, smoking between the time of commencing the march and zero-hour being strictly forbidden. And it was known to all ranks that if the enemy were to take it into his head to attack or to raid within the last half-hour, there would be no response to our S.O.S. signal except counter-battery work, though there was some consolation in knowing that this, if needed, would be sufficiently furious and effective. So the time passed slowly on through the long darkest hour before the dawn. Some relief came at 3 a.m., when bayonets, or as we have it in Rifle Brigades, "swords," were quietly drawn from their scabbards and fixed. Now only ten minutes remained.

Some of the machine-guns assisting in the protective barrage opened out a few moments before time, and the men in the assembly trenches could scarcely be restrained from setting off in response. However, the long-looked-for signal came with the almost simultaneous roar of exploding mines* and the crash of the intense artillery bombardment, upon which the 1st and 3rd Battalions advanced across No Man's Land to the assault of the Blue Line, followed closely by the 2nd and 4th Battalions. Myriads of S.O.S. rockets rose from the enemy's lines, but the answering barrage came too late, falling as it did on our old front line trenches some minutes after our troops had left them. We had no creeping barrage to cover our movement across No Man's Land, but the barrage laid in succession on the enemy's front and support lines was so effective and well-defined that our men, to use their own expression, "could lean up against it."

The two leading battalions moved abreast, each on a two-company frontage, and No Man's Land was quickly crossed. Owing to the darkness of the early hour and the smoke and dust caused by the bombardment, the keeping of direction by means of landmarks was impossible; but as all officers worked on compass-bearings they were able to check at once any tendency on the part of the little section-columns to deviate from the line laid down.

*None of these was on the front covered by the New Zealand Division; the nearest was that under Ontario Farm just beyond us to the left, while on our right one was blown opposite the centre of the 3rd Australians, and another at Factory Farm, clear of their right flank.

ORDER OF BATTLE—MESSINES, JUNE 7, 1917.

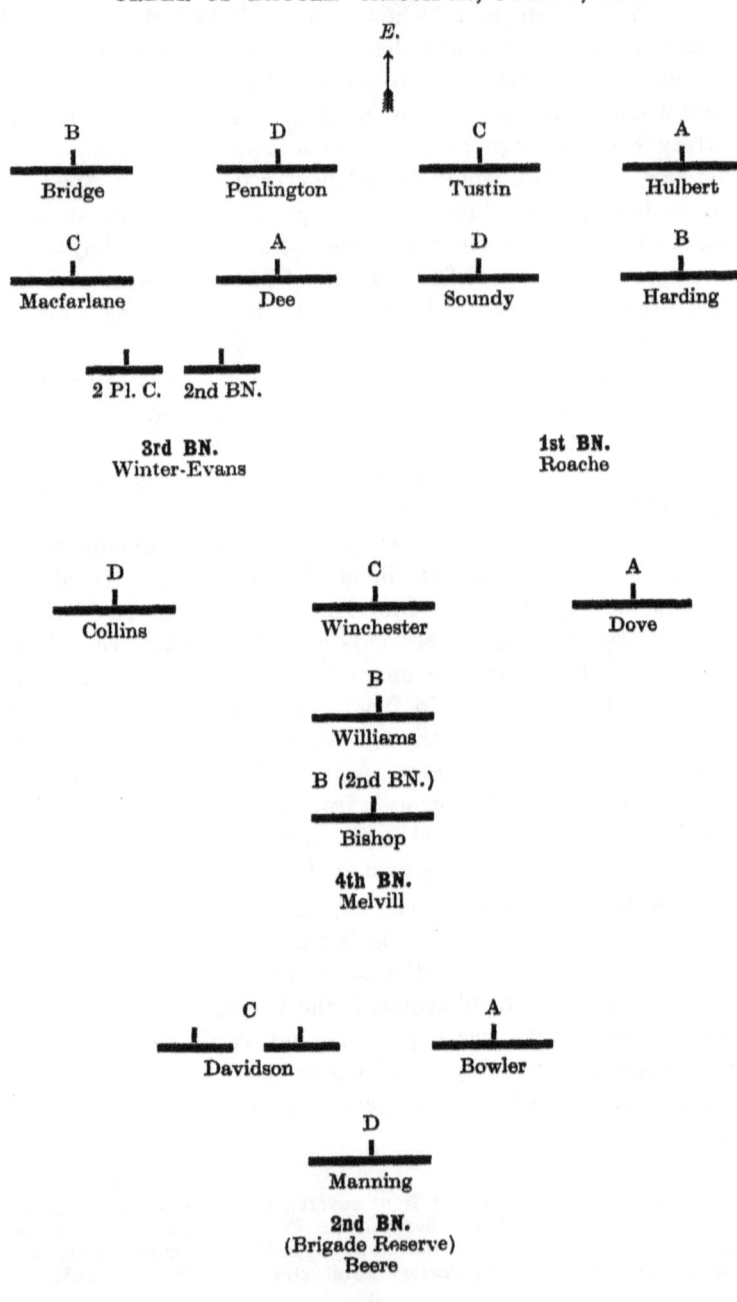

In the 1st Battalion's sector, "A" Company (2nd Lieut. E. Hulbert) was almost immediately in the enemy salient at La Petite Douve Farm, but the conclusions arrived at from the previous investigations of the 2nd Battalion raiding parties proved to be correct, and the two platoons specially detailed to deal with the Farm in case the enemy had altered his dispositions had little resistance to overcome except from isolated posts in and about the ruins and in the trenches in its neighbourhood. The remainder of the company passed on at once, cleared their section of Ulna Support and the saps leading to it, and swung the right flank up into the general alignment. "C" Company (Lieut. E. B. Tustin), on the left, passed without a check over the ruins of the German forward trench and moved steadily onward towards the support line. Fire from a machine-gun near the centre and from another towards the left flank caused no little trouble, but bombing parties promptly moved against the positions and captured both guns and crews. Near the right of the company sector Corporal H. J. Jeffrey suddenly found himself facing a dug-out from which a German machine-gunner had brought his gun and was busily enfilading the Australians advancing on our right. Without a moment's hesitation Jeffrey rushed him, but the gunner was too quick. Evading his pursuer he darted into the dug-out, and a peremptory invitation to come out not being responded to with the promptitude desirable, a bomb was thrown in. This killed five of the inmates and brought out eight others with their hands up. One of these, an officer, seizing a favourable opportunity, made as if to draw his revolver, and on being rushed made good his escape. Four more now came out of the dug-out, bringing with them a wounded companion. The twelve uninjured prisoners were handed over to the escort in charge of another batch, and Corporal Jeffrey rejoined his platoon as if nothing unusual had happened. No less inspiring was the action of Sergeant J. V. M. Cauty, who attacked single-handed and bombed out a nest of enemy sharp-shooters who were delaying the advance. There was little further opposition of any serious nature, and presently the company cleared the whole of its objective and commenced the work of putting the line gained into order as a fighting-trench.

The two leading companies of the 3rd Battalion, "D" (Capt. W. A. G. Penlington) on the right, and "B" (Lieut. C. E. Bridge) on the left, had fared equally well. Sixteen minutes had been allowed for the advance to and capture of the first objective, but before this brief period had elapsed the Blue Line, passed through to follow it up and capture the falling some little distance beyond it.

At the appointed moment the curtain of artillery fire moved forward, and the remaining two companies of the leading battalions, by this time in positions of readiness behind the Blue Line, passed through to follow it up and capture the Brown Line. "B" Company (Capt. E. A. Harding), the right of the 1st Battalion's forward companies, had a comparatively long advance, but met with little resistance. Not more than ten prisoners were captured on the way up, and the only machine-gun taken was one that had just been abandoned. On the objective itself, here further east than the remainder of the line, there were no difficulties of any great consequence to contend with. Fire from a position some little distance beyond the line caused inconvenience until a party moved out against it and brought in the garrison of twenty, the majority of whom had been found sheltering in a dug-out. "D" Company (Lieut. A. W. Soundy), on the left, was held up momentarily by parties of the enemy who had established themselves in a hedge running across the line of advance, about midway between Blue and Brown Lines. Three posts here were rushed and their garrisons bombed or bayoneted, and the cause of the delay having been thus promptly removed, the advance was continued towards the trenches of the Brown Line. These were captured with ease, for on the barrage lifting, our men made the final dash and reached their goal before the Germans could raise their heads.

In view of the greater difficulties anticipated in the capture of their section of the close defences of the southern portion of Messines, each of the two 3rd Battalion companies, "A" (Capt. G. K. Dee) and "C" (Capt. D. B. Macfarlane), had been strengthened by the attachment of a platoon from the 2nd Battalion. Until the objective was closely approached, their advance from the Blue Line proceeded swiftly, the scattered groups of the enemy everywhere surrendering freely.

For the most part, too, their allotted portion of Ulster Reserve was captured more easily than had been expected, but on the left the last stage of the forward movement was checked by machine-guns firing from positions amongst the ruins of the village. Between these guns and our men the barrage was falling with that admirable regularity and stiffness which proved to be a highly-important contributory factor in the success of the day's operations. Here, however, it was to us an obstacle, and to the Germans a protection. The awkward situation was relieved by the daring action of Lance-Corporal Samuel Frickleton. Followed by his section he moved up closer to the barrage, weighed his chances, and, seizing a favourable opportunity, dashed through to the other side. Here he proceeded at once to deal with the nearest gun single-handed. With bomb and bayonet he fell upon the crew like a fury and destroyed them all. Not content with this, he proceeded to the second gun, killed the three men serving it, and then, turning his attention to the dug-out below, he finished his work by destroying the nine men within who refused to come out. For this succession of courageous deeds, which undoubtedly prevented further casualties both to our men and to other units coming forward, and led to the completion of the capture of the objective, Lance-Corporal Frickleton was awarded the Victoria Cross. In his efforts he was gallantly supported by the survivors of his section, notably Corporal A. V. Eade and Rifleman C. J. Maubon. The former carried forward the first captured gun for the purpose of engaging another enemy gun still further ahead, but was killed while mounting it for action. Maubon followed Frickleton closely and rendered material assistance. Later on, again beyond our barrage, he himself engaged a machine-gun firing from the Institution Royale, and by daring and skilful bombing work killed the gunner and smashed the gun.

The whole of the allotted section of the Brown Line was now in our hands, the capture having been completed by the schedule time, 3.45 a.m., less than three-quarters of an hour from the time the first advance commenced. The commanders of both units attributed much of the success gained within that brief period to the excellent leadership displayed under most difficult conditions by the company officers and non-commissioned officers. According to custom, a fair proportion of the company, platoon and section commanders had been left out of the line, involving in many cases the throwing of added responsibility upon the shoulders of subordinates. Moreover, the casualties, though not on the whole heavy, were severe in the ranks of the leaders. In the 3rd Battalion alone, one company had lost all, and another company three of its officers before 4 a.m., and by the time the final objective was reached only nine officers in the whole battalion remained effective. As breaches occurred, however, they were promptly filled by juniors, and amongst those specially mentioned for fearless and skilful work in this connection were Sergeants H. Allen, F. J. Prebble, A. Taylor, G. Heard and H. Anderson, who became temporary platoon commanders; and Lieuts. F. E. Greenish, E. F. J. Reeves, and K. C. Clayton, and 2nd Lieuts. R. C. Abernethy, R. A. Bennett and J. Russell, each of whom took over the command of a company in the early stages. There were many instances of wounded officers and men remaining on duty. Major A. Digby-Smith had been entrusted with the special task of personally supervising the advance of the 3rd Battalion companies until the objective should be reached. Though severely wounded in the face at the commencement of the action, he carried on with unabated zeal and gallantry until success was assured; and it was only on the arrival of his commanding officer, who was now permitted to move forward from his headquarters in our old front line, that he consented to go out for medical attention. Similar devotion was displayed by Capt. W. A. G. Penlington and 2nd Lieut. F. S. Goulding.

The 4th Battalion, with the attached company of the 2nd, followed close up to the troops assaulting the Blue Line. Preserving their dispositions as far as possible, the troops took advantage of the shelter available and waited for the next bound of the barrage, the signal for their advance to the attack on Messines and the Yellow Line beyond. Three companies formed the forward line. "A" Company (Capt. W. W. Dove) had as its task the capture and consolidation of a zigzag section of trench just to the south-east of the village, and, working with it, "D" Company of the 1st Battalion would capture a short length in front of the right of the 3rd Battalion, thus straightening out the line in this quarter. The other two leading companies of the 4th Battalion, "C" (Lieut. E. A. Winchester) and "D" (2nd Lieut. W. E. Collins), were to capture the southern half of Messines, while "B" Company (Capt. O. W. Williams) was detailed to pass rapidly through the village and secure the trenches beyond. The fifth company, that from the 2nd Battalion, was held in battalion reserve.

Plans for the mopping-up of Messines had been worked out in great detail, and these had been communicated to the men as well as to their leaders early in May. Every man knew his particular job, and just where it was located; and to make assurance doubly sure he was provided with a specially-prepared map showing the streets and buildings as well as the dug-outs and other suspected danger-points.

Punctually to time the barrage lifted to its next position, and our men advanced. Resistance in the village proved to be much slighter than had been expected. Only those of the garrison stationed in fancied security behind their machine-guns seemed to have had any heart in their work. All above ground were speedily accounted for, and then attention was directed to the dug-outs and fortified cellars. No fewer than forty of such positions were found, constructed wholly or in part of reinforced concrete, and in most cases garrisoned. Where invitations failed and Mills bombs proved ineffective in bringing about an ejectment, recourse was had to smoke-bombs or, in more pressing cases, to Stokes mortar bombs thrown in by hand. The stiffest fight in the town raged round the ruins of the Institution Royale. The ground-floor section of this building was still standing because of the fact that it had been strongly concreted within and transformed into a fortress prepared against attack from any quarter; and it was protected by the heap of fallen rubble above from all but the heaviest of our artillery. The assault of this position, the strength of which had been suspected, fell to a platoon under Sergeant J. W. Penrose, and so fierce was the hand-to-hand struggle that only two men of the platoon survived the contest, the gallant leader himself being numbered amongst the killed. From time to time reinforcements from other parties joined in this attack on the completion of their own special tasks, and the work of

Penrose's platoon was presently brought to a conclusion by the capture of the Institution and the annihilation of the garrison. In this stubborn fight, Lance-Sergeant J. E. Thomson, who had taken up the leadership when Sergeant Penrose fell, acquitted himself no less magnificently; but he too was killed before the victory was gained.

Two hours had been allotted for the thorough mopping-up of the village, and within that time the company commanders directly responsible reported that they had finished their task. Amongst the prisoners taken was Capt. Thomas, who some time previously had been specially appointed to the permanent command of the inner and outer defences of Messines. A wounded officer volunteered the information that a tunnelled dug-out containing 200 men was situated under the Church Square, but as our search for this proved fruitless it is surmised that, if the officer's statement were correct, the entrance to the dug-out must have been blown in by our heavies and the whole of the inmates trapped within.

Meanwhile the capture of the trenches constituting the Yellow Line had been completed. The fighting here had been more severe than in the area west of the village, but all resistance on the 4th Battalion sector was quickly overcome. In the more open country to the south, the company from the 1st Battalion met with greater opposition. As the advance proceeded from point to point, the Lewis gun sections had some excellent targets both while covering their own men and while supporting the forward movement of those on the flanks. Approaching the final objective the right and the left of the leading waves of this company were held up by strong-points in the trench itself. From two concrete dug-outs fire continued to pour, and it was some time before they could be enveloped and rushed. Some five or six prisoners were taken from each; one yielded also much useful signal material, while the other, containing a quantity of explosives ready to our hand, was bombed and wrecked.

The two companies that had dealt with the village itself moved forward to the captured Yellow Line, each leaving behind a platoon to clear up any "pockets" that might have been overlooked. The village was left practically empty of troops in order to minimize casualties from the heavy enemy shelling expected to fall upon it within two hours after the opening of our attack.

Prominent amongst the 4th Battalion leaders were Lieut. D. J. Shaw, who assumed command on the loss of his company commander, and Sergeants A. J. Steer and R. Whitefield, who commanded platoons under similar conditions. As a mark of appreciation of the masterly conduct of the attack and of the fine work of the battalion under his command, Lieut.-Col. Melvill was shortly afterwards decorated with the Belgian Ordre de la Couronne.

Within thirty minutes after zero, the 2nd Battalion, less the six platoons detached with other battalions, had reached its appointed position between the Blue and Brown Lines, and had commenced to dig itself in. As Brigade reserve it held itself in readiness to move to any threatened point. On their way forward, the troops of this unit mopped-up several parties of the enemy in the Blue Line and in Ulcer Sap. During consolidation they were troubled by an enemy machine-gun firing from a concrete dug-out in the vicinity of Messines Church, but a party despatched from "C" Company promptly surrounded this position and destroyed the garrison.

Thus the Brigade's defined tasks were successfully accomplished, and nothing now remained but to push on with the completion of the consolidation of the positions gained as fighting lines, and to erect wire entanglements for their further strengthening. The casualties had been surprisingly light, and, as a consequence, the trenches of our new positions were thickly held. Though this was undesirable in view of the heavy shelling to which the enemy was sure to subject the area, yet because of the fact that operations were being continued farther forward, no thinning-out could be permitted until their success was assured. The faithful stretcher-bearers, already at work, found their labours steadily increasing. Assisting these on all parts of the battlefield was the Revd. S. Parr, Chaplain to the 3rd Battalion, who spent many hours searching for the missing, dressing the wounded, and burying the dead. The names of Riflemen H. T. Waller, A. E. Dickson, C. Ferguson, amongst the stretcher-bearers, are recalled in connection with special gallant and devoted service.

Of rescue work under fire, two striking instances may be given. Sergeant T. T. Murray, of the 3rd Battalion, finding his trench in rear of Messines subjected to particularly accurate shelling, withdrew his platoon to a flank away from the part shelled; but one of his men being reported to have been buried, he at once returned alone in the face of the continued bombardment and extricated him. Rifleman A. Dunthorne, one of the 4th Battalion men in the newly-captured Yellow Line, observed that a salvo, striking the trench, buried three of the garrison. Heedless of danger he rushed to the spot and dug out two of the three. Another crash now fell at the same spot, burying the rescued men, the concussion almost incapacitating Dunthorne himself. Struggling to his feet, he returned to the task, and by almost superhuman efforts succeeded at last in getting all three men out alive.

Maintenance of communication also was becoming increasingly difficult. The signalling personnel of Brigade, battalions and companies, amongst whom were noted at the time Sergeant A. W. M. Ohlson, Corporal A. F. Gilmour, Riflemen H. Wright, H. J. Byrne, P. Neville and W. H. F. Law, had a most difficult task, not only in laying the lines, but in locating and mending breaks caused by shell-fire. Some of the lines were repeatedly broken so badly that mending was out of the question, and entirely new lines had to be laid. In consequence of these frequent interruptions, runners had to be called upon for getting communications to the rear and to the flanks. Shell-fire and machine-guns took heavy toll of these tireless and faithful men. Rifleman A. Johnston, for instance, was the only 3rd Battalion headquarters' runner surviving the assault; while Riflemen W. R. White and A. H. Bone, of the 1st, and S. N. Managh of the 4th, after long and continuous efforts, collapsed at last from shell-shock and exhaustion.

Of the four tanks detailed for work in our Brigade area, all were late, owing to delays at bridges; one afterwards became stranded at our old front line, and two in advance of Blue Line, and the fourth moved off beyond the right flank at about 4.30 a.m. Neither the Stokes mortars nor the Vickers guns attached to battalions were called upon for action, and two of the latter were disabled by shell-fire early in the day.

The administrative arrangements generally could not very well have been improved upon. As an indication of their effectiveness, it is recorded that supplies of munitions and water reached Messines before the mopping-up of the village was complete. It is worthy of mention, too, that before the next day had dawned the Pioneers and the 1st and 2nd Battalions had dug new saps from our old front line to Messines, and that a mule-track had been carried forward well up to the neighbourhood of the village within the same period.

Troops had been ordered not to drink water found in Messines, a wise precaution in view of the reports that came in later to the effect that the water in the wells contained traces of arsenic.

The attack generally continued to go well. The 2nd Brigade troops on our left took their objectives simultaneously with us, and at this time the two assaulting battalions of the 1st Brigade which had left their assembly positions at 4 a.m. were already nearing the Brown Line, where they were to await the moving forward of the barrage still falling just beyond Messines. The guns lifted at 5 a.m., and the 1st Brigade troops advanced, 1st Auckland moving past the south, and 1st Wellington skirting the north of the village. Twenty minutes later they had secured their objective on the Black Line beyond, and had already commenced the work of consolidation. So also with the Divisions on our flanks. The swinging movement of the 3rd Australians on our right had been successfully accomplished, and the troops of the 25th Division on our left were firmly established on the Black Line. According to plan, soon after 8 a.m. a company of 2nd Auckland Battalion passed through the main line and established a series of strong posts on what was known as the Black Dotted Line, which lay from three to four hundred yards beyond. Thus the task of the Division was accomplished, and now, in accordance with instructions to facilitate the advance of the 4th Australians, another company of 2nd Auckland sent forward patrols over the country intervening between the line of posts and the Green Line. A strong counter-attack launched at 1 p.m. was checked by artillery and machine-gun fire, and at 3.10 p.m., exactly twelve hours after the morning's zero hour, the 4th Australians passed through to the assault on the Green Line. This fur-

THE PLANK ROAD FOLLOWS THE ADVANCE.

THE COLONEL-IN-CHIEF INSPECTS A DETACHMENT AT BAILLEUL.

Lieut.-Col. J. G. Roache, D.S.O.

Lieut.-Col. R. St. J. Beere, D.S.O.

Lieut.-Col. A. Winter-Evans
D.S.O.

Lieut.-Col. (Maj.-Gen.)
C. W. Melvill,
C.B., C.M.G., D.S.O.

Sergeant (Lieut.) Samuel Frickleton, V.C.,
is invested by H.M. King George V.

ther advance was successful both on our own front and also on the northern sector, but at about 9 p.m. the Germans launched a strong attack on sections of the line due east of Messines and succeeded in pushing the Australians back for some distance. The latter advanced again at 3 o'clock next morning and finally regained their position, thus completing the last main phase of the Battle of Messines, described at the time as "a model and masterpiece of modern tactics."

During the 8th the New Zealand Rifle Brigade was withdrawn from the line, the portions held by the different units being taken over by battalions of the 1st and 2nd Brigades. Our 1st and 2nd Battalions went into quarters at Hill 63, but the 3rd and 4th were held near the old front line in readiness to go forward again at short notice. All four battalions supplied strong parties for road-making and cable-burying on the 8th, 9th and 10th, working steadily through a series of high-explosive and gas bombardments.

The distastefulness of these tasks, in many respects more dangerous and less welcome than the exciting activities of front-line garrison duty or even of an actual advance, was only slightly tempered by the fine weather that prevailed; and not even the urgency of the work in hand could prevent an occasional pause to watch the issue of manœuvres at this time so frequent in the air above. On the 9th, Richtofen's squadron of eighteen aeroplanes, conspicuous by their brilliant colouring, cruised slowly up and down over our new front line at a comparatively low altitude. Immediately above the village of Messines, and flying parallel to the Germans, was a squadron of five British open-fusilage machines. The opposing formations, so unequally matched in strength, for some time maintained a respectful distance from each other, exchanging occasional bursts of machine-gun fire at long range. Presently, to the dismay of the interested spectators, a British machine suddenly swerved and crashed to earth. Almost immediately, and as if from nowhere, there appeared another British aeroplane, but this was of a vastly different type from the ponderous fighters majestically patrolling the airy spaces above the line. A light, fast machine, twisting and manœuvring dexterously, it looked quite out of place in its present company. After a few moments, spent, as it seemed, in taking stock of the position, the British scout wheeled aloft in a fast spiral, and, turning abruptly, plunged down like a meteor, alone, into the midst of that famous German squadron which was the pride of the Fatherland, and which our enemy fondly believed to be the dread of all Allied airmen. Now followed a scene of the most thrilling interest. Wheeling, twisting, turning, diving, the British machine darted hither and thither amongst the enemy 'planes, its machine-gun crackling incessantly. The Germans retaliated in kind, but finding, as it would appear, that they were firing into one another, the squadron, which had hitherto been keeping magnificent formation, broke up in disorder. From the disorganized group five machines drew off, and, mounting swiftly heavenwards, took order one above another. Then in succession they swooped down upon the lone British machine, which was still maintaining the state of confusion amongst the remaining thirteen. Each of the five endeavoured to "get on the tail" of the Britisher, but no sooner did that object appear to be within reach of achievement than the position was reversed by the prompt and skilful handling of the British aeroplane. Our men, who, in the face of this all-absorbing contest, had temporarily given up all thoughts of digging, heartily applauded each successful manœuvre on the part of the plucky pilot, and raised a derisive cheer as, thoroughly discomfited, the German squadron withdrew. They saw with satisfaction the gallant scout, now doubtless short of ammunition, turn slowly homeward, and watched with renewed interest two of the Germans, apparently emboldened by this retreat and sensing a possible defenceless victim, break back and give chase. The pursuers, however, had little heart in their work, for when the British scout turned they suddenly and finally gave up the contest. Perhaps the Germans had begun to suspect, what was indeed the case, that the pilot of the British machine was the redoubtable McCudden, whose unequalled reputation for skill and daring was well known on both sides of the Allied front.

On June 10th the Brigade came under the G.O.C. 4th Australian Division, then holding the whole of the sector from Messines forward, and on the following day moved back to Nieppe, where we rejoined the New Zealand Division, which had gone out to Corps reserve on the morning of the 9th. The

Corps Commander (General Godley) visited the Brigade on the morning of the 12th. Addressing the men, he congratulated them on their excellent work on the 7th, and was good enough to say that in the recent attack the New Zealand Rifle Brigade had proved itself second to no other Brigade in the Corps.

The captures made by the Brigade during the Messines operations included 285 prisoners, one 7.7 gun, eleven machine-guns, and one trench mortar, besides much miscellaneous ammunition, arms and specialist gear. On the whole Army front 7,200 prisoners, including 145 officers, fell into British hands, and 67 guns, 294 machine-guns, and 94 trench mortars were captured.

Our casualties during the actual attack were exceedingly light, but mainly owing to the subsequent heavy shelling of the whole area, and especially of the village of Messines, the total was rapidly increased. From June 6th to 12th the casualties were:—

	Killed.	Wounded.	Missing.
Officers	8	26	—
Other ranks	136	649	160

Brigadier-General C. H. J. Brown, D.S.O., commanding the 1st Brigade, was killed at Messines on the 8th while accompanying the Divisional Commander on a tour of inspection. Lieut.-Col. C. W. Melvill, D.S.O., then commanding our 4th Battalion, took over the command of the 1st Brigade the same evening, and Major E. Puttick thereupon assumed command of the 4th Battalion.

The following translation of an order found in Messines Headquarters will serve to indicate the importance attached by the German command to the holding of the village at all costs:

"REGIMENTAL ORDER NO. 9,447 OF 5TH MAY, 1917.

INSTRUCTIONS TO THE COMMANDANT OF MESSINES.

"1. In consequence of the importance of Messines as the southern corner post of the Wytschaete Salient, I appoint a permanent responsible commander for the outer and inner defences. Captain Thomas is detailed for this post.

"2. The outer defences consist of:—
  (a) The whole trench system of Oyster Reserve* to Ulcer Reserve—the trench round the south of Messines to Unbearable Trench and Oxonian Reserve.
  (b) The inner defences of Messines are based on five concrete works which command the lines of the streets. More of these are planned, and some are in course of construction.

"3. In the event of the outer defences being broken by the enemy, the place itself is to be defended by sectors. The main defence is five concrete dug-outs which are connected together by a close system of rubbish obstacles. Each dug-out is a self-contained strong-point, and as such is to be defended to the utmost, that is, until the place has been retaken.

The concrete dug-outs form together a mutually-supporting system of strong-points.

"4. The Commandant of Messines has the following forces at his disposal, which are to be considered as an emergency garrison. In order to distinguish them, these are to carry a white band on the left arm.

FOR THE OUTER DEFENCE:

  (a) 1 Zug (platoon) of Regimental Pioneer Company of 181st I.R. for the defensive positions north of the Wulverghem Road.
  (b) I Zug of the Oyster Reserve Company of the Reserve Battalion in Messines.
  (c) I Zug of the Regimental Pioneer Company, 134th I.R., stationed in the dug-outs of the Institution Royale.
  (d) 1 Zug of the Regimental Pioneer Company, 134th I.R., stationed in the western end of Unbearable Trench.

FOR THE MAIN DEFENCES OF THE TOWN:

  (a) The last company of the Reserve Battalion (formerly Regimental Reserve Company) which is in Messines, and battalions must arrange for the same battalion to be detailed each time; also the machine-guns as per map [not found] and the emergency gun 'Suedflinte' which is in the S.W. edge of the town.

"5. The duties of Commandant of Messines include:—
  (a) Thorough instruction of all leaders and detachments (especially machine-gunners) about their duties in case of enemy attack.

*In this translation our own trench-names are used.

(b) Practice drills in manning posts.
(c) Provisioning the dug-outs with sufficient rations.
(d) Supervision of ammunition and ration depots.
(e) Keeping ready special gear for hand-to-hand fighting, and pioneer stores at each strong-point.
(f) Regulation of Aid Posts in conjunction with the Medical Officer on duty in the Dressing Station.
(g) Control of Intelligence arrangements.

"6. Captain Thomas is authorized to make at once any necessary alteration to the disposition of the forces detailed for the defence of Messines, and is to report on same by 10th May to Regimental Headquarters.

Lieut. D. L. Spanier is detailed to assist.

"7. Captain Thomas will occupy the former battle headquarters of the Reserve Battalion Commander in the Institution Royale, and will relieve him every five days, starting 16th May.

"8. While Captain Thomas is in rest quarters in Comines, the Commander of the Reserve Battalion will be Commandant of Messines. When the definite operations start, Captain Thomas is to be continuously in Messines. The Commander of the Reserve Battalion will then be at my disposal. . . .

"(Signed) NAUMANN."

Again, General von Laffert, commanding the German 4th Corps, entrusted with the defence of the Wytschaete-Messines Ridge, issued, on June 1st, an order urging the importance of the holding of the natural strong-points of Wytschaete and Messines for the domination of the Wytschaete Salient. Inter alia, he instructed that "these two strong-points must therefore not fall, even temporarily, into the enemy's hands. Both must be defended to the utmost and be held to the last man, even if the enemy cuts connection on both sides and also threatens them from the rear." The whole of the 3rd Bavarian Division had been placed at von Laffert's disposal to support if necessary, the counter-offensive.

CHAPTER IX.
AFTER MESSINES.

PART 1.—THE ADVANCE IN THE PLOEGSTEERT SECTOR.

The German salient south of Messines—25th and New Zealand Divisions detailed to attack—Advance of the 4th Brigade's patrols—Accelerated assault by the 2nd Brigade and the 4th Battalion—In touch with the Warneton Line—2nd Battalion patrols about La Basse Ville—Out to reserve—Inspection by the Duke of Connaught at Bailleul—Command.

After the Battle of Messines the Australians, quietly exploiting their successes, pushed gradually forward from the Oosttaverne Line. This left a salient in the German forward position opposite Ploegsteert Wood, and to straighten out the line here plans were laid for an attack on June 14th. This was to be carried out by two Divisions, the 25th on the north, and the New Zealanders on the south, the River Douve forming the dividing line between the two. The line in the meantime was being held by the 3rd Australian Division as far south as St. Yves, and by the 4th New Zealand Infantry Brigade* from St. Yves to the Lys.

*The 4th Brigade was established in March, 1917, under the command of Brigadier-General H. Hart, D.S.O. It was formed mainly of fit officers and other ranks from the convalescent camps and of drafts from the 20th, 21st, and 22nd Reinforcements, the first of these latter arriving at the Brigade camp at Codford on March 30th. In addition, the commanding officers for all the new units, together with a large number of other officers and of non-commissioned officers, were despatched from the three Brigades in France; and a special party of over a hundred non-commissioned officers was sent to England from the Division for training as officers in order to meet the demands likely to be made owing to casualties.

The Brigade left for France on May 28th, and during the operations at Messines was employed on the construction and repair of roads in the battle area. It was now in the line for the first time, having taken over the sector on June 10th. It had not yet joined up with the Division, however, but was for the time being attached to the Australians.

For the proposed operation relief was to commence on the night of the 12th, when two battalions of the 2nd Brigade would take over that portion of the sector allotted to the New Zealand Division from the Douve to St. Yves. On the following night the New Zealand Rifle Brigade would come into the right sub-sector, holding the front line from St. Yves to the Warnave River with one battalion.

On the afternoon of the 12th, however, the 4th Brigade suddenly found that touch with the enemy had been lost along a considerable part of their front. Fighting-patrols were immediately sent out, and, as a result of their investigations, posts were occupied throughout the old German front line from St. Yves south to the railway line. On the 13th, further penetration to the enemy's support line was made, and posts were firmly established therein by nightfall.

As a consequence of these developments, it was now considered that the results anticipated from the larger engagement planned for the 14th could just as surely be attained by a rapid following-up of the enemy by strong patrols supported by the action of the heavy artillery. Orders to this effect were accordingly issued to the two 2nd Brigade units already in the line, and to our 4th Battalion then on its way up from Nieppe to occupy the front line and the assembly trenches selected in connection with the advance set down for the following day.

In the 4th Battalion three companies were detailed for the operation, "A" Company (2nd Lieut. D. J. Shaw) on the right, "B" (Capt. O. W. Williams) in the centre, and "C" (Lieut. E. A. Winchester) on the left. The task for each of these was the establishment of four forward posts, with a similar number in support, the new line this formed to extend for more than a mile in length from the Warnave River at the old German support line to the high ground immediately opposite the Sugar Refinery at La Basse Ville. This involved a swinging movement through an angle of thirty degrees, the left flank moving forward some 1,200 yards. "D" Company (2nd Lieut. R. M. Tolhurst) was instructed to occupy the old German support lines as battalion reserve.

The night attack commenced at 9 o'clock, half an hour after the arrival of Major Puttick's first company. Six German aeroplanes were actively reconnoitring at this time, flying low along our front line, and five minutes after the troops commenced to move an intense bombardment opened on the trenches and on the new No Man's Land. On the left, the 2nd Brigade troops were unable to gain all their objectives, but greater success attended the efforts of the 4th Battalion on the right. For the latter there had been no time for reconnaissance, and the advance in the darkness was more or less a leap into the unknown. Nothing more had been possible than to allot tasks to companies and platoons as definitely as circumstances permitted, the sequel being left to good leadership and brave following. Neither commanders nor men failed. Conspicuous amongst the subordinate leaders who did brilliantly successful work were Lieut. D. C. Armstrong; 2nd Lieuts. W. J. Organ and A. Bongard; Sergeants L. M. Blyth, H. J. Michell, and A. R. Scrivener; and Lance-Sergeants H. J. Blake and G. G. Griffiths. The whole area was swept by enemy machine-guns and artillery, and besides the difficulty experienced in establishing the posts, there remained the harder part of holding on. Posts were repeatedly blown out and their garrisons scattered, and as often the sections were reorganized and the positions once more occupied. Some amelioration of the conditions was eventually secured by direct appeal to our heavy artillery, and this night witnessed counter-battery work of the highest order. So well-directed and intense was the fire of our heavies, that at the first call the German guns were instantly silenced. They repeatedly reopened, but on each occasion the retaliation was increased in strength, till at last only a few isolated enemy guns continued their activity.

In view of the broken nature of the new line taken up, patrolling was a feature of the utmost importance, for not only was it necessary to ascertain definitely the enemy's positions, but there was also the vital need for keeping touch between our own posts. In this work the services of Corporal T. Wilson and Lance-Corporals C. H. Still and H. R. Hayes proved to be invaluable. In the early morning Corporal Wilson's patrol encountered an enemy post uncomfortably near one of our own. By a skilful flank movement Wilson drove the enemy party out, and on the vantage point thus gained established a line of snipers that during the course of the day took heavy toll of the Germans who from time to time momentarily exposed themselves in La Basse Ville.

Notwithstanding all the efforts of the runners, amongst whom Rifleman E. Vazey, S. N. Managh, and S. E. Johns were noted as having performed extraordinary feats in the open country under fire, the situation on some parts of the line remained obscure, and to clear this up a reconnaissance of the whole battalion front was made at dawn by Major Puttick, in company with Captain Purdy, Brigade Major, when the results of the operation were found to have exceeded expectations; and upon receipt of a definite report to this effect, the Corps Commander telegraphed his congratulations.

The battalion, indeed, had accomplished a noteworthy feat. There had been no general conference before the commencement of the operation. Companies had reached the jumping-off line in succession, and half an hour after its arrival each had been despatched in turn on an unexpected adventure into strange country. Yet it was found that the whole series of posts had been established as ordered, and that not one was more than twenty-five yards from the position laid down for it.

On the following night battalions of the 2nd Brigade continued the attack in the left sector and succeeded in establishing a line of posts between the Messines–La Basse Ville Road and the Douve River, west of Warneton, their operations being carried out in conjunction with an advance by the 25th Division east of Messines, from Farm de la Croix northwards. On the same night, by active patrolling, the troops of the 4th Brigade pushed their front forward to the west bank of the Lys.

The advancement of posts was equally successful along the rest of the Army front, and the British line was thus brought in close contact with the strong German defensive system known to us as the "Warneton Line."

The posts in our Brigade sector were subjected to extremely heavy shelling, Ploegsteert Wood was drenched with gas, and the enemy's machine-guns continued to be very active. The Germans still clung to two strong forward positions at La Basse Ville and Pont Rouge, on the western bank of the Lys, where patrols from the 2nd Battalion, which had relieved the 4th Battalion in the new front line on the night of 15th/16th June, had frequent encounters with those of the enemy. Lieut. H. M. Keesing, acting-adjutant of the battalion, during a special personal reconnaissance of the line while forward posts were being advanced in the neighbourhood of La Basse Ville, found the garrison at a vital point on the extreme left in difficulties. Three attempts to establish the post had failed owing to the heavy shell-fire, and casualties had been numerous. Both the company commander and the platoon commander had fallen, and the men were almost ready to give up in despair. Grasping the situation, Lieut. Keesing rallied and led them forward for a fourth attempt, succeeding at last in firmly establishing the position. On the following night Lance-Corporal P. Moffitt led a reconnoitring patrol throughout the whole battalion front, investigating the unknown No Man's Land for a distance, in some parts, of 900 yards in advance of the forward posts. Arrived at last in the neighbourhood of Pont Rouge, opposite the right of the sector, he sat down and wrote a detailed account of the results of his investigations up to that time, sent it in, and then led five men into an enemy strong-point to make certain of the position of the Germans by actual contact.

On the night of 18th/19th June the new line was taken over from the 2nd Battalion by the 3rd and 1st, the former, on the right, holding from the Warnave River to Le Gheer Road, the latter, on the left, from this point to the Messines–La Basse Ville Road. Both battalions were distributed in great depth, their reserve companies being well back in Ploegsteert village and Wood. Brigade Headquarters moved from Nieppe to Brune Gaye. The Brigade immediately commenced digging continuous front and support lines, and, by bold patrolling, gained control of the whole of the ground in front as far forward as the River Lys, excepting in the vicinity of La Basse Ville, to which point the Germans still clung tenaciously.

Another relief was carried out on the night of 24th/25th, when the 3rd and 1st Battalions were relieved by the 4th* and 2nd respectively, the units from the front line going into bivouacs on Hill 63.

*Major P. H. Bell in temporary command.

It was now noticeable that enemy activity at the Sugar Refinery in La Basse Ville, opposite our left flank, was curiously spasmodic. On June 26th this strong-point appeared to have been abandoned, and Capt. G. A. Avey and 2nd Lieut. R. Tennent, both of the 2nd Battalion, went out to make a daylight reconnaissance. These two officers reached the village, but fell into an ambush. After emptying their revolvers against the Germans they agreed to separate and endeavour to make their way back if possible unobserved. 2nd Lieut. Tennent succeeded in regaining our lines without mishap, but, finding that Capt. Avey failed to return, he concluded that his companion must have been wounded. He thereupon took a party of ten men, with a Lewis gun, and set out to find and bring him in. He selected a shorter route than that previously followed, but the party unfortunately ran against an enemy post from which they came under rifle and machine-gun fire from three directions. Our party suffered several casualties, including 2nd Lieut. Tennent, who was killed. After nightfall repeated attempts were made to recover his body, but owing to the heavy shelling and machine-gun fire, it was found impossible to approach the spot where he had fallen. It was afterwards ascertained that Capt. Avey had been surrounded and taken prisoner, and though he subsequently made several attempts to escape from prison-camps in Germany, on one occasion reaching a point within a mile of the Allied line, he remained in the hands of the enemy until the Armistice.

The New Zealand Rifle Brigade was relieved in the line by a Brigade of the 4th Australian Division on June 29th, and by the 30th had settled down in billets in the Berquin Area, with Brigade Headquarters at Doulieu. General Plumer visited the Brigade on June 21st and expressed his appreciation of the work of the troops at the Battle of Messines.

One June 26th, H.R.H. the Duke of Connaught, Colonel-in-Chief of the New Zealand Rifle Brigade, inspected a representative party from the IInd Anzac Corps at Bailleul, our Brigade sending 25 officers and 100 other ranks to this parade.

General Fulton was evacuated to the Officers' Rest House, sick, on June 16th, but returned to duty on the 25th, Lieut. Col. A. E. Stewart having taken command in the interim.

The casualties in the Brigade during the month of June, including those suffered at Messines, were:—

	Killed.	Wounded.	Missing.
Officers	7	35	2
Other ranks	157	912	163

PART 2.—WITH THE FRENCH FIRST ARMY IN NORTHERN BELGIUM.

By 'bus from Berquin to Rousbrugge Haringhe—Digging—Hospitality and appreciation—Return to the Berquin Area—In reserve—Ceremonial—Command.

The period of rest in the Berquin Area was of short duration. On July 3rd the Brigade marched northwards to Godewaersvelde, the 3rd and 4th Battalions being inspected en route by General Godley. On the following day the Brigade moved by 'bus to Northern Belgium, where we temporarily joined the French First Army. The 1st Battalion went into camp under canvas at Pollinchove, near Hoogstade; the 2nd and 3rd Battalions were located at Eykhoek, the 4th at Woesten, and Brigade Headquarters at Rousbrugge Haringhe.

In this area the Brigade was spread over a frontage of seven miles immediately opposite the Merckem Peninsula (in the flooded canal region), Houthulst Forest, Bixchoote, and other points that were soon to become famous in the Third Battle of Ypres. Pollinchove was only twelve miles from the coast at Nieuport.

Each battalion had attached to it one company of the Maori (Pioneer) Battalion, and our duties, which commenced on July 5th, consisted mainly of the preparation of roads, railways, dug-outs, emplacements and cables for the forthcoming operations. Units received their orders direct from the French Artillery Group Commanders, a system that proved to be in the highest degree satisfactory. The method of piecework was adopted as far as possible, and the working-power of our men completely surprised and mystified the French officers. Colonel Barbier, one of the Group Commanders, expressed the opinion that fifty New Zealanders could easily accomplish a piece of work for which he would ordinarily detail 250 French soldiers. In the work of cable-burying, in particular, our men, acting up to their reputation as "Diggers," progressed so rapidly that the Director of Signals found it necessary to recast his plans in order to enable him to keep up the supply of cable at the same rate as the trenches were dug. For our part, we were particularly struck with the extreme skill and thoroughness with which the French attended to the camouflaging of their works and tracks at every stage.

In the northern sector, then held by the Belgians, the front line ran along the embankment of the Yser Canal. Curiosity took one of the Maoris up to the Canal. Looking across the swamps beyond, he espied several Germans moving about in the open, and the temptation to do a little sniping proving irresistible, he raised his rifle to try his luck. His laudable intentions were, however, to his great disgust, immediately frustrated by a dozen Belgian soldiers, who promptly fell upon him and gave him to understand that the policy in that locality was, for the time being at least, one of quiescence.

During our stay here, our men were exceedingly well treated by both French and Belgian troops. The courtesies of hospitality were freely extended to us, we had a general invitation to their camp entertainments, and their regimental bands on several occasions played programmes in our camps and quarters. On July 14th, the great French National Day, the French Army sent us a special issue of wine, champagne, and cigars. On the same day General Anthoine, the Army Commander, personally thanked the various battalion commanders for what he was pleased to call the magnificent work done by their units, and decorated the Brigadier and the Brigade Major with the Croix de Guerre.

The following letters of appreciation were received and published in orders:—

> From General Anthoine, commanding the French First Army, to Sir Douglas Haig, Commander-in-Chief of the British Army:
>
> "Now that the New Zealand Troops prepare to leave the French First Army, I wish to point out the fine attitude of the British troops you have put at my disposal.

"Infantry and Pioneer Battalions and Engineers have rivalled one another in hard work and fine behaviour.

"I thank you very heartily for the precious help they gave to the First Army.

"I should be grateful if you would let them know my satisfaction."

From the General Officer Commanding the French 1st Corps to the General Officer Commanding the New Zealand Rifle Brigade:

"Now that the men of the British Army who have been put at the disposal of the French Artillery have finished doing their work, I want to thank you most sincerely for your kind and very valuable assistance.

"The New Zealand Rifle Brigade have proved to be our brothers in arms, and have shown once again how anxious they were to best our common enemy; they were as eager as indefatigable, and, thanks to them, the French Artillery will be ready to take its share in the battle at the very moment that the British superior authorities have settled.

"I feel deeply grieved by the casualties suffered by your men on account of the enemy's shelling (four killed and twelve wounded) and, as soon as we get the necessary information, the latter will be proposed for being mentioned in orders and receiving the Croix de Guerre.

"I also take pleasure in expressing to you the sincere thanks of the French First Artillery Corps."

On July 15th the Brigade returned to the Berquin Area, with Headquarters at Doulieu. The period from July 16th to 20th was spent in training. On the morning of the 21st a transport competition took place, and in the afternoon Brigade sports were held, the 4th Battalion carrying off the honours on points.

The Brigade marched to the old area near Messines on July 22nd, and became Divisional reserve. The 1st and 2nd Battalions were quartered at Canteen Corner Camp, the 3rd and 4th at De Seule and Bulford Camps, respectively, and Headquarters at Brune Gaye Camp. Here we remained until the end of the month, the units being engaged in training and in supplying parties for work under the Engineers of the Corps Troops. The transport of each battalion was in turn inspected by the Divisional Commander. The Brigade Demonstration Platoon, under Major J. R. Cowles, commenced a new term of work on the 29th. Artillery and aerial activity continued on both sides with great intensity throughout the period spent in reserve.

On July 30th General Anthoine visited the area and presented the Croix de Guerre to Lieut.-Cols. A. E. Stewart, W. S. Austin, and J. G. Roache. The ceremony was of a somewhat imposing nature, 400 of all ranks from the Brigade, under Major J. Pow, forming the guard of honour on the occasion. Major P. H. Bell, who had temporarily commanded the 3rd Battalion while serving with the French, and who was at this time in England on leave, received his decoration at a later date.

On the 22nd, General Fulton proceeded to England to take command of Sling Camp for a period of three months, and Lieut.-Col. Stewart assumed command of the Brigade pending the arrival of General F. E. Johnston, C.B. Lieut.-Col. Austin, from hospital, resumed command of the 1st Battalion on the 3rd; Lieut.-Col. Roache returned from leave on the 8th and took over the 4th Battalion; and Lieut.-Col. Winter-Evans resumed command of the 3rd Battalion on his return from leave on the 25th.

Although the Brigade had been out of the line for the whole of the month the casualties numbered 24, including five killed.

PART 3.—THE WARNETON SECTOR.

Into the line—Conditions—General Johnston killed—General Young wounded—Command—Out to reserve—General: weather; the trench-system completed; artillery and aeroplanes; casualties and sickness; command.

On August 2nd the 1st Battalion relieved the 2nd Otago Battalion in the front line opposite Warneton,* some two miles south-east of Messines, the left flank of the sub-sector being the River Douve. The main line of resistance was a continuous trench recently dug on part of the objective taken by the

*In the sector just south of us the 1st Brigade took La Basse Ville in the early morning of July 27th, but were driven back by a strong counter-attacking force. The position was, however, taken again on the 31st, and firmly held. The 4th Brigade, now permanently attached to the Division, still held the Frelinghien sector at the Lys.

2nd Brigade in the middle of June, with a series of disconnected forward posts from two to five hundred yards beyond. Battalion Headquarters were at Prowse Point in our old front line. On the same date Brigade Headquarters moved to English Farm.

The 3rd Battalion came into the line on August 4th, taking over from the 41st Australian Battalion the sub-sector north of the River Douve, with headquarters at Septieme Barn. The 2nd Battalion at the same time moved to Red Lodge, Hill 63, as support battalion, and the 4th to Kortepyp Camp as reserve.

At the time of taking over this Brigade sector the weather was wet and cold and the conditions generally were worse than those experienced on the Somme. Owing to the excessive shelling, especially on the left battalion area, which was on the forward slope of Messines Ridge, the communication-saps had been completely destroyed. The front-line trenches were for the most part thigh-deep in mud, devoid of duck-boards, and quite without shelter beyond the shallow little "cubbyholes" which had been excavated in the sides, and which possessed no other value than that they enabled those men who were not immediately on duty, and were endeavouring to snatch a little sleep, to get their legs out of the slimy mess. It would be interesting to have had from these men some expression of opinion regarding the fact, not then known to us, that Britain was piling up a huge debt to France, one that finally reached the sum of thirty million pounds, for such curious items as disturbance caused by British troops, dock dues, rent of houses and public buildings, and, most astonishing of all, rent of trenches!

General F. E. Johnston, while visiting the 3rd Battalion front during the early morning of August 7th, was killed by a sniper's bullet. Lieut.-Col. R. Young, from the 1st Canterbury Battalion, assumed command of the Brigade on the 8th, and on the following day narrowly escaped the fate of his predecessor, being dangerously wounded, again by an enemy sniper, whilst inspecting the same sector. Lieut.-Col. A. E. Stewart thereupon took over the Brigade, and on August 19th was formally appointed to the temporary command with the temporary rank of Colonel. Major J. Pow then assumed command of the 2nd Battalion.

A TRENCH IN THE WARNETON SECTOR.
Australian War Photo.

A COMPANY HEADQUARTERS IN THE FRONT LINE.
Face p. 224.

BRIGADIER-GENERAL
F. EARL JOHNSTON, C.B.

COLONEL (BRIG.-GEN.)
R. YOUNG,
C.B., C.M.G., D.S.O.

On the night of 8th/9th August the 2nd Battalion relieved the 1st in the right sub-sector, and two days later the 4th Battalion relieved the 3rd. Reliefs were effected again on the 14th and 15th. On account of enemy shelling and the difficulties of communication, the headquarters of both battalions were moved forward to old German "pill-boxes" on the River Douve near the Messines–La Basse Ville Road.

On the night of 22nd/23rd August we were relieved by a Brigade of the 4th Australian Division, the battalions moving back to their old camps at De Seule, and Brigade Headquarters to Brune Gaye Camp. Here the Brigade became temporary reserve to the Australian Division.

During the greater part of the period of our occupation of the Warneton Sector the weather conditions continued to be atrocious, and great difficulty was experienced in amending the deplorable state of the trenches. About the middle of the month the weather moderated, and the work thereafter progressed more rapidly, until, by the time we handed over to the Australians, we had connected the advanced posts into a good, continuous and well-wired front line, had greatly improved the communication-saps, and had made fair progress with a satisfactory drainage system. Other troops had been similarly active, and the efforts of the infantry, coupled with those of the pioneers, resulted in the completion by the Division, during the month of August, of a new trench system with a total of 20,000 yards of trenches and a full proportion of wiring.

Artillery and aerial activity were throughout unusually intense. In return for the enemy's incessant shelling of our trenches the heavy artillery carried out some excellent shoots on the town of Warneton; and the infantry were particularly interested in watching the rapid disclosure of German machine-gun towers as the shells of the buildings in which they had been constructed were blown away by our guns. A specially intense "dummy-raid" executed by artillery of all calibres, eventually brought about a considerable diminution of the enemy's shell-fire. The German fears of an attack on this occasion were revealed by the prolonged and magnificent display of coloured lights, and by the manner in which the enemy artillery responded, most of the hostile shelling falling along the Douve and between our lines of trenches, searching the hollows in which assemblies might be assumed to be taking place. German aeroplanes were more than ordinarily active in firing into our trenches and in bombing the roads in rear. Every morning at daybreak two enemy 'planes, painted brown and yellow, flew low along our front line. Despite our anti-aircraft shooting, from which they appeared to be immune, the pilots continued to display the utmost daring, and their visits were repeated with so much regularity and punctuality that they came to be known popularly as the "trench inspectors."

The casualties for the twenty-one days in the line were:—

	Killed.	Wounded.	Missing.
Officers	5	14	1
Other ranks	61	344	2

The officer reported as missing was Lieut. W. A. Gray, M.C., a 3rd Battalion leader who had shared in many a bold enterprise. While reconnoitring alone beyond his wiring-party in No Man's Land he encountered an enemy patrol, was severely wounded by a bomb, and captured.

Such was the condition of the weather and the state of the trenches that our sick-rate rose to 26 per cent. Lieut.-Col. Winter-Evans, 3rd Battalion, was evacuated sick on the 16th, but returned to duty on the 23rd, Major Bell assuming command in the interim. On the 17th Lieut.-Col. J. G. Roache, D.S.O.,* 4th Battalion, was similarly evacuated, his place being taken by Major Puttick. A third commanding officer, Lieut.-Col. Austin, went out through illness on the 26th, Major Bell then taking over command of the 1st Battalion.

*Lieut.-Col. Roache did not recover sufficiently to return to his unit, but from November, 1917, until May of the following year he commanded the New Zealand Rifle Brigade Reserve Depot at Brocton, and was finally invalided home.

CHAPTER X.
THE THIRD BATTLE OF YPRES.

PART 1.—DIGGING IN THE YPRES SALIENT.
First period—Appreciation—Second period—Appreciation—Condition of the troops.

After the exhausting tour in the trenches of the Warneton Sector, the Brigade rested in the camps in the neighbourhood of De Seule until the 27th August, on which date a move was made to the Waterlands-La Creche Area, north of Steenwerck, where we became reserve Brigade to the New Zealand Division. On the 30th a further move was made to the Borre Training Area, near Hazebrouck, the 1st Battalion being quartered at Caestre, Brigade Headquarters and the 2nd Battalion at Borre, the 3rd at La Creche, and the 4th at Pradelles. By this time the men, whose cheerfulness had never entirely deserted them, were beginning to regain their wonted appearance of physical fitness, and were looking forward to a comparatively enjoyable period of training. Their hopes, however, were doomed to disappointment, for a long month's digging under fire, and mostly by night, was about to commence.

On September 1st, the 2nd and 4th Battalions moved by motor-'bus to the Xth Corps Area to bury cable for the Second Army in the vicinity of Zillebeke, south-east of Ypres, going under canvas at Ridgewood Camp, near Dickebusch Lake. Three days later the 1st and 3rd Battalions went by 'bus to the 25th Divisional Area near Ypres, for cable-burying under the Director of Signals, 1st Anzac Corps. These battalions went into camp, the 1st at Chateau Segard, and the 3rd at Swan Chateau, and were employed laying cables between Hooge and Ypres.

The 2nd and 4th Battalions returned from the Xth Corps Area on September 16th, moving from Ouderdom to Caestre by rail, and thence by road to billets in the Vieux Berquin Area, the 2nd Battalion at Stein-Je and the 4th near Doulieu. They were followed on the 19th by the 1st and 3rd Battalions, the former going into billets at Vieux Berquin, and the latter at Outtersteene.

As continuous work at digging hardly tends to the maintenance of general military efficiency, that "little leaven," the Brigade School, continued in operation. Remaining with Brigade Headquarters at Vieux Berquin and later at Brandhoek, it commenced a new term under Capt. D. C. Bowler, and through it small drafts from the battalions, generally the less fit men, were passed from time to time.

The following letters of appreciation and thanks were received and their contents communicated to the troops of the Brigade:—

From the G.O.C., Xth Corps:

"It is difficult for me adequately to express to you my gratitude for the splendid work of the 1st, 2nd, 3rd and 4th Battalions, New Zealand (Rifle) Brigade, and the IInd Anzac Cyclists, in burying cable on my Corps front during the last three weeks. Their achievement in digging over 13,000 yards of cable-trench, laying the cable, and banking it from three to four feet, is an extraordinary one. The keenness they displayed is universally admired, and their skill is acknowledged to be an example to any troops. Will you please tell these gallant men how much, while I deplore the casualties they suffered, I appreciate both their valuable work and their soldierly spirit."

From the Second Army Commander:—

"The Army Commander wishes to place on record his appreciation of the work done by the 3rd New Zealand (Rifle) Brigade in burying cable to assist in yesterday's operations.* The success of the operations was in great measure due to the good communications established, to attain which results the 3rd New Zealand (Rifle) Brigade played such an important part."

After a short rest the Brigade resumed its arduous labours in the Ypres Salient. On September 21st the 2nd and 4th Battalions moved up again by motor-'bus, the former being attached to the Xth Corps Signals, and going into camp near Dickebusch Lake; the latter, working for the Ist Anzac Corps, being quartered in a camp close to Ypres. On September 26th the 1st and 3rd Battalions went up by road and rail via

*20th Sept. See page 233.

Bailleul and Poperinghe. They occupied bivouac camps, the 1st at Watou Camp, the 3rd at Hill 55, and were employed burying cable for the IInd Anzac Corps in the Vth Corps Area in the vicinity of Ypres. From the 2nd of October, the 2nd and 4th Battalions were employed with the IInd Anzac Corps, the former constructing gun-emplacements for the heavy artillery, the latter being engaged at road-making. The work went on steadily until October 7th, on which date we were relieved of this duty by the 1st Brigade and commenced preparations for active operations in the line.

In addition to miscellaneous work, the four battalions had within the whole period laid 50,000 yards of cable seven feet deep, and 10,000 yards three and a half feet deep, and had thrown up 30,000 yards of banking three to six feet high. All the cable used had to be carried by the men for an average distance of a mile.

The following communications were now received and passed down:—

From A. D. Signals,
    to Headquarters, Ist Anzac Corps:
    "I should like to bring to the notice of the Corps Commander the splendid work accomplished by the battalions of the New Zealand Rifle Brigade during the time they have been employed in burying cable for this Corps. . . . . All battalions have had an exceptionally heavy task to perform, and have got through the digging at what must have constituted a record pace. The work has frequently had to be carried on under heavy shell-fire, but the completion of each day's or night's task has never failed.

    "I am particularly indebted to the commanding officers and other officers of the battalions for the great personal interest they have taken in the work, especially as regards the preliminary reconnaissance of the routes to be dug. These officers have always surveyed the routes themselves in daylight, in addition to going up with the working parties at night, and have thus given the greatest possible assistance to the Signal Officers responsible for the construction of the lines. I much regret the casualties these battalions have suffered during the time they have been working for this Corps."

From Lieut.-General Birdwood, Commanding Ist Anzac Corps,
    to Headquarters, IInd Anzac Corps:
    "In forwarding to you the enclosed memorandum by the A. D. Signals of this Corps, I would like to express my grati-

tude for the invaluable services of the battalions of the New Zealand Rifle Brigade, and my admiration of their gallantry and devotion to duty."

It would be idle to pretend that the prospect of an engagement within a few days could be regarded with absolute equanimity. Battalion commanders knew only too well how much their men were in need of both rest and training. After the three weeks spent in the Warneton Sector under appalling conditions they had had a few days' respite; but since September 4th they had been almost continuously employed at the trying and wearing work of cable-burying and road-making, well up in the Ypres Salient. These duties had entailed long marches over difficult shell-hole country; and most of the work had been done at night, and sometimes in gas-masks under shell-fire. Exactly 200 casualties had been sustained. The weather, at first fair, became bitterly cold, and as the men had neither blankets nor warm underclothing, they had got little sleep. Throughout the period they had literally slaved at their tasks, and now they were almost worn out and certainly unready for immediate combative action.

It was expected that we should be taking part in the final assault on the Passchendaele Ridge on the 12th, following upon the capture of Bellevue Spur, which formed part of the general objective of a preliminary attack to be launched on the 9th. That would give little enough time for preparation and still less for reconnoitring, but in the sequel the conditions were to prove much more difficult than those now anticipated.

PART 2.—PROGRESS OF THE BRITISH OFFENSIVE OPERATIONS.

Opening of the summer campaign—First phase, July 31st—Second phase, August 16th—Third phase, September 20th—New Zealand Division at Gravenstafel, October 4th—Attack continued, October 9th.

It will be remembered that Sir Douglas Haig's plan of operations for 1917 comprised a spring campaign against the Ancre–Scarpe Salient and the Vimy Ridge, to be followed by a great blow on the Flanders front in the summer and autumn. The latter thrust was to be carried out by Gough's Fifth Army, supported on the right by the Second Army under Plumer, and on the left by the First French Army under Anthoine. Its object was to secure the high ground stretching north-east from Wytschaete to the Ypres-Menin Road, and thence past Passchendaele to Staden on the Ypres-Thourout-Bruges Railway. The capture of this rising ground would pave the way for a later advance on Roulers and Ghent, thus menacing the enemy's positions towards Lille and south of it, and possibly also turning his right and forcing him to give up Ostend and Zeebrugge.

We have seen that the spring operations were successful, and that the Battle of Messines had resulted in the capture of the Messines-Wytschaete Ridge, a necessary preliminary to the major attack towards the north-east.

The summer campaign proved to be a long and bloody struggle. Opening on July 31st, 1917, it continued almost without interruption till the end of the first week in November, and is officially known as the Third Battle of Ypres.

In the first phase of the battle the Fifth Army attacked on a frontage of over seven miles from the Zillebeke-Zandvoorde Road to Boesinghe, but the subsidiary attack by the Second Army on the right, together with the covering movement of the French on the left, extended the frontage from the Lys River opposite Deulemont northwards to beyond Steenstraat, a total distance of more than fifteen miles. The general objective was the crest of the high ground east of Ypres.

On July 31st, the first day of the battle, the most stubborn fighting took place in the vicinity of the Ypres-Menin Road where it crosses the crest of the Wytschaete-Passchendaele Ridge, this being the key to the enemy's position. Nevertheless the British troops pressed steadily forward through Shrewsbury Forest and Sanctuary Wood and captured Stirling Castle, Hooge and the Bellewarde Ridge. The railwaybank running towards Roulers, as well as the western outskirts of Westhoek, was also taken, but on the morning of August 1st the enemy was still clinging to Clapham Junction, Inverness Copse and part of Westhoek. Farther north the British advanced with greater ease, securing the Steenebeek ahead of Pilkem, and taking Alberta Farm, St. Julien, Pommern Redoubt and Pommern Castle. The French on the left, keeping step with our advance, took Bixschoote and Kortekeen Inn. The Second Army on the right had also progressed well in spite of fierce resistance, Hollebeke being secured by English troops, and La Basse Ville by the 2nd Wellington Battalion of the New Zealand Division after a brilliantly-conducted fight.

Unfortunately, heavy rain came on during the afternoon, and continued for several days without cessation, and this, owing to the boggy nature of the soil, brought the first phase of the Third Battle of Ypres to a close. The results, however, were so far quite satisfactory, the most important being the capture of the whole of the ridge that had for so long overlooked the British positions in the Ypres plain.

The second phase opened on August 16th, on a front extending from the north-west corner of Inverness Copse to the junction with the French south of St. Janshoek. The French were to co-operate by taking the Bixschoote Peninsula, a tongue of slightly-rising ground almost surrounded by an extensive flooded area. In this our Allies were entirely successful, and on our own left the British captured Langemarck, but elsewhere little progress could be made against the concrete forts situated in the midst of seas of mud, and protected by the swollen Hanebeek and Zonnebeke streams. It was evident that the enemy was tenaciously clinging to Nonne Boschen, Polygon, Glencorse and Inverness Woods, in order to safeguard Passchendaele Ridge, and though the British penetrated as far as the Racecourse in Polygon Wood they were unable to make good their hold at this point. Once again bad weather came on and, continuing for the remainder of the wettest August that had been known for many years, brought about a compulsory termination of the second phase of the great battle.

In making preparations for the third attack, due consideration was given to the stubborn resistance that was being maintained by the enemy on the extreme right of the Fifth Army front, and it was decided to extend the left of the Second Army northwards, the attack on the high ground crossed by the Menin Road being entrusted to General Plumer as a self-contained operation in conjunction with the advance of the Fifth Army farther north.

The weather conditions had so far improved, and the necessary rearrangements and preparations were so well advanced, as to permit of the reopening of the battle on September 20th. Ill-luck, however, still followed us, for it rained steadily throughout the night of 19th/20th, but nevertheless the attack went well. On the Second Army front the woods north of the Ypres–Comines Canal, the Tower Hamlets Spur, Inverness Copse and Veldhoek were taken. Australian troops captured Glencorse Wood and Nonne Boschen, the hamlet of Polygonveld, Black Watch Corner, and the western portion of Polygon Wood. On the front of the Fifth Army our troops captured Zonnebeke, Bremen Redoubt, and Zevenkote, and everywhere gained their objectives. During this and the following days the enemy launched an unusually large number of counter-attacks, but with the exception of temporary successes at isolated points they were repulsed with great loss.

A renewal of the advance of the Second and Fifth Armies commenced on the morning of September 26th. Australian troops carried the remainder of Polygon Wood and established themselves beyond the Becelaere–Zonnebeke Road; and British battalions captured Zonnebeke village and church, as well as strong points on both sides of the Wieltje–Gravenstafel Road. Fierce and repeated counter-attacks along the whole line of our new positions engaged attention until October 4th, when the advance was once more renewed, again in rain, after a spell of fine weather. The frontage of the attack extended some eight miles from a mile south of the Menin Road to the Ypres–Staden Railway. Reutel, Joist Farm and Noordemdhoek were captured by British regiments. Australian troops stormed Molenaarelsthoek and Broodseinde, and established themselves well to the east of the crest. The 1st and 4th Brigades of the New Zealand Division carried Gravenstafel, swept the enemy from a network of trenches and strong points on the Gravenstafel Spur, and took 1,200 prisoners from no fewer than four different Divisions. It transpired that in addition to the two German Divisions already in line in this sector, the enemy had brought up three fresh Divisions for the purpose of making an attack in strength, but our own assault anticipated his intended attack by ten minutes.

The weather continued bad, and the ground was in a deplorable condition; but balanced against this were the symptoms of confusion and discouragement in the ranks of the enemy, and the necessity of continuing operations in order to hold his reserves on this front with a view to assisting the French in their attack in the neighbourhood of Malmaison on the 23rd. It was therefore decided to deliver the next combined French and British attack on October 9th.

Notwithstanding heavy rain on the 7th and 8th, the advance commenced at 5.20 a.m. on October 9th as planned. French and British troops captured Koekuit, Veldhoek, Mangelaere, and St. Janshoek, and established themselves on their final objectives on the outskirts of Houthulst Forest. The British troops on the left were successful in taking Poelcappelle, and on the extreme right retook Reutel and captured Judge Cottage, though they could make no headway against Polderhoek Chateau, a formidable strong-point upon which, some two months later, the New Zealand troops were to try their skill with little better result.

Opposite Passchendaele the success achieved fell far short of expectations. Here the 66th and 49th Divisions operated, their section of the objective being the high ground on both sides of the Ravebeek, including Bellevue Spur. The troops of the 66th progressed satisfactorily, their advance being carried well beyond Keerselaarhoek, but the 49th on their left got no further than the first objective. The 66th, being thus exposed, were enfiladed from Bellevue, and had to fall back to a line in prolongation of that reached by the 49th. This was some 500 yards in advance of the jumping-off positions and ran roughly from the Ravebeek, through Marsh Bottom, Peter Pan, and Yetta Houses, joining up near Adler Farm with the line of the Corps on the left, where progress had been no more extensive.

PART 3.—PASSCHENDAELE, OCTOBER 12TH.

Attack to be continued, October 12th—General objective—New Zealanders and Australians put in—2nd Brigade and the New Zealand Rifle Brigade detailed for the attack—Brigade objectives—Concentration—Into assembly positions—Attack opens—An early check—Wire, concrete forts, and machine-guns—Stubborn fighting—4th Battalion troops reinforce—3rd Battalion companies come up—Line stationary except on the left—Consolidation ordered—1st Battalion up to support—Position—Situation on the flanks—Counter-attack—General conclusions—Stretcher-bearers and wounded in the bogs of Passchendaele—Casualties—Brigade Pack Train.

Prior to the action of the 9th, plans had been drawn up for a general attack on the 12th, which again was to extend from the Ypres–Roulers railway to Houthulst Forest. These plans, with such modifications as the new situation demanded, were now adhered to, and accordingly the relief of the 66th and 49th Divisions by the 3rd Australians and the New Zealanders commenced on the 10th. The New Zealand Division took over the left sector, and was thus on the extreme left of the Second Army. On its left it had the 9th Division of the XVIIIth Corps, Fifth Army.

The southern boundary line of the sector over which the Division was to advance passed some 500 yards north-west of Passchendaele Church, and the final objective was about 2,500 yards from our front line posts. Thus the capture of the village itself was included in the task set the 3rd Australians, while the main objective of the New Zealanders was the spur about Goudberg.

The 2nd Brigade and the New Zealand Rifle Brigade were detailed to carry out the attack opposite our Divisional front, the former on the right and the latter on the left.

In our own Brigade sector the capture of the successive lines, the Red, the Blue, and the Green, was allotted to the 2nd, 3rd, and 1st Battalions, respectively, and the attack was to be carried out on the "leap-frog" system. The 4th Battalion was to follow in rear of each battalion in succession, rendering assistance in the advance where necessary, and forming defensive flanks where these should be required.* On our

---

*In command of battalions on October 12th:—1st Battalion, Major P. H. Bell; 2nd, Capt. W. G. Bishop, vice Lieut.-Col. Pow, at transport lines (injured); 3rd, Lieut.-Col. A. Winter-Evans; 4th, Lieut.-Col. E. Puttick.

left the Black Watch were to advance with us to the first objective, the Seaforth Highlanders to the second, and the 6th Royal Scots to the third. The corresponding units on our right were 2nd Otago, 1st Otago, and 1st Canterbury.

During the morning of October 9th, in miserably wet and cold weather, the Brigade concentrated at "X" Camp, near St. Jean, north-east of Ypres. The Brigadier, in company with his Brigade Major and the four battalion commanders, went up to the 146th Brigade Headquarters at Gallipoli for information, and then reconnoitred the front line to be taken over. It was now learned that in the recent operations the 146th Brigade had not been able to reach the first objective. The ground conditions were awful beyond description, enemy machine-guns and snipers kept up a continuous fire on the forward positions, and the troops in the line were completely exhausted.

From the camp at St. Jean, where they had been subjected to shelling and bombing, especially during and after the action of the 9th, the battalions of the Brigade moved up on the evening of the 10th to the relief of the troops of the 146th Brigade. This in itself was no easy undertaking. The 4th Battalion, which had been detailed to hold the front line posts, had to march over five miles before reaching its destination, and the latter·part of the march, carried out in pitch darkness, was an ordeal of the utmost difficulty, for there were neither tracks nor "duck-walks," and shell-holes and mud seemed to cover the face of the earth. Lieut.-Col. Puttick personally taped routes as far as that could be done under the conditions prevailing, but at the most optimistic estimate he did not expect to get more than three-fourths of his men into position before daybreak. The companies, however, completed their movements by means of compass-bearings carefully prepared and checked beforehand, and so satisfactorily, in the circumstances, was direction maintained that the front line of posts and shell-holes was sufficiently secure by 1 a.m. on the 11th, though the adjustment of the dispositions could not be completed until the evening. As an indication of the general confusion that reigned in the sector, it is sufficient to mention that the 4th Battalion took over from troops of no fewer than six different units. In order to allow for the opening barrage of the 12th, the line finally held was placed slightly in rear of that taken over. On the whole the shelling on the forward area during the relief was not severe, but one of the 4th Battalion companies had several casualties from shell-fire on the way up. Following upon a reconnaissance of the front line by low-flying aeroplanes on the following afternoon the enemy's artillery registered on the position.

The remainder of the Brigade was disposed in depth, the rearmost battalion being over 2,000 yards from the front line. The move was completed by 6 a.m. on the 11th, and then ensued the long wait of twelve hours of daylight in such cover as could be afforded by the nature of the shell-hole positions occupied. To our weary men the prospect generally was not cheering. The shell-holes were water-logged, the weather cold, and the sky grey and threatening. Out in the open, especially in the forward area, many British wounded lay where they had fallen on the 9th, while at the aid posts were others still awaiting evacuation. Such attention as could in the circumstances be given to these unfortunate men was cheerfully rendered, our stretcher-bearers and volunteers dressing their wounds, providing them with food and water from their own rations, and, where it was impossible to pass them to the rear, placing them in less exposed positions in the shell-holes. Yet amidst all this discomfort the morale of the men remained distinctly good, though their spirits, as may easily be conceived, could not be said to have reached that high state of buoyancy which had marked their entry upon previous engagements.

During the afternoon of the 11th Brigade Headquarters moved forward from Gallipoli to an old German pill-box at Korek, just north of Gravenstafel, and at 5 o'clock next morning reports were in from all four battalions that they had reached their appointed assembly positions. As if to accentuate the hardships already sufficiently great, rain had come on at 2 a.m.

Promptly at zero hour, 5.25 a.m., the opening barrage commenced, and the 2nd Battalion moved forward towards the first objective. Within fifteen minutes it became abundantly evident that the barrage, so pitifully weak as to be barely perceptible, would be quite ineffective. It had no appreciable effect upon the German machine-guns, for these, operating for the most part from concrete "pill-boxes," immediately opened a fierce and withering fire which continued without abatement, and even increased in intensity at times, in spite of all our artillery could do. The enemy's artillery barrage was thin, and consisted almost entirely of high-explosive shell, the effect of which was to a great extent nullified by the softness of the sodden ground. Though it caused casualties amongst both the troops attacking and also those coming forward from the rear, it was nowhere as serious as it might have been had shrapnel been used in the same proportion by the German artillery as by our own. The enemy's reliance on his machine-gun barrage, however, was not misplaced, for here was a perfect example of the use of machine-guns in the defence, an intense and deadly grazing cross-fire sweeping the front of both the New Zealand Brigades.

The leading elements of the 2nd Battalion faced this without flinching, but the men fell fast. Though checked here and there by strong-posts the sections still pressed on, and, gathering impetus from the rear waves, they struggled up the muddy slopes. Wire entanglements became thicker and machine-gun pockets more numerous as the advance proceeded. Resolution and individual acts of daring, such as that of Company Sergeant-Major W. Voyle, who, moving forward alone at the head of his platoon, attacked a strongly-placed machine-gun post, killed two and captured three of the crew with their gun, and a similar exploit by Corporal A. Monkman, could avail but little against the fearful conditions prevailing, and progress became painfully slow. On the extreme right it soon ceased altogether, for here a valley ran forward, swampy and open, and so well commanded by the enemy that movement along it was impossible. The effect of this obstacle was to cause the 2nd Battalion to close in to the left in the hope of passing round by Wolf Farm and so gaining the high ground at the head of the valley. The troops of the 2nd Brigade, from whom we were now separated by a gap of nearly 400 yards, could be seen engaged in a determined attack on an enemy stronghold opposite their left flank and about 500 yards short of the first objective. Fire directed from this quarter at short range was one of the main causes of our own slow advance, and it was hoped that a successful assault here would result in more

ORDER OF BATTLE—PASSCHENDAELE, OCTOBER 12, 1917.

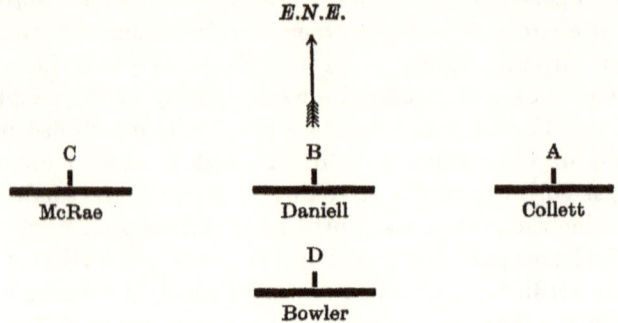

For 1st Obj. **2nd BN.** Bishop

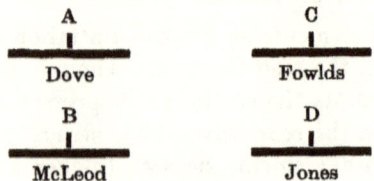

Bde. Res. **4th BN.** Puttick
(To follow each Bn.)

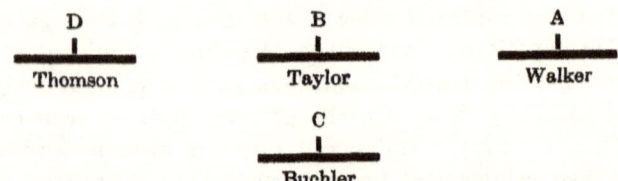

For 2nd Obj. **3rd BN.** Winter-Evans

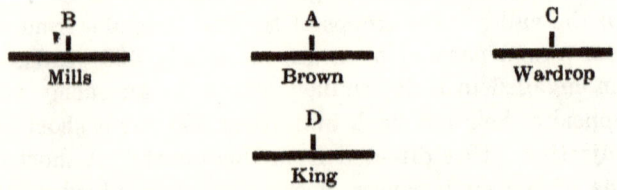

For 3rd Obj. **1st BN.** Bell

rapid progress along the whole line. The point so attacked was part of the main defences of Bellevue, and formed a section of the exceedingly strong line running north and south across the spur and protecting Passchendaele on the west. Lieut.-Col. Puttick detached two platoons, under Lieut. W. F. Fowlds, from "D" Company of his battalion, to cover the gap and to support the 2nd Brigade men with covering fire, but the position proved to be impregnable. In the great fields of wire the attackers were mown down by machine-gun fire, and the attempt failed in its main object. On our side of the spur, however, Sergeant H. M. Duston, now commanding the survivors of a 2nd Battalion company that had lost all its officers, succeeded in establishing a post with twenty men and a Lewis gun on the outskirts of Wolf Copse, thus rendering the holding of the gap practically secure.

In the meantime, the main advance of the 2nd Battalion troops was becoming more and more difficult, and presently they were directly confronted by a line of German concrete "pill-boxes," heavily wired, surrounded by a sea of mud, and strongly manned. Beyond these, again, and on slightly higher ground, stood other concrete fortresses, and the grazing fire coming from this frontal position some 500 yards ahead, as well as enfilade fire from Bellevue on the right and from Source Trench well off on the left front, was now so intense and well-directed that the general forward movement practically ceased. The centre of the line had suffered most heavily, and in consequence the left had swung up towards the Wallemolen Cemetery.

By this time the 3rd Battalion had come up, and the 1st was awaiting its turn to move. At 6.30 a.m. the leading troops of the 3rd had begun to pass through the rear companies of the 4th, but coming soon after within the zone of the machine-gun fire deluging the troops of the 2nd Battalion, they realized all too surely that the expected capture of the first objective had not been accomplished. Maintaining perfect order, they pressed on with all speed, yet, in view of the uncertainty as to what lay before them, with due circumspection and care. Advantage was taken of the little cover afforded by shell-holes, and finally, by successive bounds, the irregular line of the 2nd Battalion was reached. Efforts were at once made to carry

BOGGED IN THE PASSCHENDAELE MUD.

A PASSCHENDAELE "PILL-BOX."

Face p. 240.

LIEUT.-COL. E. PUTTICK,
D.S.O.

LIEUT.-COL. P. H. BELL,
D.S.O.

Major W. G. Bishop.

German Prisoners Carrying Wounded.

THE RUNNER SETS OUT.

SIGNALLERS LAYING TELEPHONE WIRE.

on the advance, but not all the added strength derived from the arrival of comparatively fresh troops could prevail against the deadly hail of bullets by which the line was swept. Some temporary improvement was made on the left. Lieut. F. J. L. Buchler, a 3rd Battalion company commander, pushed round the left of the Cemetery with a party of his men and succeeded in gaining a position well in advance. Here he was in touch with the Scottish troops, but presently the latter recoiled under the fierce fire from Source Trench, and Buchler and his men, now isolated and in danger of being cut off, had finally to give way and work back to the Cemetery. Elsewhere attempts, notably those by Company Sergt.-Majors F. W. H. Shepherd and C. A. Spriggs, and Sergeants L. F. Allan and T. A. Goodfellow, were made to establish advanced shell-hole posts and link them up, but these gallant endeavours resulted in no permanent advantage.

By 8 a.m. all three forward battalions were engaged, for, in addition to the two platoons of the 4th Battalion put in to cover the gap on the right, the two leading companies of this unit had, when the first serious check took place, each sent a platoon round the flank in order to help the line on, and the left of these companies had also pushed up a platoon to establish connection with the Black Watch. The line, however, still remained practically stationary except on the extreme left. Here Sergeant A. K. Coley, leading a composite platoon of men from the 2nd, 3rd and 4th Battalions, carried out a brilliant assault on an enemy strong-point still holding out in the Cemetery. Twenty-five of the garrison were killed, and three prisoners and four machine-guns captured. In this sharp fight Sergeant H. J. Langwell and Corporal J. Calderwood led their sections with great dash and skill. The whole of Calderwood's section became casualties, but, though he himself was wounded, he gathered a few more men from neighbouring shell-holes, and with this handful continued to assist till the position was won. The taking of the last strong-point in the Cemetery enabled some further general progress to be made in this quarter, and the position became of considerable importance in connection with the consolidation of the line finally held.

It was now becoming abundantly evident that our troops

were being brought to a standstill. The casualties, which included practically the whole of the 3rd Battalion Headquarters, had been extremely heavy, and many of the companies and most of the platoons were without officers. The men of three units were inextricably intermingled, and even some of the Scottish troops found themselves scattered amongst our sections. All ranks were drenched to the skin and plastered with shell-hole slime from head to foot; a large proportion of the rifles and Lewis guns were choked with mud; and, taking advantage of the decrease in the volume of our fire, the enemy was rapidly reinforcing his forward line and even placing machine-guns on the top of his "pill-boxes." To Lieut.-Col. Puttick, who made a personal reconnaissance of the position soon after 8 o'clock, the definiteness of the check and the utter futility of attempting to make further gains at once became apparent, and, being the senior officer on the spot, he ordered a cessation of the attack and gave instructions for the consolidation of the position secured. This consisted in the main of an old German trench on the farther side of the road running south-east from the Cemetery to a point slightly beyond Wolf Farm, with a few small groups of men in shell-holes about 100 yards in advance of the general line. It was thus roughly parallel to the main band of wire crossing Bellevue Spur, the lesser entanglements having been passed.

A situation report was sent to Brigade Headquarters and also to the 1st Battalion, the latter being now on its way up from its assembly position, which, in accordance with the timetable for the day's action, it had left at 8 a.m., and it was suggested that this battalion on its arrival should take up a support position in rear of the road. One of the German machine-guns captured at the Cemetery was posted on the left of the forward line covering the Brigade front, while a second was sent round to the right flank near Peter Pan to strengthen the command of the gap between us and the 2nd Brigade. At about 10 a.m. the 1st Battalion came up, and, after obtaining further information and reconnoitring the position, Lieut.-Col. Bell established a support line about 150 yards in rear of the front line, and also a strong-post with eighteen men and four Lewis guns on the right of the main position, some 200 yards east of Peter Pan.

The position now was that a more or less defined line was held, on the left 500 yards and on the right 200 yards from our original line. Practically all the advanced posts had ceased to exist, their garrisons having been withdrawn or else swept away by the withering fire. Both flanks were well held by 4th Battalion platoons placed so as to establish touch with neighbouring Brigades or to form defensive flanks. Some platoons of the 4th Battalion were in close support, while the 1st Battalion was holding a main support position, with a reserve company in readiness to move to any point. On the left we were in close touch with the Black Watch, whose commanding officer specially reported on the fearless reconnaissance work of Corporal A. McDonald of our 2nd Battalion, then on liaison duty with him. It appears that two companies of the Black Watch commencing the attack side by side had lost touch, and though both had been held up, neither knew the position of the other. Information to this effect had reached the battalion commander, and McDonald volunteered to go out to locate the companies. He conducted a perilous search in the face of our own and the enemy's fire, but succeeded at last in reaching the separated flanks in succession. He then assisted the companies to establish touch, and when this had been completed made his way back through the storm of bullets, bringing to the Black Watch headquarters a detailed report as to the situation on this part of their front.

Soon after 9 a.m. the German artillery ranged fairly accurately on the new line, and kept up an intermittent fire upon it from that time onward. The enemy machine-gun fire now decreased in volume, but any movement on our part immediately drew heavy bursts from the many commanding positions above.

The situation on our immediate flanks was no more satisfactory than with us. The 2nd Brigade's jumping-off line had been closer up to the enemy's main defensive line than ours had been, and their advance had brought them up at once against the heavy belts of wire, here, as elsewhere, broad and intact, and covered by the machine-gun positions on all the vantage-points of the slopes beyond. Further progress was found to be impossible. On the left flank, where our advance had been least unsatisfactory, the Black Watch had made a correspondingly deeper thrust, but here, as we have seen, they were no more than in touch with us.

Reports had come in, however, to the effect that farther off on the left the troops of the same Brigade had reached a position in the vicinity of their final objective, and that the Australians beyond the right flank of the New Zealand Division had also progressed well. The New Zealanders were therefore instructed to renew the attack at 3 p.m., and at one o'clock our battalion commanders were called to a conference at Kronprinz Farm. These, with their first-hand knowledge of the situation, were unanimous in their opinion as to the fruitlessness of any immediate attempt to get forward, but the orders were definite, and it was for them to carry those orders into execution to the best of their ability. By the time they had returned to their commands only half an hour remained to issue the necessary instructions. Preparatory reorganization was out of the question. Even if there had been time for this no general movement was possible, and it was arranged that the dispositions should be effected as well as might be when our barrage opened, and completed during the advance itself. At the last moment, in consequence of later reports that the general advance had been successful only on certain isolated sectors, the orders for the renewal of the attack were countermanded, and instructions were issued for holding the line.

Soon after 3 p.m. an enemy attack developed on the left flank, but this, after we had had the number of our casualties greatly increased, was driven off. Rifleman C. E. Town with his Lewis gun, and the trench mortar section under Corporal H. S. Leighton, rendered conspicuous service in this emergency. It would seem from the statements of two Germans who gave themselves up to a 4th Battalion post on the right at 7 p.m., that this attack was part of a general counter-stroke, but that for the most part their men had refused to advance in the face of the barrage, now much more effective than that of the early hours of the day, which our artillery, owing to the non-receipt of cancellation orders, had put down to cover the afternoon's attack.

After dark the adjustments required were carried out. The 3rd and 4th Battalions were withdrawn to support and reserve, respectively, and the 1st and 2nd, now occupying the forward positions gained, continued the work of consolidation.

We had come so far short of achieving our object that the attack of October 12th must be considered a failure. The direct cause of the frustration of our efforts was the presence, along the whole of the enemy front, of the exceedingly strong band, or, rather, field of wire, the existence and nature of which had not been known until the evening of the 11th, after the Division had taken over the line, it having been left to our own patrols to make the discovery. The difficulties experienced by the artillery brigades in bringing forward the batteries, though all concerned had laboured with the utmost devotion and self-sacrifice, had in most cases proved to be insuperable. The result was that a large proportion of the guns never reached their positions. Again, for many of the pieces solid platforms could not be provided, and on being fired they rapidly sank into the oozy ground and became for the time being useless. Hence the advance of the infantry was insufficiently supported, but even in the face of this disadvantage we should doubtless have won through if the wire had been dealt with. It is true that von Arnim's system of strengthening the defence by means of concealed "pill-boxes" had by now reached the last stage of perfection, and that the concrete fortresses on the Passchendaele slopes had been most skilfully sited; but positions of this nature, as we proved often enough, are not necessarily impregnable provided the infantry are able to attack them at close quarters, especially if this can be done within a reasonable time after the heavy artillery has played its part.

The failure of the attack of three days earlier had been disastrous, and now we in our turn had failed; but though downcast we were still unashamed, for surely to the New Zealanders might be applied the words of Sir Douglas Haig concerning certain earlier operations: "There was no position which the Germans chose to hold and fortify which our men could not take, even by frontal attack, when the guns had exercised their full power in the preparatory stages of the battle."

Owing to the wet weather, the broken nature of the country, and the almost entire absence of duck-board tracks, the evacuation of the wounded was a serious matter, six, and sometimes eight men being required to bring out one stretcher-case; and as the task usually took six hours to accomplish, the bearers were exhausted after one journey, and rest was imperative. As an indication of the state of the country over which these duties, sufficiently difficult even where properly-formed tracks exist, had to be performed, it may be mentioned that Riflemen W. C. Turner and M. Hennessy were specially reported upon as having, while still under fire, rescued wounded men from drowning in the shell-holes. If ever the devoted stretcher-bearers were worthy of thanks and praise, it was doubly so on the sodden field of Passchendaele, and with others Riflemen J. L. Keogh, F. K. Judd, B. Booker, F. A. Clark, F. Backholm, S. G. Stirling, D. Stevenson, F. Smith, H. F. Orpwood, F. A. Meurant and C. J. Arnold are gratefully remembered for their devotion to duty through the long dreary days and nights from the 11th to the 14th; while the bearers as well as the wounded owe much to the personal efforts of the Revd. H. Clark, Chaplain to the 2nd Battalion, who with the utmost gallantry laboured untiringly amongst them in all parts of the field. To add to our difficulties, large numbers of wounded men of the Division that had been engaged in the fighting of the 9th were still in the lines and in the regimental aid-posts. So serious, indeed, had the congestion at the aid-post at Kronprinz Farm become that early in the day word had to be sent to the advanced troops that the wounded would be safer for the time being if placed behind any sort of cover in the forward area. At one time there were as many as sixty cases, English, German and Colonial, at this one post, and as the dugout, an old German "pill-box," could hold only a comparatively small number, the rest had perforce to be laid in the open. Amongst the wounded here, now within and now without, the medical officers of the 1st and 2nd Battalions, Captains R. H. Baxter and P. B. Benham, slaved unceasingly, caring naught on their own behalf for the cold, driving rain and frequent shelling from which they were powerless to protect so many of their helpless charges.

Twelve hundred men of the 4th Brigade were employed on stretcher-bearer work in the Divisional sector during the night of the 12th/13th, besides a battalion of the 147th Brigade lent to the Division for the purpose. Even parties of the Artillery and the A.S.C. were brought up on this duty. During the 14th an informal truce existed between the British and the Germans, parties from both sides scouring No Man's Land in search of their wounded, and by the afternoon of this day all cases had been brought in.

The casualties sustained by the Brigade were 22 officers and 160 men killed, 25 officers and 873 men wounded, and 1 officer and 133 men missing.

The 3rd Battalion mourned the loss of their commander, who had been struck down early on the morning of the 12th. Lieut.-Col. A. Winter-Evans had come with the unit from New Zealand, and had led his men in all the main engagements in which the Brigade as a whole had taken part. His remarkable genius for organization was only equalled by his extraordinary gallantry under fire. In connection with the Battle of Messines, his plans for training, assembly and attack were not less notable for their minute attention to detail than for the remarkable precision which characterized their execution. When his battalion's objective had been taken on that day he was amongst his men as they laboured at the task of consolidation, and heedless of the bombardment he moved along the parapet of the trench directing and cheering them on. In like manner, at Passchendaele, as soon as it appeared that the check was more than temporary he had gone ahead to endeavour by direct personal efforts to get his troops forward, but moving from shell-hole to shell-hole amongst the scattered groups, he drew upon himself the inevitable bursts of machine-gun fire, under which, fearlessly persisting, he at last fell mortally wounded.

Mention should be made of the fact that supplies of water, rations and ammunition were maintained with excellent regularity. This was in great measure due to the fine work done by the Brigade Pack Train, under Lieut. C. M. Rout, which was employed bringing up supplies to the forward dumps. Owing to the state of the roads, wheeled transport was out of the question. The work of the men with the horses was faithfully done in the face of almost impossible conditions, and the exploits of Lance-Corporal L. C. Aldridge and his little band of volunteers called for in connection with a specially-difficult undertaking in the face of fierce shell-fire were as admirable as they were daring.

PART 4.—CONCLUDING PHASE OF THE THIRD BATTLE OF YPRES.

Opens October 26th—Canadians carry Bellevue Spur—French and Belgians take Merckem Peninsula—Canadians capture Passchendaele, November 6th.

It now only remains to recount briefly the events constituting the fourth and concluding phase of the Third Battle of Ypres, which opened on October 26th, when the Canadians attacked in the Passchendaele sector of evil memory. South of the Ravebeek they progressed well, as indeed the Australians had done on the 12th. They were, however, held up at Bellevue Spur, but made a second attempt later in the day and carried it. Satisfactory progress was also made by the Fifth Army on the left.

By the 28th the French and Belgians had taken the Merckem Peninsula in the flooded region, and thus facilitated the advance to Houthulst Forest. The Canadians made some further progress towards Passchendaele, and by the end of October 30th had taken Crest Farm, reaching to within 500 yards of the village. On the morning of November 6th they attacked and captured Goudberg, Mosselmarkt and Passchendaele.

Thus ended the gigantic struggle that had lasted for nearly four months. The total British casualties amounted to over 250,000, a number approximating the strength of the entire army at the time of the Boer War. The continuance of the conflict in the face of heavy losses and in spite of the fearful conditions of weather was justified by the unfortunate developments in Russia and in Italy. Events in these theatres rendered impossible of achievement Haig's great plan to penetrate into Belgium and act against the rear of the enemy's coast defences, but the persistence and sacrifices of the British, though shorn of their greater reward, proved to have had far-reaching and lasting effects. Not the least of these was the fact that the enemy had been compelled to use up no fewer than seventy-eight of his Divisions in the battle, of which eighteen had been engaged a second or a third time after having been withdrawn to rest and refit. It is well to remember that in the operations of Arras, Messines, Lens and Ypres, as many as 131 German Divisions had been engaged and defeated by less than half that number of British Divisions.

CHAPTER XI.

THE YPRES SALIENT.

PART 1.—AFTER PASSCHENDAELE.
Relieved at Passchendaele—Second Army Rest Area.

Two days after the Passchendaele fight we were relieved by the 4th Brigade and moved back to bivouac camps about Wieltje, where the exhausted troops rested throughout the following day.

On October 16th the Brigade marched to Ypres and entrained for Wizernes, south of St. Omer, en route to the Second Army Rest Area. On arrival at Wizernes on the following morning we were billeted in the neighbouring villages of Esquerdes, Setques and Hallines. Next day the units of the Brigade, moving independently, set off on the two days' march to their sections of the Rest Area, the 1st Battalion via Seninghem to Colembert and Le Wast; the 2nd via Affringues to Escoeuilles and Surques; the 3rd* via Coulomby to Henneveux; and the 4th via Bayenghem to Cremarest and Belle Brune. Brigade Headquarters were located at Alincthun. In this peaceful district, well to the west and about half-way between St. Omer and Boulogne, the Brigade remained until November 8th, resting, reorganizing and training. At the beginning of November approximately 1,000 reinforcements arrived. They were urgently needed, but, unfortunately, though all were of good physique and well-equipped, more than half the number had had very little training.

On November 9th the Brigade moved eastward again to the old billets at Seninghem, Bayenghem and Coulomby, and continued training in that area until the 12th.

---

*Major A. Digby-Smith assumed command of the 3rd Battalion on October 13th, vice Lieut.-Col. A. Winter-Evans, killed in action on the 12th. Lieut.-Col. Stewart was evacuated sick on November 5th, and Lieut.-Col. Puttick assumed command of the Brigade.

PART 2.—STATIONARY TRENCH WARFARE.

Return from the Rest Area—Into the Becelaere Sector—Conditions—Patrolling—Readjustment and relief—Hutment camps behind Ypres—Command—Back to the Line—Polderhoek Chateau—Snow—To Reserve—Cameron Covert—Salvage—Recreational training—Christmas dinner—Return to the Line—Enemy raid—Relief—To the Line again—Thaw, rain, trench-foot—Raid on the tank strong-point—To Reserve—Work, training, and recreation—To the Line by light railway—Enemy raid—Bombardment—Water supply—Smoke-boxes—To Reserve—To the Broodseinde Sector—The final tour—General improvements in the sector—Ruins of Ypres.

From the training-area the Brigade, on November 13th, moved up by rail to Houpoutre, near Poperinghe, and marched thence to Scottish Wood Camp, east of Dickebusch. The trains were late, all ranks were tired out when they arrived at their destination, and the camp was wet, muddy, and generally uncomfortable.

On the following day we commenced the relief of the 13th and 15th Brigades in the Becelaere Sector of the Ypres Salient, due east of the town. The 1st Battalion took over from the 1st Lincoln Regiment in support at Clapham Junction, on the Menin Road near Hooge, and the 4th Battalion relieved the 13th Northumberland Fusiliers in reserve at Railway Dug-outs, close to Zillebeke Lake. The relief was continued on the 15th, when the 4th and 1st Battalions proceeded into the front line at Reutel, taking over the right and left sub-sectors respectively. The 3rd Battalion came up to Clapham Junction in support, and the 2nd Battalion to Railway Dug-outs in reserve. Brigade Headquarters moved to Hooge Crater. Notwithstanding the long marches, the fearful state of the ground and trenches, and the heavy scattered shelling, the relief was completed by 9 p.m. with very few casualties. On our right we had the 117th Brigade, 39th Division, and on our left the 4th (New Zealand) Brigade. The 2nd Brigade was in support, and the 1st was away temporarily as a labour Brigade.

The headquarters of both front-line battalions were located in improved German tunnels in the Butte de Polygon,*

---

*The Butte is now the property of the Australian Government. It has been trimmed into regular form, and, together with an obelisk erected upon it, forms a memorial of the 5th Australian Division, whose troops had achieved such magnificent successes in this region in September. (See p. 233.)

251

a huge stump-covered artificial mound in the north-eastern corner of Polygon Wood, overlooking the Racecourse. This was a prominent landmark, and as aerial photographs would reveal the probable use to which it was put, it was subjected to almost continuous bombardment. Many tracks intersected at the Butte, and close to the neighbouring military cemetery, containing British and German dead and marked by a huge crucifix, there was an Engineers' supply dump, much disliked by our carrying parties. All was open to the view of German observation balloons, and as a result parties of men here were frequently fired upon by the enemy's artillery.

The forward part of the sector, situated on a low plateau, was swept continuously by machine-gun fire. The whole surface of the country from the front line westward was literally disintegrated by shell-fire, and every hollow converted into a loathsome bog. From the Menin Road hastily-constructed plank roads ran to Glencorse Wood and Westhoek, and from these, again, miles of duckboard tracks gave access to our trenches. These avenues of communication, of course, would show up plainly in aeroplane photographs, and consequently sections of the roads and tracks were repeatedly blown up by the German gunners. On the sides of the plank roads, in particular, there were gruesome evidences of the intensity of such shell-fire, broken transport and artillery limbers and dead animals lying all along the routes. On one stretch of 300 yards about the dreaded Jargon Cross Roads the remains of 125 vehicles were counted. Even on the Menin Road itself gangs of men had constantly to be employed filling shell-holes and clearing away wreckage, and as this road was the main artery for several sectors, it was nothing less than marvellous that casualties were not more numerous during the progress of reliefs. Such places as "Dead Mule Gully" and "Hellfire Corner" were appropriately named. The "woods" were a tangle of jagged stumps and shattered trunks, intermingled with the remains of German wire. It was with the utmost difficulty that the ruins of hamlets could be located; some, indeed, had been completely obliterated, not even a redness in the mud remaining to indicate where once brick buildings had stood. Everything, everywhere, except parts of our own works and a few German "pill-boxes," was shattered, and from any viewpoint one could get a striking example, never to be forgotten, of "the abomination of desolation." A score of tanks used in the recent advance lay derelict at various points in the area. Some had been disabled by artillery fire, and some by the new German ironclad anti-tank guns, while others had become partially engulfed and wholly immovable in the morasses that abounded. The "tank cemetery" was the appropriate name given to a certain bit of country containing several wrecks together, and this spot formed a convenient point of direction.

The Brigade immediately set to work to effect such improvements as were possible. Isolated posts in the front line were connected up, good fighting-bays were put in hand, and some attention was given to drainage. Battalions in support and reserve were employed to the utmost limit in carrying up material and in digging support and switch lines. Owing to the nature of the ground, but little advance could be made in the direction of digging communication-trenches, and for some time we had to be content with duckboard and other overland tracks right up to the front line posts.

This being new country, vigorous patrolling was necessary in order to give us our bearings, to ascertain definitely the positions and strength of the enemy's posts, and to secure a thorough knowledge of the nature of No Man's Land. Some particularly meritorious reconnoitring feats were executed through successive tours in the line by Sergeant C. C. Robertson, who was in charge of the 1st Battalion's snipers and observers and had an insatiable thirst for knowledge. Much valuable information was obtained through his fine work. After many hairbreadth escapes he was finally put out of action by a severe wound from an enemy bomb while lying up against the German wire in daylight.

On the night of 19th/20th November the 4th and 1st Battalions were relieved in the front line by the 2nd and 3rd respectively. Machine-gun and artillery fire continued unabated, Brigade Headquarters being subjected to a particularly heavy bombardment on the 20th. Enemy snipers, at first very troublesome, were now being got well under control, and a German prisoner reported that in his unit alone there were seventeen casualties resulting from the activities of our sharpshooters during the first tour in the line.

A complicated relief was carried out by midnight of the 26th November, a readjustment of the sector being effected at the same time. The 2nd and 3rd Battalions, in the line, were relieved by 1st Wellington and 3rd Otago; and one company of the latter took over from our 1st Battalion the support position at Clapham Junction. Upon completion of the relief, the 2nd and 3rd Battalions moved back to huts in Howe Camp on the Dickebusch Road, about a mile south-west of Ypres. The 1st Battalion went to Micmac Camp, some two miles west of Dickebusch, while the 4th Battalion, vacating the old reserve position, was quartered at Walker Camp, north of Dickebusch. Brigade Headquarters, on relief by that of the 4th Brigade on the 27th, also moved to Walker Camp, and our Brigade became Divisional reserve, supplying large parties for work under the Divisional Salvage Officer.

The Brigade details, including the four bands, had already moved from the sodden Scottish Wood to Dominion Camp, near Ouderdom. This contained comparatively comfortable hutments, and here facilities existed for the continuance of the intensive training of specialists and non-commissioned officers, which was carried out with conspicuous success throughout the whole period of our tours of duty in the Ypres Salient.

On November 15th General Fulton returned from duty in England, but Lieut.-Col. Puttick continued in control of the Brigade till the relief then in progress was completed. Major Digby-Smith, temporarily commanding the 3rd Battalion, was wounded on the following day, and Lieut.-Col. Puttick then took command of that unit. Major J. R. Cowles, who had assumed temporary command of the 4th Battalion on the 16th, was killed by shell-fire on the 26th, and was buried with military honours at Dickebusch. Major J. Murphy thereupon assumed command of the 4th Battalion pending the arrival of Lieut.-Col. R. St. J. Beere from duty with the Reserve Battalion in England. Lieut.-Col. Austin reported from hospital on the 20th and resumed command of the 1st Battalion, Major Bell taking over the 3rd Battalion upon the departure of Lieut.-Col. Puttick on leave on the 30th.

Our casualties for November were:—

	Killed.	Wounded.
Officers	1	5
Other ranks	40	100

We relieved the 4th Brigade in the Becelaere Sector on December 1st. The approach marches, especially that of the 1st Battalion from Micmac Camp, were very long and arduous, but the interchange was completed early and with exceedingly few casualties. The 1st Battalion relieved the 3rd Otago Battalion on the right, the 4th Battalion took over from 3rd Canterbury on the left, the 3rd moved into a new support position in Dead Mule Gully, behind Polygonveld, and the 2nd to reserve at Halfway House and Railway Wood, about a mile north-west of Hooge. The 1st Wellington Battalion was temporarily attached to our Brigade, and remained in the front line on our right. Brigade Headquarters now moved up to the Butte, which was also occupied by the Headquarters of the 1st Battalion. Headquarters of the 4th Battalion were advanced to an old German "pill-box."

We were now well settled in the Salient. Generally speaking, each Brigade had a tour of about a week in the line, followed by a similar period in support, and then went out to reserve for the same length of time. The Brigade in the line was disposed in depth, and held a battalion in rear specially detailed for counter-attacking purposes. Similarly each battalion had its counter-attacking company, and each company its counter-attacking platoon. The Brigade in support had a battalion in the front line at Cameron Covert. All through the Divisional sector, from front to rear, special Lewis gun, Vickers gun, and even trench mortar sections, were told off for the purpose of dealing with low-flying enemy aircraft; but though these did good work in warning off the venturesome airmen, there was little of the directly spectacular in their achievements.

On December 3rd the 2nd Brigade carried out from the trenches of the IXth Corps on our right an attack on the notorious Polderhoek Chateau position, which, though beyond our sector, was a constant menace to our flank posts. Owing to the concentrated machine-gun fire and the impossibility of continuing till the last moment the bombardment of the "pill-boxes" by the heavy artillery, full success was not obtained, but the front line was slightly advanced.* Particularly fine work, earning the special commendation of the Divisional Commander, was done by parties from our 2nd and 3rd Battalions in preparation for this operation. Under shell-fire and through deep mud, 650 men from these units carried 1,300 six-inch Newton bombs a distance of nearly three miles in one trek. This meant a load of 109 pounds dead-weight for each man. During the progress of the attack, 400 large gas-bombs were fired on to Becelaere from projectors set up in the lines of our Brigade. The guns of the 3rd Machine Gun Company established in our sector also assisted in the operation by repeatedly dispersing enemy counter-attacking parties moving forward on the Becelaere Road.

Heavy snow-storms commenced on December 3rd, and three days later the 2nd Battalion came into the line, taking over from 1st Wellington the Cameron Covert sub-sector on our right, between the Reutelbeek and the Polygonbeek.

We were relieved by the 2nd Brigade on the night of 9th/10th December, and became Brigade in support, with one battalion, the 3rd, in the front line holding the sub-sector previously taken over by the 2nd Battalion. Brigade Headquarters moved to Lille Gate in the southern ramparts of Ypres. The 1st Battalion went to Howe Camp, the 2nd to Otago Camp, just north of Zillebeke Lake, and the 4th to Dickebusch Camp.

The Brigade became Divisional reserve on December 15th, Headquarters and the 2nd and 3rd Battalions moving back to Walker Camp, and the 1st to Micmac Camp. The 4th Battalion remained at Dickebusch. At about mid-day on the 20th, instructions were received from Division by telephone to the effect that the enemy was attacking on the right Brigade front, and our Brigade was ordered to be ready to move up at half-an-hour's notice. Orders for assembly were accordingly issued to units, but fifteen minutes later Division announced that the attack had been driven off.

*This was the fourth attack on the Chateau. The ground gained was handed over to the troops of the IXth Corps, but nine days later the Germans, after repeated counter-attacks, succeeded in regaining their lost territory.

A PLANK ROAD IN THE YPRES SALIENT.
Australian War Photo.

DEAD-MULE GULLY.
Australian War Photo.

AN ANTI-TANK GUN NEAR THE MENIN ROAD.

THE MENIN ROAD UNDER SNOW.

THE ANCIENT CLOTH HALL OF YPRES.

AND ITS RUINS.

Band and "Bivvies" near Ypres.

"The Counter-Attack."

Face p. 257.

On December 27th the Brigade again became Divisional support, relieving the 4th Brigade, with Headquarters at Lille Gate and one battalion in the line. The 2nd Battalion moved up to Halfway House and Railway Wood, and the 3rd and 4th to the Otago and Manawatu Camps. The 1st Battalion relieved 3rd Otago in Cameron Covert.

Our position in the Cameron Covert sub-sector consisted of a number of isolated posts facing south-east, with a partially-constructed support line running behind the wood. In the wood itself and in the valley of the Polygonbeek were a number of old German concrete "pill-boxes" which we converted to our use as living-quarters. The posts overlooked the sodden valley of the Reutelbeek, and were under observation by the enemy from his position at Polderhoek Chateau, which was only 600 yards distant, and from which concealed snipers and machine-guns were unpleasantly active. Snow still lay on the ground, making movement on the forward slopes very difficult. The use of white suits for patrolling was effective, but this advantage was largely discounted by the noise of crashing ice as our men moved over the shell-holes in No Man's Land. While the ground remained frozen, progress in trench-improvement was slow, and when a thaw set in, the falling-in of the sides impeded drainage and involved much labour in the upkeep of the existing works. To mitigate, in some degree, the discomforts of the men in these conditions, parties of fifty were sent daily from the line to the Divisional Baths at Ypres for a thorough wash and a change of underclothing.

While the Brigade was in support or in reserve large parties were supplied daily for work with the Engineers or with the Divisional Salvage Officer. Scattered over the whole Divisional area was an incredible quantity of valuable material of all kinds, such as rifles, machine-guns, harness, wagons and limbers; cartridges, bombs, shell-cases and live shells of all calibres; coils of barbed-wire, stakes and tools; discarded clothing and web-equipment—the flotsam and jetsam of recent battles. Every officer and man moving towards the rear from any part of the area was expected to carry back to special dumps at least one article of equipment or clothing salvaged from the mud of the Salient. This, indeed, was a standing order, but so framed as to make obedience a point of honour.

The Divisional commander set the example by carrying out his own orders to the letter, and, serving as a prick to the conscience if one should be careless or forgetful, there were staring posters everywhere on lorries and buildings asking the pointed question, "What have you salved to-day?" How thoroughly the work was done may be judged from the statements published from time to time, that for the week ending 30th November giving the estimated value of stores salvaged by the Division at £141,768.

Recreational training became an important feature of our routine so far as it could be developed in view of the number of men required for working-parties; and so beneficial were the effects of properly-organized sports and games upon the health of the men that definite days were set apart to the different units in turn for recreational training only, and on these days no working-parties were asked for.

December 25th, with its heavy snow-storms, was a typical northern Christmas Day. Fortunately the Brigade was out of the line, and on account of the weather all special duties were cancelled. The bands of the various battalions played a programme of carols in the early morning, and, later on, the men sat down by companies to a sumptuous dinner, the major items on the menu being turkey and plum pudding. Luxuries of this kind did not, of course, come up with the rations, but were provided for out of battalion funds, subscriptions from the men, and gifts from our friends of the patriotic societies in New Zealand, and to make the necessary purchases the quartermasters scoured the country as far south as Rouen.

Our casualties during the month of December were:—

	Killed.	Wounded.
Officers	2	5
Other ranks	40	120

On January 2nd, 1918, the New Zealand Rifle Brigade relieved the 4th Brigade* in the old sector, the interchange being

---

*On January 17th, 1918, the 4th Brigade relieved the 1st as Corps Works Brigade, and early in the following month it was disbanded. Surplus troops were formed into the New Zealand Entrenching Group, under the command of Lieut.-Col. A. E. Stewart, and were organized in three battalions corresponding to the three Brigades of the Division. The 3rd N.Z. (Rifle Brigade) Entrenching Battalion was commanded by

completed by 9 p.m. The front line was now divided into three battalion sub-sectors. That on the right was named "Reutel," after the site of the village which it included; the central sub-sector was known as "Judge," from the "Judge Cross Roads" and the ruins of "Judge Cottage," both of these being German strong-points immediately opposite; and that on the left, which enveloped the remains of the hamlet of Noordemdhoek, was named "Noord." The 2nd Battalion took over Reutel sub-sector from the 3rd Wellington; the 3rd Battalion relieved 3rd Canterbury in Judge sub-sector; and the 4th Battalion replaced 3rd Auckland in Noord. The 1st Battalion in Cameron Covert was relieved by 3rd Otago, and moved to a position in the Albania Area, immediately north-west of the Butte, as battalion in support. Shelling was persistent during the relief, and we suffered several casualties. Headquarters of Brigade and of the 3rd Battalion were established in the Butte, and those of the remaining battalions in old German concrete dug-outs. The 4th Battalion Headquarters' "pill-box" was situated at the cross roads in J.5. central, a spot well known to all ranks in the Brigade as receiving much "dirty work" from the enemy artillery.

On the night of the relief the enemy attempted to raid the point of the salient at Joiner's Avenue in the 4th Battalion line. After a sharp fight the raiders were driven off, and were pursued into No Man's Land by Corporal A. Adamson and another. Unfortunately, both these men were wounded by a bomb. The corporal, however, not only succeeded in bringing his companion safely in, but also secured identifications from one of the enemy who had been killed.

Units in the forward positions worked hard to bring about some improvement in the defensive lines, and, in spite of adverse conditions, made considerable progress. The special task of the battalion for the time being in support was to assist in digging and wiring a new reserve trench, and to open

---

Capt. S. J. E. Closey. All reinforcements for the Brigade passed through the Entrenching Battalion, which thus served as an immediate source from which supplies of trained men could be drawn as required. The Entrenching Group, then commanded by Lieut.-Col. G. Mitchell, D.S.O., did good work in the trenches about Bailleul when the Germans broke through at Armentieres and Ypres in the following spring. (See p. 310.)

up emergency overland routes to the front line in preparation for meeting any possible enemy attack. During this tour the weather alternated between frost and snow on the one hand, and mist and drizzle on the other. Enemy air-craft were active, flying low over our positions. Shelling continued with varying intensity upon our trenches and tracks, and carrying-parties moving over the exposed routes suffered severely.

Early in the month a number of selected officers and non-commissioned officers were detached from the Brigade for special duty, the nature of which was at the time kept profoundly secret, though information subsequently filtered through to the effect that they had gone to join what became familiarly known as the "Hush Hush Brigade," and that the scene of their activities was somewhere in the Middle East. A note on their adventures is given in Appendix V.

We were relieved by the 2nd Brigade on January 8th, on which day there was a severe snowstorm. The 2nd and 4th Battalions were relieved by 2nd and 1st Otago, respectively, and went to the Otago Camp; the 3rd handed over to 1st Canterbury and moved to Half-way House and Railway Wood. The Brigade was now in support with headquarters at Lille Gate and one battalion in the line, the 1st Battalion having taken over Cameron Covert from 3rd Otago.

Snow fell again on the 9th, but on the following day a drizzle set in, bringing on a thaw which turned the ground everywhere into an oozy mess of mud. Conditions in the Cameron Covert sub-sector became distressingly bad, and the work of the three battalions in support, which were engaged mainly in carrying and trench-digging, was carried out under the greatest difficulties.

On January 14th, in heavy snow, the Brigade returned to the line, taking over from the 2nd Brigade. The relief was a comparatively quiet one, and was accomplished by 8.30 p.m. The 2nd Battalion relieved 2nd Otago in Reutel, the 3rd relieved 1st Canterbury in Judge, and the 4th took over Noord from 1st Otago. The 1st Battalion handed over Cameron Covert to 2nd Canterbury and went to the support position in Albania and Polygonveld, west of the Butte.

A thaw setting in on the following day, the front line and support trenches began to collapse in many places and soon became knee-deep in mud. At night rain came on, flooding the trenches and swamping the low-lying shelters. Drainage was a difficult problem, but Lance-Corporal W. G. Bowers, of the 3rd Battalion, solved it for a part of his line at any rate. Strolling out into No Man's Land one misty morning, with his spade on his shoulder, he noted the fall, selected his line, and proceeded to dig a drain back to his trench, accomplishing the task at last after an hour's steady work, with the Germans not 150 yards away.

The general conditions were such as would favour an abnormal outbreak of "trench-foot," a painful inflammatory swelling which invariably incapacitated the sufferer; but rigid attention to the supply of hot food and drinks, a daily rubbing with whale-oil or other anti-frostbite preparation, a change of socks with the same frequency, and hot baths and change of underclothing with such regularity as was possible in the circumstances,—these precautions had the effect of keeping the number of cases within satisfactory limits. The changing of socks, indeed, became a most important part of the daily routine. Every man had three pairs, one on the feet, one in the haversack, and one in "the wash." Specially-detailed "sock-men" made the rounds of the trenches every day, bringing in a pair for each man, and taking back a corresponding pair to the laundry attached to the Divisional Baths. Daily returns to Brigade were made by the non-commissioned officers in charge of the sock-men, and drastic steps were taken in dealing with any shortcomings in the various units.

One of the enemy strong-points in front of the 2nd Battalion sector consisted mainly of a derelict British tank. On January 17th this position was heavily bombarded by our artillery, and at 2 p.m. Sergeant W. B. Bowles, with four men, went forward to reconnoitre. They found twelve enemy dead inside the tank, and several dead and wounded outside. Our patrol secured identifications and brought back a light machine-gun. Enemy air-craft continued active over our front and rear lines, and on the 19th the Butte was shelled more heavily and persistently than usual.

On January 20th we were relieved by the 2nd Brigade and moved back into Divisional reserve. This proved to be a fairly easy relief, as we proceeded by light railway from Birr

Cross Roads on the Menin Road, about two miles east of Ypres. The 1st Battalion went to Howe Camp, Brigade Headquarters and the 2nd and 3rd Battalions to Walker Camp, and the 4th to Dickebusch Huts. On the whole the weather now was fine, and all ranks enjoyed to the full the short spell of comparative rest. Large parties were supplied for construction-work, carrying and salvaging, but we were able to devote a considerable amount of time to recreational and general training, battalion parades and inspections, and bathing at the Divisional Baths.

The casualties suffered during the month of January, 1918, were:—

	Killed.	Wounded.	Missing.
Officers	—	5	—
Other ranks	38	149	1

On February 1st the Brigade returned to the line, relieving the 1st Brigade in the old sector by 7.30 p.m., units having moved up by light railway as far as Birr Cross Roads. The 2nd, 1st and 4th Battalions went into the front line, and the 3rd garrisoned part of the Reserve Line then under construction east of the Butte.

Half an hour after the completion of the relief, one of the posts of the 1st Battalion captured a ration-party of five Germans who had lost their bearings. Three days later another German fell into the hands of the 1st Battalion. This man, tall, stately and middle-aged, was unarmed. He was very indignant when asked what had become of his rifle, giving us to understand that he was a "Controller," whose duty it was to visit machine-gun posts at intervals, and that one in such an exalted position was above the carrying of arms.

February 2nd was a fine, cold day, and there was great enemy artillery activity on all parts of the sector. The Butte, in particular, was subjected to a two-hours' intense bombardment with gas and high-explosive shells. In the evening a party of twenty Germans raided one of the 1st Battalion listening-posts. All four men in the post were wounded, and the raiders, under cover of bombs and revolver fire directed upon the main trench, endeavoured to remove the wounded or to secure identifications. In this attempt, however, they were smartly countered by Corporal J. G. Hart, who, after directing the fire of his section upon the raiders, dashed out to the post to protect the wounded. Under stress of the corporal's bombing and his men's rifle fire the Germans were compelled to withdraw. A patrol, taken out immediately afterwards by Sergeant J. P. Glentworth, found three enemy dead close to the wire and much blood along the raiders' line of retreat.

On February 4th, in retaliation for the enemy's bombardment on the 2nd, our artillery carried out a heavy and prolonged shelling of the enemy's sector on our front. The Germans responded with a steady bombardment of our lines with "sneezing-gas" throughout the 5th, and supplemented this with a series of "shell-storms" on the 7th.

During this tour several wells, discovered on sites of hamlets and farms near the front line, were opened up and cleaned out. By this means the supply of water to the sector was greatly improved. Hitherto all water had had to be carried very long distances, necessitating the employment of many men on this work alone.

Well out in No Man's Land, in front of the Reutel sub-sector, our observers marked down what appeared to be the ventilator or chimney-flue of an underground dug-out, and plans were on foot for dropping a Stokes bomb into this for the benefit of the people below, when, at another point, near the Butte, an old German smoke-box was discovered. In appearance it resembled a large oil-drum, containing a swinging receptacle in which there was a quantity of some chemical that still emitted fumes on being disturbed. Further investigation, by a patrol, of the mysterious "flue" revealed the fact that it was nothing more interesting than another smoke-box.

A readjustment of the Divisional sector was made on February 7th and 8th. Cameron Covert sub-sector was handed over to the 60th Division, and the New Zealand Division took over from the 66th a part of their front extending from our left boundary to the Broodseinde–Moorslede Road. This portion, together with the sub-sector held by our 4th Battalion, was taken over by the 1st Brigade, and our remaining battalions were relieved by units of the 2nd Brigade. The New Zealand Division now had two Brigades in the line. On going out on the night of 8th/9th, our Brigade went into Divisional reserve and occupied the usual hutment camps behind Ypres. The customary programme of work, training, sports and bathing was resumed. The weather, fortunately, was fine, and all ranks appreciated the short respite from the trying life in muddy trenches. On February 12th a team from the New Zealand Division played a football match with a team from the 38th, and won by fourteen points to three.

On February 14th we relieved the 1st Brigade in the Broodseinde Sector, on the left of the Divisional front, with Headquarters in a series of German concrete dug-outs in the embankment of the Ypres–Roulers Railway at Potsdam, about three-quarters of a mile east of Frezenberg. The 4th Battalion went to the right and the 3rd to the left of the front line, the 2nd to support at Garter Point, and the 1st to reserve at Hussar Camp, near Potijze, with a company in Kit and Kat strong-point.

This was a good sector, the driest and quietest occupied by our Brigade since June of the previous year. The defensive works, however, had not reached a satisfactory stage of advancement. Particularly was this so on the left, where the 3rd Battalion's front line, 1,000 yards in length, consisted only of a series of detached posts. Taking advantage of the fine weather then prevailing, a special effort was put forth by both the forward units to bring about the desired improvement. Excellent results followed. The 4th Battalion brought to completion the works that had been suitably laid out but not developed. Within a week the 3rd Battalion had dug 1,000 yards of new trench along its front, together with the necessary communication saps, had erected 500 yards of wiring and 700 yards of revetting, and had laid over 700 yards of duckwalk. But the 3rd Battalion were not content with this achievement. Sergeant J. W. Clayson with his patrol had been reconnoitring No Man's Land during daylight, and had succeeded in marking down the whole of the enemy's posts opposite the battalion front. On the information so gained a peaceful advance was planned, and in one night the battalion established four posts from 300 to 450 yards beyond its new front line, wired and garrisoned them, and linked them up with a continuous belt of wire entanglements.

The Division was now about to go out to rest as Corps reserve, and we were to be relieved by an English Brigade, which, as was now usual in the Home Army, contained only three battalions. To facilitate the relief, adjustments were made in good time, the 2nd Brigade extending to the left and our 3rd Battalion to the right, thus releasing the 4th Battalion, which now went back to the Westhoek deep dug-outs and Kit and Kat. The 146th Brigade, 49th Division, came in on February 23rd, completing a good relief by 8 p.m. The 1st, 2nd and 3rd Battalions were relieved by West Yorks units, while the positions occupied by the 4th Battalion in reserve were taken over by a battalion of the 148th Brigade, and the Brigade moved back to the old quarters in Walker, Howe and Dickebusch Camps.

So ended our series of tours of duty in the trenches of the Ypres Salient. We were destined to return for a brief period of work in the reserve systems, but never again to occupy the front line there. Our experience in the sector had been a very trying one, though in many respects not without interest. As was so often the case, we found on first coming in that very little construction work appeared to have been done, and our men were called upon, in the midst of snow, rain and mud, for almost superhuman efforts in order to make the lines habitable and fit to fight in. Engagements in this area had been so recent that here and there behind our lines both British and German dead lay unburied, and the outpost line still consisted merely of isolated advanced posts. The support positions were little better, and there was practically no reserve line, though farther back the defensive system was in a much more satisfactory state. Water, rations, and engineers' material for the front line had for a long time to be carried up by hand from dumps near Westhoek, a distance of nearly two miles, and this labour involved the expenditure of much valuable man-power. Carrying-work was rendered doubly laborious and dangerous from the fact that the duck-walks were usually ice-covered, and that these tracks were above ground and all exposed to shell-fire. Later on a great improvement was effected by the opening up of ancient wells in the forward area, and the pushing on of the light railway which eventually reached a point fairly close to the Butte. Deep dug-outs for the accommodation of support and reserve battalions were put in hand, but these were never sufficiently advanced for our occupation until just before we went out of the sector, and our men had to be content with hastily-constructed sand-bag "bivvies" which, during thaws and rains, were constantly falling in.

A glance at the trench map of the eastern and south-eastern portions of the Ypres Salient, corrected to the middle of February, is interesting and instructive. Everywhere the lines are fragmentary except the portion occupied by the New Zealand Division east of Polygon Wood. Here there is shown a complete system of front, support and reserve lines, connected up by a series of communication-trenches. The high ground in this locality projected well into the German lines beyond Becelaere; and while the striking development of trench-system may be an indication of great industry on the part of the Division, it also draws attention to the importance of the position, for it was anticipated that a German attack, expected at any moment, would develop most strongly across this plateau. During the later portion of our stay in the area, the working-parties supplied while the Brigade was in support or reserve were employed mainly in digging and wiring Divisional reserve lines and Corps support and reserve lines, constructing rear strong-points and observation posts, reversing the innumerable German "pill-boxes" by closing the original and opening new entrances, constructing artillery positions, and establishing scattered ammunition dumps. So well advanced were these works when we finally left the Salient that we fondly imagined the position was strong enough to hold up any advancing German force.

The back-country behind the Broodseinde Sector appeared to be less shell-torn than that on the Menin Road farther south but within the same distance from Ypres. The track forward from Hussar Farm, the last quarters of our reserve battalion, led through fairly intact grassy land. Where it crossed some disused trenches there was a notice-board with the legend "Old British Front Line." Standing here, one marvelled how the British, even with all their patience and doggedness, had been able to hold out in such a position. The old trenches were in low ground overlooked by those of the enemy, so much so that it would appear that the slightest movement in our lines must have been observed by the Germans, who, indeed, had had all the conditions in their favour.

Our earlier reliefs, before the extension of the light railway system, involved very long and tiring marches. The route usually ran through the battered town of Ypres, and directly past the rapidly-dwindling ruins of the ancient Cloth Hall. If the old city, so full of historic interest, evoked more than passing attention from our men, they, with their characteristic reserve, failed to display any enthusiasm they may have felt. Shell-storms still frequently fell upon the streets and ruined buildings, and it was not a place to linger in.

Before the war Ypres was a town with a population of 17,000. Its history stretches back into the dim past, and is somewhat intimately connected with that of England. The daughter of our own King Alfred the Great was the countess of a certain great Flemish lord who fortified Ypres and other towns in the same region. Ypres began to rise in importance in the tenth century, and soon became noted for its cloth manufactures, the raw material for which was obtained mainly from England. Flemish knights accompanied William the Conqueror to England, and were rewarded for their military assistance by grants of land in that new country. In the fourteenth century Ypres reached the pinnacle of its greatness, its inhabitants numbering 200,000, and producing material from 4,000 looms. It was then the leading Flemish town and the centre of the cloth trade of Flanders. Of this period of prosperity the Cloth Hall, a great and beautiful building erected by the Guild of Clothworkers, was, till its destruction in the Great War, a famous relic, while the adjoining Gothic cathedral of St. Martin, dating from the thirteenth century, was one of the most remarkable religious edifices in Belgium. Steady decline commenced with the military activities resulting from trade jealousies. In 1313 Ypres attacked Poperinghe, then a rising manufacturing town, and was in its turn attacked by Ghent towards the end of the century. As a result of these troubles many of the Ypres weavers migrated to England, where they helped to lay the foundations of the manufacturing prosperity of that country, and trade rapidly moved from Ypres and its sister towns to those nearer the seaboard. Of the former greatness of Ypres little remained in modern times, and the town had to be content with modest returns from a lace industry of no great volume, supplemented by such pecuniary benefits as might arise from the fact that here the training-school for the world-famous Belgian cavalry was established. The moat and the brick ramparts of Ypres, obsolete fortifications with which the men of the Rifle Brigade became sufficiently familiar, date back to the seventeenth century, when Louis XIV of France made the town one of the strongest fortresses in the Low Countries at that time. In the great European wars Ypres seldom escaped a siege, or at least a bombardment; in the last and greatest struggle of all hardly was one stone left upon another; and of the huge armies that strove for its possession fully half a million men, friend and foe, lie buried in the torn soil of the area in and about the dreadful Salient.

The casualties in the Brigade for the month of February were:—

	Killed.	Wounded.
Officers	1	5
Other ranks	22	87

PART 3.—IN CORPS RESERVE.
Rest and training in the Staple Area—Back to Ypres as Labour Brigade—Work and play—Sudden call to battle.

On February 24th, 1918, the Brigade left Dickebusch by rail for the Corps Reserve Area about St. Omer. Brigade Headquarters and the 2nd and 3rd Battalions detrained at Ebblinghem and went into billets in and around Staple, while the remaining units continued the journey to St. Omer and then marched to Moulle and Houlle, some four miles to the north-west.

Training was at once commenced. The men were very stiff after their long tour of nearly four months in the line, and, in addition, a large proportion of the reinforcements received since Passchendaele were raw and inexperienced. It was intended that the period in the area should extend over four weeks, with a break for construction work in the Ypres Salient. The first fortnight was devoted mainly to training of a recreational nature, and competitions in drill and sports formed a very important and highly-beneficial part of the work. The two battalions at Moulle had a five days' course in musketry and open-warfare practice on the rifle range there, and then changed over with those at Staple, the units route-marching the fifteen miles between the two areas. Though there was some rain and snow the weather generally was good; and as a result of the rest and training a marked daily improvement was noted in the state of physical and general fitness of all ranks. The scheme of sports and competitions was based on the principle of team-work, the contests being first between sections, and so progressing, until finally, when the two units returned from Moulle, battalions competed against one another. The work in all stages was closely inspected by the Divisional Commander. Larger schemes of training were to be taken up when we should have returned from the forward area, but, as we shall presently see, our next field-work in the open was to be the real thing, and not mere practice against an imaginary enemy.

On March 9th, the 2nd and 3rd Battalions, and, on the following day, the remainder of the Brigade, returned by rail to Ypres and relieved the 1st Brigade in Corps employ.* Each battalion supplied 500 men daily for work on the Corps defence line behind the Salient. The camps first occupied were somewhat scattered, West Farm being a mile and a half east of Ypres, Forrester the same distance south-west, while Halifax and Vancouver were midway between Ouderdom and Vlamertinghe, some four miles west of the city; but later a move was made to newly-constructed camps close to the south and south-east of Ypres.

The work was hard and involved long marches, but the men were now in fine form. Time was found for general recreational training. The final football match for the Brigade Championship was played off on March 19th, the 4th Battalion beating the 2nd by eight points to nil. Other final competitions were held on the 21st, the 2nd Battalion proving victorious in

*At the end of 1917 all the Australian Divisions were grouped in one formation, which was known thereafter as the Australian Corps. The IInd Anzac, now composed of the 49th, the 66th, and the New Zealand Divisions, changed its name on 1st January, 1918, to XXIInd Corps.

wiring, hand-grenade and bayonet fighting; the 1st Battalion in physical drill; the 3rd battalion in boxing; and the 4th in rifle-grenade shooting. Again, on the 22nd the 4th Battalion played a football match with the 2nd Brigade New Zealand Field Artillery, the latter winning after a finely-contested game. The Brigade School re-opened at Dominion Camp, under Capt. H. E. Barrowclough, twenty-five non-commissioned officers from each battalion attending for general training and special instruction in musketry.

On March 20th and 21st the enemy very actively shelled, gassed and bombed the area, the camps of our 2nd, 3rd and 4th Battalions being badly knocked about. Then came, on the latter date, news of the enemy push in front of Amiens, followed by orders for the Brigade to cease work in the Corps Area and to concentrate. Battalions accordingly moved back in the evening to the old camps and made the necessary preparations for taking the field at short notice.

CHAPTER XII.
THE ANCRE, 1918.

PART 1.—THE GERMAN THRUST AT AMIENS.
General situation—Expected German offensive—Opposing forces —Enemy offensive opens, March 21st—Enemy successes—Amiens threatened—Marshal Foch in supreme command of the Allied Armies—Situation on the Ancre.

When the Third Battle of Ypres ended early in November, 1917, Russian resistance in the eastern theatre of war had entirely ceased, and the situation on the Italian front was extremely grave. Already the transfer of German Divisions from the Russian to the western front had begun, and it was recognized that this movement would continue until the fighting strength of the enemy had become vastly superior to that of the Allies. The growth of the American forces in France could not be expected to keep pace with this development for some time to come. Moreover, negotiations were in progress for the taking-over by the British of some twenty-eight miles of the French front by the end of January, 1918, and for the withdrawal of the French First Army that had been co-operating with us in the recent fighting north of Ypres. It was clear that for a time the initiative must pass from the Allies to the Germans. A defensive policy was therefore adopted, and preparations were made to meet a strong and sustained hostile offensive.

By the end of February, 1918, it became evident that the enemy was about to attack our Third and Fifth Armies on the Arras–St. Quentin front, from the Sensee River southwards, with the double object of severing the connection between the French and British Armies, and advancing on Amiens and capturing that vitally important centre of communications. To meet the attack, which was expected to open on March 20th or 21st, more than half the available troops were allotted to the defence of the threatened sector; and arrangements were made for the co-operation of the French and for the rapid transport of reserves from other fronts as occasion might demand.

The Fifth Army was on the British right, and held forty-two miles of line from Barisis to Gouzeaucourt, the average frontage per Division being 6,750 yards. The Third Army held about 27 miles from Gouzeaucourt northwards to Gavrelle, with 4,700 yards as the average length of line per Division. The average for the enemy was 1,200 yards.

By March 21st the number of German Infantry Divisions in the western theatre had risen from 146 to 192, an increase of nearly one-third. On the first day of the attack on our Fifth and Third Armies the Germans employed no fewer than 64 Divisions, a number considerably exceeding the total forces composing the entire British Army in France. Opposed to this huge concentration were 29 Infantry and three Cavalry Divisions, just half the number of enemy Divisions. As the attack developed, the number of German Divisions rose to 73, and by the time his advance was held up our own numbered 49.

The long-expected assault commenced on the morning of March 21st, on a front of 54 miles between the Oise and the Sensee Rivers. Until 1 p.m. dense white fog covered the ground, rendering it impossible to see more than fifty yards in any direction. This was a double advantage to the enemy, for, while his numbers made it difficult for him to lose direction, the lack of visibility not only prevented the British artillery from distinguishing the S.O.S. signals sent up from the outpost line, but also hindered the work of the crews of machine-guns and forward field-pieces, for they were unable to pick up targets until too late to be effective. The enemy also had in his favour an advantage denied to the British in our 1917 offensive—an unusually dry spring.

The attacking forces met with immediate success at many points, and by sheer weight of numbers the enemy's advance progressed from day to day until eventually practically the whole of the Fifth Army and part of the Third were pressed back. By March 25th the British had lost most of their previous gains on the Somme battlefield, and the enemy's thrust at Amiens seemed likely of achievement. The French were as rapidly as possible taking over that part of our battle-front running from Peronne southwards. In accordance with the decision of the Governments of France and Great Britain, the supreme control of the operations of the French and British forces in France and Belgium was taken over by General Foch on March 26th.*

It is not expedient in this short history to follow in detail the developments over the whole battlefield. The New Zealand Rifle Brigade was more immediately concerned in the operations on the Third Army front in the region of the Ancre. The position there can best be understood by a consideration of the following extracts from Sir Douglas Haig's Despatch:—

"... During the night of 24th/25th March, constant fighting took place on the northern portion of the battle-front about Sapignies and Behagnies, where the enemy made determined but unsuccessful efforts to break through. On the following day, the 25th, the enemy maintained great pressure on this front from Ervillers to the south. Shortly after dawn a very heavy attack on our positions east of the Arras–Bapaume Road between Favreuil and Ervillers was repulsed with great loss, and a counter-attack by the 42nd Division drove the enemy out of Sapignies. Later in the morning the 2nd Division beat off an attack at Ligny-Thilloy, and our positions north of this point were maintained practically unchanged until mid-day.

"At noon fresh attacks developed in great force, and the right of the IVth Corps, with which the Divisions of the Vth Corps were not in touch, were pressed back. The enemy gained Grevillers, in which neighbourhood the 19th Division were hotly engaged, and also Bihucourt. North of this point our positions were substantially maintained, and at the end of the day our troops still held Ervillers. On the north bank

---

*In his introduction to the French edition of Sir Douglas Haig's Despatches, now published in book form, Marshal Foch writes a fine eulogy on the British Commander-in-Chief and his work. Referring to "the change in the decisive period when the Allies advanced to victory at the double, only to be stopped by the German capitulation at the Armistice," he states that in the Despatches "the results are briefly set forth, but their causes are not explained. All mention of the hand that guided the instrument is omitted," and goes on to say, "We may be allowed to make good this deficiency, in which the all-important part played by the British Higher Command is lost to sight." Of the momentous decision to unify the command he writes in these graceful terms: "Was it not the insight of an experienced and enlightened Commander which led him to intervene as he did with his own Government on the 24th of March, 1918, and with the Allied Governments assembled at Doullens on the 26th, to the end that the French and British armies might at once be placed under a single command, even though his personal position should thereby suffer? ...."

of the Somme, also, between the neighbourhood of Hem and Trones Wood, all the enemy's attacks were held. . . . Between Montauban and the neighbourhood of Grevillers, however, our troops had been unable to establish touch on the line to which they had withdrawn on 24th March. After heavy fighting throughout the morning and the early part of the afternoon, Divisions commenced to fall back individually towards the Ancre, widening the gap between the Vth and IVth Corps.

"During the afternoon the enemy reached Courcelette, and was pressing on through the gap in our line in the direction of Pys and Irles, seriously threatening the flank of the IVth Corps. It became clear that the Third Army, which on this day had assumed command of all troops north of the Somme, would have to continue the withdrawal of its centre to the line of the River Ancre. . . . . All possible steps were taken to secure this line, but by nightfall hostile patrols had reached the right bank of the Ancre north of Miraumont and were pushing forward between the flanks of the Vth and IVth Corps in the direction of Serre and Puisieux-au-Mont. In view of this situation, the IVth Corps fell back by stages during the night and morning to the line Bucquoy–Ablainzevelle, in touch with the VIth Corps about Boyelles. On the right the remaining divisions of the Third Army were withdrawn under orders to the line Bray-sur-Somme–Albert, and thence took up positions along the west bank of the Ancre to the neighbourhood of Beaumont Hamel. . . ."

Thus, early on the morning of the 26th, a definite gap of three miles existed between Puisieux-au-Mont and Beaumont Hamel, these places being opposite Hebuterne and Auchonvillers respectively; but the despatch goes on to say that for a further distance of two miles southward to Hamel, opposite Englebelmer, "the situation was not clear."

PART 2.—THE NEW ZEALAND RIFLE BRIGADE INTO THE GAP.

From Ypres to Amiens—March to Hedauville—1st Battalion to the Englebelmer-Auchonvillers Ridge—First contact with the Germans—Composite Brigades of the New Zealand Division—Canterbury troops pass through the 1st Battalion—1st Auckland and the 2nd Battalion prolong the line to the left—2nd Wellington and the 3rd Battalion fill the remaining gap from Euston to Hebuterne, March 27th—Congratulations.

We may return now to follow the movements of the New Zealand Rifle Brigade, which, in common with other Brigades in the Division, had received orders to concentrate and prepare to move at three hours' notice.

In connection with the general scheme of defence prepared months before to meet the expected German thrust, arrangements had been made with the First and Second Army commanders for the formation, from the troops under their command, of a special force of reserve Divisions for action as required. The New Zealand Division, then with the Second Army and in reserve at Ypres, was immediately available, and, with other troops, was therefore called upon for this service.

General Fulton being away on leave, Lieut.-Col. A. E. Stewart, from the New Zealand Entrenching Group, assumed command of the Brigade on March 22nd; and during the 24th and 25th, units entrained at Houpoutre Siding, near Poperinghe, and left for the Third Army Area.*

We were the first Brigade to move, Brigade Headquarters and the four units travelling by five different trains. The first of these, after a journey of sixteen hours, arrived at Amiens at 5 a.m. on the 25th, the others following at intervals of about four hours. The point of detrainment had been fixed for Corbie, some ten miles east of Amiens and two and a half due north of Villers Bretonneux. Divisional Headquarters had already reached Corbie, but owing to the rapid changes in the situation our immediate destination had been altered while we were en route. The 4th Battalion, indeed, because of the

---

*As an interesting instance of imperturbability, it may be mentioned that on March 23rd, the date on which the orders were issued for this move, General Russell held at his headquarters the first conference in connection with the proposed educational scheme for the Division.

bombing of the railway about Amiens, was not able to get further forward than Hangest, twelve miles to the west, which was reached after midnight.

Each unit on detraining got into fighting kit and dumped overcoats and all surplus gear. Ammunition on the man was made up to 220 rounds, that for the Lewis guns, which were now withdrawn from the limbers, up to the carrying capacity of the men of the sections, and the troops stood by waiting for the motor transport.

The first-line transport without delay went forward by road, with instructions to keep north and west of the River Ancre; and at 10 a.m., on orders from Division, Brigade Headquarters and advance parties from units proceeded by lorries to Buire, fifteen miles north-east of Amiens, arriving there at 3 p.m.

After a weary wait of nearly twelve hours the lorries arrived for the 1st Battalion, the first unit to be served, and by 8.30 p.m. on the 25th the convoy started off along the Albert Road for Buire. On arrival at Pont Noyelles, however, some six miles from Amiens, the battalion had to de-bus and complete the journey on foot, the lorries, which had been engaged on urgent work all day elsewhere, being under orders to return for the other units in succession.

The march proceeded satisfactorily until, on nearing Buire, the battalion was met by a staff car and received written orders to change direction and move on to Hedauville, six miles north-west of Albert. The men were already tired owing to the long sleepless railway journey, followed by the twelve hours' stand-to at Amiens, and an addition to the length of the march was not at all cheering. Turning off the Albert Road, the battalion passed through Lavieville, Millencourt and Senlis, and reached Hedauville shortly before 4 a.m. Except in the vicinity of Senlis the roads were good. The marching was excellent, there being only two casualties just before arrival at the destination. Night-marching with the aid of only a small-scale map is somewhat trying, and as, in anticipation of the provision of motor conveyance, all transport had been sent on ahead, there were neither horses nor bicycles available for use in marking down in good time the correct turnings in the road. Fortunately neither hitch nor delay occurred.

Fires in the direction of Albert were visible throughout the march. There were practically no signs of panic or evacuation anywhere, and no troops were seen excepting the personnel of an aerodrome making preparations for departure, and a few individual soldiers sleeping by the roadside.

The 2nd Battalion, less "A" Company, engaged on entraining duty, reached Pont Noyelles by motor lorries at 2 a.m. on the 26th. Having been apprised in good time of their correct destination they were able to make their march by a shorter route, and, leaving Pont Noyelles at 2.30 a.m., arrived at Hedauville, via Franvillers, Baizieux and Warloy, at 7 a.m.

The 3rd Battalion, less "C" Company, which was coming to Amiens by a later train, commenced the march from Pont Noyelles at 10 a.m. on the 26th. By this time there was a great deal of movement through Amiens and along the roads, streams of refugees moving back and bodies of troops marching in both directions. Hedauville was reached at 3 p.m.

The 4th Battalion marched from Hangest, and passing through Amiens, bivouacked on the Albert Road till 8 p.m. on the 26th, when they were taken to Hedauville by lorry.

In the meantime Divisional Headquarters had moved from Corbie to Hedauville, where it was established at 1.30 a.m. on the 26th. Shortly after midnight 25th/26th, Brigade Headquarters received preliminary instructions from Division to the effect that the position was obscure; that from information received it would appear a five-mile gap existed in the line from Hamel to Puisieux-au-Mont; and that the Divisional Commander intended to occupy the gap, with the 2nd Brigade on the right and the 1st Brigade on the left. Brigade Headquarters, with details and such transport as had arrived, set out for Hedauville forthwith.

On the arrival of the 1st Battalion it was warned by Division to be ready to move off again at 6 a.m. on a further two hours' march for active operations. The Brigadier and the Brigade Major presently reached Hedauville, and at 6 a.m. orders were issued to the 1st Battalion to advance through Mailly Maillet, establish an outpost line on the Englebelmer–Auchonvillers Ridge, gain touch with the 12th Division, Vth Corps, at Englebelmer, and cover the deployment of the 2nd and 1st New Zealand Infantry Brigades, which were to advance against Hamel and Serre. The line thus laid down for the battalion was nearly three miles in length, covered Englebelmer, Mailly Maillet and Auchonvillers, and had its left on the Serre Road, about 500 yards east of the Colincamps Road junction. Personal reconnaissance showed the proposed position to be good, with a fair amount of artillery in the valley in front of Mailly Maillet and in the vicinity of Englebelmer. "C" and "D" Companies (Captains K. R. J. Saxon and W. J. King) were detailed to establish the line of posts, "B" (Capt. G. P. O'Shannassy) to find advanced and flank guards for the march, to act as screen during the placing of the posts, and then to withdraw through the line into support. "A" Company (Major H. S. N. Robinson) was held in reserve.

Advanced Brigade Headquarters were established in Mailly Maillet by 9 a.m. Soon after that hour the 1st Battalion passed through the outskirts of the village, and at 11 a.m. the advanced troops gained touch with the enemy 500 yards east of Auchonvillers, where hostile patrols were engaged and driven back by Lewis gun and rifle fire. The left flank of the screen met the enemy in considerable force near the Sugar Factory and at once engaged him with the object of pushing him back beyond the position laid down for the left of the outpost line. Sharp fighting ensued and the advance of the Germans was temporarily stayed. The strength of the enemy was, however, rapidly increasing, and our men began to feel the pressure.

Meanwhile the two outpost companies moved steadily forward towards their allotted positions. The right company established its posts with little difficulty by 11 a.m. and immediately pushed out patrols, one of which went forward a distance of two miles to Aveluy Wood and the railway on the bank of the Ancre. These patrols found that the villages of Martinsart and Mesnil were in possession of troops of the 12th Division, and that troops of the 2nd Division were astride the Auchonvillers–Hamel Road. The left company's right and centre platoons established their posts without serious opposition, but the left flank platoon, joining that of the screen, became hotly engaged at 11.45 a.m. with a superior enemy force, which had by this time been considerably augmented. Fully 300 Germans were now in position across the Serre Road from

Euston on the north to Kilometre Lane on the south, and fresh troops could be seen marching rapidly westwards from Serre. Ugly rushes down the old trenches leading from the strong position in the sunken road became more and more frequent. Shouting "Give it up, Anzac; we are all around you!" the Germans closed in on the left platoon and almost succeeded in cutting it off, but 2nd Lieut. H. A. Mackenzie, who was now for the first time in action, handled his men with great dash and skill. A few moments sufficed to take in the situation. Without delay suitable positions were selected; one by one the leading sections were steadily withdrawn to the stronger line, each in turn affording covering fire for the remainder, a local defensive flank was formed, and the enemy temporarily held. In this the work of the section-leaders was admirably done. Rifleman C. A. Tucker commanded his section with great ability throughout, and when a Lewis gun team became casualties, he took over the gun himself. One rush he stopped within twenty yards of his position, and altogether he and his section accounted for 90 Germans. One of his men, Rifleman A. L. Sturmey, assisted with the gun, and in the interval plied his rifle so successfully as to have to his credit fourteen of the enemy, including two officers. The fearlessness displayed by the German leaders evoked the unbounded admiration of our men. Possibly they were unduly flushed with the victories of the past few days, for they repeatedly dashed forward with what appeared to be the utmost foolhardiness, and it was clear that a realization of the fact that they were now striking at a line practically immovable had not yet dawned upon their minds. An acknowledgment that the ability of his opponents had at least in some respects been underrated came all too late from one of the German officers, who, fatally struck by a rifle bullet at close range, cried out as he clutched at his breast, "The blighters can shoot, anyhow!"

Although the position was saved for the moment, the danger to the flank became increasingly imminent. Machine-gun fire from the north, already severe, now became alarmingly heavy. Capt. King personally took over immediate control at this threatened point. The pressure becoming rapidly stronger, reinforcements were asked for, and in response two platoons from the reserve company were sent up at about 12.30

p.m. These were followed by two Lewis gun teams from battalion headquarters' reserve sent up in ration limbers at the gallop. With the fresh troops and remnants of British sections, Capt. King bent his flank back and secured a firmly-established line in the form of a quarter-circle from Apple Tree Hill to the eastern outskirts of Auchonvillers. While the defensive flank was being formed, the enemy made a determined rush that again threatened to envelop the outer platoon, but this move was effectively countered by the fine work of the covering section under Corporal D. Osborne. Excellent support was also rendered by Lieut. R. H. Buchanan of the Canterbury Machine Gun Company, who with two guns reported at this time for duty with the battalion and took up a position covering the left flank. At 2 p.m., on account of continued pressure from the north, the whole of the support company, as well as the remaining two platoons of the reserve company, were also sent in to prolong the refused flank towards Colincamps. Between 3 and 4 p.m. the two Canterbury Battalions, advancing to the attack, passed through our line.

Shelling, which commenced at midday on the Serre Road behind Apple Tree Hill, and on Auchonvillers and the valley in rear, increased during the afternoon, but was never very heavy. The British artillery found in position in the valley in the morning were withdrawn from the forward area later in the day.

The casualties sustained by the 1st Battalion up to 2.30 p.m. were one officer wounded, nine other ranks killed and 34 wounded.

Having detailed the work of the 1st Battalion in establishing an outpost line, we now turn to the operations of the two Brigades, the deployment of which this outpost line was designed to cover.

Units from different Brigades had been arriving at Hedauville together or at short intervals, and the urgency of the position rendered it necessary to make up composite Brigades for immediate action. Thus the 2nd N.Z. Infantry Brigade became "A" Brigade, and the 1/N.Z.R.B. came under the orders of that Brigade at 4 p.m. Similarly the 1st N.Z. Infantry Brigade became "B" Brigade, and the 2/N.Z.R.B. was allotted to it.

At 12 noon on the 26th, General Young's "A" Brigade, which at that time consisted of the 2nd Brigade (less 1st and 2nd Otago Battalions) with one Machine Gun Company, moved out from Hedauville, followed later by "B" Brigade, which was simply the Headquarters of the 1st Brigade, the 1st Auckland Battalion and the 2nd Battalion of the New Zealand Rifle Brigade (less one company), together with one Machine Gun Company.

At 2.15 p.m. the troops of "A" Brigade, with 1st Canterbury on the right and 2nd Canterbury on the left, deployed out of Mailly Maillet and moved towards their objective. They passed through the line established by the 1/N.Z.R.B., pushed the Germans before them, and took up a position from the high ground overlooking Hamel on the right, to a point about 1,000 yards north-east of Auchonvillers on the left. This line was about 3,000 yards in advance of the 1/N.Z.R.B. outpost line on the right, but not more than 500 yards forward on the left, and lay along what had been the old British front line before the Somme offensive of 1916. The left flank of "A" Brigade met with considerable oppositon, the enemy strongly holding One Tree Hill, and it was decided to wait till "B" Brigade had come up on the left before pushing that flank forward.

At 4·p.m. the 1/N.Z.R.B. came under General Young's orders and was held in support to "A" Brigade. The original disposition was resumed, the two forward companies remaining in place and the others returning to their support and reserve positions. Lieut.-Col. A. E. Stewart thereupon returned to Hedauville to superintend the formation of a third composite Brigade.

General Melvill's "B" Brigade followed "A" Brigade in conformity with the scheme agreed upon. On reaching Mailly Maillet, however, reports were received that the enemy was in Colincamps, and this necessitated an alteration in the plans and entailed a delay until 4.30 p.m., at which hour the attack in this quarter was launched. It was a very small assaulting force, consisting, it will be remembered, of only two battalions, each with sections from a machine-gun company attached; but the men, although long since dog-tired, were in high spirits. It was hoped that penetration would be made as far as Serre, which lay some three and a half miles north-east of Mailly Maillet. The 1st Auckland Battalion advanced on the right, and the 2/N.Z.R.B. (Major J. Pow) on the left, the road to Serre giving the direction and forming the dividing line between battalions. For the provision of a reserve, reliance was placed on the expected early arrival of 2nd Auckland, still on the way up from Amiens.

A section of the distant Serheb Road, leading north-west from Serre to Hebuterne, was the objective for our 2nd Battalion. Of this unit, "C" Company (Lieut. W. J. Organ), on the right, and "D" Company (Capt. G. A. Mills), on the left, comprised the leading line, while "B" Company (Capt. H. M. Keesing) was detailed to form a defensive flank on the left and conform generally to the movements of the main attack. "A" Company was away at Amiens on detraining duty.

The advance in extended order from the vicinity of the railway station on the north of Mailly Maillet proceeded rapidly and steadily until the Sugar Factory, standing near the junction of the Colincamps Road with that from Serre, was reached by the right of "C" Company. Up till this time no direct opposition had been met with, though a considerable number of casualties had been caused by machine-gun fire coming from the high ground topped by a hedge and lying away on the left front. Dense smoke from a burning munition dump at the bend in the Colincamps Road, north of the Factory, had concealed the advancing platoons from frontal view, but on emerging from this, 2nd Lieut. F. W. Parry's men of the 9th platoon at once came under heavy fire from three machine-guns placed about the Serre Road, one being in a trench across the road itself, and the others in saps running parallel to and on each side of the road. It was evident that the enemy was holding strongly the one important highway from Puisieux and Serre.

On the opening of this machine-gun fire, Parry led his men forward at the double to the cover afforded by the farther bank of the road lying directly across their front and about 150 yards east of the Sugar Factory. This led northward to Euston Junction and Hebuterne, and was a continuation of that sunken road from the shelter of which the enemy had so heavily attacked the left flank of the 1st Battalion earlier in the day. As soon as the other leading platoon, under the command of Sergt. G. F. Webster, had joined up on the left, the advance was continued by sections to the next vantage-point, an old trench lying across the front. During this rush Lance-Corporal R. Ellmers and Rifleman E. H. Dodd went still further forward, passing along the sap running by the northern side of the Serre Road, where they attacked the crew of one of the machine-guns already referred to, and captured the gun. The remainder of the Germans in this section of the sap, some 40 strong, dashed across the Serre Road to the parallel sap on the south side.

The position here was now somewhat difficult, for, having its own troubles about the sunken road, the flank company of 1st Auckland was some distance back, and Parry's right was "in the air." To meet this emergency he pushed the whole of his platoon into the sap by the road, thus forming a defensive flank facing south, and opened a sniping duel with the enemy on the other side. Sergeant Webster now worked his platoon forward along another sap running parallel to Parry's, thus temporarily breaking connection with "D" Company on the left. The gap, however, was presently made good, for Webster's men fought their way into a cross trench facing east and joined up with Parry's left; and the remaining two platoons, under 2nd Lieuts. C. R. Cameron and E. R. Nutter, that had formed the company's support and reserve, cleared a series of old trenches and prolonged the line from Webster's left across to Euston Junction, where the right of "D" Company now rested.

The progress of "D" and "B" Companies had not on the whole been so successful. The line of advance of the former was crossed diagonally by a road, a railway, and a series of old but well-marked trenches, and, as is well known, troops moving across country along such a line tend to lose direction. Such, indeed, happened in the case of the platoons of this company, those on the left trending more and more to the northward, whereas the intention was that they should swing round to the east. The line was thus extended beyond its proper limits, and the advance, instead of continuing rapidly, was unduly retarded. Then, too, doubtless owing to the paucity of information regarding the enemy in the immediate vicinity of

Colincamps, the company forming the defensive flank on the left was more careful than proved to be necessary in its investigation of the area in and about that village, and this also had an appreciable effect in delaying the general movement. These two companies ultimately reached the line of trench along the side of the road running back from Euston towards Colincamps and Sailly-au-Bois.

At about 7. p.m. the left flank of 1st Auckland's line was carried forward some 300 yards and connection gained with our 2nd Battalion's right. Some slight improvements were made in our own line, which finally ran eastwards along the Serre Road to within about 300 yards of Jeremiah Hedge, thence northwards for a similar distance, and bent back in a north-westerly direction towards Euston and so on along the road already referred to. The expected junction with the 4th Australian Brigade, which had been ordered to fill the gap between Hebuterne and Colincamps that day, was not yet made.

Before nightfall the salient formed by "C" Company of the 2nd Battalion at the Serre Road was twice attacked by the enemy, but in each case his attempt failed under our steady fire. Later in the evening a motor-car came down the road from Serre and stopped at some little distance from the bend where our forward post, garrisoned by Webster and three men, was placed. An officer got out and walked quickly, and apparently all unsuspecting, towards our line. All four rifles were trained upon him, and as he failed to respond to the usual challenge he was shot dead. The driver executed an astonishing turn on the road and made off before he could be dealt with.

It is officially reported that fourteen of the new light tanks, known as "whippets," now for the first time in action, participated in this afternoon's advance and did good service on the left flank. This reference is probably to some activity about Colincamps and Hebuterne earlier in the day, for though one had rendered some assistance to the 1st Battalion on the Serre Road they took no part in the 2nd Battalion's attack. During the next two or three days Lewis-gun teams from the tanks were attached to certain of the New Zealand battalions holding the line.

Our 2nd Battalion was relieved by 2nd Auckland before daybreak on the following morning, the 27th, and went back to Courcelles-au-Bois, just behind Colincamps.

Meanwhile the remaining Brigade, under the command of Lieut.-Col. A. E. Stewart, had been concentrating at Hedauville as a reserve, and finally comprised Headquarters of the New Zealand Rifle Brigade, the 3rd Battalion N.Z.R.B., 2nd Wellington and 2nd Otago Battalions, and the Wellington Machine Gun Company. It was decided to push the reserve Brigade into the gap on the left, but as the troops, some of whom had marched by road from Hangest, a distance of 27 miles, were too exhausted to move at once, their departure from Hedauville was delayed for some hours.

Our 4th Battalion arrived at 10 p.m., but for the time being it was held in Hedauville to form part of a new Divisional reserve being constituted as units came up. 1st Wellington and 1st Otago subsequently joined this last reserve, as did also the Engineers, Pioneers, Trench Mortar Batteries, etc.

Just before midnight on the 26th, Lieut.-Col. A. E. Stewart's composite Brigade of three battalions received orders to move via Mailly Maillet to Colincamps and occupy a line along the Auchonvillers–Hebuterne Road between the 1st N.Z. Infantry Brigade ("B" Brigade) and the right of the 62nd Division. The 4th Australian Brigade (temporarily attached to the 62nd Division) was reported to be holding the line round the south-eastern outskirts of Hebuterne, and, as the left of "B" Brigade was at Euston, the position to be attacked was some 2,500 yards in length.

The move from Hedauville commenced at 1 a.m. on the 27th. The night was fine and cool, with moonlight so brilliant that by its aid maps could be read with considerable ease. For some time the column was accompanied by a huge German bombing-aeroplane flying comparatively low and clearly visible to our men; but, probably because of the exhaustion of its supply of bombs and machine-gun ammunition, the troops on the march were not molested. There had been no time for the issue of detailed orders for the operation in hand. Before marching out from Hedauville the battalion commanders were allotted their respective tasks by the Brigadier, and the necessary tactical plans were elaborated and communicated to company commanders at the regulation clock-hour halts by the road-side. In a similar manner the details were worked out by company commanders with their junior officers, who, in their turn, marching in the midst of their platoons, explained the nature of the enterprise to the men and mapped out the duties of the different sections. How well the adaptability of all ranks proved itself in the face of these novel methods, and in spite of lack of information regarding this unknown country and the position and strength of the enemy to be encountered, will be shown in the sequel.

As the column emerged from Mailly Maillet the 2nd Otago Battalion pushed out advanced and flank guards, and when the main body reached Colincamps, where Brigade Headquarters were now established, the same unit formed a temporary outpost line east and north-east of that village. While this screen got into position the two attacking battalions broke up into artillery formation about the scattered buildings. By this time the moon was setting, and in order to take full advantage of the poor visibility during the hour remaining before the dawn, the 3rd Battalion (Lieut.-Col. Puttick) was held only some fifteen minutes in Colincamps. Moving with all speed these troops took the road leading directly north-east towards Hebuterne, "D" Company (Capt. H. C. Meikle) leading, followed by "A" and "B" (Captains F. E. Greenish and H. W. Slater) at suitable intervals. Each company found its own flank guards, the first providing in addition an advanced guard of one platoon.

The refused right flank of the Australians curved round Hebuterne to a point some 800 yards south-west of the village, and the instructions issued to "D" Company provided that as soon as the advanced guard should gain touch with the Australians the company was to halt, turn to the right, and advance eastwards in attack formation. "A" Company was to act similarly, prolonging the attack to the right, while "B" was to form a support line in a defensive position 100 yards east of the road and covering the whole battalion section.

Save that, owing to ground mist, "A" Company overstepped its turning-point, an error that was speedily rectified, the operation was carried out with clock-like precision. Advancing in perfect order against machine-gun and rifle fire of moderate intensity, "D" Company pushed forward to its objective some 600 yards distant, its left being secured by a defensive flank formed by two Lewis gun sections facing north. The breaking dawn gave sufficient light for rapid movement, and in six minutes the company gained the crest of the ridge. Both flanks were immediately extended, the northern to gain touch with the true right of the Australians at Hebuterne, and the southern to assist "A" Company, whose leading lines were at the moment 400 yards short of their goal. By 6.45 a.m. the whole of the battalion sector of the objective was in our hands.

Numerically the enemy was greatly superior to the attacking troops, but on the whole the fighting was not severe. Here and there, however, local encounters were sufficiently sharp. Lance-Corporal J. N. O'Donnell's section was at one time entirely surrounded by the enemy and called upon to surrender. The lance-corporal's silent reply was some busy personal work with the bayonet, and he and his men speedily cleared up the situation. Another lance-corporal, B. T. Smith, being troubled by a sniper, set out to stalk him, but unexpectedly he came upon a machine-gun enfilading the trench. Enlisting the support of one other man he rushed and killed the crew and captured the gun. W. G. Bowers, also a lance-corporal, experienced a similar surprise, for, pushing down an enemy sap to secure two wounded Germans as prisoners, he ran against a party of twelve of the enemy, all hale and hearty. He was fired at and wounded, but, rushing boldly forward, he attacked the dozen single-handed and succeeded in capturing two and driving off the remainder.

The determining factors in the successful issue of the operation were the rapidity and regularity with which it had been conducted. That the enemy had been completely taken by surprise was evidenced by the weak resistance offered, the disorderliness of his retreat, and the great quantity of equipment and tools left scattered about the whole front.

In the meantime the 2nd Wellington Battalion, whose objective lay on the right of that of our 3rd Battalion, moved out of Colincamps in an easterly direction, and coming under heavy rifle and machine-gun fire from the hedge west of La Signy Farm, was held back for some time. The right, however, eventually got forward into touch with 2nd Auckland at Euston, and the left had secured its objective before our own right company was up; but the centre was delayed and had to dig in on a line of posts 300 yards west of the Hebuterne Road.

Thus, by 9 a.m. on March 27th, the great five-mile gap was closed. The enemy, as we shall see, continued for many days his efforts to sweep away the obstacles in his path, but although beyond both our flanks he made some slight gains, such as the capture of Hamel* on the south and Rossignol Wood on the north, and on our own front succeeded in temporarily enlarging his small salient from the line of the Hebuterne Road, his advance was definitely held up. The following message received from General Harper, commanding the IVth Corps, is indicative of the fact that the situation was now regarded as eminently satisfactory:—

"The Corps Commander congratulates the 42nd, 62nd, and New Zealand Divisions and the 4th Australian Brigade on their magnificent behaviour during the last few days' fighting. Numerous heavy attacks by the enemy have been completely repulsed with heavy loss and the capture of prisoners and machine-guns. He heartily thanks the troops for their courage and endurance, and is confident that they will continue to hold the line against all attacks."

PART 3.—STRAIGHTENING THE LINE.

Brigade formations restored—Counter-attacks—Enemy enlarges the salient at La Signy Farm—3rd Battalion holds its ground—4th Battalion takes over from 2nd Wellington at the salient, March 27th/28th—4th Battalion companies attack, March 28th, and clear the salient by March 31st—Congratulations—The new Line—Disaster to Brigade Headquarters: General Fulton mortally wounded, and Major Purdy killed—Command.

From time to time, as opportunity offered, the units of the composite organizations were interchanged and restored to their proper Brigades. After the successful advance of our 3rd Battalion on the morning of the 27th, 2nd Otago passed from Lieut.-Col. Stewart's command to Divisional reserve, and

*Owing to the extreme length of the line held by the New Zealanders, Hamel had been handed over to the Division on our right.

BRIGADIER-GENERAL A. E. STEWART, C.M.G., D.S.O.

Face p. 288.

Lieut.-Col. J. Pow,
D.S.O.

Lieut.-Col. L. H. Jardine,
D.S.O., M.C.

A Captured German Machine-Gun in use in the Front Line near La Signy Farm.

Another Part of the Front Line near the Farm.

A "Whippet."

A Derelict Tank.

moved back to help dig and garrison a section of a new trench-system known as the Purple Line, sited on the high ground behind Colincamps and extending north-eastwards towards Hebuterne. On the previous night, 26th/27th, our 2nd Battalion had been relieved by the 2nd Auckland and had gone back to Mailly Maillet in support to "B" Brigade. It moved to Courcelles on the evening of the 27th, and at 4.30 a.m. on the following day came forward to Colincamps and rejoined the New Zealand Rifle Brigade as battalion in reserve. The 1st Battalion was still detached from the Brigade. Relieved on the morning of the 27th by 1st Otago, it moved from the support position behind the Canterbury battalions and was to be placed in Divisional reserve at Colincamps; but owing to uncertainty regarding the situation beyond our right flank it was retained by General Young as reserve, and stationed at Englebelmer. It did not rejoin the Brigade till the evening of the 29th, going then into the Purple Line as part of Divisional reserve. With this last move the re-establishment of the normal formation of all three Brigades was completed. The available artillery had been strengthened by the arrival of a considerable number of New Zealand guns, four 18-pounder Batteries and one Howitzer Battery having reached Hedauville by the evening of the 27th. Stokes mortar ammunition came to hand on the following day.

On the 27th the enemy launched a series of counter-attacks on the newly-established line, but, save at one point, these all proved abortive. At 6 a.m., while the 3rd Battalion attack was still in progress, a strong enemy concentration about the Serre Road was broken up by our artillery. In the middle of the forenoon a force of about the strength of two battalions was mown down by machine-gun fire as it came into view at "16 Poplars," east of Hebuterne. At this time the enemy's artillery, now evidently reinforced, commenced a light but steady bombardment of the whole area. The gunfire increased in intensity towards noon, when the massing of troops at various points in the distance was observed. Infantry attacks presently developed against the 2nd Auckland position about the Serre Road, and against the two Canterbury battalions opposite Beaumont Hamel, but though these were pressed with great determination they were everywhere held.

At about 3 p.m. it was seen that the front of attack was again extending northwards, involving 2nd Wellington, our own 3rd Battalion, and the Australians south-east of Hebuterne. Against this section of the line the Germans advanced steadily in numerous short columns, small red flags being carried by the leaders, whose whistle signals could be heard from our lines. As they came within range our rifles and Lewis guns opened rapid fire, and the advance against both the Australians and the 3rd Battalion was checked. The men of "A" Company welcomed the good targets at short range, of which they had to some extent been deprived during the early morning, and amongst the busiest of them all was probably one of the cooks, whose ordinary duties, as may well be understood, had not yet commenced. He certainly made very good practice, and the truth of his declaration, repeated as each new clip of cartridges was pressed into the magazine, that he had mistaken his vocation, may be conceded; for if he had concocted his stews as magnificently as he was then handling his rifle he would probably have been kept carefully under cover.

But while the situation in front was thus far satisfactory, developments on the right flank of the battalion were giving cause for anxiety. Just prior to the advance of the enemy infantry our right company commander had received word from the troops on his right that they had had orders to fall back in the event of a serious attack. As the enemy assault developed it was seen that 2nd Wellington were in difficulties, for the Germans on their front, having the initial advantage of the small salient on which they had maintained their hold, were making full use of their superiority of position, and under stress of enfilade as well as frontal fire, our immediate neighbours were compelled to give ground, leaving our flank exposed. To meet this danger, 2nd Lieut. A. J. Beehan, who was in command of "A" Company's support line, was ordered to form a defensive flank with one of his platoons. While reading his instructions he fell a victim to the storm of machine-gun bullets coming across from the high ground about La Signy Farm; but his platoon-sergeant, Sergeant W. Cumming, promptly acted on the order and at once despatched a platoon under Corporal J. Dean to carry out this difficult task. The corporal's management of the affair was to the last degree admirable. Under the cover of Sergeant Cumming's Lewis gun fire, he skilfully rushed his men to a small isolated trench beyond his flank. There he was faced by a German machine-gun only 200 yards away. As though at target practice on the rifle range, Dean gave his men careful and detailed instructions and calmly awaited his opportunity. With the first renewed splutter from the gun he gave the object, distance, and the order for three rounds rapid fire. Thus he accounted for the gun team. The gun was re-manned, and again the procedure was gone through, with a like result. Yet again this was repeated, and this time he had the satisfaction of putting the gun out of action altogether. He now devoted his attention to other guns firing from the vicinity of a timber dump on the right, and was successful in considerably reducing the volume of fire coming from that point.

Thanks to the skill and daring of Dean and his men the threatened envelopment of the support positions failed, but the enemy was having greater, though but temporary success in that long straight trench by the road where the front line troops were stationed. Sergeant A. C. Goodhue, "A" Company's Lewis gun sergeant, was sent up to the front line to co-ordinate the work of the Lewis guns there in dealing with the attack, but meanwhile the Germans had rolled up our line for a distance of about 100 yards to where a small sap led diagonally from the main trench, and a German officer with twelve men, under cover of rifle and revolver fire, was advancing along the parapet towards the handful of our men at this point. Just as Sergeant Goodhue arrived he heard the German officer call out in English: "Come along, you New Zealanders; you will have to surrender!" With a characteristic expression voicing derision of the idea of surrender, Goodhue brought a Lewis gun to his shoulder and discharged the whole drum at the party, killing the officer and six of his men. The remainder, some of whom were wounded, made good their escape.

Earlier in the day, when the attack seemed imminent, bombs had been ordered up. These arrived from the transport speedily enough, but not one was detonated, the transport having been on the move continuously for some time. The whole of the battalion headquarters' staff thereupon set to work to insert the necessary detonators, and a goodly supply was ready for the bombing party, which, under Lieut. J. Russell, now worked to the right and cleared the enemy from the last stretch of front-line trench.

After dusk, there being no improvement in the situation beyond our right, a platoon from the reserve company was sent up to reinforce the hard-pressed men on the flank. Fortunately "C" Company (Lieut. F. J. L. Buchler), which had been detained on duty at Amiens, arrived from Hedauville at 7.30 p.m. Three of its platoons were immediately pushed in on the exposed flank, which was thus strengthened and securely held; and this extension enabled touch to be gained with the left of 2nd Wellington, now about 500 yards back from the original line. 2nd Wellington, assisted by our covering fire, launched a counter-attack at 8.50 p.m. with the object of regaining the lost ground. The results, however, were inconsiderable, and the situation in our immediate neighbourhood remained practically unchanged.

Capt. (Temp. Major) A. Thomson, acting Second-in-Command, took over control of the battalion just after noon, Lieut.-Col. E. Puttick, D.S.O., having been wounded.* His conduct of the operations following the capture of the general objective was characterized by much skill, and his coolness in the face of the difficult situation that developed had a markedly steadying effect upon all ranks. Major P. H. Bell, from the 1st Battalion, assumed command of the 3rd Battalion on the following day.

During the night (27th/28th) the 4th Battalion marched from Hedauville to take over from 2nd Wellington, but as the latter unit was engaged in fighting for the lost ground, the relief was not completed until near daylight. "B" Company (Capt. W. F. Fowlds) went in on the right, "C" Company (Capt. A. L. McDowell) on the left; "D" Company (Capt. M. H. R. Jones) was placed in support, and "A" (Capt. W. W. Dove) in reserve.

*This morning's fight marked the close of Lieut.-Col. Puttick's active service in France. He commanded the Reserve Depot at Brocton from the end of May until a month after the Armistice, when he left for New Zealand on duty.

The enemy was holding 1,200 yards of the Hebuterne Road from 400 yards north of Euston to the flank of the 3rd Battalion, with a series of posts pushed well forward. He was strong in machine-guns, and from his commanding position on the ridge had the whole battalion frontage under observation and fire. A night reconnaissance was made, but as the sector was otherwise unknown it was impossible to make a general attack on the salient at once. Some slight gains had been made, however, even before the relief was actually complete, for at 5 a.m. a platoon of "B" Company, under 2nd Lieut. G. Malcolm, fought their way forward against heavy odds and established posts in old gun-pits below the road. It was a stiff struggle, and in the hand-to-hand fighting the platoon-commander was killed. Then, again, at 7 a.m. 2nd Lieut. A. French led a section from "C" Company in a bombing attack along one of the main saps leading directly up to the road above. The trench was strongly held, but the Germans were driven back fifty yards, and the section established a post covering the ground gained. Beyond effecting certain necessary adjustments in the various posts and reconnoitring the position, nothing more was attempted in the meantime.

Away on the left flank of the 3rd Battalion, Capt. H. C. Meikle's company had, during the night and early morning, been thoroughly patrolling the saps and country to its front; and as a result of the investigations made it was decided to attack the enemy's position in a series of quarries some little distance in front of the centre of the company's sector. Supported by Australian trench mortars and machine-guns, the attack was made during the afternoon. All resistance was quickly beaten down, and the position, large enough to hold a company, with good quarters and an excellent well, fell into the hands of the enterprising "D" Company. As on the previous morning, the Germans left behind a great quantity of tools, equipment, rifles and bombs. The captured position gave a wide field of observation extending over 3,000 yards, and formed an excellent advanced post covering our line for some distance to the north and south.

At 11.30 a.m. Lieut.-Col. Beere received the expected orders for an attack at 4 p.m., with the object of pushing the enemy off the high ground and establishing touch with the 3rd

Battalion, whose front line troops were to assist by bombing southwards. Little artillery support was available, and the covering barrage was feeble. The attack was made by "B" Company on the right and "A" on the left, "D" Company moving back into the reserve position. The right of "B" Company was successful in gaining the objective on the crest, but its left flank was held up by the enemy strongly entrenched about the huge timber dump. Here, however, a platoon established a post in one of the old gun-pits. The left company made similar progress, the two platoons on its inner flank being held up, and the remainder gaining the ridge, but the machine-gun fire had been so fierce that when the objective was reached only two officers and twelve men were left. This small party was confronted by fifty Germans fighting fiercely to retain their hold on the trench. The enemy were driven out, however, and no fewer than six machine-guns and two Lewis guns were captured. Touch was gained with the 3rd Battalion, whose platoon under Lieut. D. George had given splendid support to the 4th Battalion men. In this platoon Rifleman J. H. Bromley led a handful of men to the attack on a strong-point containing a machine-gun. They killed the garrison, secured the gun, and, moving on with it, repeated the exploit at the next post.

It was during the progress of this fighting that a young Saxon came over and surrendered to one of the 3rd Battalion companies. Quite unnerved and practically inarticulate, he kept on repeating hysterically the same six words, of which our people, ignorant of the language, could make nothing except that there appeared to be some reference to Prussians and Saxons. Presently an officer was found who, though his knowledge of German was decidedly limited, succeeded in eliciting from the deserter the information that in his post were twenty Saxons under a Prussian officer. The man was plied with cigarettes and other comforts with the object of rendering him more loquacious, but this treatment had little result. The company commander was now struck with the brilliant idea of securing the whole garrison of the post without cost to ourselves, and with the few words that constituted his stock of German, aided by many gesticulations, gave the deserter to understand that he was to go back and persuade his fellow-

Saxons to return with him. Ominous wavings of a revolver made it clear that a terrible fate awaited him if he should fail to report again either alone or with his comrades, and with a final objurgation given in dumb show he was sent off on his mission. Apparently the iron discipline of his Prussian officer was considered preferable to the frightfulness of the New Zealanders, for he was not heard of again.

Though the efforts of the 4th Battalion on the evening of the 28th had resulted in a considerable reduction in the extent of the enemy salient, full success had not been attained, and after daylight next morning an attempt was made to complete the work. Gallant endeavours were made by bombing-parties led by Capt. J. L. McAlister from the flank, and by Lieut. J. G. Greenwood from the front; but though they each drove the enemy from 200 yards of trench, their supplies of bombs ran out before they could make good their gains.

A third attack by the 4th Battalion was planned for the afternoon of the 30th in conjunction with 2nd Auckland on the right, the main objective there being Jeremiah Hedge, running north-west from the Serre Road to the Hebuterne Road beyond La Signy Farm, and standing on high ground giving an almost uninterrupted view eastward. The 2nd Battalion, which had relieved the 3rd overnight, would co-operate by assisting the forward groups of "A" and "D" companies to bomb along to the right. "B" and "C" companies were detailed for the principal task of the 4th Battalion, and each of these was strengthened by the addition of a platoon from the 3rd Battalion as a reserve. The attack, preceded by a bombardment,* opened at 2 p.m. under a satisfactory barrage. A portion of the right company gained the hedge in touch with the 2nd Auckland troops, but its left flank could make little progress against the position at the dump. "C" Company had severe hand-to-hand fighting, captured 23 prisoners, and pushed the enemy back for some distance. The Germans stuck to their new position, however, and our men had to be content to dig in, still short of their objective. So also with the composite party on the right of the 2nd Battalion. The enemy at first gave ground, but only to take up a stronger

*Supplies of ammunition having now become available, three Stokes guns assisted, firing on the posts about the timber dump.

fighting position. He was fought here till our supplies of bombs were exhausted, but could not be dislodged. The attack was continued that night, when the 3rd Battalion platoon attached to the right company moved up through the Auckland position, and, gallantly led by 2nd Lieut. H. T. Marshall, bombed their way along the trench by the hedge to a position abreast of the timber dump.

Preparations were now made for a renewed effort. The 2nd Battalion extended its flank to the right, setting free the little group of exhausted 4th Battalion men there, and Lieut.-Col. Beere replaced his "C" Company on the left with the comparatively fresh "D" Company. At 3 a.m. on the 31st, soon after this preparatory adjustment had been completed, patrols reported that the enemy had evacuated his strong-point about the dump, whereupon "B" Company moved up and occupied the coveted trench on the ridge as far along as the cross-roads. From the position thus taken ten machine-guns were captured, and the number of German dead that lay about the trenches testified to the severity of the long struggle. Of the salient there remained now only that part opposite "D" Company, whose platoons moved up the slope at 5.15 a.m. Their advance was swift, resistance being slight except on the crest itself, and in a few minutes they had beaten down this opposition and were in possession of the trench.

In this closing stage of their protracted fight the 4th Battalion men were materially assisted by their comrades of the 2nd. Capt. H. E. Barrowclough, with two platoons of "A" Company, commanded respectively by Sergeants C. P. Hine and H. J. Laurent, set out southwards along the crest trench with the object of reducing the enemy's salient by attacking it from flank and rear. Progress was satisfactory until the leading men reached Palestine Hedge, running eastwards from the Hebuterne Road. Here some slight noise must have aroused the suspicion of the enemy, for two star-shells suddenly shot into the air; but the raiders instinctively crouched into the shadows and remained still for some time, and the expected burst of machine-gun fire was not sprung upon them. Creeping steadily forward again, our men silently approached the position thus revealed, and the first hostile shot was the signal for a rush from our side. Rapid fire was opened on the startled

ORDER OF BATTLE—COLINCAMPS, MARCH, 1918.

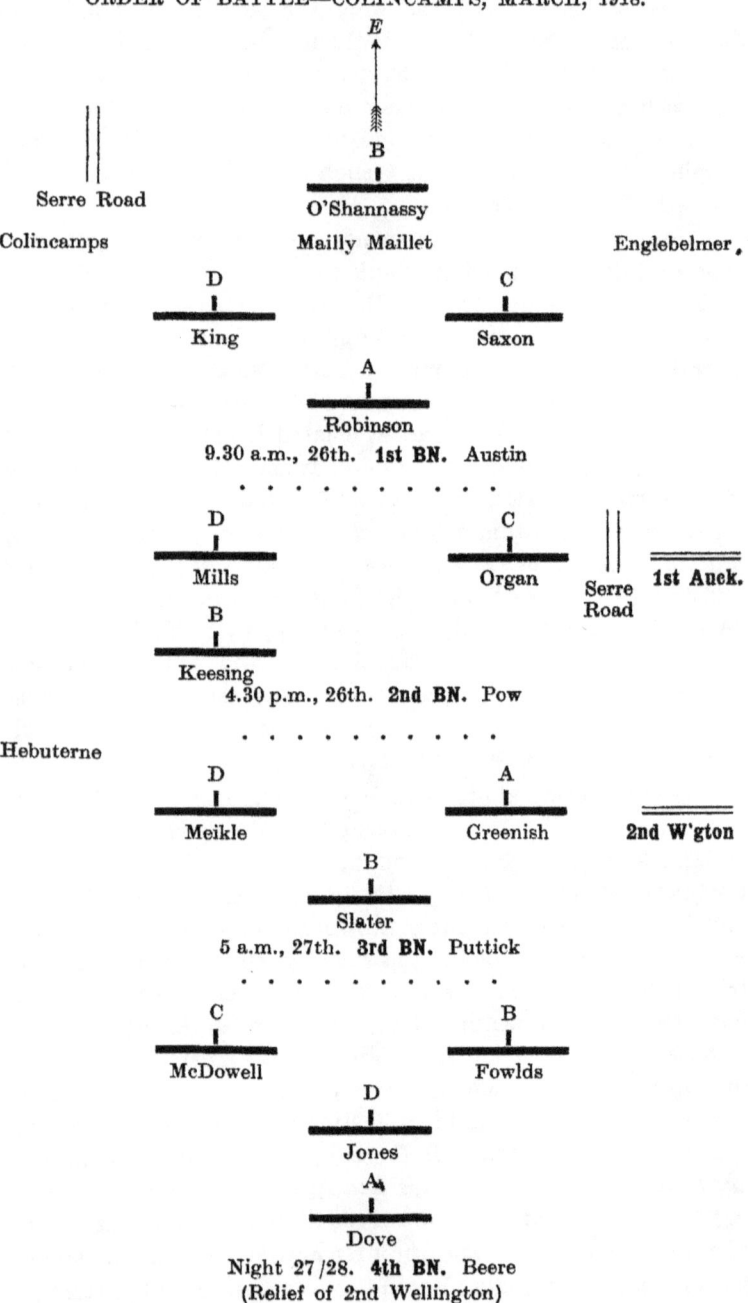

Germans, who, thus enfiladed, were thrown into confusion. They retreated in disorder and were mown down as they ran. Sections previously detailed for the purpose pushed along the main trench to deal with those of the enemy still to be found there, while others followed up those escaping by the saps. The whole attack was an affair of hand-to-hand encounters. Excellent leadership was displayed by Corporals Pram and Waterhouse. Firing at point-blank range, Lance-Corporal Grover with his Lewis gun annihilated a machine-gun crew. Rifleman Scaife, while bombing down a sap, suddenly ran into a burly German at a junction. Bombs at such close quarters being useless, he "went for" his opponent with his fists, and was making a good showing when the contest was brought to a sudden close by one of Scaife's party, who now came up with a rifle. Twenty-two prisoners and sixteen machine-guns were captured in this brilliant operation, while of Capt. Barrowclough's men only two were wounded. An important position was gained and the advance from the front greatly facilitated; for, when the 4th Battalion men finally reached the crest, they found the 2nd already in possession of a considerable stretch of the original objective.

So ended the 4th Battalion's stubborn struggle. Against an enemy strongly holding a position having all the advantages, his last bit of high ground to which he clung with the utmost determination, they had, through four long days of heavy rain, struck and struck again, until at last success had come. To both sides it had been a costly contest. The captured saps and trenches were found littered with dead and wounded, while the casualty list of the 4th Battalion included three officers and fifty other ranks killed, and five officers and 139 other ranks wounded.

The long line held by the three Brigades was now approximately regular and continuous, and being on high ground the advantage gained was invaluable. Observation was good throughout, particularly on the northern half from One Tree Hill to Hebuterne, for from this portion we almost completely overlooked the enemy. Many congratulatory messages were received by Division, amongst these being one from General Plumer, commanding the Second Army from which we had become detached when we moved down from Ypres.

We were now able to reflect with some degree of satisfaction upon the Brigade's share in the notable successes achieved by the Division during the past six days. Of this we had every reason to be proud, but the natural feeling of elation was damped by the disaster that had fallen upon Brigade Headquarters. During the heavy shelling on the night of the 28th, the cellar in Colincamps occupied by the Brigade staff was struck by a shell and demolished. Brigadier-General H. T. Fulton, C.M.G., D.S.O., who had returned from leave on the previous evening, was mortally wounded, and Major R. G. Purdy, M.C., the Brigade Major, was killed. The Staff Captain (Major G. C. Dailey), the Signalling Officer (Lieut. C. R. G. Bassett, V.C.), and the Grenade Officer (Lieut. K. E. Luke) were wounded, and no fewer than nine other ranks killed and eleven wounded. General Fulton succumbed to his injuries on the following morning whilst being conveyed to the casualty clearing station at Doullens. To the Brigade this catastrophe came as a severe blow. General Fulton had been entrusted with the organization and training of the Brigade from its inception, and during practically the whole of its existence it had been under his command. He jealously guarded its interests, but ever aimed at a high standard of efficiency. He was a strong disciplinarian and a stern taskmaster, yet every officer and man under his command knew that a somewhat gruff exterior but thinly concealed a kindly and sympathetic nature, and, infected by his intense pride in the Brigade, learned to discharge every task as if it were a personal service as well as a public duty.

Major Purdy, an officer of the New Zealand Staff Corps, had also been closely identified with the Brigade from its birth. In the 1st Battalion he had been in succession Platoon and Company Commander, and for a period Adjutant, serving in each of these capacities with conspicuous ability. Later he became Staff Captain and then Brigade Major, and won the esteem of all for the extreme thoroughness with which he discharged his duties, not less than for the self-sacrificing manner in which he gave his personal attention to the smallest details, however trying the conditions might be. He was fearless in the presence of danger, and every inch a soldier.

Lieut.-Col. A. E. Stewart, of the 2nd Battalion, again assumed command of the Brigade, with Major R. Logan, N.Z.S.C., of the 2nd Brigade, as temporary Brigade Major; and Lieut. E. Zeisler took over the duties of Staff Captain. Major J. Pow succeeded Lieut.-Col. Stewart in the command of the 2nd Battalion.

PART 4.—THE GERMAN ATTACK, APRIL 5TH.

Improving the Line—Daylight patrols—Advancement of posts—Readjustment of sector—Opening of the attack—Intense bombardment—German infantry everywhere held—Attack dies away by noon—3rd Battalion advance the Line—Local enemy counter-attacks—Congratulations—Enemy success about Armentieres, Messines, and Passchendaele.

The heavy rain that had drenched the men of the 4th Battalion throughout their long uphill fight continued on the 31st, but every effort was put forth to clear the lines and consolidate the position gained. After dark the 1st Battalion took over the sector, the 4th going into Divisional reserve at Courcelles.

Both battalions in the line now commenced a vigorous policy of improvement. The main position ran for the most part along the hedge and the Hebuterne Road, the garrison occupying an old trench with posts pushed forward along the saps leading eastward towards the German lines. Although we were on the crest of the ridge, it was found that there was much dead ground immediately in front. We were thus at some disadvantage, and as a preliminary step towards amending this state of affairs, daylight patrolling was at once put in hand in order to secure information as to the forward positions of the enemy.

On the 1st Battalion front Lance-Corporal R. McMurray pushed out alone, and, after much patient manœuvring, succeeded in pouncing upon a sentry, whom he brought in. From this man we gained sufficient information to enable us to capture and occupy two posts in the neighbourhood during the evening. Not content with this, McMurray moved on and marked down a third post, and on the following day continued his reconnaissance until a considerable stretch of the enemy's line was located with certainty. In the course of his wanderings he drew fire from an enemy machine-gun which we afterwards silenced with artillery-fire. Capt. Saxon and Lieut. C. C. Best gave special attention to the mysterious La Signy Farm, and without great difficulty succeeded in investigating the hedge on its northern and eastern sides during daylight. Fighting-patrols actively engaged the enemy on the 2nd Battalion front, and as a result of these combined efforts our forward posts were pushed into positions giving uninterrupted close as well as distant observation. These posts were strengthened, wired, and eventually connected up with a continuous trench, and, where required, further saps were dug.

This advantageous adjustment of the greater part of the line brought sections of it within fairly close touch with the enemy's advanced posts, and the necessary wiring was carried out at even greater risk than usual. One party engaged at this hazardous occupation near La Signy Farm came almost within bombing range, and when the Germans found that bombs failed to cause any appreciable check to their activities they opened fire with a machine-gun, an action that compelled our men to take cover with due promptitude. Then the usual flares went up again from the vicinity of the German post, and the illumination revealed the fact that the whole party of six men had sought the protection of the one small shell-hole within reach. They had, however, done little better than the ostrich, for, though their heads and shoulders were safely under cover, the greater part of their bodies remained exposed above ground round the rim. Fortunately they lay sufficiently still to escape enemy observation, and no casualties were sustained.

The 1st Brigade on our right established posts to the east of La Signy Farm on the night of 3rd/4th April, but these were not destined to be held for very long.

A readjustment of the sector was made on the night of 2nd/3rd April. The 4th Australians took over that part of the front line so smartly captured by our 3rd Battalion on 27th March, the 1st Battalion extended its front northwards to junction with the Australians, and the 2nd Battalion, thus relieved, went into support at Colincamps. Again, on the night of 4th/5th the 1st Brigade was withdrawn from the centre of the Divisional sector, our Brigade taking over from them the front line from One Tree Hill northward. The Brigade now held a front of well over 3,000 yards, with three battalions in the line. The 3rd held from One Tree Hill to the Serre Road; the 4th the centre, with its left on the hedge to the north of La Signy Farm; and the 1st the left from this point to the right of the Australians. Brigade Headquarters had by this time moved to safe quarters in a deep dug-out near the Colincamps–Sailly Road.

During the night the enemy's patrols displayed no unusual activity, though one consisting of an officer and ten men was discovered fumbling with the wire in front of a 1st Battalion advanced post held by a Lewis gun section under Lance-Corporal S. W. Toms. The lance-corporal dashed out and, covering the officer with his revolver, endeavoured to take him prisoner. The officer resisted, however, and was shot dead, and his party was dispersed with Lewis gun fire.

At 5 a.m. on 5th April, an intense enemy bombardment opened on the front line and continued for three hours over the whole area. Heavy shelling fell upon Colincamps and Courcelles and extended farther west towards Bus and Bertrancourt. Two battalion headquarters in the cellars of Colincamps narrowly missed destruction from 12-inch shells which placed a line of huge craters along each side of the main street of the village. All signal wires were immediately cut. At 8.30 a.m. the barrage on the front line lifted to the hollow and ridge in rear, and shortly afterwards the enemy were seen through the haze advancing to the attack all along the line. The infantry moving against the 2nd Brigade's sector on the right were checked by artillery-fire, and the advance in that quarter was not renewed. On our 3rd Battalion front there was no serious development except on the left flank at the Serre Road, where, however, the enemy was effectually held. Farther north the attack was stronger, but under the withering fire of rifles and machine-guns and bombing sorties in the saps, it nowhere reached nearer than thirty yards of our posts. On our left the Germans were driven back, but renewed the attempt at about 10 a.m. Against the salient at La Signy Farm the pressure was strongly maintained, and a 4th Battalion ad-

ORDER OF BATTLE—COLINCAMPS, APRIL 5, 1918.

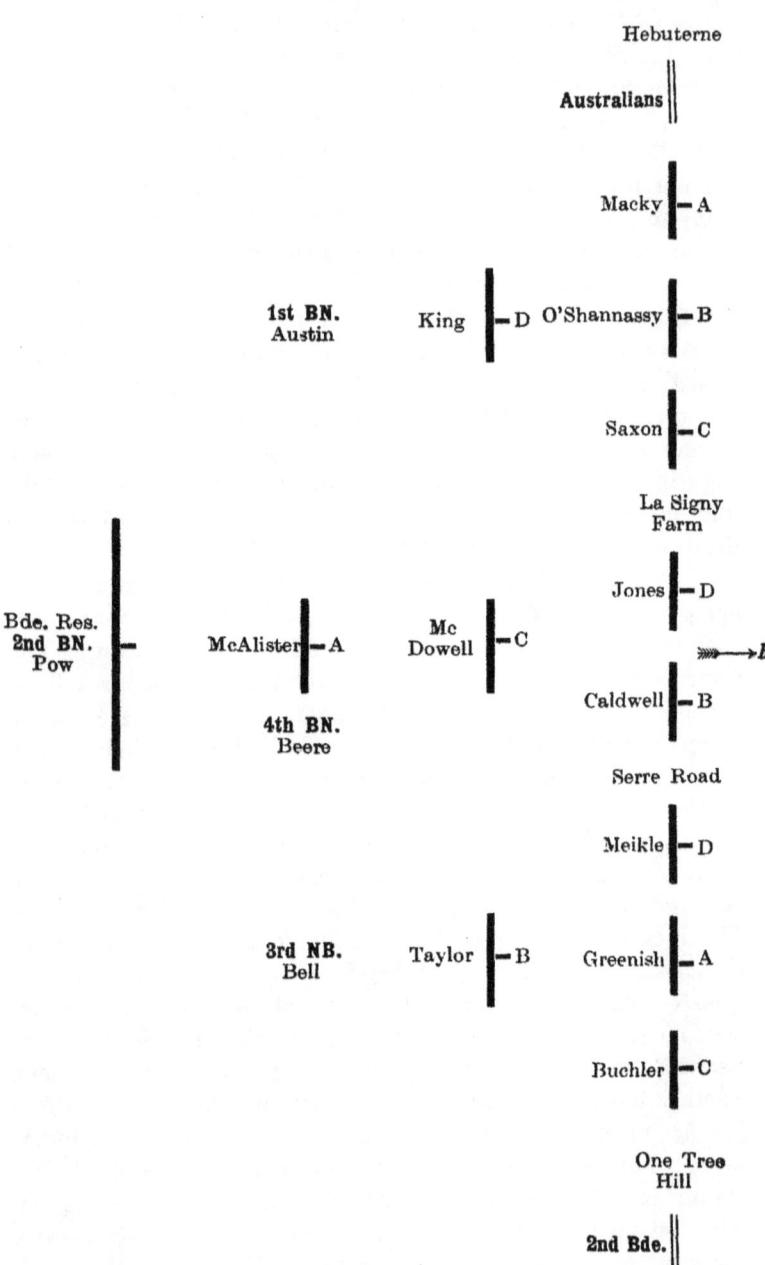

vanced post east of the Farm, one of those recently established here by the 1st Brigade, was captured. Pushing on after this slight success, the enemy overran the Farm and attempted to assault the 4th Battalion's main line, but the forward posts here had the situation well in hand, and after sustaining heavy casualties from our men the enemy gave up any further attempt to advance at this point. Never before had the Lewis gunners of the 4th Battalion had such targets as on this day, and of their opportunities they made full use, but they yield pride of place to Sergeant Lines, both for the magnificent handling of his team and for his own personal exploits with the gun.

On the well-defined front line of the 1st Battalion the preliminary bombardment fell with great intensity, particularly on the trenches held by the right company. Capt. Saxon, however, took his garrison forward to a position between the front line and the line of advanced posts. When the Germans had gained ground at the Farm they had this company's position enfiladed, and they thereupon endeavoured to exploit the advantage by working northward. Capt. Saxon immediately met the situation by promptly placing two sections of riflemen along the hedge running out past the Farm, and by ordering a platoon to form a defensive flank across the main line in case the enemy should succeed in breaking through from the front. Particularly gallant work on this flank was done by Sergeant B. L. Dixon, who took the place of his fallen platoon commander. Similarly, Lieut. M. A. Stedman, commanding the platoon holding the forward posts of this company, finding the Germans had pushed past his flank and were firing into the rear of his position, took out one of his sections of riflemen and lined the hedge, thus continuing the line already placed in position by his company commander. Notwithstanding heavy trench mortar and machine-gun fire this flank was securely held.

In the meantime the forward posts farther to the left were holding their own. Two attacks on the left company and three on that in the centre were boldly pressed, the enemy, finding his attack over the open unsuccessful, making determined efforts to reach our posts by way of the saps, but all his assaults were beaten off. Early in the day Rifleman R. C. Shannon, one of a Lewis gun team that had made some fine shooting against the advancing waves, was wounded by a shell that put his gun out of action. He at once attached himself to a neighbouring post guarding a sap. Up this trench fully a hundred Germans, led by an officer, were advancing rapidly against the post, when Shannon rushed out across the open, bombed the enemy at close range, killed the officer and two men near him, and wounded five others. A Lewis gun brought to bear on the remainder completed the rout of this assaulting party. Lieut. J. McL. Roy's platoon occupied a prominent salient which bore the brunt of repeated attacks from which it suffered severely. When the enemy abandoned the open and took to pushing up the saps, Lieut. Roy suitably laid a Lewis gun and then personally led a bombing section forward beyond our wire and forced the Germans back. Those who stuck to the trench were vigorously bombed, while those who rushed across the open to escape from the bombing were mown down by the Lewis gun. These forward movements were common features of the morning's work, and without doubt proved more effective in beating off the attack than mere fighting from the trenches. As leaders in such sorties, Capt. H. W. Kennedy, Lieut. R. J. Grant, Lance-Corporal G. A. Papworth and Rifleman A. L. Peters were conspicuous.

By noon the situation was again normal. Our casualties were not heavy. They were very slight in the 3rd Battalion; the 4th had one officer and 25 men killed, and one officer and 45 men wounded; while in the 1st, two officers and 26 men were killed, and one officer and 50 men wounded. A conservative estimate of the enemy's casualties opposite our immediate front places the number at over 500.

This attack was unique in the respect that it was the only one of major importance that the New Zealand Division ever sustained. It was launched with great determination, and wave after wave of advancing troops added strength and weight to the leading lines striking vainly at our posts. The enemy's immediate objective was that long stretch of high ground to our rear on which Colincamps stood, and along which the construction of our defensive system known as the Purple Line had already been commenced. This was made clear from pencilled sketch-maps which were found on the bodies of German officers and non-commissioned officers, and which were drawn with so much detail as to show the positions in our territory that had been fixed upon as his battalion and brigade headquarters. Add to this the circumstance that his men advanced to the attack wearing full packs, and the fact is at once apparent that a successful issue was, in his mind, a foregone conclusion.

Throughout the day the fighting spirit of our men was exceedingly good, and probably the sentiment expressed in the concluding passage of a situation report sent in during the morning by a company commander, in which he says: ".... We have beaten off two attacks by the Hun and are wanting him to put in a third," would have been subscribed to heartily by every man in the trenches. Doubtless the success of the operations from March 26th onward had much to do with the maintenance of high morale, while the novelty of dealing with an attack in force, and the unusual experience of fighting from a superior position, were important contributing factors.

An unusual bit of fearless reconnaissance is worthy of record. When the bombardment opened in the early morning, Corporal L. J. Whisker, of the 1st Battalion, took a patrol through the barrage and well out into No Man's Land to watch for possible developments on the part of the enemy infantry. From his point of observation he sent back to his company commander valuable information of enemy movements, while he himself remained out until the certainty of an advance became evident, rendering on his return a clear and definite report regarding the strength of the hostile force and the probable points of attack.

It should be mentioned, too, that in one battalion at least the cook-house staffs, whose usual orderly routine had been sadly disturbed by the early morning's fighting, brought up supplies of hot tea which they took round to the hard-pressed men of the front line while blows were still being exchanged; and that the Padre, the Revd. C. B. W. Seton, welcome everywhere, but appearing to have a special preference for positions of danger, spent the whole of the forenoon visiting the posts on his battalion front, assisting the stretcher-bearers in their labours, dispensing comforts to the garrisons, and shedding abroad that heartening influence which he to an eminent degree possessed.

The sub-sector taken over by the 3rd Battalion on the night of the 4th/5th was in some respects unsatisfactory. The line was not continuous, the posts were situated in old fragmentary trenches and communication saps, and for the most part the observation was poor. The enemy attack on the following morning had delayed the preparation of general plans for the improvement of the position, but throughout the ensuing night local attempts were made to push back the German bombing-posts in the communication trenches, and to clear out troublesome machine-gun nests still clinging to a salient between "C" Company (Lieut. F. J. L. Buchler), on the right, and "A" Company (Capt. F. E. Greenish), in the centre. Some progress was made in the saps, but the attack on the machine-guns succeeded only in pushing the nearer gun slightly back.

On the morning of the 6th, while the two company commanders were reconnoitring the position with a view to a more definite attack on the machine-gun positions and the clearing of the salient, Lieut. Buchler was killed by a shot from a sniper, the same bullet also accounting for a sentry stationed in the shallow trench near him. Later in the day a strong enemy counter-attack developed in this locality. The Germans were particularly bold and enterprising, and there was long-continued hand-to-hand fighting in practically every sap held by the 3rd Battalion. Our artillery action, however, prevented enemy reinforcements from coming up, and not only were the attackers everywhere forced back, but fresh ground was gained at all points.

The position was not yet satisfactory, however, for, in spite of the progress made, the enemy still had the advantage of the higher ground with its commanding view. During the next two nights our bombing-attacks continued, and yard by yard the posts were advanced. On the afternoon of the 8th, a general advance was made by the three forward companies. The men of "D" Company (Capt. H. C. Meikle), on the left, had very stubborn fighting. The two main communication trenches in their sector were held with great determination, and the bombing parties were unable to make progress until rifle-grenades and a Stokes mortar had been brought into use. Success eventually crowned the efforts of all three companies, and the higher ground was gained throughout. The front line here was now from 150 to 200 yards farther east than the original position, and for us dead ground no longer existed. After nightfall the digging of a continuous front-line trench was commenced, and by the time the battalion was relieved this work, with the exception of a gap of fifty yards near the centre, was completed.

Throughout the fighting of the last three days on the 3rd Battalion front, excellent service was rendered by a platoon from the support company temporarily attached to that in the centre of the line. The platoon, commanded by 2nd Lieut. H. T. Marshall, took more than its full share in the various attacks, and its work against the strongly-held salient was particularly daring and successful.

Apart from the local activity on the part of the 3rd Battalion companies the situation on the Brigade front continued comparatively quiet. On the night of 8th/9th the two flank battalions extended inwards, enabling the centre unit to be withdrawn and held in Brigade reserve. This alteration being completed, we were relieved by the 1st Brigade on the following night.

This tour in the line had been a particularly strenuous one, for in addition to the heavy fighting there were the effects of the long-continued rain to contend with. In the 3rd Battalion sector especially, because of the constant local encounters, little attention could be given to the drainage of trenches, and these were almost everywhere thigh-deep in liquid mud. Yet even under such conditions our men found some slight compensation, for prisoners and enemy dead yielded up generous supplies of expensive brands of cigarettes, looted, doubtless, from the British canteens during the rush towards the Channel.

Major J. Pow, D.S.O., was severely wounded on the 6th, and Major L. H. Jardine, M.C., assumed command of the 2nd Battalion. Major Pow was promoted Lieut.-Colonel in the following month, but never recovered sufficiently from his injuries to return to the unit. Major Jardine had been transferred to the Brigade from the Wellington Regiment at the end of 1917, from which time he had occupied the position of Second-in-Command of the 4th Battalion, except for a brief interval while in temporary command of the 2nd.

The attack on 5th April was the enemy's final attempt to prevent the French and British line in this region from becoming stable. On the previous day he had launched an attack with massed troops against the British front south of the Somme, but failed to make any appreciable impression. On 5th April the principal German effort was made north of the river, the attack being delivered on practically the whole of this front from Dernancourt to beyond Bucquoy. Except that he gained the eastern portion of the latter village, the enemy's attempted stroke was entirely without result. "His troops, held or driven back at all points, lost heavily, and any hope that he might have entertained of opening the road to Amiens at the eleventh hour ended in an exceedingly costly rebuke."[*]

The following message of congratulation was received from General Harper, commanding the IVth Corps:—

"The Corps Commander desires to congratulate the New Zealand Division on their fine record since coming into the line in the Corps. By a brilliantly-executed attack they captured a large number of prisoners and machine-guns. They have held their ground successfully against numerous attacks and have caused the enemy very severe losses. The organization of their troops for the defence of the line has been extremely well carried out."

On April 9th the enemy delivered a second great blow, this time on the Lys front held by the First and Second Armies. Striking first at the 2nd Portuguese Division, he rapidly extended his attack and overran all the old sectors held in succession by the New Zealand Rifle Brigade on our first coming to France and after our return from the Somme in 1916. It was disconcerting to read of the loss of such pleasant "homes" (for so, looking backward, we had come to regard them) as the Armentieres, Bois Grenier, Rue du Bois, Fleurbaix and Cordonnerie Sectors, and such billeting towns and villages as Armentieres, Estaires, Laventie, Vieux Berquin, Outtersteene, Sailly-sur-la-Lys and Bac St. Maur, where we had lived in comparative comfort in the old days. It was more distressing to learn that most of our gains at Messines and Passchendaele were rapidly being recovered by the enemy,

[*] Sir Douglas Haig's Despatches.

who was sweeping past Neuve Eglise, Merville, Bailleul and Kemmel, and was threatening the railway centre at Hazebrouck. To us the only bright spot in the otherwise gloomy picture was the brilliant work done by the New Zealand Artillery, Mounted Rifles, Cyclist Battalion, 2nd Entrenching Battalion* and Tunnellers, in an endeavour to hold up the enemy's advance, which was finally brought to a standstill on April 30th.

PART 5.—STATIONARY TRENCH WARFARE.

In the "Purple Line" as Divisional reserve—Back to the Line, new sector—Patrols—Snow—To reserve—The "Red Dinks"—Rear defence systems — Sound-ranging apparatus -- Fighting strength—To the old sector of the front line—Enemy raids—Relief—Band returns from Amiens—Training—To the Hebuterne Sector—Patrols and raids—Casualties from hostile shelling—Americans—A midsummer month in reserve about St. Leger—General and recreational training—Horse Shows—Concerts—Details' Camp at Marieux Wood—Into the front line east of Hebuterne—Patrols—2nd Battalion's silent advance.

On being relieved in the line by the 1st Brigade, the New Zealand Rifle Brigade became Divisional reserve, with Headquarters at Bus-les-Artois. The 1st and 2nd Battalions garrisoned the Purple Line, behind Colincamps, and the 3rd and 4th went into a bivouac camp north-west of Courcelles-au-Bois. The two forward units supplied 300 men each daily for work on the reserve lines under the Engineers. Divisional Baths were already in operation, and every man had a much-needed bath and a change of underclothing.

The Brigade went into the line again on the night of 13th/14th April, during very heavy rain. The 1st Battalion relieved 2nd Otago in the right sub-sector of the front line, and the 2nd Battalion took over the left sub-sector from 2nd Canterbury. The 3rd Battalion went into support, and the 4th to reserve, relieving 1st Canterbury and 1st Otago, respectively.

*The 1st and 3rd Entrenching Battalions had been sent south to follow up the Division at the end of March; the 2nd rejoined the Group at about the middle of the following month.

This was a new sector, the front line of which lay about 1,500 yards beyond the outpost positions taken up in front of Englebelmer and Auchonvillers by the 1st Battalion on the morning of the memorable 26th of March. It overlooked Hamel on the right, and faced the famous St. Pierre Divion; to our right front, beyond Hamel, were Thiepval Ridge and Wood, while "Y-Ravine" projected towards the centre of the position. The trenches occupied were mainly those of the old British front line as it existed before the 1916 offensive. A Brigade of the Naval Division was in line on our right, and the 1st Brigade, occupying the sector we had last held, was on our left. Brigade Headquarters were in the Chateau on the southern outskirts of Mailly Maillet. Naturally enough the trenches were in bad order, but the subsoil being of chalk, they rapidly improved in condition as our work developed, especially so on the right, where drainage could be carried out with some degree of ease.

The period on the whole was quiet. At the outset unusual movement amongst the troops on the opposite ridges gave rise to suspicion, but no action followed. In addition to the usual constant night patrolling in No Man's Land, there were several daylight reconnaissances by officers' patrols operating down the old saps. By this means accurate information regarding the position and strength of the enemy's posts was obtained, either from close observation or by drawing the fire of the garrisons. These expeditions were not without their exciting incidents. Sergeant R. Fogarty was a member of a patrol consisting of one officer and two other ranks that had discovered a somewhat advanced enemy post. In order to estimate its strength they took up a position in a shell-hole and threw a bomb into the post. The enemy replied with rifle-fire, followed by a shower of stick-bombs. One of the latter fell fairly into the shell-hole, and as Fogarty stood up to throw it back it exploded, wounding him slightly in the hands and face. The patrol then moved to a trench to engage the post with rifle-grenades. After firing the first round they found they had inadvertently left the remainder of their supply in the shell-hole. These were retrieved by Fogarty, and after some very satisfactory shooting the patrol returned, well pleased with their morning's work. Next day Fogarty went out on patrol again, and this time had the misfortune to be blown up by a shell-explosion; but, though badly shaken, he remained out till the patrol had accomplished its mission.

The 3rd and 4th Battalions interchanged with the 1st and 2nd on April 18th, the relief being completed by midnight. The 2nd Battalion went to support and the 1st to reserve. The cold, wet weather continued throughout the 18th and 19th, snow falling heavily during the forenoon of the latter date. A spell of fine weather commenced on the 20th, and on the following day the enemy heavily shelled the sector, particularly the reserve positions in the vicinity of Englebelmer Wood.

During the nights 23rd/24th and 24th/25th April the Brigade was relieved by the 35th and 36th Brigades, and Headquarters removed to Bus-les-Artois on the 25th. The 1st Battalion, relieved by the 7th Royal Fusiliers, went to the bivouac camp north-east of Acheux on the 23rd, and on the following day cleared up this camp and moved to Coigneux, where they bivouacked in the grounds of Rossignol Farm. The 2nd and 3rd Battalions, on handing over to the 7th Royal Sussex and the 5th Royal Berks, moved back, the former to the Purple Line at Beaussart, and the latter to Bertrancourt. The 4th was relieved by a battalion of the 35th Brigade, and went to the Purple Line near Sailly-au-Bois. These various moves were entailed by a redistribution of the forces on this part of the battle front. The Vth Corps to the south of us extended its left, the Australians were withdrawn from the Hebuterne Sector, and the New Zealand Division side-stepped to the north, holding now a sector extending from One Tree Hill to the east of Hebuterne. The other Divisions of the IVth Corps, the 42nd and the 37th, were on our left in that order.

The Brigade supplied the usual large parties daily for work under the Engineers on support and reserve lines. The Brigade School reopened at Louvencourt on April 30th, twenty-five men from each unit, and also all officers in excess of twenty-five per unit, being drafted to it for special training, and remaining there while the Brigade was in the line.

Encamped at Coigneux and Couin we found battalions of the 170th Brigade that had relieved us in the Cordonnerie Sector in February, 1917, and we were glad to renew acquaintanceship with the "Red Dinks," as our fellows nicknamed the men of those units, from the red diamonds, squares and triangles worn by them on the sleeve as distinguishing marks.

In this reserve area we were able to observe something of the marvellously rapid and extensive development of the systems of defensive trenches and other works that had so recently been put in hand. In the forward area, immediately following upon the consolidation of the new front line at the end of March, we had assisted in the construction of Brigade and Divisional support and reserve lines, a work in which the Maori Pioneer Battalion had, as usual, set the pace.* Here, however, we found under construction, well behind the Purple Line, a great system running roughly north and south through Souastre, Coigneux and Louvencourt. This Reserve Corps System, known as the Red Line, had its own front, support and reserve trenches, communication saps, strong-points, and

---

*The admiration of our men for the Maoris of the Pioneer Battalion was unbounded, and they will heartily applaud the words of commendation in the following letter from the Divisional Commander to the Minister of Defence on the departure of the unit for New Zealand in March, 1919:—

"I have just heard that the Maori Pioneer Battalion is on the eve of embarking on its return to New Zealand. Having had the honour and good fortune to have the Maoris under my command, both as the Maori Contingent on Gallipoli and later in France as the Pioneer Battalion of the New Zealand Division, I should like to express my appreciation, which I know is shared by all ranks of the New Zealand Expeditionary Force, of the fine qualities shown by the Maoris during the war. On Gallipoli, where they took a full share in the initial operations on the 6th August, 1915, in the Battle of Chunuk Bair, and later in the fighting on Hill 60, the Maoris proved themselves true representatives of those fighting tribes from which they are descended. In France their work as Pioneers may not have been so dramatic, and therefore perhaps not so easily recognized by the public. But those of us who have benefited by the labours of the Pioneer Battalion—not only on the Somme in 1916, at Messines, at Ypres, and on the battlefields of 1918, but also during the monotonous months of trench warfare—will readily acknowledge what we owe to this Battalion. I am not going too far when I say that their work on communication-trenches and in the preparation of defence lines has saved the Division many lives; and this work was carried out under conditions as arduous and as dangerous as those attending any other duty which soldiers are called upon to perform, while their opportunities for rest and relief were fewer than is the case with Infantry in the line. . . . . . Right through their period of active service the Maoris have shown themselves to be brave and well-disciplined, and to possess in a very marked degree that cheerful and willing spirit which goes so far towards the making of a good soldier. I am confident that I speak for the whole Division when I say we are proud of the Maoris as our countrymen and as brothers-in-arms."

machine-gun positions; was interlocked with other systems by means of numerous switch trenches, and was provided with concealed tank-traps in the shape of long and very broad excavations cunningly sited. The work was being carried out by French and British units. In rear of this, again, was another complete system known as General Headquarters' Line, passing through Authie, Marieux and Beauquesne, from seven to twelve miles behind the front line. In this back area Chinese labour was extensively used.

At Coigneux our officers had an opportunity of inspecting in operation the sound-ranging apparatus of the Heavy Artillery. The main station was in electrical communication with observation-posts in the forward area, and the records coming through from these were so analysed and combined by the ingenious apparatus that the precise locality of any hostile battery in action at the moment was ascertained with absolute certainty. By this means counter-battery work was carried out by our Heavy Artillery with that accuracy so dreaded by the German gunners.

Our total casualties for the month of April were:—

	Killed.	Wounded.	Missing.
Officers	5	12	—
Other ranks	102	357	3

The fighting-strength of units at the end of the month was:—

	Officers.	Other ranks.
1st Battalion	28	860
2nd Battalion	25	858
3rd Battalion	23	840
4th Battalion	26	797

"Fighting-strength" is not to be confounded with "trench-strength." The former denotes the total number available for fighting in an emergency, and includes all men at schools, details at the transport lines and with the quartermasters, and so forth. "Trench-strength" represents the number of men actually taken into the line in ordinary circumstances.

The Brigade went into the trenches of the old La Signy Sector, east of Colincamps, on the night of 30th April, with headquarters in the dug-out by the sunken road south of Sailly-au-Bois. The 2nd Battalion relieved 1st Canterbury in the right sub-sector of the front line, and the 1st relieved 1st Otago in the left sub-sector. The 3rd Battalion went to support in relief of 2nd Canterbury, and the 4th took over the reserve positions from 2nd Otago.

The position of both battalion fronts was generally satisfactory except in the vicinity of La Signy Farm. Here the enemy occupied a small salient, and steps were taken to reduce his area of occupation by pushing forward our own posts and trenches; but before this improvement had proceeded far, the Germans attempted to raid a post which the 1st Battalion had brought close up to the hedge on the northern side of the Farm. At 3.30 a.m. on May 2nd, after a hurricane bombardment by artillery and trench mortars, about sixty of the enemy attacked this position in four parties. The situation was capitally handled by that Lance-Corporal McMurray who, a month before, had so distinguished himself in single-handed patrol work in the same locality, but who was now a sergeant with a D.C.M., and in charge of the platoon forming the garrison. Possibly he felt more than ordinary interest in the position, seeing that he had been mainly instrumental in its establishment; at any rate he dealt with the attack without calling for artillery support, and succeeded in driving off the raiders after inflicting heavy casualties. The only German, an officer, who entered our trench, was promptly killed. Our listening-post here was driven in, but was immediately re-established. In the repulse of the raiders particularly gallant work was done by Lance-Corporal M. Willets, who was in command of one of the sections. Though severely wounded during the bombardment, he continued the active direction and control of his men, carrying out to the letter the instruction to hold on at all costs. Three days later the enemy made a similar attempt on a neighbouring post, but this also was a complete failure.

The 4th and 3rd Battalions changed over with the 2nd and 1st, respectively, on the night of 6th/7th May, during heavy rain. The weather cleared on the following morning and continued fine for the remainder of the tour, and, as a result, a considerable advance was made in the improvement and strengthening of the front and support lines, a work in which parties from the support and reserve battalions assisted.

On the early morning of the 7th a strong party of the enemy succeeded in overwhelming an advanced Lewis gun post on our extreme right. While one section of the raiders attacked the position from the front, another entered the communication-sap in rear unobserved. We immediately retook the post, but the enemy carried off five prisoners.

Throughout this tour of duty we on our part frequently subjected the German trenches to like attentions; and although our minor sorties failed to yield a similar haul of prisoners, yet important identifications and other valuable information were almost invariably obtained. In these small raids the support of the trench mortar sections attached to battalions was a special feature, the entry into the enemy's line being effected after a short concentrated bombardment of the point selected for investigation.

The period otherwise was uneventful. On May 12th we were relieved by the 1st Brigade, and moved into Divisional reserve. The 1st and 2nd Battalions went into the Purple Line east and south of Sailly-au-Bois, the 3rd Battalion to Rossignol Farm, and the 4th to the bivouac camp north-west of Courcelles-au-Bois. Brigade Headquarters were at Bus-les-Artois.

The 1st Battalion Band now rejoined the Brigade, after an absence of three weeks on duty as baggage-guard. It will be remembered that on arrival at Amiens or in its vicinity on March 25th, all units discarded overcoats and other gear surplus to the fighting-kit. The extra clothing and material belonging to the three battalions that had succeeded in reaching Amiens was handed over to the care of the band, and was, appropriately enough, stored in a twine and cordage factory containing a stock of New Zealand hemp.

The bandsmen were able to render considerable service to the Maire and the Town Major, and the first few days of their stay in the city were not without their stirring events. Piteous streams of refugees passed through from the forward area, and spies were arrested on every hand. On March 26th German aeroplanes heavily bombed the place, inflicting severe casualties. On the following day the Maire ordered the civilian population of 90,000 to evacuate the city, and in the subsequent entraining operations our men worked unceasingly in the assistance of the unfortunate people. These brought with them the usual strange collection of household gods, from which they could not be parted. There was little time for ceremony. One poor family arrived at the station with its belongings heaped upon a donkey-cart, and in a twinkling the burly Riflemen lifted the whole outfit, donkey and all, and placed it in the truck amongst its owners and their friends. March 28th saw the city completely emptied of all but soldiers and those few civilians who, as was so often the case, preferred to remain by their own hearths till the bitter end. A brighter side of the picture was the passing through of English, French and Australian troops bound for the firing-line.

Motor lorries arrived from Division on the 27th, and in these the great-coats were sent up to battalions. Some days later the remainder of the equipment was taken forward by train to Beauval, in the vicinity of Doullens, and some fourteen miles west of Colincamps. Here the remainder of the kits of the Division had been stored, awaiting the turn of events. In the meantime the men were exceedingly glad to have their coats again, for the weather then was still cold. Certainly the New Zealanders had been fortunate enough to happen upon a store of waterproof coats in Colincamps, apparently part of the equipment of some vanished Labour unit; but unluckily the supply was limited, and not a large proportion of the find came the way of the men of the Rifle Brigade.

On May 14th the Divisional Commander held with the Brigadier and battalion commanders a conference regarding the scheme for a counter-attack in case of a possible enemy advance, and traversed the programme of tactical exercises to be carried out by battalions while the Brigade was in Divisional reserve.

Attack in open warfare was practised by the 4th Battalion on the 15th, and by the 3rd Battalion on the 16th. The Corps Commander (General Harper) watched these exercises, and at the conclusion of each reviewed the work done. The weather was hot and bright, and the ground over which the battalions manœuvred, being in the vicinity of the Heavy Battery positions, was subjected to much disconcerting attention from the enemy's long-range guns.

We moved into the line again on May 18th, this time relieving the 2nd Brigade in the northern sector of the Divisional front. The 4th Battalion went into the right sub-sector south of Hebuterne, while the 3rd held the village and the trenches to the east. The 2nd Battalion was in support and the 1st in reserve, with Brigade Headquarters in Sailly-au-Bois.

This being for us a new locality, both battalions in the line at once embarked upon an active policy of patrolling with a view to gaining first-hand knowledge of No Man's Land and of the enemy's position.

On the first night after coming into the line, a 3rd Battalion patrol of two non-commissioned officers, working down the sunken road leading eastward towards Puisieux, located a number of enemy posts, and at two o'clock next morning 2nd Lieut. M. Macdonald, with a party of ten men, moved out to raid the nearest of these and secure prisoners for purposes of identification. After assembling in No Man's Land they discovered some twenty Germans extended across their front. The latter threw bombs at our men, scattered, and returned to their line, from which heavy machine-gun fire was directed upon the assembly point. Not to be denied, 2nd Lieut. Macdonald brought his party back, increased the strength to thirty, and set out again to renew the attempt. The position was successfully rushed, seven Germans were killed, and three prisoners and the two machine-guns brought in. The remainder of the garrison of thirty succeeded in making good their escape. The fine work of Sergeant B. J. Pemberthy contributed greatly to the success of this undertaking. In the German trench he attacked one of the gun-crews singlehanded, and, though wounded, covered the withdrawal of the party when their object had been attained.

On May 21st Sergeant W. Methven, also of the 3rd Battalion, went out in daylight with one companion and succeeded in rushing an enemy sentry-post and capturing two prisoners. Again, at 3 p.m. on the 24th, this sergeant, with two men, worked through the wire and entered a post occupied by three Germans, two of whom were shot and the third taken prisoner.

The alarm had been given, however, and from a trench behind the crest some thirty of the enemy moved up towards the post. The prisoner now gave trouble and had to be shot. Methven ordered his two companions back, held up the pursuers with bombs and revolver-fire, and finally succeeded in making his way back to our lines. The Stokes mortars, which had been trained upon the post, opened fire as soon as the patrol was clear, and one bomb was observed to land fairly in the midst of a group of twelve Germans. The discomfiture of the enemy was completed by the fire of their own light field guns and trench mortars, which was now directed upon the point raided.

On the last morning in the line still another prisoner was taken by the 3rd Battalion, but not from the enemy's trench; for twelve Germans came out from Fusilier Trench to meet our raiding party of one sergeant and nine men. There was a sharp fight here and also on the flank, where the covering party came in contact with a listening-post. In addition to the capture of the prisoner, some eight of the enemy were accounted for, our raiders on the other hand coming through unscathed.

The 4th Battalion patrols and raiding parties were similarly active. Their most successful minor operation was that conducted on the night of 21st/22nd May by 2nd Lieut. A. O. Williams and twenty men, who attacked under cover of a trench mortar bombardment. While flanking patrols with Lewis guns worked down the Jean Bart and Nairn Street saps, the main party got into position in Home Avenue, and on the cessation of the trench mortar fire, which was expected to rake the enemy forward from the suspected post in the sunken road, rushed the position. Here they found the strong-point battered to pieces, and two Germans buried up to the neck in the debris. Fifteen others were kept back by rifle fire while the two were dug out, and our men then worked back to the line. Besides the casualties caused by rifle and Lewis gun fire, it is estimated that of the thirty of the enemy engaged at wiring near the sunken road, and caught by the barrage, the greater number were killed. On our own side only one man was wounded, his injury being caused by a flying fragment from a Stokes mortar bomb.

On the night of May 25th/26th, the 1st and 2nd Battalions relieved the 3rd and 4th in the front line.

Hostile shelling throughout the month was on the whole below normal, the enemy confining himself in the main to periodical shell-storms. On the 8th the 4th Battalion aid-post near the Sugar Factory was wrecked by a heavy shell, both the medical officer, Capt. A. M. Tolhurst, and the chaplain, the Revd. A. Allen, being killed. During a bombardment of Sailly-au-Bois a week later, two eight-inch shells fell upon one of the 1st Battalion headquarters' dug-outs, killing all the occupants, including the Lewis gun sergeant, the signalling sergeant and a number of signallers.

Brigade Headquarters in the village were bombarded on the morning of the 31st, when the Brigade Major, Capt. P. W. Skelley, N.Z.S.C., was mortally wounded.* The most serious shelling took place on the 25th and 26th, the enemy seeking to divert attention from his great thrust of the 27th against the French near Rheims.† On these two days the whole of the Third Army front was subjected to counter-battery work, shelling of rear areas by high-velocity guns, gas-shelling of villages, and fierce bombardment of forward trenches. Except in the case of those units in the line close to Hebuterne, our casualties were not heavy.

Two officers and one non-commissioned officer of the American Expeditionary Force, and six officers of the 74th (British) Division, were attached to the Brigade on May 26th for the purpose of gaining experience in trench warfare.

Lieut.-Col. Austin was evacuated, sick, on May 20th, Major H. S. N. Robinson, N.Z.S.C., assuming command of the 1st Battalion until the arrival of Major N. F. Shepherd‡ from the 4th Battalion on the 23rd.

The casualties suffered by the Brigade during the month of May were:—

	Killed.	Wounded.	Missing.
Officers	3	11	—
Other ranks	55	203	6

*The duties of Brigade Major were taken over later by Major D. E. Bremner, M.C., N.Z.S.C., from the Divisional Staff.

†See p. 342.

‡Major Shepherd had recently been transferred to the Brigade from the Canterbury Regiment.

DIGGING THE PURPLE LINE.

RIFLEMEN WITH THEIR TROPHIES FROM THE GERMAN TRENCHES EAST OF HEBUTERNE.

THE PADRE'S FREE CANTEEN IN A FORWARD TRENCH.

A BURIAL PARTY.

On the evening of June 1st we were relieved in the front line by the 1st Brigade, and moved back to Divisional reserve, with headquarters at St. Leger. The 1st Battalion went to billets in this village, and the 2nd to Rossignol Farm, while the 3rd and 4th occupied bivouac camps in Warnimont Wood.

We were now out for what was virtually a month's midsummer holiday, for in less than a week the Division went into Corps reserve and was not due for its next tour in the line until the beginning of July. There was certainly a considerable amount of movement, but never farther forward than the Purple Line. This we occupied for three days, from June 4th to 6th, taking over from the 111th Brigade when the 37th Division moved for active operations farther south, and then handing over to the 1st Brigade. We went into the same defensive position from the 14th to the 22nd, coming for the time being under the command of the 42nd Division, now in the line. The trench-system itself was held by two battalions at a time, the remainder of the Brigade being in billets or camps about Courcelles, Rossignol Farm and Warnimont Wood. When not in occupation of the defensive lines, we were comfortably quartered in the billets of St. Leger, Authie, Couin and Henu, or in the bivouac camps of Warnimont and Authie Woods. The Woods were delightful spots, and the days spent therein were in the main quiet and peaceful; but even this remote area was occasionally searched by the German long-range guns, and an unlucky shell from one of these fell upon the 4th Battalion's transport lines, destroying a large number of the horses and mules.

The programme of training was comprehensive and thorough. Units availed themselves of every opportunity for holding the smartening-up drills usually found so necessary after a long period in the line, but on the larger scale the work was based on definite and detailed operation orders issued as to the part to be played by the reserve troops in connection with an expected enemy attack on Colincamps and Hebuterne. This involved frequent practices in manning the Purple Line, or in occupying the Reserve Corps system in rear to meet the exigency of a breach of the former. Much attention was also given to tactical exercises in open warfare, both by individual battalions and by the Brigade as a whole. Except for occasional showers, the weather was fine throughout the month, and the training proceeded practically without interruption on this score.

The signallers were able to put in some fine practice, for they had the opportunity of working in conjunction with the 59th Squadron, Royal Air Force,* especially in contact-aeroplane work introducing the new signalling panel. An evening lecture was given by an officer of the squadron, and one by an officer of the Tank Corps.

Recreational training bulked large in the syllabus, and to sports of all kinds, based mainly on the principle of team-work, section competing against section, platoon against platoon, and so forth, much time was devoted. One whole day was set aside for Divisional sports. The programme, excellent in all respects, was carried through in admirable style, and the day was one long round of enjoyment.

Then there were two Horse Shows, one held by the Brigade alone, and one by the whole Division. At both of these our 3rd Battalion came an easy first for the best transport. Brigade show-day was not one of unalloyed pleasure. It entailed a long route-march to and from Vauchelles, followed by a further march in the evening, for on that day, June 6th, we were relieved in the Purple Line by the 1st Brigade, and it was a very tired lot of Riflemen that finally settled down in the billets of Henu and Couin.

Evening concerts were frequent. In addition to programmes played by the regimental bands, always a delight, performances were given by the "Kiwis," the "Tuis," and parties from the 1/7th Lancashires and the Entrenching Group. At the Divisional Band Contest, held at St. Leger on the 27th, the 2nd Canterbury band took first place, followed by the band of our 2nd Battalion. In this competition, which was judged by Capt. Williams, of the Grenadier Guards, no fewer than thirteen bands took part. That of the 1st Battalion, which had been confident of an easy victory, had to withdraw at the last minute owing to the ravages of influenza. The bands of the 2nd and 3rd Battalions came first and second in drill.

*The Royal Air Force had only just come into being as such, the Naval and Military air services having been combined under that name in April. Even these were of no very great age, the R.N.A.S. dating from four and the R.F.C. from two years before the war.

Just before the close of our rest period the Rt. Hon. W. F. Massey and Sir Joseph Ward inspected the Brigade at a parade in Warnimont Wood, and on the last evening all officers attended a lecture given by the Corps Commander.

Now that we were to move again to the forward area, the Brigade School and "B Teams" were detached under the command of Major J. Murphy, who established a camp at the hangars and huts in Marieux Wood. Capt. D. W. McClurg was placed in charge of the instruction at the school. Life in the Details' Camp was by no means a soft and easy one, for training there was carried out with the utmost vigour, and the hours were long. The general conditions, however, were usually good, and the men were able to enjoy to the full that great blessing temporarily denied to their less fortunate comrades in the line,—the music of the bands.

It was at Marieux that our own pierrot troupe was organized, its personnel being drawn mainly from the members of the bands, augmented by other vocalists of the Brigade. A piano for its use was provided by the New Zealand War Contingent Association; while the costumes, including a specially-designed black-and-green dress for the inevitable "lady," were presented by the Y.M.C.A.

In many respects the New Zealanders deserved their reputation for silence; but as far as music was concerned, excepting always the absence of singing on the march, they surely made no little noise in the world. The Artillery, the Entrenching Group, and each of the twelve infantry battalions in France had its brass band; two of the latter rejoiced in the possession of pipe bands in addition; and there were, of course, the bands of the Base in France and of the Depots in England. Then, too, the New Zealanders produced at least five pierrot parties, each with an orchestra, that had a more or less lengthy lease of life,—the "Kiwis" of the Division (a development from the original 3rd Field Ambulance orchestra), the "Tuis" of the 4th Brigade (now attached to the 2nd), the "Guns" of the Artillery, the "Eyes Front" of the Entrenching Group, and the "Dinks" of the Rifle Brigade. Our own party came into being much too late to achieve lasting fame; for, soon after its establishment, the old order of stationary trench-warfare gave place to the new and more desirable fighting mainly in the open, and the conditions which then obtained were not favourable to the full development of a troupe of entertainers.

The period of comparative rest, extending throughout the month of June, and spent amidst pleasant surroundings in glorious weather, served to reinvigorate us all after the trying activities in the line since the 26th of March. The only drawback of moment was an outbreak of influenza which temporarily decimated our ranks. The epidemic fell earliest and most heavily upon the 1st Battalion, whilst the unit was in camp at Authie Wood, and soon nearly a hundred of its men were down with it. The medical officer, Capt. S. H. Ward, collected the sufferers in isolation tents, in the hope that by this expedient the necessity of sending them out to hospital would be obviated; but when the battalion was ordered forward he was at a loss to know how his scheme would fare. Desiring to have the experiment carried to a conclusion, he interviewed Col. McGavin, the A.D.M.S. of the Division, with the object of obtaining permission to continue the isolation at the Details' Camp in Marieux Wood, and of securing the services of a medical officer from the Ambulance to watch the patients, at the same time suggesting that infected men from the other battalions of the Brigade might be collected in the same camp and similarly treated. The request was at once acceded to, and the scheme was extended to cope with the outbreak throughout the whole Division, the isolation camp in the Wood being given a full staff of medical officers and orderlies. A great saving in man-power was thus effected, for, in the ordinary course of events, patients formerly evacuated to hospital had, on their recovery, to pass through the Reinforcement Base and the Entrenching Group before rejoining their units, a procedure entailing a considerable loss of time; whereas, by adopting the new isolation system, the interval of absence was reduced to a period covering the duration of the infection together with a short rest at the Details' Camp.

On 'July 2nd, the Brigade returned to the front line, relieving units of the 152nd and 172nd Brigades in the IVth Corps' centre sector. The new Brigade front covered Hebuterne, while on our right the 42nd Division occupied the old New Zealand sector south of the village. The 1st Brigade was on our left, and beyond that again was the 37th Division. The

2nd Battalion took over the right, and the 3rd the left subsector of the front-line trenches, the 4th was in support behind Hebuterne, and the 1st in reserve at Sailly-au-Bois. Brigade Headquarters occupied the Catacombs, a deep dug-out and cave on the outskirts of the latter village. Part of the work that fell to the lot of the support and reserve battalions here was the harvesting of crops on the abandoned land forward of the Purple Line, from which zone many loads of fine rye and clover were sent back.

We were now close up to the northern angle of the salient caused by the German advance in March. Beyond the Gommecourt–Puisieux Road, which, at the front-line trench, marked our left boundary, the 1st Brigade's front ran roughly east and west, with a salient pushed down past the eastern side of Rossignol Wood.

When the great Somme battle had opened on 1st July, 1916, Gommecourt, directly to the north of Hebuterne, was in a German salient that successfully withstood a powerful subsidiary attack launched with a view to holding part of the enemy's reserves. Now it was so far within our lines as to be behind the main trench of the Purple System, and the old German front and support lines along the south-western face of the original salient were now used by our left battalion as communication trenches. The immense quantity of rusty wire lying about the trenches of Gommecourt village and park, as well as the large number of deep dug-outs that abounded there, testified to the great strength in which this locality had been held. To the south-east of Hebuterne the British front line of pre-Somme days was well over in German territory.

Our front line battalions commenced a minute investigation of the sector, now for the first time occupied by us. No Man's Land was closely reconnoitred, and, as no identifications had been secured for some time past, small fighting-patrols were sent out with the object of entering the enemy's line, dealing with his posts, and taking prisoners. Our men found, however, that much wire had recently been erected in the open and piled up in the old saps, and their efforts were not attended with the usual success; but the information obtained, especially by those patrols that went out by day, indicated the possibility of advancing the line held by the 2nd Battalion.

This operation was silently carried out by that unit on July 5th. From the right of the 2nd Battalion line a spur jutted forward into the enemy's territory. It obstructed the view and did not appear to be strongly held. Nicholson Sap, an old communication-trench, ran up the slope from our front line to Carency Trench, which crossed the spur. During the morning a patrol reconnoitred both of these, finding little trace of enemy occupation in either; and in the afternoon a platoon pushed up the sap, and with no opposition beyond heavy sniping, occupied Carency Trench. After dark the position gained was put into fighting order, the old saps improved, and a close support trench dug.

The advance thus made greatly improved the observation, and brought our right within a few yards of the enemy's line, into which, however, no entry could then be made owing to the amount of new wire recently put out. But our men were not to be denied. Three days later the howitzers hammered this point, which was at the junction of Carency and Pasteur Trenches, and following the bombardment a party of fourteen 2nd Battalion men under the intelligence officer, 2nd Lieut. T. A. Snelling, rushed the post situated there. The struggle with the garrison was short. After three Germans had been shot the remainder made off to the rear, but in the ensuing chase one of these was caught and brought back in triumph; and from him, the first prisoner taken in the neighbourhood for a period of five weeks, information of the utmost value was obtained.

On July 5th each unit sent a party of seventeen men to Paris to represent the Brigade with the New Zealand Divisional contingent taking part in the French National Day celebrations on the 14th.

The 1st and 4th Battalions relieved the 2nd and 3rd in the front line on July 10th, taking over the right and left subsectors, respectively. Lieut.-Col. Austin, from hospital, had resumed command of the 1st Battalion at the beginning of the month; the 4th was under the temporary command of Major H. E. Barrowclough, Lieut.-Col. Beere being on leave.

CHAPTER XIII.
THE BEGINNING OF THE ADVANCE TO VICTORY.

German spring offensive temporarily at a standstill at the end of April—Strength of opposing forces—Policy of active defence and preparation—1st and 4th Battalions attack at Hebuterne, July 15th—General Stewart wounded—German report on the fight—German appreciation of the New Zealand Division—2nd Brigade take Rossignol Wood—To reserve about Couin—Back to the line, northern sector—Enemy raid—American troops—Patrols and raids—To reserve.

By the end of April, 1918, as we have seen, the German spring offensive had been brought to a standstill on both the Somme and the Lys fronts. Everywhere the enemy had failed definitely to break the British line or to sever our army from that of the French, but he had stretched the resources of the Allies almost to the breaking-point. On the British front there remained only forty-five infantry Divisions available for operations; most of these had been much reduced in establishment, and all were urgently in need of rest. The French reserves were required behind their positions south of the Somme and north of the Lys; and the American forces, though rapidly increasing in number and efficiency, were still far from being able to affect the situation very materially. On the other hand it was known that the Germans now held no fewer than seventy-five Divisions in reserve on the Western Front. The War Office, it is true, took immediate steps to pour into France all available reinforcements then in England, as well as bodies of our troops serving in other theatres; but to accomplish these movements, and to complete the necessary training, equipment, assimilation and acclimatization, precious time was required.

In view of the position of the Allies as compared with that of the enemy, it was decided that we must be content with a policy of active defence until August at the earliest, by which time it was expected that we should have tided over the necessary period required for that growth of the American Armies and assimilation of our own reinforcements which would enable us to regain the initiative and pass to the offensive.

During this interval spent on the defensive, every opportunity was taken to rest and train Divisions; and, while their strength and efficiency were being restored, to execute, with ever-increasing frequency and scope, such minor operations as would maintain the fighting spirit of the troops, and at the same time effect local improvements in the line in readiness for the day when the Allied Armies could once more attack in strength.

One of such operations was that carried out east and south-east of Hebuterne by the 1st and 4th Battalions of the New Zealand Rifle Brigade on July 15th, following on the silent advance made by the 2nd Battalion ten days previously.

The objective for the 1st Battalion was Fusilier Trench,* which ran roughly parallel to the front line recently improved by the 2nd Battalion. The taking of this involved an advance to a depth of from 100 to 200 yards on a frontage of over 1,000 yards.

It was arranged that, as a preliminary to the attack, an unostentatious artillery shoot should be carried out for some three or four days along the whole Divisional front to conceal wire-cutting and the destruction of enemy posts. During this period, both by day and by night, patrols worked with great boldness and persistence, exploring thoroughly the intervening stretch of No Man's Land with its numerous old saps, marking down with exactness the location of posts, and noting the progress of wire-cutting by the artillery. The information so obtained, especially that brought in by Sergt. A. J. Cunningham, who on the night of 14th/15th July closely inspected the whole of the objective, was of material value, both in the preparation of the plans and in the execution of the assault.

Two companies, "A" (Lieut. R. J. Grant) and "B" (Capt. G. P. O'Shannassy), were detailed for the attack, each to go over with a strength of not more than three officers and 100 other ranks.

For some hours before zero, which had been fixed for 4 p.m., sections of the attacking companies were dribbled down

---

*This is shown on some maps as Lier Trench.

at intervals to their selected positions in the front line, then occupied by the other two companies, and apparently no unusual movement was noticed by the enemy. At zero minus three minutes, when the intense covering bombardment opened, the attacking sections moved out from our trenches and worked up well under the barrage. At zero the artillery fire moved forward, and our men closed on their objectives. The garrisons of posts about the centre and on the flanks, though taken by surprise, put up a good fight, but from the intervening sections of the trench the Germans fled in disorder towards their rear, our men firing on them as they ran. Unfortunately, owing to the number of old saps affording cover, a good proportion succeeded in making their escape. At zero plus twelve minutes the first platoon signal for "Have secured our objective" was seen from advanced battalion headquarters, and at the same time prisoners were observed on their way towards our lines. Soon afterwards the whole of Fusilier Trench, except the extreme right, was in our hands. The latter point was very stubbornly held, and it was not till forty minutes later that the enemy was driven from this last stronghold.

Independent observers from various points reported that the attack, excellently led, was carried out in fine order and with great dash. The artillery support was perfect; the wire entanglements were well-broken, the barrage clearly defined, and the front and right flank securely covered. On the left flank, about the 16 Poplars, where the objective was too close to our front line for safe artillery work, a rifle-grenade barrage was put down with good effect. Twenty-four prisoners and ten machine-guns were captured, and 28 enemy dead were counted in or near the objective. Our own casualties were one officer and fourteen men slightly wounded.

While the mopping-up and consolidation were in progress, patrols were sent down the numerous saps leading forward from the captured trench, and the enemy was followed up so rapidly that very little resistance was encountered. The patrol led by Sergeant W. Bray came in contact with a party of Germans, five of whom were killed and the remainder driven back. Another, under Rifleman B. Radcliffe, fell upon a group attempting to re-organize; these broke and ran, but Radcliffe, giving chase, succeeded in bayoneting two.

As a result of the activities of the various patrols, both companies pushed forward a further distance of from 200 to 500 yards beyond their original objective. Ford Trench, now occupied by "B" Company, was an old British front-line trench running north and south; while "A" Company's new front was part of Jena Trench, running roughly at right angles to Ford, and facing the south; and by this second advance the length of trench held by the two companies was increased from 1.000 to 1,500 yards. As soon as consolidation had progressed sufficiently, patrols went out again. Those from the left company discovered that the country on their front was clear to a depth of about 200 yards, the Germans now occupying part of their old front line as it existed prior to the first Somme battle. The men of "A" Company, on the right, found themselves not so favourably situated, for it was ascertained that the continuation of Jena Trench, from the right post westward to the 42nd Division's front line at the Quarries, was strongly held by the enemy. The right flank was thus "in the air;" and as this part of Jena Trench was beyond our Divisional boundary, a consultation was held with the commanding officer of the 5th East Lancashires, the regiment holding the line there, with a view to concerted action by bombing parties, which would work inwards and clear the trench. This course was accordingly arranged and put into execution; but as from neither end could any impression be made on the strong-points encountered, it was decided to hold over further action till daylight. The indomitable Sergeant McMurray, who had displayed such conspicuous ability in the trenches near La Signy Farm during the previous April, was mortally wounded while leading in one of the fierce bombing-fights in Jena Trench.

The renewed attempt was timed for 4.30 a.m., but at 3 a.m. the enemy commenced a heavy bombardment of our forward posts, and half an hour later counter-attacked in strength and with great determination. The two posts on the right were forced back along the saps towards Fusilier, and the Germans regained some 200 yards of Jena, capturing one of our men who had been disabled by a bomb while covering the withdrawal of his party.

"A" Company, however, had done too well to endure this slight set-back for long. The Stokes mortars were brought into requisition. After a short bombardment, the garrison of the withdrawn right posts moved down and engaged the enemy from the front; and while his attention was so held, another party, led by 2nd Lieut. W. Henning, worked along Jena and attacked him from the flank. A sharp fight ensued, but eventually the lost territory was regained. Pursuing the enemy still further, Henning and his men attacked the German post beyond our flank, accounting for a number of the enemy and capturing a machine-gun. Thus by 4.30 a.m. our posts were restored and an additional length of trench was added to the former gains.

In the meantime the remainder of Jena was being dealt with. Owing to the great length of our new line, this task had been entrusted to "C" Company (Capt. K. R. J. Saxon), then in support in the old front line. Taking up the running from "A" Company's right, a section under Lieut. M. A. Stedman fought their way westward for a distance of 250 yards until held up by a strong post from which machine-gun fire was directed along the trench. Here a double block was established, and by 6 a.m. the stretch of trench gained had been consolidated. Once more the Stokes mortars were called upon for support, and, after a few rounds on the machine-gun post, the latter was rushed by Capt. Saxon and five of his men. This was the last point at which the enemy made any determined resistance, for, as Capt. Saxon and his party of five pressed rapidly along the trench, the few remaining Germans scuttled off down the saps. By noon the whole was clear, and soon afterwards the consolidation of the line was complete and a portion handed over to the East Lancashires.

Shortly after noon on the 17th, the garrison of one of the posts covering a sap leading out into No Man's Land saw to their astonishment one of our own men crawling slowly towards the line. He proved to be the wounded prisoner captured by the Germans on the previous morning. He had been taken to a dug-out in Jean Bart Trench with several of their own wounded. Here he was carefully attended to, but the enemy during the night vacated that locality, leaving him behind. Acting on the information thus obtained, our patrols at once extended their field of observations, and presently ascertained that the enemy's main line was now fully 500 yards distant from Jena, with only a few posts slightly in advance of that line.

In the subsidiary operations on the morning of the 16th, our casualties numbered three killed and ten wounded. Two machine-guns were captured and twenty of the enemy killed.

The operation carried out by the 4th Battalion coincident with that of the 1st Battalion at 4 p.m. on July 15th, consisted of a bombing attack almost at right-angles to the advance of the latter.

Running out eastward from the right of the battalion sector was a spur similar to that along which the 2nd Battalion had advanced the line on the 5th. From this the Germans overlooked the greater part of our forward positions to the northwards, and the object of the attack was to displace the enemy from the commanding ground and establish our own front line there. The actual objective was not a broad one, not much more than 400 yards, in fact, but the advantage to be gained was ample in the meantime, for it would enable us to threaten from the flank the enemy's front line running northwards along the lower ground towards Rossignol Wood. The old German front and support lines extending along the south-western face of the original Gommecourt salient, and now used by the 4th Battalion as communication trenches, have already been referred to. These continued across No Man's Land into the present German lines, and, bending southwards, formed the enemy's new position facing the 1st Battalion's left company when the latter drove him out of Fusilier and Ford on this same evening. These two trenches were known as Nameless Trench and Nameless Support. Still another sap, Snuff Alley, ran out from our front line, roughly parallel to the others, and a trench intersecting the three formed that part of the German line to be assaulted.

The 4th Battalion men were well acquainted with the ground over which they were to advance, for most of them had patrolled it. Lance-Corporal J. Sillifant, in particular, knew every inch of it up to within twenty yards of the objective, and, in addition, could state exactly where the enemy's posts were situated. He had, by the way, added sniping to his other duties, and during the past four days had accounted for ten of the enemy, a score that he was to increase considerably this afternoon.

The attack was carried out by two platoons and two sections of "A" Company. No. 4, platoon, under 2nd Lieut. C. H. Adams, bombed up Nameless Trench; No. 3 platoon, under 2nd Lieut. W. Skelton, similarly dealt with Nameless Support; while two sections of No. 1 platoon, under Sergeant A. J. Officer, attacked along Snuff Alley.

The operation was entirely successful, though strong resistance was met with at all three points attacked. At two of these the destruction or capture of the garrisons followed swiftly, but at the third our men were temporarily held up till Corporal A. Corbett, dashing through the barrage of the longer-ranged German bombs, got to close quarters with his bayonet and disorganized the garrison. His section followed up and completed the capture of the position, which was found to contain no fewer than four machine-guns. Covering-patrols were pushed down the saps while the new line, now 100 yards beyond the original objective, was consolidated in readiness to meet a counter-attack. The enemy, however, had been so badly hit that he made no attempt to regain his lost positions. Eight prisoners and seven machine-guns were captured, while our own losses were two men killed and six wounded.

During the night the 4th Battalion attacked again with the object of pushing forward another 300 yards and establishing posts in that part of Owl Trench lying between Nameless and Nameless Support.

For the task of carrying out this second advance a platoon of "C" Company, under 2nd Lieut. R. Whitefield, was detailed. The plans were quickly made, and at 1.20 a.m. the commander led a party, consisting of half his men, down Nameless Support. Little opposition was encountered until the junction with Owl Trench was reached. Here the enemy held a strong bombing-post, and there ensued a stiff contest for its possession, but the Germans were eventually driven along the trench to the left, and blocks were established to hinder his return. The enemy made three counter-attacks on the post from Nameless Support, and one from Owl Trench, before the morning dawned, but all were repulsed. The second party, under Sergeant Hamilton, operated along Nameless Trench, and, some fifty yards from our line, came in contact with the Germans, who, after a brisk exchange of bombs, retreated. Pressing on towards Owl Trench, Hamilton's men came to a post similar to that which was engaging the attention of the left party. It was an awkward point, and the Germans, holding in strength, put up a good fight, but these also were pushed out. While blocks were being established, the enemy counter-attacked from a flank, but failed to make any impression upon the stranger within his gates. He tried again, however, this time endeavouring to reach the post by bombing up Nameless Trench, but meeting with no better success from this quarter, he finally gave up the attempt. Thus the platoon's mission was accomplished. The actual capture of the two posts occupied only some forty minutes, and the attack and consolidation cost no more than five men wounded. The trophies included one machine-gun and two trench mortars.

These combined operations of the two battalions were, within their scope, probably the most successful hitherto carried out by the Brigade. They were brilliantly executed, and individual instances of initiative and daring were unusually numerous and striking, awards for gallantry being granted to no fewer than three officers and thirteen other ranks. Our men had entered upon the engagements fully confident in their ability to carry them through, and the success, exceeding as it did all expectations, engendered a high elation which not even the pouring rain, the muddy trenches, and the abominable filth of the German quarters could dampen. Those who had not been privileged to participate were equally affected. The mopping-up of the first objective had not been fully completed before the carrying-parties were on their way forward with wiring-material, and other parties were at work on the communication-trenches leading towards the captured positions. Hot tea and stew were delivered to the forward posts before dark; and company commanders in their reports specially stressed the fact that throughout the following days the rations never failed to reach the men, though in many exposed places the carriers had to worm their way through the mud, flat on their faces, dragging the food-containers after them.

There was cheeriness everywhere, arising from the feeling that what had been done was but an earnest of still better developments yet to come. Unfortunately, General Stewart, while inspecting the new front line on the morning of the 17th, was wounded by a sniper.*

Lieut.-Col. Austin assumed command of the Brigade pending the arrival of Brigadier-General H. Hart, C.M.G., D.S.O., from England, on the 22nd.

The following extracts, taken from a copy of a captured German intelligence summary, refer to the operations described above. The exaggeration in the strength of our attacking parties will be noted. In the translation, our own names are given to the trenches referred to in the original:—

"INTELLIGENCE SUMMARY NO. 1, OF THE 28TH RESERVE DIVISION.
"Period 14/7/18 to 17/7/18.

"ENEMY INFANTRY.—On the 15/7/18, at 4 p.m., the enemy infantry attacked in strength of 800 to 1,200 men, penetrating into the north sector of the Div. (6th Coy.) after very heavy artillery fire. They penetrated our outpost line in several places, and established themselves in it.

"During the night the enemy, bringing up fresh forces, penetrated the 'D' Coy. Sector of 119th R.I.R. and broke through 'A' Coy. in Fusilier Trench, to the main line of resistance. In the sector of 180 I.R. he attempted repeatedly to roll up the northern flank from the point of penetration. He was repulsed after heavy fighting. He only succeeded in entering the southern flank of 'B' Coy. in Nameless Trench and Nameless Support.

"We counter-attacked at 3 a.m. on 16/7/18 with the 7th and 8th Coys. and remnants of 1st and 2nd Coys. 119 R.I.R., and succeeded in clearing the sector of 'B' Coy. in Jena Avenue. The enemy still held the sector of 'A' Coy. in the eastern half of Jena.

"At 4.30 a.m., after heavy artillery and trench-mortar fire, the enemy renewed his attack with overwhelming forces. After heavy fighting he succeeded in again penetrating Jena

---

*General Stewart was the fourth of our Brigadiers to become a casualty, two having been killed and two wounded. He did not return to the Brigade, but on his recovery was appointed to the command of Sling Camp, remaining in control there from September 27th, 1918, until April 4th of the following year.

Avenue and into the positions of 'B' Coy. in that trench. The southern half of 119 R.I.R. sector was slightly withdrawn on account of the seriously-threatened flank.

"The attempts of the enemy to advance further on the evening of the 16th were repulsed.

"On the 17/7/18, at noon, an attack on the 'C' Coy. Sector of 180 I.R. was repulsed.

"119th R.I.R. took several English prisoners during the counter-attack on the sector of 'C' Coy., who, however, again fell into the hands of the enemy through their strong counter-attack. According to statements of the Englishmen, and the title N.Z.R.B. on the shoulder-strap, they belonged to a battalion of New Zealand Rifles. The southern flank of the New Zealand Division, therefore, extends further south than we had hitherto assumed.

"Enemy artillery activity was normal on the 14th and morning of the 15th. It rose occasionally to great intensity in the evening of the 15th and night of 15th/16th in connection with enemy attacks. At noon and in the afternoon of the 16th heavy crashes fell on the sector of 180 I.R. and 119 R.I.R., overlapping on to the sector of the northern flank division. During the night of 16th/17th harassing fire increased.

"Our artillery engaged two enemy batteries with aeroplane observation, and, on observing the flares of the infantry, put down barrage and destructive fire in front of the threatened sectors. We also liberally bombarded the portions of our outpost zone occupied by the enemy......

"Our light and medium trench mortars fired on the enemy trenches and on barrage fire during the enemy attacks.

"Enemy aircraft were very active over our front line during the fighting, and over the roads and villages in our back areas. The enemy dropped a large number of bombs......"

The same intelligence summary contains the following information concerning the New Zealand Division:—

"PARTICULARS OF THE NEW ZEALAND DIVISION.

"Commander: Sir Andrew Russell.

"Order of Battle—Infantry.

3rd N.Z. Rifle Bde.	2nd N.Z. Inf. Bde.	1st N.Z. Inf. Bde.
I/N.Z. Rifles.	I/Canterbury Regt.	I/Auckland Regt.
II/N.Z. Rifles.	II/Canterbury Regt.	II/Auckland Regt.
III/N.Z. Rifles.	I/Otago Regt.	I/Wellington Regt.
IV/N.Z. Rifles.	II/Otago Regt.	II/Wellington Regt.

"The companies appear, in addition, to carry special names, e.g., those of II/Wellington Regiment are Taranaki, West Coast, Hawke's Bay, Ruahine. The existence of a Fourth Brigade is possible.

"MACHINE-GUNS: New Zealand Machine Gun Bn. consists of 4 companies, each of 16 Vickers guns. 5 light machine-guns [Lewis guns] have recently been identified with infantry companies, but their number has probably since been increased; an attempt is made to train all men in the use of the light machine-gun.

"FIELD ARTILLERY: 1st and 2nd Brigades.

"PIONEERS: 1st and 2nd Field Companies (Field Coys. Royal Engineers).

"WORKING BATTALION: 1st Bn. N.Z. Pioneers (Maoris).

"ENTRENCHING BATTALION: I, II, III. This is a sort of convalescent unit which is employed mostly behind the front and frequently outside the Divisional Area.

"HISTORY: The Division was in rest in the St. Omer area at the end of March, 1918, and was transferred south and put into the rearguard battle west of Bapaume. It remained in the Colincamps Sector continuously until the 10th of June, and then went into rest (probably in the area north of Pas). The losses during the period in line were at times not inconsiderable. Since the 10th of July the Division has been in line in the Hebuterne sector.

"REINFORCEMENTS: White New Zealanders.

"The Battalion of N.Z. Pioneers is composed of natives (Maoris), who are a light brown people of the Polynesian race. The infantry reinforcements are chiefly drafted to the Entrenching Battalions and drawn from these as required by the fighting troops.

"Losses incurred during the last period in line were made up quickly by small parties drawn from this unit. The company fighting strength is estimated at about 150 men.

"In New Zealand a limited system of compulsory service has been introduced. The reinforcements consist almost entirely of young, strong men.

"BADGES AND EQUIPMENT: In addition to the steel helmet, a khaki-coloured hat with coloured bands is worn, that of the infantry being khaki and red, the artillery dark purple and red, the Pioneer Companies khaki and blue-black, A.S.C. khaki and white. Shoulder straps have a flap of the same colour. On the collar of the coat there are brass letters; those of the 1st and 2nd Brigades have N.Z.R., the Rifle Brigade

N.Z.R.B.. the Pioneer Companies N.Z.E. Coloured cloth badges are carried on the back (possibly on both arms?) and on the hat band.

[NOTE.—A complete illustration with colours of the patches of all the regiments follows here. All these are correct with the exception of 1st Canterbury and 1st Otago, which apparently were unknown. A footnote adds that the patches of the 1st and 3rd Brigades had not been confirmed for a long time.]

APPRECIATION OF THE DIVISION.

"A particularly good assault Division. Its characteristic is a very strongly developed individual self-confidence or enterprise typical of the colonial Englishman, and a specially-pronounced hatred of the Germans. . . . .

"(Sgd.) WALTHER, Colonel.

"Distribution to Companies and Batteries."

Similar minor operations were carried out by the 2nd Brigade in the sector just north of us, where for some time fighting-patrols and raiding-parties had been feeling the strength of the enemy defences of Rossignol Wood. The Wood was found to be strong in wire, "pill-boxes" and machine-guns, but on the evening of the 15th July, following on our own advance in front of the village, troops of the 1st and 2nd Canterbury Battalions attacked and gained a footing in the northwestern projection. Four nights later the enemy relinquished his hold on the Wood, and at daylight on the morning of the 20th, 2nd Otago, now in line in this sector, advanced through it and dug in beyond its eastern edge. The 1st Brigade battalions which had relieved us in our advanced sector on the night of the 17th immediately followed suit, and in their turn moved forward, 1st Auckland on the left capturing the remainder of Owl Trench and gaining touch with 2nd Otago at the Wood, and 2nd Wellington pushing on from Jena to Chasseur Hedge beyond Jean Bart. Further gains were made on the 24th, when Hawke Trench was captured. Beyond our right, again, the troops of the 42nd Division had improved their position by capturing La Signy Farm on the 16th.

On relief by the 1st Brigade on July 17th, we moved back to Divisional reserve, with headquarters at Couin and the 1st Battalion in the neighbouring Wood. The 2nd Battalion took over a section of the Chateau de la Haie Switch, while the 3rd occupied bivouacs and billets at Rossignol Farm, and the 4th the Coigneux billets.

Our period of eight days in reserve passed pleasantly enough. The quarters on the whole were good, the canvas camps in particular being an agreeable change from the "cubby-holes" and dug-outs of the front line trenches. Practically the only drawback was the uncomfortable proximity of our heavy batteries, which drew a considerable amount of fire from the enemy's long-range guns. German 'planes occasionally bombed the area, but only once succeeded in causing damage, a bomb dropped on Couin Wood wounding the Brigade bandmaster, Lieut. P. E. Cole, and six men. The usual working-parties were supplied by battalions, but as these were engaged no farther forward than Chateau de la Haie Switch, where they were employed excavating deep dug-outs for the platoons of the garrison, no great hardship was felt. During the long evenings, too, we had the pleasure of listening to open-air performances given by the Divisional Pierrots, who set up their temporary stage in the Wood.

The Brigade returned to the line on the night of July 25th/26th, relieving the 2nd Brigade in the left sector, east of Rossignol Wood, with headquarters in a dug-out just south of Fonquevillers. The 3rd Battalion took over the right subsector from 2nd Otago, and the 2nd Battalion the left from 1st Otago. The 1st Battalion went to support, relieving 2nd Canterbury, and the 4th took over the reserve position from 1st Canterbury.

During the relief, the enemy attempted to raid the trenches held by 2nd Otago. The attack, made by three companies, was driven off, leaving 30 prisoners in our hands. The prisoners gave it as their opinion that the three assaulting companies had been completely destroyed.

The heavy rains of the 25th and 26th had a very bad effect on the recently-captured trenches, which soon became knee-deep in mud and water. The conditions, which were little better than those at Passchendaele, made the labours of working and carrying parties extremely arduous. For the Americans, two platoons of whom were attached to each battalion in the line for experience, this introduction to trench-life was somewhat unfortunate. The Americans, however, adapted themselves with admirable readiness to the novel conditions, made light of the discomforts, and ceaselessly voiced their one desire "to get at the Hun and on with the war."

Lieut.-Col. Beere returned from leave and resumed command of the 4th Battalion on July 21st. It having been decided that the Details' Camp of each Brigade should be commanded when possible by a battalion commander, Lieut.-Col. Austin took over our camp at Maricux from Major Murphy on July 25th. Major Shepherd thereupon assumed temporary command of the 1st Battalion.

On July 22nd, the 2nd Battalion band was detached for duty with the IVth Corps School for a fortnight.

The casualties for the month of July were:—

	Killed.	Wounded.
Officers	1	9
Other ranks	23	153

On the night of 2nd/3rd August the 1st and 4th Battalions relieved the 3rd and 2nd in the front line, the two latter units going to support and reserve respectively.

The enemy artillery bombardment of the area, and especially of Rossignol Wood, continued steadily day by day, frequently rising to great intensity, and this was supplemented by trench mortar activity on our front trenches.

At 2.30 in the afternoon of August 7th, a remarkable raid was carried out by 2nd Lieut. J. A. McL. Roy, intelligence officer, and Rifleman A. H. Perry, both of the 1st Battalion. The enemy was known to be holding a post close to our line southeast of Rossignol Wood, and, after a few rounds from our Stokes mortar, the little party of two slipped down an old communication-trench and came upon a German listening-post. In the side of the enemy's trench was a dug-out with an oil-sheet hanging over the entrance. The lifting of this revealed within two Germans, who made a considerable outcry when they found a revolver within a foot of their faces. On being signalled to come out they did so with alacrity, and were taken back to our lines. Deciding that more prisoners might possibly be obtainable, Lieut. Roy and his companion went across again, and, pushing further down the enemy trench, came to a fork with Germans in both branches. On one side two were seen with a machine-gun which they were making ready to fire. These, on being rushed, immediately threw up their hands, and were promptly escorted to our lines. Once again the gallant pair returned to the German trench, and, after some difficulty, secured and brought back the machine-gun. No casualties were suffered on our side. A German officer who attempted to bomb the raiding-party from a flank was shot through the head by a sergeant in our front trench.

On the same date a night patrol of one officer and four men from the 4th Battalion was suddenly confronted by a party of thirty of the enemy, who opened fire. The patrol took cover and, under instructions from their officer, the men made their way back individually to our lines. As the officer failed to return, Corporal R. T. Corsbie and Rifleman C. V. Murray went back into No Man's Land to search for him. He was at last discovered lying in a shell-hole severely wounded. Thinking they were safe from observation, the two rescuers raised their unconscious officer with the object of carrying him back. Unfortunately, however, the loud groans of the sufferer brought the enemy again upon the scene. These were now engaged single-handed by Rifleman Murray, who with bombs and rifle-fire kept them at bay whilst the corporal bound up the officer's wounds. Seizing a favourable moment they rapidly withdrew, bringing their officer with them, thus not only saving his life but preventing the enemy from gaining identifications.

On the evening of August 10th we were relieved in the line by the 1st Brigade, going back to reserve in our old quarters about Couin and in the Chateau de la Haie Switch. Here we spent a brief but enjoyable period of rest. The weather now was fine and warm, and the calls for working-parties being less exacting than usual, recreational and general training went on with little interruption.

On August 16th, Major A. H. Carrington temporarily took over the duties of Brigade Major, vice Major Bremner, evacuated sick.

CHAPTER XIV.
THE BATTLE OF BAPAUME.

PART 1.—THE GENERAL SITUATION.
Ready for a vigorous offensive—Opposing forces—The turning point—Renewed German thrust towards Paris—Foch's counter-stroke, July 18th—Allied plans—Battle of Amiens, August 8th, and advance to the edge of the old Somme Battlefield—Attack transferred north of the Somme—The New Zealanders' pressure at Hebuterne—Plans for the Battle of Bapaume.

It was now becoming abundantly evident that on the Western Front the Allies were drawing near to the close of the stage of transition from the period of active defence to that of vigorous offence. The interval of comparative quiet since the holding up, at the end of April, of the German advance, had effected a striking improvement in the condition of the British Armies. Despite our losses in guns during March and April, we were now stronger in artillery than ever we had been. Drafts from England and reinforcements from abroad had been absorbed and trained, with the result that the number of effective Divisions had increased from forty-five to fifty-two. Reinforcements for the French Armies had been largely augmented; and with the arrival of a million troops despatched from America on July 2nd, the opposing forces were rapidly approaching an equilibrium in strength. Harassing operations had been carried on steadily on the Lys front and east of Amiens throughout May, June, and the early days of July, resulting not only in the improvement of our positions, but in a very great aggregate loss to the enemy in men and material.

The turning-point in the year's campaign was marked by the Allied counter-attack on July 18th near Soissons. The enemy's second great offensive had opened on May 27th, when with twenty-eight Divisions, supported by tanks, he attacked the French Sixth Army on a front of thirty-five miles north-west of Rheims. In this thrust on Paris he took Soissons, and for the second time reached the Marne. On July 15th the enemy launched his third great offensive, directing his attack east and south of Rheims. He succeeded in crossing the Marne, but was held by the French, American and Italian forces. These enemy thrusts had been expected, and Marshal Foch had completed his preparations for a great counter-stroke. This he delivered on July 18th with such definite success as to effect a complete change in the whole military situation. The enemy's ambitious offensive collapsed. The bulk of his accumulated reserves had been used up, and the period of maximum strength was past. Plans were immediately made for a converging advance, the French and Americans towards Mezieres, the British towards Maubeuge, two great railway centres near the Belgian frontier. If these operations should be successful, and the advantage fully exploited, the German lateral communications in this region would be cut, and those in Flanders seriously threatened.

The British attack opened with the Battle of Amiens on August 8th, when the Fourth Army, with which the French First Army co-operated on the right, struck on a front of over eleven miles from the Amiens–Roye Road to Morlancourt. The object was to free the main Paris–Amiens railway and then to cut the enemy's communications by seizing the important railway centre of Chaulnes. The troops employed were the Canadian Corps on the right, the Australian Corps in the centre, and the IIIrd Corps on the left. Behind the British line, the British Cavalry Corps, a special mobile force of two Motor Machine Gun Brigades, and a Canadian Cyclist Battalion, were placed in readiness to exploit successes. The attack was a complete surprise, and resulted in a series of brilliant victories. By nightfall on August 12th the advance had reached the line of the original Roye–Chaulnes defences on the edge of the old Somme battlefield. The French had also made rapid and deep progress, and had taken Montdidier in their stride.

The enemy was now found to have heavily reinforced this front, and, while our pressure was steadily maintained in order to deceive, the front of attack was transferred north of the Somme, where the Third Army was ordered to operate in the direction of Bapaume, and so turn the line of the old Somme defences from the north.

Opposite the sector held by the New Zealand Division east of Hebuterne, the enemy's line formed a small salient, the area of which we had reduced considerably by the minor operations in July already described. Disappointment had been felt when we were not permitted to exploit these successes. The reason for thus holding our hands now became apparent, for on August 14th, after the Battle of Amiens, the enemy began to withdraw from this salient voluntarily, and the role of the 1st and 2nd Brigades, then in the line, was merely to follow him up, keep touch, and continue such pressure as would hasten his movement.* This was maintained with such vigour that by evening the Divisional front had advanced to the line Serre–Box Wood–Fork Wood, and by the 17th to the western outskirts of Puisieux-au-Mont.

On August 18th the New Zealand Rifle Brigade relieved the 2nd Brigade and details of the 3/317th American Regiment in the right sub-sector, and next day took over the whole Divisional front extending from a point about 1,000 yards south of Puisieux to a point a similar distance south of Bucquoy. The maximum strength of units in the line was fixed at 640, any surplus being sent back to the Details' Camp.

The great series of engagements extending over the period of twelve days from August 21st to September 1st, and known as the Battle of Bapaume, was about to commence. The object of this attack, in a south-easterly direction on the front between Albert and Arras, was to turn the line of the Somme south of Peronne, thus constituting a step forward towards the strategic objective St. Quentin–Cambrai.

The general plan was for the Third Army to deliver, on August 21st, a limited attack north of the Ancre, to gain the enemy's main line of resistance on the Arras–Albert Railway. On the following day the Fourth Army would swing forward its left flank between the Somme and the Ancre, and then on August 23rd the main attack would be delivered by the Third Army and those Divisions of the Fourth Army which were north of the Somme. Following upon the success of the Third Army, the First Army was to extend the frontage of the attack

---

*At about the same time, as a further result of the Amiens reverse, the enemy prepared to abandon the salient on the Lys front also.

as far north as the Sensee River, and, by turning the western extremity of the Hindenburg Line, compel the enemy to make a further retreat.

PART 2.—PUISIEUX-AU-MONT, AUGUST 21ST.

Objectives for the New Zealand Rifle Brigade—First phase: 3rd and 4th Battalions capture Puisieux—Second phase: 3rd Battalion clears the triangle towards Miraumont—Germans counter-attack the 42nd Division—3rd Battalion troops advance the line—Success elsewhere.

In the opening battle of August 21st the task for our Brigade, the only one of the New Zealand Division engaged, was divided into two phases. In the first phase, we were to advance abreast of the 42nd Division on the left, to the general Blue Line which, opposite us, ran approximately north and south about 500 yards east of the centre of the village of Puisieux-au-Mont. In the second phase, the 5th Division was to pass through the 37th and our left on the Blue Line, and, carrying on the advance in conjunction with the 42nd Division, gradually pinch us out. Our role in the second phase was to secure, by means of fighting-patrols, the triangular area formed in this pinching-out process and extending some 2,000 yards in advance of our Blue Line; and also to assist the 42nd Division in the capture of Beauregard Dovecote, an outstanding feature in their general objective, on a hill-top north-west of Miraumont.

The capture of our portion of the Blue Line, some 3,000 yards, was entrusted to the 3rd Battalion (Lieut.-Col. Bell) on the right, and the 4th Battalion (Lieut.-Col. Beere) on the left. The battle opened at 4.55 a.m. in a heavy mist which did not lift until 10 a.m.

An excellent barrage rested for ten minutes on a line well in advance of our trenches, and under its cover the assaulting troops moved out into No Man's Land to escape the answering bombardment and to ensure an orderly arrangement in prosecuting the advance. The 3rd Battalion worked on a three-company frontage, "C" (Lieut. T. G. Robertson) being on the right, "D" (Lieut. J. H. Irvine) in the centre, and "B" (Lieut. A. L. Martin) on the left. "A" Company (Lieut. J. Russell),

ORDER OF BATTLE—PUISIEUX-AU-MONT, AUGUST 21, 1918.

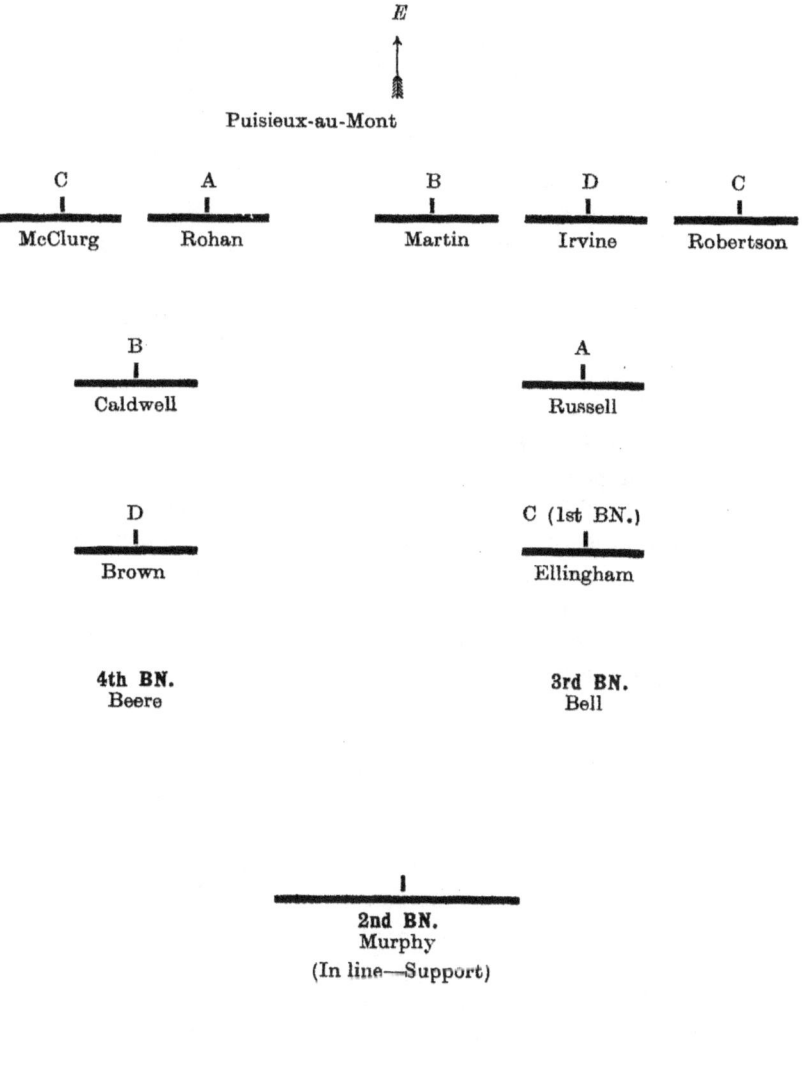

was to pass through the Blue Line and complete the battalion's task, while "C" Company of the 1st Battalion (Lieut. H. A. Ellingham) was attached as reserve. The 4th Battalion employed as attacking troops "A" Company (Capt. M. D. Rohan) on the right, and "C" (Capt. D. W. McClurg) on the left. "B" Company (Major K. S. Caldwell), in support, detailed a platoon under 2nd Lieut. C. Darling to mop up the northern fringe of Puisieux. "D" Company (Capt. A. E. Brown) was in reserve. On our right were the 5th Lancashires, while on the left the 4th Manchester Regiment was in touch with the 4th Battalion.

From the outset the infantry attack went well. The 4th Battalion reached its objective with the loss of only seventeen men wounded, having met with little stubborn resistance except on its flanks. On the left, Lance-Corporal H. A. Matheson and Rifleman J. McLure did admirable work in assaulting a machine-gun post and exterminating its crew; while on the right, after a stiff struggle in the eastern outskirts of Puisieux, a Lewis gun section under Corporal N. C. Neilson succeeded in capturing two machine-guns and twelve prisoners. During the consolidation of the line an odd adventure befell a 4th Battalion runner. Returning to the forward position after delivering a message to his company headquarters, he missed his way in the fog and walked straight into a German post. Here he was promptly disarmed and sent off to the rear under guard of a party moving back. His journey towards Berlin had not proceeded far, however, before he was overtaken by a tank manned by Australians, who promptly reversed the position, placed the runner in charge of his erstwhile captors, and shepherded the whole back to the former's proper destination.

The 3rd Battalion had a complicated task to perform. Its section of the objective was shorter than that of the 4th Battalion, but it had a greater portion of the village to deal with. Moreover, beyond the right flank there was a hill-top higher than any other ground in the neighbourhood, and from which our position on the Blue Line could be directly enfiladed; and although this was situated in the area over which troops of the 42nd Division would pass in their swinging movement towards the south-east, yet it was deemed necessary to detail a platoon to assist in the capture and clearing of this dominating position, and thus render the flank secure. Again, to the 3rd Battalion fell the work of clearing the triangle referred to above, and of assisting in the capture of the Dovecote. That the whole of this intricate series of operations was successfully carried through by noon, notwithstanding the constantly changing situation and the difficulty of keeping touch with the two Divisions on the flanks, was largely due to Lieut.-Col. Bell's cool handling of his companies, following upon his personal reconnaisance of the positions at the different stages of the action.

At the opening of the battle the 3rd Battalion's movements were planned to coincide with those of the 42nd Division; and as the front line south of the village was nearer the objective than was the section to the north, the 3rd Battalion commenced the advance a little later than the 4th. The left swept through the southern part of the village without a check, and, extending northwards, established touch with the right of the 4th Battalion on the Blue Line. The right moved over open, exposed ground and suffered some casualties from the sweeping fire of machine-guns operating apparently from a shell-torn road just short of the objective. Guided only by the sound, for through the fog nothing could be seen, the leading sections rushed the position, which was found to consist of four machine-gun posts. The crews were killed and the advance continued, but the troops immediately came under more intense fire from another gun directly to their front. The rush was repeated, and a fifth machine-gun silenced and captured. This brought the men of the right company to a second road about a hundred yards beyond the objective; and here, protected by shell-hole posts established 150 yards in front, they consolidated their position. The centre company met with strong opposition from a series of old trenches about 200 yards short of the objective. From the greater part of this position the Germans were quickly cleared; but further advance was held up by a concealed machine-gun post, which was finally rushed from a flank by Riflemen C. W. Batty and J. Lowe, who captured the guns as well as the garrison of one officer and ten men.

The movements of all the attacking companies of both battalions, notwithstanding temporary checks, were well timed, the forward line kept close to the barrage throughout, and by 6 a.m. Puisieux was in our hands and the troops were well established on the Blue Line. During this hour's fighting we took nearly 100 prisoners and several machine-guns, our own casualties being comparatively nominal.

The fog which had proved of advantage in covering our movements was not an unmixed blessing, for, besides obscuring landmarks, it rendered establishment and maintenance of touch exceedingly difficult. Thus, Sergeant W. Motion, of the 4th Battalion, in charge of a section on the flank, found on reaching the objective that the neighbouring unit had failed to join up. Going out alone under fire he succeeded in eluding the enemy, located the nearest section, and then returned and led a number of his own men to a position from which the gap could be held. Rifleman A. Dalzell, of the 3rd Battalion, going out on a similar mission, had a more exciting time. He found the intervening area still in possession of the enemy, but without pausing to consider their possible strength he attacked them single-handed, bombed a number of dug-outs, and captured five prisoners. At the same time he marked down the position of a machine-gun actively firing. Having brought in his five prisoners and handed them over, he took three men and with them went back to deal with the machine-gun post. After some preliminary manœuvring for position the little party rushed the post, killed the crew, and carried off the gun.

Soon after the taking of the Blue Line the second phase of the day's action commenced. The 5th Division troops passed through our 4th Battalion on their way towards securing a predetermined position from which they were to launch their attack on Achiet-le-Petit. This position they were expected to gain at 7.30 a.m.; and shortly before that time the remaining company of the 3rd Battalion moved out to capture the triangle and fill the narrowing interval between the 5th and the 42nd Divisions, the general objective of the latter being a line running north-east through the Dovecote, and extending to the valley of the Ancre. Owing to the fog, Lieut. Russell's company advanced warily, and failing to gain touch with the 5th Division after having moved forward some 500 yards, our men were halted and a temporary line was formed. Small fighting-patrols were now sent out, and these having located the flank of the 5th Division at about 8 a.m., the advance towards the south-east was continued. When the fog lifted, soon after 10 a.m., our left platoons found themselves in advance of their objective and in a position on the exposed face of a spur under full observation by the enemy. They were swept by machine-gun fire coming from the high ground beyond the Ancre valley on their left, and there were no friendly troops on that flank. They were therefore withdrawn slightly to conform to the line of the 5th Division; and at noon the two remaining platoons, maintaining touch with the Division on the right, came up into alignment, which was now unbroken throughout. Here the company proceeded to dig itself in, in preparation for an expected counter-attack. The position occupied faced the south-east, with the outskirts of Miraumont 1,500 yards away and directly to the front. Immediately below was the bottom of the valley through which a light railway ran westward towards Serre, and beyond the valley the ground sloped up to the Dovecote, 1,000 yards distant. During the afternoon and evening the posts were strengthened and improved and patrols worked through the bottom of the valley and about the slopes on either side. Thus ended an excellent day's work. With the loss of some sixty killed and wounded the Brigade had carried out all its tasks, and the forward posts of the 3rd Battalion were 2,000 yards east of Puisieux. The toll of prisoners had risen to 235, and the number of captured machine-guns to 30.

The men of "A" Company had had a particularly strenuous time. During the heavy shelling that fell on their assembly positions a few minutes before zero, Captain R. J. S. Seddon and some of his platoon were killed and others wounded. Two hours later, 2nd Lieut. S. N. Managh, D.C.M., while leading his platoon to the jumping-off position on the Blue Line, was shot by a sniper still lurking in Puisieux. Then during the forenoon 2nd Lieut. A. Hart, while manœuvring to outflank a machine-gun post holding up the advance of his men, fell under a burst of fire at point-blank range. Lieut. Russell was thus left without a single officer, but the non-commissioned officers, notably Company Sergt.-Major F. Slevin, rose splendidly to the occasion, promptly assumed leadership, and, as we have seen, carried on the operation to a successful issue.

No fewer than ten machine-guns were captured by this company alone, and the prisoners taken numbered sixty-six, including two officers.

The night passed fairly quietly, but at five o'clock next morning, the 22nd, the enemy in great strength counter-attacked from Miraumont with the object of regaining his lost position of vantage on the high ground about the Dovecote. The 3rd Battalion's sector of the line was not directly involved; but as the left of the 42nd Division fell back under the weight of overwhelming numbers, our own right flank was uncovered. As the leading party of the enemy's flanking troops appeared over the skyline, Lance-Corporal R. Milne rushed with his Lewis gun to the crest and there engaged them at point-blank range, killed twelve, disabled a further eight, and sent in five prisoners with four machine-guns. This dashing deed prevented the enemy from occupying a commanding position from which he could have rendered an important section of our line untenable; and beyond the bending back of our extreme right to form a defensive flank, the line, which had been strengthened on the previous evening by an additional platoon from the support company, remained unaltered.

The enemy succeeded in regaining possession of the Dovecote, but an attempt to follow up this success by advancing still further across the spur resulted in fearful slaughter amongst the advancing waves. Coming under close range fire from eight New Zealand machine-guns handled by sections that had taken up an excellent forward position, they were literally mown down. Fully 400 were killed, and a further 250 surrendered at once to a platoon of the Gloucester Regiment that had overlapped our front during the night.

During the forenoon the support company of the 3rd Battalion, less the platoon already sent forward, passed through the advanced posts and established a new line well down the slopes overlooking the railway. This forward movement took place in conjunction with the advance of the troops of the 42nd Division in a further but only temporarily successful attack on the Dovecote.*

*In the afternoon the 1st Brigade concentrated between Gommecourt Park and Rossignol Wood, and a squadron of the Royal Scots Greys was attached to the Division ready to assist in the advance.

As to the advance as a whole, the battle had gone well, the attack having come as a complete surprise to the enemy. The general objective, the Arras–Albert Railway, had been secured on practically the whole front, and the British troops had gained the required positions from which to launch the principal attack. Early in the morning of August 22nd, the IIIrd Corps captured Albert and advanced the line between the Somme and the Ancre well to the east of the Bray–Albert Road.

PART 3.—MIRAUMONT, AUGUST 23RD.

Main operation commences August 23rd—1st Battalion's preliminary advance with the 42nd Division to secure the Dovecote, 2.30 a.m.—Enemy counter-attack—1st Battalion's main advance, 11 a.m.—General results.

The main operation opened on August 23rd, and consisted of a series of strong assaults along the greater part of the front of 33 miles from the junction with the French at Lihons, near Chaulnes, to Mercatel, near Arras.

In our vicinity, the 5th and other Divisions on our left were to advance at 11 a.m. on August 23rd, with the object of capturing Irles, Achiet-le-Petit, and Achiet-le-Grand, and we were to co-operate by advancing 800 yards to take a sector of about 1,500 yards of railway immediately north-east of Miraumont. But the jumping-off line was unsatisfactory while the enemy still held the Dovecote position, and to remedy this defect a preliminary attack was planned for the early hours of the morning. For this action the 1st Battalion came into line during the previous evening, relieving the 3rd; and the southern boundary of the Division was moved 800 yards nearer the Dovecote, with its direction modified so that it ran south-east.

The objective for the 1st Battalion, which was to attack in conjunction with the 42nd Division, was some 500 yards in length, and for the taking of this section, "C" Company (Lieut. H. A. Ellingham) was detailed. At a perilously late hour an additional length of 700 yards to the north was added in order to ensure closer contact with the 5th Division. Hurried orders brought two platoons of "B" Company, under

Brigadier-General H. Hart, C.B., C.M.G., D.S.O   *Face p. 352.*

PRISONERS FROM PUISIEUX.

A GERMAN OBSERVATION-POST, BAPAUME.

Lieut. B. C. Kirk, into a position of readiness to cope with this extension, and well before zero the attacking troops had formed up on the broad slopes in bright moonlight, awaiting the signal to advance. This came at 2.30 a.m., with the opening burst of the barraging guns of the 5th Division, which gave us perfect support throughout. The opposition encountered was nowhere sufficiently stubborn to cause a check of any consequence, and the objective was reached well within the time allotted.

The final line ran north-east and south-west some 400 yards from the main railway-line, its left near the eastern point of the triangle patrolled but not wholly held by the 3rd Battalion during the fighting of the previous two days. On the right, which was slightly bent back, connection was made with the flanking troops of the 125th Brigade, who had now succeeded in finally pushing the enemy back from the much-contested position at the Dovecote.

As these same platoons of the 1st Battalion were to attack again at 11 a.m., in connection with the main advance, there was little time or opportunity for consolidation beyond some strengthening of the shell-hole positions gained. Careful reconnaissance was all-important, and some excellent work in this connection was carried out by Lieuts. Kirk and Ellingham down the exposed slopes across which the troops they commanded were to pass. For the special confirmatory information of headquarters, too, Sergeant C. R. Wilson, of the battalion scouts, under continuous fire from machine-guns and snipers, made a complete reconnaissance of the new line, and supplied an accurate report as to the exact locality of each advanced post. Our line was very much exposed, and all through the forenoon machine-gun fire was heavy, especially from the high ground to our left beyond the valley. There appeared to be no serious attempt to launch a general counter-attack, but, from 9 a.m. onwards, parties of the enemy repeatedly advanced against the right company. One of these, coming forward with considerable boldness under cover of the long grass, was held in check by one man, Lance-Corporal G. Hunter, who was in a shell-hole in advance of the line. Four of the enemy fell to his rifle, and the Germans took cover and brought machine-gun fire to bear upon him; but, though wounded three times, he still held his ground and maintained his fire, and here, as elsewhere, the enemy failed to make any impression on our line.

When the detailed orders for the main attack were received by the battalion just before 8 a.m., Major Shepherd found to his dismay that the opening barrage would fall upon two platoons that had, in the previous attack, advanced far beyond the objective, and being now in a valley dominated by a ridge occupied by the enemy, were quite unable to move in daylight. Fortunately, though at the last moment, efforts of Brigade Headquarters to have the barrage line advanced proved successful.

The task allotted to the six attacking platoons was somewhat peculiar. The 5th Division, after sweeping through Achiet-le-Petit and across the slopes to the south of it, was to increase the frontage of its attack so as to extend southwards across our front and take in Irles. We, on our part, were to render that extension safe by clearing the valley immediately to our front, keeping touch throughout with the 5th Divison, and then forming a defensive flank facing south-west. This involved a swinging movement through slightly more than a right-angle.

The action opened with a good barrage, which moved down the railway-line from left to right in lifts of 100 yards every four minutes. The artillery supplying immediate covering-fire for the 1st Battalion was that New Zealand formation known as the 2nd (Army) Brigade; and the Otago Machine Gun Company gave additional support by barraging the farther slope of the valley through which the railway ran. "C." Company advanced on a two-platoon frontage, while the two platoons of "B" Company on the left, moving round in echelon, maintained touch with "C," and at the same time conformed to the movements of the right flank of the 5th Division. Machine-gun fire throughout was intense, and considerable opposition was met with, especially by the sections on the left, but the operation was successfully completed within the time laid down. Excellent leadership and dashing gallantry were displayed by Sergeants W. B. Timmins, R. J. Sinclair and P. G. Craig as temporary platoon commanders on the loss of their officers. A heavy trench-mortar, seven machine-guns, and 76 prisoners were captured, the greater part of the spoils falling to the "B" Company men as they cleared up the area about the railway line.

On this day brilliant results were everywhere obtained. Irles, Achiet-le-Petit, Achiet-le-Grand, Bihucourt, Gomiecourt, Ervillers, Boyelles and Boiry Becquerelle were taken, and the British forces were in position astride the Arras-Bapaume Road. There was still a pronounced salient on the Thiepval Ridge, but the position of the German Divisions there was becoming extremely perilous. The attack made earlier in the day both north and south of the Somme had met with equal success, and evidences were abundant that along the whole of the front the enemy was becoming disorganized and confused.

PART 4.—BAPAUME, AUGUST 26TH TO 29TH.

New Zealand Division carries on the attack towards Bapaume, August 24th—1st Brigade captures Loupart Wood and Grevillers —2nd Brigade captures Biefvillers and closes in on Bapaume— General results of the four days' fighting—1st and 2nd Brigades continue the attack on Bapaume, August 25th—New Zealand Rifle Brigade to continue the attack, August 26th—Concentration—Plans and objectives—An unexpected first objective—Partial success: Beaugnatre Road secured—Attack continued 6 p.m. —Cambrai Road gained and lost—Railway secured—Bapaume entered and line established beyond, August 29th.

At 4 p.m. on August 23rd, warning orders were received that the New Zealand Division would sidestep slightly to the northward and carry on the attack towards Bapaume. Just before dawn on the following morning the 1st Battalion was, after much difficulty, relieved by the 7th Manchester Battalion of the 42nd Division, and joined the remainder of the Brigade in the bivouac area north of Puisieux. By this time the Brigade was under orders to move at half-an-hour's notice, for the operations of the 24th had commenced.

For these the New Zealand Division had been put in on the left of the 5th Division, and at 4.15 a.m. the 1st Brigade, with the 2nd Brigade in support and the New Zealand Rifle Brigade in reserve, advanced and took Loupart Wood and Grevillers. During the forenoon the 2nd Brigade moved up

ORDER OF BATTLE—BAPAUME, AUGUST 26, 1918.

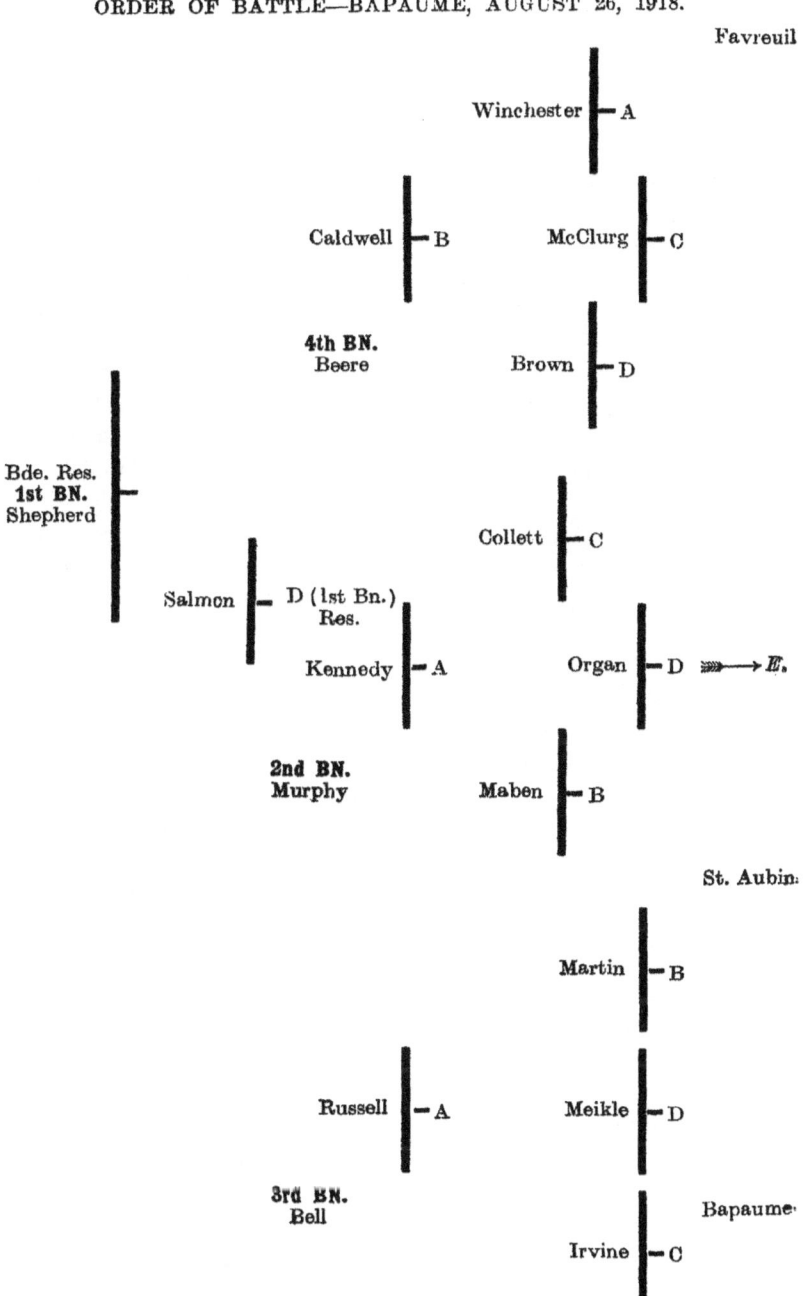

356

on the left of the 1st, and, having assisted the 37th Division, then operating on its left, by the capture of Biefvillers, pressed forward towards Bapaume. The New Zealanders, however, had moved more quickly than their neighbours; and as their position now formed a pronounced salient, a further extensive advance was not possible until flanking Divisions came into alignment. At noon our Brigade was brought up to a position near Divisional Headquarters between Bucquoy and Achiet-le-Petit, and, while it continued in reserve, sent reconnoitring parties forward frequently to study the country and to keep touch with the general situation as it developed.

By the end of the day the 42nd Division, in the old sector, had captured Miraumont and Pys; while farther south the Thiepval Ridge had been carried, as had other old Somme strong-points such as Pozieres, Courcelette and Martinpuich.

In the four days* since August 20th, the advance made by our Corps—the IVth—exceeded seven miles. Its general direction was at right-angles to that along which we had fought in the Somme Battle of 1916, and we were now well behind the shell-blasted forward zone of the enemy's trench-system. The roads were good, horsemen could ride everywhere without difficulty, and, owing to the rolling nature of the country, transport could be brought with ease within a mile of the battle-line. As for the fighting, this was entirely different from that of all earlier battles in which we had participated in France. Advances were deeper and on much wider frontages, troops were not so densely packed, and there was greater scope for initiative and leadership. There was a diminution of the gruesomeness and horror of trench warfare, and all ranks were affected by a peculiar calmness, giving place at times to a distinct feeling of "the joy of battle." In one very important respect fortune favoured us: the enemy for once had lost his old allies, rain and mud.

At 5 a.m. on August 25th the 1st and 2nd Brigades continued the attack on Bapaume, but the enemy's stubborn defence of the town could not be entirely broken down. The

---

*The casualties throughout the Brigade during this period were:—

	Killed.	Wounded.
Officers	4	3
Other ranks	20	97

former, operating to the south, made some progress east of Grevillers, but did not succeed in taking more than a short section of the Albert Road. To the north, the 2nd Brigade had better fortune, for, after a long and bitter fight, they took Avesnes, a suburb of the town, and a considerable stretch of the Arras Road as far north as the Monument at the crossroads near Favreuil. A further effort was made by the 2nd Brigade at 6.30 p.m., after a heavy bombardment of Favreuil. The objective was the high ground to the north of Bapaume, and it was expected that the Bapaume–Beugnatre Road would be reached.

Half an hour after the opening of this evening attack, the New Zealand Rifle Brigade commenced to move forward to take over the northern sector from the 2nd Brigade and make ready for a continuance of the advance next day. By 10 p.m., after a trying march across country in profound darkness and through a tropical downpour of rain, concentration between Biefvillers and Grevillers was completed. Definite plans for the attack, depending as they did on the results of the enterprise of the 2nd Brigade, could not be drawn up until after midnight, and at 1.30 a.m. on the 26th these were communicated orally to battalion commanders, who had been called to advanced Brigade headquarters for the purpose.

The frontage of attack being over 2,500 yards in length, three battalions were detailed for the operation, the 3rd, 2nd, and 4th, in that order from the right. From the position of the 2nd Brigade on the Beugnatre Road they were to advance in a south-easterly direction for about 1,500 yards, thus partially encircling Bapaume and securing a position due east of the town. Part of the objective lay slightly beyond the great highway running eastwards towards Cambrai, while a defensive flank would stretch northwards to connect with the 5th Division, which had relieved the 37th during the night. Co-operating on the flanks, the 1st Brigade would maintain touch with our right, send patrols into Bapaume, and, if the enemy's hold were found to be weakening, mop it up, while on the left, the 5th Division would assault Beugnatre and the system of trenches about its outskirts. The attack, timed to commence at 6.30 a.m., was to be carried out without a barrage and with no assistance from tanks. One section of the Auckland Machine Gun Company, and one of the 3rd Light Trench Mortar Battery, were placed at the disposal of the respective battalion commanders, who each had also at call a battery of the New Zealand Field Artillery for the provision of covering fire. Battalion commanders had taken the precaution to bring their company commanders with them to the conference, and, the necessary plans having been discussed on the spot, the latter moved off to pass down the orders to their subordinates. The concentration area was some two miles behind the jumping-off line, but in good time the attacking units got forward into position immediately behind the line held by the 2nd Brigade. Here it was found that practically the whole of the Beugnatre Road was still in the hands of the enemy; and this formidable position, for the most part sunken and strongly held, had now to be taken as an unexpected first objective. This necessitated some modifications in the plans previously adopted, and threatened to entail vexatious delay.

The line ran slightly east of north, roughly parallel to and about 1,000 yards west of the Beugnatre Road, the right being opposite the centre of Bapaume, and the left close to Favreuil. The outskirts of Bapaume extended northwards for about half a mile along the Beugnatre Road, and the northern extremity of this collection of houses was known as St. Aubin. Here there was a network of railway sidings, together with a number of huge dumps of timber and other engineers' supplies, the whole covering an area of some thirty acres on the western side of the village. This position lay almost on the dividing line between the sectors to be operated over by the 3rd and 2nd Battalions, and the reports as to its being strongly held by the enemy were confirmed in no uncertain way by the volume of machine-gun fire that issued from it whenever our men moved.

Lieut.-Col. Bell employed three companies for the attack on his sector. "C" Company (Lieut. J. H. Irvine) on the right was instructed to press eastwards towards Bapaume by means of fighting patrols; "B" Company (Lieut. A. L. Martin), on the left, was given the task of dealing with St. Aubin and the dumps; while "D" Company (Capt. H. C. Meikle) would link up between the two and establish a line of posts facing Bapaume from the north. In the 2nd Battalion, "D"

Company (Lieut. W. J. Organ) was to capture the allotted portion of the first objective on the road, with "B" (Lieut. K. M. Maben) and "C" (Capt. H. C. Collett) disposed in echelon on the flanks, the former being specially detailed to watch St. Aubin and its neighbourhood. On the left of the line, the 4th Battalion had two companies detailed for the capture of the objective, "D" (Capt. A. E. Brown), on the right, and "A" (Capt. E. A. Winchester), on the left. "C" Company (Capt. D. W. McClurg) had moved up earlier to take over the sector from the 2nd Brigade troops, and the remaining company was held in reserve.

When the general attack opened at 6.30 a.m., the absence of a barrage was felt at all points, for at the first forward movement, machine-gun fire poured in upon our men from front and flank. The 3rd Battalion's right patrols were held up almost at once, their position being completely dominated from the buildings of Bapaume. The left company made considerable progress towards St. Aubin, clearing by a series of hand-to-hand fights the greater part of the dump and siding area, but the machine-gun posts in the village itself were too strongly placed and could not be taken. The centre company came under heavy crossfire from Bapaume and St. Aubin, but pressed steadily forward and finally succeeded in gaining a position beyond the Arras Road, thus advancing the investment of the town by one more step.

The 2nd Battalion had slightly better success. The leading company, after an hour's steady fighting, pushed its way eastward to the road, and with a final rush succeeded in clearing its portion of this objective. The company's right flank was "in the air," however, for the supporting company had swung out too much to the right and was carrying out an attack on its own account against St. Aubin, finally digging in facing the south and south-east close up to the village and dumps. It was pinned down here by the accurate sniping and short-range machine-gun fire.

Meanwhile, in the 4th Battalion's sector, Capt. McClurg's company had gone on with the original programme. Advancing through the wood by Favreuil under the storm of shellfire to which the enemy was subjecting the whole area, it reached the 2nd Brigade posts on the Favreuil Road, where it was now learned for the first time that the Beugnatre Road as well as the intervening country was still held by the Germans. Capt. McClurg decided to press on at once to secure the jumping-off line for the attacking companies,—a perilous undertaking in view of the obscurity of the situation on the flanks. The men were ably led, however, 2nd Lieut. W. Skelton and Corporal E. J. McInnes doing brilliant service in this respect, and they pushed steadily up the slope towards the road. They were exposed to machine-gun fire from the huts about the south-east corner of Favreuil and from Beugnatre, and presently came into full view of the enemy posts in the aerodrome huts near the road forming their objective. Advancing upon these in V-shape formation, the company secured a footing in the road and steadily extended its gains right and left till the position was won. Here it was decided to consolidate for the time being, the miniature hollows in the roadbanks from which spoil had been removed forming ready-made cover from enfilade fire. Presently the scouts of "A" Company approached the position. Capt. Winchester had been wounded, and 2nd Lieut. C. Darling was now in command. Capt. McClurg acted with promptitude. Taking over direction of the forward operations pending further instructions, he placed "A" Company on the left to form a defensive flank. Similarly, he arranged with Capt. Brown to place "D" Company on the right to continue the main line southwards, and, though some stiff fighting lay before both these companies, it was not long before the position was comparatively secure. Soon afterwards the troops of the 2nd Battalion gained touch on the right, but the left was still "in the air." The wisdom of the precautionary measures taken for the safeguarding of this flank was demonstrated early, for during the forenoon the enemy, a half-battalion strong, counter-attacked from Beugnatre. Severe fighting took place, and the 4th Battalion had many casualties; but the flank company stood fast, and the enemy finally withdrew to the village. 2nd Lieut. L. C. L. Averill displayed exceptional gallantry and fine leadership during the struggle in this quarter.

The first objective was thus only partially gained, and for that reason the hostile artillery fire on the new line was, for the moment, practically negligible. Such casualties as we had suffered from shell-fire had occurred on the way up to the position of deployment, and these included a considerable proportion of the personnel of the 2nd Battalion headquarters' section, which was twice struck. The enemy, however, had the situation sufficiently well in hand. Still holding in strength Bapaume and Beugnatre on the flanks, as well as the commanding position at St. Aubin, he was able to pour streams of machine-gun bullets upon the whole length of the Beugnatre Road and over the country in the vicinity. The heavy rain had ceased before daybreak, giving place to bright clear weather, and the German gunners in the high buildings, unmolested by our heavies, could pick up their targets with ease. The situation beyond the left flank remained unsatisfactory; Bapaume, of course, was not being assaulted; and neither the 3rd Battalion company on the west nor that from the 2nd Battalion on the north could make any satisfactory impression on the awkward St. Aubin salient. In these circumstances an immediate continuance of a local attack was out of the question, and, shortly before 10 a.m., orders were issued to the forward units of the Brigade to sit tight and await further instructions.

At noon General Hart held a conference with commanding officers at the 2nd Battalion headquarters to discuss plans for the resumption of the attack.* All were agreed that the advance could be carried on successfully provided a satisfactory artillery barrage could be arranged for, especially if the guns concentrated on St. Aubin and the two flanking towns even though for a very brief period. For the moment, however, no definite orders could be issued. It was clear that any action must be made in concert with the troops of the 5th Division, but these were still held up at Beugnatre, and no instructions for the next move had as yet been received. These indeed did not reach General Hart until some three hours later, and as zero hour was to be 6 p.m., he at once issued orders by telephone. The evening attack was to be supported by a barrage, under cover of which the 2nd Battalion was to ad-

---

*Lieut.-Col. R. St. J. Beere, commanding the 4th Battalion, was wounded while on his way to attend this conference, and the command was taken over by Major H. E. Barrowclough. Major J. Murphy was in temporary command of the 2nd Battalion, Lieut.-Col. Jardine being absent on leave.

The 3rd Battalion on the right would conform, and send patrols vance to the original final objective on the Cambrai Road. into Bapaume from the north; while the 4th Battalion, swinging forward its right into a north and south line, would link up between the left of the 2nd Battalion and the right of the 5th Division, the latter being ordered to continue the attack on Beugnatre.

Major Murphy sent for his company commanders, but these were not able to assemble until 4.45 p.m. The original plans were modified to the extent of putting in "C" Company on the right of "D," leaving "B" in its present position to continue the pressure on St. Aubin. "A" Company was to act in support, and "D" Company of the 1st Battalion was brought up in reserve. In view of the brevity of the time now remaining, the company commanders pressed for a short respite to enable them to perfect their arrangements, but the action not being an isolated one it was impossible to alter the zero hour. Orders got down to platoon commanders only twenty minutes before the opening of the barrage, and it speaks well for the adaptability of our men that, though little could be done beyond giving them the objective and the direction, they "shook themselves into their formations as the advance progressed, and moved forward in excellent style."

"C" Company suffered rather heavily in skirting St. Aubin. "D" Company's line of advance was crossed diagonally by the strongly-wired Bancourt Trench, but this was cleared of its garrison by a section of the right platoon after fourteen rounds had been thrown into it from the Stokes mortars, and both companies approached the railway running along the broad valley towards Bapaume. The resistance met with here was speedily overcome, though the troops suffered from machine-gun fire sweeping across from the spur to the left front. From the railway the advance was continued towards the Cambrai Road, here 500 yards ahead. The barrage, however, moved too slowly, and the German machine-guns on the road, as well as those on either flank, had not yet been reached by the artillery. Under the withering fire our men fell fast. "D" Company lost two of its platoon commanders, and "C" Company all its officers. The objective was reached but could not be held. The road was enfiladed from both flanks, and presently, from a sunken road leading to the old Sugar Factory, the Germans poured into the gap between the two companies. At the opening of the evening attack the platoons had mustered only from twenty to twenty-five bayonets, and by this time, 8 p.m., our numbers had been too greatly reduced to withstand this all-round pressure. The remnants of the two companies were thus compelled to give ground, and they eventually dug in by the railway, from the little branch known as Gun Spur, along to St. Aubin, which still held out. The 3rd Battalion patrols working round the north of Bapaume made progress, but were unable to reach the Cambrai Road. They were held up by the steady machine-gun fire from the Brickyard and the Shrine situated on their objective, besides being enfiladed from both flanks, and had to be content with a line of posts close to the northern outskirts of the town. The 4th Battalion, keeping touch with the 2nd, moved forward some 500 yards to the high ground east of the road. The company on the outer flank had a sufficiently difficult time maintaining connection with the troops of the 5th Division as they strove with the enemy in and about the village. It was involved in considerable fighting long after the remainder of the Brigade had proceeded to consolidate, for the Germans were not driven from Beugnatre until late that night. Here Corporal W. J. Patching distinguished himself by his fine handling of a platoon on the loss of his sergeant, and later by carrying out an excellent reconnaissance, in which, as at Puisieux on the 21st, he gained accurate information concerning not only the position of the flanking posts on our side, but also the location and strength of the enemy's line in the vicinity.

The night of the 26th/27th was spent in re-organizing and consolidating, the troops close to Bapaume devoting much attention to the construction of overhead protection from machine-gun fire which the enemy, from his elevated positions, was able to direct into the trenches. During the 27th the situation remained unchanged. Our new posts were heavily shelled and the German machine-gunners renewed their activities, but there were no further attempts to counter-attack. In view of the contemplated advance from the north against the Cambrai Road and Fremicourt by the 1st and 4th Battalions, in conjunction with the 2nd Brigade on the left, the 3rd Battalion was withdrawn to reserve on the night of the 27th/28th, relief being effected by the 2nd Battalion and the 2nd Brigade extending their inner flanks. The projected operations were postponed, however, and the opportunity was taken to bring the cookers further up and supply the troops with a welcome hot meal.

The night of the 28th/29th was quiet. Patrols had continued their operations unceasingly, some having succeeded in reaching the rest-billets near Fremicourt. The enemy was found to be everywhere alert, and not a few casualties were sustained during the progress of this reconnaissance work. After dawn on the 29th, however, a diminution of his watchfulness was noted, and about Bapaume contact could not be gained. Reports were quickly got back, and the 3rd Battalion came up to prosecute further investigations. Capt. Meikle's company was organized into strong patrols, and at 8.30 a.m. these entered Bapaume by the Arras Road and worked eastwards through the northern half of the town. Troops of the 1st Brigade simultaneously moved through the southern half. Soon afterwards the remaining line battalions took up the movement. The 2nd Battalion advanced to the Cambrai Road, and then swung up its right in touch with the 3rd Battalion as the latter moved steadily eastward. A large number of machine-guns were captured by both units, the 3rd Battalion claiming in addition as part of its spoils a fine haul of telephone-exchange instruments, some horses, and two ten-inch howitzers. The 4th Battalion was not able to advance to the same extent, the enemy continuing to hold in strength the system of railway sidings opposite the centre of its position. Against the posts at the sidings two whippets dashed out from the Beugnatre Road, only to bring down upon themselves a storm of artillery fire from all the German guns in the neighbourhood, and their plucky attempt was cut short before they had gone 200 yards. By 2 p.m. the new line had been established 1,500 yards east of Bapaume and the Beugnatre Road, and was within about the same distance of Bancourt and Fremicourt. From the latter village machine-gun fire continued to pour upon our posts, but from Bancourt the enemy was seen to be retiring in haste. Battalion commanders pleaded for permission to advance further and occupy the latter village, but the initial forward movement had not been carried out to the same depth on the flanks, and sanction was reluctantly withheld. This was unfortunate, for presently the enemy troops began to filter back again, and there was to be some stiff fighting before the village, a veritable strong-point elaborately entrenched and wired, finally passed into our hands.

PART 5.—FREMICOURT, AUGUST 30TH TO SEPTEMBER 1ST.

Advance continued, August 30th—1st Battalion takes Fremicourt and the ridge beyond—1st Brigade takes Bancourt—1st Battalion's flanks exposed—Withdrawal down the slope—Counter-attacks—Advance to the crest again, September 1st—General results—End of the second stage of the British offensive.

Preparations were at once put in hand to exploit the successes so far gained. The enemy had withdrawn to a fine defensive position on the high ground to the east, and the line taken up included a number of villages already fortified, while crossing it diagonally lay the strongly-wired Beugny trench system. To prevent completion of consolidation it was proposed to press the attack on the following day. The Brigade's objective was the village of Fremicourt and the ridge 800 yards to the east of it. The 1st Brigade on our right was to take Bancourt and a section of the same ridge, while the 5th Division on our left was to capture the system of trenches known as the Beugny Line. On the right of the New Zealanders was the 42nd Division, which had Villers-au-Flos as its objective.

The Brigade's task was entrusted to the 1st Battalion,[*] then in reserve behind Monument Wood south-west of Favreuil. General Hart was not able to issue warning orders before 9 p.m., nor detailed instructions until after midnight. As companies had a distance of nearly two miles to march before

[*] Lieut.-Col. Austin was recalled from the Brigade Details' Camp and resumed command of the 1st Battalion on the 29th. On the following day Major Bremner, from hospital, again took up the duties of Brigade Major.

reaching the position of deployment, they moved off at 3 a.m. Guides had been expected, but as these did not report in time company commanders had to rely on their maps and compasses, and without mishap they gained their appointed places. "A" Company (Lieut. R. J. Grant) was on the right, astride the Cambrai Road leading from Bapaume through Fremicourt; "D" Company (Capt. P. E. A. Salmon) on the left; "C" (Lieut. M. A. Stedman) in support; and "B" (Capt. G. P. O'Shannassy) in reserve. The leading companies were extended over a line 1,000 yards in length, lying due north and south about 1,500 yards west of Fremicourt. "D" Company had been detached to the 2nd Battalion as reserve during its latest fighting, and owing to some misunderstanding, two of its platoons were still absent engaged as carrying party. They rejoined their company in the thick of the fight, thanks to their own pluck and perseverance and to the excellent leadership of Sergeant W. L. Free.

At 5 a.m. the artillery and machine-gun barrage opened, and after six minutes advanced due east by lifts of 100 yards every three minutes. Both the attacking companies met with stiff opposition from machine-gun posts established in the huts of the rest-billets on both sides of the road just beyond the line of the first barrage. These, enclosed within the usual thick earth banks built up as a protection against aeroplane bomb splinters, formed ready-made strong-points and gave considerable trouble. They were, however, smartly outflanked, and the line was able to move steadily forward with the barrage. The trench behind the billets was cleared at the point of the bayonet, and our men were within touch of Fremicourt.

In accordance with instructions, each of the leading companies skirted the village, leaving its mopping-up to the support company. "A" Company progressed steadily, clearing without serious difficulty some isolated buildings and a trench system running round the south of the village, and then, pressing forward up the slope, carried the final position with a rush. Except for some stiff fighting in the sunken road marking its left flank, and a sharp struggle about a dug-out position confronting the centre when half-way up the rise, this company, during the concluding stage of its advance, nowhere found the enemy's direct resistance sufficiently stubborn to cause a check, but as they approached the crest the men fell fast under the enfilade fire coming in from the right. On the left, "D" Company struck further trouble when in line with the nearer outskirts of Fremicourt. Here, just beyond the north-west corner, was situated a large camouflaged strong-point containing three machine-guns, but, by keeping close to the barrage, the leading sections were able to rush and capture this without casualties. As the forward companies passed on, "C" Company, in support, approached the village. Shells from one of our heavy howitzers, still crashing down upon its western edge, threatened to block the way; but three platoons passed round to the north, and one to the south, and from the sides they entered the village and dealt with its garrison.

In the meantime "D" Company was meeting with new and unexpected difficulties, for it was beginning to lose touch with the flank of the 5th Division, which was drawing away northwards. To ensure its own safety "D" Company's left had to extend correspondingly, and this brought it against strong enemy posts at a large railway dump. In clearing the position here, fifty prisoners were taken, but by the time the task was completed the barrage had passed on. The right of the company, however, was already on its objective; and by 8 a.m. the left came up in line with it and secured a strong position with its outer flank on the railway-cutting. This final stage was not completed without a stiff contest, and the lack of support from troops beyond the railway was felt as a serious handicap. Fortunately a tank arrived on the scene, and the struggle ended with the taking of the cutting and the capture of another fifty prisoners.

Both companies were now in position on the final objective on the ridge, but the flanks were "in the air." The 1st Brigade's extreme left was digging in 300 yards behind "A" Company's right; while on the left, although we had extended 300 yards into our neighbours' territory, there was still a considerable gap between us and their nearest troops. The support company, having completed the mopping-up of the village, passed on clear of the houses and dug in at the pre-arranged position astride the highway and abreast of the cemetery. Its "bag" of prisoners consisted of seven officers and 110 other ranks. Of these, no fewer than five officers and

76 other ranks had been hoodwinked into surrender by the clever tactics of Corporal E. Sheldrake with a section of five men.

The reserve company also had its adventures. At 6.30 a.m., one platoon was sent up to strengthen the left flank of "D" Company. The remainder, while waiting near the road, about half-way between Bapaume and Fremicourt, were fired on by our advancing tanks, whose crews, however, presently made amends by assisting the men of this company in the rooting out of some nests of machine-guns, which had been passed over by the advancing troops and were now firing from positions south of the old rest-camp.

On our right, the 1st Brigade took Bancourt, two companies of our 2nd Battalion assisting in the mopping-up of the village, in which they captured 34 prisoners; but the 42nd Division, operating beyond them, did not succeed in the endeavour to take Reincourt, and consequently the further advance of the 1st Brigade was checked. Similarly, on the left, Beugny was to have fallen to the troops of the 5th Division, but it was still beyond their grasp.

A somewhat prolonged and agitated telephonic discussion with regard to the situation now commenced between Brigade Headquarters and that of the 1st Battalion. The unit had sent in the usual urgent reports concerning its own position and that of the flanking troops, these being based on the information furnished by its forward companies. It would appear, however, that as to certain details the reports did not coincide with those supplied to Division by the formations on either hand, and Brigade Headquarters promptly advised the battalion of the fact; but by this time the unit's intelligence section had made their special reconnaissance, and confirmation of the previous statement was as promptly presented. Nevertheless this did not end the matter, for apparently the information in the hands of Divisional Headquarters was still conflicting, and presently a curt intimation to this effect was sent down to the battalion. Affairs were now becoming serious, for, in view of a counter-attack in strength, which was to be expected in the ordinary course of events, the artillery were awaiting those definite particulars which would enable them to give effective support. To set the matter at rest, the adjutant, Lieut. L. J. Rowe, set out to make a close investigation of the position. In the face of heavy machine-gun fire, now becoming increasingly intense, he passed along the line, visited in turn all of our own posts and in addition those immediately adjoining, and had the satisfaction of reporting that in no case was the location of our positions incorrectly given.

Occupying as it did a salient with two exposed flanks, the 1st Battalion soon found its position an exceedingly perilous one. The line was subjected to continuous heavy rifle and machine-gun fire, not only from the higher ground to the right, but also from Beugny. Soon after midday the enemy counter-attacked, and succeeded in driving in the right flank and a post on the left. Casualties throughout the morning had been severe. 2nd Lieut. H. Ellen found himself the only surviving officer of his company, Sergt. R. J. Sinclair's platoon was reduced to himself and eight men, and another platoon was carrying on bravely under Rifleman C. J. Ball; and, as no further advance had been made by the troops on our flanks, the remaining posts on the crest were quietly withdrawn during the afternoon and the line re-established some 200 yards down the western slope. The three platoons of the reserve company were moved from the west of the village to the north, in order to meet any further attack that might develop on the exposed left flank, and a company from the 3rd Battalion was attached as reserve in its place. At nightfall the Vickers guns were also sent up to this flank to cover the road from Beugny. The seriousness of the position in this quarter had been observed by the 4th Battalion. Soon after the enemy had inaugurated his return thrust, "C" Company of that unit, under Capt. McClurg, came over from the Beugnatre Road and established itself, with its two attached Vickers guns, on a spur northwest of Fremicourt, and in view of the uncertainty of the situation their presence in the near neighbourhood was a source of some considerable comfort to the troops of the 1st Battalion.

At 5 a.m. on 31st August the enemy barraged our front line, and half an hour later launched a strong counter-attack. As the advancing Germans approached the line from the crest above, it was seen that they were accompanied by tanks, a new experience for our men. The S.O.S. rocket went up, but apparently the signal was not seen, for the attackers reached the posts before our barrage could be brought down. Two tanks, working together, breached the line on the right and moved on towards Fremicourt, but the German infantry had not learned the art of co-operation, and the tanks were poorly supported. Approaching "C" Company's position on the east of the village, the tanks drew heavy rifle and Lewis gun fire, and, turning southwards, they moved on towards the 1st Brigade's line. "C" Company thereupon strengthened its defensive flank, but was not further molested. Both tanks fell into the hands of the New Zealanders two days later.

The lost positions on the right of the front line were presently regained, for the remaining posts had succeeded in holding up the infantry attack without great difficulty. Indeed the whole situation appeared to be eminently satisfactory; but at daylight two parties of Germans, each about fifty strong, were discovered in rear of our left flank, having worked their way in between our left and the right of the 5th Division. The first party was sighted by Sergt. A. J. Cunningham, of "B" Company, who was now to add yet another achievement to the fine score already standing to his credit. Taking with him no more than a section, he moved out at once to engage the Germans, and so skilfully did he handle his men that within a few minutes the little operation was over and 46 prisoners were on their way to the rear. The second party of Germans moved on till they reached the position held by the Vickers gun section and the detached platoon of "B" Company on the north of the village. Here they received short shrift, for, making no response to the command to surrender, they were raked by our rifles and machine-guns, and the handful of unwounded Germans remaining gave themselves up.

During the afternoon, orders were issued for an advance on the following morning, September 1st,* in conjunction with the 1st Brigade and the 5th Division, with the object of regaining the advantage of view and command afforded by the position on the crest of the ridge. In accordance with in-

---

*The total casualties to the Brigade from the opening of the great battle on August 21st were, up to the end of the month, 14 officers and 114 men killed, and 34 officers and 499 men wounded, together with 40 men unaccounted for. During the earlier part of the month they numbered one officer and eight men killed, and four officers and 61 men wounded.

structions, however, fighting patrols went out during the night to test the enemy's strength, and, if found feasible, to gain the desired objective without having recourse to the proposed set action. Their investigations showed that the crest was too strongly held to be taken by this means, and it was accordingly decided to carry out the larger scheme.

At 4.55 a.m. the barrage came down promptly, and shortly afterwards "C" and "B" Companies passed through the outposts of the other two companies and pushed up the slopes. In spite of heavy machine-gun fire from the flanks, the leading platoons gained their objectives by 5.30 a.m., capturing 75 prisoners and a number of machine-guns and trench-mortars. Touch was established with the 1st Brigade troops, who had come up on the right, but the flank company of the Brigade on our left did not arrive in time to participate in the attack. Eventually the company moved as far forward as was possible in the daylight, and in the evening, under cover of darkness, completed the advance and filled the gap.

The number of prisoners captured by the 1st Battalion from 30th August to 1st September was over 400, including a battalion commander and his staff, this total being greater than our own unit's trench strength. The battalion also took two 77 mm. guns, nine minenwerfer, six anti-tank rifles,* and thirty machine-guns. Our front line was now thirteen miles east of Hebuterne.

At 7 a.m. on September 1st, Lieut.-Col. Austin was wounded by a shell-splinter and was evacuated,† Capt. G. P. O'Shannassy assuming temporary command of the 1st Battalion until the return of Major Shepherd from the Details' Camp.

In the evening the Brigade was relieved by the 2nd Brigade, and went into the area between Bapaume and Favreuil as Divisional reserve.

*These were the first anti-tank rifles captured on this front. They were long, clumsy pieces, apparently too heavy to fire with accuracy except from a rest. The bore was much larger than that of an ordinary rifle. It was curious to note that the sling, cartridge-belt and pouches were woven, like our Mills equipment, and that the material was of twisted paper, similar to that used by the Germans for their sand-bags.

†Lieut.-Col. Austin did not return to the Brigade.

During these closing days of the Battle of Bapaume the fighting had gone well along the whole front of the Fourth and Third Armies. By the night of August 30th, their line north of the Somme ran along Clery, Marrieres Wood, Combles, Les Bœufs, Bancourt, Fremicourt, Vraucourt, to the western outskirts of Ecoust, Bullecourt and Hendecourt. By the fighting of the following two days the line was pushed still further eastward and embraced Mont St. Quentin and Peronne, which were taken by the Australians.

So ended the second stage in the British offensive. In the first stage Amiens was freed. In the second, the Third and Fourth Armies, comprising 23 British Divisions, had in ten days driven 35 German Divisions from one side of the old Somme battlefield to the other, thereby turning, as had been intended, the line of the River Somme, inflicting an enormous number of casualties, and capturing over 34,000 prisoners and 270 guns. It now appeared that the enemy would for a time stand on the line of the Somme River and the high ground about Rocquigny and Beugny until he could with safety withdraw behind the Hindenburg Line.*

*Owing to the local pressure on the Lys front, and to the reverses south of Arras, the enemy gave up all hope of reaching the Channel ports, and began, early in August, to withdraw from the Lys Salient. At the end of the month his retrograde movement became more rapid and extensive, and by the 6th September our forces in that area were once more back on the general line Givenchy-Neuve Chapelle-Nieppe-Ploegsteert-Voormezeele, the salient having now entirely disappeared.

CHAPTER XV.
THE BATTLE OF THE SCARPE.

Third stage of the offensive—First Army extends the front of attack northwards — First Army's preparations — First Army strikes at the outworks of the Hindenburg Line, September 2nd —Third and Fourth Armies prolong the attack southwards—2nd Brigade pushes forward to a depth of a mile—Enemy begins to fall back to the Canal du Nord—New Zealand Division follows—2nd Brigade maintains contact—New Zealand Rifle Brigade in Divisional Reserve—2nd Brigade captures Metz and clears Havrincourt Wood by dawn on September 7th, and is relieved by the New Zealand Rifle Brigade.

The time had now arrived for the opening of the third stage of the offensive, when the front of attack should be extended northwards by the First Army, which, in accordance with the general plan of operations* was to follow up the successes of the Third and Fourth Armies by suddenly striking at the western extremity of the Hindenburg Line.

During the last week of August, the First Army, by driving in the enemy salient formed east of Arras by the advance of the Third and Fourth Armies, had been preparing for this blow. The troops of the First Army were now within assaulting distance of the strong trench-system known as the Drocourt–Queant Line, which ran from the Hindenburg Line at Queant to the Lens defences about Drocourt.

On September 2nd the Canadian Corps, together with the XVIIth Corps of the Third Army, successfully attacked this system, stormed the maze of trenches at the junction with the Hindenburg Line, and thereby caused the enemy to commence a precipitate retreat along the whole front to the south of it. The Third and Fourth Armies prolonged the line of attack as far south as Peronne.

The pressure on the enemy opposite our Divisional front this day was maintained by the 2nd Brigade, which pushed forward the line to a depth of a mile.

*See p. 344.

During the night of 2nd/3rd September, the enemy fell back rapidly on the whole of the Third Army front, as well as on the section facing the right of the First Army; and by the evening of the 3rd he had taken up positions along the general line of the Canal du Nord, which passes through or near Peronne, Ytres, Hermies, Inchy-en-Artois, Ecourt St. Quentin, and so on to the Sensee River east of Lecluse. This movement was followed by a withdrawal, on the 4th, from the east bank of the Somme south of Peronne. By September 8th the enemy was holding the general line Vermand, Epehy, Havrincourt, east bank of Canal du Nord. South of the Somme, the French pushed him back beyond Ham and Chauny to the line of the Crozat Canal.

Everywhere, as the enemy withdrew, our troops pressed forward to keep in touch with him. On September 3rd the 2nd Brigade had to move forward nearly four miles to maintain contact, and there was a corresponding advance of the whole Division, General Russell now establishing his headquarters at Fremicourt. The countryside was alive with infantry, artillery of all calibres, transport, tanks, whippets, all moving eastward—a truly stirring sight. Even the observation balloons, still floating high, made a corresponding advance.

On September 4th the New Zealand Rifle Brigade, as Divisional reserve, moved to the area between Favreuil and Fremicourt, reconnoitring parties going east as far as Bertincourt to keep battalions informed as to the ever-changing situation. Transport lines and quartermasters' stores were brought up to the north side of Bapaume.

We relieved the 1st Brigade in support on September 6th, Brigade Headquarters being established at Villers-au-Flos, in what had been a Corps Headquarters before the March retreat. The 1st Battalion was quartered in Haplincourt Wood, the 2nd Battalion east of Barastre, the 4th in a trench-line farther east, and the 3rd, temporarily attached to the 2nd Brigade, which was still in the line, in the trenches south-west of Bertincourt. Lieut.-Col. Jardine returned from leave and resumed command of the 2nd Battalion.

The 2nd Brigade, having taken Neuville on the 5th September, completed its fine work by capturing Metz-en-Couture and clearing Havrincourt Wood by dawn on the 7th. That afternoon we relieved the 2nd Brigade, but, owing to the changing situation, took up a line well to the eastward, with the 2nd, 3rd and 4th Battalions in the front line, in that order from the right, and the 1st in reserve. We held the whole Divisional front of 3,000 yards.

Lieut.-Col. P. H. Bell, D.S.O., commanding the 3rd Battalion, was wounded while reconnoitring the front,* and on his being evacuated, Major Murphy was transferred from the 2nd Battalion to command the 3rd.

*This was Lieut.-Col. Bell's last reconnaissance. He was still in hospital when the Armistice was declared, and did not rejoin the Brigade.

CHAPTER XVI.
THE BATTLE OF HAVRINCOURT AND EPEHY.

PART 1.—TRESCAULT SPUR, SEPTEMBER 9TH.

Situation—Object of the main battle set down for September 12th—Preliminary action, September 9th—Objectives—2nd Battalion attacks African Trench and African Support—3rd Battalion forms a defensive flank to the north—Counter-attacks.

The enemy's main line of resistance north of Havrincourt was the Canal du Nord, and south of the village it was the Hindenburg Line. His position behind the Canal was strong, whereas on the British side of it the ground sloped gradually down and was, for the most part, open to and swept by his machine-guns on the eastern bank. It was clear that nothing but a carefully-organized attack would succeed in driving him from such a position. Again, the main line of resistance running south-east from Havrincourt was covered by formidable positions about Havrincourt and Epehy, and before a final attack on the Hindenburg Line itself could be undertaken, it was first necessary to clear this strongly-held forward zone.

Operations to this end were planned for the 12th of September, when the IVth and VIth Corps of the Third Army were to attack on a front of five miles in the Havrincourt sector.

As a preliminary to this attack, however, a subsidiary action was ordered for the 9th, with the double object of feeling the strength of the enemy and weakening his hold on the Trescault Ridge and Spur. In this operation the Vth Corps on our immediate right was to attack the high ground to the west and south-west of Gouzeaucourt, while the New Zealanders were to assist by prolonging the Vth Corps' line slightly and establishing a strong defensive flank back to the projecting south-eastern corner of Havrincourt Wood.

The position held by the New Zealand Rifle Brigade was some little distance in advance of an old British trench running roughly north and south. In front of us the ground sloped to the bottom of the Trescault Valley, in the southern end of which was Gouzeaucourt Wood. Across the valley the ground rose again to the crest of the Trescault Spur, which jutted out northwards from Gouzeaucourt to Trescault. Along this crest was another old British system, consisting of a main trench and a reserve trench, the former being about 2,000 yards from our position, and the latter from 300 to 500 yards nearer to us. On the southern section opposite our front they were known as African Trench and African Support, and on the northern section as Snap Trench and Snap Reserve. A portion of this system formed the main part of the objective for the day's operations, and the task for the New Zealand Division was allotted to our 2nd and 3rd Battalions, the former being detailed to capture that portion of African Support and African Trench lying directly opposite its front, and the latter to establish a defensive flank running diagonally back from the left of the 2nd Battalion's objective, through a sunken cross-roads known as Dead Man's Corner, and so on to our original line. The 4th Battalion, on the left, was to remain in position for the present. A moving barrage was provided for the advance of the 2nd Battalion, and a standing barrage was to be placed along the enemy trench in front of the 3rd; while the heavies were instructed to bombard Gouzeaucourt and the trenches and sunken roads running along the eastern slopes of the Spur. Machine-guns were also to place a standing barrage on selected trenches and roads.

Part of the line finally taken up by our Brigade on the afternoon of September 7th lay along the western edge of Gouzeaucourt Wood, and, as the latter presented a possible serious obstacle to the intended advance, patrols went out at daybreak on the 8th to ascertain the position and strength of the enemy posts within it, and to report on the feasibility of moving the line forward to the eastern edge. One of these, led by Rifleman J. C. Dibble, working beyond the southern boundary, had an encounter with an enemy party just on the point of rushing one of the 17th Division's posts on our right, Dibble's arrival and prompt action averting what threatened to be certain disaster to the garrison. The Wood was found to be strongly held, and although a few posts were actually established on the forward edge, they were, on account of their comparative isolation, withdrawn in the evening.

The attack on the 9th opened at 4 a.m., and it was soon evident that the enemy's tired rear-guards had been replaced by fresh troops determined to maintain to the last their hold on the valuable spur. His artillery response to our opening barrage was heavy and well-directed, while the country over which our advancing troops were to pass was swept by the heaviest machine-gun fire yet experienced.

The 2nd Battalion moved forward under the barrage with "A" Company (Lieut. D. Kennedy) on the right, and "B" Company (Lieut. H. B. Pattrick) on the left. "C" Company (Capt. W. C. I. Sumner) was in support, and "D" Company (Capt. G. A. Mills) in reserve. A platoon of the support company, under Lieut. G. W. Morice, was attached to "A" to act as immediate support. Anticipating the enemy barrage, "A" Company, on a three-platoon frontage, made the passage of the Wood with all speed, two platoons moving by the sunken Gouzeaucourt Road and the remainder through the thick Wood itself, here fortunately somewhat narrow. Arrived on the eastern edge, the three leading platoons deployed and pushed smartly up the slope. Hand-to-hand fighting in the various posts encountered about the scattered trenches and along the road commenced at once, and soon 42 prisoners were on the way back. Queen's Cross, a sunken cross-roads near the right flank, was found to be strongly held, but the right platoon quickly overcame the opposition here as well as in the encircling and radiating trenches in the vicinity, and our men passed on to the more defined trench-line beyond. This was systematically assaulted and was presently captured. The advance had proceeded so swiftly that there was as yet little light, and as a well-formed trench had already been crossed, Lieut. Kennedy was under the impression that he was on his final objective, and it was some time before he discovered that the position occupied was really part of African Support, and not the main trench. However, it was also ascertained that both his flanks were " in the air," and he decided to stand fast in the meantime. The support platoon was placed in position forming a defensive flank on the right, for the troops of the neighbouring Division had been held up, and the Ger-

ORDER OF BATTLE—TRESCAULT SPUR, SEPTEMBER 9, 1918.

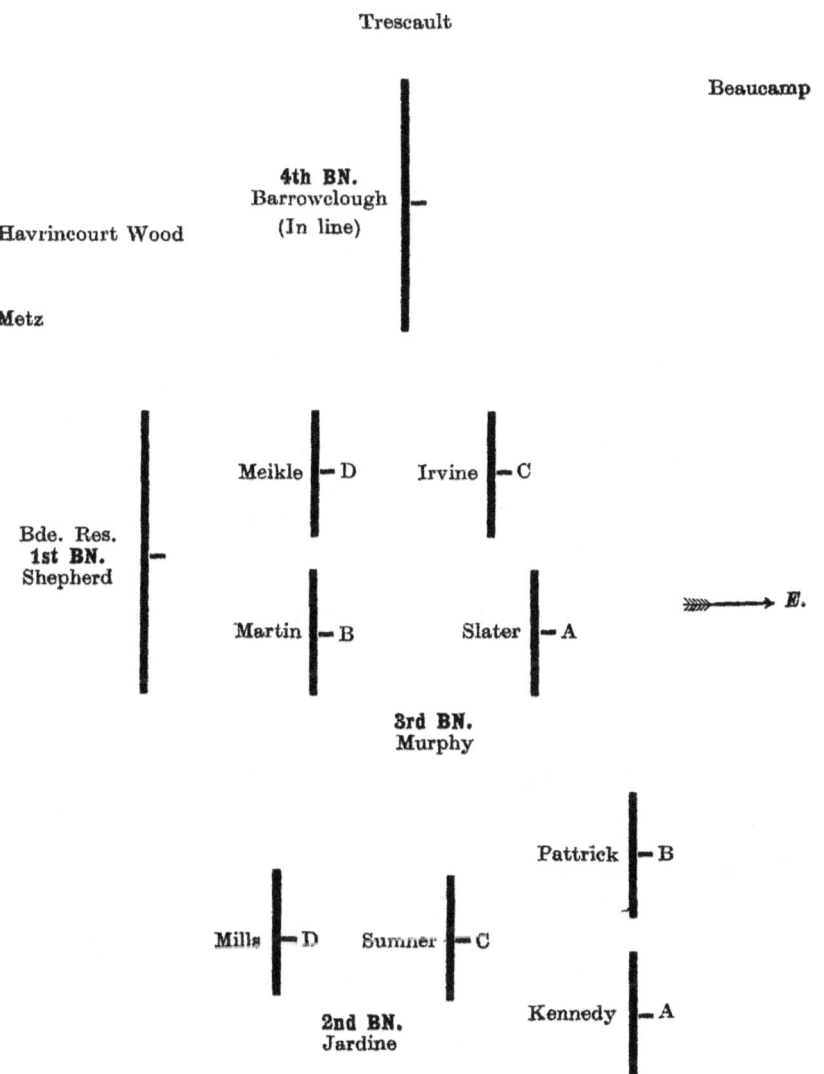

mans were holding a trench by the south-eastern edge of the Wood 500 yards behind Kennedy's right. On the left, "B" Company's platoons had met with extraordinary difficulties. They had first to deal with a section of the Wood, then an awkward switch trench in the open, and finally another stretch of the timbered area which curved southwards and covered their first objective. The intense machine-gun fire from these positions proved too severe for rapid movement, and the company was pinned down for some time. Now the support company appeared upon the scene. The task of mopping up the Wood had been long and difficult; casualties had been very heavy, and Capt. Sumner was the only officer left. As soon as it was realized that "B" Company had been held up and that part of African Support was still held by the enemy, Capt. Sumner sent forward a half-company, now under the command of Sergeant-Major G. F. Webster, for a further effort. The two platoons, one led by the sergeant-major and the other by Sergt. T. R. Kennerley, dashed gallantly across the open country and carried the position on "A" Company's left, capturing a number of machine-guns after an exceptionally severe struggle. It was now about 7 a.m., but not all of the allotted portion of African Support was as yet in our hands. Further sections of "C" Company were brought up, and, after the position had been strengthened, an attempt was made to bomb along the trench towards the strongly-held Dead Man's Corner, from which the enemy was not only enfilading our forward troops but was still holding up the men of "B" Company. Three successive attacks of this kind were led by Corporal G. Fruin, each resulting in the taking of an additional length of trench and the capture of several machine-guns. From the new line fighting-patrols also worked along the forward saps to test the strength of the enemy's hold on African Trench; but these activities, in which Corporal Fruin was again conspicuous, caused the enemy to send up the S.O.S. signal, and the patrols were checked by the answering barrage. Some of "B" Company's sections, taking advantage of the distraction caused by this fighting, rushed forward under the leadership of 2nd Lieut. R. G. Bates and captured their objective on the left, but an immediate counter-attack drove them out, and Dead Man's Corner remained in the enemy's hands. The remainder of the line held out through this onslaught and against repeated attempts by frontal and flank attacks. The bombing-fights had been so frequent that the shortage of supplies, which had proved our undoing on the left, was being seriously felt elsewhere. Sergeant-Major P. A. Scully, commanding a platoon in the new support company, rendered Lieut. Kennedy's hard-pressed men a double service. With one man to help him he crawled forward from the Wood to the front line with a welcome supply of bombs. On his way back he marked down a machine-gun firing actively from a flank. The two manœuvred carefully into position, and under 'cover of his comrades' rifle-fire the sergeant-major rushed the post, bombed the crew, and secured the gun. Pressure from the right rear was not relieved till 1 p.m., at which hour troops of the 17th Division got forward and secured touch with the 2nd Battalion at Queen's Cross.

The objective for the 3rd Battalion, on the left, was roughly parallel to Snap Reserve, a continuation of African Support, but here bending back slightly towards the west. Elements of both the leading companies, "A" (Capt. H. W. Slater) on the right, and "C" (Lieut. J. H. Irvine) on the left, succeeded in reaching this, but the advancing troops, as well as reinforcements sent up to their assistance, melted away under the fierce machine-gun fire from Dead Man's Corner and Snap Reserve. A counter-attack drove the remains of the left company back to the vicinity of their original position, and the left of the right company had to swing back to conform. On the ground lost, three of our wounded were plainly visible to their comrades, now 200 yards away. Desperate efforts were made to bring them in, but every movement was the signal for a fresh burst of machine-gun fire from the slopes above. Sergeant J. Keatley, having been wounded in the face, was sent back to receive attention and to take a despatch to company headquarters. Disdaining his injuries, however, he returned to the outpost line and at once went out to endeavour to rescue the wounded. He succeeded in bringing in Rifleman C. Soar. A second journey was made, and, despite continuous machine-gun fire, he brought in Rifleman A. T. Oliver. His errand of mercy was repeated yet once more, but when he reached the third man, Rifleman A. W. Cooper, he found that the later had been struck again and was now past all help.

The line now firmly held by the 3rd Battalion ran roughly along the northern edge of Gouzeaucourt Wood, with the right in touch with the 2nd Battalion. Casualties had been heavy, and the toll was steadily increased throughout the morning. The machine-gun fire continued with unabated intensity, the enemy's artillery steadily bombarded the line of posts, and even aeroplane bombs were dropped upon it. As if this were not sufficient, the much-tried men were harassed in a manner new and strange. At 9.30 a.m. the Germans projected upon the line two salvos each of about 300 spherical bombs slightly larger than an orange. These exploded as they fell, throwing out shrapnel and gas, and as the clouds drifted away it was seen that the grass had been burnt black.

At about 7 p.m., after a heavy bombardment with gas and high-explosive, the enemy counter-attacked along our whole line. He was everywhere held up except at one point, but the post he succeeded in driving in here was immediately re-established. During the night the 3rd Battalion companies slightly advanced their line and improved their positions.

In the fighting of this day we took over a hundred prisoners, a large proportion of whom were from Jager regiments, regarded as amongst the best fighting troops in the German Army. They stated that they had been warned to expect an attack that morning, the investigations of their aeroplane observers flying low behind our lines on the previous day having revealed unmistakable signs of immediate action.

The following two days passed fairly quietly. The weather was fine, but disagreeably cold and windy. There was a diminution in enemy artillery activity, which was mainly confined to drenching with gas the village of Metz-en-Couture, lying just behind our position. In the early evening of the 11th, a patrol under Corporal N. G. Stone worked forward, bombed the enemy out of Dead Man's Corner, and occupied it. At 6 p.m. the enemy again counter-attacked in strength, but he was everywhere repulsed except at Dead Man's Corner, from which he drove the little party of six that had so recently captured it. The fine covering work of Rifleman W. H. McMillan enabled Corporal Stone to withdraw his men without casualties.

PART 2.—TRESCAULT SPUR, SEPTEMBER 12TH.

Main action—Troops—Objectives—Barrage—2nd, 1st and 4th Battalions advance—Full success denied—Signallers, runners, stretcher-bearers—Sergeant Harry John Laurent, V.C.—New Zealand Division to Corps Reserve—Main battle continued—Results—New Zealand Rifle Brigade resting and training—Visits to Flers and other old Somme battlefields—Warned for action.

Preparations for the more important action on the morrow were now well forward. The IVth and VIth Corps of the Third Army were to attack on a front of about five miles. The IVth Corps Divisions to be employed were, in order from the right, the New Zealanders and the 37th. Our right flank was to be safeguarded by troops of the 38th Division, Vth Corps. North of the 37th, the 62nd Division of the VIth Corps would attack Havrincourt,* while the New Zealanders and the 37th would assault Trescault Spur.

The task of the New Zealand Division was entrusted to our Brigade, and that of the 37th Division to the 111th, while on our right the 115th Brigade was to operate. Our own objective was some 3,000 yards of the crest northwards from the main Gouzeaucourt Road, and three battalions were to be employed. The 2nd Battalion, on the right, would take African Trench as its only objective; the 1st Battalion, in the centre, would pass through the 3rd and capture a sector of Snap Reserve as the first objective and Snap Trench as the second. The 4th Battalion, on the left, had a somewhat similar task, only that its second objective was some distance beyond Snap Trench, on a line running more nearly north and south. Excellent artillery support was provided. No fewer than six field artillery brigades were in position to provide the creeping barrage, which was to move forward by lifts of 100 yards every three minutes, but pausing for a longer period just beyond each of the two objectives. The 4.5 howitzers had their successive lines of targets ahead of those of the field guns, and three batteries of 6-inch howitzers were laid on the enemy's battery positions and other selected targets in the valley be-

---

*By a curious coincidence the 62nd Division had made a similar attack in exactly the same manner in the successful Cambrai offensive of the previous October; and from this same locality, too, the enemy had opened his no less successful counter-attack only one week later.

Lieut.-Col. N. F. Shepherd, D.S.O.

Major J. Murphy.

Sergeant (2nd-Lieut.) Harry John Laurent, V.C.

yond the ridge. General Hart had four 6-inch Newton mortars at his disposal, and these he detailed to bombard Dead Man's Corner and a similar sunken cross-roads 500 yards to the north, two strong-points lying in the line of the 1st Battalion's advance; and, in addition, six light trench mortars were employed to supplement the guns providing the moving barrage. Three machine-gun companies were detailed to assist, two of these plus one section to take part in barraging the Brigade front, and the remaining three sections to accompany the attacking troops, one section with each battalion.

An hour before dawn all three battalions were in position for the attack. Following was the order of battle: In the 2nd Battalion, "A" Company (Lieut. D. Kennedy) was on the right, and "C" Company (Capt. W. C. I. Sumner) on the left; "D" (2nd Lieut. R. O. C. Marks) and "B" (Lieut. H. B. Pattrick) were in support, but from each of these, two platoons had been detached to the forward companies as immediate reserves. The 1st Battalion had "B" Company (Capt. G. P. O'Shannassy) on the right, "C" Company (Lieut. E. B. Tustin) on the left, with "D" (2nd Lieut. H. Ellen) and "A" (2nd Lieut. D. L. Crooks) in support. "C" and "B" had attached to them one platoon from "A" Company. The two leading companies of the 4th Battalion were "D" (Capt. M. H. R. Jones) on the right, and "B" (Capt. B. McLeod) on the left; while "A" (Lieut. H. S. Kenrick) and "C" (Capt. D. W. McClurg) were in support. The 3rd Battalion, in Brigade reserve, held two companies in readiness at the call of Lieut.-Col. Jardine and Major Shepherd, and before the day had well advanced both were sent forward. Later on still another company was called upon by the centre battalion.

On the opening of the barrage at 5.25 a.m., the leading elements of the two attacking companies of each unit pushed forward close to the line of bursting shells. Keeping pace with the lifts, our men advanced up the slopes towards the first objective on the crest. The 2nd Battalion's advance, though stiffly contested, was short, and its appointed length of African Trench was quickly taken. As far as this unit was concerned this was also its final objective; but its troubles were by no means ended, for "A" Company, on the right, found that the company of the 115th Brigade which was to advance

ORDER OF BATTLE—TRESCAULT SPUR, SEPTEMBER 12, 1918.

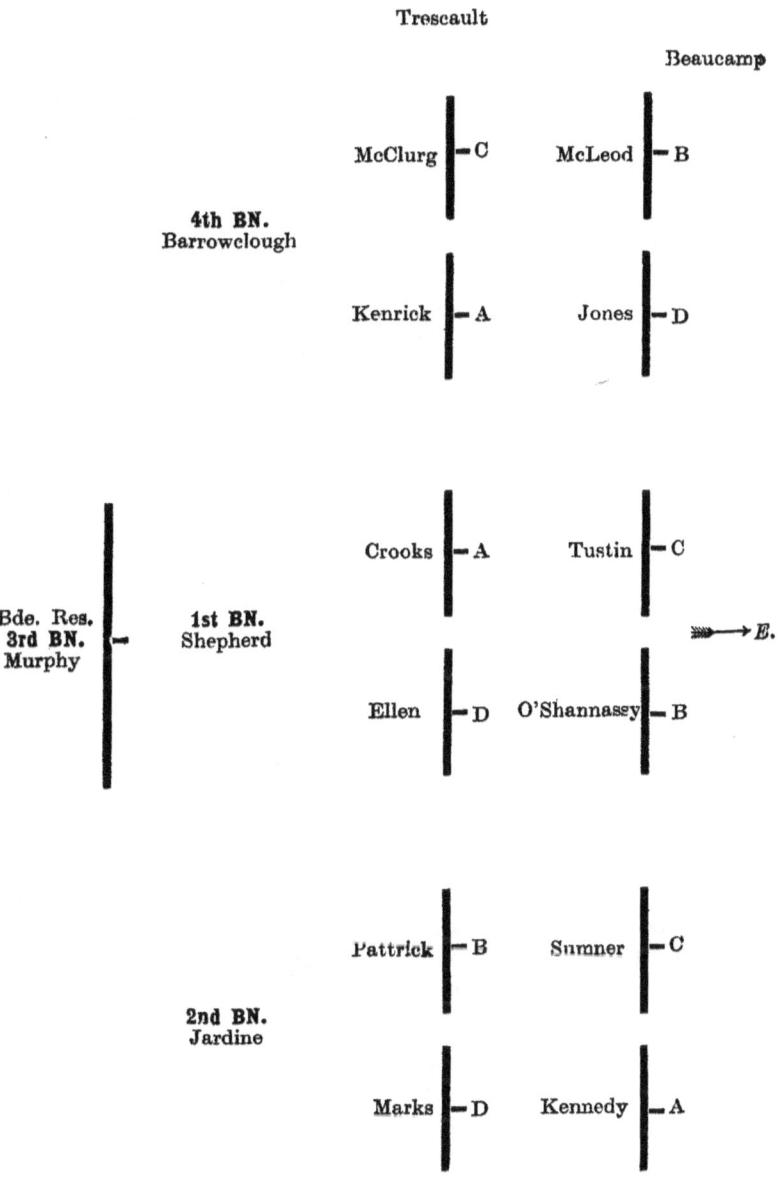

and cover the flank had failed to come up. Similarly, "C" Company, on the left, discovered that the 1st Battalion troops, after clearing Dead Man's Corner, had eased away northwards in moving forward to the main trench beyond. The Germans seized the advantage in both cases, and after a long struggle the flanks of the 2nd Battalion's line had to be bent back; but these were eventually firmly held by sections from the support company who fought their way forward under the skilful leadership of 2nd Lieut. W. E. McMinn, Sergeants F. J. Peters and A. I. Batty. As an indication of the enemy's strength, it may be mentioned that the party commanded by Sergeant Batty took 26 prisoners and seven machine-guns. Sergeant F. Ellery, who had led a platoon of "A" Company in the attack, found himself with a handful of men almost cut off on the right flank, but he successfully held out against repeated attacks until the battalion was finally relieved after nightfall. In this long-continued contest he was aided most gallantly by Corporal W. S. O'Brien, who was in charge of one of the Lewis gun teams.

In the meantime the remaining two battalions had had a sufficiently hard struggle to gain their first objective in the face of the heavy machine-gun fire that swept the broader stretch of country over which they had to pass. Sergeant C. K. Jennens, of the 1st Battalion, completed the first advance in charge of a company, all the officers having been struck down. Approaching Snap Trench he personally and successfully led a small party against a machine-gun post which was delaying the advance. At another point Rifleman C. T. Stevens carried through a similar exploit, using enemy bombs when his own gave out, and then, when the post was taken, bringing the captured German gun into action. He was materially assisted by Rifleman J. Donn, who, after killing the crew of a gun on his own account single-handed, jumped into the trench and attacked this second crew from the other flank.

Riflemen F. Smith and A. Gillam, two 4th Battalion men, carried a post containing three machine-guns, and killed the garrison of three officers and ten men, thus relieving pressure that had for a time proved serious and costly. Further along the line, Rifleman W. F. Turner with a Lewis gun worked across the open to the flank of a strong-point from which the enemy with two machine-guns was holding up his platoon. He succeeded in forcing down the heads of the German gunners, and so enabled the platoon to rush and capture the post. A similar feat, no less daringly essayed, was successfully accomplished by Rifleman E. Mellor.

With equal promptitude all opposition elsewhere was crushed, and the first objective for the two battalions was secured well up to time. Reorganization was proceeded with as rapidly as possible during the longer rest of the barrage in front of the line gained, and the platoons detailed for the purpose made ready to carry on towards the final goal.

The innumerable German machine-guns had our line only too well marked, however, and when the barrage moved on it at once became certain that the continuance of the advance across country was utterly impossible. There remained the saps leading forward, and up these avenues parties of our men immediately began to bomb their way, but the Germans, strongly posted at every vantage-point therein, clung to their positions with the greatest determination. After most strenuous efforts, in which 2nd Lieut. H. Ellen, the only remaining officer of his company, and Sergt. E. S. Ellingham, who led a handful of men in four successive bombing attacks, were most conspicuous, three posts were established in the southern end of Snap Trench by the 1st Battalion, and this was the only part of the second objective that fell into our hands. Farther north, the left company had to be content with the establishment of blocks to hold the enemy beyond bombing distance from Snap Reserve.

Despite the most persistent efforts, the 4th Battalion, with the broader area to cross in the second advance, and with Snap Trench lying midway between the first and second objectives, could make little progress. On the extreme left, a small party moving swiftly and with extreme boldness succeeded in actually reaching the objective; but, finding themselves entirely isolated, they had to fall back again in the face of superior numbers. For the rest, nothing more could be done than to establish advanced posts in the saps and await a more favourable opportunity to improve the situation.

The cold, driving showers which commenced at 9 a.m., after a bright morning, became more frequent and heavy as the day advanced, and movement in the muddy trenches became increasingly difficult. During the afternoon the 1st Battalion, having brought up fresh supplies of bombs, commenced a series of attacks along the saps leading forward to Snap Trench and along this latter trench itself. Some progress was made, notably by sections led by Corporal E. C. Fletcher and Riflemen G. A. Papworth and W. McIntyre, but the gains did not materially improve our hold on the forward trench. The pressure from the repeated local counter-attacks on the advanced posts on the battalion's front proved most exhausting; and that the garrisons were able to maintain their hold at all was in large measure due to the fine example and gallant leadership of 2nd Lieut. A. G. Holder, who came up from support to take over the command of one of the companies that had lost all its officers. One by one Capt. O'Shannassy's subalterns had gone down under the deadly hail of bullets and showers of bombs, and when he at last fell the direction of affairs devolved upon his Company Sergt-Major, E. J. Reeve, who, under the trying conditions prevailing, acquitted himself magnificently. On the open slopes of Trescault Ridge, indeed, the warrant officers were unusually prominent in leadership and in personal service; and of their number was Company Sergt.-Major S. Smith, of the 4th Battalion, whose dash and vigour, apparently inexhaustible, proved to be a source of inspiration during repeated bombing-fights.

At 7 p.m. the 4th Battalion launched a fresh attack under an artillery barrage, the 1st Battalion co-operating; and, though they failed to achieve the full success they sought, by 7.30 p.m. the whole of Snap Trench was in their hands, and on the extreme left a post was established well forward and close to the second objective. Here touch was established with the troops on the flank.

During the fighting on the left, Riflemen E. L. Cullen and J. J. H. Wilson, each in charge of a section, proved themselves remarkably dashing and fearless leaders in a succession of assaults upon enemy strong-points. Of the many enterprises by bombing-parties, that carried out by 2nd Lieut. R. Whitefield's platoon from the flank support company was prosecuted with more than the usual insistence and boldness, but the attackers were opposed by Germans no less stubborn in their determination to hold on, and the fight proved long and strenuous. The men were splendidly led, and the efforts of the leader were skilfully seconded by his platoon-sergeant, Sergeant Hamilton; but probably the factor which at last turned the scale in their favour was the valorous action of the battalion commander himself. Major Barrowclough was up with his forward troops at the time, superintending this local assault, and, observing the fact that the platoon was in danger of being held up while still short of the desired goal, he seized a rifle and a supply of bombs, dashed up the shallow trench to the head of the attack, and laid about him with such effect that the well-nigh exhausted men, thus spurred on to fresh efforts, regained the ascendancy, and shortly afterwards had the satisfaction of beating down all opposition and securing the favourable position for which they had striven.

The counter-attacks that had fallen upon the men of the 2nd Battalion throughout the day, particularly those at 6 a.m. and 2 p.m., had made their impression on the flanks of their sector, but they still clung tenaciously to a considerable stretch in the central portion of the trench originally captured, and continued their endeavours to regain further lengths of this line. In these efforts Rifleman R. C. Naismith was conspicuous until, after leading successive bombing-parties as first bayonet-man, he was severely wounded by a bomb. Corporal G. Fruin, who had so distinguished himself in a series of most gallant attacks on the 9th, was mortally wounded while similarly leading on this day. With their refused flanks strengthened by sections brought up from their supports, the leading companies were well established in such a position as would prevent the development of a turning movement on the part of enemy troops moving from Gouzeaucourt, and with this they had now to rest content.

At 10.30 p.m. the enemy launched his last counter-attack in strength. The stroke fell for the most part upon the much-tried forward posts in the salient of the 1st Battalion's sector, and these were pushed back to the road running north from Dead Man's Corner, leaving Snap Trench in this vicinity finally in the hands of the enemy; for though bombing-fights continued throughout the night they did not result in any material gains. The right company of the 4th Battalion was also affected, though to a less extent. All its officers with the exception of the company commander had been either killed or wounded, and now its right post was lost for the third time. So heavy had been the casualties that the platoon here was by this time almost completely annihilated, and a platoon had to be brought up from the support company to re-establish the post. When Capt. Jones was finally relieved his company consisted of himself, one lance-corporal, and a handful of men.

So ended this day of fierce struggle. A competent authority has stated that there was more long-sustained close fighting on the 12th of September than the Division had experienced on any other single day since Gallipoli. We had opposed to us fresh troops from two of Germany's finest Divisions, including the Jagers, specially brought in to hold this important ground; and, all things considered, the achievement of the Brigade in securing the greater part of the line of vantage on the crest of Trescault Spur was one of which we had no small reason to be proud. The enemy had held his sector in great strength and had suffered correspondingly. A careful estimate of the enemy dead alone puts the number at not less than 300, quite apart from the casualties he must have suffered in his rear lines from shell-fire, while the toll of prisoners taken reached a total of 502.*

On the sectors to the north of us, Trescault was taken by the 37th Division and Havrincourt by the 62nd. Hence on this part of the front the desired favourable position for the grand attack on the Hindenburg Line was now secured.

The full tale of the work of the subsidiary sections of the Brigade throughout this day with its fluctuating fortunes would in itself make a moving story of gallant service and extreme devotion. The discharge of their duties was a matter of sheer self-sacrifice, for though they had all the dangers to face they had not the thrill of hand-to-hand conflict to sustain them, nor the satisfaction of being able to return blow for blow. Sergeant W. J. Clifford and Riflemen G. Burgess, J. S.

*Our total casualties during the fighting from 1st to 12th September, including those at Fremicourt, were:—

	Killed.	Wounded.	Missing.
Officers	7	19	—
Other ranks	121	458	15

Mathias and W. Stockdale are remembered for their efforts in laying and repairing the telephone lines, exhausting duties which exposed them to constant danger from shell-fire and gas. So also are Riflemen W. H. Jowers, H. Heath, E. McGrath, T. J. Senn, D. G. Irvine, W. H. Corbett and E. J. White, as representing that wonderful band of battalion and company runners, upon whose skill and faithfulness in bearing messages to and from the front line so much of the success of an operation depends. It is characteristic of the runners that they never give up till outraged Nature knocks them off their feet; and it must be borne in mind that in the execution of their duties they have frequently to pass through the enemy's barrage. Rifleman Jowers, for instance, is credited with twelve such runs in this one day. They gain an uncanny knack, a sort of new sense, by which they are able to foresee, nine times out of ten, where the next shell will fall; but in this respect they are not infallible, and every time they go out they take their lives in their hands, but in the face of it all they smile and "carry on." Riflemen W. J. Allason, D. A. McKie, J. A. Jones, G. Skatt and T. W. Voss were amongst the stretcher-bearers who survived. Some of these devoted men continued at their labours for eighteen hours on end, and in many instances they crept out into No Man's Land to bring in wounded who had fallen as the line swayed to and fro. Even the men of the transport had deeds of daring to their credit, as, for instance, Rifleman J. R. Gould, of the 2nd Battalion, who took his limbers through a barrage and brought bombs and ammunition to within 500 yards of the front line.

Of the combatant officers all will willingly yield pride of place to Lieut. D. Kennedy, M.C., of "A" Company, 2nd Battalion, to the influence of whose brilliant reconnaissance work and brave and skilful leadership on the 9th, and again on the 12th, the fine advances and stubborn resistance of his company on both those days were in great measure due. He advanced to the attack on the 12th with a company-strength of 50, and went out on relief with two officers and 23 men. The unusual award of the Distinguished Service Order granted to Lieut. Kennedy was richly earned.

To complete the account of this day's doings there remains one of its earliest events, an astonishing adventure that possesses many of the features of an independent operation. In accordance with the general instructions for the attack on the 12th, each battalion detailed beforehand certain sections for the duty of exploiting the success gained. These sections were to form reconnoitring patrols which, immediately after the capture of the final objective, were to work forward and maintain touch with the enemy. One of such patrols from "A" Company, 2nd Battalion, consisting of twelve men with a Lewis gun, under Sergeant Harry John Laurent, moved forward from African Trench on its special mission. Strangely enough, for the Germans were sufficiently numerous elsewhere, the patrol failed to make that instant contact with the enemy which from their experience of the 9th they had good reason to expect, and Sergeant Laurent led his men cautiously but steadily forward, taking advantage of such little cover as was available. Machine-gun bullets and shells were falling unpleasantly thick, but there was still no sign of the enemy infantry. As the patrol continued their advance down the slope they were presently able to make out a trench, afterwards ascertained to be some 750 yards east of African Trench, lying at right angles to their line of advance, and strongly garrisoned. Laurent was seeking contact, and he now determined to get it with a vengeance. A few moments sufficed for the necessary dispositions, and, with a shout of exultation, Laurent, followed by his mere handful of men, dashed at the trench. Rifleman M. Healey found himself alone on a flank, where with bayonet and bomb he killed ten of his opponents, and presently accounted for a senior officer who was frantically working the telephone. Corporal E. W. Wood moved along the parapet firing his Lewis gun from the hip into the trench. An attempt on the part of a German machine-gun crew to bring their gun into action was nipped in the bud, and the enemy, now thoroughly demoralized by the suddenness and fierceness of the onslaught, threw up their hands, but not before our men had accounted for some thirty killed and wounded. The prisoners were unceremoniously marshalled and conducted as expeditiously as possible to our lines, bringing with them our casualties, consisting of two dead and two wounded. They numbered in all an officer and 111 non-commissioned officers and men, and proved to be the survivors of a whole support company. The position they had occupied, partly trench and partly sunken road, was extremely strong, with many concrete emplacements each mounting a heavy and a light machine-gun; while in the close vicinity were field guns firing over open sights. Sergeant Laurent, as the leader in this extraordinary enterprise, was awarded the Victoria Cross.

During the night of 12th/13th September, in pouring rain, we were relieved by the 1st Brigade,* and went into Divisional support near Ytres. On the 14th the Division became Corps reserve, being relieved by the 5th Division, and the New Zealand Rifle Brigade moved to the area about Favreuil, Biefvillers and Sapignies.

The battle for the forward positions on our right was continued on the 17th, when the Australian and IXth Corps captured Massemy and Holnon Village and Wood, and again on the 18th, when the Fourth and Third Armies attacked on a front of seventeen miles from Holnon to Gouzeaucourt, penetrated to a depth of three miles, and captured the important positions about Epehy.

In this fourth stage of the offensive, fifteen British Divisions defeated twenty German Divisions, took 12,000 prisoners and 100 guns, and secured all the positions required for a great attack on the main Hindenburg defences.†

The New Zealand Rifle Brigade remained in Corps reserve from 15th to 27th September, during which time training, including battalion and company tactical exercises, was carried out. Except for a few thunderstorms the weather was fine throughout the period, and, despite some bombing of the bivouac area from time to time, all ranks enjoyed to the utmost the rest and change.

A Brigade Church Parade was held on the 15th, Bishop Gwynne, late of Khartoum, conducting the service. His Lord-

---

*On the following night the Germans, using liquid fire, attacked the two southern battalion sectors and succeeded in driving the garrisons back to African Support. African Trench was not regained till the 28th, when troops of the 25th Division secured it after two strong attacks.

†Throughout this period, the French Armies kept up their pressure and made important advances. The Americans also were making their presence felt; on September 12th their First Army dealt a smashing blow, driving the enemy out of the St. Mihiel Salient and inflicting severe losses in prisoners and guns.

ship spoke of the good work done by the New Zealand Division since the commencement of the war, and congratulated the Brigade on its fine record during the recent operations. General Harper, General Russell and the Brigadier were present at the parade, and took a march past at its conclusion.

On the same day a Special Order was issued by General Hart, congratulating all ranks upon their splendid work, and praising the gallantry, skill, determination and assurance displayed throughout the operations just concluded. The order recalled that, during a period of twenty-two days, the Brigade had taken part in eight engagements, capturing 1,281 prisoners and very large quantities of war material.

Units, with their transport, were inspected by the G.O.C. Division, who took the opportunity to congratulate the battalions on their achievements in the great advance, and to compliment the men on their fine appearance and bearing so soon after the strenuous times they had just passed through. While on route marches the different battalions visited the old battlefields of the Somme, in particular Flers and its vicinity.

Reconnoitring parties kept constant touch with developments in the forward zone. On September 25th the Brigade received a warning-order to be ready to move at short notice in support of operations to be carried out by the IVth Corps, and on the 28th moved to a position of readiness east of Bertincourt, replacing the reserve brigade of the 42nd Division.

CHAPTER XVII.
THE BATTLE OF CAMBRAI AND THE HINDENBURG LINE.

PART 1.—THE GENERAL ATTACK.

Object—General line—Plan of operations—Nature of the German defensive position—Attack opens September 27th—Continued 28th and 29th—New Zealanders engaged—1st and 2nd Brigades penetrate to the Escaut Canal—Continued September 30th and October 1st—1st Brigade forces the Escaut Canal and takes Crevecoeur.

The hour had now come for striking the blow at the Hindenburg Line with the object of breaking a way through in the direction of the great strategic objective, the railway centre of Maubeuge.

The Fourth, Third and First Armies, in the order named, occupied a line running from the village of Seleney (west of St. Quentin) through Havrincourt and Moeuvres, and thence along the west side of the Canal du Nord to the Sensee River at Ecourt St. Quentin. The enemy occupied the Hindenburg Line as far as the vicinity of Havrincourt. South of that village he still held some formidable positions forward of the main defensive system. To the north he held equally strong positions between the Nord and Scheldt Canals. Thus the approaches to Cambrai were well covered, while the bend in the enemy's line made it difficult to carry out, to the best advantage, an attack by the three armies simultaneously. It was therefore decided to open a very heavy bombardment of the whole line during the night of 26th/27th September, to be followed on the morning of the 27th by an attack on the left by the Third and First Armies only. Then, if success should attend these efforts, the Fourth Army would join the battle and strike at the remainder of the Hindenburg defences on its front.

The Canal du Nord, which was under construction at the outbreak of the war, runs northward about six miles to the east of Cambrai. The Scheldt Canal is also known as the Escaut Canal, or the St. Quentin Canal. It is the canalized Escaut River, and runs northward in a circuitous course to within four and a half miles of Cambrai. Here it takes a wide sweep to the west, and then back to the western outskirts of the town. Between St. Quentin and the village of Bantouzelle, some eight miles south of Cambrai, the principal defences of the Hindenburg system lay in parts to the west, but more generally to the east of the Scheldt Canal, which afforded cover to resting troops and to the garrisons of the main defensive trench lines during bombardment. About midway between St. Quentin and Cambrai the canal passes through the now famous Le Tronquoy Tunnel, 6,000 yards long, which was connected by shafts with the trenches above. The whole series of defences known as the Hindenburg Line, with the numerous defended villages and deep cuttings contained in it, covered a belt of country varying from 7,000 to 10,000 yards in depth, organized by the employment of every available means into a most powerful system, well meriting the great reputation it had gained. One of the outstanding characteristics was the skill with which it was sited so as to deny to the attacking forces effective artillery positions from which to bombard it.

The attack carried out on September 27th, as planned, met with instant and striking success. By the end of the day the British troops had passed the Canal du Nord, had reached the general line Beaucamp–Ribecourt–Fontaine-Notre-Dame and thence northward to Oisy-le-Verger, and had taken 10,000 prisoners and 200 guns. On September 28th, the advance on this front was continued and the line pushed forward in places to the Escaut (Scheldt) Canal immediately south-west of Cambrai.

On September 29th, the front of attack stretched from Marcoing, about four miles south-west of Cambrai, away south to St. Quentin. On this day, Sunday, the Vth and IVth Corps of the Third Army opened the attack at 3.30 a.m., in the moonlight, on an eight-mile front between Vendhuille and Marcoing. On the right, the Fourth Army attacked two hours later on a twelve-mile front between Holnon and Vendhuille, and the line of attack was continued in the St. Quentin sector by the French First Army. Of the New Zealand Division (IVth Corps, Third

Army) the 1st and 2nd Brigades were employed. Their attack on Welsh Ridge, La Vacquerie village, and Bonavis Spur, the last of the high ground west of the canal on our front, met with marvellous success. They penetrated a distance of from 5,000 to 6,000 yards into the intricate Hindenburg system, and reached points on the Escaut Canal, capturing 1,450 prisoners, 44 guns, and hundreds of machine-guns, yet suffering only 200 casualties.

Equal success crowned the efforts of other Divisions all along the line. To the Third Army fell the village of Masnieres and the crossings of the Escaut Canal between that village and Cambrai. On the Fourth Army front the capture of Bellicourt and Bellenglise stands out conspicuously.

The attacks on all fronts were continued on September 30th, when the gap in the Hindenburg Line was enlarged by the capture of Thorigny and Le Tronquoy Tunnel. The enemy, threatened with envelopment about Villers Guislan and Gonnelieu, south-west of the sector captured by our 1st and 2nd Brigades on the previous day, abandoned those villages and withdrew behind the Escaut.

On October 1st a great advance was made in the St. Quentin sector, many villages as well as the town of St. Quentin being taken by the French and Australians. In the Cambrai sector, our 1st Brigade took Crevecoeur after forcing the passage of the Escaut Canal, while the 3rd Division captured Rumilly. North of Cambrai the Canadians exploited their successes of the previous day, cleared the high ground west of Ramillies, and entered Blecourt.

By a series of minor operations the battle was completed on October 5th, by which date the right of the Third Army was able to cross the canal and occupy the Hindenburg Line to the east of it, thus greatly simplifying arrangements for the next great attack.

PART 2.—CREVECOEUR, OCTOBER 5TH.

New Zealand Rifle Brigade relieves 1st Brigade at Crevecoeur—Heavy shelling—Patrols—Canterbury and 4th Battalion companies cross the Canal and advance towards Masnieres Switch—Stiff fighting—1st Battalion's fighting patrols to the Old Mill and the village of Lesdain—3rd Battalion's patrols north of Crevecoeur—General results of the main battle.

In the minor operations just referred to, the New Zealand Rifle Brigade took part.* On the night of 30th Sept./1st Oct. the Brigade, in Divisional reserve, was disposed in an area actually in the Hindenburg Line two miles east of Trescault, and during the afternoon of 1st October we moved eastward to a position of readiness two miles south of Marcoing, transport being up with battalions.

On the following day our reconnoitring parties went forward to study the ground, beyond Crevecoeur, over which the Brigade was expecting to attack shortly. We relieved the 1st Brigade during the night of 3rd/4th October, taking over the left of the Divisional front through the village of Crevecoeur. The 4th Battalion replaced 2nd Auckland in the right sub-sector, part of which was on the western side of the canal; the 1st Battalion relieved 2nd Wellington in the salient through the eastern edge of the village; and the 3rd took over 1st Auckland's positions on the left, along the road running north towards Cambrai.† The 2nd Battalion was in reserve. South of us, 2nd Canterbury, still on the western bank, held the whole

---

*Lieut.-Col. R. C. Allen, D.S.O., assumed command of the 1st Battalion on September 30th, and Major Shepherd left for the United Kingdom on duty. Lieut.-Col. Allen, formerly of the Auckland Regiment, had been wounded at Messines. He had been invalided to New Zealand, but had now returned to the front. Major Murphy having gone to Aldershot for the Senior Officers' course, Major A. H. Carrington assumed command of the 3rd Battalion until the arrival of Major G. W. Cockroft on October 4th.

†At Crevecoeur, two Maoris of the Pioneer Battalion unofficially attached themselves to one of the companies of the 3rd Battalion. They expressed great dissatisfaction at being retained on non-combatant duties in the rear area—"Te big men having to sweep te roads"—and exclaimed, "Why, Tommy he see us te big fellow sweeping, and he laugh! No good to us. We join te Dinks!" Notwithstanding a refusal to take them on the strength, they remained. Both, by the way, had amassed enough food to last at least a week. One was afterwards badly wounded on patrol. To the medical officer he remarked: "Just out for te walk on patrol. I stop one. But I get well—I join te Dinks again."

399

of the 2nd Brigade's front, and on the right, again, was the 37th Division. On our left the 3rd Division, VIth Corps, was in line.

There had been very heavy shelling on Crevecoeur during the morning of the 2nd, and again during the evening of the 3rd, while the relief was in progress; and on the following morning there were signs that the enemy was about to deliver a counter-attack against the village. The expected action did not follow, however, and our patrols began to feel cautiously forward to ascertain the position and strength of the enemy with a view to a possible peaceful penetration.

Along our Brigade front the enemy was found to be very alert, but at 9 a.m. on the morning of the 5th, 2nd Canterbury reported unmistakable signs of the slackening of his hold on the eastern bank of the canal in the sector to the south of us. Major Barrowclough passed on the information to Brigade Headquarters and at once proceeded to essay the crossing on his own front. His left company, "C," under Capt. D. W. McClurg, was already on the eastern side, holding a position immediately south of Crevecoeur. "A" Company (Lieut. H. S. Kenrick) was on the western bank in occupation of two bridge-heads, while "D" and "B" were in support and reserve, respectively. On receipt of orders Lieut. Kenrick promptly commenced the forward movement, sending 2nd Lieut. C. W. Rule's platoon against the northern bridge, while 2nd Lieut. V. R. Bernard was instructed to force that to the south. It was at once evident that if the enemy had really commenced a withdrawal it was not his intention to retire to any great distance. Rule's men crossed with comparative ease. Bernard's platoon, however, was confronted with a machine-gun post established in the lock-keeper's house, but this was successfully dealt with, and the garrison of eighteen men with their two machine-guns was captured and sent to the rear. The initial stage thus successfully completed, the leading platoons, followed by the third (for at this time the company, being only ninety strong, was organized in three platoons) pressed on with the object of gaining a footing in Masnieres Switch, a strongly-wired trench running due south from Crevecoeur, and lying from 1,000 to 1,500 yards to their front. They had not gone far before intense machine-gun fire opened up from Masnieres Switch, as well as from vantage-points at the Factory by the railway-sidings to the north and at Bel Aise Farm to the south; and to this fire "D" Company, following in support under Capt. A. E. Brown, was also subjected as its foremost sections reached the bridges. Nevertheless the advance proceeded well, and, with the support of Capt. McClurg's men, who co-operated by working down the trench from the north, the leading lines effected an entry into the Switch at various points. On the right, however, the position was far from satisfactory, for the Canterbury troops, who had also crossed, were not in touch, and a counter-attack from the south appeared to be imminent. To meet this danger, Lieut. Kenrick took his supporting platoon up the sunken road leading to Bel Aise Farm, and with them formed a defensive flank, strengthening this with a platoon drawn from Capt. Brown's company.

Now came the inevitable direct counter-attacks on the two forward platoons in the Switch. The casualties, already heavy, became increasingly severe. 2nd Lieut. Rule was killed, his acting platoon-sergeant, Lance-Corporal A. M. Hyland, was mortally wounded, and two Lewis guns were disabled. Under the repeated blows the remnants were compelled to relinquish their hold and take up a position on the slopes some 200 yards to the west. Their advance had been greatly aided by the bold action of a Lewis gunner, Rifleman P. Manderson, who, working in the open, engaged the enemy machine-guns firing within 100 yards. Manderson now remained behind to cover their retirement, and, though heavily fired on, he succeeded both in this and in rejoining them later with his gun. The garrison of the new line, now so thinly held, was strengthened by the addition of the remaining two platoons of "D" Company; and the Canterbury troops, having driven the enemy from Cheneaux Wood, came up on the right, thus relieving us of further anxiety regarding the security of that flank.

In the meantime the 1st Battalion, in the centre, and the 3rd, on the left, had joined in the thrust forward. Under cover of patrols sent out by "A" Company, 1st Battalion, then on the forward edge of the village, two platoons of "D" Company advanced to attack a strong enemy position about the Old Mill of Lesdain, some 300 yards to the east. This was on a slight eminence with a double escarpment, the first of which was successfully taken and held. Attempts were made to blind the position with smoke bombs, but it proved impossible to reduce materially the steady machine-gun fire, and the advance here was definitely hung up. The two platoons suffered 30 casualties. An attempt was now made to secure Lesdain, a village on the other side of the Escaut River to the south-east, with its nearer outskirts not more than 700 yards from those of Crevecoeur. For this task "A" Company was detailed. One platoon, under 2nd Lieut. W. Williams, worked down a small valley leading to Lesdain and took up a covering position. Two platoons then followed and were making ready to deploy for the rush forward through them, when a wounded runner crawled back with a message that 2nd Lieut. Williams and several of his men had been killed, and that the remainder were unable to move in any direction owing to the intense machine-gun fire which had suddenly opened up from the high ground to their right. Investigation showed that the platoons intended for attack could now do nothing but cover the retirement of their comrades, and even this latter operation could not be completed until after dark.

The ill-luck attending the efforts of the 1st Battalion had its effect also on the 3rd, whose patrols had made a fine advance of over 500 yards, for, both flanks being exposed, part of the ground captured had now to be given up.

Thus, except on the 4th Battalion's front, where useful deploying ground had been gained on the far side of the canal, the results of this attempted "peaceful penetration," which had been more or less spontaneous on the part of the units engaged, were inconsiderable. The information secured as to the enemy's dispositions and strength was, however, to prove of great value in the next set battle.

The casualties had been comparatively heavy, and the stretcher-bearers, amongst whom Riflemen J. G. Langrish, A. G. Smith and W. R. Douglas were conspicuous, had a trying time bringing in the wounded from exposed positions during daylight. Langrish himself was twice blown off his feet by shell-fire. Rifleman A. O. Williams, a 4th Battalion runner taking an important message to an advanced post, was severely wounded in the leg long before he reached his destination, but, though suffering great pain, he dragged himself slowly forward, and at last reached the post, fainting from loss of blood as he handed over the communication. A similar act of supreme devotion was performed by another 4th Battalion runner, whose name, unfortunately, has not been recorded. He was in "C" Company, and was a late reinforcement man who had only recently joined up. Sent back from his platoon with an urgent message to company headquarters, he was struck on the way by a shell which tore off one of his arms from the shoulder. Incredible as it may seem, he not only accomplished his mission but expressed his intention of returning with the answer! He was taken to the rear at once for medical attention, but sank and died before the dressing-station was reached.

The nine days' fighting, from 27th September to 5th October, had brought great results. Thirty-one British and two American Divisions had engaged thirty-nine German Divisions, had stormed the line of the Canal du Nord and broken the Hindenburg Line, taking over 36,000 prisoners and 380 guns.*
"The enemy's defence in the last and strongest of his prepared positions had been shattered. The whole of the main Hindenburg defences had passed into our possession, and a wide gap had been driven through such rear trench systems as had existed behind them. The effect of the victory upon the subsequent course of the campaign was decisive. The threat to the enemy's communications was now direct and instant, for nothing but the natural obstacles of a wooded and well-watered countryside lay between our Armies and Maubeuge."†

*During the same period a great victory had been gained on the Flanders front. On September 28th a force commanded by the King of the Belgians, and comprising the Belgian Army, some French Divisions, and all of the artillery and certain Divisions of Plumer's Second Army, attacked from Dixmude on the left to a point five miles south of the Ypres–Zonnebeke Road on the right. By the end of the day the British Divisions had passed well beyond the farthest limits of the bloody battles of 1917, while the Belgians had made a corresponding advance on their front. By the evening of October 1st the line had been carried past Ploegsteert Wood and Messines, and was close up to Wervicq, Gheluwe and Ledeghem; and on the left the Belgians had gone beyond the line Moorslede–Staden–Dixmude. On October 2nd the enemy in the region of the Lys began to fall back before General Birdwood's Fifth Army on the whole front from Lens to Armentieres.

†Sir Douglas Haig's Despatches.

CHAPTER XVIII.
FROM CREVECOEUR TO LE QUESNOY.

(THE BATTLE OF LE CATEAU AND THE BATTLE OF THE SELLE RIVER.)

PART 1.—LESDAIN AND BEYOND, OCTOBER 8TH.

Object of the Battle of Le Cateau—Front of attack—New Zealand Division engaged—New Zealand Rifle Brigade takes Lesdain and advances beyond—2nd Brigade captures Esnes—General success—Cambrai entered.

With the object of compelling the enemy to evacuate Cambrai, the Third and Fourth Armies on October 8th attacked on a front stretching seventeen miles southwards from the southern outskirts of the town. On the right, again, the French troops extended the line of attack as far south as St. Quentin, while, still farther south, the French and Americans attacked east of the Meuse and in Champagne. The action on the British front is known as the Battle of Le Cateau, and marks the commencement of the fighting in open country.

On the IVth Corps' front the 2nd Brigade and the New Zealand Rifle Brigade attacked in conjunction with the 37th Division on the right and the 3rd Division on the left. The task of the New Zealand Division was to establish itself just west of Esnes, and on the Esnes-La Targette Road to the north of the village. This meant a thrust to a depth of over 4,000 yards on a front of 3,500 yards, and would constitute the longest advance under a barrage the New Zealanders had yet made.

Crevecoeur is only about four and a half miles almost due south of Cambrai; and as the main object of the attack was to turn the enemy's position at Cambrai, the general direction of the advance was now to bend slightly north of east.

Our Brigade held a small salient, the most easterly point of the whole British front, round the eastern outskirts of

Crevecoeur, and had the village of Lesdain immediately opposite its right flank. The attacking battalions were the 4th, 1st and 2nd, in that order from the right, and the assault of Lesdain thus fell to the 4th Battalion. The advance of the 2nd Brigade was planned to overlap, some distance east of Lesdain, the frontage of the 4th Battalion, which thereafter was to confine itself to mopping up the area in and about Lesdain, as well as some 1,500 yards of the deep valley to the eastwards, through which flowed the Torrent of Esnes, and on the completion of this task was to assemble as battalion in support. The 3rd Battalion was to reduce its front line garrison to one company during the night, and immediately after zero, when the troops of the 3rd Division and the 2nd Battalion would have passed through the line, this company was to rejoin its unit in Brigade reserve.

A field-gun barrage was provided, to move forward by lifts of 100 yards every four minutes, to the Seranvillers trench-line forming the first objective some 2,000 yards ahead, beyond which it was to pause for half an hour and then advance again by similar lifts every three minutes to the final objective. This barrage was strengthened by the fire of the 32 guns of the Auckland and Wellington Machine Gun Companies; and heavy artillery would bombard selected points. After assisting in the opening barrage, four Stokes mortars were to go forward with the attacking troops, two with the 1st Battalion and two with the 2nd. To each of these units, also, eight guns of the Otago Machine Gun Company were attached, and the remaining sections of this company were directed to follow to positions from which covering fire could be directed to protect the flanks of each objective when taken. Four tanks from the 12th Tank Battalion were detailed to assist the 4th Battalion in the mopping-up of Lesdain. The 3rd Division was to have similar assistance in dealing with Seranvillers.

Our opening barrage-fire commenced at 4.30 a.m. The attacking battalions were in their assembly positions long before this time, and to avoid the enemy shelling which in response was expected to fall most heavily on Crevecoeur, they had got well forward of the village. Owing to the rapidity of the previous advance, our own artillery had not been able to complete their dispositions and ranging in sufficient time to ensure that accuracy of fire which had characterized their covering work in previous engagements, and the short-shooting of one or two guns caused some slight confusion amongst the waiting troops. The first lift came four minutes later, and the three battalions advanced to the attack.

In the 4th Battalion's sector, "C" Company (Capt. D. W. McClurg), moving in touch with 2nd Canterbury, captured the strongly-held factory buildings and dump on the boundary just in front of the starting-line, and then passed on, pushing the enemy from the network of railway sidings immediately beyond. At this early stage of the advance there occurred an incident exemplifying the value of close co-operation between the flanks of different bodies of troops. During the sharp fighting about the Factory, it was observed that the Canterbury men were suffering heavily from the sustained firing of a machine-gun posted on the slope beyond the buildings. Lance-Corporal Davidson, of the 4th Battalion, marked down the position, and, with three of his section, worked round to the rear of the post and rushed it, captured the garrison, and effectually removed an obstacle which had threatened seriously to impede our neighbours' progress, but from which we ourselves had experienced no great inconvenience.

The forward movement continued steadily until the western outskirts of Lesdain were reached. From this point one platoon moved along the southern edge of the village and took up a position on the east of it. A second followed half-way and held the southern edge, while a third, when these had been firmly established, passed along the northern fringe, cleared out the Chateau position, and faced the south. At the pre-arranged moment all three platoons entered the village simultaneously and proceeded to mop it up. This task was speedily accomplished and many prisoners were taken, especially from the strong dug-outs at the cross-roads on the far side. Amongst the spoils were six minenwerfer and two anti-tank rifles. "B" Company (Capt. B. McLeod), on the left, keeping pace with the barrage, had already passed along the north of the village, had cleared part of its outskirts, and was engaged in dealing with the enemy in the valley of the Torrent of Esnes. The platoons of this company had difficult country to work over, and met with considerable resistance throughout their advance. The whole of the battalion's task was, however, completed in good time, and in all 324 prisoners, including 19 officers, were sent back. From this comparatively small area no fewer than thirty machine-guns were taken.

In the centre of the Brigade sector the 1st Battalion had a frontage of 1,000 yards. For the capture of the first objective, "A" Company (Capt. N. L. Macky) and "D" Company (2nd Lieut. C. A. Spriggs) were detailed, the former on the right and the latter on the left. "B" Company (Lieut. H. J. Thompson) would follow in support, and "C" (Lieut. H. A. Ellingham) in reserve, and then pass on to the assault of the second objective. Immediately opposite the right company was the strong enemy position about the Old Mill of Lesdain, which our patrols had vainly attempted to storm on the 5th; but it was subjected to a hurricane bombardment by our Stokes mortars during the four minutes devoted to the opening barrage fire, and this was followed up so swiftly by the leading platoons that both the Mill and the posts along the road running north from it were cleared at a stride. That danger zone passed, the companies advanced steadily eastward up the broad whale-back spur towards the Seranvillers Trench. A succession of sunken roads lying across our line of advance, and held by the enemy, had to be taken, but the checks, though frequent, were never seriously prolonged. As so often happens, the advancing troops moving in the dim light of dawn had overlooked a concealed enemy post, and from this nest machine-gun fire was opened upon our men as they passed. Sergeant R. J. Sinclair, following his company with the headquarters section, rushed the position single-handed, killed the crew and captured the gun. When abreast of Lesdain the right flank was threatened by heavy fire from the edge of the cliff. To this point Sergeant P. A. Thompson led a small party, but was for a time held up by the intensity of the fire. The sergeant and Rifleman A. E. Strong, covered by the fire of the remainder, worked round the flank, shot the crew and captured the gun, which was now turned on parties of the enemy observed moving in the valley. This flank met with trouble again from a strong-point in a quarry further east. Corporal C. A. Rowe, taking a party of six men, rushed the quarry,

ORDER OF BATTLE—LESDAIN AND BEYOND, OCTOBER 8, 1918.

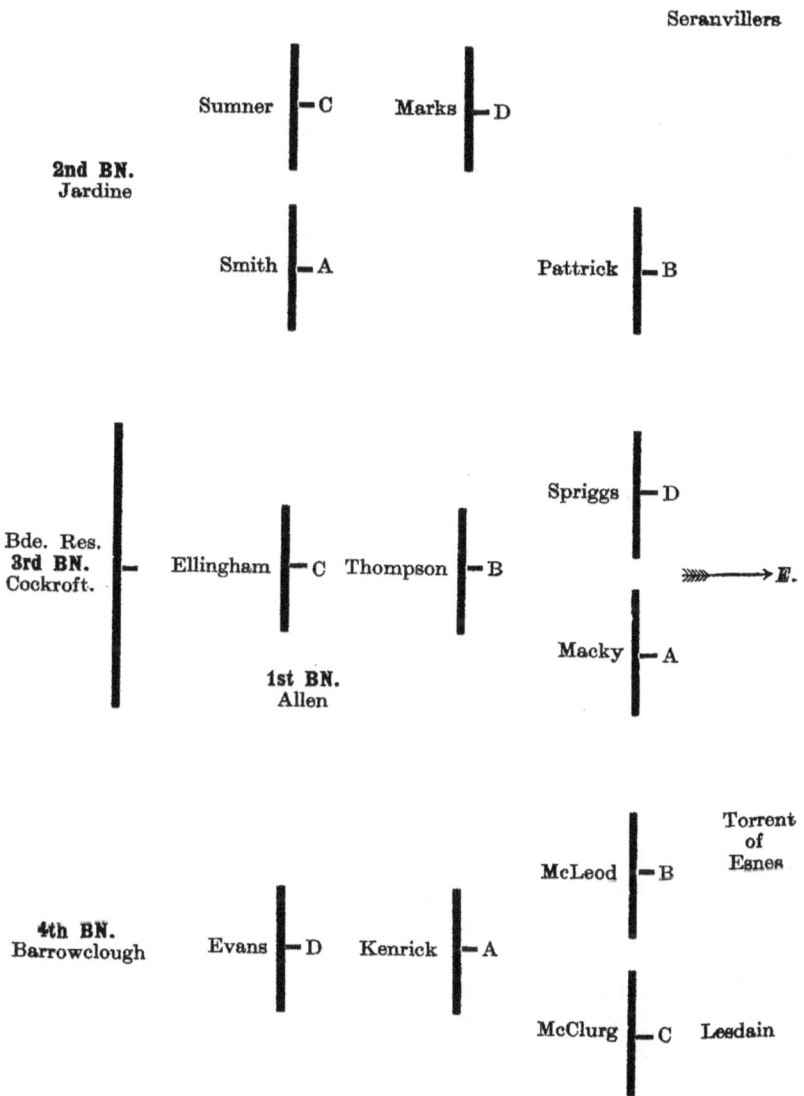

killed a number of the garrison, and took twenty prisoners. The advanced troops of the battalion were now steadily approaching the first objective, and as the barrage, by no means regular or intense, passed beyond this, machine-guns opened up on our men from various points in the trench. The leading sections crept up close to the wire, which was broad and strong, though fortunately breached in several places. Through these gaps an entry was forced, and bombing sections, working right and left, eventually cleared up the trench.

The 2nd Battalion had a frontage of only 500 yards at the commencement of the advance, though this widened somewhat near the first objective. It had more difficult country to work over, however, with scattered trench elements between the roads and on the flank. It advanced with "B" Company (Lieut. H. B. Pattrick) leading, "D" Company (2nd Lieut. R. O. C. Marks) following in close support to watch the left flank and to assist the forward line where required. "A" Company (Lieut. M. D. Smith) and "C" (Capt. W. C. I. Sumner) were detailed for the capture of the second objective, with "D" on the flank as before. The Northumberland Fusiliers were to be in touch to the first objective, and the Suffolks to the second. Throughout the first advance several checks were experienced, but all were of short duration. One machine-gun post was attacked from the flank by Rifleman A. E. Forsyth, who, with a Lewis gun, forced the enemy to retire over the open, thus exposing them to the fire of the remainder of his section, by whom they were all shot down. At another point, as the leading troops approached the first objective, intense machine-gun fire swept down the valley running up towards Seranvillers, causing many casualties on the left. Corporal S. J. Sapsford, a Lewis gunner, located the enemy guns, two of which were seen to be in action. Calling upon two other Lewis gun teams to follow him, he dashed across the open to a commanding position, and still under fire, directed the three guns upon the enemy post, which was speedily and effectually silenced. A short length of double trench lying directly across the advance and a little distance from the objective held up the line completely for a time; but the situation was smartly cleared up through some clever work on the part of Sergeant T. O'Neill, now in charge of a platoon in the place of his officer, who had fallen. Quickly grasping the situation, he made the dispositions for the sections of his platoon, brought both Lewis guns into effective action, and then personally led a bombing section against the flank of the position, killed several of the enemy holding it, and caused the rest to surrender. The troops on the left were thus enabled to get forward, and, aided by sections sent up from the support company as the front widened, they entered the trench forming the first objective. The right, however, was still held up by a strongly-held section of the trench from which machine-guns were firing forward upon the 2nd Battalion and also enfilading the 1st. This hornet's nest was dealt with by a bombing party led from the flank by Sergeant H. L. Moyle of the 2nd Battalion, who, by his furious attack, compelled the surrender of forty Germans with several machine-guns. The whole of the first objective was now in our hands, and touch was gained with the troops on the left. For the moment, the 4th Battalion's line ran back from the right of the 1st Battalion at right-angles, and joined up with that of 2nd Canterbury some little distance to the east of Lesdain.

It was now 5.30 a.m., and while the protective barrage rested just beyond the trench, the 1st and 2nd Battalions completed their dispositions for the next advance towards the final objective some 1,500 yards ahead. This was the tree-lined highway running from Esnes in a north-westerly direction to Cambrai. It rose steeply from Esnes to the Mill on the crest, and then dropped beyond down a longer and gentler slope to La Targette on the eastern outskirts of Seranvillers. As before, a number of intersecting roads and trench elements lay between us and our goal; and while, during the advance, the left would be in touch with the 3rd Division, the right would be exposed and unsupported; for, as will be remembered, the left of 2nd Canterbury's temporary line was, according to plan, by Lesdain, 1,500 yards west of us.

Now the barrage lifted and the advance was resumed. The 1st Battalion's companies had become somewhat intermingled. but they pressed steadily up the spur, the centre line of their advance leading directly towards the Mill on the sky-line. For the most part the enemy's resistance was easily overcome; the Mill was enveloped, and this position, as well as the greater part of the objective along the road, fell speedily into our hands. Most of the casualties sustained were caused by machine-gun fire from the flanks, particularly from Esnes, which lay close to our right, and from which those of our sections clearing the banks and tracks and sunken roads on the steep southern slope were clearly visible and within short range. On the right of the objective the enemy had a strongly-wired trench system projecting from the village and looping across the road. Three machine-guns firing from this temporarily held up the right flank. Here Rifleman M. J. Mulvaney, who was in charge of a Lewis gun section, set to work to relieve the situation. Taking up a position on a point of vantage, he opened fire to cover a flanking movement, thus drawing fire upon himself. Marking down the nearest gun and watching his opportunity he succeeded in killing the crew. Soon afterwards he silenced the second gun in the same way, and then forced the crew of the third to take cover. Now, without a moment's hesitation, he dropped his gun, seized a rifle, and with one of his men dashed forward into the trench. A few minutes' exercise with the bayonet sufficed to complete his work, and the remainder of the garrison of the trench surrendered. The 1st Battalion was thus in possession of the whole of its allotted section of the objective. Consolidation was at once proceeded with, and a defensive flank formed facing the north-west of Esnes till the 2nd Brigade troops should come up.

While the digging was proceeding, the left forward company of the battalion was shelled by a German battery of field guns which were firing at short range from their position in a sunken road just beyond the objective. 2nd Lieut. A. L. McCormick was the only officer left, and, under stress of the accurate shelling, some of his men fell back. McCormick thereupon personally led parties of Lewis gunners forward to attack the battery from a flank. They engaged the field-gun crews at point blank range, but were driven back, and McCormick rallied his men for a second attempt. In this they were supported by Corporal F. R. Cormack, who had reorganized the men driven back from the trench, and who, under cover of Lewis gun fire directed at the battery from the front, was bringing them forward again. The attention of the Germans being thus momentarily distracted, Corporal L. G. McLean, in charge of one of the teams working under the lieutenant, dashed from cover, raked the German gunners, and occupied the battery position till consolidation was completed. The officer in command of the battery scuttled off to the rear, but he was promptly run to earth and brought back.

The advance of the 2nd Battalion on its broadening front had been equally successful, but the troops had suffered somewhat heavy casualties from machine-guns sweeping the open slopes about Seranvillers. Rifleman S. Fatt, a Lewis gunner, who with his team had been detailed to establish close liaison with the troops of the 3rd Division on the left during the two advances, had a remarkable series of adventures with successive enemy machine-gun positions. Two field-guns abandoned by the enemy were passed midway between the two objectives. Further casualties occurred as the 2nd Battalion companies crossed the sky-line on the spur behind the La Targette Road, for here they formed a good mark for the battery presently silenced by 2nd Lieut. McCormick and his Lewis gunners. However, all but the extreme left of the battalion's objective was taken without serious delay. On this flank two of "D" Company's sections under the command of Corporal F. L. Cross and Rifleman W. A. Mackinder, respectively, met with considerable resistance and were held up by a machine-gun post. The two leaders, working in co-operation, handled the position skilfully. One held the front while the other took his men to a flank, and, closing in, they cleared the position with a dashing rush, taking twenty prisoners and two machine-guns. This completed the advance, the whole line being in our possession shortly after 8.30 a.m. By this time the 2nd Canterbury troops had gained touch on our right and were looking down on Esnes from the high ground close to the north-western edge of the village.

As soon as the barrage had died down sufficiently, each battalion sent forward reconnoitring patrols to maintain touch with the enemy; but strong hostile machine-gun fire from the ridge above Longsart seemed to indicate that the expected rapid retirement had not yet commenced. Indeed, we were to have convincing evidence of enemy activity nearer home, for before the "D" Company men, on the left of the 2nd Battalion, had got well started with their digging-in, their position was threatened by two tanks that came lumbering down the road leading straight to our line from Wambaix. They proved to be two of our old female tanks* that had been repaired and painted by the Germans. There now ensued an exciting fight between these two tanks and a German field gun on the one hand, and a New Zealand Lewis gun section on the other. For Rifleman R. C. Ramsay, of the 2nd Battalion, had gone out along the Wambaix Road in advance of our line to engage with his Lewis gun an isolated enemy field gun firing from a position south of the village. Despite the approach of the tanks, Ramsay continued firing on the field gun until he had silenced it, and then turned his attention to the tanks, which were now within 150 yards of the position held by his section. Steadfastly holding their ground, he and his men kept up a steady fire upon these moving fortresses, but the odds were doubly against him, for, safe behind the stout steel plates, the German crews were returning his fire with their captured Lewis guns. At this critical moment two of our own male tanks came upon the scene from Seranvillers. Moving up to the Cambrai Road, they shelled the enemy tanks at close range and completely disabled both in quick succession. Not a few of our men have reason to remember 2nd Lieuts. H. H. Sherratt and F. Clarke, of "C" Company, 12th Battalion, Tank Corps, for their prompt support on this morning of October 8th.

The situation beyond our left flank was still somewhat obscure, and we had not established touch with the 3rd Division. Moreover, machine-gun fire was falling upon our left rear. To secure definite information as to the situation on this quarter, Corporal J. C. Dibble, of the 2nd Battalion Scouts, was sent off with three men in the direction of Seranvillers. He eventually pushed on into the village itself, searched the roads and houses, and finally marked down enemy posts still clinging to the north-eastern outskirts. He then located the two right posts of the 3rd Division, reported to them the results of his investigations, and returned to his own battalion headquarters with the information gained.

*Briefly, the distinction between the female and the male tank lay in the fact that the former was provided with machine-guns only, while the latter had in addition two six-pounder Hotchkiss quick-firing guns.

At 9.30 a.m. the 2nd Brigade troops advanced from their second objective 700 yards west of Esnes, and without much difficulty captured that village. Exploitation patrols now moved forward from the whole Divisional front and cleared up the country as far eastward as the "Green Dotted Line" beyond which, in accordance with orders for the day, no further advance was permitted. This line ran north-west midway between Esnes and Haucourt, and about 1,200 yards east of the Cambrai Road. Here we had to halt until the artillery, now rapidly moving forward, got into such positions as would enable them effectively to cover a further advance next day.

The whole operation had been most successful. Our Brigade had advanced nearly three miles, and had captured seven 77 mm. guns, a howitzer, 89 machine-guns, the usual proportion of trench-mortars, and nearly 900 prisoners.

The casualties in both the forward battalions had been somewhat severe, especially in the 1st Battalion, whose list of wounded included its commanding officer and adjutant. As soon as the first objective had been taken, Lieut.-Col. Allen moved his headquarters forward from Crevecoeur to the captured line. Passing on to note the progress of the final stages of the second advance, he was in time to witness McCormick's contest with the field-guns. Satisfied that all was well in the new line, he presently returned to his advanced headquarters. Shells were falling about this position and a move was being discussed, when a burst of high explosive disabled the greater portion of his party. The adjutant, Capt. E. Baxter, M.C., an officer of exceptional ability and with a long period of distinguished service in various capacities to his credit, was mortally wounded. While attending to the comfort of Capt. Baxter, Lieut.-Col. Allen was himself wounded, but, though suffering severely from his own injury, he remained at his post personally superintending the evacuation of the casualties, and only consented to go out when the day's operation was completed. He was temporarily succeeded in the command by Capt. E. A. Harding, but returned from the casualty clearing-station next day with his arm in a sling.

During the afternoon the enemy began to feel back cautiously to ascertain the position of our line, and patrol encounters were frequent. At about 5 p.m. he launched a strong counter-attack against the Division on our left. As the left flank of the Germans moved across from Wambaix towards Seranvillers they came into full view from our line. The machine-gun section attached to us took full advantage of the excellent targets offering, as they had done during the advance earlier in the day when they sighted the enemy's batteries within good range, and our advanced artillery also joined in the shooting. The enemy was successful in occupying part of Seranvillers, and our left flank had to be refused accordingly. Two hours later our neighbours recovered their lost ground, and the line thereafter remained stable.

PART 2.—THE ADVANCE TO THE SELLE RIVER.

Advance continued, October 9th—The Guards, the 2nd Brigade, and the 3rd Battalion to the Cambrai Railway—3rd Battalion patrols to Fontaine-au-Pire—General success—Cambrai taken—Pressure continued, October 10th—1st and 2nd Brigades to the Selle—Immediate result of the Battle of Le Cateau—Effects farther north—Ostend and Lille taken.

On October 9th the whole advance was continued. Our 3rd Battalion, attacking in conjunction with the 2nd Brigade on the right and the Guards' Division on the left, had for its objective a section of the St. Quentin–Busigny–Cambrai Railway. The advance, starting at 5.20 a.m., proceeded with practically no oppositon, and outposts were established well beyond the objective. Patrols from the 3rd Battalion were finally checked on the outskirts of Fontaine-au-Pire, while those of the Guards were held up at Estourmel. A cavalry patrol passed through the new line at 10 a.m. with the object of exploiting the gains of the infantry, but was driven back by machine-gun fire pouring from Fontaine.

The 3rd Battalion now became attached to the 2nd Brigade, which took over responsibility for the whole front of the Division. It was relieved during the night, however, and returned to Brigade.

Elsewhere also the advance had been a complete success. The close defences of Cambrai had been partially broken by the Canadians and the 57th Division on the 8th, and on the following day the town fell and the British troops passed on to a line three miles to the east of it. We were now within two miles of the important centre of Le Cateau.

Progress continued on October 10th, the enemy's resistance stiffening as he reached the Selle River* in his retreat. It soon became evident that he intended to stand behind the general line of the Selle, and, save for minor operations, the fight was broken off while communications were improved and other preparations completed for an assault in strength.

The 1st and 2nd Brigades took part in the advance of the 10th. The latter, passing beyond Beauvois and Caudry, captured the railway running north to Quievy. The 1st then leap-frogged through the 2nd and advanced to the Selle, some of the troops actually securing a footing on the farther side of the stream, just south of Solesmes. The 1st Brigade continued its pressure here till the 12th October, when the New Zealand front was taken over by the 42nd Division.

The immediate result of the Battle of Le Cateau was the capture of the important lateral double line of railway running from St. Quentin through Busigny to Cambrai. The toll of prisoners taken amounted to 12,000, and the captures included no fewer than 250 guns. Incidentally, the enemy's withdrawal before Lens was hastened, and by October 13th British troops had reached the western suburbs of Douai. Similarly, under this pressure from the north, combined with local French attacks, the enemy was forced to evacuate his positions in the Laon salient, and by the same date Laon itself had fallen to the French.

The effects of the advance in the Cambrai sector were also being felt on the Flanders front, where the enemy was being constantly pressed. Here, on the whole front from Comines to Dixmude, he was attacked in strength on October 14th by the forces, British, Belgian and French, under the command of the King of the Belgians; and so successful was the attack that by October 17th Ostend was captured and three days later the northern flank of the Allied line rested on the Dutch fron-

---

*The Selle River is a small winding stream flowing slightly west of north through Le Cateau, Neuvilly and Solesmes, and joining the Escaut between Cambrai and Valenciennes. Solesmes is about eighteen miles due east of Cambrai.

Lieut.-Col. R. C. Allen, D.S.O.

Major G. W. Cockroft.

TOWING A CAPTURED TANK.

A RUINED FACTORY—SMASHED, NOT BOMBARDED.

tier. The advances on the northern and on the southern fronts left the flanks of the Lille defences exposed, and these the enemy began to evacuate on October 15th; but he was pressed so hard that he was given no time to complete either the removal of his stores, the destruction of roads and bridges, or the evacuation of the civil population. Douai was taken on the 17th, and Lille on the 18th; and by the evening of October 22nd the Britsh troops had reached the general line of the Escaut from Valenciennes northwards to Avelghem, north-east of Roubaix.

PART 3.—THE BATTLE OF THE SELLE RIVER.

New Zealand Rifle Brigade in billets at Esnes—A freed town—Inspections—The Prince of Wales—The battle opens, October 17th—Enemy driven from the river, October 20th—Patrols to the Harpies River—The great attack of October 24th—2nd Brigade advances four and a half miles—2nd Brigade advances again to within a mile of Le Quesnoy, October 24th—The New Zealand Rifle Brigade keeps pace in reserve.

The New Zealand Rifle Brigade, after the successful actions of October 8th and 9th, went into billets at Esnes on the 10th. These were real billets in houses, and this was the first time the whole Brigade had occupied such quarters since the preceding February, when we were in the Staple area for training. For the past three months we had been almost constantly on the move, the "bivvy," the dug-out, and occasionally the dilapidated hut, being the extent of our luxuries in the matter of shelter from the elements. We were now in new country almost entirely undamaged by shell-fire. The villages, though deserted, were intact, and stoves and the heavier articles of furniture, and even the precious feather beds, remained in the houses. To the delight of everyone, vegetables in plenty were found growing in the gardens, and we were thus able to provide a welcome addition to the rations which it had been impossible to augment in any way for six weeks past. That the same quarters had been occupied by the German troops was evident from the filth that abounded.

On the afternoon of the 10th, one of our senior officers going forward to reconnoitre the front took the opportunity of visiting Caudry, which had been taken during the morning. He thus describes the town as it appeared immediately after evacuation:—

"Caudry is a large factory-town and had been occupied continuously by the Germans since the Mons retreat, when our British 'Contemptibles' were forced back over this ground. The place had not been knocked about by the Germans until a few days ago, when parties of men were specially detailed to go through the factories and deliberately and methodically smash the machinery with hammers. I saw for myself the results of their activity. Everywhere cog-wheels were shattered, and I could quite understand how half a dozen men could utterly ruin the machinery of a huge factory in one half-day. Even in private houses clocks, ornaments, furniture and windows had, in many cases, received equally thorough attention.

"Between 2,000 and 3,000 inhabitants and refugees, women, children, and old men, were still in the town. The Germans had lived there so long that most of these unfortunates had learned to speak the language. Before the oppressor left he concentrated them all in one street, every house in which he marked with a red cross flag, so that, if we had not harassed him onward, he would have been able to shell the remaining part of the town. All men between the ages of fifteen and sixty had been taken away. At various times during the past four years most of the population had been induced by threats or specious promises to leave the town for employment in munition works or on roads and railways. The people were not starved, for they had succeeded somehow in cultivating their crops and vegetables in order to keep themselves in food. They were delighted to see us. The tricolour was flying from nearly every window, and the people waved their hands, doffed their caps, threw kisses, shook hands, and showed, by smiles and signs and every other possible means of expression, how grateful they were at their deliverance from veritable slavery.

"The roads in and around Caudry had been blown up at all junctions and other important points, this destruction being effected by binding together half a dozen minenwerfer bombs or large shells and exploding them by means of electric batteries. 'Booby-traps' were placed in dug-outs, houses, roads and wells to catch the unwary; but, wisely enough, we now keep German prisoners whom we send to these places first to remove the traps safely or otherwise. . . ."

The Division being now out of the line, the battalions of the Brigade commenced at once to reorganize and refit, and to carry out recreational and general training. For some reason, our reinforcements were coming forward very slowly, and all units were sadly under strength. On Sunday, October 13th, a Brigade church parade was held. The Corps Commander, General Harper, was present, and after the service presented ribands to twenty-seven recipients of awards recently made. He also spoke in warm terms of the Brigade's good work during the past operations. His Royal Highness the Prince of Wales, who was on a visit to the New Zealand Division, inspected the Brigade during training on the 14th, and was shown over the scene of the latest fight.

The repair of roads, railways and other communications on the Le Cateau front was so far advanced as to warrant the recommencement of larger operations on October 17th, on which date the Fourth Army attacked on a ten mile front extending from Le Cateau southwards. The French First Army co-operated by attacking farther south. The enemy was holding his line in great strength, and during the first two days' fighting his resistance was obstinate; but by the end of the 19th the French had driven the enemy across the Sambre Canal as far north as Catillon. From that village the British front followed the course of the Richemont stream to its junction with the Selle, north of Le Cateau.

This operation was followed by an advance at 2 a.m. on the 20th October, when the Third Army launched an attack on the line of the Selle River north of Le Cateau. The resistance offered by the enemy proved very serious. His position, naturally strong, had, during the delay caused by our difficulties in completing communications, been further strengthened by the erection of extensive wire entanglements. The attack succeeded, nevertheless, and the enemy was driven back from the river, British patrols reaching the Harpies River three miles east of Solesmes.

The capture of the Selle positions paved the way for a greater attack with the object of gaining the line Sambre Canal–Mormal Forest–Valenciennes. The major assault was opened at 1.20 a.m. on October 23rd by the Fourth Army, and was extended at a later hour by the Third Army. The New Zealand Division was engaged in this fight.* Led by the 2nd

*It had been intended to employ the New Zealand Rifle Brigade for this undertaking, but, owing to our numerical weakness, the task was given to the 2nd Brigade.

Brigade, it passed through the 42nd Division at 8 a.m. The day went well, and the 2nd Brigade made a record advance of four and a half miles. The enemy had strong positions but a faint heart, and, tackled at close quarters, he surrendered freely. Next day, October 24th, the First Army prolonged the front of attack northwards to the Escaut; on our own front the 2nd Brigade attacked again, and by the evening the line had been carried forward another mile and a half, being now within a mile of Le Quesnoy.

In the Selle Battle, thus brought to a victorious close, twenty-four British and two American Divisions, though opposed by thirty-one German Divisions, had made a deep advance and had taken over 20,000 prisoners and 475 guns.

Keeping up with the general advance, the New Zealand Rifle Brigade had moved, on October 19th, to Beauvois, about a mile north-west of Caudry, where it lay in readiness if required for the attack on the 20th. Owing to the great amount of destruction done to railways, roads and bridges, the traffic on the few available avenues was greatly congested. Time after time the railway was blown up by clockwork devices, often as long as a week after the enemy's retirement, and for several days transportation of ammunition and supplies had to be carried out entirely by motor lorries. Railhead was established at Beauvois on October 22nd. On the morning of the 23rd the Brigade went forward again, marching eastward some seven miles to the reserve position on the farther bank of the Selle River, just south of Solesmes. Here the 4th Battalion was attached to the 2nd Brigade as reserve during the day's fighting. The 3rd Battalion joined the 4th in the afternoon, and the two units moved up to Vertigneul, where they were held in readiness for action at half an hour's notice. Movement was now becoming so rapid and extensive that that part of the first line transport carrying ammunition, bombs and tools was ordered up to accompany the respective battalions, and the remainder was brigaded within easy reach. Next morning, following upon the further advance of the 2nd Brigade, another eastward march was made, the 1st and 2nd Battalions moving to Vertigneul and Romeries, and the 3rd and 4th to positions about midway between those villages and Beaudignies.

CHAPTER XIX.
LE QUESNOY AND THE ARMISTICE.

(THE BATTLE OF THE SAMBRE.)

PART 1.—MINOR OPERATIONS.

The New Zealand Rifle Brigade takes over the line at Le Quesnoy—3rd and 4th Battalions advance the line—2nd Battalion attack on the Orsinval Road—Withdrawal to the Railway—Increase in enemy artillery activity—Readjustment of the line—Notable patrols and raids—Assembly for the attack—Conditions—The town of Le Quesnoy.

On the night of 24th/25th October we relieved the 2nd Brigade in the line at Le Quesnoy. The 3rd Battalion took over the right battalion sector of the front line from 1st Otago, and the 4th Battalion the left sector from 2nd Canterbury. The 1st and 2nd Battalions were in right and left support positions, relieving 2nd Otago and 1st Canterbury respectively. Relief was completed before midnight. The Otago Machine Gun Company, one troop of the Otago Mounted Rifles, and the 3rd Field Company of the Engineers were now attached to us. The support battalions were on the Beaudignies Road at the St. Georges River, some two miles behind the front line, but, with Brigade Headquarters, moved forward to Beaudignies on the afternoon of the 25th.

The main line of resistance taken over ran from south-east to north-west, and lay about 700 yards ahead of the outskirts of Beaudignies. The outposts were established from 300 to 500 yards in advance of this, and at the nearest point were 1,000 yards from the south-west angle of the outworks of Le Quesnoy. The left post was on the Ruesnes-Le Quesnoy Road, some 1,500 yards from the ramparts. This was the whole front of the sector held by the New Zealand Division. On our right we had the 37th Division, and on our left the 3rd.

The trench-strength of units at this time was as under:—

1st Battalion.	21 officers,	435 other ranks.
2nd	,,	23	,,	450	,,
3rd	,,	20	,,	448	,,
4th	,,	20	,,	434	,,
Total . . .		84		1,767	

Thus, numerically, the man-power of the Brigade, available for immediate action, was considerably less than 50 per cent. of the normal strength.

The usual policy of active patrolling was ordered, with the twofold object of keeping touch with the enemy and advancing the line. During the afternoon and evening of the 25th, the right battalion swung its line forward through an angle of about 45 degrees into a north and south position, bringing its left post within 500 yards of the outworks of the town. The 4th Battalion troops moved forward also, and prolonged this line northwards. They overcame without serious difficulty all opposition on the right half of their front, but they found the enemy so strong along the railway running north-west from Le Quesnoy, and in the great triangle at the junction with that running south, that they had to be content with a line bent back on the left along the Precheltes stream. Throughout its whole length the Brigade's line of posts was now from 300 to 600 yards on the near side of either one railway or the other.

During the early morning the two commanders of the line companies of the right battalion, while making the preparatory reconnaissance for this advance, found that the buildings of de Beart Farm had been set on fire by the enemy shelling. The old farmer and his daughter stood weeping on the doorstep, while the flames rapidly spread through the upper rooms. It was hoped that the farm-house might have been used as a headquarters, but it was clear that the place was doomed. An aged civilian, who had already given valuable information regarding both the French and the Germans in Le Quesnoy, and was now acting as guide, took the officers forward to his little cottage on the eastern margin of the farm, which he hoped would serve as well. In this were found seven men, seven women, and three children, and although the house was actually between two of our front-line posts, and the German machine-gun bullets were chipping the tiles on the roof, the civilian inmates did not wish to leave. After the usual embraces had been submitted to, the cottage was inspected. It was found to possess two cellars, one below the other, and was accordingly settled upon as a headquarters. The four-course lunch that presently appeared may have been a determining factor in arriving at this decision. The civilians were evacuated next day, but apparently the interpreter who had the matter in hand had not been informed that the house was in the front line, for he went gaily forward on horse-back along the road towards Le Quesnoy. A burst of machine-gun fire greeted his appearance, and the horse, taking fright, careered along No Man's Land at a gallop, and was not got under control until a wood to the north was reached. Fortunately neither horse nor rider was hit, though a bullet passed through the saddle.

Renewed efforts were made during the night to swing up the left of the line across the railway, but against the intense machine-gun fire and showers of bombs the 4th Battalion fighting-patrols could make little headway except at the Orsinval Road Level Crossing. Here a party led by Lance-Sergeant H. Moscroft, after a stiff and prolonged fight, succeeded in establishing a post and holding it against a determined counter-attack launched against it at 2 o'clock next morning under cover of a sharp bombardment. The post was practically isolated, however, with the enemy pressing strongly on both flanks, and shortly afterwards it was withdrawn.

Deeds in the forward zone of the battle area are apt to overshadow the less spectacular but no less important services of the non-combatants slaving behind the lines, but even here those duties are not unattended with difficulties to be overcome and dangers to be faced. Of the faithfulness of the transport-drivers, for example, the story will never be fully told, and of their many daring exploits only too few examples have been recorded. To escape heavy shelling in the back areas, foot-soldiers on the move may pass across the fields, but the transport must stick to the highway. On October 25th, while the companies up in the line were pushing forward, Rifleman C. H. Nailer, a 3rd Battalion transport-driver, was "doing his bit" bringing up the rations to the accompaniment of the usual shelling on the roads. At a cutting he came to a water-cart from which the wounded team had been cut adrift, and around which the shells were still falling. Driving coolly on he delivered his rations, but, learning that the non-arrival of the water-cart meant shortage of water for the men of his unit, he returned with his horses to the cutting, hitched them to the abandoned vehicle, and, facing the shelling again, started off once more towards the front. This time he was wounded, but he persevered in his undertaking, finally bringing back his team and limber to the transport lines without further misfortune. Mention might be made here, too, of a fine act performed in the face of great danger of a particularly fearsome kind. The Brigade forward dump of ammunition, grenades and Stokes mortar bombs, located at Beaudignies, was struck and set on fire during a heavy shelling of the village. Rifleman M. Hickey, of the 3rd Battalion, then in charge of the dump, rushed from shelter, and, ignoring both the bursting shells and the possibility of a devastating explosion, dragged out the burning boxes one by one and threw them into a neighbouring ditch.

The operation of October 25th was made in conjunction with the 3rd Division on the left. The latter, meeting with less resistance, had a correspondingly greater degree of success. Their left had swung well across the railway, and they were now improving their positions preparatory to an advance eastwards against Orsinval and the villages to the north of it. This attack was to be made at dawn on the 26th, and we were to co-operate. The major part of the task assigned to our Brigade was allotted to the 2nd Battalion, then in support. This battalion was to extend our general line northward for about 1,200 yards along the Orsinval Road from the Level Crossing to the cemetery, advance eastward to the Le Quesnoy–Orsinval Road, and push out patrols to operate against the north and north-west of Le Quesnoy. The 4th Battalion was to have prepared the way by securing the Level Crossing during the night of 25th/26th, but, as we have already seen, the Crossing position was abandoned before the 2nd Battalion could arrive.

Through storms of high-explosive and gas shells, the 2nd Battalion moved northwards from Beaudignies at about midnight, and battalion headquarters were established close to the outskirts of Ruesnes, on the Le Quesnoy Road. At 3 a.m., 26th October, "C" and "D," the leading companies, began to work forward to their assembly positions on the Precheltes stream. At zero, 5 a.m., "C" Company (Capt. G. R. Jamieson) was to cross the railway, push up the Orsinval Road and establish itself on its allotted section. "D" Company (Capt. J. C. McKillop) would move past "C," capture the remainder, and secure the flank. Movement eastwards would follow with the assistance of "B" Company (Lieut. T. H. Denniston), while "A" Company (Lieut. F. T. Bennington) was held in reserve. There was a possibility that the operation would prove to be comparatively easy, for the enemy was reported to be withdrawing from the sector on our left, and a section of the Otago Mounted Rifles was attached to the 2nd Battalion and one to the 4th, to exploit successes if our penetration should be deep. No barrage was provided, but the attacking battalion had at its disposal two trench mortars and a machine-gun.

The intensity of the machine-gun fire experienced by the two leading companies as they approached their positions on the stream was a sufficient indication that, contrary to expectations, the railway ahead of them was not clear from the junction on the right to the reported "pocket" beyond the left. Definite information as to the true situation was soon forthcoming, and the change in the plan of action was arranged accordingly. This involved a preliminary attack on the whole section of railway from the junction along to the left boundary; and the necessary dispositions were made with such expedition that, after a preliminary bombardment of the junction and the crossing by the trench mortars, the leading platoons were able to advance to the attack within a few minutes of the original zero-hour. Thick fog hung over the ground, but intense machine-gun fire, started, no doubt, in response to our own trench mortar and machine-gun covering activities, poured upon the leading troops from the front, and with even greater volume from both the high ground in the triangle and the railway embankment on their right rear. Frontal and enfilade fire took heavy toll, but our men pressed on; and before 6 a.m. posts were established on the railway right across our front, from the left boundary to the junction.

A further vigorous push half an hour later carried the line of posts 400 yards beyond the railway, the right post being on the sunken Orsinval Road, and the left in touch with the 3rd Division.

An attempt was now made to continue the penetration down the Orsinval Road. Taking advantage of the fog, a platoon under 2nd Lieut. R. J. Richards moved across the railway at 7 a.m., and worked forward some 800 yards, but, coming to a straight stretch in the road, they encountered a steady stream of machine-gun fire from the front. This caused heavy casualties amongst the men of the leading section, and the remainder thereupon left the road and dashed across the open country on their right towards a bank in the vicinity of a belt of trees. By this time, however, the enemy had recovered from his surprise and was beginning to press in strength upon all our forward posts. The men of Richards's platoon came under a hail of bullets as they rushed to cover, and found when they reached it that they could neither advance nor retire. The commander was wounded in the jaw and neck, and the Lewis gun was put out of action. The platoon-sergeant, A. Ashby, received a bullet in the thigh, but succeeded in dragging himself back to the road with information as to the plight of his comrades; and a scout sent out from one of the forward posts to reconnoitre the position reported that only dead and wounded were visible, but that owing to the intensity of the machine-gun fire he had not been able to cross the open to get in touch with the platoon. At about 8 a.m. artillery fire opened upon the belt of trees, the railway junction and the Level Crossing, and the enemy struck at all our posts beyond the railway. Under pressure from overwhelming numbers the platoon in the sunken road was withdrawn, the men working steadily back under cover of the fire from the posts in rear, but 2nd Lieut. Richards and his handful of survivors were trapped. From the high ground above, machine-guns barraged the road behind him, and another gun, brought up under the covered approach afforded by a dry ditch, suddenly appeared close up to his right flank, swept his line from end to end, and every man was hit.

In the meantime, pressure from the railway triangle towards the post at the junction had steadily increased, and the garrison there, weakened from the effects of the fierce artillery fire directed upon that point, was at last compelled to fall back to the Level Crossing at 9.30 a.m. During the next hour the enemy bombardment became increasingly violent about this post, and presently a strong counter-attack developed from the triangle. This was pressed with the utmost determination, and we came near to losing the post at the Crossing. The Germans worked right up to the keeper's house, under the shelter of which they prepared to rush to the western side. Our Stokes mortar and rifle-grenade barrage proved to be too strong and too well-directed, however, and the rush never came. The leader of the party did indeed dash across, but he was immediately shot down, and the attack faded away. The attempt was repeated at 4.30 p.m. after a hurricane artillery and trench-mortar bombardment, and though the Germans again reached the crossing-keeper's house, they failed to break down our defence.

Through all the attacks of the day, Lieut. R. T. Carlyon's platoon had maintained a stubborn hold on the forward posts established in and about a little square wood situated to the left of the Orsinval Road and some 400 yards north of the railway; but in view of the changed situation these were now considered to be too isolated to be of great value, and at nightfall the platoon was withdrawn. Sergeant W. P. McGillan and five men had occupied the spearpoint of this position and had beaten back repeated assaults. They were willing enough to remain in spite of the danger of being cut off, but this was not permitted. They covered the retirement of the others, however, finally working back safely to our main line late at night.

During the night our hold on the section of railway was strengthened, and the forward posts just beyond dug themselves in securely. Those troops of the 3rd Division still behind the railway swung forward, and their boundary was moved about 500 yards to the right. The 4th Battalion drew in its left, handing over to the 2nd the sunken road from the Precheltes stream to the Level Crossing.

A great increase in enemy artillery activity was noticed in connection with our minor operations and the ensuing counter-attacks. At times shell-fire from guns of all calibres was intense; as on previous occasions our opponents sent over gas-shells to a considerable extent; and an unusually large number of minenwerfer were used. Altogether there was every evidence that the enemy intended to resist to the utmost any attempt on our part to make further headway.

The swinging forward of our line on the left had had the result of increasing the Brigade front to more than two miles in length. On the night of 28th/29th October, the frontage was readjusted, some 500 yards of the line being handed over to the Brigade of the 37th Division on our right. The 1st and 2nd Battalions took over the remainder, the former on the right and the latter on the left, the 3rd Battalion going to support and the 4th to reserve.*

Patrolling and raiding, by night and by day, in parties varying from three men to a half-company, went on without cessation. By this means we not only caused many casualties and secured numerous prisoners, affected the enemy's morale and kept him in a state of unrest, but we gained an intimate first-hand knowledge of his strength and dispositions, and our activity precluded any possibility of his slipping away unobserved if, perchance, he should decide to retire.

A patrol had definitely marked down an enemy post on the embankment of the railway forming the western side of the triangle opposite the 2nd Battalion front. It was known to have two machine-guns, and its garrison was estimated to number sixteen. Against this post Sergeant S. Hartley volunteered to lead a raiding party. Arrangements were hastily made, the sergeant selected ten men, told them off for their respective duties, and led his party out into No Man's Land just before 2 a.m. on October 29th. After a Stokes mortar bombardment lasting two minutes the post was rushed, but the garrison at once fled, scattering over the railway line. Our men pursued, shot three, took a fourth prisoner, and with him returned to our lines without having suffered any casualties. Not content with this success, Sergeant Hartley conducted a second raid on the evening of the same day, this time against an enemy post in the sunken Orsinval Road north of the Level Crossing. His plan was similar to that followed in the morning raid. By 9 p.m. he and his nine men were out in position

---

*Major Barrowclough, commanding the 4th Battalion, went to the transport lines, sick, on October 25th; and Major K. S. Caldwell, who thereupon assumed command, was wounded on the following day, Capt. B. McLeod succeeding him. Major Barrowclough, however, returned at the beginning of November.

waiting for the pre-arranged Stokes bombardment. This was short and sharp, and when it ceased our men could hear the enemy running off down the road. Now ensued another chase. Some 250 yards from our line Hartley's men caught up with the rearmost Germans, who turned and wildly fired their revolvers and ran again. Along the banks of the road were the usual numerous cubby-holes, mostly deserted, and littered with rifles and equipment; but some were still occupied. Our men paused to deal with the Germans cowering in these, and with others firing from the banks, and then resumed the pursuit. This was carried on for another 250 yards, when further progress was blocked by a bombing post. The party now worked their way back, disappointed at not being able to bring in at least one prisoner, but otherwise well satisfied with an exploit which had been carried out so successfully without loss to themselves.

Another small raiding-party from the 2nd Battalion went out in the early morning of the 30th. This was composed of Sergeant G. A. Jarvis, Corporal M. Kerrigan, and six men, and their objective was a double post close to the little wood occupied by us as a forward position on the 26th but vacated the same night. Kerrigan knew the ground well, for he had been one of the garrison holding the copse throughout that long day. Protected by a covering party with Lewis guns, put out to prevent their being cut off from a flank, the raiders crept out silently at 1.30 a.m. and gradually separated into two parties. As they rushed the post both parties were met with showers of stick-bombs, but they succeeded in killing every man of the garrison except one, whom they took prisoner and sent back at once to our lines. While making sure that the work had been well done and that there were no Germans left, our men were bombed from posts on either flank. These posts were now rushed in turn, and their occupants killed or put to flight. Of the thirty Germans seen, fully fifteen had been despatched, five having fallen to Kerrigan alone, but we on our side had also suffered. Four of our party had been wounded, including the sergeant, who had been struck in the chest by a bomb. Declaring his wound to be fatal, he insisted on the others returning to our lines as best they could with the less severely wounded. This was accordingly done. Corporal Kerrigan immediately went back with a stretcher-party to bring in the sergeant, but was unable to approach the posts, for the enemy had now re-occupied them in strength.

Opposite the 1st Battalion, on the right, the enemy's front line along the railway embankment was practically straight and even. Patrols had got into touch with the Germans at various points, but no outstanding features were discovered such as might be dealt with by small parties. During the forenoon of the 30th, 2nd Lieut. M. G. Luxford and two men went out to reconnoitre a wood in No Man's Land, and to discover how strongly the enemy held the section of the railway in the vicinity of this. The patrol thoroughly searched the copse, and reached its eastern edge at noon. Two machine-gun posts were found, empty, but with fresh cartridge shells lying about; also a house, then unoccupied, but evidently, like the other two positions, used at night. Four enemy posts were definitely located on the railway, which, it was ascertained, was held in strength. The patrol spent three hours in this useful reconnaissance, and although they drew fire from each of the occupied posts, the party returned without mishap.*

This was followed by an enterprise carried out at 3.30 a.m. on the 31st, in co-operation with the Somersetshires, our neighbours on the right. Two platoons were employed in each case, and the objective was a stretch of the enemy's line some 600 yards in length.

The 1st Battalion's party, drawn from "A" Company, was commanded by 2nd Lieut. H. Blackburne, and, as it was expected that most of the work would be carried out with the bayonet, only one Lewis gun accompanied it. Two Vickers gunners went over as specialists to deal with enemy machine-guns captured. Artillery, trench mortars and machine-guns provided a light but sufficient barrage. The operation was an

---

*Apparently the German patrols had been similarly active and not less successful; for, from one of the officers of the party captured on the railway by the 1st Battalion's reserve company during the advance on November 4th was taken a German map giving the exact disposition of practically the whole of the Brigade, including the precise positions of the front-line posts. From the fact that the same map showed how the remainder of the Division was placed, we were inclined to ascribe the exactitude of the information to the activities of spies as well as to the enterprise of the enemy's patrols. It is interesting to note that the same German officer had in his possession a document, similar to that captured at Hebuterne in the previous July, giving a detailed description of the Division. (See p. 336.)

instant and complete success. The enemy put down no answering barrage, and so great was the surprise that the garrisons of the enemy posts fired no rifles and threw no bombs, and only one hostile machine-gun opened up. The enemy's position was an excellent one, his posts being dug in along a hedge at the bottom of the railway embankment, here from eight to ten feet high. Our men penetrated his line without meeting with more than slight opposition, and as the sections worked right and left along both sides of the railway, all but the few Germans who were taken in an isolated post scurried over the bank and into the plantation beyond. After the lapse of the fifteen minutes allowed for the occupation of the enemy's line the raiders returned, bringing with them three prisoners and two machine-guns. Only four of the enemy were known to have been killed, and on our side there were no casualties. Similar success attended the attack made by the Somerset men on their half of the objective, and the information gained during the little operation was of particular value in connection with the plans now being worked out for the next advance.

On this same day the 2nd Battalion completed the long series of brilliant raiding exploits for which that unit was deservedly famous throughout the Division. Its earliest enterprise of this kind, carried out in the Armentieres sector in the middle of 1916, only a month after its first introduction to trench warfare, was an achievement of the highest order; and now an officer with a handful of men was to round off the wonderful record with a dashing adventure as successful as it was daring.

The nearer railway line of the notorious triangle passed, as it approached the junction, through a cutting which, as we well knew, was very strongly held. During the forenoon a patrol consisting of Rifleman W. A. Wilson and two others worked down this line and located a strong enemy post, and, on their return with the report on the position, plans were set on foot to bombard the post with trench mortars and at the same time to send out a fighting-patrol to watch the result. If circumstances were auspicious, the patrol would attack the garrison. The trench-mortar shoot opened shortly after noon, and 2nd Lieut. W. E. McMinn, who had arranged with a neighbouring Lewis gun post to give him covering-fire on the right, moved down the line with Lance-Corporal F. H. Phillips and five men with a Lewis gun. Arrived at a point beyond the junction, the party divided. The lance-corporal and two men crawled along the main line under cover to a point opposite the post. They were followed by Rifleman W. A. Wilson and the remaining two men with the Lewis gun. Wilson, who, as the result of his experience with the reconnoitring patrol during the forenoon, knew his ground well, manœuvred his gun into position at the bend so as to enfilade the line where it ran straight on. The forward party, having advanced another 150 yards, now worked across the high ground to the top of the cutting. Looking down, they discovered a large number of the enemy sheltering in small dug-outs in the opposite bank. The corporal and his two men at once stood up and opened fire on the couching figures, and Wilson supported them with bursts from his Lewis gun on the flank. 2nd Lieut. McMinn, from his position farther back, whence he had been directing the operations of his men, now saw that his forward party was hopelessly outnumbered, and, fearing that they might be cut off, he dashed along the line to their assistance. Joined by one of the Lewis gun team as he passed, he fell upon the enemy, shooting the nearest with his revolver. The patrol ahead slipped down the bank and continued the fight with the bayonet, and within a few moments the Germans threw up their hands and were hurried along the railway to our lines. Other parties of the enemy farther along the cutting were engaged by the Lewis gun as our party withdrew, and finally the Lewis gunners also worked back without mishap. Our men suffered no casualties. Their "bag" of prisoners consisted of one officer and thirty-seven men.

Towards evening a strong 2nd Battalion fighting patrol attempted to work up the Orsinval Road from the Level Crossing, but the enemy was found to be more than ordinarily alert at this much-contested point. His rearward line of posts was bombarded by our howitzers and field guns, and the road itself by trench mortars, but the enemy's S.O.S. call brought down his answering barrage almost simultaneously with our own. The patrol pushed out, however, but was presently held up by a pair of machine guns firing directly down the road, and a third which closely swept the banks. Under cover of this fire the enemy essayed a counter-attack upon the patrol, but, when

AEROPLANE PHOTOGRAPH
OF
LE QUESNOY
AND NEIGHBOURHOOD.

Inset p. 432-3.

three of the leading Germans had been shot, his effort died away. All attempts to outflank the machine-gun positions proving fruitless, our patrol was recalled.

The raids of October 31st were the last of the New Zealand Division's operations of this kind. Patrolling was continued, but this was entirely for the purpose of keeping close touch with the enemy on all parts of the line. No premeditated encounters with the enemy's posts were now permitted, for warning orders in connection with the forthcoming attack on Le Quesnoy were already out, and the necessary preparations, which claimed all our attention, had begun.

The total casualties for the month of October were:—

	Killed.	Wounded.	Missing.
Officers	6	25	1
Other ranks	93	551	142

During the night of 1st/2nd November the 4th Battalion relieved the 2nd, the latter going back to reserve for a well-deserved and much-needed rest. On the following night the Divisional front was again adjusted, the 1st Battalion taking over some 700 yards from the 37th Division, and the 4th Battalion handing over to the 62nd Division that part of their line on the railway running back from the Level Crossing. At dusk on the evening of the 3rd the 2nd Battalion returned to the line, the garrison of which was thereupon rearranged in readiness for the following morning's advance, the 1st Battalion holding the right, the 4th the centre, and the 2nd the left. The 3rd Battalion concentrated about Saint Roch, just behind the right of the 1st Battalion.

The weather was, and had been for a long time past, well-nigh perfect. The nights were chilly and the early mornings often misty, but when the sun burst through it shone glorious and warm. The part of the country which we had now reached was exquisitely beautiful. It was mostly rolling, cultivated down-land, dotted over with many orchards, and the copses about the villages shone in all their autumn glory. Before us were the ancient walls and tall buildings of Le Quesnoy, seemingly untouched by the devastating engines of war. It is not surprising that into the otherwise dry-as-dust official records of one of our battalions there should have crept the statement that "More than one 'Digger' for a moment forgot the horrors of war, the crash of artillery, and the clatter of machine-guns, as he contemplated the rolling countryside with its brown and gold hedges and woods, and the tree-crowned ramparts and rising towers of the promised land of Le Quesnoy.''

Le Quesnoy is an ancient fortress town of some 5,000 inhabitants, supported for the most part by a few minor manufactures. Any great interest attaching to it is mainly historical, it having changed hands frequently in the many wars throughout the centuries from the 15th to the 18th. Mons is twenty miles to the north-east.

Its fortifications, no longer proof against artillery, nor, indeed, as the sequel will show, against determined infantrymen without the aid of siege guns, consist mainly of a wide and deep moat, and a rampart consisting of a solid brick wall backed by a broad bank of earth, both completely encircling the town. The moat, banked on the outer side, is from 200 to 300 yards in width, and its bottom is about fifteen feet below the general level of the surrounding land. The rampart, from thirty to forty feet high, is in outline of the form of an irregular eight-sided polygon, and at the angles is carried out to form bastions giving flanking fire along the intervening sides. Within the moat is a series of detached bastions, irregularly placed. These are faced with brick or stone, and their tops, rising to a height of from twenty to thirty feet above the ground-level of the moat, are crowned with trees and undergrowth. Their outer faces are perpendicular, but in rear the earth bank slopes away more or less gradually. At the foot of the main rampart itself there is a narrower but deeper moat, which could be filled to the brim by letting in the water from one of the two lakes just outside the town on the south-east. Ordinarily the outer moat is dry, save for seepage water which forms ponds here and there. In some respects the defences may be likened to a trench position, the moat taking the place of the wire entanglements, the detached bastions that of the outposts, and the inner ramparts serving as the main line of resistance. The ''lofty islets'' were indeed strongly garrisoned as outposts by German machine-gunners and snipers.

Of the three roads which enter Le Quesnoy, one comes from the railway station on the east, one from Orsinval on the north, and one from Jolimetz and the Mormal Forest on the south-east. Roads from other directions junction with these as they approach the town, and there is no gate on the western side.

PART 2.—THE CAPTURE OF LE QUESNOY, NOVEMBER 4TH, 1918.

Condition of the enemy—Opening of the Battle of the Sambre—Preliminary attack: Valenciennes taken—Main attack, November 4th—Conditions—Task of New Zealand Division—New Zealand Rifle Brigade orders for the capture of Le Quesnoy—Attack opens 5.30 a.m.—1st, 4th and 2nd Battalions clear the railway and reach the first objective—3rd Battalion companies pass through the 1st and gain the second objective south of the town—3rd Battalion advances to the final objective—1st Auckland from the north links up—Le Quesnoy completely encircled, 9.30 a.m.—Repeated attempts to enter the town, 3rd Battalion from the east, 2nd Battalion from the north, 4th Battalion from the west—4th Battalion's assault successful—The rampart scaled at 4.15 p.m.—Le Quesnoy mopped up.

The cumulative effect of the heavy blows that had been rained upon the enemy in rapid succession was now becoming more and more apparent in the lowered morale of his fighting men. His losses in men and material had been huge. Turkey and Bulgaria had capitulated, and the collapse of Austria was daily expected. Germany was undoubtedly beaten, and it only remained to strike such a blow at a vital centre as should prevent the enemy from shortening his lines and protracting the struggle over the winter.

In our position before Le Quesnoy we were fifteen miles almost due west of the great railway centre of Maubeuge, which, it will be remembered, was the main objective of the British offensive. The city of Valenciennes, however, still in German hands, lay nine miles north-west of Le Quesnoy, and its capture was a necessary preliminary to the continuance of the main British attack. On November 1st, therefore, the Third Army delivered an assault on six miles of the enemy's front south of Valenciennes, and made such a successful advance that during the second day of the fighting the Canadian Corps of the First Army without great difficulty took the city and made progress beyond it. Thus began the series of engagements officially styled the Battle of the Sambre.*

On various sections of the front there were signs of approaching enemy withdrawal, but our preparations for a decisive attack were complete, and the blow fell on the morning of November 4th, when the Fourth, Third and First Armies delivered an assault on a thirty-mile front from Oisy to Valenciennes.

"The nature of the country across which our advance was to be made was most difficult. In the south, the River Sambre had to be crossed almost at the outset. In the centre, the great Forest of Mormal, though much depleted by German wood-cutting, still presented a formidable obstacle. In the north, the fortified town of Le Quesnoy, together with several streams which cut across the line of our advance, offered frequent opportunities for successful defence. On the other hand, our troops had never been so confident of victory or so assured of their own superiority."†

The task of the New Zealand Division was to envelop the town of Le Quesnoy and carry the line forward a total distance of five and a half miles on a frontage of 3,000 yards. The capture and mopping-up of the town was allotted to the New Zealand Rifle Brigade, the advance beyond being entrusted to the 1st Brigade. On our right we had the 37th Division, and on our left the 62nd. The 1st Brigade assembled in rear by Beaudignies, to pass through as the attack developed. As this proved to be our last fight, the Brigade orders for the attack are here recorded in detail.‡

---

*The canalized Sambre River leaves the valley of the Oise near Longchamps, about twenty miles south of Le Cateau. It takes a winding course to the north until it approaches the latter town, where it turns north-east, passing behind the Mormal Forest, and so on through Maubeuge.

†Sir Douglas Haig's Despatches.

‡The various task-maps referred to are not reproduced.

3RD NEW ZEALAND (RIFLE) BRIGADE.

Order No. 197.

Ref. Maps:
Sheet 51A, S.E.
Sheet 51, S.W.

Headquarters,
2nd November, 1918.

1. The Fourth, Third and First Armies are resuming the advance on November the 4th. ZERO HOUR will be 05.30 hours, November 4th.

2. The New Zealand Division, in conjunction with the 37th Division (on the right) and the 62nd Division (on the left), will attack and establish itself on the line FRANC A LOUER (M.36.a.)–HERBIGNIES–TOUS VENTS (M.24.a.) and, if opportunity offers, will exploit success Eastwards through the FORET DE MORMAL towards the SAMBRE RIVER.

3. (a) Objectives and boundaries will be as shown on the attached Map "A."

(b) The town of LE QUESNOY will not be attacked, but troops moving North and South of it to the BLUE DOTTED and GREEN LINES will form a flank to encircle the RAMPARTS, which will be screened by smoke.

4. The attack will be carried out by the 3rd New Zealand (Rifle) Brigade Group, on the right, and the 1st New Zealand Infantry Brigade Group, on the left.

Battalion tasks are as shown on attached Map "A."

The attack will be carried out in five phases as under:—

(a) PHASE 1.

The 3rd New Zealand (Rifle) Brigade Group will attack at ZERO and capture the BLUE LINE. The timing of the advance South of LE QUESNOY will be co-ordinated to conform with that of the 37th Division, viz.:—1st lift, ZERO plus 4 minutes, followed by seven lifts of 100 yards in 4 minutes, then at the rate of 100 yards in 6 minutes. The rate of advance North of LE QUESNOY will be for 3 lifts of 100 yards in 3 minutes, and then at the rate of 100 yards in 4 minutes. After reaching the Protective Line for the BLUE LINE, the barrage will search the RAMPARTS of LE QUESNOY for 15 minutes, and then cease on the West and Northwest faces while patrols push forward to ascertain if the town is still occupied; if patrols are unable to penetrate the RAMPARTS, smoke will be fired intermittently from P bombs and No. 36 Rifle Grenades from ZERO plus 60 minutes until ZERO plus 180 minutes.

(b) PHASE 2.

The 3rd Battalion, N.Z.R.B., will advance from the BLUE LINE South of LE QUESNOY to the DOTTED BLUE LINE, in conjunction with the 37th Division, at ZERO plus 119 minutes.

Troops will be on the BLUE LINE by ZERO plus 100 minutes.

Rate of barrage, 100 yards in 6 minutes.

The 1st Battalion, N.Z.R.B., will, immediately after the advance to the DOTTED BLUE LINE, take over the frontage facing towards LE QUESNOY from R.36.a.7.2. to M.31.b.7.6.

The 1st New Zealand Infantry Brigade Group will pass one battalion through troops of the 62nd Division and 3rd N.Z. (Rifle) Brigade Group, on the front R.18.c.2.0.-R.18.a.0.0., at ZERO plus 141 minutes, and, in conjunction with the 62nd Division, will advance and establish itself on the DOTTED BLUE LINE, forming a flank facing LE QUESNOY as it progresses.

Rate of barrage, 100 yards in 3 minutes.

For the purposes of this operation the Inter-Divisional boundary will run from R.18.a.00.00. to M.14.d.20.00.

A smoke screen will be put down on the line R.24.a.8.0.-M.20.c.3.2.-M.20.d.5.3. to cover this advance.

(c) PHASE 3.

The 3rd Battalion, N.Z.R.B., will continue the advance from the DOTTED BLUE LINE to the GREEN LINE, in conjunction with the 37th Division, at ZERO plus 197 minutes, at the rate of 100 yards in 6 minutes, until its right reaches the GREEN LINE, when it will swing up to the GREEN LINE, the rate of the barrage on the left conforming with the lifts of the barrage covering the 1st New Zealand Infantry Brigade Group.

The 1st N.Z. Infantry Brigade Group will move forward two battalions to advance in conjunction with the 62nd Division, from the DOTTED BLUE LINE, at ZERO plus 206 minutes, to the GREEN LINE. The barrage will move at the rate of 100 yards in 3 minutes, and will pick up the barrage covering the 3rd N.Z. (Rifle) Brigade Group at the corner of the Lake, M.26.c.65.80.

Junction between the 1st N.Z. Infantry Brigade and the 3rd New Zealand (Rifle) Brigade will be effected at Cross Roads M.26.d.1.9. and at M.27.c.1.5.

On reaching the GREEN LINE, the 1st New Zealand Infantry Brigade will extend its right flank to the Southern Divisional boundary in readiness to continue the advance; troops may be moved South of LE QUESNOY for this purpose if desired.

(d) PHASE 4.

The 1st New Zealand Infantry Brigade Group will, at ZERO plus 290 minutes, continue the advance from the GREEN LINE to the RED LINE, under a barrage of all available artillery, moving at the rate of 100 yards in 3 minutes.

This barrage will die out on reaching the limit of the range of the guns, and the advance will be continued without a barrage, but supported by Forward Sections or Batteries.

The 3rd New Zealand (Rifle) Brigade will mop up LE QUESNOY.

(e) PHASE 5.

Should enemy resistance weaken on reaching the RED LINE, patrols will be pushed forward to secure the DOTTED RED LINE, whence the 2nd New Zealand Infantry Brigade Group from Divisional Reserve will continue the advance.

Should opposition be met with, a definite line will be established by the 1st New Zealand Infantry Brigade Group, and artillery brought forward preparatory to an attack by the 2nd New Zealand Infantry Brigade Group during the afternoon.

5. (a) The attack will be carried out under a Field Artillery barrage, for which barrage-maps and instructions will be issued separately.

(b) The IVth Corps Heavy Artillery are co-operating in the attack by bombardment on special points to be notified later.

(c) One Forward Section, Field Artillery, will accompany the 3rd Battalion, N.Z.R.B., going forward to the GREEN LINE. (This section will be supported as soon as possible by batteries and brigades which will be moved forward on completion of their barrage tasks.)

(d) The attack on the BLUE LINE will be carried out covered by twelve 6-inch Medium Trench Mortars and two batteries of Light Trench Mortars, the 2nd New Zealand L.T.M. Battery having been placed at the disposal of the 3rd New Zealand (Rifle) Brigade Group for this purpose.

Tasks: 2 guns, 3rd L.T.M. Battery, will be attached to the 3rd Battalion, N.Z.R.B., and will report at 3rd Battalion Headquarters at 17.00, 3rd November. The 3rd Battalion, N.Z.R.B., will detail two carriers to accompany each gun.

Tasks of remainder of 2nd and 3rd New Zealand L.T.M. Batteries and "X" and "Y" Medium T.M. Batteries are as shown on attached Map "B."

Barrages of M.T.M.'s and L.T.M.'s will conform to and keep 300 and 100 yards respectively in advance of the Field Artillery barrage.

The 3rd New Zealand L.T.M. Battery will, in addition, detail the following to accompany Battalions after completion of the barrage task:—

    1st Battalion, N.Z.R.B., 2 guns.
    4th Battalion, N.Z.R.B., 1 gun.
    2nd Battalion, N.Z.R.B., 2 guns.

6. The advance of the 1st Battalion, N.Z.R.B., will be covered by the OTAGO Machine Gun Company, opening on line R.35.c.6.6.–R.29.c.6.6., conforming to the artillery barrage to full range, and then ceasing, except those guns covering Square R.30., which will place a barrage on the Southern outskirts of LE QUESNOY.

Upon completion of the barrage tasks the O.C. Otago M.G. Company will place 1 section at the disposal of the O.C. 3rd Battalion, N.Z.R.B., to accompany the battalion in its advance to the GREEN LINE.

The advance of the 2nd Battalion, N.Z.R.B., will be covered by a barrage by the AUCKLAND Machine Gun Company, which will open on line R.23.d.00.70.–R.17.d.00.60, conforming to the artillery barrage to full range, and then ceasing.

In addition, two sections (8 guns) of the CANTERBURY Machine Gun Company will carry out the special task of enfilading the streets and RAMPARTS of LE QUESNOY from ZERO to ZERO plus 30 minutes.

On conclusion of the above tasks, the AUCKLAND Machine Gun Company will be placed at the disposal of the 1st N.Z. Infantry Brigade Group, and the two sections CANTERBURY Machine Gun Company will rejoin the 2nd N.Z. Infantry Brigade Group.

7. (a) "Q" Special Company, R.E., is arranging to project oil drums on to the RAMPARTS of LE QUESNOY at ZERO hour.

(b) No. 5 Special Company, R.E., is arranging to fire smoke on to:—

    1. R.29.d.0.9., from ZERO plus 15 minutes to ZERO plus 35 minutes, and from ZERO plus 110 minutes to ZERO plus 140 minutes.

    2. R.23.d.4.2., from ZERO to ZERO plus 20 minutes.

8. The C.R.E., New Zealand Division, will arrange for the following:—
> (a) A proportion of N.Z.E. and Tunnellers to investigate for mines, etc., in LE QUESNOY. A party of 1 N.C.O. and 6 Sappers will be attached from the 3rd Field Company, N.Z.E., to each of the 2nd and 4th Battalions for this purpose.
> (b) A similar party to work in the area East of LE QUESNOY.
> (c) Field Companies, N.Z.E., and Pioneers (less parties detailed above) to be concentrated in the vicinity of BEAUDIGNIES by ZERO plus 2 hours, in readiness to commence work on Roads and Bridges as soon as the situation permits.
> An Officer will be detailed to keep touch with the situation at Headquarters, 3rd New Zealand (Rifle) Brigade.
> (d) A special party to prepare crossings for Field Artillery over the Railway in R.35.c.

9. For the above operations the 3rd New Zealand (Rifle) Brigade Group will be constituted as follows:—
> 3rd New Zealand (Rifle) Bde.
> Otago Machine Gun Company.
> 2 sections O.M.R.
> Detachment N.Z.E. and Tunnellers.

10. The 59th Squadron, R.A.F., is arranging for a Contact Aeroplane at the following hours:—
> ZERO plus 110 minutes; ZERO plus 170 minutes; ZERO plus 270 minutes; and at intervals of 2 hours afterwards.
> A counter-attack machine will also be in the air during the hours of daylight.

11. Liaison with 37th Division will be established at Road on BLUE LINE, M.31.d.

12. Watches will be synchronized on November 3rd at Headquarters, 3rd New Zealand (Rifle) Brigade, X.2.a. central, at 16.00 hours.

13. Battle Headquarters will be as follows:—
> Brigade Headquarters: R.28.c.3.6.
> 1st Battalion, N.Z.R.B.: R.28.c.7.4.
> 2nd Battalion, N.Z.R.B.: R.16.d.6.0.
> 3rd Battalion, N.Z.R.B.: M.31.b.7.5.
> 4th Battalion, N.Z.R.B.: R.22.d.30.75.

14. Brigade Headquarters will close at present location at 22.00 hours on the 3rd November, and re-open at FME du FORT MARTIN, R.28.c.3.6., at the same hour.

15. The strictest measures will be taken to maintain secrecy.

All movements of troops and dumping of ammunition will take place in darkness. There will be no increase or decrease of artillery fire.

16. ACKNOWLEDGE.

D. E. BREMNER, Major.
Brigade Major.

Issued at 23.00 through Signals:

	Copy No.		Copy No.
Brigadier	1	63rd Inf. Brigade	17
1st Bn., N.Z.R.B.	2	187th Inf. Brigade	18
2nd Bn., N.Z.R.B.	3	1st N.Z. Inf. Bde.	19
3rd Bn., N.Z.R.B.	4	2nd N.Z. Inf. Bde.	20
4th Bn., N.Z.R.B.	5	C.R.A., N.Z. Divn.	21
3rd L.T.M. Batt.	6	C.R.E., N.Z. Divn.	22
2nd L.T.M, Batt.	7	1st Bde., N.Z.F.A.	23
Otago M.G. Coy.	8	3rd Bde., N.Z.F.A.	24
Auckland M.G. Coy.	9	2nd (A) Bde., N.Z.F.A.	25
Canterbury M.G. Coy.	10	Signals	26
"X" M.T.M. Batt.	11	Intelligence Officer	27
"Y" M.T.M. Batt.	12	Staff Captain	28
N.Z. M.G. Bn.	13	Liaison Officers	29, 30
3rd Field Coy., N.Z.E.	14	War Diary	31/33
New Zealand Division	15, 16	File	34

Briefly stated, the operation was to be conducted as follows. The three battalions in the line would advance simultaneously and capture the railway line running roughly parallel with their front. This would bring the 4th Battalion, in the centre, to its appointed sector of the first objective, its front exactly corresponding in length to the width of the town and earthworks. The two flank battalions had much more to do before their first phase would be completed. The 1st Battalion, to the south, would pivot on its left flank near the railway, bringing up its right to the Landrecies Road, so covering the town from the south-west. The stiffest task confronted the troops of the 2nd Battalion, on the left, for, swinging on their right flank, they had to clear up, not only the railway triangle of evil fame, but also an area of similar shape and size north of the main railway, and including a stretch of the Orsinval Road. This would bring them facing the town from the northwest. Thus half the encircling operation would be completed.

Now the 3rd Battalion, coming forward, would pass through the right of the 1st and continue the advance eastwards eventually to the Green Line, moving, of course, in co-operation with the troops of the southern Division, first with the 13th Rifles, and then with the 1st Essex. To the north of the town a battalion of the 1st Brigade, starting about half an hour later than the 3rd Battalion, would pass through the left of our 2nd Battalion there, swing round and close in near the railway on the north-east. Fresh troops of the 1st Brigade would pass through to the Green Line, take over the whole of the Divisional front, and continue the advance. This would leave our 3rd Battalion free to join with the rest of the Brigade in the task of mopping-up Le Quesnoy, which by this time would be isolated and completely enveloped. Excellent artillery support was provided. The advance was to be covered by a creeping field artillery barrage of a density of one gun to thirty yards, but no artillery fire was to be directed on the buildings of the town.* Twelve light and twelve medium trench mortars would fire on selected targets from zero hour, ceasing when the troops approached the limits of trench mortar range. In addition, heavy artillery would bombard special points of resistance eastward of the town; and three hundred drums of burning oil were to be projected on to the western outworks at zero. We were also to have a fine machine-gun barrage. Two machine-gun companies were to put down a creeping barrage covering the advance of the two flank battalions at a density of one gun to sixty yards of frontage; and an additional eight Vickers guns would direct their fire on the principal streets of the town, and then lift for a considerable time to the eastern exits to prevent the garrison from running away.

As the Brigade was, as we have seen, considerably under strength, companies were, for the forthcoming operation, organized on a three-platoon basis, the platoons averaging twenty-eight bayonets. It was arranged that companies should

---

*During the whole period of our activity about Le Quesnoy, every care was taken, as far as was possible, to avoid causing any damage to the houses or injury to the civilian population of the town. The burning, some two or three days before the 4th, of a building with a tall tower from which our line could be overlooked, was a mysterious occurrence of which the records give no explanation.

attack with two platoons in line and one in support, the platoons advancing with three sections in line, extended to four paces, with one section in support.

All adjustments in the line were completed in good time during the evening of November 3rd. Enemy shelling was normal except on the northern battalion sector, where it repeatedly became intense. Here eleven men of a platoon of the 2nd Battalion moving into the line were killed by one shell. A hot meal was served during the early hours of the 4th. The rain, which had come on at 6 o'clock on the previous evening, ceased at 3 a.m., and there was every promise of favourable weather. The usual patrols were out during the night, and their reports showed that there had been no diminution in the enemy's strength and activity. Half an hour before zero our forward posts were withdrawn clear of the barrage line, swords were fixed, the final muttered orders and cautions given, and, with spirits high, our men awaited the signal to advance.

At 5.30 a.m. there burst forth the first part of our reply to the sackful of peace propaganda dropped on our lines from a German aeroplane on the previous afternoon. This took the form of a deafening crash of artillery and an opening barrage, almost perfect in density and alignment, falling between us and the railway. Immediately after the commencement of the artillery fire a sheet of flame rushed skywards from behind the waiting troops, and following a pause during which a mighty rushing noise seemed to drown all other sounds, huge flames burst from hundreds of points beyond the railway and about the outworks of the town. This was the special burning-oil bombardment which, though it resulted in little material damage to the enemy's position or to his men, had, nevertheless, a most important moral effect on both attackers and defenders.*

After resting on its first position for three minutes the barrage passed on with its appointed lifts, and our leading

---

*The oildrums were fired each from a separate tube fixed in the ground at the required angle, the projecting charge being exploded electrically. The same method was employed when a concentrated discharge of gas was required on a particular spot at some considerable distance within the enemy's line, as, for example, when Becelaere was so bombarded during the 2nd Brigade's attack on Polderhoek Chateau in December of 1917.

sections followed closely to the assault of the enemy's front line along the embankment.

In the 1st Battalion's sector two companies led, "A" (2nd Lieut. V. G. Hunter) on the right, and "B" (Capt. E. A. Harding) on the left. The railway was not carried without considerable fighting, but, for the most part, the positions of the posts on the railway were well known, the plans had made special provision for dealing with each, and on the whole there was no undue delay in the advance of the forward companies. Emergencies were well handled. Near the centre, Corporal M. J. Mulvaney was in charge of a Lewis gun section. His own advance was proceeding satisfactorily, but he discovered a machine-gun firing across the front of the company on his right, and at once took action to remove the obstruction. Directing the fire of his men upon the position, he himself worked round to a flank and presently rushed it, capturing four prisoners. A similar fine piece of work stands to the credit of Sergeant R. L. Fergusson, whose whole company was being held up by a machine-gun firing from a flank.

Soon the railway was passed, and, as "A" and "B" moved forward again, "C" Company (2nd Lieut. L. M. Blyth) advanced to complete the mopping-up of the railway and establish itself there as battalion reserve. As "C" Company approached the position, a machine-gun that had not been discovered by the leading companies suddenly burst into activity, and for some time succeeded in holding up one of the platoons. This pressure, however, was relieved by the fearless action of one man, Rifleman E. W. Hallett, who with a Lewis gun moved on alone, fired a long burst upon the post at close quarters, and then, dropping his gun, dashed in and captured the whole of the crew at the point of the revolver. The only German who fell to his weapon was one who at this moment blundered into the post with his rifle at the ready and made no response to the usual demand. There was little other opposition during the process of clearing up the line generally, and the company was soon disposed in readiness for further action as required.

"B" Company, passing rapidly through the extensive orchard immediately beyond the railway, cleared out the machine-gun nests in the whole of that area, and dug in along the forward hedges. Part of the company thus faced Le

ORDER OF BATTLE—LE QUESNOY, NOVEMBER 4, 1918.

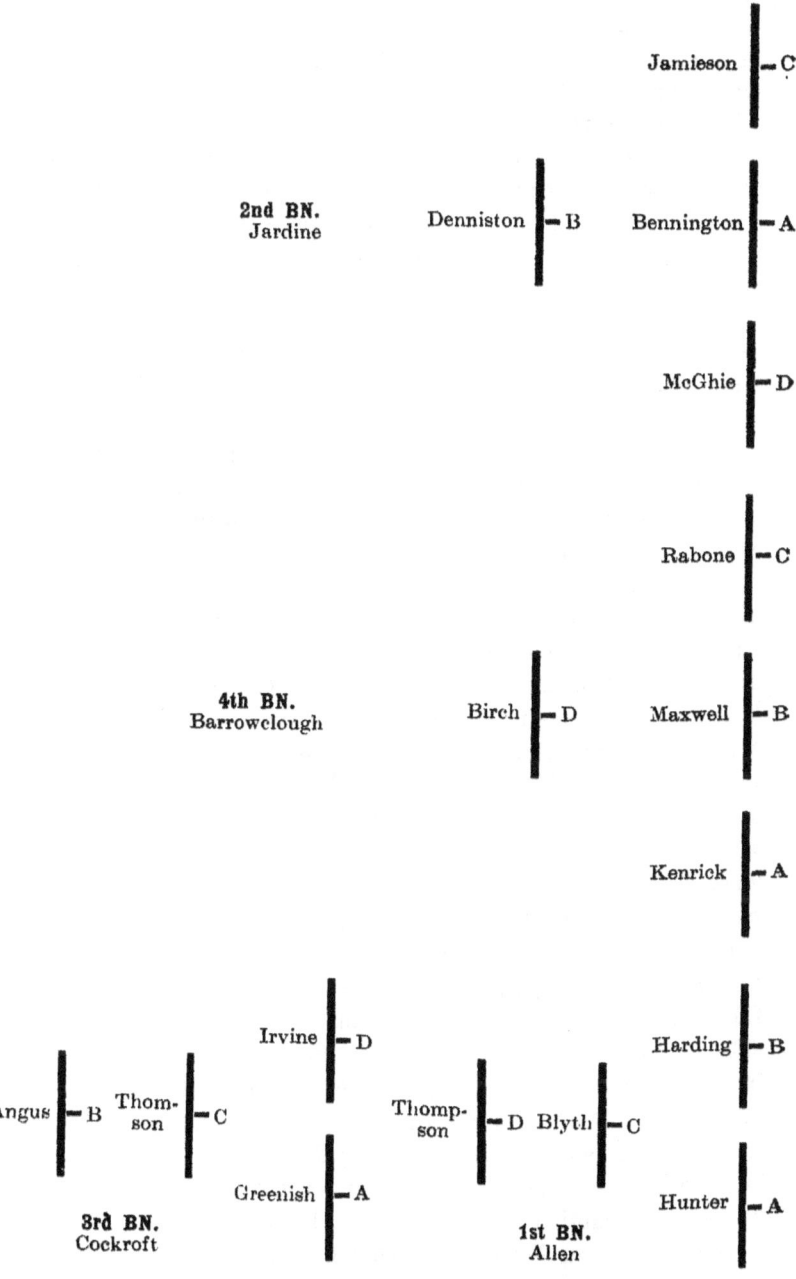

Quesnoy and part was ready to meet any counter-attack from the south-east. Meanwhile, "A" Company, skirting the southern edge of the orchard, was moving eastward to capture a section of the Ghissignies Road beyond the Drill Ground. Here considerable trouble was experienced in dealing with machine-guns in the house at the road-fork and in the two groups of orchards along the main road, but the task was accomplished with satisfactory speed and the company consolidated its position along the hedges facing south-east.

It was now the turn of "D" Company (Lieut. H. J. Thompson), whose immediate objective was the remainder of the battalion's portion of the Blue Line between the Ghissignies and Louvignies Roads. Moving through "A" Company's positions in the small orchards, "D" Company advanced across the open country beyond. As soon as the leading platoons emerged from the cover of the hedges, they came under heavy fire from machine-guns operating at close range. It was a steady, sweeping fire, in the face of which the advance was continued with great difficulty; and, mingled with the rattle of the machine-guns, the crack and boom of the guns, and the crash of bursting shells, was a peculiar "clink-clink," the nature of which was altogether new and mysterious. The morning mist, combined with the smoke of the barrage, made it impossible to see more than a few yards ahead; but if satisfactory progress were to be made it was imperative that the troublesome machine-guns should be bombed and silenced. The situation was ably handled by the company commander, who, getting his men down into such poor cover as existed, went forward himself to reconnoitre. His investigations revealed the fact that the fire was directed from a number of houses standing close together on the far side of the Louvignies Road, just beyond which our barrage was then falling, and that in the neighbouring orchard was a considerable number of the enemy. A few moments sufficed to take in the details of the situation and to formulate plans for dealing with it. While the posts in the houses were engaged from the front, a Lewis gun section under Rifleman J. H. Mason got into position on the flank, and under cover of their fire a platoon commanded by 2nd Lieut. J. L. Brown worked round to the rear of the houses. Peering through the back door of the first of these, 2nd Lieut. Brown discovered two Germans with a machine-gun busily firing through a hole in the wall. These he promptly despatched, and the gun being silenced, a loud chattering revealed the presence of a number of the enemy in the cellar beneath. Orders to come up not being obeyed, a smoke-bomb was thrown down and the platoon passed on to deal with the remaining houses. No fewer than four posts, each equipped with a heavy machine-gun, were cleared from this row of buildings. An interesting experience now fell to the lot of Rifleman Mason and his companions on the flank. In the intervals of their firing they could still distinguish that curious and mystifying clinking sound, but whether the cause of it, whatever it might be, were near or distant, it was impossible to determine. Suddenly the fog lifted, and from the ditch by the roadside where they had taken up their position they saw, not ten yards away, a light field gun standing out in the open and being served and fired with great rapidity. But Mason's men were discovered also, and in a twinkling the gun was trained upon them. Mason was too quick for his opponents, however, and a burst from his Lewis gun settled the contest. Some little distance along the road a second field gun was still in action, the gunners all unconscious of the fate that had befallen their friends. Upon these Mason moved stealthily until a favourable point was reached, and, bringing his Lewis gun to bear once more, laid the whole crew low. In the clearing of this position about the road, a remarkably fine achievement in which Company Sergeant-Major E. Olsen played a distinguished part, no fewer than forty unwounded prisoners were taken; and the successful issue enabled the company to complete with little further trouble the capture of the whole of its objective on the Blue Line.

It was now about 7 a.m. Half an hour later a flank patrol from the reserve company, working southwards along the railway into the area of the 37th Division to establish touch, made the discovery that our neighbours had either been held up or had left an extensive gap. Arrived at the first bend, they were startled to see a body of the enemy moving up the line towards them with the apparent intention of counter-attacking from the flank. Word was at once got back to

The Front Line Before Le Quesnoy.

A Reserve Company on the Railway, November 4th.

The Inner Ramparts of Le Quesnoy.

The Ramparts at another Point.

MAJOR H. E. BARROWCLOUGH,
D.S.O., M.C.

THE 4TH BATTALION IN THE SQUARE OF LE QUESNOY: A WET PARADE.

PRISONERS FROM ABOUT LE QUESNOY.

THE NEW ZEALAND FLAG PRESENTED TO LE QUESNOY.

the company commander, who despatched a platoon under 2nd Lieut. D. C. Guthrie to deal with the situation. Their action was swift, and, thanks largely to the skilful leading of Corporal C. Taylor, who commanded a flank section, the Germans were forced into a position from which they readily surrendered, over 100 prisoners, including five officers, being sent back, and two more machine-guns added to the number already taken. In view of further possibilities of the kind, one of the trench mortars attached to the battalion was now placed on this flank, which was further strengthened by posting there a section of the Otago Machine Gun Company.

The 4th Battalion, in the centre of the brigade front of attack, reached its first objective over the railway without difficulty. The three forward companies were in their normal order from the right, and "D" Company was held in reserve. As soon as the movement of the barrage permitted, patrols worked forward over the narrow stretch of ground between the Blue Line and the western outworks of the town. Streams of machine-gun bullets and even shell-fire from the 77 mm. guns posted on the ramparts, were a sufficient indication that the garrison had no intention of quitting the town, and that our attempts to enter it would be strenuously resisted.

On the left the 2nd Battalion advanced against the railway triangle, which maintained its sinister reputation. The three leading companies were, in order from the right, "D," "A" and "C," under the command, respectively, of Lieuts. J. G. McGhie and F. T. Bennington and Capt. G. R. Jamieson. "B" Company (Lieut. T. H. Denniston) was in reserve, with orders to follow in fairly close touch with the leading companies. The battalion followed the barrage in good order, but on nearing the first railway line the centre company met with disaster. Machine-guns brought enfilade fire to bear upon the leading line, almost annihilating the right platoon. A section from the support platoon worked round to deal with the guns; and when the remaining sections were called for to reinforce the front, they too were found to have shared the fate of the forward platoon. Thus, within the first few minutes, this one company had lost more than a third of its strength. In the endeavour to close the gap, Sergeant J. Grubb, of the left platoon, extended his right section and at once proceeded to deal with two machine-gun posts on his immediate front. These he succeeded in silencing, but the advance of the company was still being held up by the enfilading post. Rifleman C. Birch, of the trench mortar battery attached to the battalion, now came up to locate this nest. This done, he brought a Stokes gun to bear upon it and reduced its fire to fitful bursts. With Rifleman W. Ferguson, another of the gun team, he advanced to the position bombarded, took prisoner the whole garrison, consisting of an officer and twenty-seven men, and captured its three guns. By this time, however, Lieut. L. H. Denniston, on observing the disorganization of "A" Company, had brought his reserve company forward, passed through the centre company, joined up with those on the flanks, and pressed on with them towards the objective. The right company also had to fight hard to gain ground and, in rooting out the many machine-gun posts on the nearer railway line, suffered somewhat heavy casualties. Despite the fact that one platoon lost direction almost as soon as the advance commenced, the company reached its goal in good time, and pushed out patrols to the sunken road curving round the outworks of the town. "C" Company, on the left, had first to clear the area about the well-known railway junction and then swing round to complete the advance eastward to the Orsinval–Le Quesnoy Road. Several enemy posts were dealt with in succession, but, fortunately, in nearly every case resistance was so slight that the garrison surrendered on closer approach. Near the extreme left, however, one machine-gun post held out with grim determination. Against the post, Sergeant W. P. McGillan, moving across the open, brought his gun to bear; but under this pressure the garrison, instead of surrendering, retired smartly to a house in rear. McGillan, not to be outdone, followed up as quickly, rushed the house, and bombed the inmates; and when five had been killed the remaining fourteen gave up the contest. Thus the 2nd Battalion, like the others, had secured its objective within the time limit, and all along the Divisional front the Blue Line was securely held. Shortly after the left company had got into position, the troops of the 62nd Division came up and established contact.

The stage was now set for the opening of the second phase of the battle. To the south, the 3rd Battalion troops had left their assembly position just west of the railway in sufficient time to enable them to follow closely in rear of the attacking companies of the 1st Battalion. Some gas-shelling just before the advance made it necessary to wear respirators for some little time, and during the forward movement from the railway the smoke of the barrage rendered the keeping of direction so difficult that compasses had to be used. Lieut.-Col. Allen, of the 1st Battalion, with 2nd Lieut. R. A. Ridley, his intelligence officer, had gone forward to reconnoitre the positions taken up by his companies, but, bearing away too much to the south, he found himself slightly beyond the flank of his line. Here the two almost ran into some fifty Germans, who promptly opened fire from the cover of a hedge, and they dropped into a shell-hole to discuss their predicament. The possibility of a successful charge was being considered, but at the crucial moment a company of the 3rd Battalion reached the position. These, coming under a brisk fire, also lay down. One of the men, however, immediately afterwards rose to his feet and moved calmly forward with his pipe in his mouth and his rifle at the "ready." Alternately raising and lowering his rifle as though stalking a rabbit, he advanced to the hedge, and to this one rifleman the whole party surrendered.* The incident caused but a few moments' delay, and in good time the 3rd Battalion was in position on the Blue Line and ready to commence its advance. "A" Company (Capt. F. E. Greenish) was on the right, and "D" Company, plus two platoons of "B" (Lieut. J. H. Irvine) on the left; "C" Company (Capt. A. Thomson) in support, and "B" Company, less two platoons (Lieut. A. J. C. Angus), in reserve.

At 7.29 a.m., covered by a good barrage, the battalion advanced to the capture of the Dotted Blue Line, which lay across the middle of a stretch of country 1,000 yards deep, almost entirely covered with small orchards, and intersected by a maze of hedges. Hardly had the forward line moved than an adventure befell this battalion, strangely similar to that which at the same moment was lending interest to the otherwise colourless task of the 1st Battalion's reserve company on the railway. Major Cockroft, with his intelligence

---

*Lieut.-Col. Allen was shortly afterwards wounded, and Capt. E. A. Harding assumed command of the 1st Battalion.

officer, 2nd Lieut. E. C. Drummond, and two runners and a signaller, was in a forward position awaiting progress reports momentarily expected from the companies ahead, when out of the smoke there appeared a strong party moving, not eastwards, but northwards from the area of the Division on our right. It soon became clear that they were part of a hostile force that had been overlooked by our neighbours. The situation was awkward alike for Major Cockroft and his party and for the reserve company now coming forward over ground which they naturally expected to be clear. Decision was quickly made, however, and at a word our headquarters' party opened out fan-wise and charged the Germans, who, dumbfounded by the suddenness of the attack, yielded without a struggle. One of their machine-gunners had his gun trained, but, apparently because no order came, he did not open fire. This "bag" of prisoners numbered eighty men and four officers, and they had with them one of our 1st Battalion runners, who, on his way back to Brigade Headquarters with a situation report, had lost direction and had fallen into their hands.

The short advance to the Dotted Blue Line was accomplished without great difficulty, and there now ensued a wait to allow for the completion of the 1st Brigade's more extensive movement round the north of the town in continuation of our 2nd Battalion's line. Promptly at the appointed time, 8.47 a.m., the three forward companies of the 3rd Battalion advanced again towards the Green Line some 1,500 yards to the eastward. All efforts to secure touch with the troops of the 37th Division having failed, the support company watched the flank in case it should prove to be exposed. Considerable resistance was met with in the remaining stretch of orchard land. "A" Company, on the right, encountered particularly heavy machine-gun fire from the Chateau Montout and the high ground beyond. The Chateau position was, however, skilfully enveloped by the two platoons under Capt. Greenish's personal direction, and the momentary check was overcome. Both companies now pushed forward to the Jolimetz Road, sweeping up some posts in the hedges on the way. Beyond the road the country was more open, with awkward glacis-like slopes on the hilly, ploughed land. By this time, too, the barrage, hitherto good, had thinned out considerably, and it was clear, from the volume of machine-gun fire coming from the direction of Jolimetz, that the right flank was "in the air." After a brief pause about the road, during which Lieut. Irvine disposed his two attached platoons across the south-eastern exit of Le Quesnoy to provide against a possible sortie against the rear of his company, the advance was continued in short rushes across the open country. Here the main difficulty was to locate the machine-gun posts, for, once marked down, they were dealt with promptly enough, and much had to be left to good leadership in the various sections. Corporal W. Linton accomplished a brilliant feat with his Lewis gun team, outflanking and capturing a strong post containing two machine-guns. At another point Rifleman J. Currie, who was in charge of the battalion scouts, on his own initiative took forward three of his men and rushed an awkward nest, killing twelve of the garrison and capturing three guns. Again, Rifleman N. Coop, the No. 1 of a Lewis gun team, despairing of otherwise locating a troublesome machine-gun, moved out into the open to draw the fire upon himself, and the plan worked so successfully that his No. 2, Rifleman Pedersen, was able to bring such a burst of fire upon the enemy as effectually to silence the gun. On the extreme right of the line the flank platoon of "A" Company swung out beyond the boundary line and dealt with the enfilading gun down the Jolimetz Road, thus enabling the company to hasten its advance. Almost immediately it was confronted by posts about the Maison Goffart. The sight of a few German helmets here led to an exciting chase by the company runners, who, however, proved less fleet of foot than their quarry. The house itself was found to be unoccupied, but two machine-gun posts in the vicinity held out for some time. They were eventually cleared by parties under Sergeants J. T. V. Snowden and J. H. Williams, but not before both these leaders had been wounded. The resistance thus smartly overcome, "A" Company swept onwards and established itself on the final objective. "D" Company had a somewhat greater distance to cover, and at one stage was temporarily held up by the sweeping fire from machine-guns concealed in a dip on the far side of an extensive ploughed field. These had to be dealt with by a flanking movement by two sections sent round the left through the cover afforded by the orchards. Noting "D" Company's delay, Capt. Thomson promptly took his company forward from the support position and prolonged "A" Company's line towards the left, thus enabling Irvine's men, though still under heavy fire from the high ground about the railway, to move forward with greater freedom, and presently "D" Company, by a final rush, completed the capture of the Green Line. Touch on the left was soon afterwards made by troops of the 1st Brigade, but connection with the 1st Essex on our right was not secured for some time. Apparently, maintenance of direction had been difficult; a tank, sent up to assist the Essex men in rooting out machine-gun nests about Jolimetz, even went so far astray as to crash its way into the garden of the Maison Goffart, where our right company commander was calmly writing his situation report after the taking of the objective. Two of our battalion runners, Riflemen J. Jenkins and W. A. Craven, were sent out to locate the nearest troops. This they were unable to do, but instead they encountered fire from an enemy machine-gun. Their errand was not entirely fruitless, however, for they attacked the post, killed some of the gunners, and brought back to battalion headquarters the four survivors and their gun.

Meanwhile, as the advance to the Green Line progressed, "B" Company worked up to its position close in to Le Quesnoy, mopping up a triangle of considerable area in doing so. Linking up with the two platoons previously detached, it was finally established astride the Jolimetz Road leading into the town, with posts close· up to the twin lakes south-east of the outworks, and the centre opposite the Landrecies Gate. On the right, the troops of this company were in touch with 1st Auckland, and on their own left they joined up with the right of "D" Company of the 1st Battalion, which had also moved up to this general inner line and was facing the town.

Thus, by 9.30 a.m., four hours after the opening of the battle, Le Quesnoy was completely and securely invested. The 1st Brigade now extended to the right, and at 10.20 a.m. continued the advance along the whole Divisional front, the next objective being the Red Line, about a mile and a half to the east.

Our task, however, was not yet finished. The orders read: "The New Zealand Rifle Brigade will mop up Le Quesnoy," but Le Quesnoy was objecting strongly to being mopped up; as our men put it, the garrison "hadn't got the war news up to date." The 1st Battalion's positions were from 500 to 800 yards from the outer bank of the moat, and every attempt to trickle men across the intervening ground, utterly devoid of cover, was at once frustrated by heavy machine-gun fire. The line of the 3rd Battalion was 700 yards away, and there was no means of approach but by the single main road between the two lakes. Patrols, hoping against hope, repeatedly endeavoured to negotiate this passage, only to be caught in the withering fire from the machine-gun which guarded it. One of the earliest of these, consisting of two men, worked its way through the outer gate and, creeping from doorway to doorway of the houses that lined the causeway on either side, moved towards the main entrance of the town. In one of these houses they came upon a medical officer holding a sick-parade, some forty or fifty Germans being present under inspection. The whole party was captured and was being brought back to our lines, when from the inner walls machine-gun fire opened on friend and foe alike. Both our men were wounded. One with a broken leg took shelter in a house, while the other succeeded in getting back with his report. Persuasion was tried with no better result. Soon after 10 a.m., when the town was completely encircled and the troops of the 1st Brigade were commencing their triumphant march eastward towards the Mormal Forest, "B" Company sent a German officer into Le Quesnoy with an oral message explaining the position and advising instant surrender, but there was no diminution in the fire from the walls, and the messenger did not return. Again, at 3 p.m., two other prisoners were sent in with a written message to the Commandant. Whether or not the message was actually delivered is not known, but the prisoners returned with the information that though the men realized the hopelessness of the situation and were willing to give in, the officers were obstinate and refused to yield. No better response was made to the offer of higher authorities, who, half an hour earlier, had sent over an aeroplane to drop the following message within the walls:—

"To the Commandant of the Garrison of Le Quesnoy:

"The position of Le Quesnoy is now completely surrounded. Our troops are far east of the town. You are therefore requested to surrender with your garrison. The garrison will be treated as honourable prisoners of war.

"The Commander of the
"British Troops."

Closer approach had been made by the 2nd Battalion on the north. All three companies had pushed patrols forward into the sunken road close up to the moat. "B" Company, at first in reserve, but now holding the centre of the line, succeeded in getting a patrol of four men across the moat to the outer ramparts at about 8 a.m. Here they held on for a time, but were finally driven back by machine-gun fire, though not before they had taken and thrown down into the moat one of the German guns. The attempt was repeated shortly afterwards by a platoon from the same company, who, covered by a platoon of "D" on the right, forced their way into the moat; but intense fire caught the covering platoon in their exposed position and not only compelled their withdrawal, but also pinned the advanced platoon down till late in the afternoon. At 9.30 a.m. the Factory, where the enemy, now within our lines, had stubbornly held out since daybreak, was cleared, yielding seventy-five prisoners. Half an hour later, a party from "C" Company, on the left, under 2nd Lieut. J. H. Boles, moved eastward to attempt to approach the ramparts by means of the road-bridge over the railway. The bridge had been mined by the enemy, but the Engineers attached to the battalion, working under heavy and sustained fire, safely withdrew the charges, and Boles and his men seized the bridge and a section of the road beyond. The German machine-gunners, however, had this prominent position well commanded; the fire proved to be too hot, and further forward movement was blocked. At 1 p.m. another small party from this company, under 2nd Lieut. B. Kingdon, secured the Orsinval cross-roads close up to the moat, and a prisoner they held was sent into the town with a demand for surrender. It was now considered possible to rush the northern gate, for the bridge leading to it was found to be intact. All available men were concentrated about the cross-roads for this effort at 1.45 p.m., but, when everything was ready for the assault, the enemy blew up the span nearer the gate. A dash was essayed, however, and one man actually made his way across by means of a plank, reached the gate, and shot one of the garrison, but this forlorn hope was otherwise without result. The hostile machine-gun fire from this quarter continued to be intense, though the effect of the steady fire from our Lewis guns and from the Stokes mortar at the railway triangle was becoming more and more marked. One of the mortars was now brought round to a position opposite the gate, and at 3.30 p.m. fire was opened upon the ramparts on either side. From this moment the hopes of the 2nd Battalion men rose as rapidly as the volume of hostile machine-gun fire diminished; but it was getting late in the day, and the persistent efforts of the 4th Battalion on the western side were beginning to bear fruit.

Our account of the movements of the 4th Battalion left those troops approaching the outer defences of the town after the capture of their section of the railway, "A," "B" and "C" Companies being in the leading line and "D" in reserve along the railway bank. "C" Company (Lieut. C. N. Rabone) on the left succeeded in establishing itself in that sunken road reached later by patrols from the 2nd Battalion, but when the kindly smoke-barrage, under cover of which the company had made this advance, drifted away, the enemy machine-guns so swept the open ground both before and behind them that the men were prevented from making any further movement either forward or backward. Here they were pinned down for the rest of the day, and had to be content with engaging as fully as might be the attention of the enemy troops on the fortifications to their immediate front.

The scouts of "B" Company (Lieut. V. F. Maxwell) in the centre reached the outer edge of the moat, and were followed by Major Barrowclough, who went up to make a personal reconnaissance. As a result of the investigation it was seen that for the time being the best position was this outer bank, and "B" Company was accordingly brought up at once. Smoke and fog were still thick, and the advance was made without much difficulty, the few occupied rifle-pits in the level ground being quickly cleared. The garrison of one post, followed into the moat itself by 2nd Lieut. F. M. Evans and a handful of men, eluded capture by passing in rear of one of the bastions and mounting to the commanding position at the top. On the right, "A" Company (Lieut. H. S. Kenrick) had a longer advance, but presently joined up with "B," 2nd Lieuts. P. A.

Lummis and L. C. L. Averill leading the way and bringing with them a party of seven German machine-gunners whose activities had been delaying the advance of the company. This capture had been neatly effected by the two officers with the assistance of a runner, Rifleman W. E. Lowe, the barrage-smoke enabling them to execute a flanking movement and a final dash without being observed.

"C" Company in the sunken road was now visited, and it was found that beyond the continuance of the holding-attack no further assistance in the general assault could be expected from these troops, for in addition to machine-gun and rifle fire they were now experiencing a smart bombardment from minenwerfer and a 77-mm. gun firing from the walls. Clearly any further advance must be made from the position occupied by "A" and "B" Companies, whose men were enjoying a near view of the obstacles still to be overcome. Before them lay the broad outer moat with its maze of low, intersecting banks and its many bush-crowned "lofty islets"—those disconnected bastions, shaped in some cases like the head of a broad-arrow, in others like the familiar flat-iron; and beyond these again were the deep waters of the inner moat, and finally the sheer forty-foot walls of the main ramparts. Truly the prospect was not cheering, and the problem as to how they might circumvent the machine-gun posts stationed upon all the important high points and ultimately scale the inner defences seemed to bristle with difficulties.

In company with his intelligence officer, 2nd Lieut. Averill, and a runner, Major Barrowclough now set out on a close investigation of the ground between "B" Company's position and the inner wall, the smoke still hanging about the trees on the floor of the moat rendering this movement fairly easy of accomplishment. Two Germans encountered were taken prisoner, and one was persuaded to lead the little party towards a suspected entrance to the town. The route taken, however, wound about so circuitously amongst the criss-crossed walls and banks that suspicion, quite unfounded, as it transpired, was aroused as to the guide's real intentions, and the mission was abandoned. The way back had to be made through heavy shelling which the enemy now directed upon the area, but fortunately his own people in the locality frantically sent up their signal lights for a lengthening of the range, and from that time onward his artillery ceased to give trouble here. At this stage, however, the smoke barrage began to thin out, and the reconnoitring party came under hot machine-gun fire from several quarters.

Major Barrowclough now bethought him of the cork mats and the scaling-ladders that had been provided by the Engineers for the passage of the moat and wall. Fortunately the floats would not be required, but it was certainly possible to put the ladders to immediate use. His conscience pricked him as he recalled that at the preliminary Brigade conference he had lightly scoffed at this provision, and had laughingly put forward a request for a spare copy of "Ivanhoe" so that the ancient mode of assault might be closely studied. For it was just the old-fashioned plan, to be prosecuted with the aid of modern weapons, that was finally decided upon. It was evident that if a general advance were made towards the walls, the attacking troops would inevitably be drawn in between the outlying bastions and enfiladed while meeting fire from the front, and the commanding officer determined to avoid this by capturing these same outworks one by one and making use of them to cover his further advance. This involved a series of frontal attacks on positions presenting to our men sheer faces of masonry from thirty to forty feet high, and to secure a footing on the tops the attackers must needs follow the example of the mediæval men-at-arms and use the scaling-ladders. While the necessary dispositions were being made the ladders were sent for, but it was found that all but one had been destroyed by shell-fire at the opening of the battle. An additional drawback lay in the fact that the one trench mortar attached to the battalion had been similarly put out of action. However, it was decided to carry on and make shift with the means available.

From the moat-bank the top of the nearest island bastion was raked with Lewis gun fire, and at shorter range bombarded with rifle-grenades; and at a given signal a platoon from the centre company, led by 2nd Lieut. F. M. Evans, a dashing young officer who had but recently been commissioned in the field, rushed forward with the ladder. They gained the summit without further opposition, for the garrison had hastily retreated, leaving behind a portion of their machine-gun equipment and a large quantity of ammunition. Evans was anxious to push on, but was not permitted to do so until two neighbouring positions had been similarly captured. This accomplished, he moved with characteristic boldness against the bastion immediately to his front, but, passing beyond with his platoon to take the position from the rear, he lost touch with his company. Barrowclough and a party of men scaled this bastion soon afterwards, but could neither see Evans nor get into touch with him, and no further action could be taken in this direction for fear of firing inadvertently into his platoon. It was afterwards ascertained that Evans and his men had pushed on right up to the inner wall, where, however, they came under such intense cross-fire that they were compelled to take cover in a slight hollow from which they were unable to escape for many hours. Any movement brought upon them a shower of bullets, but Evans, fretting at this inactivity, de-decided to seek a way out. Together with his runner, he wormed his way up to the edge of the hollow, only to be met there by a burst of fire in which this gallant officer and his devoted companion perished.

The uncertainty as to the position of Evans's platoon, together with the increasing activity of the enemy machine-guns and minenwerfer, made it necessary to hold over any further exploitation of the partial success gained at this point. The right company could for the moment do little to assist, and upon a survey of the whole situation it seemed clear that to persist in the endeavour to force an entry was to take risks not altogether justifiable. The noon hour was approaching, and the defenders as well as the attackers knew that the town was practically isolated and must presently fall without direct assault. The battalion had done all that it had been asked to do, and more, and the final task of mopping-up Le Quesnoy would follow in due course. Still, it was a provoking business. Moreover, the officers of the artillery were becoming importunate, for, owing to the general success of the advance they were now anxious to get their guns forward, but all roads in the Divisional area led through or closely skirted Le Quesnoy, and it was useless to attempt to pass while fire poured from the walls. Partly for this reason, and partly out of sheer doggedness, Major Barrowclough determined to renew the attempt to enter the town.

Reconnoitring patrols had as a matter of course continued their activities, those from "A" Company being especially successful; and from information received it was considered probable that success might attend an attempt to penetrate the inner fortifications at a point between the two prominent main bastions on the south-west corner. It had been ascertained that in this locality two of the disconnected bastions lay directly one behind the other, and that, situated behind these again, was a number of comparatively low walls and banks which appeared to form a means of approach to the wall of the inner rampart, as they would afford considerable cover for strong fighting patrols. Movement along this line, from the projecting angle of the moat to the wall itself, meant an advance of nearly three hundred yards against a succession of strong posts having a commanding situation, and covered, further, by machine-gun fire from the two prominent salients of the principal fortification; but the favourable features had a compensating value where determined men were concerned, and preparations were at once set on foot for the prosecution of an assault in accordance with this plan.

The reserve company, Lieut. C. Birch, was brought forward to the general line along the moat, and with them a Stokes gun and crew that had till now been attached to the 1st Battalion. Under a barrage of Stokes mortar bombs and rifle-grenades, Lewis gun sections detailed for the purpose worked forward with the ladder, drove the enemy back, and occupied the two principal "lofty islets" and one of the higher of the subsidiary walls beyond. These, as well as the sections in rear, directed their fire upon the top of the inner rampart, while the mortar bombarded the two great salients on either side, and by 2.30 p.m. the hostile fire had so far been reduced as to warrant a further advance.

2nd Lieut. Averill, with a Lewis gun section from the centre company, was accordingly despatched to reconnoitre forward towards the wall. Carrying with them the precious scaling-ladder, the party moved on to a mass of earth and masonry beyond the two nearer "islets." This they scaled, and from their new vantage-point they discovered that nothing lay between them and the last rampart but a few low banks and the deep inner moat. The Lewis gun section took up its position here, and Averill passed down to a bank near the edge of the moat, where he joined 2nd Lieuts. Lummis and E. P. Canavan, who, with a strong patrol from "A" Company, had worked up under cover from the right and had just reached the same spot. Fortune seemed to smile upon these intrepid advanced parties, for, just at this point, a narrow masonry wall crossed the inner moat and led along the sheer wall beyond to the opening of a stairway which evidently passed up through the rampart and so gave access to the town. Apparently the masonry structure was the wall of a dam by means of which the flow of water in the moat was regulated, for it was provided with a sluice-gate, and the stairs no doubt served for the convenience of the attendants. Closer scrutiny, however, disclosed the fact that the stairway had been hastily but effectively blocked with baulks of timber thrown down from within. There remained the scaling-ladder, which, given a footing, precarious though it might be, on the narrow causeway, might reach to the top of the wall, here somewhat lower than elsewhere. Cautiously the party, led by 2nd Lieut. Canavan, moved out from cover to place the ladder in position and try their fortune; but, taking advantage of a momentary decrease in our covering fire, a party of Germans returned to their post immediately above, and a shower of stick-bombs caused our men to drop the ladder and dash back to cover.

This was not encouraging, but on the whole the situation was considered to be very satisfactory. All the platoons of the three companies had been steadily working forward and were now close at hand under cover, and the supporting fire had already effected a very noticeable diminution in the enemy's resistance. Every Lewis gun in the battalion, with the exception of those with the fire-harassed "C" Company in the sunken road, was now trained on the summit of the inner wall, which was "combed" with intermittent bursts of fire. The effect of this, supplemented as it was by frequent volleys of rifle-grenades, soon became most marked. The hostile fire rapidly diminished, and the enemy at this point was finally driven from the rampart and compelled to seek shelter in the underground barracks which had been constructed beneath. A platoon from the reserve company, under 2nd Lieut. H. W. Kerr, was detailed to continue the operation, the plans for which were carefully worked out. The platoon was divided into three parties, one of which would secure the position on the rampart about the head of the ladder, and then the two others, working right and left from this, would seize and hold the two flanking bastions. This done, a firing-line would be built up under cover of the bank of earth which rose to a height of five or six feet above the brickwork of the wall, and from this position a final rush would be made down the slope into the streets of the town. Further rifle sections were posted in commanding positions to augment the volume of covering fire, the Stokes mortar was brought within closer range of its important targets, and shortly before 4 p.m. all preparations were complete.

Our Lewis guns and rifles opened intense fire, sweeping the bank along the top of the rampart; the trench mortar bombarded the point to be assaulted and then directed its attention to the salients; and under cover of this fire the storming-party, led by Averill and Kerr, took forward the ladder to the moat. Working calmly, yet swiftly, our men laid the ladder with its foot over its appointed place on the causeway. Two men weighted and steadied this end, and the others, with a running lift, had it erect in a twinkling. Averill was half-way up the ladder before the top reached its resting-place on the wall. A moment later he was clambering over the grassy bank, where he was met by an astonished German who turned and ran for the dug-outs below. Joined instantly by Kerr and two men with a Lewis gun, he followed in the fugitive's tracks and rounded up the party to which he belonged. Now the light and flimsy ladder was being severely tested, for, following closely upon the heels of the assaulting platoon, the whole available portion of the battalion, led by its commanding officer, who had personally directed these operations to their conclusion, was passing up in one continuous stream in single file. Platoons were rapidly reformed and steps taken to deal with any resistance, but these precautions proved to be quite unnecessary, no serious opposition being anywhere encountered. Telephonic communication with Brigade Headquarters had been maintained throughout, and at 4.15 p.m. Major Barrowclough, on stepping from the ladder, sent a message stating that he had just entered Le Quesnoy. At this time also Lieut.-Col. Jardine's men on the north were reaping the fruit of their long and persistent effort, and at 4.30 p.m. they stormed the Valenciennes Gate and set foot within the walls.

The systematic mopping-up of the town now claimed attention, and in this we were both aided and hindered by the civilian population. They gladly pointed out the known hiding-places, but, unable to restrain their expressions of joy at deliverance, they repeatedly broke into the ranks, thrust flowers and cakes and flags upon our men, and freely embraced them in the manner peculiar and common to the French, but most embarrassing to the stolid New Zealanders. Even these difficulties were finally overcome, however, and the place, now gay with innumerable tricolour flags, which fluttered from every window, was cleared up by nightfall. The German commander with 100 men surrendered with full ceremony to one of the 4th Battalion officers. Others were added to these from time to time, till eventually the number of prisoners assembled in the square reached the total of 711. Parties of Germans were organized into bucket brigades to extinguish the many incendiary fires they had started, and into squads for the removal of mines and booby-traps; and when these duties had been satisfactorily completed the prisoners were drafted off in batches to the Divisional cage, where they joined the 532 that had been captured by the Brigade at the first objective. Five 77-mm. guns, twelve minenwerfer, eighty machine-guns, two anti-tank rifles, a travelling-kitchen and a number of horses were taken, together with a whole limber-load of optical instruments, mainly telescopic periscopes, to say nothing of an unusual number of field-glasses and revolvers unofficially collected by the men as souvenirs. Amongst the 77-mm. guns was one captured while still engaged in firing into the lines of the New Zealanders to the east of the town. Curiously enough, this eventually found its way to Dunedin, where it was identified by Lieut. H. S. Kenrick, whose men had captured it.

The faithful cooks of the 4th Battalion were not long in following their victorious comrades into Le Quesnoy; for when word was got back that the place had been taken they immediately set off with their travelling-kitchens, which, after the manner of a triumphal procession, presently passed through the streets with full steam up, and a hot meal was ready before the rounding-up of the garrison had been fully completed. That night discipline was relaxed to the extent of permitting the men to find billets where they chose, and the grateful citizens saw to it that these were the best the town had to offer.

The day's operations cost the Brigade 6 officers and 37 men killed, and 13 officers and 238 men wounded.

PART 3.—CONCLUDING STAGE.

1st Brigade five miles to the east of Le Quesnoy by the evening of November 4th—2nd Brigade troops pass through and advance a further four miles, November 5th—New Zealand Division relieved—The Division's recent achievements—General advance continued—Maubeuge taken, November 9th—Canadians take Mons, early morning, November 11th—The Armistice, 11 a.m., November 11th, 1918.

The advance of the 1st Brigade, followed by the 2nd, had continued methodically throughout the day, all resistance being quickly overcome, and by evening these troops were five miles east of Le Quesnoy. Taken altogether the 4th of November was probably the most successful day for the New Zealand Division during the war. There had been a total advance of six miles; in addition to Le Quesnoy, the villages of Ramponeau, Villereau, Potelle and Herbignies had been taken; and the captures included nearly 2,000 prisoners, sixty field-guns, and several hundred machine-guns.

At daybreak on the 5th, the 2nd Brigade passed through the outpost line of the 1st Brigade and continued the advance through the Mormal Forest, the troops fighting their way from tree to tree until eventually, when night fell, they established the line along its north-eastern fringe, having by this time covered four miles of difficult country.

So far as the infantry were concerned this was the New Zealand Division's last fight. Towards midnight the 42nd Division commenced to take over the sector from our three Brigades, but the artillery, remaining in line to cover the relieving Division, did not return till the 11th.

The achievements of the 4th and 5th of November constituted a fitting crown to the New Zealanders' record of activity during the great advance to victory: Between August 21st and November 5th the Division had captured nearly 9,000 prisoners, 145 guns, 3 tanks and 1,263 machine-guns, besides vast quantities of other war material; and of the total advance of 56 miles on the Corps' front, commencing with the thrust in front of Hebuterne in the middle of July, its troops had fought through no less than 49 miles.

The enemy now began to fall back at all points of the line; and throughout the following days the British infantry and cavalry pressed forward with scarcely a check, maintaining always close touch with the rapidly retreating Germans. On November 7th the outskirts of Maubeuge* were reached, and that city was entered by the Guards and the 62nd Division on the 9th. The Canadians were approaching Mons, in the neighbourhood of which the enemy was offering strong opposition; but early on the morning of November 11th that historic town fell to the Canadian Division, the whole defending force being either killed or taken prisoner. This, the last engagement of the war, was fought on almost precisely the same site as that battle in which the "Old Contemptibles" first impressed upon the Germans the fact, afterwards repeatedly emphasized and now completely demonstrated, that to prosecute ambitious plans of conquest and subjugation without reckoning on the spirit with which the British people are instinct is a policy fraught with danger, short-sighted in the extreme, and indicating a total disregard of those lessons which stand out clearly from the pages of the nation's history.

At 11 a.m. on November 11th hostilities were suspended.

"The military situation on the British front at that hour can be stated very shortly. In the fighting since November 1st our troops had broken the enemy's resistance beyond possibility of recovery, and had forced on him a disorderly retreat along the whole front of the British Armies. Hereafter, the enemy was capable neither of accepting nor of refusing battle. The utter confusion of his troops, the state of his railways, congested as they were with abandoned trains, the capture of huge quantities of rolling stock and material, all showed that our attack had been decisive. It had been followed on the north by the evacuation of the Tournai salient, and to the south, where the French forces had pushed forward in conjunction with us, by a rapid and costly withdrawal to

*See p. 343.

the line of the Meuse. The strategic plan of the Allies had been realized with a completeness rarely seen in war. When the armistice was signed by the enemy his defensive powers had already been definitely destroyed. A continuance of hostilities could only have meant disaster to the German Armies, and the armed invasion of Germany.''*

*Sir Douglas Haig's Despatches.

CHAPTER XX.
TO THE RHINE.

PART 1.—AFTER LE QUESNOY.

Back to Solesmes and to Fontaine-au-Pire—Celebrations at Le Quesnoy—The New Zealand Division's service of thanksgiving —Training and recreation—Liberated British prisoners.

At the conclusion of the successful attack on Le Quesnoy the Brigade became Divisional reserve, and spent the night of 4th/5th November in billets and bivouacs in and around the captured town; but as the New Zealand Division was handing over the sector to the 42nd, we moved back on the following afternoon to billets in Solesmes, a march of eight miles in pouring rain.

Before leaving Le Quesnoy, the 4th Battalion paraded in the square and received from the Maire an address of welcome and thanks on behalf of the people of the town. As the battalion was to march past General Hart on its way out of the square, the Maire begged permission for himself and his councillors to follow behind the troops. They were, however, placed in front, and just as they came abreast of the General there was a sharp word of command, and with wonderful precision off came the hats in salute. That every head so uncovered was bald was curiously startling, yet one more reminder of the sacrifice the younger men of France were making in the service of their beloved country.*

At Solesmes the Brigade immediately commenced refitting, reorganizing and training. By the 8th the weather had cleared somewhat. The following day broke fine and sunny, and there commenced a most enjoyable period of fine, sharp weather. Recreational training formed a considerable proportion of the Brigade syllabus of work, and many stiffly-contested inter-company and inter-battalion football matches were played under almost ideal conditions.

*Lieut.-Col. Beere having returned from hospital, the command of the battalion was now handed over to him, and Major Barrowclough was transferred to the 1st Battalion, of which unit he assumed command, vice Lieut.-Col. Allen, wounded on the 4th.

All personnel of the Brigade Details were recalled on November 10th, on which date we marched back, via Quievy, Bevillers and Beauvois, to billets in Fontaine-au-Pire, some fifteen miles south-west of Le Quesnoy.

At an early hour on November 11th, a telegram, on the ordinary pink field-message form, was received from Division, conveying the instruction: "HOSTILITIES CEASE AT 11 A.M. TO-DAY." The conditions of the armistice were received and promulgated on the following morning. The great news was received with extraordinary calmness by all ranks; there was no excitement whatever, and training went on without interruption. After parade hours the terms of the armistice and the prospects of an early and certain peace were quietly discussed by little knots of men, who left unspoken their deeper thoughts of thankfulness.

On the afternoon of the 10th there had been a combined civil and military function at Le Quesnoy on the occasion of the visit of President Poincaré. The New Zealand Divisional Staff, the G.O.C. Brigade, and the various battalion commanders were present, and New Zealand troops formed the guard of honour. The French President was received by the Maire of Le Quesnoy in the Place d'Armes, and, having inspected the guard, he warmly thanked General Hart on behalf of France for the good services rendered by the Brigade. A short address to the assembled populace brought the brief but enthusiastic ceremony to a close, and the President hurried off to visit other liberated towns.

The Brigadier had, on the previous day, received from the Maire a French flag with an autograph letter of thanks for the deliverance of the city. This compliment was reciprocated on the 14th, when General Hart, in company with his four commanding officers, motored to Le Quesnoy to present to the town a New Zealand flag to commemorate the victory of November 4th.[*] Our party was received in state by the

---

[*] The New Zealand Division was not given to much waving of bunting, and some difficulty was experienced in finding flags for these unusual ceremonies. At the moment only two could be unearthed, and these, it would appear, had been gifts from the Otaki electorate in New Zealand, one to the Division and one to the Maori Pioneer Battalion. The latter was flown over the town to signalize its capture by the New Zealanders, while the former was placed at our disposal for presentation to the Maire.

Maire in the presence of a great assemblage of townspeople, by whom the Brigadier's address was received with enthusiastic applause. The Maire was deeply moved, and on receiving the flag he caressed its folds and pressed it to his lips. In his remarks on formally accepting the gift, he stated that one of the principal streets of the town had been renamed in honour of the New Zealanders, and that an application had been made to the proper authorities for permission to add the New Zealand fern-leaf to the coat of arms of the city, this being the highest honour that it was in their power to confer. He mentioned, further, that the three guns captured by us in the vicinity and also presented to the Maire by the Brigadier on behalf of the New Zealand Division, were to be mounted above the three entrances to the town as a lasting memorial of the forcing of the ramparts.*

On Thursday, 14th, the whole Division held near Estourmel a service of thanksgiving in connection with the signing of the armistice. It was a beautiful day, and the occasion was one of more than ordinary solemnity, but the impressiveness of the ceremony, conducted in the open air, was marred somewhat by the pranks of a great number of aeroplanes which joyfully darted hither and thither immediately overhead. On the following Sunday the 1st and 2nd Battalions held their divine service in the Fontaine Church, kindly and freely offered for the purpose by the curé, who further honoured the New Zealanders with his presence.

On account of the changed outlook the amount of definite military training was now largely reduced. For the purpose of maintaining smartness and physical fitness a formal parade

---

*The last of the four war memorials erected by New Zealand in France has been placed at Le Quesnoy. It takes the form of a great marble panel let into the wall itself at the spot where the entry was made, and on this is sculptured the winged figure of Peace Triumphant, with palm and laurel-wreath, and a representation of the section of wall with New Zealand soldiers passing up a ladder to its top. The inscription, in English and in French, reads: "In honour of the men of New Zealand, through whose valour the town of Le Quesnoy was restored to France, November 4, 1918." An ornamental garden and shrubbery, in which flax, toi-toi, veronicas, olearias, manuka, and other of our characteristic native plants predominate, and which will be under the constant care of the people of Le Quesnoy, has been arranged as a setting; and on the marble balustrade erected on the opposite side of the moat has been engraved, as if in reply to the oft-repeated enquiry, "Whence come these men?" the legend: "From the uttermost ends of the earth."

lasting two hours was held each morning, while on two half-days in each week long route-marches were carried out. The afternoons were devoted to football, general sports, and other forms of recreational training; and twice weekly a regular programme of athletic competitions was worked through on the team system by the whole Brigade. Each night there were two cinema and two pierrot entertainments, and, as ever, the Y.M.C.A. provided refreshment for body and mind. The educational scheme was now rapidly developed, so much compulsory study, mainly along vocational lines, being imposed upon all ranks without exception.

Major Barrowclough was detached to Divisional Headquarters on November 20th as Assistant Educational Officer, and on the 23rd Major H. C. Meikle, released from duty at Havre, assumed command of the 1st Battalion until the return of Lieut.-Col. Allen from hospital on the 30th.

After the signing of the armistice, French civilians passed through our area daily in ever-increasing numbers on their return from the hands of the Germans. They had many harrowing tales to tell of the frightfulness of their treatment in captivity. It was noticed that they were wearing sabots or clogs, and it transpired that the Germans, before their retreat, had collected every make, shape and size of boots and shoes from civilians, issuing the more clumsy substitute in their place. Liberated military prisoners, too, were drifting back by every road, and we organized parties to meet them and bring them to our quarters, where they were provided with uniforms and supplied with food until they could be sent down to the coast. Without exception they were pinched and pale, and clad in every possible variety of ragged clothes. The English prisoners captured since March had, it seems, been treated with more than ordinary cruelty; exposed to all weathers and to shelling and bombing; neglected, insulted and beaten.

PART 2.—THE MARCH TO GERMANY.

We leave the IVth Corps, November 28th—Earlier stages—The King and the Prince of Wales at Bavay—Rest at Thuin—Across the frontier, December 21st—By train to Cologne—Over the Hohenzollern Bridge to the billeting areas, December 22nd.

The New Zealand Division was detailed to form part of the Army of Occupation across the Rhine, and on November 28th left the IVth Corps and commenced the long march to Germany, where we were to join the IInd Corps of the Second Army.

The New Zealand Rifle Brigade, starting from Fontaine-au-Pire at 8.30 a.m., moved north-east through Caudry, Bethencourt, Viesly and Briastre, and, after a march of thirteen miles in heavy rain, arrived in the area north of Solesmes at about 1 p.m., settling down in billets about Beaudignies and Haussy. As the Brigade passed the billeting areas of our old IVth Corps friends, the 37th Division, their bands played us through, and their men lined the route to give us farewell cheers.

We moved again at 8.30 a.m. on the 29th, passing north of Le Quesnoy and billeting in Wargnies-le-Petit and Wargnies-le-Grand. For some battalions this was a very long march, our previous billeting areas having been greatly scattered. The roads, however, were good, notwithstanding the long stretches of cobbles, and all units finished up in fine style, even those arriving so late as 3.50 p.m. having suffered no casualties.

On the following day the march was continued to La Longueville, four miles from Maubeuge, via St. Waast and Bavay, the new billets proving very comfortable. The weather was now good, seasonably cold, with fogs in the early morning. At this stage we were forty miles from our first starting-point. All the unfit having been sent to base before the march began, and the remainder being in good form after their recent training, we were spared the unpleasant experience of having exhausted men falling out by the way. March discipline was very strictly adhered to, and the clothing, equipment, and packs were worn with absolute uniformity; and altogether we were convinced that there was no finer looking Brigade then on the move anywhere in Europe.

For the next two days we rested in the La Longueville area, and the opportunity was taken to effect repairs to boots and clothing. His Majesty the King, with the Prince of Wales and Prince Albert, attended our divine service at Bavay Church on December 1st.

On December 3rd the Brigade moved forward a short stage to Bussois and Recquignies, passing by the northern outskirts of Maubeuge and through Assevant on the way. The 2nd Battalion continued the march to Solre-sur-Sambre, where next day they were joined by the remainder of the Brigade. The frontier between France and Belgium was crossed about two miles before this destination was reached.

We arrived at Thuin at mid-day on December 5th. As we approached the town it was realized that we had left behind the region of battered villages, ruined factories, broken bridges, and mined cross-roads, and were entering a different world. We had seen much of famished refugees, ill-nurtured children, and other piteous accompaniments of the battle zone. Now we passed to the area only a few days since occupied by the enemy's reserves. Here the land was well-tilled and cropped, and to all outward appearance the people were as prosperous as if war had never been. The children, in whom is visible the first evidence of general contentment, appeared happy; the mills were working, the shops well-stocked, and generally the atmosphere of naturalness pervaded the countryside. Towards noon, in brilliant sunshine, and with bands playing, we commenced the descent, from the high ground along which the road had passed, into the valley of the Sambre. Before us was spread a magnificent panorama. On our left, across the valley, was the quaint village of Lobbes with its ancient monastic church, while at the bottom of the slope lay the fine old abbey with its cloistered courtyard and symmetrically-arranged garden. Soon our road led us across the stream and then up to Thuin, which rose straight above us. As we tramped up the steep main street, the people poured from everywhere and gave us an overwhelming welcome, and during our short stay of two days treated us with remarkable kindness and hospitality. The good folk of the town were impressed with the physique of the New Zealand Division, which they considered the best they had ever seen.*

We were on the road again by 8 a.m. on December 7th, moving from Thuin, via Gozee, over the high ground to Montignies-sur-Sambre, just east of Charleroi. The tram-service between the village and the city was placed at the use of our men free of charge, and this privilege was taken advantage of to the full. In Charleroi, which is the centre of an important mining district, business appeared to be proceeding exactly as under peace conditions; the mines, electric lighting, trams and railways all running, and cinemas in full swing. At this point in the march, steel-helmets, entrenching tools and greatcoats were discarded, and for the remainder of the journey the only extra clothing in the pack was the leather jerkin and a change of underclothing, together with the ground sheet. Two blankets per man were carried on motor lorries and distributed each evening.

Velaine, about midway between Charleroi and Namur, was reached at 1 p.m. on December 8th; and next day we marched in warm, drizzly weather, to scattered billets in the St. Denis–Rhisnes area north of Namur. The 1st Battalion was quartered at Rhisnes, the 2nd and 4th at Meux, the 3rd at Bovesse, and Brigade Headquarters at St. Denis. Here we rested on the 10th, when, notwithstanding the heavy rain, visits were paid to Namur, some fifteen kilometres distant. General Hart departed on leave to Italy on December 9th, and Lieut.-Col. R. C. Allen assumed command of the Brigade, Capt. E. A. Harding taking over the 1st Battalion.

The march on December 11th brought us to the Leuze area, north of Namur. On the following day we moved eastward to Burdinne, and again, on the 13th, eastward still to Vinalmont. We had rain on all three days and the roads were rather bad. We rested in this area for another three days,

---

*At Thuin, as at Caudry and Boussois, our officers learned at first-hand something of the horrible barbarities and atrocities practised on the inhabitants in the early days of frightfulness. It is not right that we should turn away from these things, but some of the statements, solemnly vouched for by citizens whose word appeared to be absolutely reliable, are too dreadful to be recapitulated here. Innumerable cases of similar nature are recorded in the report of Lord Bryce's Committee on Alleged German Atrocities, a document published as a Parliamentary Paper in 1915, and obtainable from booksellers.

during which time the men got baths and a change of underclothing. Lieut.-Col. Jardine went on leave to the United Kingdom on December 16th, Major W. C. I. Sumner assuming command of the 2nd Battalion.

The trek was continued on December 17th, when the Brigade accomplished a fourteen-mile march down the valley of the Meuse to the Flemalle area, close to the outer fort-line of Liege. The weather was dull but dry, and the billets proved to be very good. The next stage, carried out on the 18th in showery weather, brought us to the Chenee area, immediately south of the city, which, being within easy reach, was freely visited. Moving up the valley of the Vesdre by a long march on the 19th, we reached Verviers. Of all our marches this was perhaps the most pleasant, leading as it did through the most beautiful scenery imaginable. On either side of the narrow valley the hills rise very steeply, leaving but little room for the road, the railway, and the swiftly-running Vesdre stream. The winding roadway led us repeatedly across both river and rail. A few miles short of Verviers the valley gradually widened out into a broad basin in which the town was situated. Here we received our most hearty welcome. At every point the citizens greeted us with enthusiastic cheers. The battalions were billeted in schools or large factories, and every effort had been made to render these quarters as comfortable as possible, but families vied with one another in their endeavour to secure one or more of our men as private guests. We rested here during the following day, enjoying to the full the public and private hospitality extended to us. Spa, the late Headquarters of the German General Staff, was only some ten miles away, and, being accessible by train, was freely visited.

On December 21st, in cold, unsettled weather, the Brigade moved out from Verviers for its last march in Belgium. As battalions from their billets converged on the starting-point, the whole town seemed to have turned out, lining the footpaths five and six deep. During the short wait here the warm-hearted people seized the opportunity to bedeck wagons, horses and men with the colours of the Allies, and there was hardly a rifle without a miniature bit of bunting stuck in its muzzle. As the gay column moved off with the bands playing the Belgian national anthem, "La Brabançonne," the multitude united in one long last cheer, and waved and gesticulated until at length we disappeared from view.

We had now had experience of both the Fleming and the Walloon. With the former we had long been in contact nearer the British battle zone, and now we had lived for some time amongst the latter. There is a very marked difference between the two races, which need not here be enlarged upon. There is also a decided antipathy between the two, and we know that upon this the German worked his hardest for his own ends; but happily there was a strong tie that to a large extent held them united—the intense loyalty to the person of their Sovereign, whom both sections almost worship.

Just before noon on December 21st the head of the column reached a highway running north-west along the frontier. Into this we turned, and had on our left hand Belgium and on our right Germany. Surely this was a stirring moment, but probably the thought uppermost in our minds was, "What will the billets be like?" Soon we entered Herbesthal, whence we were to entrain for Cologne on the following day. Half the population of this town is German and half Belgian, and the street along which we marched separated the two. To the left every doorway and window was gay with Allied flags, and as we passed by we were enthusiastically greeted by old and young; but to the right there was dulness and silence. The railway station was an example of the thoroughness of German methods. Elaborately-planned sidings were everywhere, and in all cases they appeared to be arranged for the sole purpose of facilitating the despatch of military personnel and material.

December 22nd was a miserably cold day. The ever-faithful representatives of the Y.M.C.A. were at the entraining point with abundant supplies of coffee, biscuits, cigarettes and chocolates, and at the journey's end we found them awaiting us with similar comforts. We moved from Herbesthal to Cologne in five trains, the first departing at 4 a.m. and the last at 11.15 p.m. The journey, lasting over four hours, proved on the whole rather uninteresting.

Arrived at Ehrenfield, on the western outskirts of Cologne, the various units set out on their last march of some twelve miles to the billeting areas. The route lay through the centre of the city of Cologne, across the great square, past the walls of the famous cathedral, and over the Rhine by the

Hohenzollern Bridge. With quick and sprightly step our men swung along with the proper air of conquerors, disdainful alike of the discomforts of the pouring rain and of the fact that the passage of their column was dislocating the city's excellently-conducted tramway system.

Brigade Headquarters were established at Holweide, but on January 4th were moved to Haus Mielenforst, Delbruck. The 1st and 2nd Battalions were billeted at Bensberg in an enormous "schloss" large enough to hold a Brigade, and used in pre-war days as a college for German cadet officers. The 3rd and 4th Battalions were quartered at Delbruck and Dunwald, respectively. The billets were found to be very comfortable. Every man had a paillasse, and, where there was no central heating, every room was provided with a fire. Where further conveniences or luxuries were desired, from tableware to pianos, a requisition on the Burgomaster always resulted in the production of the necessary articles. There were few signs of the stress of war, and the people were neither under-fed nor ill-clad. They were very docile, looked upon us more in sorrow than in anger, and implicitly obeyed all orders and proclamations, which, however, were designed to disturb as little as possible the normal routine of their civil life.

PART 3.—THE END.

Education — Christmas dinner — The Prince of Wales — Demobilization commences, December 26th—1st and 2nd combine as "A" Battalion, and 3rd and 4th as "B" Battalion, January 15th—Absorbed into the 1st and 2nd Brigade Groups, February 4th, 1919.

The Brigade now settled down to an easy time of training and recreation. Plans for the defence of the Cologne bridgehead were got out at once, and all ranks were instructed and practised in their duties in this respect in case the unexpected should happen. Morning parades were held for the purpose of maintaining and improving smartness and efficiency, the afternoons being devoted to sports and other amusements. Regular trips to neighbouring places of interest, such as the cities of Cologne and Bonn, were arranged, as were frequent river-outings on the beautiful Rhine. It must be recorded that there were many unauthorized shoots over the forests owned by local barons and by the ex-Kaiser; but only in this mild way did our men "spoil the Egyptians." For evening entertainment there was the choice of the Y.M.C.A. "sing-song," the Divisional cinema, the innumerable city picture shows and music-halls, and the grand opera magnificently staged and beautifully rendered in German. At the earliest moment the educational scheme was put on a proper working basis. The compulsory section comprised either two subjects in general education, or agriculture, or engineering; and, in addition, attendance was expected at lectures on economics and hygiene on alternate afternoons. The troops, however, were hardly in the frame of mind for this new form of training. Their fighting-days over, they longed for the conclusion of the whole matter; and while some entered upon their studies with eagerness, to the majority the return of school-days was but a weariness and vexation of spirit.

General Hart returned from leave and resumed command of the Brigade on December 29th.

Owing to the shortage of supplies caused by transport difficulties, the usual Christmas dinner was postponed till New Year's Eve, when the various units held a double celebration. The menu of the 4th Battalion, here reproduced, will serve to indicate the nature of these festivities.

"Soyes Ferme."

4th N.Z.R.B.

XMAS, 1918.

Dunwald, Cologne.

N.Z. Div.
Press.

TOASTS.

The King.

Our Guests.

Absent Friends.

"A Merry Xmas and a Happy New Year."

Our Padre.

MENU.

POTAGES.
Consommé à la Royale
Potage Anglais

ENTRÉE.
Curried Salmon.

POULTRY.
Roast Turkey, seasoning.

JOINTS.
Roast Beef, Yorkshire Pudding.

VEGETABLES.
Potatoes, Baked and Boiled.
Cabbage, Carrots, Turnips.

SWEETS.
Xmas Pudding, Cognac Sauce.
Apple Pie, Custard.
Compôte Figs.

SAVOURY.
Cheese Straws.

HONOURS.

1916. Egypt.
Armentieres.
Somme.
Fleurbaix.

1917. Ploegsteert Wood.
Messines.
Dixmude.
Passchendaele.

1918. Colincamps.
Hebuterne.
Puisieux.
Favreuil.
Trescault Ridge.
Lesdain.
Le Quesnoy.

His Royal Highness the Prince of Wales visited the Brigade on January 18th. After being shown round the Brigade area he attended a rifle meeting, took part in a competition, and at its conclusion presented the prizes.

The end was now rapidly approaching. Demobilization had begun on December 26th, when the first draft of our men left for England, en route for New Zealand. By the end of January, drafts from the Division were leaving at the rate of 1,000 men per week; and a further 40 men per day were being despatched to England on leave, on completion of which they reported to the Depots and did not return to Germany. On January 15th the battalions of the Brigade were organized on a two-company basis, and then the 1st and 2nd were combined to form what was known as "A" Battalion, under the command of Lieut.-Col. R. C. Allen, and the 3rd and 4th were similarly amalgamated into "B" Battalion, commanded by Lieut.-Col. Jardine. The last act came on February 4th, 1919, when "A" Battalion was absorbed into the 1st Brigade Group, and "B" Battalion into the 2nd Brigade Group, and the New Zealand Rifle Brigade ceased to exist.

The First Stage of the March to Germany: Departure from Solesmes.

THE HOHENZOLLERN BRIDGE OVER THE RHINE.

H.R.H. THE PRINCE OF WALES AT BRIGADE HEADQUARTERS, MIELENFORST NEAR COLOGNE.

THE LONGUEVAL MEMORIAL ON THE FLERS BATTLEFIELD.

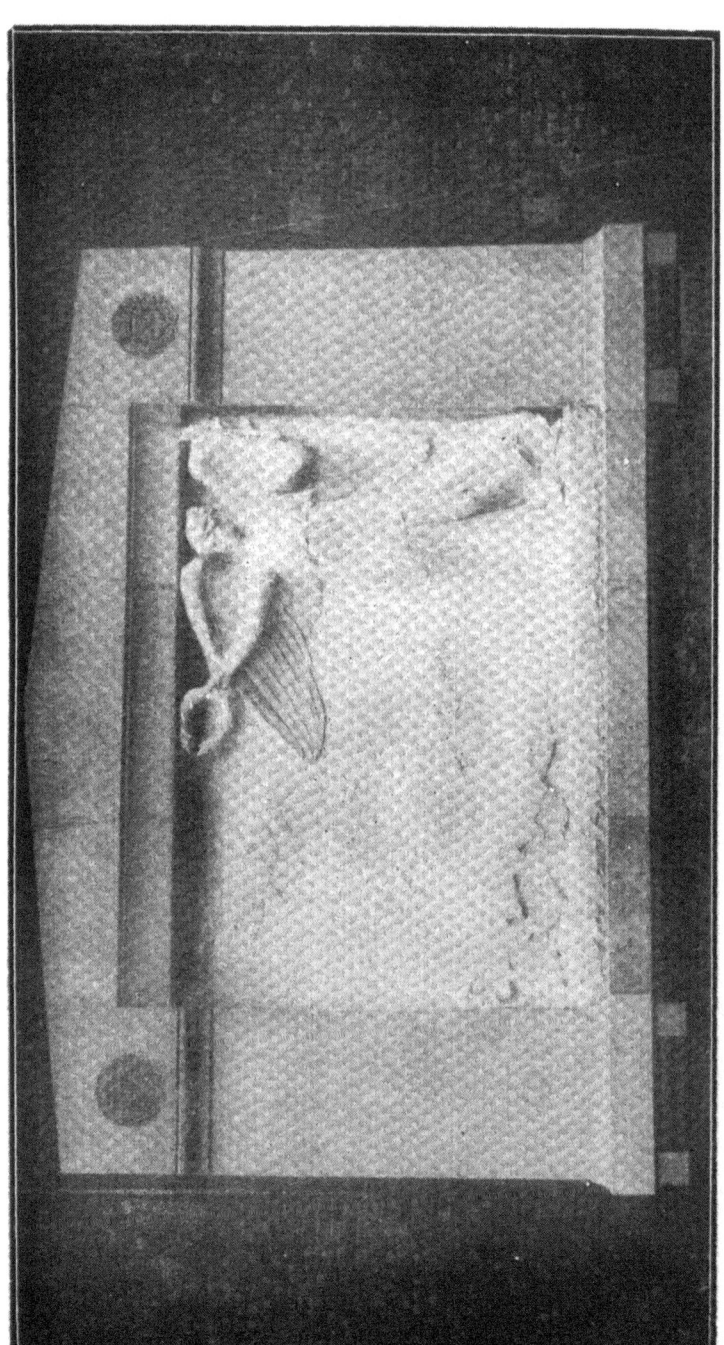

The Memorial at Le Quesnoy.

APPENDIX I.

HONOURS AND AWARDS.

In formal recognition of specially gallant conduct and meritorious service in the Great War, the following honours and awards were conferred upon or granted to members of the New Zealand Rifle Brigade and other soldiers serving at the time with the Regiment.

THE VICTORIA CROSS.

6/2133 Frickleton, Lance-Corporal Samuel.
24/213 Laurent, Sergeant Harry John.

COMPANION OF THE ORDER OF THE BATH.

10/133 Hart, Brig.-Gen. H., C.M.G., D.S.O.
15/35 Melvill, Brig.-Gen. C. W., C.M.G., D.S.O.

COMPANION OF THE ORDER OF ST. MICHAEL AND ST. GEORGE.

23/1 Fulton, Brig.-Gen. H. T., D.S.O.
15/35 Melvill, Brig.-Gen. C. W., D.S.O.
24/1 Stewart, Brig.-Gen. A. E., D.S.O.

BAR TO DISTINGUISHED SERVICE ORDER.

12/3538 Allen, Lt.-Col. R. C., D.S.O.
10/1049 Jardine, Lt.-Col. L. H., D.S.O., M.C.

THE DISTINGUISHED SERVICE ORDER.

23/2 Austin, Lt.-Col. W. S.
24/16 Barrowclough, Major H. E., M.C.
24/3 Beere, Lt.-Col. R. St. J.
23/27 Bell, Lt.-Col. P. H.
26/11 Winter-Evans, Lt.-Col. A.
— Hastings, Major W. H., M.C.
10/1049 Jardine, Lt.-Col. L.H., M.C.
26/56 Kennedy, Capt. D., M.C.
4/310 Macnab, Major A. A.
24/1268 Massey, Capt. F. G., M.C.
15/35 Melvill, Lt.-Col. C. W.
23/8 Pow, Lt.-Col. J.
23/5 Puttick, Lt.-Col. E.
25/1215 Richardson, Maj. H. M. W., M.C.
23/1263 Roache, Lt.-Col. J. G.
6/821 Shepherd, Lt.-Col. N. F.
24/25 Digby-Smith, Major A.
24/1 Stewart, Lt.-Col. A. E.

THE ORDER OF THE BRITISH EMPIRE (OFFICER).

23/3 Kay, Major W.

THE ORDER OF THE BRITISH EMPIRE (MEMBER).

26/1212 Eastgate, Capt. H.   25/1200 Magnay, Capt. C. R. A.

BAR TO MILITARY CROSS.

25/954	Greenish, Capt. F. E., M.C.	23/10	Purdy, Capt. R. G., M.C.
26/194	McMinn, 2/Lt. W. E., M.C.	36839	Roy, Lt. J. A. McL., M.C.
	26/17 Saxon, Capt. K. R. J., M.C.		

THE MILITARY CROSS.

14185	Abernethy, 2/Lt. R. C.	24/23	Inglis, Capt. L. M.
26/8	Armstrong, Lieut. D. C.	26/12	Jones, Capt. M. H. R.
46219	Averill, 2/Lt. L. C. L.	24/1303	Keesing, Lieut. H. M.
24/19	Avey, Lieut. G. A.	26/56	Kennedy, Lieut. D.
24/16	Barrowclough, Capt. H. E.	24/1546	Kennedy, Capt. H. W.
23290	Baxter, Lieut. E.	18911	King, Capt. W. J.
3/2594	Baxter, Lieut. R. H. (N.Z.M.C.)*	57315	Kirk, Lieut. B. C.
		23/336	Lewer, 2/Lt. E. E.
3/1122	Benham, Capt. P. B. (N.Z.M.C.)	23/490	Luxford, 2/Lt. M. G.
		23/25	McAlister, Capt. J. L.
12115	Best, Lieut. C. C.	24/235	McClurg, Capt. D. W.
15290	Bongard, 2/Lt. A.	23/334	McCormick, 2/Lt. A. L., D.C.M.
24/55	Bongard, 2/Lt. J. R.		
14025	Bowler, Lieut. D. C.	23/2053	Macdonald, 2/Lt. M.
9/1391	Brown, 2/Lt. J. L.	26/16	McDowell, Capt. A. L.
10951	Brown, Lieut. T.	23299	McGhie, Lieut. J. G.
12931	Clark, Revd. H. (C.F.)	26/10	McLeod, Capt. B.
25/15	Closey, Capt. S. J. E.	26/194	McMinn, 2/Lt. W. E.
23/9	Cowles, Capt. J. R.	23/1286	Macky, Lieut. N. L.
7/36	Dailey, Capt. G. C.	24/1906	Manning, Lieut. L. I.
24/1270	Davidson, Lieut. C. J. H.	40154	Marshall, 2/Lt. H. T.
3/2877	Dempster, Capt. N. H., M.C. (N.Z.M.C.)	9/445	Marshall, Lieut. V.
		23/1533	Martin, Lieut. A. L.
14538	Denniston, Lieut. L. H.	24/1268	Massey, Lieut. F. G.
26/5	Dove, Capt. W. W.	26/13	Meikle, Capt. H. C.
8/3242	Drummond, 2/Lt. E. C.	25/30	Mollison, 2/Lt. B.
15/202	Eastwood, Capt. T. R.	15937	Murray, 2/Lt. T. T., M.M.
10/212	Edwards, Lieut. E. B.	22731	Organ, Lieut. W. J.
6/2401	Ellen, 2/Lt. H., M.M.	3/2180	Parr, Revd. S. (C.F.)
23108	Ellingham, Lieut. H. A.	3/800	Pattrick, Lieut. H. B.
26/20	Emery, Capt. L. A. J.	24/8	Powley, Capt. A. J.
26/4	Fowlds, Capt. W. F.	23/10	Purdy, Capt. R. G.
26/42	Goulding, 2/Lt. F. S.	23/1786	Reeves, Lieut. E. F. J.
33125	Goulding, 2/Lt. A. M.	25/1215	Richardson, Capt. H. M. W.
15836	Gow, 2/Lt. G. V.	25/6	Rogers, Capt. S. D.
12171	Grant, Lieut. R. J.	18020	Rowe, Lieut. L. J.
25/955	Gray, Lieut. W. A.	36839	Roy, 2/Lt. J. A. McL.
25/954	Greenish, Capt. F. E.	13095	Russell, Lieut. J.
26/23	Greenwood, Lieut. J. G.	26/17	Saxon, Capt. K. R. J.
24/13	Harding, Capt. E. A.	22732	Senior, 2/Lt. S. E.
24/172	Harrison, 2/Lt. W. G.	60393	Seton, Revd. C. B. W. (C.F.)
11376	Henning, 2/Lt. W.	15981	Slevin, C.S.M. F. R.
27664	Holder, 2/Lt. A. G.	23261	Snelling, 2/Lt. T. A.
23/23	Holderness, Capt. H.	24/1248	Stedman, Lieut. M. A.
18/12	Houchen, Revd. C. (C.F.)	23288	Taylor, Capt. L. J.

THE MILITARY CROSS—(Continued).

25/12	Thomson, Capt. A.	24/6	Wilkes, Capt. T. M.
15834	Thompson, Lieut. H. J.	23/1875	Williams, Capt. O. W.
36504	Webster, C.S.M. G. F.	26/9	Winchester, Lieut. E. A.
26/643	Whitefield, 2/Lt. R.	12338	Zeisler, 2/Lt. E.

BAR TO DISTINGUISHED CONDUCT MEDAL.

25/708	Anderson, Sgt. H., D.C.M.	39681	McMurray, Sgt. R., D.C.M.

THE DISTINGUISHED CONDUCT MEDAL.

25/708	Anderson, Sgt. H.	24/815	Kennerley, Sgt. T. R.
24/345	Bates, Sgt. G.	23/1088	Keogh, Rfm. J. L., M.S.M.
40485	Batty, Sgt. A. I.	45217	Kerrigan, L/Cpl. M.
25/92	Berry, L/Cpl. M.	23/1431	Langrish, Rfm. J. G.
36944	Birch, Rfm. C.	24/654	Latimer, Sgt. R. T.
23/366	Boles, C.S.M. G. H.	23/483	Lepper, Cpl. R.
12/3257	Bowers, L/Cpl. W. G.	26/462	McConachy, Sgt. W.
23/94	Cherry, Sgt. W. R.	23/334	McCormick, Q.M.S. A. L.
26/733	Coley, Sgt. A. K.	36472	McGillen, Sgt. W. P.
26/730	Conlon, R.S.M. E. J.	39681	McMurray, L/Cpl. R.
33312	Corsbie, Cpl. R. T.	22824	Managh, L/Sgt. S. N.
23/399	Cunningham, Sgt. A. J., M.M.	15390	Manderson, Rfm. P.
		24/502	Marks, Sgt. R. O. C.
23/1029	Daniell, C.S.M. L. T.	29966	Mulvaney, Cpl. M. J., M.M.
26/299	Davis, C.S.M. F. H.	35123	Nailer, Rfm. C. H.
24/763	Densem, L/Sgt. J.	23/536	Nimmo, Rfm. T.
26/768	Dickey, Rfm. A.	36479	O'Connor, Rfm. T. R.
26571	Dibble, Cpl. J. C.	24/875	O'Neill, Sgt. T.
53765	Douglas, Rfm. W. R.	23/246	Ohlson, Sgt. A. W. M.
26/1161	Douglas, Rfm. W. T.	38866	Olsen, C.S.M. E.
26/766	Dunthorne, Rfm. A.	24/659	Perry, L/Sgt. L.
20512	Ellery, Sgt. F.	24/888	Price, Sgt. H. W.
36742	Ellingham, Sgt. E. S.	24/1189	Scully, C.S.M. P. A.
24/1983	Ferguson, Rfm. W.	13822	Shannon, Rfm. R. C.
40200	Fleming, Rfm. A.	25/71	Sheppard, C.S.M. F. W.
25/429	Fraser, Sgt. H. C.	40724	Sillifant, L/Cpl. J.
33144	Free, Sgt. W. L.	26/474	Smith, C.S.M. S.
23/973	Gair, Sgt. C.	25/69	Spriggs, C.S.M. C. A.
38525	Gaskell, L/Cpl. F. A.	33128	Steele, Sgt. J. H.
28874	Gillam, L/Cpl. A.	23/923	Struthers, Sgt. H.
24/157	Grubb, C.Q.M.S. J.	48107	Sturmey, Rfm. A. L.
24/942	Haddow, R.S.M. R. W.	13824	Taylor, Cpl. C.
25/1232	Hansen, Rfm. J.	12294	Toms, Cpl. S. W.
24/451	Hartley, Sgt. S.	23/1224	Tucker, Rfm. C. A.
24/186	Healey, Rfm. M.	24/1323	Voyle, C.S.M. J. W., M.M.
34368	Hunter, L/Cpl. G.	26/1554	Williams, Cpl. C. J.
22808	Jeffery, Cpl. H. J.	25765	Williams, L/Cpl. L. S.
25/887	Keatley, Sgt. J.	26/951	Williamson, Sgt. W. J.
	23/1239 Wilson, Sgt. C. R. C.		

BAR TO MILITARY MEDAL.

26/710	Baker, Cpl. G. H., M.M.	25/239	Simmers, Sgt. R., M.M.
25/1760	Hammond, Cpl. S. A., M.M.	23/598	Sinclair, Segt. R. J., M.M.
36646	Methven, Sgt. W., M.M.	26/927	Thom, Sgt. W. N., M.M.
44306	Papworth, L/Cpl. G. A., M.M.	14884	Timmins, Sgt. W. B., M.M.

THE MILITARY MEDAL.

23/2143	Adams, Rfm. J.		24/1350	Clarke, Cpl. F. A.
23/1366	Allan, Sgt. H.		25/1119	Clayson, Sgt. J. W.
32286	Allan, Rfm. J.		23346	Clinker, Rfm. H. S.
18924	Allan, Sgt. L. F.		18621	Cochrane, Sgt. R.
28946	Allason, Rfm. W. J.		26/1180	Collins, L/Cpl. W. J.
41066	Allison, Rfm. A. J.		48456	Coop, Rfm. N.
25/1650	Ansin, Rfm. F. W.		26/736	Corbett, Cpl. A.
23/664	Apperley, L/Cpl. H. W.		14764	Corbett, Rfm. W. H.
28951	Arnold, Rfm. C. J.		54472	Cormack, Cpl. F. R.
24/676	Ashby, Sgt. A.		15348	Courcy, Sgt. H. P. de.
17169	Atherfold, Cpl. L. J.		24346	Craig, Sgt. P. G.
25/89	Backholm, Rfm. F.		42050	Craven, Rfm. W.
24/1332	Bagley, Rfm. E.		39767	Cross, Cpl. F. L.
23/2503	Bailey, Rfm. G.		24/996	Crowther, Sgt. W. J.
26/710	Baker, L/Cpl. G. H.		12356	Cullen, L/Cpl. E. L.
20949	Baker, L/Cpl. H.		20108	Cumming, Sgt. W.
69745	Ball, L/Cpl. C. J.		23/399	Cunningham, Sgt. A. J.
23/356	Ballantyne, L/Cpl. J. M.		25676	Currie, Rfm. J.
25/162	Bassett, L/Cpl. E.		65747	Dalzell, Rfm. A.
26/155	Bathurst, Sgt. H. C.		24/113	Dean, Sgt. H.
46871	Batty, Rfm. C. W.		26570	Dean, Cpl. J.
26/385	Beaton, Rfm. A.		24/738	Dewar, Sgt. J. L.
24/48	Bedggood, L/Cpl. W. W. C.		25/1162	Dickason, Rfm. A. E.
23474	Bell, Sgt. A.		25824	Dixon, Sgt. B. L.
25666	Berghan, Rfm. A. J.		23/734	Donn, Rfm. J.
23/968	Blackman, Sgt. A. R.		26/1161	Douglas, Rfm. W. T.
26/388	Blake, L/Sgt. H. J.		48709	Drury, Rfm. F. B.
24/1940	Blenkinsopp, Rfm. J.		52073	Duff, Cpl. A.
26/332	Blyth, Sgt. L. M.		24/413	Duston, C.S.M. H. M.
22542	Boles, Sgt. J. H.		25/614	Duthie, Cpl. E. D.
23/77	Booker, Rfm. A. B.		25/749	Eastgate, L/Cpl. H. S.
23/686	Booth, Cpl. G. R.		18640	Edwards, Rfm. W. H.
25/938	Bower, Sgt. F.		23/1381	Elliott, L/Sgt. A. C.
12/3257	Bowers, L/Cpl. W. G.		24/746	Ellmers, L/Cpl. R.
24/978	Bowles, Sgt. W. B.		20979	Everitt, Rfm. A.
24/1944	Brakhage, Rfm. C.		26/1151	Fatt, Rfm. S.
36736	Bray, Sgt. W. T.		20980	Ferguson, Rfm. C. C.
41069	Bromley, Rfm. J. H.		37797	Fergusson, Sgt. R. L.
32297	Brown, L/Cpl. C. D.		48929	Few, Cpl. F.
44682	Brunton, L/Sgt. J. S.		26/775	Finlay, L/Cpl. C. P.
42032	Burgess, Rfm. G.		24/144	Fitzgerald, Sgt. N. E.
21777	Burgess, Cpl. J. W.		41434	Fletcher, Cpl. E. C.
24/704	Burton, L/Cpl. L. A.		23/136	Fletcher, L/Cpl. F. N.
23/89	Butler, Rfm. W. H.		26/556	Flett, L/Cpl. A.
25/1195	Byrne, L/Cpl. H. J.		23/1048	Fogarty, Sgt. B.
25/316	Calderwood, Cpl. J. H.		31119	Forsyth, Rfm. A. E.
23/697	Caldwell, Sgt. R. T.		25/626	Fox, Cpl. H.
23/699	Campbell, L/Cpl. A. K.		26086	Fraser, Rfm. J. S.
24/990	Campbell, Rfm. E. H.		25/178	Fruin, Cpl. F. G.
26/1209	Campbell, Rfm. W. C.		25/1227	Fruin, L/Cpl. F. L.
26/725	Cashmore, Cpl. F. R.		26/98	Fulcher, Sgt. A. E.
23/381	Cauty, Sgt. J. V. M.		24/431	Gaffaney, Sgt. P. M.
23/1345	Chambers, Rfm. W. V.		24/430	Gallagher, Sgt. A. W.
26042	Cheeseman, Rfm. J. H.		26/447	Gardner, L/Cpl. G. W.
26/93	Ciochetto, Sgt. C. V.		26/993	Geaney, Rfm. D. P.
15873	Clark, Cpl. A. C.		23/760	Gibson, Rfm. L. V.

THE MILITARY MEDAL—(Continued).

23/762	Gillespie, L/Sgt. O. A.		24/821	Le Comte, L/Cpl. H. E.
23/1402	Gilmore, Cpl. A. F.		25/505	Leighton, Cpl. H. S.
23/1403	Glentworth, Sgt. J. P., M.S.M.		26638	Lewis, L/Cpl. A.
			39606	Linton, Cpl. W.
25/323	Goodfellow, Sgt. T. A.		30956	Lowe, Rfm. J.
25/871	Goodhue, Sgt. A. C.		74877	Lowe, Rfm. W. E.
25/109	Gorton, Sgt. A. E.		47157	Lund, Sgt. W.
24/1058	Gould, L/Cpl. J. R.		54542	Lyford, Rfm. L.
24/432	Gowers, Rfm. H.		21873	McClure, Rfm. D. J.
13752	Gradwell, Rfm. G. H.		10962	McClure, Sgt. W.
25/108	Grainger, Sgt. J. C.		24/1433	McDonald, Cpl. A.
31837	Gray, Rfm. C. A.		24/524	McGrath, Rfm. E.
25408	Green, Cpl. W. J.		26/610	McInnes, Cpl. E. J.
25/430	Gribble, Cpl. W.		45610	McIntyre, L/Cpl. W.
12174	Griffiths, L/Sgt. G. G.		24383	McKeegan, Sgt. C.
54501	Hallam, Rfm. W. E.		48992	McKie, Rfm. D. A.
63601	Hallett, Rfm. E. W.		24/1420	Mackinder, Rfm. W. A.
33081	Hamilton, L/Cpl. L. R.		24/1145	McLean, Rfm. A.
25/1760	Hammond, Cpl. S. A.		44141	McLean, Cpl. L. G.
24/776	Hanson, L/Cpl. S. F.		24/1439	McMillan, L/Cpl. W. H.
21835	Hart, Cpl. J. G.		24/865	McQuillan, Cpl. J.
24/176	Hartigan, Rfm. H. H.		21047	Martelli, Rfm. C. R. S.
25/1080	Harwood, Rfm. J. R. B.		23/1433	Mason, Rfm. J. R.
15899	Hayter, Rfm. R.		23/495	Mathias, L/Cpl. J. S.
26/1551	Heard, Sgt. G.		32868	Matheson, L/Cpl. H. A.
39810	Heath, Rfm. H.		24282	Maubon, Rfm. C. J.
24/783	Henley, Sgt. N. G.		55072	Mellor, L/Cpl. E. E.
23/1407	Hennessy, Rfm. M.		23/825	Menzies, Sgt. J. W. C.
25/984	Hickey, L/Cpl. M.		36646	Methven, Cpl. W.
11875	Hill, Cpl. E.		11072	Meurant, Rfm. F. A.
26619	Hill, L/Cpl. J.		26/1014	Michell, Sgt. H. J.
15293	Hine, Sgt. C. P.		27100	Milne, L/Cpl. R.
26/103	Hine, Sgt. H. S.		25912	Moar, Rfm. H.
24/639	Hodgson, Sgt. F. J.		24/848	Moffitt, L/Cpl. P.
7/967	Holyoake, Rfm. F. T.		24/1124	Monkman, Cpl. A.
74912	Hooker, Rfm. A. C.		26/858	Moscrop, Sgt. H.
38534	Hutchins, Rfm. F. G.		26/1648	Motion, Sgt. W.
24/472	Ingpen, Rfm. N. L.		15295	Moyle, Sgt. H. L.
23/791	Irvine, Rfm. D.		29966	Mulvaney, Cpl. M. J.
21512	Irvine, Rfm. W. C.		26/584	Munro, Rfm. J. M.
24/806	Islip, L/Cpl. E. E.		25/529	Murray, Sgt. A. W.
26/1177	Jeffreys, Sgt. H. D.		63644	Murray, Rfm. C. V.
25885	Jenkins, Rfm. F.		23/837	Murray, Rfm. R. N.
38865	Jennens, Sgt. C. K.		15937	Murray, Sgt. T. T.
22809	Jepsen, Sgt. O. O.		24/843	Murray, Sgt. W. J.
25/646	Jesse, Rfm. P. W.		23/1127	Myers, Rfm. R.
15/108	Johnston, Rfm. A.		13080	Naismith, Rfm. R. C.
23/795	Johnstone, Cpl. R. M.		25/898	Nankivell, Sgt. L.
49678	Jones, Rfm. J. A.		26/1666	Negus, Rfm. F.
44483	Jowers, Rfm. W. H.		26/1129	Neilson, Sgt. N. C.
25887	Judd, Rfm. F. K.		25/558	Neville, Rfm. P. J.
23/2515	Kelk, C.S.M. G.		12242	Newberry, Rfm. J.
11056	Keys, Rfm. J.		24448	Nicholson, Rfm. N. A.
23/2576	Lane, Sgt. T.		36880	O'Brien, Cpl. W. S.
25/771	Langwell, Sgt. H. J.		48063	O'Donnell, L/Cpl. J. N.
26/273	Larsen, Cpl. H.		26/1019	O'Driscoll, Rfm. C.

THE MILITARY MEDAL.—(Continued).

54576	O'Halloran, Cpl. M. J.		54164	Somerville, L./Cpl. W.
23/2582	O'Neill, Rfm. P.		28554	Staite, L./Cpl. O.
26/1020	Orpwood, Rfm. H. F.		20575	Stevens, Rfm. C. T.
15955	Osborne, Cpl. D.		25/677	Stevenson, Rfm. D.
26/1191	Pain, Sgt. J. C.		26/421	Still, L/Cpl. C. H.
26/1074	Paine, Sgt. W.		25/912	Stirling, Rfm. S. G.
44306	Papworth, L/Cpl. G. A.		23/605	Stockdale, L/Cpl. W.
38208	Park, Sgt. J. W.		13129	Stone, Cpl. N. G.
26/1045	Patching, Cpl. W. J.		26708	Storry, Rfm. W.
26/1677	Patrick, Rfm. V.		40463	Strong, Rfm. A. E.
24/1167	Pearce, L/Cpl. V. W.		23/295	Taylor, Sgt. A.
65186	Peat, Rfm. A. G.		24/1838	Taylor, L/Cpl. A.
25/403	Pemberthy, Sgt. B. J.		26/481	Taylor, Sgt. W. G.
51497	Perry, Rfm. A. H.		26/927	Thom, Sgt. W. N.
23/1465	Peters, Rfm. A. L.		25754	Thompson, Sgt. P. A.
15411	Peters, Sgt. F. J. F.		23/1217	Thomson, Sgt. D. M.
12465	Phelan, Rfm. E. M.		33068	Thomson, Sgt. G. W. G.
21532	Phillips, L/Cpl. F. H.		56486	Thomson, Rfm. M. A.
23/882	Poole, L/Cpl. S. H.		23/301	Thorn, Pte. B. (N.Z.M.C.)
23/883	Prebble, Sgt. F. L.		14884	Timmins, Sgt. W. B.
65448	Prince, L/Cpl. F.		26/1103	Tomlinson, Sgt. C. G.
14149	Quinn, Rfm. J. M.		25/1150	Town, Rfm. C. E.
26/248	Quinn, Rfm. J. P.		23/941	Turner, Rfm. W. C.
68794	Radcliffe, Rfm. B.		17851	Turner, L/Cpl. W. F.
60314	Ramsay, Rfm. R. C.		26718	Vazey, Rfm. E.
26/1689	Ray, Rfm. R.		38239	Voss, Rfm. T. W.
21097	Roberts, Rfm. R. P.		24/1323	Voyle, L/Cpl. J. W.
24/1183	Rosanowski, L/Cpl. H.		43119	Wake, L/Cpl. A. A.
46245	Rowe, Cpl. C. A.		23/1503	Walker, Rfm. W. R.
31893	Rudkin, Sgt. A. R.		23/948	Waller, Rfm. H. T.
24/1492	St. George, L/Cpl. F. C.		39128	Walles, Rfm. C. W.
24/643	Samson, Cpl. C. O.		24/1850	Warren, Rfm. N.
26/1707	Sapsford, Cpl. S. J.		20583	Watts, L/Cpl. G. R.
25/1019	Sheat, Rfm. C. M.		26/940	Welch, Sgt. H. C.
25/239	Simmers, Sgt. R.		23/953	Whisker, Cpl. L. J.
23/598	Sinclair, Sgt. R. J.		25/248	White, Rfm. A. E.
38234	Skett, Rfm. G.		51938	White, Rfm. E. J.
44787	Smith, Rfm. A. G.		23/1502	Whyte, Sgt. W. A.
25/1024	Smith, L/Cpl. B. T.		31003	Willetts, L/Cpl. M. W.
15427	Smith, Rfm. F.		48217	Williams, Rfm. A. O.
34929	Smith, Rfm. F.		55215	Wilson, L/Cpl. J. H.
2/2264	Smith, Bomb. H. P.		52670	Wilson, Rfm. J. J. H.
44316	Smith, Rfm. S.		26/227	Wilson, Cpl. T.
29097	Smith, Rfm. W. K.		65644	Wilson, Rfm. W. A.
14501	Somerville, Rfm. J.		31917	Wood, Cpl. E. W.
		26/429	Youle, Rfm. H.	

THE MERITORIOUS SERVICE MEDAL.

18941	Adamson, Cpl. A.		25/732	Colebrook, R.Q.M.S. E. S.
23/2540	Askenbeck, Sgt. A.		25/858	Croft, R.S.M. F.
23/68	Beattie, Sgt. J. N.		24/729	Crook, Sgt. T. W.
25/81	Berry, Sgt. W. K.		24/739	Dewar, Rfm. W.
26/719	Bray, S/Sgt. B. R.		20130	Fairbairn, Rfm. F.
25/1073	Clark, Q.M.S. T. G.		23/1403	Glentworth, Sgt. J. P.

THE MERITORIOUS SERVICE MEDAL—(Continued).

25/628	Green, Sgt. J. F.	24/1919	Marr, L/Cpl. E. T.
24/1177	Harvey, Rfm. L. J.	23/2506	Mayne, S/Sgt. C. H.
23/778	Henty, Sgt. C. J.	24/1116	Mercer, Sgt. W. J.
25/984	Hickey, Rfm. M.	30965	Moles, Cpl. W. T.
25/1645	Hunt, Sgt. R. E.	25/213	Morison, S/Sgt. H. B.
25716	Jeffs, Sgt. E. C.	62616	Nash, Sgt. B.
25/1217	Jones, Sgt. B.	25/226	Porteous, R.S.M. J.
24/1915	Kingdon, Sgt. B.	26/617	Power, Q.M.S. S. A.
25/121	Kivell, Cpl. C. L.	49004	Rattray, Rfm. J. McH.
23/1431	Langrish, Rfm. J. G.	23/2076	Rice, Rfm. P. J.
26/675	Law, Rfm. W. H. F.	25/813	Richards, L/Cpl. W. H.
24/655	Lomax, R.S.M. R. H.	23/583	Robertson, Sgt. C. C.
24/1134	McDonald, Sgt. E. J.	24/296	St. George, Sgt. G. L.
24/239	Macdougall, S/Sgt. A. H. D.	23/2278	Shaw, Cpl. L.
32983	McGregor, S/Sgt. J.	23/1261	Shardlow, Bandmaster B. J.
12455	McIvor, S.S.M. J. E.	26/473	Smith, L/Cpl. T.
10973	McKay, Cpl. J.	25/1033	Spencer, C.Q.M.S. N. B.
	58425 Whittington, Rfm. C. E.		

MENTIONED IN DESPATCHES.

23/49	Aickin, S/Sgt. T. R.	23/36	Clark, Sgt. P. J.
12/3538	Allen, Lt.-Col. R. C., D.S.O. (3)	23/2128	Colbeck, Lt. W. S.
		23/9	Cowles, Maj. J. R., M.C.
26/1288	Arden, 2/Lt. N. H.	12/2255	Crann, Cpl. S.
23/2	Austin, Lt.-Col. W. S., D.S.O. (2)	26/767	Dalhousie, Cpl. R. H.
		26/299	Davis, Sgt. F. H.
23/670	Bader, Cpl. T.	25/616	Day, Sgt. J. E.
24/361	Bailey, Sgt. A. L.	24/11	Dee, Capt. G. K.
20078	Bailey, Cpl. A. R.	25/20	Dudson, R.S.M. L. C.
13722	Bailey, Sgt. S. G.	15843	Eade, Cpl. A. V.
26/44	Ball, Sgt. D. G.	26/1212	Eastgate, Capt. H.
25/42	Barr, Sgt. G. W.	15/202	Eastwood, Maj. T. R., M.C. (4)
24/16	Barrowclough, Maj. H. E., D.S.O., M.C.	36742	Ellingham, Sgt. E. S.
23290	Baxter, Lt. E., M.C.	26/1036	Emmerson, Rfm. J.
24/3	Beere, Lt.-Col. R. St. J., D.S.O. (3)	26/11	Winter-Evans, Lt.-Col. A., D.S.O. (2)
23/27	Bell, Lt.-Col. P. H., D.S.O. (3)	24/2125	Farthing, R.Q.M.S. H. E.
		26/551	Fisher, Sgt. G. D. McN.
24/370	Bennett, Lt. R. A.	26/4	Fowlds, Capt. W. F.
23/1300	Bishop, Capt. W. G.	13748	Gifford, Rfm. P. H.
3/534	Bogle, Capt. G. V. (N.Z.M.C.)	23/762	Gillespie, Cpl. O. A. (2)
		26/42	Goulding, Lt. F. S.
18608	Bone, Rfm. A. H.	12171	Grant, Lt. R. J., M.C.
24/9	Bowring, Capt. W. A.	26/23	Greenwood, Lt. J. G.
26/82	Boyle, S/Sgt. J. P.	25/640	Halliday, Sgt. R.
25/945	Breach, Sgt. S. F.	24/779	Harvey, Sgt. H. W.
68666	Brown, Cpl. C. H. T.	—	Hastings, Maj. W. H., D.S.O. (3)
23/18	Brydon, Capt. R. O.		
23/1575	Buchler, Lt. F. J. L.	26/59	Hawkes, Sgt. E. T.
18611	Burr, Rfm. T. G.	23/23	Holderness, Capt. H., M.C. (2)
25/16	Burrows, Lt. E.		
10/2386	Carrington, Maj. A. H.	3/1671	Holmes, 2/Lt. J. G.
24/24	Christie, Capt. W. E.	3/3286	Horsburgh, Capt. P. G. (N.Z.M.C.)
54330	Clarke, L/Cpl. F. J.		

MENTIONED IN DESPATCHES—(Continued).

54750	How Chow, Rfm. E. K.	24/1269	Prescott, Lt. J. L.
23/789	Howell, Cpl. W. S.	23/5	Puttick, Lt.-Col. E., D.S.O. (2)
24/182	Hunter, Sgt. A.		
23/460	Iorns, Cpl. A. W.	26/278	Quinn, Sgt. J.
10/1049	Jardine, Lt.-Col. L. H., D.S.O., M.C.	25/1215	Richardson, Maj. H. M. W., M.C.
26/1625	Jensen, Sgt. A.	23/1263	Roache, Lt.-Col. J. G., D.S.O. (2)
25/119	Johanson, Sgt. W. G.		
26/56	Kennedy, Capt. D., M.C.	23/1303	Robinson, Capt. E. C. N.
26/675	Law, Rfm. W. H. F.	39715	Robinson, Maj. W. L.
26/583	Leathley, Rfm. R. P.	25/6	Rogers, Capt. S. D.
23/483	Lepper, Cpl. R.	27692	Rohan, Lt. M. D.
23/334	McCormick, 2/Lt. A. L., M.C., D.C.M.	24/1183	Rosanowski, L/Cpl. H.
		13095	Russell, Lt. J.
23/1315	McDonald, C.Q.M.S. F. E.	26/905	Sache, L./Cpl. E. P.
24/239	MacDougall, S/Sgt. A. H. D.	4/230	Salt, 2/Lt. C. H. (2)
14305	McKenzie, Rfm. J.	25/684	Sampson, Rfm. W. B.
23/2244	McLeod, C.S.M. N.	25/9	Scoular, Capt. S. G. (2)
4/310	Macnab, Maj. A. A.	26/62	Scrivener, Sgt. A. R.
29056	McSkimming, Sgt. R.	25/59	Shearer, Sgt. A.
23/1286	Macky, Capt. N. L., M.C.	6/821	Shepherd, Lt.-Col. N. F., D.S.O. (2)
40591	Malam, Rfm. W. H.		
24/1906	Manning, Lt. L. I., M.C.	41235	Skelley, Capt. P. W.
26/1043	Marchant, Cpl. J. A. A.	23/981	Smith, Sgt. A.
9/445	Marshall, Lt. V.	24/25	Digby-Smith, Maj. A., D.S.O. (2)
26/1043	Martin, Cpl. J. A.		
24/1268	Massey, Capt. F. G., D.S.O., M.C. (3)	24/1	Stewart, Brig.-Gen. A. E., C.M.G., D.S.O. (2)
46527	Mauger, Sgt. E.	26/224	Stewart, S/Sgt. J. B.
15/35	Melvill, Brig.-Gen. C. W., C.M.G., D.S.O. (4)	9/781	Strang, Capt. J. D. K. (2)
		23/1831	Sumner, Lt. W. C. I.
19022	Milne, Rfm. W. D. H.	25/12	Thomson, Capt. A.
37044	Murphy, Maj. J.	39123	Toon, L/Cpl. W. A.
23/529	Murray, Sgt. A. W.	25/525	Turner, 2/Lt. H. A.
24/843	Murray, Sgt. W. J.	24/6	Wilkes, Capt. T. M. (2)
23/536	Nimmo, Rfm. T.	23/644	Wilkie, 2/Lt. G.
23/545	Oxenbridge, Sgt. E. W.	—	Wilson, Maj. H. M., D.S.O. (2)
25/1795	Pascoe, Rfm. A. E.		
23/8	Pow, Lt.-Col. J., D.S.O. (3)	23/960	Wood, Sgt. O.

MENTIONED FOR HOME SERVICE.

(The names of the following were brought to the notice of the Secretary of State for War for valuable services at Home towards the successful conduct of the war.)

24/3	Beere, Lt.-Col. R. St. J., D.S.O.	41438	Jones, Sgt. E. J.
		25/1200	Magnay, Capt. C. R. A.
25/858	Croft, S.M. F.	25/226	Porteous, R.S.M. J.
24/24	Christie, Capt. W. E.	23927	Ridling, Lieut. R. G.
23/1998	Harris, Sgt. H. S.	78255	Shires, Rfm. F. W.
78757	Hockey, Rfm. L. W. F.	18914	Trevethick, Lt. H. J.
	59171	Tyerman, L/Cpl. N. R.	

THE ALBERT MEDAL.

(Awarded in recognition of gallant conduct in saving life at bombing practice, Brocton Camp, 19.4.18.)

23927   Ridling, Lt. R. G.

FOREIGN DECORATIONS.

FRENCH.

CROIX DE GUERRE.

23/2	Austin, Lt.-Col. W. S. D.S.O.
24/16	Barrowclough, Capt. H. E., M.C.
23/27	Bell, Maj. P. H.
10/2386	Carrington, Maj. A. H.
23/1	Fulton, Brig.-Gen. H. T., C.M.G., D.S.O.
15888	Furby, Rfm. S. R.
33061	Jones, Sgt. T.
22685	Loughlin, Rfm. A.
35214	McDonald, Rfm. T. C.
25/448	McNaught, Rfm. G.
38564	Moore, Rfm. J.
23/10	Purdy, Capt. R. G., M.C.
26/623	Rillstone, Sgt. M. J.
23/1263	Roache, Lt.-Col. J. G., D.S.O.
25/59	Shearer, Sgt. A.
14163	Shellam, Rfm. H.
24/1	Stewart, Lt.-Col. A. E., D.S.O.
12502	Sturgess, Rfm. S. C.
23281	Warren, Rfm. C. H.
24/324	Wilson, Rfm. W. K.
24/938	Wotten, Rfm. F. C.

MEDAILLE MILITAIRE.

25754   Thompson, Sgt. P. A.

MEDAILLE D'HONNEUR AVEC GLAIVES EN VERMEIL.

24/535   MacKay, R.S.M. J.

MEDAILLE DE BRONZE.

23/340   St. Leger, Sgt. R. W.

RUSSIAN.

MEDAL OF ST. GEORGE, 2nd Class.

25/239   Simmers, Sgt. R.

BELGIAN.

ORDRE DE LA COURONNE (Officier).

15/35   Melvill, Lt.-Col. C. W.

BELGIAN CROIX DE GUERRE.

23/363	Bickford, C.Q.M.S. T. E.
26/77	Bolton, Rfm. G. M.
10/2386	Carrington, Maj. A. H.
26/730	Conlon, R.S.M. E. J.
24/389	Coupland, C.Q.M.S. A. J.
26571	Dibble, Sgt. J. C.
26/75	Gothard, C.S.M. K. B.
23/1058	Grant, Sgt. P. L.
25/326	Hooper, Rfm. S. N.
6/1319	Hyland, Sgt. F.
15/35	Melvill, Lt.-Col. C.W., D.S.O.
25/445	Moulding, Sgt. J.
23/572	Reeve, C.S.M. E. J.
25751	Senn, Rfm. T. J.
48099	Smith, Cpl. F. R.
25/838	Watkins, Sgt. W.

APPENDIX II.

The Honoured Dead.

In the following list are the names of members of the New Zealand Rifle Brigade who were killed in action or who died of wounds or of sickness contracted while on service in the Great War. Except where rank is mentioned, all were Riflemen.

Abbreviations: (d) = Mentioned in Despatches.
[F] = Foreign Decoration.

BRIGADIER-GENERAL HARRY TOWNSEND FULTON, C.M.G., D.S.O.
(d) [F].

General Fulton was the son of the late Lieut.-Gen. John Fulton, R.A. Born at Dalhousie, India, on August 15th, 1869, he came to New Zealand at an early age, and as a young man served for some time as Lieutenant in the Dunedin High School Cadets, and for four years with the same rank in the Dunedin City Guards Rifle Volunteers. Before reaching the age of 23 years he received a commission in the Imperial Army, being appointed 2nd Lieutenant in the Argyll and Sutherland Highlanders on April 9th, 1892. Towards the end of that year he transferred to the West Yorkshire Regiment. Two years later he joined the Indian Staff Corps, and was attached, first to the 26th Madras Infantry, and then to the 39th Bengal Infantry (Gharwal Rifles). In December, 1897, he was appointed to the 2nd Battalion of the Prince of Wales's (now King Edward's) Own Gurkha Rifles, in which unit he served for a year as a company officer, and two and a half years as Quartermaster. In May, 1901, he was appointed Adjutant of his battalion, was promoted Captain two months later, Major in April, 1910, Second-in-Command in January, 1917, and received brevet-rank of Lieutenant-Colonel in the following June.

With the Gurkhas the late General (then Lieutenant) Fulton fought in the Indian frontier war of 1897/98, serving with the Malakand and Mohmand Frontier Forces (medal with clasp), and participated also in the Tirah Campaign of the same period (clasp). At the outbreak of the Boer War in 1899 he was in New Zealand on sick-leave from the Indian Army, and in accordance with the usual custom volunteered for service with the New Zealand forces. He was appointed Captain of No. 9 Company (afterwards "A" Squadron) of the 4th Contingent, and served with it in Carrington's Rhodesian Field Force in the operations about Ottoshoop and Malmani. At the latter place he received a severe wound, from the effects of which he was never afterwards entirely free. His service in the South African War carried with it the award of the Queen's Medal with three clasps, and was marked by the honour of Mention in Despatches and the decoration of the Distinguished Service Order.

General (then Major) Fulton was on furlough in New Zealand when the Great War broke out, and again, on 5th August, 1914, offered his services to the New Zealand Government. Six days later he joined the Samoan Expeditionary Force, and on his 45th birthday sailed with that body in command of a composite battalion, with the rank of Lieutenant-Colonel. In March of the following year he returned with the relieved troops to New Zealand, and was given command of the 4th Reinforcements due to sail for Egypt in three weeks' time. With these troops he embarked on April 16th, but was next day withdrawn to take command of the new regiment, the formation of which had just been decided upon. The training and the general management of the first two units of this regiment, soon to be known as the New Zealand Rifle Brigade, were placed entirely in his hands, and with them he sailed on active service in October. On the formation of the New Zealand Division in March, 1916, and the arrival in Egypt of the remaining two battalions, he was given command of the Brigade and promoted from the New Zealand rank of Lieutenant-Colonel to that of Brigadier-General.

In connection with the fighting in France, General Fulton was twice mentioned in Despatches, was created a Companion of the Order of St. Michael and St. George on 1st January, 1917, and was awarded the Croix de Guerre in December of the same year.

General Fulton was mortally wounded on March 28th, 1918, at Colincamps on the Somme, and was buried at the Doullens Military Cemetery.

At the close of the war the balance of the officers' mess funds, including that of the mess at Brocton, was voted to the Governors of the Otago Boys' High School, where the late General Fulton had received his early education, for the purpose of founding a scholarship in his memory, to be known as "The General Harry Fulton Bursary," and of placing in the hall of the school a tablet drawing attention to the career of one of its former scholars.

On the occasion of the unveiling of the memorial erected in St. Matthew's Church, Dunedin, by the late General's widow, Sister A. H. Fulton, R.R.C., the following lament, composed by a former schoolmate and close personal friend, was recited. It fittingly expresses the sentiments of his other friends, the men of the New Zealand Rifle Brigade.

Chant Funèbre.
In Memoriam.
Brigadier-General Harry Townsend Fulton, C.M.G., D.S.O.
Obiit 29th March, 1918.

Peal, organ; make great music; lo, a bier
We bear in spirit to the resting-place
Of that which royally served a shining Soul.
In France that marred form lieth. France is here!
Love, loyalty the envious leagues efface,
And scorn the watery wastes between that roll.

Love, loyalty we bear him; he is ours;
We shared his boyhood bright, his laughing youth,
Bade him God-speed when, following his Star,
As true men must, with swift-unfolding powers
He gave himself, whole, one, in simple truth,
To soldier service in a field afar.

Wide, wide is England; they who love her ask
But that they serve her; very careless where;
Yet Destiny, His Will Who rules supreme
Over His subject Worlds, decrees the task,
Pushes her ignorant pieces here and there,
Making man's dream a fact, man's fact a dream.

So, though he left us, though he passed from view
Of outer eyes, though scarce we hoped to see
Him ever again on his adopted shore,
Fate brought him hither when the trumpets blew,
Forth-calling all our Island chivalry
To help in England's warring—ours once more.

Ours, with the wisdom of the years apart
To make his joyous giving rich and warm—
Ask veldt and kopje; ask the men that learned
In war's remorseless testings what gr at heart
Beat 'neath the cool, collected, expert form;
What flame of brotherly love within it burned;

Love never hardship, love not wounds, nor yet
The dread of living death could quench or dim;
Softness and strength his secret; depth and height
In exquisite union none will soon forget.
Long shall we thrill at sudden thought of him,
Our Age's "very perfect, gentle knight."

War's flare died down; peace came again; and he
We loved again bade us a gay adieu,
Passed from our loving vision to his place
On the great Frontier, bending faithfully
To the day's burden midst his Hillmen true,
His by a deeper bond than Faith or Race.

Years lapsed, when lo, the mutterings, the peal,
The loosened levin—all the World in arms!
Not England's fight but Freedom's; and again
By subtle unseen turn of Fortune's wheel
Our hero, resting with us, at the alarms
Sprang to his post, strong leader of strong men.

Samoa saw him; and the Training Ground,
Whence many a levy, moulded by his hand,
Went forth to battle by his spirit fired;
Then the bars fell; an open path he found,
And forth himself at last, in high command,
Fared, as the lion heart of him desired.

Triumph on triumph followed, bay to bay
He added, as his Rifles played their role
On that blood-boltered stage; and did and dared,
And did and dared, from day to glorious day—
Graved deep on Fame's imperishable scroll,
Deep, deep their names, and ours their life that shared.

Loved, trusted, ever staunchly following
Even as followed; neither with success
Made arrogant, nor by reverse downcast;
Thankt of his People, honoured by his King—
What could the starry Soldier further bless
Save that God take him to Himself at last?

We weep not, for we know he riseth still
From height to height; all of him that hath died
We reverently leave beneath the sod.
Heaven needed him some onerous post to fill;
He lives! our hearts supremely satisfied,
Trust the superb economies of God.

Peal, organ; make great music; fill the Fane
With phrases magical, on which our praise
And prayer soft to the throne of God may rise—
Prayer that Earth's sacrifice be not in vain,
That God from the wreckt World a nobler raise;
Praise that beyond Earth's best His Wonder lies!

MARSYAS.

JOHNSTON, BRIGADIER-GENERAL F. EARL, C.B., (d) [F].
Killed immediately after taking over the command of the Brigade,
7th August, 1917.

41461	Abbott, G. 12.10.17	53299	Allan, R. G. 28.10.18
14182	Abernethy, 2/Lt. K. S. 16.8.17	48144	Allen, Revd. A. (C.F.) 8.5.18
55293	Abernethy, T. M. 12.9.18	15857	Allen, A. G. 3.1.17
26/655	Ackers, E. L. 15.9.16	55191	Allen, R. H. 23.11.18
25/304	Adams, L/Cpl. A. 15.9.16	31798	Allen, R. W. 7.6.17
65525	Adams, C. G. 11.5.18	25/1196	Alley, F. 13.12.17
26/700	Adams, G. 18.11.17	49683	Allwill, J. R. 26.8.18
23/47	Adams, J. T. 15.9.16	13719	Almond, W. 16.1.18
19100	Adams, R. B. 7.6.17	22915	Alquist, C. A. 7.6.17
23/336	Adamson, F. V. 31.10.18	26/706	Ambridge, C. T. 14.12.16
25778	Ahern, L. J. 1.6.17	28411	Amner, R. 1.6.17
24/2140	Ahern, W. 26.7.16	23/1319	Ander, E. F. 22.9.16
65092	Aherne, T. 8.10.18	54316	Andersen, O. 15.1.18
59180	Ah Keong, A. 9.9.18	22914	Andersen, N. 12.10.17
24/670	Aitken, Sgt. E. B. 10.9.16	25/578	Anderson, A. 15.9.16
70211	Aiton, A. 29.8.18	26/432	Anderson, A. 24.9.16
56704	Alberthsen, B. 14.9.18	11/1629	Anderson, A. R. J. 12.10.17
24/957	Aldridge, A. 17.6.17	23/989	Anderson, C. 15.9.16
26/1561	Aldridge, T. B. 12.9.16	27192	Anderson, D. W. 11.8.17
24/1926	Aldridge, W. 27.11.16	71546	Anderson, E. 3.11.18
26/45	Alexander, L/Cpl. (T/Cpl.) F. J. 4.11.18	24/2503	Anderson, J. B. 26.8.18
		15302	Anderson, J. R. 13.11.16
45338	Alexander, G. 8.1.18	25/709	Anderson, Cpl. L. H. 16.12.18
31796	Alexander, G. A. 14.6.17		
24/1324	Allan, A. 8.10.18	65524	Anderson, R. C. 26.8.18
45644	Allan, A. 10.12.18	54317	Anderson, R. W. 5.8.18
25/164	Allan, C. 15.9.16	58720	Anderson, T. 26.8.18

55892	Andrew, F. P. 17.12.17		61982	Babbage, F. R. G. 30.10.18
25/1155	Andrew, J. 18.7.16		22750	Bacchus, J. H. 15.9.16
25781	Andrew, P. R. 16.10.17		22751	Bacchus, R. L. 15.9.16
21952	Andrews, F. J. 26.8.18		23/365	Backman, O. 26.3.17
32929	Andrews, L/Cpl. H. G. 30.9.17		38484	Baikie, R. S. 28.3.18
			53755	Baildon, L/Cpl. W. 5.2.18
25/155	Angell, C.S.M. H. W. 7.6.17		62482	Bailey, R. M. 9.5.18
			24/1334	Bailey, P. E. 1.6.16
25/481	Annals, F. J. 15.9.16		13722	Bailey, Sgt. S. G. (d) 12.9.18
23/53	Annand, A. L. 10.9.16			
19224	Annett, J. 7.8.17		23/992	Bain, H. 15.9.16
23/991	Anniss, E. 13.11.16		75352	Bain, J. 8.10.18
72052	Anson, R. W. 8.10.18		28268	Baines, W. E. 20.5.18
26/331	Anstis, L/Cpl. P. 15.9.16		42619	Baird, A. 24.10.18
25782	Appleyard, Sgt. D. 30.7.18		23/671	Baird, W. 8.8.17
48889	Appleyard, J. 24.10.18		20080	Baker, Cpl. E. T. 12.10.17
15858	Archer, E. 7.8.17		44246	Baker, F. C. 8.12.17
25/574	Archibald, D. 21.5.16		23/672	Baker, H. 23.8.18
25/302	Archibald, J. 1.10.16		52359	Baker, J. 21.4.18
23/1288	Arden, Capt. N. H. (d). 4.10.17		24804	Baker, J. R. 12.10.17
			25/1669	Balero, J. 16.11.17
26/49	Armit, Sgt. R. L. 15.9.16		61983	Bales, S. E. 20.5.18
25/577	Armitage, H. 15.9.16		31107	Ball, H. E. 26.5.18
26/381	Armitage, T. W. 15.9.16		24/679	Ballagh, Cpl. R. 18.6.17
18581	Armstrong, Lt. P. F. 6.4.18		23/1321	Bamsey, A. H. 15.9.16
			68588	Barber, W. J. 16.7.18
56213	Armstrong, P. T. 9.9.18		22752	Barclay, F. 25.9.16
53995	Arnott, R. H. 4.'1.18		24/41	Barclay, L/Cpl. W. G. 14.7.16
28951	Arnold, L/Cpl. (T/Cpl.) C. J., M.M. 21.4.18			
			28954	Barker, G. T. 5.4.18
25/930	Arrol, J. 15.9.16		44960	Barker, T. E. 12.10.17
70080	Arthur, L. G. 5.10.18		24/964	Barlow, A. J. 29.9.16
24/36	Ashton, Sgt. H. 22.9.16		8/1398	Barlow, E. E. 1.7.18
18960	Ashwell, J. 13.9.18		68925	Barlow, F. 12.9.18
26/433	Ashworth, F. R. 15.9.16		52928	Barlow, H. 19.11.17
40175	Askew, W. R. 9.9.18		26767	Barlow, Sgt. P. 15.5.18
25/959	Asquith, H. D. 18.6.17		53626	Barnacle, H. A. Y. 7.12.17
24/1331	Astridge, Cpl. W. G. 12.10.17		3/1899	Barnard, A. 22.8.18
			24/647	Barnard, C. V. 25.11.17
25/482	Atkins, T. F. 15.9.16		47962	Barr, L/Cpl. J. W. 30.8.18
23331	Atkinson, H. 15.9.16		25/309	Barrett, Cpl. (T/Sgt.) C. R. 12.10.17
26530	Atkinson, J. T. 7.6.17			
25/28	Atkinson, Sgt. L. A. 22.9.16		12128	Barrett, J. H. 4.10.18
			23/994	Barris, L/Cpl. P. 24.6.17
14714	Atkinson, Lt. (T/Capt.) S. A. 5.6.17		25/1658	Barron, P. 12.10.17
			15327	Barrow, N. 6.8.18
53746	Atwood, E. 8.1.18		56410	Barrowman, J. 9.9.18
24/339	Austin, E. M. 15.9.16		38482	Barry, J. P. 12.10.17
23/2148	Austin, F. H. 8.6.17		26/384	Barson, G. E. 4.1.18
23/669	Austin, Cpl. H. R. 13.9.16		56717	Bartholomew, K. M. 29.3.18
32283	Austin, J. J. 7.6.17			
40271	Autridge, C. 12.10.17		24/2146	Bartlett, P. N. 24.9.16
24/675	Avery, A. G. 3.10.16		49865	Bartley, J. 8.10.18
23/1929	Avis, J. 11.9.16		58724	Bartley, R. 9.9.18
23/58	Ayling, 2/Lt. A. B. 4.11.18		12/2638	Bartley, W. 10.10.18
64982	Ayling, F. 12.11.18		24/40	Bartrum, Cpl. C. F. 5.4.18
56209	Ayling, J. 1.6.18		26/83	Bason, F. 15.7.16

23/1325	Bassett, A. E. 30.8.18		19950	Benjamin, H. T. 11.6.17
40176	Bassett, E. 28.12.17		57013	Bennett, C. 17.3.18
25/162	Bassett, Sgt. E., M.M. 23.11.17		65278	Bennett, E. A. 26.8.18
28416	Bassett, I. G. 14.6.17		24326	Bennett, 2/Lt. E. B. 12.10.17
23/65	Bateman, H. A. 15.9.16		24/972	Bennett, H. E. E. 15.9.16
26/709	Bateman, H. O. 15.9.16		21142	Bennett, 2/Lt. J. L. 12.10.17
45182	Bateman, T. H. 7.1.18			
24/345	Bates, 2/Lt. G., D.C.M. 4.11.18		25/91	Berendt, L/Cpl. G. P. 31.3.18
24/633	Bates, H. L. 30.9.16		21/42	Bernard, 2/Lt. V. R. 4.11.18
69395	Bates, W. 30.8.18			
23290	Baxter, Lt. E., M.C. (d) 12.10.18		36392	Berrett, Cpl. B. 8.10.18
			32295	Berry, A. E. 21.6.17
33815	Baxter, E. G. 5.4.18		23/362	Berry, 2/Lt. A. J. F. 12.10.17
72393	Baylee, J. C. 1.10.18			
48896	Bayne, J. J. 27.3.18		64195	Berry, A. L. 31.8.18
26/78	Baxter, L/Cpl. E. 19.9.16		47110	Berry, J. 26.3.18
25/259	Beachen, F. J. 13.3.17		27767	Berry, J. A. 12.10.17
45030	Beale, L/Cpl. G. H. 15.10.18		24/43	Berry, T. 30.9.16
			26/487	Best, H. P. 24.9.16
12968	Bean, C. W. 7.6.17		68104	Bettridge, W. 4.11.18
25/163	Bean, Cpl. W. E. C. 19.7.16		25794	Beverley, D. 5.5.17
23/2154	Beaton, J. 9.6.17		28466	Bevins, D. 12.2.18
33057	Beattie, B. O. 2.10.18		47966	Bewley, J. 5.4.18
22919	Beattie, L/Cpl. D. 8.4.18		24/356	Bicknell, L/Cpl. C. R. 15.9.16
26/434	Beattie, Sgt. L. F. 9.9.18			
38797	Beattie, 2/Lt. P. M. 4.11.18		23/1332	Biondi, L. 25.5.17
41718	Beatty, L/Cpl. G. 30.3.18		53121	Birchall, L/Cpl. A. V. 28.3.18
15862	Beaumont, C. 23.12.16			
25/85	Beaumont, T. A. G. 15.9.16		54724	Birch, J. F. 5.4.18
74852	Beaurepaire, L. J. 4.11.18		23/364	Bird, A. J. 15.9.16
24/690	Beaven, L/Cpl. W. H. G. 18.6.17		44083	Bird, F. 12.10.17
			26/52	Birss, 2/Lt. A. C. 12.10.17
20485	Beck, G. 17.10.17		25/49	Bisset, G. E. 7.6.17
24/2150	Beckett, C. D. 12.10.17		49226	Bissett, N. 26.8.18
24/971	Beckett, M. 28.5.16		68590	Bisphan, W. C. 26.8.18
10988	Becroft, W. C. 12.10.17		45031	Black, 2/Lt. C. L. P. 30.7.18
24/48	Bedggood, Cpl. W. W. C., M.M. 25.9.16			
			12/2215	Black, J. S. 7.6.17
26/1056	Beechey, H. W. A. 18.1.18		24/2156	Blackall, R. S. 2.10.16
24/1337	Beechey, L/Cpl. L. F. 10.5.17		25/948	Blackham, J. 26.9.16
			23/681	Blacklock, G. 22.9.16
22909	Beehan, 2/Lt. A. J. 27.3.18		23/968	Blackman, 2/Lt. A. R., M.M. 9.9.18
26535	Beeson, L/Cpl. C. B. 8.9.18			
31108	Behm, W. E. 1.5.18		32934	Blackmore, W. E. 7.6.17
8/2405	Behrent, L/Cpl. A. E. 28.8.18		23/682	Blaikie, R. G. 28.1.16
			26/79	Blaikie, Sgt. S. J. 24.9.16
70929	Bell, J. 25.10.18		12346	Blair, R. E. 7.6.17
22753	Bell, L. 20.9.16		15865	Blair, L/Cpl. W. W. 24.11.17
24/1255	Bellamy, W. J. 19.7.16			
26/437	Belliss, R. H. 6.4.18		57020	Blake, G. W. 3.12.17
24/1937	Belsham, W. J. 8.7.16		23/2544	Blanchard, C. 15.9.16
22930	Belton, E. L. 12.10.17		26/48	Bland, Cpl. H. G. 15.9.16
25/1564	Benbow, E. 22.9.16		25/1191	Blatch, J. R. 15.9.16
18948	Benbow, T. H. 7.6.17		22757	Blinks, R. G. 6.1.17
22754	Bendall, G. E. 10.9.16		47970	Bloxham, C. G. 5.10.18

18607	Bloxom, T. G. 9.11.17		25/945	Breach, 2/Lt. S. F. (d) 8.10.18
24/67	Blundell, Cpl. F. W. 4.1.18			
22932	Blyton, L/Cpl. S. 5.4.18		31803	Brearton, L/Cpl. T. H. 1.6.18
25802	Boddy, T. 3.1.18		21778	Breen, T. J. 12.10.17
22760	Bodley, D. 15.9.16		26/656	Bremner, C. 31.7.16
3/534	Bogle, Capt. C. V., (d), (N.Z.M.C.). 17.9.16		32808	Brennan, J. 12.10.17
			25800	Breuer, J. C. 8.8.17
47497	Bollinger, H. 15.3.18		25/530	Brewer, Cpl. E. A. 12.9.16
38115	Bolton, A. 15.10.17		26/40	Brewer, L/Sgt. H. E. 1.10.16
21774	Bond, R. 4.8.17			
24/56	Bonner, R. 15.9.16		13688	Bridge, G. I. 7.6.17
23/77	Booker, A. B., M.M. 31.10.17		24332	Bridge, Cpl. H. D. 25.11.17
			31110	Bridge, W. H. 12.10.17
45587	Booker, S. A. 15.1.18		25/82	Bridgeman, L/Cpl. A. C. 7.6.17
26/291	Boon, L/Cpl. R. D. 12.7.17			
24/1342	Booth, Cpl. A. W. 20.9.16		57022	Bridger, W. 23.8.18
21485	Booth, L/Cpl. C. F. 7.9.17		64935	Briggs, G. E. 6.8.18
20960	Booth, G. H. 4.2.17		23/1941	Briggs, J. 15.9.16
24/60	Borrows, Bugler A. L. S. 15.9.16		3/1687	Briggs, Pte. R. A. E. (N.Z.M.C.) 25.8.18
75078	Boswell, D. W. 5.10.18		24/1344	Bright, H. S. 15.9.16
54460	Bottcher, L. H. 3.11.18		23/1002	Brightling, A. R. 20.7.16
40766	Boucher, H. 11.8.17		40502	Brindle, F. J. 20.10.17
23/1327	Boulden, G. E. 15.9.16		41213	Brittan, 2/Lt. H. R. 5.4.18
25/159	Boundy, Sgt. S. T. W. 15.9.16		24/693	Broadbridge, T. C. 11.11.16
			30340	Broadmore, L. F. 12.10.17
18954	Bourke, G. H. 7.6.17		25/1067	Brodie, R. 15.9.16
22928	Bowden, E. R. 12.10.17		6/1788	Brook, L/Cpl. J. 29.3.18
23/2155	Bowe, D. 15.9.16		12/600	Brook, Lt. J. C. 2.9.18.
14025	Bowler, Lt. (T/Capt.) D. C., M.C. 12.10.17		71054	Brooke, J. F. 10.10.18
			47114	Brooks, J. C. 12.10.17
24/978	Bowles, Sgt. W. B., M.M. 6.4.18		21480	Broomfield, L/Cpl. W. W. 28.11.17
56407	Bowman, H. F. 12.9.18		23/2548	Brown, E. 26.9.16.
24/9	Bowring, Capt. W. A. (d) 24.9.16		48698	Brown, E. C. 12.10.17
			23/1526	Brown, E. L. S. 6.8.17
24/695	Boyce, L/Cpl. A. A. J. 7.6.17		72229	Brown, J. 15.10.18
			42624	Brown, J. D. 18.7.18
24/694	Boyce, D. S. 15.9.16		41306	Brown, J. F. 10.11.17
43911	Boyce, J. S. 28.3.18		25/937	Brown, M. L. 24.10.16
54225	Boyd, A. 8.10.18		12122	Brown, N. P. 14.10.17
24/1942	Boyd, A. 12.9.16		14056	Brown, L/Cpl. P. J. 14.6.17
24/355	Boyd, Sgt. A. A. 12.10.17			
25/1662	Boyd, J. 1.10.16		53312	Brown, L/Cpl. R. 4.11.18
23/367	Boyer, Sgt. A. S. 15.9.16		10051	Brown, Lt. T., M.C. 23.8.18
19227	Boyle, J. F. 8.10.18		53752	Brown, W. 6.4.18
44439	Braddock, J. L. 5.12.17		26/1572	Browne, C. B. 29.10.16
23/79	Bradford, H. M. 31.1.17		23128	Bruce, Cpl. J. 14.8.17
28968	Bradley, J. 4.8.17		28424	Bruce, W. B. 7.6.17
26027	Braithwaite, L/Cpl. H. W. 16.2.18		54226	Brunning, J. W. 30.8.18
			28425	Bryan, W. H. 11.9.17
24/1944	Brakhage, C., M.M. 14.11.18		55906	Bryant, J. E. 8.2.18
			24/57	Bryden, L/Cpl. A. J. 19.7.16
42622	Brand, C. 12.10.17			
71178	Braniff, T. J. 9.10.18		45341	Bryden, T. J. 12.10.17
31770	Brasell, A. 16.8.17		23/18	Brydon, Capt. R. O. (d) 16.9.16
20487	Bray, J. 13.6.17			

26/1570	Buchanan, G. 11.9.16	25/260	Cameron, R. A. 9.9.18
23/1575	Buchler, Lt. (T/Capt.) F. L. 6.4.18	48701	Cameron, R. H. 12.10.17
		69572	Cameron, R. W. 10.10.18
69567	Buck, H. E. 12.9.18	25/1698	Cameron, T. 30.4.18
25/796	Pacey-Buck, H. F. 15.9.16	23342	Cameron, T. C. 15.9.16
42030	Buck, W. H. 4.11.18	23/1947	Campbell, A. 12.10.17
23/1944	Buck, W. 12.9.18	65099	Campbell, C. 30.3.18
25/41	Buckeridge, D. W. 26.8.18	55208	Campbell, C. 9.11.18
27747	Buckley, J. 12.2.17	22770	Campbell, C. E. 15.9.16
26/386	Budd, L/Cpl. F. W. 25.9.16	25/727	Campbell, Cpl. D. P. 15.9.16
25/308	Budge, L/Cpl. J. A. 29.8.18		
69801	Buglass, G. Y. 26.8.18	14061	Campbell, G. H. 8.6.17
38863	Bunt, Cpl. G. A. 9.9.18	24339	Campbell, Sgt. H. W. 3.2.18
41964	Bulfin, G. F. 5.4.18	14063	Campbell, J. 7.12.17
24/982	Bull, G. R. 7.6.17	48908	Campbell, J. C. 2.5.18
59187	Bull, H. E. 16.7.18	62012	Campbell, N. C. 5.10.18
38491	Bullingham, L/Cpl. S. V. J. 26.10.18	23/377	Campbell, P. 15.9.16
		25805	Campbell, R. 8.8.17
68506	Burborough, H. R. 12.9.18	23/376	Campbell, W. J. 15.9.16
32294	Burgess, G. B. 12.10.18	26/92	Canton, W. I. 15.9.16
25/939	Burgess, J. 6.8.17	26/339	Capper, R. 15.9.16
33828	Burgess, J. 12.9.18	23/702	Cardno, G. A. 15.9.16
65339	Burgess, J. 4.11.18	57028	Carlson, R. 5.4.18
25361	Burgess, W. J. 7.6.17	23/93	Carlyon, L/Cpl. J. 10.12.17
26/1571	Burkhardt, A. P. 15.9.16	56734	Carman, B. T. 17.10.18
24/702	Burnell, R. H. 24.9.16	23/1340	Carman, H. E. 15.9.16
23/86	Burnett, G. F. 5.4.18	35158	Carmody, W. 12.10.17
27059	Burns, E. 12.10.17	46289	Carn, W. 10.9.18
64887	Burns, J. 17.7.18	39724	Carncross, 2/Lt. C. C. 12.10.17
27066	Burns, J. 7.6.17		
23/694	Burrell, F.W. 15.5.18	24/396	Carney, J. 15.9.16
75282	Burridge, H. W. 29.10.18	25/165	Carr, L/Sgt. C. O. 25.5.16
25/16	Burrows, Lt. E., (d). 22.9.16	36406	Carr, L/Cpl. E. M. 27.3.18
		14755	Carr, W. J. 6.1.18
25/724	Burton, A. B. 15.9.16	14227	Carroll, Cpl. F. 30.3.18
40504	Busby, W. H. 20.1.18	24/991	Carson, J. 15.10.17
62008	Butler, D. J. 31.10.18	27070	Carson, W. J. 13.12.18
25/935	Butler, J. 2.10.16	47977	Carter, G. A. 7.1.18
26/86	Butler, L. 8.7.16	10997	Carter, H. S. 12.10.17
38426	Butler, D. 12.10.17	26556	Carthy, V. C. 7.6.17
44251	Butler, T. 12.10.17	24/74	Casey, F. J. 15.9.16
18958	Butler, W. J. 14.6.17	25/493	Casey, P. 15.9.16
24/62	Butler, Wm. 9.10.16	53476	Cassidy, F. C. 7.5.18
23/2551	Byrne, J. M. 15.9.16	69681	Cassidy, F. W. 4.11.18
26/1085	Byrnes, R. J. 15.9.16	31814	Cassidy, P. 12.10.17
58230	Byron, G. H. R. 8.10.18	65620	Cassin, H. 29.8.18
		24/22	Castle, Lt. A. P. 15.9.16
65343	Cain, W. T. 2.8.18	24/382	Cate, W. G. 15.9.16
65053	Caird, J. S. 10.7.18	24/2159	Cattanach, W. 6.5.17
15871	Cairncross, J. 28.2.17	25/419	Catton, H. E. 14.9.18
24/989	Calder, Sgt. J. 12.10.17	21492	Causer, W. 21.6.17
23/1005	Callaghan, L. H. 5.8.16	51333	Cavanagh, J. 4.10.18
23/91	Callaghan, M. 24.9.16	23/1259	Cavanagh, T. N. 5.5.17
24/1950	Cameron, L/Cpl. H. 13.6.17	12987	Caven, J. 15.6.17
46518	Cameron, J. 26.3.18	25/1685	Chadwick, J. W. 3.12.18
13689	Cameron, 2/Lt. McR. C. 10.9.17	42285	Chadwick, N. 12.10.17
		21489	Chalmers, F. W. 21.6.17

23/1344	Chalmers, G. G. 8.10.18	22776	Clark, W. 8.6.17
39604	Chalmers, R. 27.6.17	53318	Clark, W. M. 6.4.18
24/383	Chamberlain, Sgt. L. O. 26.8.18	54007	Clarke, G. A. 19.5.18
		53475	Clarke, J. C. 31.3.18
24/384	Chambers, C. S. 2.10.16	26560	Clarke, J. R. 8.6.17
23/1011	Chammen, A. 15.9.16	26561	Clarke, W. J. 8.10.18
37767	Chance, J. 28.9.17	45668	Clarke, W. W. 12.10.17
23147	Chandler, F. J. 7.1.17	44930	Clausen, W. E. 2.5.18
24762	Chandler, S. E. 16.11.17	25/1119	Clayson, Sgt. J. W., M.M. 9.9.18
49692	Chaplin, J. C. A. 26.5.18		
24/76	Chapman, A. 17.7.16	26/1577	Clegg, L. 26.9.16
24/77	Chapman, G. 19.7.16	65353	Clemens, W. H. 8.10.18
24/2160	Chapman, H. 31.12.16	26048	Clementson, L/Sgt. C. E. 12.9.18
12977	Chapman, L. H. 12.10.17		
33301	Charleston, J. 15.3.18	68239	Clinker, G. F. 8.10.18
24/721	Chapman, R. 14.11.16	25/600	Clive, B. 2.10.16
45312	Charlton, Lt. A. H. 3.2.18	26/729	Cloke, L/Cpl. J. 26.9.16
69573	Chase, G. E. 8.10.18	30346	Clothier, C. A. 26.3.18
25/925	Chermside, D. J. McB. 7.6.17	22708	Clough, A. R. 31.10.18
		47989	Clough, G. L. 14.12.17
26/1573	Cheyne, G. 15.9.16	45479	Coate, Sgt. H. L. 26.8.18
53903	Cheyne, G. B. 5.4.18	25/262	Cobbe, 2/Lt. E. 12.10.17
25807	Cheyne, J. M. 7.7.17	44254	Cochrane, H. J. 26.8.18
24/2	Childs, Maj. A. J. 15.9.16	53737	Cochrane, J. 27.3.18
21791	Childs, C. 19.5.17	18621	Cochrane, Sgt. R., M.M. 3.8.18
52951	Chirnside, J. W. 1.5.18		
40883	Chirnside, L/Cpl. R. J. 29.8.18	25813	Cockburn, A. 12.10.17
		25/602	Cockburn, L/Cpl. E. 19.8.17
53145	Chisholm, J. 12.7.18		
10998	Chitty, J., (d). 7.6.17	18970	Coffey, T. 27.6.17
39759	Christensen, Cpl. A. B. 10.5.18	25/495	Cogle, J. F. 15.9.16
		52831	Cole, F. A. 23.12.17
26044	Christensen, E. 7.6.17	38260	Coleman, A. J. 19.7.18
24/385	Christiansen, E. 15.9.16	25/857	Coleman, C. C. 4.7.16
24/80	Christiansen, L/Cpl. H. 1.10.16	20500	Coleman, J. 8.6.17
		32941	Colgan, H. 7.6.17
64939	Christie, W. A. 29.7.18	25/1689	Collett, S. B. 5.4.18
24/713	Christie, L/Cpl. W. J. 15.9.16	57034	Collinge, F. P. 26.8.18
		31398	Collington, O. 22.6.17
23/382	Christmas, P. J. 15.9.16	67520	Collins, A. P. 1.9.18
24/7	Christophers, Capt. H. H. 2.6.16	24/93	Collins, Cpl. H. C. 14.7.16
		23109	Collins, 2/Lt. W. E. 7.6.17
32506	Chuck, G. H. 12.10.17	51646	Collinson, C. 23.11.17
27781	Church, J. S. 12.10.17	23/2131	Collis, D. L. W. 15.9.16
42041	Churches, E. G. 12.10.17	24/649	Coltman, Sgt. C. W. 14.7.16
25/1694	Claasen, H. 15.9.16	56416	Comport, H. 8.10.18
24/81	Clapham, H. A. G. 15.9.16	26/294	Comrie, J. M. 21.9.16
13855	Clare, L/Cpl. C. H. J. 30.3.17	18967	Condon, W. F. 3.4.18
		24/94	Congdon, A. E. 15.9.16
24/84	Clark, C. R. C. 15.9.16	40299	Connell, J. 25.5.18
25/738	Clark, J. 15.9.16	49874	Connelly, J. T. 26.4.18
38120	Clark, J. R. 17.11.18	28979	Conway, D. 21.6.17
23/1016	Clark, P. 2.10.16	53730	Conyngham, J. 10.9.18
46224	Clark, 2/Lt. P. G. 26.8.18	10/1057	Cook, F. 29.8.18
25/17	Clark, 2/Lt. R. C. 4.10.16	32303	Cook, J. 7.6.17
26/746	Clark, L/Cpl. R. McG. 14.10.17	29914	Cook, J. Y. 30.8.18
		48703	Cook, S. G. M. 12.10.17

53320	Coombe, G. 10.12.17		32507	Cresswell, G. H. 12.10.17
45191	Coombes, J. L. 4.5.18		23/719	Cresswell, L/Sgt. (T/Sgt.) J. K. 9.1.18
32820	Cooney, J. V. 12.10.17			
23/99	Cooper, A. R. 15.9.16		44258	Cresswell, J. T. 12.10.17
53901	Cooper, A. W. 9.9.18		26/90	Crighton, Cpl. J. H. 3.10.16
31819	Cooper, G. J. 7.7.17			
25/1161	Cooper, L/Sgt. W. A. 7.6.17		38497	Cripps, A. C. 21.6.17
			56741	Cripps, V. G. 6.4.18
48916	Cooper, L/Cpl. W. L. 11.9.18		14232	Cronin, M. 12.10.17
			1/607	Cronin, T. 30.3.18
24/1254	Copland, R. D. 19.9.16		12143	Crook, H. N. 28.12.16
55916	Copp, J. H. 19.2.18		25/535	Crook, J. 2.10.16
56246	Corbett, E. 17.7.18		23/1023	Crooks, L/Cpl. W. J. 8.6.17
52959	Corbett, L/Cpl. K. 26.8.18		25819	Cross, A. S. 7.6.17
26566	Corbett, H. A. 15.6.17		23/396	Cross, G. H. 6.5.16
63829	Corbishley, C. A. 9.9.18		25/263	Cross, J. 1.10.16
26/739	Corden, E. 17.9.16		24/1360	Crozier, A. H. 15.9.16
25/1238	Corin, W. H. 27.3.18		39180	Crozier, W. 23.11.17
46438	Cork, J. Y. 20.10.17		20107	Cruickshank, J. H. 8.5.17
32939	Corkhill, C. R. 13.8.17		31401	Cruller, H. A. B. 12.10.17
26/235	Corkhill, E. J. 16.9.16		23/1960	Cule, J. 15.9.16
54472	Cormack, Sgt. F. E., M.M. 4.11.18		23/1961	Cumberland, Sgt. A. C. 12.10.17
24/386	Cornes, W. C. A. 30.9.16		59801	Cumming, W. M. 28.11.18
24/2173	Corney, Cpl. C. K. 5.10.18		11237	Cummings, D. P. 12.9.18
33312	Corsbie, Sgt. E. T., D.C.M. 8.10.18		23/720	Cummins, P. E. 15.9.16
			13739	Cunliffe, R. L. 4.12.17
25815	Cosgrave, E. 19.8.17		23/110	Cunningham, C. 25.5.17
24/1004	Coton, F. W. 12.10.17		14761	Cunningham, F. P. 7.8.17
53647	Cotter, M. 7.1.18		24/1534	Cunningham, L/Cpl. J. 2.5.18
58745	Cottingham, H. J. 5.4.18			
24/70	Couch, J. R. 22.8.16		23/1365	Cunningham, Sgt. W. 29.10.18
62021	Coulson, E. 6.8.18			
24/387	Coulson, S. 30.9.16		47410	Curkovitch, P. 8.12.17
56747	Courtney, R. 5.4.18		25/963	Curline, H. N. 1.10.16
23/9	Cowles, Maj. J. R., M.C., (d). 25.11.17		24/1008	Currie, Sgt. E. 9.6.17
			25/533	Curry, A. J. 2.10.16
25/740	Cox, R. J. 7.6.17		25/744	Curry, O. J. 29.9.16
25/605	Cox, S. G. 24.9.16		39183	Curtis, G. 12.10.17
24345	Coyle, Sgt. F. J. 18.8.17		26/47	Curtis, L/Sgt. K. O. 11.8.16
25/168	Crabbe, Sgt. J. B. 17.4.16		45343	Cuthbertson, J. P. 12.10.17
65359	Craig, A. A. 27.9.18			
23/715	Craig, A. C. 8.8.17		65364	Daily, M. 12.9.18
40301	Craig, A. W. 8.10.18		24/731	Dale, A. E. 10.10.16
59098	Craig, T. P. 4.11.18		41073	Dale, R. J. 1.10.17
52385	Craig, W. R. 9.5.18		44259	Daniels, J. E. 4.11.18
21799	Craighead, H. 15.3.17		25/1120	Danzey, H. 23.6.17
23/1359	Cran, J. 20.9.16		14191	Darling, 2/Lt. C. 26.8.18
14765	Crann, P. 3.5.18		58748	Darragh, T. W. 30.8.18
57036	Craven, N. E. 30.8.18		28991	Dass, E. 2.7.17
23/392	Craw, L/Cpl. G. 6.8.17		25/1711	Dath, J. 15.9.16
27076	Crawford, D. 7.6.17		24/1365	D'Ath, W. J. 15.9.16
24/1963	Crawford, G. P. 5.4.18		18030	Daulton, R. F. 12.9.18
72236	Crawford, H. 4.11.18		25/377	Davenport, L/Cpl. D. 6.10.17
23/1362	Crawford, R. 8.3.17			
46440	Creamer, L. 18.4.18		23/113	Davey, L/Cpl. D. 12.10.17
23/394	Crean, L/Cpl. P. L. 26.7.16		57581	Davey, A. G. 8.10.18

22158	Davey, J. M. 7.12.17		25/618	Dick, J. 15.9.16
23/1370	Davey, Cpl. L. 5.10.18		23/1374	Dick, R. J. 15.9.16
24/734	Davey, S. E. 15.9.16		26/26	Dickey, 2/Lt. C. V. 12.10.17
25/101	David, E. J. 21.10.17			
15877	Davidson, A. 10.11.16		26/753	Dickey, J. D. 15.9.16
56913	Davidson, A. 12.9.18		15853	Dillon, E. T. 3.7.17
65622	Davidson, J. 21.8.18		24/404	Dinan, J. H. . 14.11.16
24/1964	Davidson, J. A. 8.11.16		23/38	Dines, Sgt. G. W. 15.9.16
44260	Davidson, R. N. 20.11.17		23/1373	Divehall, C. W. J. 15.9.16
24/1366	Davies, Cpl. C. H. 15.9.16		47997	Dix, G. 12.10.17
23/1033	Davies, F. 15.9.16		53764	Dixon, C. W. 6.2.18
45671	Davies, P. S. 12.10.17		24/1025	Dixon, L/Sgt. J. F. 15.11.16
65768	Davies, T. H. 12.9.18			
71389	Davies, W. J. F. 26.10.18		26068	Dixon, R. J. 23.2.17
23/402	Davis, E. N. 25.12.15.		25/1045	Dixon, S. J. 26.8.18
24/1965	Davis, F. L. 9.9.18		12158	Dobson, Sgt. J. 5.4.18
24/733	Davis, Cpl. G. H. 7.6.17		25684	Dobson, J. 8.10.18
44261	Davis, H. H. W. 12.10.17		54336	Dodd, L/Sgt. E. H. 11.9.18
24/1018	Davis, H. W. 15.9.16		53329	Doggett, A. C. 29.3.18
23/116	Davis, Cpl. L. H. M. 20.6.17		42479	Doherty, C. 7.4.18
26/761	Davis, S. 23.9.16		20118	Doherty, L/Cpl. E. 26.8.18
64989	Davison, L. P. 26.8.18		23358	Doherty, J. W. 7.11.18
18900	Davy, 2/Lt. E. B. 12.10.17		24/125	Doig, P. W. 7.9.17
26/757	Daw, L/Cpl. A. G. 6.11.18		25688	Donaldson, I. D. 5.4.18
69576	Dawkins, V. L. 9.10.18		25/747	Donaldson, J. 15.9.16
42633	Dawson, J. H. 12.10.17		23/1254	Donaldson, S. J. 5.5.17
23/726	Dawson, V. 9.10.18		70095	Donn, C. A. 27.10.18
20507	Day, D. W. 3.5.17		15882	Donn, E. 7.6.17
53763	Day, F. 26.8.18		23/734	Donn (T/Cpl.), J., M.M. 8.10.18
26/541	Day, M. D. 20.9.16			
24/2179	Dear, F. E. 15.10.17		73327	Donn, R. 17.10.18
20115	Death, A. S. H. 19.8.17		15350	Donn, Cpl. S. 9.9.18
38137	De Blois, W. J. 9.9.17		23929	Donnan, 2/Lt. A. V. 10.6.17
24/11	Dee, Capt, G. K., (d). 8.6.17			
			44263	Doran, J. J. 21.11.17
52835	Deed, E. T. 15.7.18		41315	Dorricott, W. 12.10.17
44836	Deeney, T. J. 15.8.17		41274	Douglas, F. W. 19.11.17
31403	Delaney, G. I. 12.10.17		47127	Douglas, K. 11.11.18
53328	Delaney, W. T. 30.3.18		26/665	Douglas, K. J. K. 7.6.17
12148	Dellow, L/Cpl. A. J. 5.4.18		52970	Douglas, P. O. 10.11.18
25/382	Dempsey, H. 24.9.16		38133	Douglas, R. 16.6.17
24/1021	Denbee, Cpl. T. W. 19.7.16		25/612	Douglas, W. K. 12.10.17
24/401	Denby, Sgt. W. H. 15.9.16		70386	Dove, L/Cpl. J. C. 26.10.18
15349	Denize, L. C. 7.6.17		32831	Dow, J. 12.10.17
24/115	Denniston, J. A. 12.10.17		51356	Dowd, J. 26.3.18
24/736	Densem, 2/Lt. J., D.C.M. 26.8.18		53330	Doull, J. 5.4.18
			24/2521	Dowdle, F. E. 17.9.16
35110	Denston, G. H. 8.10.18		23/409	Downer, W. B. 1.5.10
54477	Dent, T. J. 23.8.18		36430	Downes, W. 12.10.17
20974	Derbyshire, L/Cpl. W. F. 28.3.18		24/126	Downie, Cpl. A. 16.9.16
			20508	Downs, C. H. 12.10.17
24/414	Derrett, Cpl. T. L. 15.9.16		25/21	Doyle, 2/Lt. H. T. 10.10.18
23/729	Devening, L/Cpl. T. F. 20.9.16		38136	Doyle, J. 12.10.17
			49879	Doyle, T. F. 31.3.18
26/759	De Ville, P. 18.7.16		62276	Dray, W. A. M. 26.8.18
26067	Dewar, L/Cpl. W. 12.10.17		24/1373	Drew, F. 19.6.16
24/740	Dey, A. A. 18.6.17		26580	Drummond, F. T. 7.6.17

45195	Drummond, P. 9.4.18		25993	Eggleston, Cpl. W. D. 30.3.18
24/107	Drummond, W. G. 19.9.16			
23/122	Dryden, L/Cpl. J. W. 27.9.18		24/2523	Eisfelder, F. 2.10.16
			45373	Elford, W. F. 15.2.18
4/95A	Drysdale, 2/Lt. T. J. H. 6.4.18		47129	Ellen, G. E. C. 31.5.18
			17772	Ellery, L/Cpl. S. G. 12.10.17
45346	Dudfield, A. J. S. 12.10.17			
25/20	Dudson, 2/Lt. L. C. (d) 28.10.18		51360	Elliot, J. A. 22.11.17
			15352	Elliott, H. 3.6.17
26/1590	Duff, C. A. 15.9.16		52974	Ellis, A. D. 11.9.18
23/739	Duffey, Sgt. F. 5.4.18		11010	Ellis, J. P. 3.10.16
12362	Duffy, G. 7.6.17		41078	Ellis, P. 12.10.17
65960	Duffy, J. 9.10.18		44102	Ellis, W. J. 16.1.18
40913	Duggan, P. J. 4.2.18		23/1979	Ellison, A. R. 7.6.17
59101	Duke, G. 31.8.18		24/746	Ellmers, Sgt. R., M.M. 26.8.18
39778	Dumbleton, L/Cpl. D. H. 12.10.17			
			73330	Elvin, J. V. 5.10.18
41077	Duncan, C. W. 12.10.17		51831	Emmett, A. 31.8.18
25/173	Duncan, Cpl. J. 28.12.17		23/745	Emmett, A. 18.9.16
56568	Duncan, J. 29.3.18		15886	Engelbrecht, Cpl. J. 29.3.18
47716	Dungey, A. H. 12.4.18		26076	Englet, T. H. L. 7.6.17
27681	Dunlop, A. 18.6.17		17853A	Ensor, C. H. 6.6.17
26583	Dunn, E. J. 7.6.17		38831	Entwistle, C. J. 3.11.17
24/408	Dunn, E. R. T. 15.9.16		53335	Epplett, H. E. 7.12.17
55931	Dunne, F. H. 12.10.18		62037	Espiner, L/Cpl. P. G. 12.9.18
31826	Durie, W. A. 3.12.17			
24/1033	Dupeyron, C. L. 12.10.17		26/11	Winter-Evans, Lt.-Col. A., D.S.O., (d). 12.10.17
42639	Durrant, J. D. 7.11.17			
52393	Durrant, R. 30.5.18		65709	Evans, E. L. 8.10.18
39031	Durey, G. F. 3.9.18		20316	Evans, F. 7.6.17
24/121	Duthie, 2/Lt. D. K. 7.8.17		26/67	Evans, 2/Lt. F. M. 4.11.18
64474	Dyer, H. 26.10.18		64873	Evans, G. R. 22.8.18
23/1970	Dyer, J. A. 15.9.16		28996	Evans, L/Cpl. H. H. 14.2.18
40786	Dynes, D. J. 21.2.18		23/747	Evans, Cpl. (T/Sgt.) L. 15.9.16
25/58	Eade, C.S.M. A. L. 21.9.16			
15843	Eade, Cpl. A. V., (d). 7.6.17		23/418	Evans, P. W. E. 10.9.16
			32835	Evans, T. H. 30.3.18
23114	Earnshaw, G. F. 7.7.17		48822	Everest, T. D. 4.11.18
23/125	East, L/Cpl. H. E. 2.12.17		20979	Everitt, Cpl. A., M.M. 7.8.18
53161	Easton, W. P. 16.11.17			
42309	Ebbitt, G. 5.4.18		40107	Everton, C. F. L. 12.10.17
23/2308	Ede, J. P. 7.6.17		25/426	Every, H. R. 15.9.16
6/3308	Edgar, Cpl. J. 27.4.18		59102	Evinson, F. R. 23.8.18
33318	Edgecombe, C. 23.6.17		26/992	Ewart, S. 19.7.16
52175	Edmonds, E. W. 8.10.18		22960	Ewen, L/Cpl. (T/Cpl.) G. T. 7.4.18
23/1040	Edmonds, J. 24.9.16			
23/1509	Edwards, A. 10.9.16		22164	Excell, L/Cpl. A. 3.11.17
41517	Edwards, L/Cpl. A. G. 2.5.18		35497	Eyles, A. 29.10.17
			22610	Eyres, L/Cpl. F. G. 12.10.17
38140	Edwards, Cpl. M. S. 20.11.17			
			25/176	Fabling, J. 5.4.18
31832	Edwards, R. L. 7.6.17		24/416	Fairbairn, W. A. 27.9.16
26/169	Edwards, L/Cpl. W. A. E. 7.6.17		32836	Fairweather, J. 12.10.17
			24/1039	Fairweather, O. S. 8.10.16
33051	Edwards, Cpl. W. T. 26.5.18		41137	Farland, Cpl. C. T. 30.8.18
			12998	Farmar, L/Cpl. N. W. 20.11.17
25/103	Egarr, N. S. 29.7.18			

45374	Farmer, W. P. 12.10.17		18642	Fleming, V. 3.1.17
15887	Farnie, S. C. 5.5.17		26/556	Flett, Sgt. A., M.M. 12.9.18
3/1699	Farnsworth, 2/Lt. E. E., M.M. 12.9.18		18980	Flett, W. 7.6.17
25/750	Farrell, L/Sgt. D. F. 15.9.16		25/1722	Flewry, J. C. 3.10.16
			38516	Flood, T. F. 12.10.17
23/2560	Farrell, J. T. 15.9.16		25/754	Flower, F. E. 15.9.16
39039	Faulkner, C. E. G. 12.10.17		21503	Flower, H. R. 7.6.17
26/174	Faulls, W. M. 15.9.16		25/539	Flowers, L/Cpl. F. L. 15.9.16
24/1376	Fearon, A. E. 21.9.16		56758	Floyd, A. 20.5.18
24/1982	Fearon, T. P. 15.9.16		22788	Flute, H. H. 5.12.17
51363	Feil, R. B. J. 8.8.18		26/99	Flynn, F. J. 19.9.16
12164	Fenton, Sgt. E. I. 8.10.17		26/263	Foley, J. 15.9.16
24/428	Fergie, D. H. 28.9.16		40671	Foley, J. 5.2.18
48711	Ferguson, A. G. E. 3.1.18		25/1724	Foley, W. H. 16.12.16.
26/402	Ferguson, Cpl. C. D. 15.9.16		15355	Fonseca, L/Cpl. J. 9.9.18
20133	Ferguson, D. H. 6.12.17		24/2198	Forbes, G. 15.9.16
23/972	Ferguson, 2/Lt. E. C. 2.10.16		58753	Forbes, W. R. 9.9.18
			18644	Ford, H. 7.6.17
24/138	Ferguson, Sgt. J. 12.10.17		48933	Ford, L/Cpl. L. F. 26.8.18
29918	Ferguson, J. A. 7.6.17		18983	Ford, R. E. 7.6.17
26/963	Fernandez, C. J. 16.9.16		24/147	Ford, S. R. 11.8.17
12165	Ferriday, Sgt. H. 20.5.18		65516	Foreman, A. F. 26.8.18
32837	Field, T. S. 27.6.17		20320	Foreman, E. L. 6.1.18
45684	Fife, J. 19.12.17		65844	Forrest, A. 26.8.18
53768	Fifield, E. 14.4.18		30104	Forrest, Lt. H. A. 12.10.17
24/427	Finch, L. 15.9.16		21814	Forsyth, Cpl. (T/Sgt.) F. 8.10.18
47016	Findlater, A. W. 26.10.18			
40922	Findlay, J. A. 12.10.17		23/2183	Forsyth, I. A. 15.9.16
23/422	Findlay, T. S. 15.9.16		40927	Forsyth, J. 16.8.17
36856	Finnerty, J. H. 26.8.18		39791	Forward, C. 12.10.17
26/555	Finnerty, T. 22.11.16		24/1047	Foss, T. J. 30.9.16
23367	Fisher, D. M. 3.2.18		68783	Foster, F. J. 9.9.18
24/2193	Fisher, G. 29.6.17		54734	Foster, H. A. 1.9.18
25/753	Fisher, R. A. 15.9.16		26/1090	Fothergill, J. S. 19.7.16
25/105	Fitness, L/Sgt. J. 15.9.16		26/100	Fougere, L/Cpl. L. G. 16.9.16
15354	Fittall, C. F. 2.3.17			
53168	Fitzgerald, E. 30.3.18		24/2197	Fowler, R. G. 2.10.16
39040	Fitzgerald, R. H. 2.4.18		53171	Fox, B. 5.4.18
48931	Fitzgerald, L/Cpl. T. B. 12.9.18		24/191	Jackson-Fowler, R. P. 8.9.18.
14095	Fitzpatrick, L/Cpl. F. 27.11.17		24/756	Frampton, Cpl. L. H. 31.7.16
24/1137	Fitzsimmons, W. 24.9.16		23/1052	Francis, Cpl. E. J. 5.10.18
49237	Flack, A. 6.8.18		52185	Frankham, W. E. 4.4.18
34049	Flanagan, J. 12.10.17		62045	Fraser, A. 28.7.18
24/2196	Flannagan, Cpl. W. D. 31.8.18		40929	Fraser, F. S. 8.10.18
			45318	Fraser, 2/Lt. M. 9.1.18
45200	Flannery, P. 12.10.17		25/757	Frater, W. 23.12.16
45685	Flavell, H. 6.12.17		48011	Fredrickson, J. B. 25.8.18
26083	Fleming, A. 7.6.17		24/141	Freebairn, J. 19.5.16
12167	Fleming, L/Cpl. F. J. 6.4.18		23/1984	Freeman, S. 7.6.17
			62539	Freeman, T. W. 21.8.18
71006	Fleming, J. S. 4.11.18		14096	Freeth, C. L. 1.1.17
25/7	Fleming, Lt. R. L. G. 7.6.17		42646	French, J. 14.10.17
			38148	French, P. W. 6.8.17
			31120	French, L/Cpl. T. 9.9.18

20986	French, W. G. 9.6.17		26/1149	Gibbings, A. G. 12.9.16
25/623	Frew, D. 15.9.16		26/792	Gibbon, H. 8.5.17
26595	Friar, W. B. 5.11.17		33347	Gibbons, L/Cpl. E. 12.9.18
74940	Friedrich, L. T. 10.10.18		35667	Gibbs, B. 5.10.18
25/557	Friend, Sgt. G. S. 18.2.18		46577	Gibbs, J. E. 26.8.18
65211	Frood, J. 9.9.18		53773	Gibbs, J. E. 6.4.18
28457	Frost, V. A. 17.8.17		22790	Gibson, E. P. 13.9.16
25/178	Fruin, Cpl. F. G., M.M. 16.9.18		24/438	Gibson, J. T. 12.11.16
			20987	Gibson, R. 23.2.17
26/98	Fulcher, A. E., M.M. 13.8.17		23/1053	Gibson, L/Cpl. R. 15.9.16
			15893	Gibson, Cpl. S. H. 18.10.17
42075	Fullerton, W. 17.9.18		26597	Giddens, L/Cpl. K. C. P. 8.6.17
24/1048	Furnival, Sgt. F. W. 20.5.18		23370	Gieson, W. L. 27.6.17
48936	Fuss, V. J. 4.1.18		13748	Gifford, P. H., (d). 1.1.17
59200	Futter, J. 1.9.18		70672	Gilchrist, W. C. 12.9.18
			74961	Giles, H. 4.11.18
24/1050	Gadd, G. 15.3.18		38524	Giles, T. C. 5.8.17
24/431	Gaffaney, Sgt. P. M., M.M. 5.4.18		38153	Gill, H. 5.4.18
			23167	Gillespie, W. 26.8.18
28458	Galbally, J. O. 7.6.17		31839	Gillett, A. H. 12.10.17
44637	Galbraith, J. C. 12.10.17		26/1166	Gillice, J. R. 12.3.17
26/1181	Galbraith, W. G. 7.7.17		39394	Gillman, L/Cpl. E. J. 11.9.18
23/141	Gallagher, J. 15.9.16			
25/541	Gallop, A. 15.9.16		51518	Gillon, W. 13.12.17
24/1381	Galloway, H. W. 19.7.16		26/1597	Gilmour, Cpl. F. D. 1.8.17
24/1383	Gandy, J. H. 28.9.16			
18986	Garbett, A. H. 7.6.17		69689	Gilmour, R. J. 8.10.18
26/994	Garbett, A. L. 15.9.16		31122	Girvin, J. 12.10.17
41139	Garden, L/Cpl. A. L. 8.12.17		26/445	Gordon-Glassford, J. D. 12.10.17
25/179	Gardner, S. 15.9.16		11020	Glavas, M. 7.6.17
12376	Gardner, T. 8.5.17		25855	Gledhill, T. W. 9.8.17
49239	Garrick, J. 31.3.18		45688	Gleeson, F. H. 12.10.17
34358	Garry, Cpl. L. 9.9.18		25/762	Glover, C. H. 2.10.16
34468	Garry, Cpl. S. 12.9.18		25/107	Goddard, S. V. 15.9.16
55741	Garvey, M. A. 30.8.18		25851	Godfrey, E. F. 5.4.18
38525	Gaskell, Sgt. F. A., D.C.M. 28.8.18		25852	Godfrey, F. A. 7.6.17
			53490	Goer, E. J. 7.12.17
24/151	Gasson, L/Cpl. C. H. 15.9.16		23/1391	Goggin, Cpl. J. 12.10.17
			25/1737	Going, A. H. 1.9.18
23/430	Gasson, Cpl. E. W. 7.6.17		25/870	Going, P. S. 15.9.16
25696	Gavin, Cpl. A. 12.10.17		23/1990	Goldie, Cpl. (T/Sgt.) J. 14.10.17
21816	Gawler, W. T. 17.7.18			
41188	Gaylor, H. C. D. 27.3.18		54349	Goldsmith, J. R. 5.4.18
31121	Gaze, D. V. 27.6.17		56277	Goldsworthy, L. B. T. 26.5.18
26/993	Geaney, D. P., M.M. 27.7.16		33351	Goldthorpe, H. 1.6.18
24805	Gear, D. 26.9.17		44271	Gollan, T. 17.9.17
26/793	Geard, Sgt. A. G. 7.6.17		26/561	Gonley, L/Cpl. D. 12.10.17
42649	Geary, F. 12.10.17			
44970	Geddes, A. 12.10.17		58762	Gooch, E. T. 31.8.18
26/790	Gemmell, Sgt. C. V. 7.6.17		25850	Good, M. I. 12.10.17
			21818	Goodall, R. H. 12.10.17
13000	Geoffrey, J. 17.6.17		26/1119	Goodey, J. H. 15.9.16
25/631	George, E. 7.6.17		66064	Goodhue, L. E. 8.5.18
61091	Gerrie, W. 21.5.18		54741	Goodwin, R. C. 5.4.18

8/2924	Gordon, 2/Lt. A. R. 26.8.18		18653	Groves, W. C. 25.6.17
24/1056	Gordon, Sgt. A. T. 25.5.16		23/1059	Grundy, W. 10.10.16
26/795	Gordon, Sgt. H. T. 29.3.18		25/180	Gudgin, L/Cpl. L. A. 1.12.17
25/1744	Gordon, J. 15.9.16		22451	Gudsell, S. J. 7.6.17
26/562	Gordon, J. 13.11.16		20993	Guild, D. G. 4.12.16
65055	Gordon, J. 11.9.18		18919	Guild, L/Cpl. W. A. 7.6.17
26091	Gordon, R. J. 7.6.17		21820	Guilford, W. 27.3.18
55945	Gorham, J. 22.11.17		24/1267	Guiness, Capt. W. J. P. 17.11.16
36779	Gorrie, L/Cpl. W. 20.5.18			
36440	Goulds, L/Cpl. W. 21.10.18		5/166	Guinness, 2/Lt. A. G. 12.10.17
23371	Goulton, C. 26.8.18		12385	Gullery, L. H. 12.10.17
24/769	Graham, L/Cpl. A. E. 12.10.17		24/773	Gunn, C. 18.6.16
			25/320	Gunn, Sgt. R. B. 1.10.16
46519	Graham, F. J. 5.4.18		15364	Gurnett, T. 12.10.17
23/435	Graham, Cpl. G. 5.8.17		24/159	Gurney, D. A. 15.9.16
18650	Graham, L/Cpl. G. H. 6.4.18		44638	Gurr, Cpl. F. 29.3.18
53350	Graham, H. 5.4.18		51987	Gutheridge, J. F. 7.1.18
26/1602	Graham, J. 30.5.18		26/784	Gutterson, C. W. 3.10.16
69024	Graham, T. 5.10.18			
46019	Graham, W. 17.9.18		48020	Hackett, F. 9.12.17
26/264	Grahame, L/Cpl. W. G. 15.9.16		18656	Haddrell, S. H. 12.10.17
			41083	Hadler, W. J. 8.10.18
20140	Grant, J. 11.8.17		24/173	Haigh, G. M. 15.9.16
32321	Grant, J. W. 12.8.17		11/1439	Hainsworth, Cpl. A. E. 22.4.16
23/1400	Graves, J. H. 20.6.16			
24/1991	Gray, A. 4.10.16		24/452	Hair, W. H. C. 15.9.16
26/448	Gray, Cpl. G. C. 4.11.18		25/195	Hales, L/Sgt. C. H. C. J. 15.9.16
23/1397	Gray, G. H. 15.9.16			
30935	Gray, J. 26.7.18		41789	Haliburton, G. L. 26.10.18
26/1165	Gray, J. C. W. 10.10.17		26/1193	Hall, L/Sgt. C. 19.10.17
15361	Gray, T. 8.6.17		33877	Hall, C. N. 3.10.18
44273	Gray, T. 12.10.17		25/1190	Hall, G. A. 31.7.16
23/1399	Gray, W. E. 15.9.16		41084	Hall, H. 12.10.17
26/787	Greatbatch, 2/Lt. E. P. 20.10.16		24/949	Hall, H. C. 7.10.16
			32952	Hall, T. 20.8.17
28465	Green, A. F. 7.6.17		24/1065	Hall, W. G. 19.11.16
39605	Green, A. S. 16.11.17		26607	Hallett, H. H. 10.10.17
54499	Green, E. 29.3.18		49892	Hallett, J. S. 12.9.18
24/441	Green, J. 8.10.18		48021	Halley, J. 11.12.17
41324	Green, R. 9.10.18		24/469	Halley, L/Cpl. W. 12.10.17
45334	Green, W. J. 12.10.17		28469	Halligan, L/Cpl. W. 12.10.17
25/321	Green, W. J. 7.6.17			
24/2212	Greenlees, B. 15.9.16		26/1613	Ham, F. 12.10.17
47424	Greer, L/Cpl. S. P. 10.10.18		38169	Hamilton, D. 27.6.17
27081	Grieve, D. 8.6.17		23/160	Hamilton, J. 24.9.16
74911	Griffin, E. A. 8.10.18		26/1001	Hamilton, J. 8.10.18
24/2209	Griffin, Cpl. H. F. 7.6.17		23/1273	Hamilton, J. 12.9.18
18654	Griffen, P. J. 6.1.18		39803	Hamilton, J. H. 12.10.17
23/1393	Griffen, R. 17.6.16		66092	Hamilton, L. 26.8.18
18993	Griffin, R. J. 12.10.17		75238	Hamilton, N. A. 8.10.18
20992	Griffith, A. G. 7.6.17		20999	Hamilton, L/Cpl. R. 24.1.18
24/1063	Griffiths, G. A. 8.3.17		53361	Hamilton, R. M. 26.8.18
25/110	Grigg, A. 19.8.17		20531	Hamilton, T. H. 10.1.17
36862	Grimwood, H. R. 8.10.18		22792	Hamlin, F. E. 15.9.16

25/8	Hammond, Capt. E. J. 31.7.16	3/939	Harvey, Pte. D. (N.Z.M.C.) 12.10.17
39047	Hampton, D. L. 6.12.17	30368	Harvey, F. C. 25.10.17
46521	Hampton, T. V. 9.12.17	23/449	Harvey, H. J. 17.8.17
26/106	Hancock, L/Cpl. S. F. 12-14.10.17	31126	Haskell, W. A. 12.10.17
24/453	Hanlen, A. 24.9.16	25/388	Hassell, T. 15.9.16
64926	Hanley, P. 30.8.18	44111	Haughey, S. F. 20.6.18
26/806	Hanna, A. 29.5.16	13011	Havill, F. G. 7.6.17
26611	Hanna, W. H. 12.10.17	11041	Hawke, E. A. 15.3.18
47058	Hanna, W. J. 31.10.18	25/980	Hawker, E. R. 15.9.16
44639	Hannam, D. 19.11.17	26/808	Hawker, H. J. 5.6.16
58766	Hannigan, J. 11.9.18	72028	Hawkey, L. G. 8.10.18
27130	Hanrahan, R. J. 7.6.17	12196	Hawkins, C. T. 21.8.18
18659	Hansen, C. 28.6.17	51838	Hawkins, J. S. 15.2.18
25869	Hansen, C. S. 7.6.17	32331	Haworth, L/Cpl. G. B. 8.10.18
31849	Hansen, H. C. 17.8.17	26/308	Hawthorne, L/Cpl. T. A. 25.11.17
59205	Hansen, O. 4.5.18		
25/327	Hardie, Cpl. L. G. 9.10.18	23/166	Hay, A. 1.1.16
26612	Harding, G. F. 12.10.17	13019	Hay, F. V. 7.6.17
24/950	Harding, Cpl. P. B. 16.9.16	15906	Hay, H. F. 24.11.17
15366	Hardwick, L. J. 8.6.17	26/449	Haycock, A. 5.4.18
45507	Harley, W. J. 18.2.18	24/1070	Hayes, A. E. 24.9.16
53187	Harlow, J. L. 12.9.18	26/999	Hayes, Cpl. H. R. 9.12.17
49392	Harneiss, L/Cpl. R. 26.8.18	59807	Hayes, L/Cpl. J. 5.10.18
21833	Harney, D. J. 5.4.18	26/815	Hayes, Cpl. J. N. 26.9.16
25/74	Harper, Sgt. A. B. 7.6.17	8/4347	Hayes, W. J. 27.3.18
26/1188	Harper, Cpl. (T/Sgt.) L. A. 5.4.18	26615	Haylock, A. R. 12.10.17
		26/1615	Haylock, A. W. 25.9.16
49895	Harper, L. T. 11.12.17	32849	Haynes, T. W. 12.10.17
9/1856	Harper, Cpl. M. R. 30.8.18	54745	Hayter, L/Cpl. A. 4.11.18
14808	Harper, L/Cpl. W. C. 12.10.17	38533	Hayward, L/Cpl. H. 8.10.18
15368	Harris, A. J. S. 7.6.17	55882	Hazell, G. I. 14.7.18
23/448	Harris, C. 15.9.16	26/306	Heale, G. S. 12.9.16
23/1997	Harris, C. A. 15.9.16	25/390	Healey, L. J. 15.9.16
29012	Harris, H. 12.10.17	41948	Healey, W. 12.10.17
24/167	Harris, H. E. 7.6.17	51723	Heaps, F. P. 10.9.18
22978	Harris, H. R. 5.4.18	26/1551	Heard, Sgt. G., M.M. 22.11.17
26/1041	Harris, Cpl. J. A. 15.7.16		
24451	Harris, L. J. 12.10.17	40148	Heaton, E. D. H. 28.3.18
51639	Harris, M. 1.9.18	23/455	Hebenton, R. W. 8.6.17
36972	Harris, W. E. 24.9.17	24/1072	Heckler, L/Cpl. W. H. 25.7.18
32330	Harrison, B. 16.8.17	32332	Hegan, G. W. T. 6.4.18
40116	Harrison, J. R. 29.7.18	23/40	Heldt, Cpl. E. R. 5.6.16
21836	Harrison, L/Cpl. N. D. 16.12.17	14727	Helem, A. W. 13.8.17
		56777	Heley, Cpl. K. H. 12.9.18
17781	Harrod, S. 29.8.18	24/1523	Helm, L. 5.10.16
23/2200	Harrop, E. J. 15.9.16	24/793	Henderson, C. J. 12.10.17
23/165	Harrop, G. A. 27.7.16	23/168	Henderson, C. W. 10.9.16
41976	Hart, 2/Lt. A. 21.8.18	45693	Henderson, E. A. B. 4.11.18
35201	Hartley, H. 14.9.18		
23/1411	Hartley, S. C. 15.10.16	38530	Henderson, W. 12.10.17
25/437	Hartnett, D. 15.9.16	25/638	Henderson, W. L. 15.9.16
24/2216	Hartnett, D. 5.10.16	11034	Hendriksen, H. I. 26.8.18
47139	Harvey, A. P. 8.10.18	26/1770	Hendry, A. 15.9.16

20527	Hendry, Cpl. A. B. 12.9.18	24/471	Hodder, L/Cpl. B. R. 15.9.16
23180	Heney, G. 3.10.16	26/1618	Hodder, H. 12.9.16
23/1407	Hennessey, M., M.M. 21.11.17	48030	Hodge, M. J. 2.5.18
11376	Henning, 2/Lt. W., M.C. 13.9.18	25/1757	Hodges, T. 26.9.16
		26/305	Hodgkinson, Sgt. W. 26.10.18
46233	Henry, Cpl. E. S. 9.10.18	53359	Hodgson, R. E. 23.8.18
24/785	Henry, H. M. 21.9.16	24/1393	Hodgson, T. H. 30.12.16
25/1167	Henry, R. 17.8.16	28480	Hogg, F. 8.10.18
24/1392	Hensman, A. 3.10.16	22030	Hogg, J. 5.7.18
44278	Hepburn, Cpl. C. J. H. 29.8.18	24/797	Holdaway, F. C. 10.7.16
40749	Herbert, C. L. J. 1.4.18	39696	Holder, L/Cpl. J. C. 12.9.18
22797	Hertz, A. J. 6.6.17	24/447	Holland, J. P. 29.3.18
25/188	Herzog, Cpl. C. M. 25.5.16	68788	Hollobon, J. T. 26.8.18
39051	Hewitt, A. F. 5.4.18	26/452	Holman, W. 22.5.17
54364	Hewson, V. W. L. 7.4.18	23/2004	Holmes, L/Cpl. L. 27.7.16
29922	Heydon, L. 5.6.17	23176	Holmes, Sgt. M. 29.8.18
26/810	Hickey, J. J. 6.5.17	72359	Holmes, W. E. 9.10.18
28478	Higgie, M. 12.10.17	49959	Holst, P. E. 12.5.18
62063	Higgins, J. 22.8.18	25/881	Holwell, Cpl. J. H. 28.12.17
26/1076	Higgins, L/Sgt. P. J. 8.7.16	42104	Honore, F. W. 26.10.18
24/2004	Highsted, F. L. 8.6.17	24/1081	Holyoake, A. 2.6.16
15901	Hight, C. M. 12.10.17	48032	Hood, J. 26.5.18
15902	Hight, L. H. D. 12.10.17	46454	Hood, O. E. 31.8.18
41331	Hildreth, D. 12.10.17	26/490	Hook, C. F. 19.7.16
25/549	Hill, Cpl. D. O. 24.11.17	23383	Hooker, Cpl. A. W. 29.10.18
23/780	Hill, E. W. 15.9.16	65815	Hooker, K. A. 28.8.18
21834	Hill, G. 7.6.17	23/784	Hookings, L. G. 23.1.16
36619	Hill, L/Cpl. J. 4.10.18	23/1677	Hooper, A. E. 11.9.18
14822	Hill, J. G. 12.10.17	45694	Hooper, L/Cpl. C. 13.1.18
55966	Hill, J. H. 29.10.18	23/2205	Hooper, G. S. 15.9.18
48719	Hill, O. 15.7.18	42666	Hope, T. A. 4.11.18
24/787	Hill, Sgt. S. 26.8.18	3/1774	Hopkins, Pte. L. G., M.M. (N.Z.M.C.) 12.10.17
60371	Hill, S. D. 30.6.18		
24/2221	Hill, W. C. 17.9.16	23/785	Hopkins, 2/Lt. V. P. 21.3.18
14205	Hillier, Sgt. A. L. 12.10.17	26621	Horan, J. 16.4.18
47888	Hills, C. F. R. 4.11.18	24/2223	Horn, A. 30.9.16
26/451	Hills, C. W. 24.9.16	25876	Horsefield, C. B. 26.6.17
26/1607	Hillson, C. 7.6.17	51731	Horsman, A. F. 6.11.18
23/458	Hilton, J. P. 15.9.16	25/1052	Hosie, W. G. 15.9.16
44279	Hindrup, F. J. 26.8.18	45770	Hosking, A. 12.9.18
53013	Hine, F. J. 5.2.18	23/1072	Houghton, Sgt. G. 5.5.17
26/102	Hine, L/Cpl. H. 16.11.17	26/809	Houghton, H. C. 24.9.16
24/465	Hinkley, T. 24.9.16	38924	Hoult, V. P. M. 22.8.18
44845	Hinton, W. 8.12.17	24/2224	Howard, B. 15.10.16
51842	Hintz, A. 6.4.18	52610	Howard, J. M. 21.4.18
26/1183	Hintz, G. 5.6.16	48956	Howe, A. 30.8.18
17788	Hislop, A. 11.6.17	23/2006	Howe, L. A. 15.9.16
71400	Hitchcock, A. 26.10.18	12183	Howe, T. H. 12.10.17
49710	Hitchman, L/Cpl. W. G. 27.10.18	24/2007	Howes, J. 15.9.16
		70698	Howie, R. B. 26.10.18
42854	Hoare, E. 5.10.18	11039	Howland, J. H. 30.8.18
11042	Hockey, L/Cpl. C. H. 8.3.18	44283	Hoult, L. C. W. 3.9.18
		38527	Houston, A. C. 24.8.18

25/884	Hubbard, L/Cpl. A. C. 15.9.16		23/464	Jack, Cpl. D. L. 15.9.16
24/1547	Hudson, 2/Lt. A. 14.7.16		26/516	Jack, R. 15.9.16
23/1074	Hudson, A. J. 15.9.16		13681	Jackson, Capt. A. 5.9.18
61946	Hudson, 2/Lt. E. G. 9.9.18		25883	Jackson, L/Cpl. A. 18.10.17
26/1000	Hughes, E. H. 8.5.18		64208	Jackson, A. R. 10.8.18
25/1051	Hughes, H. 20.9.16		21023	Jackson, E. J. 22.8.18
44935	Hughes, 2/Lt. L. M. 27.3.18		24/2229	Jackson, G. 15.9.16
62573	Hughes, M. 6.4.18		31287	Jackson, J. 29.3.18
25/1752	Hughes, W. 7.11.16		40957	Jackson, J. H. H. 18.11.17
12191	Hughes, Cpl. W. A. A. 8.6.17		46459	Jackson, R. G. 12.10.17
21017	Hullten, J. G. 30.3.18		26/817	Jacobson, L/Cpl. W. V. 12.10.17
23/2007	Hume, J. 1.10.16		54643	Jaffray, L/Cpl. T. H. 26.8.18
24/460	Hume, M. 6.5.17			
26/30	Hunt, Q.M.S. A. E. 7.2.17		41203	James, C. D. 6.8.17
72246	Hunt, J. R. A. 26.10.18		26/108	James, L/Cpl. F. 22.7.16
53020	Hunt, R. H. W. T. 5.4.18		22992	James, F. J. 8.6.17
22984	Hunter, A. H. 12.10.17		22806	James, J. C. 1.10.16
23/176	Hunter, R. 7.6.17		23/2209	James, R. 8.5.17
37066	Hunter, R. C. 12.10.17		22717	James, T. W. 23.3.17
44550	Huntington, 2/Lt. S. H. 6.4.18		26/453	James, W. 22.9.16
44284	Hutchinson, B. M. 3.12.17		26/348	James, W. 9.2.17
45600	Hutchinson, R. 12.10.17		26/454	Jamieson, Sgt. J. G. 30.3.18
25/927	Hutchison, L/Cpl. W. W. 23.2.18		23/2012	Jamieson, R. 15.9.16
27502	Hutton, C. G. 30.8.18		47146	Jamison, J. 10.11.17
53022	Hutton, D. L. 7.7.18		24/474	Jarrett, 2/Lt. O. G. 8.10.18
26/404	Hutton, W. A. 15.9.16		22807	Jarrett, W. A. 16.8.17
13022	Hyland, L/Cpl. A. M. 6.12.17		24/478	Jarvis, Sgt. H. E. 2.10.16
			22808	Jeffery, Cpl. H. J., D.C.M. 20.6.17
24/1397	Ingram, J. F. 5.7.16		13656	Jeffery, Sgt. J. C. 26.8.18
45212	Ingram, T. E. 16.7.18		25/1199	Jenkin, C. P. 23.9.16
15911	Inwood, E. J. 23.11.16		40149	Jenkins, L/Cpl. C. G. 7.1.18
12399	Inwood, L/Cpl. G. A. 12.10.17		56303	Jenkins, K. 30.8.18
30592	Irons, L/Cpl. N. C. S. 27.10.18		12402	Jenkins, W. S. 14.5.17
40816	Ironside, L/Cpl. A. 30.8.18		38174	Jensen, Cpl. A. P. 9.9.18
38837	Irvin, V. C. 12.10.17		24/809	Jenson, E. M. 30.12.16
26/819	Irvine, L/Sgt. J. S. 29.3.18		26/1624	Jervis, D. G. 8.10.16
23388	Irving, A. 7.6.17		15307	Jess, Cpl. T. 12.10.17
23/463	Irving, Sgt. C. 5.4.18		65791	Jobe, J. 30.8.18
26/1114	Irving, D. J. O. 12.9.16		25/119	Johanson, Sgt. W. G., (d) 7.6.17
59810	Irving, J. 12.9.16		3/1113	Johns, Maj. F. N., M.C. (N.Z.M.C.) 25.8.18
24/805	Irving, L/Cpl. J. 12.10.17			
40326	Irwin, F. 9.9.18		12408	Johns, H. 18.12.16
24/804	Isbister, W. 17.9.16		25/551	Johns, Sgt. W. 3.6.18
40956	Isitt, C. G. 5.12.17		24/475	Johnson, A. C. 15.9.16
12400	Isitt, W. W. 31.10.16		25/392	Johnson, C. B. 23.9.16
24/806	Islip, Cpl. E. E., M.M. 19.5.17		59208	Johnson, E. G. 4.11.18
			47895	Johnson, Cpl. H. 4.11.18
26/571	Israel, L/Cpl. (A/Cpl.) G. E. 10.10.16		38540	Johnson, H. G. 15.10.17
			25712	Johnson, J. 7.6.17
53500	Izett, A. S. 5.4.18		54048	Johnson, W. G. 8.10.18

32955	Johnston, L/Cpl. A. H. 5.4.18		53788	Kearney, M. 5.4.18
24/480	Johnston, 2/Lt. A. J. 3.8.18		25/1771	Kearse, B. E. 16.7.18
			12412	Keating, A. J. 27.2.17
25/333	Johnston, A. W. 3.11.16		72406	Keating, S. C. 4.11.18
24/1095	Johnston, Cpl. C. F. 12.10.17		26/831	Keay, D. S. 15.9.16
			15915	Keay, L/Sgt. T. 30.11.17
4/120	Johnston, 2/Lt. C. G. 7.6.17		25717	Keay, W. R. 5.8.17
			39059	Keeley, G. C. 12.10.17
12404	Johnston, G. S. 23.2.17		38178	Keeley, H. 28.7.17
23186	Johnston, L/Cpl. J. 12.10.17		44119	Keetley, E. H. 10.9.18
			60342	Keightley, R. 26.10.18
23/466	Johnston, L/Cpl. J. E. 10.11.16		44292	Keightley, T. F. 1.9.18
			49715	Keith, J. G. 12.9.18
19004	Johnston, J. E. 12.10.17		24/1407	Kelly, A. 1.10.16
25714	Johnston, J. S. 12.10.17		52617	Kelly, L. 26.8.18
64960	Johnston, L. D. 30.8.18		24/2013	Kelly, T. C. 8.10.18
42113	Johnston, M. R. 12.10.17		25/1766	Kelly, W. 12.9.16
24/199	Johnston, Cpl. P. T. 12.10.17		20168	Kemble, L/Cpl. C. R. 7.6.17
25/1034	Johnston, S. J. 26.8.18		32859	Kemp, C. 7.6.17
47022	Johnstone, L/Sgt. H. O. 29.10.18		25/395	Kemp, L/Cpl. R. M. 12.10.17
23/467	Johnstone, J. T. 27.12.15		27146	Kendall, G. 19.4.17
23/975	Johnstone, Cpl. (T/Sgt.) R., M.M. 27.9.18		20169	Kennedy, J. McM. 7.6.17
			39058	Kennedy, S. 6.4.18
47149	Joli, H. A. 12.10.17		47023	Keogh, J. S. 12.10.17
44288	Jones, A. D. 29.3.18		38180	Kerambrun, J. 2.1.18
15374	Jones, E. 7.6.17		24/485	Kerr, L/Cpl. A. V. 23.3.17
65663	Jones, L/Cpl. E. M. 4.11.18		24/1099	Kerr, W. 19.7.16
			13040	Kerr, W. G. 28.3.18
23/2016	Jones, Cpl. F. 12.10.17		42123	Keymer, G. E. 12.10.17
48964	Jones, F. 5.12.17		10979	Keyworth, O. 6.11.16
65664	Jones, F. P. 8.10.18		74914	Kidd, L/Cpl. R. D. 5.11.18
40819	Jones, G. A. 19.8.17		25/337	Kiddey, Sgt. F. 24.11.17
23/468	Jones, J. 15.9.16		44123	Kiely, Cpl. R. D. 29.3.18
20166	Jones, N. K. 7.6.17		47152	Kiely, T. 29.3.18
33381	Jones, R. L. 4.11.18		25/1770	Kilford, E. S. 9.9.17
33061	Jones, Sgt. T. [F]. 12.7.17		24/206	Kilgour, Cpl. J. D. 12.10.17
26/346	Jones, T. A. 15.9.16		24/688	Killoch, J. 25.5.16
68535	Jones, W. R. 1.9.18		41818	Kilmister, T. 2.1.18
24/482	Jordan, Cpl. S. C. 12.10.17		42125	Kinahan, E. 26.3.18
			59126	King, A. W. 5.4.18
26/272	Jowett, W. M. 17.9.16		42672	King, C. 30.8.18
25/199	Joyce, W. 15.9.16		23/472	King, J. 15.9.16
74874	Jury, V. R. 5.11.18		55978	King, K. L. 15.5.18
			26115	King, L. 26.10.17
26113	Kane, F. W. 12.10.17		35169	King, T. 30.3.18
23/798	Kappely, H. 20.9.16		52226	Kingsford, A. J. 2.5.18
54644	Katterson, J. 2.4.18		24/1705	Kingston, C. H. 15.9.16
24/203	Kavanagh, L/Sgt. V. C. 9.8.17		12415	Kinzett, A. 7.8.17
			59128	Kinzett, C. T. 20.5.18
48512	Kayes, J. E. 24.11.17		24/1410	Kinzett, L/Cpl. I. 12.10.17
23/799	Kean, P. 4.11.18		41090	Kirk, W. 19.7.18
26629	Keane, G. W. 31.3.18		54532	Kirkwood, F. W. 6.1.18
18671	Keaney, P. 7.3.17		28494	Kitchen, A. 12.10.17
45700	Kearney, J. C. 29.3.18		35170	Kite, Cpl. W. 12.9.18
			24/1707	Kitson, W. C. 3.1.18

26/826	Kittcho, N. 5.6.16			59210	Lean, H. W. 8.5.18	
25/203	Kivell, Sgt. C. M. 12.10.17			45353	Lean, W. 12.10.17	
26/832	Kjoller, J. 19.6.16			62587	Leatham, G. 26.8.18	
25890	Klink, L/Cpl. C. A. 27.3.18			25896	Leaper, W. 23.8.18	
25/648	Kloogh, G. F. O. 12.10.17			23/807	Leckie, A. 15.7.16	
33386	Knapp, C. W. 15.9.18			1/691	Le Cren, 2/Lt. H. E. 26.8.18	
10960	Knapp, R. H. 23.6.17			74998	Lee, J. W. 10.10.18	
23193	Knight, L/Cpl. A. R. 8.10.16			23/188	Leeds, C. L. 30.5.18	
45602	Knox, J. T. 10.10.17			15924	Lees, F. 14.8.17	
48040	Knuckey, J. 30.8.18			15925	Lees, L/Cpl. H. J. 27.3.18	
22816	Koerner, E. J. 15.9.16			26/1633	Legg, R. 19.8.17	
60365	Kreger, H. 23.8.18			66098	Leggoe, R. S. 30.8.18	
55979	Kupli, M. 29.3.18			65849	Leighton, C. 9.9.18	
70500	Kyle, W. G. 9.10.18			55513	Leighton, W. 12.9.18	
				26/353	Lelievre, Cpl. C. E. 7.6.17	
69857	Labroome, W. T. 8.10.18			54901	Lello, G. 25.11.18	
52844	Lacey, E. 13.4.18			44975	Lemon, W. D. 14.10.17	
15921	Laffey, J. T. 29.3.18			26/839	Lennan, A. 10.5.17	
32862	Laing, Cpl. J. D. 30.3.18			29037	Leonard, P. 16.7.17	
25/1169	Laitila, K. 15.9.16			23/2024	Le Quesne, J. A. 15.9.16	
22630	Laloli, L/Cpl. J. H. 12.10.17			44645	Leslie, J. F. 12.10.17	
				44646	Leslie, J. G. 12.10.17	
23/803	Lamb, Sgt. N. J. 15.5.18			24/1106	Leslie, K. G. 27.6.16	
17793	Lambert, G. F. 15.10.17			21515	Leslie, T. 12.8.17	
53792	Lambeth, T. B. 8.10.18			24/214	Leslie, L/Cpl. W. F. 4.2.18	
25/396	Lancaster, G. C. 17.3.18					
31418	Land, A. F. 26.3.18			23/190	Lester, L/Cpl. H. 4.11.18	
62086	Lander, F. 9.9.18			72109	Lester, W. A. 5.11.18	
36459	Lane, E. T. 26.8.18			44126	Lever, O. D. 13.1.18	
26/1094	Lane, H. W. 24.9.16			12419	Levinge, L/Cpl. M. 17.3.17	
24/1544	Lang 2/Lt. H. 20.7.16			23/484	Levy, A. N. 15.9.16	
21029	Lang, L/Cpl. W. G. 18.10.18			36749	Levy, Sgt. T. 12.10.17	
				24/1917	Lewis, D. M. 12.10.17	
23/1092	Langdon, F. 5.10.18			24/824	Lewis, L/Cpl. R. 24.9.16	
31419	Langford, Sgt. A. 1.9.18			23/809	Lewis, S. 22.9.16	
24/2017	Langford, Sgt. W. 8.10.18			22906	Lewis, 2/Lt. S. E. 5.4.18	
38552	Langley, H. T. 16.11.17			26121	Lewis, W. E. 28.3.17	
28497	Langridge, H. M. 7.6.17			24/10	Liardet, Capt. L. M. 3.10.16	
12208	Langrish, G. G. 26.6.17					
24/1105	Langrish, T. F. 24.9.16			64995	Lilly, A. H. 30.8.18	
58778	Large, A. 26.8.18.			21034	Linder, L/Cpl. C. 21.8.18	
34385	Lauer, Cpl. T. 4.11.18			39835	Lindsay, A. M. 12.10.17	
34386	Lauer, Sgt. W. 29.10.18			23/194	Lindsay, W. 19.7.16	
23/481	Laurie, L/Cpl. E. G. 8.10.18			23/811	Lindsay, W. J. 19.9.16	
				33389	Lines, L/Cpl. R. H. 4.1.18	
25/772	Laurie, P. 18.9.16			23/1529	Lines, W. A. 1.9.18	
47043	Laverty, J. 30.3.18			21035	Lingar, A. J. 15.6.17	
24/497	Lavery, M. J. 12.10.17			39069	Linklater, J. G. 12.9.18	
54055	Lawlor, J. 16.7.18			24/1418	Linn, J. R. 15.9.16	
23/1428	Lawlor, T. H. L. 4.8.16			57104	Lister, O. H. 30.8.18	
24/1415	Lawson, D. M. 7.6.17			56444	Litchfield, M. P. 21.5.18	
21031	Lawton, L/Cpl. N. A. 29.3.18			47227	Little, W. 23.8.18	
				26/836	Liversedge, F. 8.1.18	
57100	Leach, C. E. 9.5.18			48974	Lloyd, R. R. J. 30.9.17	
12209	Leah, L/Cpl. H. L. 29.3.18			69412	Loader, W. J. 28.8.18	
54058	Leal, T. 4.1.18			25/654	Loan, R. 15.9.16	

32019	Lochhead, L/Cpl. T. L. 26.8.18		42758	McCarthy, L/Cpl. E. 12.9.18
26/113	Locke, J. E. 28.3.18		23/1448	McCarthy, J. F. 31.1.17
23/1424	Lockhart, J. B. 21.10.16		26/1657	McCartney, M. 14.7.16
38914	Lofts, J. 12.10.17		24/2542	McCaul, H. 21.9.16
24/218	Long, J. 15.9.16		23/840	McCaw, W. 15.9.16
14187	Long, J. L. 12.10.17		23/1449	McCleary, D. 13.9.16
25719	Long, S. J. 7.6.17		23/2521	McColl, J. 15.9.16
23/814	Lonsdale, 2/Lt. W. 19.9.16		20556	McClelland, W. 20.3.17
23/489	Loper, E. C. 17.7.16		23/222	McCollum, E. 2.7.16
44295	Lord, E. S. 26.8.18		15401	McCollum, A. N. 10.8.17
23/1430	Lory, T. S. 4.8.17		26/873	McCollum, V. A. 26.9.16
26/116	Lothian, S. O. 14.8.17		26/862	McConnell, A. J. 19.7.16
23/197	Lowry, H. 15.9.16		25/447	McConnell, J. 15.9.16
71231	Lovatt, T. 8.10.18		29049	McConnell, Cpl. R. J. P. 12.10.17
26/1632	Love, L/Cpl. D. 2.4.18			
53374	Love, G. J. 17.11.17		22171	McConnell, Cpl. W. N. 12.9.18
41192	Love, J. P. 23.11.17			
26/1634	Lovelock, G. F. 15.9.16		20202	McConville, P. R. 18.6.17
38187	Low, A. J. 12.10.17		42689	McCorkindale, A. B. 12.10.17
24/830	Lowe, R. A. 15.9.16			
23/1097	Lowen, L. M. 24.6.17		42690	McCorkindale, M. 2.12.17
12/2019	Lowther, A. E. 2.4.18		54563	McCracken, A. 26.8.18
24/2240	Lucas, L/Cpl. H. A. 19.9.16		21058	McCracken, L/Cpl. J. 12.10.17
23/1511	Luck, R. 15.9.16		48737	McCulloch, D. 12.10.17
54667	Ludbrook, L/Sgt. H. R. 8.9.18		52252	McCulloch, G. W. 26.8.18
			20203	McCullough, J. A. 26.8.17
13049	Lugsdin, C. 23.9.16		18691	McCullough, R. 25.12.16
65628	Luke, J. H. 26.5.18		53244	McCurdy, A. 21.2.18
23/1723	Lunan, C. 15.9.16		23/502	McCurdy, L/Cpl. C. 15.9.16
52847	Lunan, J. 12.9.18		42692	McCutcheon, J. 18.9.17
24431	Lund, A. 30.12.16		41988	McDermott, Sgt. N. A. L. 1.6.18
14120	Lusk, A. R. 6.6.17			
15927	Lyall, G. G. 7.6.17		31878	McDonald, A. 12.10.17
24/499	Lynam, P. L. 15.9.16		53380	MacDonald, A. 4.12.17
23/199	Lynch, Cpl. C. P. 3.9.18		25/1176	McDonald, A. D. 19.7.16
26/841	Lynch, E. 21.9.16		40603	McDonald, A. K. 11.12.17
26/965	Lynch, R. W. 30.9.16		29693	MacDonald, D. 7.6.17
23/816	Lynch, T. 8.8.17		24/517	McDonald, G. L. 15.9.16
12423	Lynn, J. J. 13.11.16		13076	MacDonald, J. 16.10.17
24/2029	Lyon, G. E. 12.10.17		26/514	McDonald, Sgt. J. 28.8.17
48976	Lyons, G. M. 29.3.18		26/121	McDonald, 2/Lt. J. D. C. 25.10.18
48145	Lyons, W. 17.2.18			
			26/1658	MacDonald, N. 12.10.17
			26/606	McDonald, A/Cpl. S. R. 23.9.16
26/314	McAllan, Sgt. J. 20.10.17			
26/1010	McAllister, G. 23.2.17		35214	McDonald, T. C. 14.7.17
23/220	McAnally, A. G. 6.8.16		13068	McDonald, T. F. 1.10.16
21055	McAnnally, H. J. 8.5.17		23012	McDonnell, J. 4.5.18
47028	McArthur, J. F. 5.4.18		48731	MacDougall, I. B. 23.11.17
24/533	McArthur, P. 15.9.16		3/1179	McDougall, Cpl. M. A. 7.10.18
14846	McArthur, R. 6.6.17			
41344	McAughern, W. J. 21.8.17		39547	McDowell, J. 27.10.18
26/1656	McAvoy, F. 15.9.16		51859	McFadden, J. E. 27.3.18
55603	McBride, A. 26.8.18		56814	McFadyen, J. U. 16.7.18
26137	McBride, D. J. 7.6.17		53795	McFarlane, D. 12.9.18

23/7	Macfarlane, Capt. D. B. 7.6.17		24/525	McKenzie, Sgt. D. 9.9.17
72073	Macfarlane, D. P. 5.10.18		18693	McKenzie, Sgt. F. 30.8.18
56454	McFarlane, W. H. 5.5.18		32880	McKenzie, J. 12.10.17
25/29	McGahan, Sgt. C. W. 15.9.16		37002	McKenzie, J. 30.3.18
			44647	MacKenzie, K. W. 21.4.18
53383	McGavin, A. M. 9.1.18		24/526	McKenzie, Sgt. M. 7.6.17
52253	McGill, J. R. 9.5.18		45641	McKenzie, Q. 4.11.18
42141	McGill, W. A. 10.9.18		40608	McKenzie, T. W. 8.10.18
12441	McGillivray, Cpl. H. 12.10.17		47034	McKenzie, W. 30.3.18
			45225	McKenzie, W. A. 12.10.17
24/1434	McGinn, J. H. 15.9.16		27098	McKenzie, W. T. C. 12.10.17
54565	McGovern, J. P. 4.1.18			
48989	McGowan, C. 2.12.17		54768	McKeown, J. 6.8.18
21866	McGregor, Cpl. A. 18.11.17		24/242	McKichan, L/Cpl. A. McL. 15.9.16
55998	McGregor, C. J. 28.8.18			
24/1138	McGregor, D. 15.9.16		15387	Mackie, L/Cpl. R. 27.8.18
24766	McGregor, J. 9.12.17		12238	McKinley, G. K. 3.10.16
55610	McGregor, W. 7.10.18		23016	McKinnon, E. 1.1.17
24/1140	McHugh, J. 7.6.17		25/1788	McKinnon, J. 15.9.16
17807	McIlroy, Cpl. A. H. 12.10.17		52259	McKinstry, L/Cpl. E. F. 12.9.18
24311	McIlroy, Lt. G. T. 12.10.17			
35216	McIlroy, H. F. 6.5.18		23/229	McKinstry, G. L. 29.5.16
26/610	McInnes, Cpl. E. J., M.M. 29.8.18		40714	Mackintosh, D. 17.10.17
			25/665	McKone, L/Cpl. J. 1.10.16
45776	McInnes, M. L. 12.10.17		23022	McKoy, G. G. 12.10.17
26658	McIntosh, A. 9.6.17		23/233	MacLachlan, Cpl. A. 4.11.18
19029	McIntosh, D. M. 14.2.17			
23/511	McIntosh, J. 12.10.17		53711	McLachlan, C. R. 18.4.18
12443	McIntosh, S. H. 29.3.18		47746	McLachlan, D. 24.10.18
25/658	McIntosh, Cpl. W. 17.9.18		25923	McLachlan, L. 22.11.17
55081	McIntosh, Cpl. W. G. 5.4.18		46236	McLaren, W. W. 5.4.18
53050	MacIntyre, J. P. 2.2.18		25922	McLarnon, F. T. 21.5.17
45610	McIntyre, Cpl. (T/Sgt.) W., M.M. 4.11.18		26/1173	McLaughlin, H. J. 27.5.16
			26/1655	McLean, A. J. 21.9.16
26/1642	Mack, R. 28.9.16		23/1105	McLean, D. 10.10.16
23402	Mackay, A. 6.4.18		14730	McLean, Sgt. D. 8.6.17
53710	McKay, A. D. 30.8.18		25/510	MacLean, L/Cpl. D. B. S. 6.9.17
26/1662	McKay, A. P. 4.11.18			
62117	Mackay, D. 29.3.18		38200	McLean, F. 15.10.17
23/1310	McKay, Cpl. D. E. C. 9.6.16		24/527	McLean, F. A. 15.9.16
			26/601	McLean, H. 6.7.17
23/1454	Mackay, J. 15.9.16		24/1437	McLean, J. W. 12.10.17
51415	Mackay, J. 4.12.17		23/1444	McLean, R. 16.6.17
21526	McKay, J. 26.10.18		23/514	McLean, Sgt. W. E. 12.10.17
11065	Mackay, L/Cpl. J. M. 8.1.18			
			23/2243	McLellan, J. 15.9.16
25/661	Mackay, J. R. 15.9.16		41103	McLeod, A. 2.12.17
12435	Mackay, S. A. 7.6.17		19032	McLeod, A. G. 7.6.17
26/496	McKay, L/Cpl. W. 28.9.17		23/2052	McLeod, F. J. 15.9.16
26660	McKechnie, J. 12.10.17		23/1106	McLeod, L/Cpl. G. M. 22.9.16
25/216	McKechnie, R. D. 17.9.16			
23/2247	McKee, T. 7.6.17		42696	McLeod, J. 7.4.18
46891	McKenna, A. E. 12.10.17		41347	McLeod, J. A. 17.8.17
26145	McKenzie, A. E. C. 7.6.17		42697	McLeod, J. K. 12.10.17
26752	MacKenzie, A. N. D. 12.10.17		24/858	McLeod, J. T. 24.6.16
			31875	Macleod, L. 15.4.18

24/857	McLeod, Sgt. R. 30.9.16	26643	Maitland, Sgt. R. 29.8.18
36836	McLeod, Cpl. W. E. 5.4.18	23/818	Makeham, 2/Lt. C. E. 12.9.18
56820	McLuckie, A. A. 12.9.18		
24/2541	McMillan, Cpl. A. W. 12.10.17	24/222	Makeig, L/Cpl. C. D. 5.12.16
53638	McMillan, D. 11.9.18	41981	Malcolm, 2/Lt. G. 28.3.18
26148	McMillan, J. D. 7.6.17	19019	Malcolm, W. 19.8.17
24/246	McMinn, S. V. 15.9.16	42681	Maley, T. 16.9.17
26/195	McMinn, T. 15.9.16	70779	Mallett, Revd. C. A. (C.F.) 30.9.18
23416	McMullan, W. 13.2.17		
39681	McMurray, Sgt. R., D.C.M. 20.8.18	27715	Mallinson, P. J. 7.6.17
		41597	Maloney, T. 23.11.17
20211	McMurrick, D. 12.10.17	24/835	Mancer, A. E. 9.11.18
22846	McNaughton, W. A. 5.5.17	14831	Maney, M. A. D. 12.11.16
58783	McNeil, A. 20.4.18	44976	Mangin, J. T. 8.10.18
26/1176	McNeil, A. A. 31.5.16	44130	Mangos, W. 26.8.17
26/193	McNeil, J. 12.10.17	42682	Mann, E. 12.10.17
23/234	McNeil, J. P. 19.9.16	23/202	Manning, A. 30.5.16
27096	McNoe, L/Cpl. W. A. 6.4.18	23/1906	Manning, Lt. L. I., M.C., (d). 26.8.18
26/1659	McNulty, L/Cpl. V. J. 9.8.17	23/1513	Mansell, L/Cpl. F. 27.9.18
		45709	Mansell, F. J. 12.10.17
26661	McOnie, C. 7.6.17	24/2031	Manson, S. R. 12.10.17
23417	McPeak, A. J. 20.5.17	23/1434	Marchant, A. B. 27.3.18
24/1441	McPhee, J. 25.6.16	26/844	Marrian, J. 15.9.16
26/864	McPhee, K. McK. 15.9.16	26/363	Mars, J. 15.9.16
41211	Macpherson, Lt. A. E. 26.8.18	25/891	Marsack, Sgt. C. W. 6.6.17
		23404	Marsh, G. H. 15.9.16
54769	McPherson, J. 30.8.18	26/592	Marshall, Cpl. (A/Sgt.) A. A. 14.7.16
70116	McQuarrie, D. 22.8.18		
23/1108	McQueen, Cpl. W. A. 26.3.18	53376	Marshall, D. M. 8.12.17
		25/994	Marshall, L/Cpl. F. G. 24.9.16
24/2246	Macrae, A. 15.9.16		
35673	McRae, L/Cpl. A. F. 8.10.18	62605	Marshall, G. A. 22.5.18
		39264	Marshall, J. A. 15.10.17
25/1002	McRae, Sgt. A. P. 7.6.17	25/123	Marshall, T. 5.10.16
38199	McRae, A. 5.5.18	21857	Marshall, G. R. 7.6.17
24/15	McRae, Capt. P. F. 12.10.17	69354	Marslin, W. T. 12.9.18
		12436	Marten, C. 29.3.18
25/215	McRae, S. A. 15.9.16	26/1043	Martin, Sgt. J. A., (d). 15.9.16
32883	McWatt, W. 12.10.17		
25/776	Mackwood, J. H. 17.7.16	21499	Davie-Martin, J. E. 23.3.17
18913	Maben, Lt. (T/Capt.) K. M. 26.8.18	42160	Martin, T. 28.12.17
		25/996	Martin, W. H. 31.5.16
41844	Mace, L/Cpl. G. G. 29.3.18	54210	Masefield, R. T. 12.9.18
44296	Madden, F. 26.10.18	65426	Mason, H. 8.10.18
39262	Madden, Sgt. J. F. 9.9.18	24/1112	Mason, J. 16.9.16
52237	Madill, Cpl. H. A. 26.8.18	25/507	Mason, L/Sgt. W. 29.3.18
26/585	Maffey, S. A. 15.9.16	26/1652	Mason, W. A. 7.6.17
41341	Maher, J. S. 22.11.17	24/2243	Mason, W. P. 5.4.18
38843	Mahoney, E. J. 9.10.18	67631	Masson, R. R. 4.11.18
14200	Mahoney, Sgt. J. 8.6.17	41984	Matchett, R. J. 12.9.18
23/2029	Maides, Sgt. A. B. 15.9.16	25/129	Mather, Sgt. C. W. 30.6.16
		14654	Mather, Sgt. R. 17.3.18
23205	Main, J. 10.6.17	36874	Matheson, J. W. 12.10.17
26/846	Mair, J. 12.5.18	4/288	Matheson, L/Cpl. N. McL. 29.12.17
15389	Maisey, J. 7.6.17		

32869	Matheson, T. A. 7.8.17	38845	Milne, Cpl. A. C. H. 2.5.18
12426	Mathews, T. R. 2.11.16	58786	Milne, R. F. 9.9.18
24/836	Matthews, F. N. 10.9.18	52352	Milne, S. S. 21.1.18
40227	Matthews, W. J. 2.5.18	53393	Milne, Cpl. T. A. 5.4.18
26127	Mattingley, F. A. 23.2.17	19022	Milne, W. D. H. 28.12.16
30106	Maude, Lt. E. A. 17.8.17	14352	Missen, A/Cpl. D. C. 7.1.17
52851	Maule, J. 16.4.18	71517	Mitchell, A. 30.10.18
23/498	Mawhinney, R. 20.6.17	23/209	Mitchell, A. 4.1.18
26/35	Mawley, Lt. G. 12.10.17	23/1119	Mitchell, A. M. 8.6.17
15928	Maxwell, C. 28.3.18	41253	Mitchell, A. R. 21.8.17
18685	Maxwell, H. 7.6.17	33572	Mitchell, F. 26.8.18
23/823	May, D. 20.9.16	23/1118	Mitchell, T. F. 22.9.16
23006	May, L/Cpl. D. G. 23.9.17	26/1067	Mitchell, V. 12.9.16
25/780	Mayell, C. J. 15.9.16	13066	Mockford, T. D. 30.9.17
21521	Meaney, A. 26.8.18	45712	Mohan, E. 26.3.18
26/586	Meffin, G. 7.6.17	25/30	Mollison, Lt. (T/Capt.) B., M.C. 21.3.18
26/123	Mehra, R. C. 3.12.17		
21159	Melhuish, W. H. 7.8.17	29045	Molloy, Cpl. D. P. 6.10.18
26/589	Meliar, B. 22.9.16	51053	Moorby, T. W. 26.8.18
18687	Mellar, L/Sgt. A. H. 19.10.18	46471	Monaghan, R. C. 8.10.18
		15940	Monaghan, T. 23.6.17
23/2225	Melling, T. 15.9.16	23406	Monds, F. W. 7.6.17
20187	Mellor, P. 7.6.17	24/1124	Monkman, Cpl. A., M.M. 12.10.17
29825	Melrose, L/Cpl. R. M. 26.8.18		
		38193	Monson, L. W. 23.10.17
25/779	Menzies, D. 27.3.18	23/212	Montagu, Sgt. E. C. D. 5.4.18
23/979	Menzies, L/Cpl. S. 15.9.16		
23/825	Menzies, C.S.M. J. W. C., M.M. 31.8.18	44652	Montgomery, E. 21.11.17
		41096	Moore, A. K. 29.3.18
39270	Metcalfe, E. 28.4.18	24/1125	Moore, D. 30.1.17
36344	Metcalfe, R. 5.10.18	50028	Moore, F. G. 6.8.18
33913	Mettam, T. H. 12.10.17	24/229	Moore, G. F. 26.5.16
21158	Meuli, C.S.M. L. 22.8.18	44943	Moore, 2/Lt. R. C. 12.9.18
65228	Mewhinney, R. J. 9.10.18	25/212	Mordin, J. H. 26.8.18
65229	Mewhinney, S. C. 26.10.18	25/208	Mordin, W. J. 27.5.16
21854	Meyenberg, L/Cpl. W. R. 12.9.18	52852	Morey, L/Cpl. L. 21.8.18
		25/997	Morgan, Sgt. A. 7.6.17
26/1013	Michell, A. E. 28.9.16	23082	Morgan, L/Sgt. A. J. 28.9.17
15395	Middleton, W. 7.2.17		
10370	Midgley, Sgt. H. L., M.M. 7.11.18	25915	Morgan, E. 10.5.18
		12/1465	Morgan, 2/Lt. H. L. 8.12.17
25/782	Milburn, Sgt. C. L. 12.10.17		
		22348	Morgan, J. E. 12.10.17
45231	Milburn, Cpl. L. S. 15.1.18	22634	Morgan, L. C. 7.6.17
24/1121	Miles, L. F. 26.8.18	54553	Morgan, R. 30.3.18
39074	Millar, J. 5.4.18	25/446	Morgan, S. 12.10.17
18018	Millar, 2/Lt. J. 12.10.17	26/857	Morgan, V. 7.6.16
39271	Millar, J. S. 12.10.17	41599	Moriarty, M. 27.11.17
13060	Miller, A. C. 23.3.17	15934	Morland, P. 6.6.17
21051	Miller, R. S. 8.5.17	23/1441	Moroney, J. H. 15.9.16
25/207	Milligan, D. 12.10.17	55991	Moroney, P. 7.4.18
59214	Milligan, W. 4.10.18	72129	Morris, A. 9.9.18
26/1639	Milligan, W. G. 15.9.16	37123	Morris, J. 31.7.18
23/521	Millis, A. J. 2.10.16	23/833	Morris, O. 19.9.16
25/206	Millman, W. H. 1.10.16	23/215	Morrison, L/Cpl. A. L. 2.5.18
62610	Mills, W. 7.9.18		
27717	Milne, A. 16.8.17		

513

R

55158	Morrison, E. F. 15.5.18	25/1086	Nelson, J. H. 16.9.16
26/315	Morrison, J. H. 4.11.18	34119	Nelson, J. P. 26.8.18
17799	Morrison, L/Cpl. J. R. 14.10.17	20216	Ness, T. P. J. 30.1.17
24791	Morrison, R. E. 8.6.17	26153	New, P. J. 28.3.17
31134	Morrow, F. R. 4.11.18	24/2549	Newcombe, R. 17.9.16
11078	Mort, W. A. 16.6.17	48558	Newell, C. R. 31.8.18
72265	Morton, D. 31.10.18	56825	Newell, F. L. 2.5.18
23/525	Mouldey, J. E. 15.9.16	21877	Newlove, C. 7.6.17
23/42	Mowlem, Sgt. J. 15.9.16	23/242	Nicholas, A/Cpl. E. O. 15.9.16
24/230	Moyle, T. 23.9.16	47924	Nicholas, H. 9.9.18
24/849	Muff, N. D. 4.1.18	29058	Nicholas, L. 7.6.17
45714	Muir, D. 12.10.17	12458	Nicholson, A. 3.10.16
30968	Mulholland, Cpl. R. F. 30.8.18	24/2266	Nicholson, E. 16.12.16
49925	Mullan, C. 1.1.18	23418	Nicholson, J. A. 27.12.16
24/2045	Mullany, J. 6.4.18	23419	Nicholson, W. 5.3.17
29935	Mulley, R. 12.10.17	54073	Nicol, W. J. 12.9.18
44004	Mumford, A. 14.10.17	51890	Nicolson, D. 31.3.18
44005	Mumford, H. E. 12.10.17	53803	Nicolson, Cpl. F. J. 8.10.18
26/1541	Mumford, H. G. M. B. 29.8.18	26152	Nielsen, G. M. 12.10.17
38556	Mundy, H. R. 12.10.17	15069	Nielsen, L/Cpl. P. 9.8.17
31869	Munro, J. D. 16.6.17	38574	Nightingale, C. M. 12.10.17
60336	Munro, W. 9.5.18	64968	Noble, F. H. 9.9.18
62614	Munyard, H. A. 9.9.18	25/223	Noble, S. J. 15.9.16
24/850	Murdoch, A. G. 10.7.16	71253	Nolan, R. J. 19.10.18
69616	Murdoch, W. 21.11.18	26/1015	Noonan, L/Cpl. J. P. 15.9.16
24/532	Murfitt, L/Cpl. E. G. 31.8.18	44142	Norman, A. E. 16.1.18
31528	Murray, A. J. 27.9.18	29061	Norquay, D. S. 21.6.17
63644	Murray, C. V., M.M. 27.8.18	24/1151	Norrie, 2/Lt. R. D. 15.9.16
25/1783	Murray, J. J. 1.10.16	23/1135	Norris, A. J. 15.9.16
13/2599	Murray, L/Cpl. M. 28.3.18	41004	Norris, H. W. 12.10.17
24/530	Murray, W. S. 8.2.17	26/687	North, H. S. 15.9.16
59216	Murrell, J. R. 8.9.18	23/1136	North, M. S. 22.9.16
23/2580	Murton, J. H. 11.3.17	21073	Norton, A. 12.10.17
23/1127	Myers, Cpl. R., M.M. 19.6.17	24/872	Norton, Cpl. W. H. 12.10.17
		26/197	Noyce, Cpl. C. H. 15.9.16
		62619	Nugent, E. 8.5.18
		38849	Nutter, 2/Lt. E. R. 30.3.18
65435	Nairn, S. H. 15.7.18		
15067	Neame, A. A. 7.6.17	25/667	O'Brien, A. J. 12.10.17
23/1906	Napier, Lt. (T/Capt.) D. G. 16.9.17	62621	O'Brien, F. T. L. 7.11.18
23081	Nash, Sgt. F. H. 5.4.18	56011	O'Brien, J. 26.8.18
25/556	Nathan, Cpl. B. C. 15.9.16	41869	O'Brien, J. P. 12.10.17
26/1665	Naughton, H. L. 15.9.16	29846	O'Brien, W. 26.8.18
15404	Neal, W. L. 10.10.18	51891	O'Connell, J. J. P. 26.8.18
41001	Neave, S. H. 12.10.17	23/386	O'Connell, Cpl. W. M. 27.5.18
26/1096	Nee, J. 14.8.17	47176	O'Connor, D. 12.10.17
49102	Neely, A. 1.9.18	12462	O'Connor, J. 25.3.17
36753	Nees, 2/Lt. F. A. 1-2.9.18	36883	O'Connor, M. 20.4.18
32884	Neil, J. A. 8.6.17	11095	O'Connor, P. M. 15.9.16
22690	Neilson, Lt. A. R. 28.3.18	44984	O'Connor, T. J. 13.10.17
47071	Neilson, M. 7.12.17	26/1018	O'Donnell, J. 3.1.17
39087	Nelson, D. 5.11.17	48063	O'Donnell, L/Sgt. (T/Sgt.) J. N., M.M. 3.11.18
18695	Nelson, D. 12.10.17		

24/254	O'Donohue, Sgt. E. J. 15.9.16.	69719	Palmer, J. 10.9.18
26/1019	O'Driscoll, C., M.M. 12.10.17	25/454	Palmer, J. 23.5.18
		24/877	Palmer, R. 12.10.17
		23/872	Palmer, W. W. 22.9.16
62706	O'Gorman, C. 28.8.18	51495	Park, T. J. 4.11.18
23/1457	O'Hara, Sgt. P. C. 11.4.17	32961	Park, W. H. 24.10.18
23/1187	O'Kane, R. H. 4.12.17	42385	Parker, Cpl. C. A. 31.7.18
52873	O'Keefe, L./Cpl. W. 8.10.18	53735	Parker, J. 27.7.18
		48069	Parkinson, H. 6.12.17
24/874	O'Leary, J. W. 1.10.16	59278	Parkinson, J. 26.8.18
23/865	O'Meara, J. 29.3.18	24/1158	Parkinson, L. E. 12.10.17
54583	O'Sullivan, J. C. 27.8.18	24/1457	Parry, L./Cpl. P. L. 15.11.16
55616	O'Sullivan, P. 5.4.18		
19039	Officer, W. J. 8.5.17	52877	Parslow, A. V. 6.1.18
23036	Oglethorpe, L./Cpl. E. A. 2.4.17	25/903	Parsons, J. A. 12.10.17
		26/73	Partridge, Sgt. F. J. 8.9.16
27132	Okey, J. T. 12.10.17	24/878	Passell, Cpl. J. 5.12.17
20560	Old, C. R. 7.6.17	58800	Patchett, E. E. 29.3.18
56831	Oldridge, T. S. D. 27.3.18	28529	Patching, E. W. J. 3.6.17
40715	Oldfield, F. W. 12.10.17	41353	Patterson, J. H. 5.10.17
46478	Olds, H. 12.10.17	62631	Patterson, S. H. 21.8.18
23/864	Oliff, W. J. 2.2.18	26/132	Patterson, L./Cpl. S. H. F. 25.9.16
23234	Oliver, D. A. 8.10.16		
23/1141	Oliver, J. R. 15.9.16	18698	Patton, A. 12.10.17
25/1184	Oliver, R. J. 29.8.18	11/120	Patton, A/Cpl. A. C. (N.Z.M.C.) 5.5.17
41010	Oliver, T. F. 6.4.18		
65906	Oliver, W. M. 29.8.18	47072	Patton, F. J. 27.5.18
26/1021	Olsen, A. 15.9.16	25/1198	Patton, W. C. 12.10.17
23037	Olsen, A. J. 25.5.17	24/1165	Pauwels, Sgt. L. C. 12.10.17
24/1153	Olsen, L./Cpl. E. 15.11.16	48840	Payne, W. 12.10.17
25736	Olsen, H. R. 16.2.17	52268	Peake, F. R. 8.4.18
31427	Olsen, J. O. 11.6.17	70329	Peake, H. S. 6.10.18
38207	Olsen, K. 8.10.18	25/349	Pearce, J. W. 12.10.17
26/1672	Olsen, O. 18.11.16	17816	Pearce, L. G. 12.10.17
41871	Olson, N. S. 12.10.17	24/1167	Pearce, Cpl. V. W., M.M. 26.3.18
25/452	Orchard, C. L. 20.9.16		
23/248	Ormsby, L./Cpl. W. G. 15.9.16	48677	Pearce, W. G. 26.5.18
		25/565	Pearpoint, Cpl. H. S. 1.10.16
14314	Orr, E. 7.6.17		
23/1143	Orr, L./Cpl. H. W. 8.6.17	24/2552	Pearson, J. J. 12.9.18
23/867	Orsborn, J. 6.10.18	52878	Pearson, R. 10.9.18
67897	Osmond, G. J. 8.10.18	24/1539	Peck, A. G. 8.6.17
30398	Owen, A. 7.1.18	24/1460	Pedder, G. C. P. 10.10.16
51494	Owen, J. 9.12.17	26/368	Peers, R. T. 17.9.16
14853	Owen, W. 29.3.18	23/554	Pegden, H. G. 15.9.16
29586	Owens, A. 21.6.17	56844	Penberthy, H. A. 26.10.17
23/545	Oxenbridge, Sgt. E. W, (d). 14.10.17	23/254	Pendergrast, J. 15.9.16
		24/1461	Pennefather, O. F. 10.7.16
		21085	Pennell, A. McC. 4.1.18
41106	Pacey, W. 27.3.18	23/2256	Penney, G. L. 29.9.16
26/967	Page, T. A. 7.6.17	23/556	Penney, T/Sgt. R. C. 15.9.16
51893	Page, T. A. J. 5.4.18		
45731	Page, W. 19.11.17	26671	Penny, S. E. 15.11.17
21080	Pain, H. S. 25.7.18	26/200	Penrose, Sgt. J. W. 7.6.17
61759	Pallesen, T. G. 5.10.18	24/1462	Pepperell, L. F. 12.7.16
23/1145	Palmer, C. C. 26.9.16	62633	Perchard, P. H. 9.5.18
54584	Palmer, C. R. 1.6.18	49168	Percy, A. 4.11.18

69033	Percy, A. T. 12.9.18		26892	Potter, G. 15.9.16
65606	Perfect, J. H. 9.9.18		24/1464	Potts, C. H. 8.10.18
23/1151	Perfect, S. 15.9.16		26/1023	Potts, J. W. 12.10.17
56017	Perrin, F. D. 15.5.18		43926	Potts, W. R. 30.5.18
42570	Perry, J. 6.4.18		21534	Povey, J. 30.4.17
25/1229	Perry, L/Cpl. S. 15.9.16		24434	Powell, A. 30.5.17
20224	Perry, T. 7.6.17		36484	Powell, G. W. 4.10.18
10/1617	Perry, L/Cpl. W. A. 28.3.18		14677	Powell, W. M. 22.11.17
23/255	Perry, W. J. 10.7.16		24/8	Powley, Capt. A. J., M.C. 20.9.16
38211	Persen, E. 27.6.17		26169	Powley, J. C. 7.6.17
29071	Peryman, Cpl. L. W. 6.4.18		41013	Powley, J. T. 30.8.18
24/2070	Peters, L. F. 15.9.16		23/2264	Pratt, E. 7.6.17
26672	Peters, W. 1.10.17		69878	Preacher, J. 5.10.18
24/2071	Peters, W. 2.11.16		41091	Prebble, L/Cpl. E. K. 31.3.18
23/558	Petersen, A. 23.9.16		23/883	Prebble, C.S.M. T. L., M.M. 7.11.17
23/878	Petersen, Sgt. G. V. 15.9.16			
20562	Petersen, H. L. C. 7.4.18		19/221	Preen, E. G. 12.10.17
24/881	Petersen, R. 15.9.16		22175	Preston, W. G. 19.12.16
23/879	Petersen, W. 13.9.16		49261	Prictor, J. A. 28.3.18
25934	Peterson, J. 7.6.17		44152	Priest, E. J. 29.3.18
24/1168	Peterson, J. P. 2.10.16		9/1478	Priest, L/Cpl. G. W. 23.8.18
12465	Phelan, E. M., M.M. 7.6.17			
56839	Phelan, J. McD. 26.8.18		40049	Priest, J. P. 20.1.18
65799	Phelan, P. P. 8.10.18		21090	Probert, T. 18.10.17
46486	Philipps, F. E. 12.10.17		14718	Prouting, L/Sgt. W. J. 9.8.17
25/1007	Phillips, C. C. 1.10.16			
26/888	Phillips, Sgt. R. 4.8.18		26/57	Pruden, S.M. A. F. 15.9.16
32962	Phillis, L/Cpl. F. J. 29.3.18		52884	Prujean, H. A. 9.9.18
23/1464	Phillpots, J. 15.9.16		40130	Pryor, A. 4.12.17
38307	Pickering, G. 12.10.17		23/566	Pryor, R. 15.9.16
68748	Pidgeon, W. H. 9.9.18		15319	Puckridge, H. D. 20.6.17
26167	Pierce, E. H. 9.9.17		24/262	Pugh, Cpl. F. G. 25.9.16
24/2074	Pierce, J. 19.7.16		41877	Pugh, S. W. 15.8.17
52882	Pierson, C. 15.7.18		15414	Pulford, J. 27.11.16
14858	Pierson, F. 5.4.18		55085	Pullar, J. 6.4.18
49053	Pilcher, Cpl. F. W. 8.10.18		41014	Pullin, R. J. 3.5.18
23/560	Pimm, Cpl. W. H. 15.6.16		15962	Purcell, L/Cpl. A. R. 12.10.17
18700	Pinhey, S. N. 23.6.17			
55621	Pinkerton, R. 27.3.18		23/567	Purcell, L. A. 17.9.16
12249	Plummer, D. A. 2.10.16		25/1231A	Purcell, R. 21.9.16
25139	Poll, A. I. 12.10.17		23/10	Purdy, Capt. (Temp. Maj.) R. G., M.C., [F]. 28.3.18
23245	Pollard, W. F. 30.12.16			
41992	Pollock, Cpl. W. 30.8.18		23/884	Purkis, C.S.M. R. C. 25.12.15
38868	Polson, 2/Lt. C. 26.8.18			
24/559	Pool, C. 12.10.17		24/2275	Putman, W. 24.9.16
24/260	Poole, F. A. 15.9.16		56841	Putt, C. F. 7.1.18
13802	Poole, Cpl. F. E. 2.12.17		25/228	Pycroft, C. 15.9.16
46243	Poole, L/Cpl. S. J. 4.11.18		21091	Pye, B. G. 6.2.17
36790	Porteous, L/Cpl. T. 27.3.18		12254	Pyke, J. 10.6.17
25586	Porter, G. 7.6.17			
24/2075	Porter, J. 15.9.16			
25/1009	Porter, J. T. 23.11.16			
3/507	Porter, Cpl. W. C. (N.Z.M.C.) 14.10.17		55622	Quayle, J. J. 18.8.18
			25/669	Quinn, L/Cpl. C. H. 21.5.18
23/562	Posha, A. 12.10.17		41109	Quinn, M. C. 12.10.17
30402	Potroz, B. 12.10.17		54607	Quirke, M. 23.8.18

25/44	Radcliffe, Sgt. J. V. 25.5.16	24/1472	Roberts, L/Cpl. C. C. 15.9.16
24/2078	Radcliffe, W. H. 15.9.16		
41355	Radford, R. C. 30.3.18	32901	Roberts, J. P. 7.6.17
12/3453	Rae, 2/Lt. T. H. 4.11.18	23/2268	Roberts, J. S. 15.9.16
28534	Rafter, J. 16.10.17	26/470	Roberts, P. G. 27.3.17
42708	Raines, E. B. 16.1.18	51443	Robertson, C. 20.11.17
47076	Rainey, W. J. 21.8.18	25944	Robertson, D. H. 30.8.18
41110	Rains, L/Cpl. W. H. 9.5.18	64929	Robertson, E. H. 30.8.18
12256	Ramsay, Sgt. A. 8.10.18	25/672	Robertson, J. 6.5.17
14209	Ramsey, J. H. 7.6.17	59990	Robertson, Cpl. J. 22.10.18
18704	Randal, E. S. 8.8.17		
54080	Randall, B. R. 19.4.18	39424	Robertson, J. A. 28.9.17
23/1467	Rathbone, W. L. 15.9.16	18709	Robertson, T. 12.10.17
26/204	Raxworthy, T. A. 15.9.16	39721	Robertson, Lt. T. G. 22.8.18
26/1687	Ray, H. 15.9.16	47038	Robertson, W. J. 20.4.18
26/1689	Ray, R. M.M. 30.3.18	23/45	Robertson, W. R. 15.9.16
12/4255	Rayner, C. H. 28.8.18	15418	Robinson, L/Cpl. A. 16.11.17
26/205	Rayner, Cpl. J. 3.8.18		
26/137	Rea, M. J. 7.6.17	24/1921	Robinson, A. A. 15.9.16
23/888	Read, W. 23.6.17	26/207	Robinson, Sgt. A. G. 15.9.16
26/1179	Reddy, T. M. 27.3.17		
70124	Redmond, B. 5.10.18	23/2080	Robinson, A. J. 8.8.17
21094	Redshaw, W. E. 7.6.17	23/897	Robinson, Sgt. E. F. 3.6.16
55624	Rees, D. H. 27.9.18		
30407	Reeve, G. S. 6.4.18	75290	Robinson, G. W. 5.10.18
24/660	Reeve, 2/Lt. W. A. C. 29.3.18	3/964	Robinson, Pte. H. (N.Z.M.C.) 23.9.16
21095	Reeve, W. C. L. 7.6.17	56027	Robinson, J. 2.2.18
51317	Reeve, L/Cpl. W. L. 26.5.18	26/895	Robinson, O. H. 23.11.17
		23/584	Robinson, T. A. 7.6.17
42709	Reid, J. 19.4.18	72080	Robinson, W. A. 15.10.18
25/24	Reid, Sgt. S. 23.12.16	26/624	Robjohn, W. F. 7.6.17
53814	Reid, S. B. 20.5.18	24/1474	Robson, A. C. 24.12.16
45737	Reid, W. B. 30.11.17	65039	Rodger, A. 26.8.18
41889	Reside, W. 12.10.17	25/459	Rodger, Cpl. J. C. 23.9.16
53413	Reynolds, G. S. 26.3.18	26/1111	Rodwell, Sgt. J. A. 12.9.18
24/574	Rice, S. 15.9.16	48570	Rogers, C. E. 19.4.18
25/1801	Richards, C. 1.10.16	24/1475	Rogers, F. 1.10.16
69727	Richards, D. C. 4.11.18	55161	Rogers, F. T. 2.5.18
23/892	Richards, Cpl. S. 30.9.16	23440	Rogers, G. G. 12.10.17
26/1690	Richardson, C. S. 12.10.17	27692	Rohan, Lt. (T/Capt.) M. D., (d). 22.8.18
39101	Richardson, G. K. 11.9.17		
23433	Richardson, N. C. 9.8.17	14867	Roil, A. L. 20.2.17
32900	Richardson, W. 9.8.17	52888	Roper, H. E. 30.1.18
25/1111	Rickerby, B. 15.9.16	60270	Rosa, H. 29.3.18
54084	Ricketts, A. D. 27.10.18	15846	Rose, Cpl. E. L. 4.11.18
3/3031	Riddell, Pte. D. (N.Z.M.C.) 12.9.18	13097	Rose, Cpl. W. R. 12.10.17
		49006	Ross, C. 12.10.17
24/2558	Riddle, J. T. 7.6.17	26182	Ross, D. 26.5.18
72271	Ridland, A. J. 5.11.18	20239	Ross, F. 12.10.17
29083	Ridley, J. W. L. 12.10.17	47086	Ross, J. 21.5.18
25739	Rigden, G. A. 7.6.17	23/1166	Ross, J. 19.8.17
23436	Riordan, J. 11.10.16	24/1476	Ross, J. 8.7.18
20235	Ritchie, J. T. 18.8.17	53812	Ross, J. A. 22.2.18
23437	Rivers, J. P. 7.4.18	23/900	Ross, P. R. 15.9.16
41885	Rivett, G. 12.10.17	42711	Ross, R. J. 20.2.18
41358	Roach, Cpl. E. R. 12.9.18	54601	Ross, R. M. 5.4.18

41888	Ross, S.	4.11.18
25741	Ross, W.	8.10.18
40717	Ross, W. A.	12.10.17
41362	Rossiter, H.	12.10.17
25947	Roughan, E. T.	2.9.18
56031	Roulston, H. L.	5.4.18
23/1168	Rout, E.	3.10.16
26690	Rowe, S. W.	12.6.17
19049	Rowell, J. J.	10.6.17
26/1147	Rowland, C. K.	19.7.16
31895	Ruck, L/Cpl. F. T.	30.3.18
41022	Rudd, H.	6.12.17
70651	Rudkin, E. R.	13.9.18
56032	Rudkin, E. S.	9.12.17
23256	Rudkin, G.	12.10.17
26/902	Rule, 2/Lt. C. W.	5.10.18
39722	Rule, Lt. W. B.	12.10.17
59230	Rundle, E. A.	11.9.18
46905	Rundle, Cpl. W. A.	2.5.18
13808	Ruscoe, H. G.	12.10.17
24/1310	Russell, L/Cpl. G. B. E.	15.9.16
23/589.	Russell, R.	15.9.16
25949	Russell, R. S.	12.10.17
38590	Russell, T.	26.8.18
26179	Ryan, L/Cpl. A. E.	12.10.17
46664	Ryan, T.	28.8.18
26181	Ryan, T. F.	1.9.18
24/272	Ryan, Cpl. (T/Sgt.) T. H.	1.10.18
55093	Ryan, T. P.	23.8.18
26/1712	Saies, A.	23.9.16
20242	Salisbury, L/Sgt. C.	9.9.18
15086	Salt, Cpl. J.	12.9.18
37884	Sampson, A. C.	1.9.18
23/2085	Samson, Sgt. W.	20.6.17
25/685	Samuel, Sgt. D. A.	26.8.18
25/1808	Samworth, C. H.	15.9.16
31437	Sanderson, E.	14.10.17
24/1805	Sands, A.	15.9.16
14330	Sangster, W.	5.12.17
25/5	Sare, Capt. H. K.	16.9.16
14872	Sargent, H. R.	8.8.17
26185	Sargent, S. S.	7.6.17
23/275	Sarratt, Sgt. W.	2.8.17
18710	Satterthwaite, L/Cpl. T.	12.9.18
56859	Scadden, C. T. A.	10.4.18
38074	Scanlan, W. W. W.	5.4.18
25/1021	Scarf, H.	7.11.16
26/321	Schaeffer, L.	18.9.16
54604	Schreck, W.	12.9.18
20573	Schulz, A. A.	2.5.17
15979	Sclater, T. S.	12.10.17
25/1015	Scott, A. E.	15.9.16
66030	Scott, C. W.	9.11.18
30413	Scott, F. H.	29.3.18
27111	Scott, G.	6.9.17
20572	Scott, G.	12.10.17
51905	Scott, G. E.	7.1.18
23/591	Scott, J. A.	26.10.18
15978	Scott, R.	30.8.18
25951	Scott, R. P.	23.2.17
26/418	Scott, W.	28.9.17
60301	Scott, W. C.	12.9.18
40379	Scott, W. K.	6.4.18
24/946	Scoullar, 2/Lt. W. A.	6.4.18
25/1146	Scudamore, L. T.	15.9.16
69381	Scullion, P.	1.9.18
24/1189	Scully, C.S.M. P. A., D.C.M.	4.11.18
14162	Seal, J.	12.10.17
23/1179	Searchfield, R.	15.9.16
57384	Seddon, Capt. R. J.	21.8.18
38599	Sefton, H.	23.6.17
26/275	Sellars, N.	14.6.16
3/2874	Serpell, Capt. S. L., M.C. (N.Z.M.C.)	15.12.17
23/277	Sewart, Cpl. (T/Sgt.) H. Y.	2.8.17
25/143	Sewell, J. H.	15.9.16
23/278	Sexton, J. B.	15.9.16
55242	Shanahan, L.	12.9.18
12280	Shand, J. T.	24.2.17
19056	Shankland, J.	29.3.18
59732	Sharman, C. R.	26.10.18
71285	Sharp, A.	4.11.18
62645	Sharp, H.	21.4.18
26/254	Sharpin, R. C.	4.11.18
14023	Shaw, Lt. D. J.	30.3.18
26/638	Shaw, G. D.	15.9.16
15/65A	Shaw, Dvr. J.	1.6.17
52473	Shaw, J. M. F.	4.2.18
22874	Shaw, N.	26.10.18
21904	Shaw, R.	28.9.17
58816	Sheehan, J. M.	26.8.18
70349	Sheeran, F.	2.9.18
20249	Shellam, A.	27.4.17
45245	Shennan, J. J.	23.4.18
29943	Shepherd, H. G.	12.10.17
32079	Shepherd, Cpl. M. W.	19.7.18
41028	Shepherd, P. J.	4.11.18
46532	Shepherd, L/Cpl. R. F.	27.3.18
27116	Shepherd, T. L. A.	21.6.17
41115	Shiel, V. P.	18.9.17
51995	Shields, A.	18.2.18
22215	Shirley, Sgt. J. W.	7.8.17

25/1065	Shortland, E. G. O. 15.9.16	23/1532	Smith, G. A. 5.5.17
25/463	Shute, A. V. 13.9.16	39110	Smith, G. A. 12.8.17
48096	Sibbin, G. R. T. 21.5.18	24/286	Smith, Cpl. (T/Sgt.) G. A. E. 15.9.16
38610	Sigglekow, F. H. L. 10.10.18	27785	Smith, G. C. 29.6.17
40724	Sillifant, L/Cpl. J., D.C.M. 9.9.18	62160	Smith, G. D. 2.5.18
39713	Simm, J. C. 12.10.17	29096	Smith, H. 7.6.17
70547	Simmons, G. J. 4.11.18	26/1708	Smith, H. M. 3.10.16
25953	Simms, W. 2.10.17	71413	Smith, J. H. 11.10.18
23/2281	Simpkin, C. H. 19.1.18	23/1814	Smith, L. W. 14.4.17
39107	Simpson, A. 28.6.17	51906	Smith, N. B. F. 7.5.18
56860	Simpson, J. G. C. 3.1.18	45260	Smith, O. J. 6.12.17
26/216	Simpson, L/Cpl. J. W. 5.4.18	29584	Macleod-Smith, N. 12.10.17
		46666	Smith, L/Cpl. P. D. 9.9.18
44315	Sims, E. L. 26.8.18	44165	Smith, R. 27.3.18
40725	Sims, R. J. 12.10.17	27115	Smith, L/Sgt. R. M. 5.10.18
72427	Sinclair, A. J. 4.11.18	56038	Smith, S. 9.9.18
15425	Sinclair, R. M. 7.4.18	53273	Smith, W. 5.4.18
26/914	Skeet, B. H. 15.9.16	25/1816	Smith, W. D. 11.3.17
41235	Skelley, Capt. P. W., (d). 9.6.18	69731	Smith, W. H. C. 28.10.18
		23/912	Smith, L/Cpl. W. J. 1.9.18
23/1186	Skelton, A/Cpl. R. A. E. 15.9.16	29097	Smith, W. K., M.M. 12.10.17
48576	Skinner, G. L. 22.11.17	66037	Smith, W. L. 12.9.18
23/281	Skivington, E. (N.Z.M.C.) 28.5.17	54091	Smylie, R. J. 8.5.18
		55633	Smyth, J. 7.12.17
3/3018	Slade, Pte. G. A. (N.Z.M.C.) 6.1.19	70688	Smythe, J. K. 9.9.18
		25/690	Sneddon, A. D. 3.2.17
54089	Slatter, D. H. 22.11.17	40655	Snell, A. G. 12.10.17
74498	Slattery, J. 8.10.18	23300	Snell, Cpl. G. D. 29.3.18
25769	Slaymaker, L/Cpl. C. 12.10.17	32388	Snelling, J. M. 11.8.17
		42718	Snodgrass, L/Cpl. (T/Cpl.) W. J. 7.4.18
23/282	Sloss, R. 10.9.16	38615	Snowden, B. 12.10.17
24/1487	Small, Sgt. C. R. 14.10.17	25/359	Sole, E. 31.5.16
23/283	Small, L. E. 28.3.18	14501	Somerville, J., M.M. 24.6.17
13110	Small, L. R. 23.2.17	54164	Somerville, Cpl. W., M.M. 12.9.18
25/1813	Smart, W. 12.10.17		
41368	Smeed, E. 19.4.18	25956	Sorensen, H. 24.6.17
22378	Smith, A. 12.10.17	60316	Sorenson, M. J. 9.4.18
59469	Smith, A. 25.5.18	11126	Sotnikoff, P. A. 12.10.17
14716	Smith, Lt. A. D. 12.10.17	23/1193	Southcombe, H. H. 15.9.16
19063	Smith, A. H. 7.6.17	25957	Southgate, J. 7.6.17
23/2287	Smith, A. T. 8.10.18	24/590	Spark, Cpl. R. T. 15.4.18
14156	Smith, C. 12.10.17	51500	Speck, H. J. 5.4.18
22377	Smith, Sgt. C. 6.4.18	46398	Speedy, A. L. 15.11.18
65679	Smith, C. L. 4.5.18	23/914	Speer, R. J. 20.10.17
75208	Smith, C. T. 8.10.18	68905	Speid, W. E. 8.10.18
26/1702	Smith, D. F. 7.10.17	39343	Spence, J. 12.10.17
74231	Smith, E. B. 8.10.18	24413	Spence, 2/Lt. R. 12.10.17
26702	Smith, E. J. 15.2.17	56484	Spencer, D. 12.9.18
26/239	Smith, E. P. 12.9.16	48744	Spittle, J. W. 8.10.18
29702	Smith, 2/Lt. E. S. 12.10.17	72429	Spratt, T. A. 28.10.18
23/910	Smith, F. L. 30.3.18	25/69	Spriggs, 2/Lt. C. A., D.C.M. 8.10.18
39109	Smith, F. P. C. 11.9.17		
12273	Smith, G. 30.5.17	23/289	Sprott, G. 8.10.18

23/603	Spurden, E. W. 19.7.16		23/607	Stokes, E. J. 17.8.17
41936	Squire, E. G. 12.10.17		26/219	Stone, J. 24.2.17
25/360	Squires, W. 1.10.16		25/1819	Storey, L/Cpl. W. 12.6.17
25642	Stables, L/Cpl. W.G. 18.6.17		35049	Stow, E. J. 4.11.18
			51916	Stowe, E. 21.8.18
26/1102	Staff, L/Cpl. A. 15.8.17		29947	Strachan, G. 12.10.17
21898	Stalker, W. D. 5.5.17		23/1204	Strachan, L/Cpl. J. T. 7.6.17
66148	Stanley, L. J. 12.9.18			
26/7	Stansell, Capt. L. B. 4.6.16		25/1815	Strachan, J. D. 1.10.16
39907	Staub, W. R. 12.10.17		39115	Strachey, R. C. 4.8.17
49937	Staunton, J. F. 12.4.18		9/781	Strang, Capt. J. D. K., (d, 2). 15.9.16
24/291	Stayte, Sgt. E. O. 11.1.18			
26/107	Stead, G. W. G. 22.8.18		40849	Street, L/Cpl. D. 4.11.18
42871	Steel, A. 12.10.17		15984	Street, J. 7.6.17
25/681	Steel, J. 19.8.17		26/211	Streetley, Cpl. R. E. 2.5.18
12278	Steele, Sgt. A. 26.8.18		25/1212	Stretton, W. 21.9.16
68762	Steele, L. C. 8.10.18		25/825	Strong, H. H. 15.9.16
41116	Stenning, J. A. 12.10.17		45249	Strong, S. R. 20.5.18
53434	Stephens, J. 30.3.18		23/922	Stroud, D. S. 3.7.16
25/1016	Stephens, S. 6.12.17		46497	Stroud, W. R. 12.10.17
25/686	Stephenson, R. 19.7.16		48582	Strude, W. 22.11.17
69301	Stevens, A. 12.9.18		54785	Struthers, S. H. 9.9.18
26/1148	Stevens, C. F. 15.9.16		23/293	Struthers, W. W. 15.9.16
24/2098	Stevens, F. 20.6.17		26/282	Stuart, C.S.M. A. 5.4.18
44318	Stevens, J. C. 12.10.17		25/1113	Stuart, L/Cpl. A. M. 16.9.16
14880	Stevens, L. G. 5.11.16			
24/586	Stevens, R. J. 9.8.17		28556	Stuart, J. A. 8.6.17
26/139	Stevens, S. 23.9.16		26/1719	Stuart, W. 7.6.17
65745	Stevens, W. A. 31.8.18		56042	Stubbings, R. J. 2.2.18
26/472	Stevens, 2/Lt. W. E. 15.8.17		24415	Stubbs, 2/Lt. T. E. 12.10.17
			24/292	Styants, Sgt. A. F. 15.9.16
26/218	Stevenson, A. C. 15.9.16		18714	Sullivan, J. 12.10.17
72430	Stevenson, A. J. C. 4.10.18		21899	Sullivan, J. 23.3.17
45774	Stevenson, J. 12.10.17		23/1474	Sutherland, A/Cpl. C. E. 16.11.16
23/291	Stevenson, J. 18.9.16			
26197	Stevenson, R. 13.10.17		52702	Sutherland, O. R. 30.3.18
25958	Stevenson, R. E. 8.8.17		39912	Sutherland, W. D. 11.10.17
44319	Stevenson, W. 29.3.18		34166	Sutherland, W. R. 12.10.17
26/221	Stewart, A. J. 12.5.18		38608	Sutton, H. 30.10.18
26/637	Stewart, L/Cpl. A. W. 27.10.18		41957	Sutton, W. 12.10.17
			25/682	Sutton, L/Cpl. W. 22.11.17
24/1202	Stewart, Cpl. D. 8.7.16		46498	Swadling, J. C. 3.5.18
66042	Stewart, F. B. 4.8.18		25047	Sweetapple, Cpl. E. T. 30.3.18
26199	Stewart, G. L. 16.11.17			
18429	Stewart, 2/Lt. H. 12.10.17		23/2097	Swenson, Cpl. J. C. 12.10.17
41041	Stewart, J. A. 4.11.18			
42719	Stewart, J. W. 6.4.18		25/1137	Swift, W. 15.9.16
26/627	Stewart, L/Sgt. W. B. 28.5.16		36693	Swinney, Cpl. W. T. 7.4.18
			29101	Sykes, F. S. 7-8.6.17
44320	Stewart, W. H. 12.10.17		13124	Sykes, J. W. 18.10.18
24/1492	St. George, Cpl. F. C., M.M. 9.8.17		23/614	Symonds, A. H. 15.9.16
			42423	Symons, J. 9.5.18
26/421	Still, Sgt. C. H., M.M. 28.9.17		45752	Symons, N. 8.10.18
34939	Still, J. 26.10.18		23/2591	Taaffe, E. R. 21.6.17
6/4151	Stobie, 2/Lt. G. L. 26.8.18		25/470	Taffs, E. A. 4.11.18

71139	Taggart, C. 8.10.18		24/2109	Thomas, W. F. 25.2.17
38236	Tait, E. F. 29.8.18		39499	Thompson, F. 7.10.17
21909	Talbot, L/Cpl. H. L. 26.7.18		37038	Thompson, G. 16.4.18
			32798	Thompson, Cpl. H. 12.10.17
62173	Talbot, J. E. 23.9.18		44803	Thompson, L/Cpl. J. L. 4.11.18
41371	Talbot, R. McI. 27.10.18			
26/1127	Tansey, F. E. F. 15.9.16		32972	Thompson, O. C. 29.3.18
24/1494	Tantrum, J. 23.10.17		23/299	Thompson, L/Sgt. W. 6.4.18
17835	Tarrant, C. R. 12.10.17			
13144	Tarrant, L/Cpl. E. N. 3.8.18		26/917	Thompson, W. L. 5.6.16
			26208	Thomsen, N. 13.9.17
46402	Tate, F. 24.11.17		44565	Thomson, 2/Lt. A. 27.8.18
25/410	Tate, L/Cpl. G. W. 29.7.18		42723	Thomson, A. D. 19.8.17
44986	Tate, J. A. 19.8.17		25/472	Thomson, L/Cpl. G. C. 15.9.16
20262	Tattersall, A. 12.10.17			
38769	Tattersall, W. J. 12.10.17		26/1733	Thomson, Ian. 3.1.17
23/295	Taylor, Sgt. A., M.M. 23.6.17		26/284	Thomson, L/Sgt. J. E. 7.6.17
24/307	Taylor, A. W. 9.9.18		18719	Thomson, L/Sgt. L. 16.7.18
34169	Taylor, Sgt. C. W. 31.10.18		23/1305	Thomson, Sgt. S. B. 12.10.17
13136	Taylor, D. L. 12.10.17			
62176	Taylor, D. W. 8.10.18		25/692	Thomson, Sgt. W. 15.9.16
44169	Taylor, E. 8.1.18		25651	Thorburn, C. S. 28.3.18
23/1212	Taylor, E. J. 10.6.16		23/301	Thorn, B., M.M. (N.Z.M.C.) 20.11.17
30991	Taylor, E. J. 15.5.18			
54650	Taylor, G. B. R. 7.12.17		55101	Thurston, V. H. C. M. 5.2.18
51926	Taylor, H. F. 29.8.18			
56511	Taylor, J. 28.8.18		49942	Thurston, W. P. 5.4.18
23452	Taylor, J. H. V. 15.9.16		23/1852	Tickner, A. 15.9.16
24/1209	Taylor, L. M. 1.6.16		24/312	Tiernan, L/Cpl. E. 2.10.16
23/1518	Falconer-Taylor, R. 15.9.16		38238	Tilzey, R. 13.10.17
23/931	Taylor, Cpl. V. J. H. 5.10.18		14338	Timperley, V. E. 6.10.17
			62177	Tindle, G. W. 9.10.18
26/696	Taylor, W. F. 14.6.17		14701	Tiney, K. 5.2.17
41909	Teal, N. 10.10.17		49030	Tobeck, L. W. 27.3.18
49024	Teape, W. H. 12.10.17		24/920	Tobin, T. 18.6.17
23/2140	Telford, R. 15.9.16		42724	Tobin, W. McI. 8.4.18
13132	Telford, T. 2.2.17		56871	Todd, Cpl. D. 26.10.18
15320	Tennent, 2/Lt. R. 26.6.17		23/626	Todd, J. M. 25.12.15
12510	Terras, Sgt. R. M. 12.9.18		3/746	Tolhurst, Capt. A. M. (N.Z.M.C.) 8.5.18
52899	Terrill, W. F. 5.12.17			
24/916	Tetley, G. 20.7.16		48748	Tombs, R. 6.12.17
25/365	Thackwell, H. W. 11.9.17		40727	Tonkin, L. J. 29.10.17
26/925	Thirlwall, P. 17.10.16		54094	Tooley, D. D. 5.2.18
28560	Thistlewaite, Cpl. H. 9.9.18		62178	Toon, W. L. 5.10.18
26/1175	Thom, G. G. 15.9.16		25/244	Torkilsen, J. 15.9.16
23/933	Thom, J. 7.6.17		23/1222	Tornquist, J. E. 26.3.16
26/928	Thomas, C. B. 24.9.16		38617	Torr, A. C. V. 5.8.17
14505	Thomas, C. E. 12.11.16		23/2292	Torrens, A. J. 18.9.16
21911	Thomas, G. 7.6.17		39124	Torrens, J. 1.9.18
26/375	Thomas, J. H. 24.3.17		25/1150	Town, Cpl. C. E., M.M. 27.3.18
44171	Thomas, R. 9.8.17			
19069	Thomas, R. E. 2.4.17		45575	Townsend, F. C. 17.11.17
26207	Thomas, S. 14.1.18		26/515	Tozer, E. C. 16.9.16
23/296	Thomas, A/Cpl. S. E. 16.9.16		53445	Tracey, A. 30.8.18
			25752	Trail, W. H. 7.6.17

49031	Travis, W. C. 19.11.17		46500	Viall, S. R. 12.10.17
25/831	Treadgold, L/Cpl. C. H. 6.8.17		26720	Vieira, M. 12.10.17
25/1831	Treadwell, A. 16.9.16		25/835	Vile, F. C. R. 27.7.16
25/691	Treadwell, W. J. 15.9.16		25758	Vipond, H. G. 1.10.17
24/599	Tregilgus, S. 15.9.16		11557	Vogel, J. J. 9.5.18
23/1488	Treleaven, C. J. 19.9.16		12304	Volkert, C. A. 3.10.16
47097	Tremain, R. J. 21.8.18		30999	Vosper, L/Cpl. J. H. 12.9.18
24/1502	Trim, H. M. 15.9.16			
23/938	Triplow, H. 15.9.16		23/2112	Wainwright, Cpl. F. W. 26.8.18
55651	Trischler, J. J. S. 16.9.18			
29107	Trolan, M. 26.9.17		52701	Satterth-Waite, J. M. 30.7.18
69321	Trotter, A., 4.11.18			
62179	Trotter, C. A. 4.5.18		19074	Wakefield, A. McP. 12.10.17
27135	Troulard, L. D. T. 2.5.17		23283	Wakeford, J. 7.6.17
25832	Trounce, C. H. 16.9.16		47650	Wakelin, H. 29.8.18
44174	Trower, E. W. 7.4.18		24/1511	Wakelin, L/Cpl. L. T. 30.3.18
23/307	Truscott, L. 9.10.16			
75010	Tuck, A. S. M. 7.10.18		26/482	Walden, H. 13.6.17
14886	Tucker, E. C. 12.10.17		2/3650	Waldin, I. D. 9.9.18
54616	Tucker, L. 5.4.18		21124	Walker, A. 6.2.17
26/34	Tuckey, Cpl. A. 19.7.16		55229	Walker, A. H. 12.9.18
23/940	Tuke, H. 16.7.18		24/608	Walker, L/Cpl. C. R. 17.7.16
24/1216	Tunnicliffe, D. McK. 26.9.16			
40088	Tuohy, A. 6.4.18		26721	Walker, E. H. 7.6.17
45264	Turnbull, C. M. 5.4.18		15437	Walker, E. V. 3.1.18
26/1030	Turnbull, D. M. 15.9.16		44886	Walker, H. S. 5.12.17
29951	Turnbull, J. L. 10.5.18		26/327	Walker, P. 12.9.16
24/1504	Turner, P. J. 18.9.16		46504	Walker, R. D. 1.11.18
23/1489	Turvey, J. 15.7.16		53645	Walker, R. K. 17.11.17
42726	Tweed, J. O. 12.10.17		42727	Walker, W. 5.4.18
23272	Tweedie, D. 16.10.17		41055	Walker, W. 5.4.18
42231	Twidle, Sgt. V. S. 4.11.18		23/984	Wall, Sgt. M. 10.9.16
25/1827	Twigger, H. 29.9.16		56885	Wall, P. 28.3.18
20582	Twomey, J. O. 13.9.17		52517	Wallace, D. 3.5.18
25/833	Tye, A. J. 5.4.18		38463	Wallace, L/Cpl. D. N. 12.9.18
57173	Tyer, W. E. 31.8.18			
12/1815	Tyrie, A. 12.10.17		21917	Wallace, J. N. 6.12.17
			15315	Wallace, K. J. 12.10.17
11136	Udy, H. 9.8.16		14889	Wallace, R. 8.3.17
18508	Urwin, L/Sgt. F. C. 12.10.17		68776	Waller, E. 26.8.18
			72155	Wallis, P. R. 12.10.18
			23/2305	Walsh, F. 15.9.16
			57175	Walsh, L. M. 6.7.18
21915	Vague, W. E. 29.3.18		24/1923	Walsh, 2/Lt. M. F. 23.12.16
13145	Varney, A. C. 12.10.17		65759	Walsh, T. H. 21.5.18
24/1507	Vaughan, G. H. 15.9.16		4/1482	Walsh, 2/Lt. T. P. 4.5.18
56875	Vaughan, J. 29.3.18		24/2114	Walters, C. 15.7.16..
18021	Vaughan, 2/Lt. R. P. 12.10.17		59768	Wanstall, A. J. 26.8.18
			68910	Ward, A. A. 12.9.18
23/2594	Vaux, H. 16.9.17		14890	Ward, A. C. 16.8.17
33106	Vavasour, 2/Lt. G. M. 12.10.17		70428	Ward, J. C. S. 8.10.18
			28565	Ward, W. A. 7.6.17
24/1508	Vercoe, P. F. 15.9.16		39918	Ward, W. J. 5.4.18
24/1251	Vernon, Bglr. A. A. 15.9.16		10982	Ward, L/Cpl. W. R. 12.10.17
49946	Vernor, J. R. 12.9.18			

26/329	Warden, L/Cpl. J. R. 11.9.17	23/317	Westerholm, N. B. O. 19.9.16
23/12	Wardrop, Capt. C. L. 12.10.17	26/328	Westlake, G. E. 11.9.16
		44327	Weston, J. E. 7.4.18
20588	Ware, J. 2.4.17	24/607	Wetherall, F. J. 19.5.17
14340	Ware, Cpl. J. W. 21.11.17	40855	Wetherall, R. G. 13.9.18
23280	Warnock, J. E. E. 16.9.16	13159	Whearty, P. 12.10.17
35136	Warren, J. 4.11.18	60016	Wheatley, J. 8.12.18
26/936	Warren, L/Cpl. L. A. 7.6.17	40734	Wheeler, C. D. 12.10.17
		29114	Wheeler, H. E. 9.6.17
41914	Warren, W. H. 23.10.17	23/2114	Whetton, C. H. 25.5.17
39129	Warring, L/Cpl. J. 12.10.17	23/953	Whisker, L. J., M.M. 21.4.18
25974	Wasson, R. 12.9.18	25/1840	Whitaker, F. S. 12.10.17
23/310	Watchorn, E. L. 16.9.16	26/1158	White, J. L. 15.7.16
33787	Waters, F. V. 12.9.18	55658	White, R. F. 24.5.18
26/484	Watkins, C. R. 2.1.18	26225	White, P. 22.11.17
58948	Watkins, R. W. 29.3.18	26726	White, W. C. 12.10.17
26/1107	Watson, J. W. B. 8.12.18	23/642	White, L/Cpl. W. D. H. 24.3.17
56891	Watson, T. 4.11.18		
24/317	Watson, W. 19.7.16	25/249	White, J. 1.10.16
53453	Watson, W. C. 5.4.18	21129	Whitehouse, Cpl. C. P. 25.11.17
65006	Watson, L/Cpl. W. H. 6.11.18		
25/299	Watson, L/Cpl. W. W. 25.5.16	45626	Whitelock, R. A. 24.2.18
		25/839	Whiting, Cpl. H. F. V. 11.6.17
36502	Watt, W. 8.10.18		
26/61	Watts, 2/Lt. E. J. 3.12.17	24/1228	Whiting, Cpl. J. W. 26.8.18
15881	Watts, J. S. D. 6.10.18	31449	Whyman, H. 9.9.18
24/2115	Watts, T. A. 15.9.16	25/367	Wicks, Sgt. H. J. 1.10.16
25657	Watts, W. J. 12.10.17	23/1235	Widdowson, L/Cpl. G. A. 15.9.16
48119	Way, P. H. 12.10.17		
21626	Weaver, W. 23.3.17	72961	Wigg, E. A. 11.10.18
32917	Webb, A. R. 7.8.17	26953	Wightman, H. 26.10.18
24/2116	Webb, Sgt. C. E. 26.8.18	26/1760	Wighton, D. McP. 14.10.17
31914	Webb, G. 12.10.17	24/1231	Wilce, Sgt. G. 11.8.17
56877	Webb, G. F. 27.5.18	15440	Wild, A. H. 27.3.17
56055	Webley, A. 7.12.17	42245	Wile, A. 10.8.17
25771	Webster, F. E. 7.8.17	47189	Wiles, T. A. 5.4.18
14892	Weekes, H. 8.6.17	42243	Wiley, B. C. 25.8.18
26/285	Weekes, T. L. 23.11.16	23/2123	Wilkins, S. T. 15.9.16
23/639	Weeks, R. 27.8.18	22898	Wilkins, T. F. 6.5.17
41202	Weenink, H. W. 12.10.17	23/678	Beresford-Wilkinson, Cpl. E. C. 25.12.15
49038	Weir, A. 18.2.18		
34762	Weir, F. 21.4.18	25/1027	Willcox, G. H. C. 19.7.16
26/645	Weir, L/Cpl. F. R. 11.9.16	20269	Williams, L/Cpl. C. E. 22.8.18
51935	Weir, H. 27.3.18		
23/314	Weir, Sgt. S. F. 25.12.15	25/151	Williams, D. 19.5.18
25/699	Welch, A. V. 15.9.16	26/1750	Williams, D. C. 13.9.16
26/939	Welch, G. C. 3.10.16	23/955	Williams, 2/Lt. F. B. 17.9.16
26/940	Welch, Sgt. H. C., M.M. 10.5.17		
		23/2302	Williams, F. P. 1.5.17
21923	Welsh, J. 12.10.17	21927	Williams, H. L. 7.6.17
26/1763	Wells, W. M. 15.9.16	20270	Williams, J. W. 28.4.17
55268	Westbrook, F. V. 23.4.18	25765	Williams, Cpl. L. S., D.C.M. 12.10.17
23/1233	Westbury, H. J. 15.9.16		

20271	Williams, Cpl. P. L. 19.8.18		65486	Witt, J. W. 26.8.18
30416	Williams, R. 7.6.17		13147	Wohlers, Cpl. H. W. 31.7.18
45583	Williams, R. H. 27.3.18		26/1	Wolstenholme, Maj. A. E. 3.7.16
23/323	Williams, 2/Lt. W. 5.10.18		41960	Wood, A. 16.11.17
42441	Williams, W. H. 12.10.17		25/920	Wood, L/Cpl. C. 15.9.16
39133	Williams, W. H. 7.1.18		24/621	Wood, Cpl. E. A. 26.8.18
55190	Williams, W. R. 2.9.18		26228	Wood, F. R. 13.9.17
44667	Williamson, F. 10.10.17		23/959	Wood, H. E. 15.5.18
71309	Williamson, J. 4.11.18		24/665	Wood, R. E. 30.9.16
21948	Williamson, J. M. 15.6.17		44809	Wood, Cpl. W. H. 4.9.18
25/152	Williamson, S. J. 16.9.16		23/1246	Woodford, P. 15.9.16
26/2596	Willing, C. 15.9.16		25/1030	Woodfield, F. 24.9.16
23/350	Willis, Sgt. C. N. 7.12.17		55576	Woods, L/Cpl. L. S. 4.11.18
19081	Willis, E. J. 10.2.18			
32975	Willis, F. S. 7.6.17		12337	Woods, Lt. (T/Capt.) S. J. 5.12.17
74301	Willis, G. E. 1.10.18			
59177	Willis, W. H. 28.3.18		47104	Woods, W. J. 18.2.18
23/1499	Willoughby, A. E. 15.9.16		18736	Woodward, J. 4.11.18
23/651	Willoughby, W. 31.3.17		23/352	Woollatt, Cpl. A. 25.12.15
23/1500	Wills, C. C. 15.9.16		23/34	Wootton, Sgt. P. J. 7.6.17
66054	Wills, J. P. 10.5.18		49759	Worker, R. 2.11.18
25/368	Wills, R. F. 31.5.16		40736	Worsford, Cpl. R. P. 30.5.18
25/369	Wilson, A. 9.8.17			
39135	Wilson, A. 29.3.18		24/938	Wotten, F. C., [F]. 13.7.17
13649	Wilson, Cpl. G. 4.11.18		18514	Wright, A. J. 23.12.16
24/327	Wilson, G. C. 12.10.17		25/374	Wright, E. 23.11.16
65832	Wilson, G. C. 6.8.18		46420	Wright, E. W. 9.11.18
1/310	Wilson, Sgt. H. W. 3.10.18		23/1248	Wright, F. B. 12.10.17
39594	Wilson, J. 8.1.18		18515	Wright, H. 23.12.16
52120	Wilson, J. 5.4.18		25/154	Wright, H. W. 8.6.17
24/1234	Wilson, 2/Lt. J. 12.9.18		59178	Wright, J. 5.4.18
41121	Wilson, J. 16.11.17		54631	Wright, L. T. 31.8.18
23/956	Wilson, L/Cpl. R. J. 21.10.16		53830	Wright, R. E. 27.5.18
			26/950	Wright, Cpl. S. 15.9.16
26/946	Wilson, V. H. G. 5.6.16		12/3881	Wright, 2/Lt. W. H. 7.10.18
21134	Wilson, W. 7.6.17			
26/948	Wilson, L/Cpl. W. 18.2.18		40172	Wyatt, 2/Lt. S. J. 18.3.18
65644	Wilson, W. A., M.M. 4.11.18		42247	Wylie, W. H. 9.9.18
			71417	Wyllie, J. 1.10.18
50789	Wilson, W. F. C. 5.12.17			
39385	Wilson, L/Cpl. W. J. 6.4.18		53736	Yearbury, F. W. 5.4.18
			48133	York, F. W. 20.11.17
26/423	Wilton, H. R. 15.9.16		23/657	York, T. F. 25.12.15
26/424	Wilton, S. T. 15.9.16		49957	Young, J. 16.2.18
66074	Windram, G. 12.9.18		49958	Young, J. 10.4.18
60341	Wing, F. C. 29.8.18		42858	Young, L. S. 31.3.18
25/919	Winnard, H. 15.9.16		8/2192	Young, N. 8.6.17
39136	Winter, A. C. 4.8.17		26/43	Young, Sgt. O. M. 4.10.16
29124	Winwood, H. L. 18.1.18		20593	Young, W. E. 12.10.17
26/147	Wise, F. C. 15.9.16		15318	Young, W. S. 12.10.17
24/329	Wisely, H. O. 15.9.16		24/2308	Young, W. W. 15.9.16
23085	Wiseman, Cpl. J. A. 26.8.18		39927	Youngson, Cpl. (T/Sgt.) W. G. 6.10.18
23/2118	Wishnowsky, H. H. 15.9.16			
62192	Witt, C. H. 10.5.18		41926	Zillwood, P. W. 16.11.17

THE CROSS OF SACRIFICE.

The Stone of Remembrance.

APPENDIX III.

THE NEW ZEALAND RIFLE BRIGADE TRAINING BATTALION.

As first laid down, the establishment of a training battalion provided for a commanding officer, adjutant, quartermaster, sergeant-major, quartermaster-sergeant, on the regimental headquarters; a company commander, two subalterns, a sergeant-major, quartermaster-sergeant, three sergeants and five corporals, for each company; and ten riflemen for cookhouse and other duties. These formed the cadre whose duty it was to complete the training and equipment of reinforcements and of convalescents found fit for further service. The personnel of the training cadre were seconded from, and borne as supernumerary to, the establishment of the Brigade, to which transfers were to be made on the principle that, after a period of training duty, officers and men should be given the opportunity of service with the parent unit in the line.

When Major W. Kay, the first commanding officer, moved out from Brigade at Ismailia towards the end of March, 1916, to take over his new duties, he found there was little to be done in the meantime beyond preparatory work, for in the formation of the Division practically every man, including all the Reinforcements from the 2nd to the 9th, had been absorbed. Even his own training cadre was not up to strength. Each of two company establishments was one officer short, and beyond the regimental sergeant-major and the quartermaster-sergeant, there were as yet no non-commissioned officers detailed for duty with him. The total strength of riflemen was eleven, one being the orderly-room clerk, and the remaining ten those laid down in the establishment for permanent duties about the quarters.

The earliest reinforcement draft to be received was the 10th. This arrived early in April, but was not held in Egypt for a longer period than was required to equip it. The despatch of the 11th Reinforcements to France was similarly hurried.

On April 18th, 1916, the training base was moved from Moascar to Tel-el-Kebir, where the battalion remained for some six weeks. It was now decided to transfer the whole of the New Zealand Expeditionary Force training base to England, as being more suitable for troops destined for service in France. The units accordingly embarked at Alexandria on May 31st, and, arriving at Plymouth on the 9th of the following month, proceeded at once to Sling Camp, Salisbury Plain. Here the troops were accommodated in groups of hutments according to Brigades. Training at Sling Camp was carried on with considerably greater vigour and for much longer daily periods than had been possible in Egypt; and after the inevitable sickness following upon the sudden change of climatic conditions had passed, the health of the troops was found to be much more stable than it had hitherto been.

The 13th Reinforcements were the first to join the battalion in England, the 12th having been held for a time in Egypt. Thereafter drafts arrived in regular order. Early in August the number of officers and men assembled at Sling had become so great that the unit was divided into two battalions, but on the 22nd the old order was reverted to, an increase in the number of companies being held as a suitable means of providing for the efficient handling of an abnormal number of personnel. On this date the name of the formation was changed to the "5th (Reserve) Battalion, New Zealand Rifle Brigade," and the command was taken over by Lieut.-Col. W. W. Alderman, C.M.G., of the Auckland Regiment, Major Kay proceeding overseas to join the Brigade. Capt. J. Bishop became Second-in-Command, and was succeeded as Adjutant by Capt. C. R. A. Magnay, who continued in that office until the battalion's activities finally ceased in 1919.

On May 3rd, 1917, His Majesty the King held his second inspection of New Zealand troops quartered in the Salisbury Plain camps, the first review having been held in October of the previous year; and on June 19th, a cinema film of the troops was taken for exhibition in New Zealand.

Sling Camp was now becoming overcrowded, and on August 15th the New Zealand Rifle Brigade reserve troops, about 2,000 strong, moved out and established a canvas camp at Tidworth Pennings, some four miles to the north. By this time General Fulton was in charge of the New Zealand section of Sling Camp, and Lieut.-Col. Alderman had taken up the duties of Staff Officer under him. The Tidworth Pennings Camp was under the command of Major R. St. J. Beere, and the troops there were again formed into two battalions, under Capt. O. W. Williams and Capt. W. W. Dove, respectively. In addition there was a special company of instructors commanded by Capt. K. R. J. Saxon. Hitherto the training had been carried out on the "bull-ring" method, which had been initiated by General Braithwaite while in command at Sling. By this system the men, after the ceremonial assembly each day, were drafted off in groups which, in accordance with a set time-table, passed in succession through the hands of instructors specially qualified in certain branches of military work. Under instructions from General Fulton this system was modified in order to throw more responsibility on the shoulders of the officers, and to introduce a more definite feeling of corporate life such as would prevail when the drafts should presently move over to the battalions in France; and at Tidworth, accordingly, the company of instructors was absorbed into the two battalions, whose commanders were now to take over the personal direction of the training of the troops under their immediate control.

The canvas camp was situated amidst delightful surroundings, and the training grounds were admirable. Within the camp itself special attention was directed towards securing the maximum comfort for the men as far as the general conditions permitted. The tents were fitted with wooden floors, and in addition to a liberal issue of blankets each man was provided with a paillasse and bolster. Even hot shower-baths for general use were fitted up in a number of tents. Indeed, as the result of the unceasing labours of Capt. W. E. Christie, than whom there was probably no more efficient quartermaster in the British Forces, the camp at once took its place as the model for the whole of the Southern Command, and General Slater, commanding in the south, on more than one occasion sent representative officers to observe the working of the camp generally, and in particular to note the methods and devices introduced in the quartermaster's branch. Tidworth Pennings was, however, essentially a summer camping-ground, and, as the season was now far advanced, preparations were made for a further move. A general inspection was held by the Colonel-in-Chief, H.R.H. the Duke of Connaught, and on September 27th our reserve troops entrained for the permanent camp at Brocton, in Staffordshire. The strength at that time was 1925, for, though heavy drafts had been sent to France, the 27th Reinforcements had marched in some ten days previously.

Brocton Camp was a section of the great Rugeley Camp, officially termed "The Cannock Chase Reserve Centre," at that time commanded by Major-General H. R. Davies, C.B., a former New Zealand officer.* The greater proportion of the

---

*General Davies had commanded one of the contingents in the South African War, and later became Inspector-General of the Forces in New Zealand. Being in England at the outbreak of the Great War, he was given a British Brigade on active service, and afterwards rose to the position of Divisional Commander. He was invalided to England after the second battle of Loos. General Davies frequently expressed

troops at this centre formed a Reserve Division, composed for the most part of British youths as yet too young for the field; and close to our section of the camp was that in which some 2,500 German prisoners were housed. The latter appeared to be healthy and comfortable enough. It is safe to say that they were fed on a more generous scale than that which obtained in the prison-camps of Germany, and on the whole they were amenable to discipline and for that reason easily handled. On one occasion, however, a mild strike over some food trouble necessitated a display of force, our men being ordered out under arms, and machine-guns placed in position covering the prison enclosure.

For local administrative purposes Brocton Camp came under the control of the Cannock Chase Reserve Centre, but in respect to both general administration and training it was virtually an independent command, responsible direct to the New Zealand Headquarters in London. For the sake of co-ordination, formal connection was maintained with the Reserve Group at Sling, whose commanding officer paid periodical visits of inspection. In control of the Northern Command was General Sir John Maxwell, under whom we had served in Egypt, and who now frequently visited the camp.

Brocton Camp was situated on a somewhat bleak and dreary upland surrounded by a charming countryside dotted with quaint old-time villages. Some four miles away was the historic county-town of Stafford, whose people proved to be eminently kindly and hospitable. The camp itself was thoroughly equipped for all branches of general and specialist training, the open spaces afforded ample scope for extended-order work, while the climatic conditions, combined with the nature of the soil, gave a realistic touch to the frequent rehearsals in trench routine and attack and defence.

On October 12th, Major Beere was promoted Lieutenant-Colonel, and a month later proceeded to France to rejoin the Brigade. The command was now taken over by Lieut.-Col. J. G. Roache, D.S.O.

With the opening of the year 1918, a slight change was made in the organization. The troops were re-grouped into one unit known henceforth as the 5th (Reserve) Battalion, while the camp became the New Zealand Rifle Brigade Reserve Depot. Lieut.-Col. Roache was appointed to command the

his pleasure at once more having New Zealand troops under his care, and his admiration of their work was shown in a definite way, the whole of the troops under his command having twice been paraded to view our model platoon carrying out attack practice. General Davies' kindly interest in the welfare of the New Zealanders was keenly appreciated by all ranks, and his death on May 17th, 1918, was felt as a personal loss.

Depot, the battalion being placed under the direct control of Capt. H. C. Meikle. On May 22nd, Lieut.-Col. Roache was invalided to New Zealand, and Lieut.-Col. E. Puttick, D.S.O., assumed command.

The striving towards the attainment of a high ideal which had hitherto characterized the New Zealand Rifle Brigade during its short career, was the outstanding feature in its training-camps as well as in the field. At Brocton this reached its highest development. Directed in succession by selected commanding officers from battalions in France, each thoroughly familiar with the requirements of modern war and with the special needs of the parent Brigade, the training reached a standard of excellence frequently commended in the warmest terms by inspecting officers of wide experience. The instructors were, without exception, war-seasoned men of outstanding ability, whose power lay in inspiration rather than in driving force; while the material in their hands, whether untried recruits or older soldiers from the convalescent camps once more preparing to take their place in the firing-line, was second to none that the Empire had to offer. A spirit intensely keen pervaded the barrack-square, the training-fields, the lecture-halls, and the camp activities generally; while a gratifying sense of attainment served to preserve that desirable spirit of the regiment upon which it is impossible to set full value. The general training covered such subjects as formal drill, protection against gas, wiring, construction of trenches, bayonet-fighting, physical training, musketry, tactical schemes, and all-night occupation of trenches. Nor was this all. Experience had shown not only the value of such specialists as Lewis-gunners, signallers, scouts and bombers, but also the difficulty of replacing casualties in their ranks; and to the training of men along the lines required for this purpose more than usual attention was given. In one period of six months during the extraordinary activity of 1918, some 2,000 officers and men were transferred from the Depot to France, and of every hundred of these no fewer than fifteen were highly-trained specialists.

On the administrative side the conduct of the camp was equally efficient. The work of the quartermaster and his staff, already established at a high standard, was raised still further until it became a fine art. At Brocton Camp waste was unknown. Crumbs and stale bread were baked in the huge ovens and sold to Birmingham manufacturers of calves' food; bones, fat, marow, cracklings, meat-residue, swill, and even paper, were disposed of for good money in the best markets. In this connection the following statement taken from the general record will be of interest. It covers a period of four months in the middle of 1918, and shows the monetary value of the by-products sold, as well as the daily cost of food per man.

Month.	Cost of food per man per day.	Fat. £ s. d.	By-products. Swill. £ s. d.	Others. £ s. d.	Total. £ s. d.	Average daily strength
May	1/7½	45 9 0	15 6 6	33 19 10	94 15 4	1,438
June	1/8¾	33 1 6	11 7 0	29 11 8	74 0 2	1,460
July	1/6	77 1 10	13 14 6	34 3 7	124 19 11	2,020
August	1/3½	35 0 0	18 13 0	78 7 7	132 0 7	2,484

Economies of this kind, as well as the steadily-rising returns from the "wet" and "dry" canteens, made it possible to extend the provision made for the comfort and general welfare of the men. The food-ration, supplemented in various ways, was well-prepared by expert cooks in model kitchens, and the dining-halls were provided with central stoves serving not only to warm the room, but, by means of a camp invention in the form of an ingenious rack built round the flue, to heat the dinner-plates as well. Excellent recreation halls, well-furnished billiard parlours, and comfortable reading rooms were provided, and a cinematograph entertainment was given nightly.

In common with other camps, Brocton had its worthy representatives of the Y.M.C.A., who are gratefully remembered for their many-sided activities, and more particularly for their labours in arranging a long series of concerts and lectures and other forms of evening amusements. In this connection, too, the band, under Sergeant-Major Shardlow, calls for special comment, not only as being a highly important aid to the wellbeing of the troops, but also as affording a means of making some small return for the generosity and kindliness of the people of the neighbouring towns.

It is a significant fact that, notwithstanding the rigours of the Staffordshire climate, only one New Zealand camp in England, that at Boscombe, had a lower sick-rate than had Brocton. Indeed, until the onset of the influenza epidemic at the end of June, 1918, the general health was uniformly excellent. The first wave of this scourge came in a comparatively mild form, and, being expected, was met by complete and effective arrangements for the protection of the men. A large portion of the camp was set aside as a hospital, and permanent orderlies were detailed to attend to the inmates. Into this area every influenza patient, on his complaint being recognized, was despatched, and all contacts were isolated. These measures, together with other necessary precautions, resulted in the restriction of the epidemic to a small proportion of the troops, amongst whom there were no serious cases, and in the stamping out of the disease within the comparatively short period of two weeks. A second visitation later in the year proved more severe, but this was successfully countered in the same manner.

As on the one hand no pains were spared in the endeavour to seek out devices which might serve to increase the general efficiency, so also on the other hand every care was taken to guard against the development of weaknesses in unsuspected quarters. It is the common experience in all camps which have been established for some time that the staff, as well as the men employed on camp duties generally, tend to become more or less firmly fixed in their positions. Brocton was no exception to this rule, and although provision was made for the replacement of officials by men from France who had recovered from the effects of wounds or sickness, it was found advisable in addition to conduct a definite periodical overhaul to ensure that no one had been employed at the camp beyond the term laid down. As a further safeguard, and as a check on the records, each man was required to report in writing when he had been on duty as a camp official of any kind for a period of three months.

The relations of the Riflemen with the neighbouring British troops and with the civilian inhabitants of the district were of the most cordial nature, and the excellent discipline and gentlemanly deportment of all ranks won for them a high place in the esteem and regard of the people generally. The interchange of hospitality was a marked feature, and camp concerts, which were open to all, appear to have been appreciated as heartily by our visitors, as the town and village entertainments, particularly the dances, both indoor and on the village greens, were enjoyed by the New Zealanders. General Davies, as well as his successor, General Wanless O'Gowan, were frequent visitors to the officers' mess and to the concerts in the camp, as were many commanders of the British brigades and battalions in the vicinity, and such visits were freely returned.

Lieut.-Col. Puttick relinquished command of the Depot on returning to New Zealand on duty, and on October 11th was succeeded by Major N. F. Shepherd. By this time the 42nd Reinforcements had reported in camp.

Following upon the cessation of hostilities at the front, the amount of definite military training at Brocton was gradually reduced, being finally established at that standard sufficient only for the maintenance of sound health and general smartness. Its place was to a large extent taken by educational work, partly voluntary and partly compulsory, but the constant changes resulting from the reception of drafts from Germany and the despatch of others to New Zealand, combined with the natural restlessness of the troops, greatly militated against the success of the educational scheme. The general direction of this side of the work was in the hands of Capt. H. M. Keesing, M.C.

In the third week of January, 1919, the Depot was re-organized to the extent of establishing four "provincial" companies according to the New Zealand centres of demobilization. At the beginning of February the first of the larger drafts, numbering 1,000 men, arrived from Cologne. Owing to transport difficulties the evacuation of the troops was a slow process, and on May 17th, there were 31 officers and 315 other ranks still in camp.

On May 10th the 5th (Reserve) Battalion formally bade farewell to the people of Stafford. At this ceremony a full parade was held, and Major (now Lieut.-Col.) Shepherd, on behalf of the New Zealand Rifle Brigade, presented to the Mayor a New Zealand flag, receiving in return the Union flag and the flag of New Zealand, both in silk, to be brought to this country as a token of goodwill from the citizens of Stafford. These gifts have been supplemented by the presentation to the Brigade of a handsome musketry challenge-shield of local workmanship, in sterling silver, to serve as another tangible sign of that invisible link of affection forged during the Riflemen's sojourn at Brocton Camp. Unlike other regiments, a Rifle Brigade does not possess colours, and it was in lieu of these that the challenge-shield was presented. The flags will doubtless find a final resting-place in some suitable building; the shield is in the custody of the Defence Department, and, with the concurrence of the trustees of the New Zealand Rifle Brigade, serves at present as an important trophy in connection with the rifle-shooting of the Territorial Forces. Some little time before the Armistice, the officers of the New Zealand Rifle Brigade at Brocton had handed to the representatives of the Rifle Brigade (British Army) a challenge cup of considerable value, the hope being expressed that the trophy might stand as a perpetual reminder that the Dominion formation had been proud to be associated with the honoured Homeland Brigade, in close touch with which it had been privileged to fight on more than one occasion.

The end came on June 14th, when, after handing over to the General Officer Commanding the Cannock Chase Reserve Centre the large-scale model of Messines, which our men had constructed in the camp lines for instructional purposes, the evacuation of Brocton was completed, and the last detachment of the 5th (Reserve) Battalion of the New Zealand Rifle Brigade left for Codford Camp, where they joined the small body of troops then awaiting despatch to New Zealand.

APPENDIX IV.

DRESS REGULATIONS OF THE NEW ZEALAND RIFLE BRIGADE, 1918.

The following Dress Regulations were issued in 1918. They embody the final modifications.

1. BADGE.—The badge of the New Zealand Rifle Brigade is the crest of the Earl of Liverpool, the Hon. Colonel of the Regiment: On a chapeau a lion rampant supporting a Man-of-War's Church pennant proper, with the motto "Soyes Ferme."

2. JACKET.—A pair of badges, facing inwards, will be worn on the collar as follows:—

(a) Officers: On the lapel above the step, the centre line of the badge to bisect the angle formed by the bottom edge of the collar and the seam. The bottom of the badge to be half an inch from the base of the step.

(b) Warrant Officers, N.C.O.'s and Riflemen: The standard of the badge will be two inches from the front edge of the collar and at right angles to the top of the collar, and the centre line of the badge will be midway between the top and bottom of the collar.

3. SHOULDER TITLES.—A black metal "N.Z.R.B." title will be worn on each shoulder-strap of the jacket and greatcoat. The base of the title will be ¼-inch from the shoulder seam. The "N.Z.R.B." wil be 2½ inches by ⅜-inch.

4. BLAZE.—Each Unit has a distinctive blaze of Black Melton Cloth.

BRIGADE HEADQUARTERS: An eight-pointed star of two superimposed squares of 1½ inches.

FIRST BATTALION: A square, 1½ inch side, worn as a diamond.

SECOND BATTALION: A square of 1½ inch side.

THIRD BATTALION: An equilateral triangle, with a perpendicular height of 1½ inches, having the apex uppermost.

FOURTH BATTALION: An equilateral triangle, with a perpendicular height of 1½ inches, having the base uppermost.

FIFTH BATTALION (The Reserve Battalion): A diamond 2¾ inches by 1¾ inches, the longer axis perpendicular.

The blaze will be worn on both sleeves of the jacket and of the greatcoat, the top to be 1½ inches below the shoulder seam, the centre line of the blaze being in line with the centre line of the shoulder strap.

5. BUTTONS.—Black horn "Rifle" buttons; large, 37 lines; small, 27 lines.

OFFICERS: Jackets,—four large buttons down front; six small buttons, four for pockets and two for shoulder straps. Greatcoats.—eight large buttons in two rows of four each down the front, and seven small buttons, three for coat strap, two for shoulder straps, and two for vent at back.

OTHER RANKS: Jackets,—Five large buttons down front; six small buttons, four for pockets and two for shoulder straps. Greatcoats,—five large buttons down front; and seven small buttons, three for coat strap, two for shoulder straps, and two for vent at back.

6. BELTS.—Officers and First Class Warrant Officers will wear brown Sam Browne Belts. All other ranks will wear Webb equipment belts.

7. BOOTS, PUTTEES AND LEGGINGS.

(i) All ranks will wear puttees and black boots. Mounted Officers in certain order of dress will wear brown boots and brown leggings. (See 12 and 13 below).

(ii) The tops of puttees will be turned down over the tapes. The tops of puttees, when so turned down, to be not more than four inches below the centre of the knee-cap. When it is found necessary to cross puttees, the crossing must be done at the back of the leg.

8. SPURS.—Mounted Officers will wear spurs. Transport sergeants and drivers will wear spurs with black spur straps.

9. TROUSERS, BREECHES, ETC.—Riding breeches will be worn by Officers, transport sergeants, drivers, and officers' grooms. All other ranks (including all Warrant Officers) will wear trousers. The leg of the trouser will be worn turned down three inches over the top of the puttee.

10. TIES.—Officers will wear khaki knitted ties.

11. COLLARS AND SHIRTS.—Collars and shirts will be of the Regulation service coloured flannel.

12. DRILL ORDER AND COURT MARTIAL.

OFFICERS—Mounted: Brown gloves, belts, boots, gaiters, and spur straps.

OFFICERS.—Dismounted: Brown gloves and belts, khaki puttees, black boots.

13. MARCHING ORDER.

OFFICERS—Mounted: Web equipment without packs, khaki puttees, black boots and black spur straps.

OFFICERS—Dismounted: Web equipment with packs, khaki puttees and black boots.

14. BADGES OF RANK—OFFICERS.

(a) Jacket: Badges of rank will be worn on the sleeve only.

(b) Greatcoats: Black metal badges of rank will be worn on the shoulder strap. Size, ·8 inch.

15. SLOUCH HATS.—Slouch hats will be worn peaked, with the brim flat, and with brown leather chin straps, width, ·35 inch. Caps will not be worn by any ranks at any time.

16. PUGGAREE.—Regulation issue puggaree will be worn by officers and other ranks, and will be sewn to the hat.

17. HAT BADGE.—A black badge, lion facing to the right of wearer, will be worn in front of hat, the bottom of the badge touching the upper edge of the puggaree.

18. GREATCOATS.—Greatcoats when worn must be properly buttoned up.

APPENDIX V.

THE DUNSTERFORCE EXPEDITION.

It is well known that in making her bid for world-domination Germany expected Asia Minor would fall easily into her hands and form a convenient halfway house on the road to India. With the driving of the Turks from southern Mesopotamia and the capture of Baghdad by the British in March, 1917, the route by the Berlin–Baghdad Railway was blocked; but the Russian military collapse, followed by the Bolshevik triumph and the signing of the shameful treaty of Brest-Litovsk, opened the alternative route through the Caucasus to Baku, across the Caspian Sea to Krasnovodsk, and so on by the railway extending through Russian Turkestan to within easy reach of the Afghan border. In order to bar this way also, the War Office proposed to despatch a small secret force of some 100 officers and 200 non-commissioned officers to the Caucasus, where they were to organize the Georgians, Armenians, and those remnants of Russian Corps still loyal to the old regime, and with these hold that cold mountainous region for the Allies and link up with the exposed right flank of the Mesopotamian Force. This adventurous mission, it should be explained, was organized quite apart from the latter force, for these already had their hands sufficiently full, and Baku is 800 miles from Baghdad.

The officers and non-commissioned officers for the mission were, with few exceptions, selected from Canadian, South African, Australian and New Zealand regiments then operating on the Western Front. They were chosen for special ability in the field, and it was made clear to them, while their destination was still withheld, that their new duties would be of such a hazardous nature that few could hope to come through the experience alive. The unknown risks were cheerfully accepted. The little band of stalwarts, of whom their commanding officer afterwards wrote, "It is certain that a finer body of men have never been brought together," included 11 officers and 23 non-commissioned officers from the New Zealand Division, and numbered amongst them the following from the New Zealand Rifle Brigade: Lieut. S. G. Scoular and Sergeants T. B. Smith and R. B. Clarke, 3rd Battalion; and Lieut. G. E. F.

Kingscote and Sergeants W. O'Connor and A. N. Wilkins, 4th Battalion.

Leaving France on 12th January, 1918, while the Division was in the Ypres Salient, the detachment spent a fortnight billeted at the Tower of London, outfitting in fur-lined coats, caps, gloves, and so forth, and laying in stocks of medical stores and equipment necessary for extremes of climate. The veil of secrecy which had hitherto shrouded the expedition was partially lifted when General Sir William Robertson came down from the War Office and in an intimate talk with the personnel traversed the political situation in the Middle East. He here named the expedition the "Dunsterforce," after the brilliant soldier selected to command it, Major-General L. C. Dunsterville,* of the Indian Army. When, soon afterwards, twelve Russian officers of the Tzarist Army joined up with the detachment, speculation as to its ultimate destination gave place to approximate certainty.

This portion of the "Hush Hush Brigade," to give it its more familiar name, now numbering 68 officers and 110 sergeants, left Waterloo Station on January 29th, and was despatched with all speed via France, Italy and the Suez Canal to Basra, on the Persian Gulf, and passed on at once up the River Tigris to Baghdad, where small detachments from Salonika, Palestine and Mesopotamia were already assembled. Here, owing to some hitch in the negotiations between the War Office and General Headquarters of the Mesopotamian Force, there ensued a long wait, and it was not until April 19th that the first party, comprising half the whole detachment and most of the New Zealanders, left Baghdad, crossed the Persian border, and commenced their long winding trek on foot through a famine-stricken land via Kermanshah to Hamadan, some 350 miles to the north-east, where they were welcomed by General Dunsterville and a small party of officers who had preceded them.

The spread of Bolshevism, the covert hostility of the Persians, and the quarrels between the peoples that it was desired to assist, had already practically sealed the fate of Dunsterville's scheme of organization. A semi-independent and hostile tribe of Persians, officered largely by Germans and Austrians, held the road to Enzeli, on the southern shores of the Caspian, and so for the time being rendered impossible a dash to Baku; and the Bolsheviks holding the latter city, while denying to the Turko-German forces a passage by the Trans-Caspian route to Afghanistan, resolutely declined all assistance from the British.

*The original of "Stalky" in Kipling's "Stalky and Co."

The Turks now changed their line of advance and commenced to move south-east by way of Tabriz. General Dunsterville thereupon shifted his headquarters forward to Kasvin, and rushed off two parties with instructions to occupy strategic positions on the two main routes, and to organize bodies of irregulars and train levies to aid in holding up the advancing Turks. The first party, numbering 15 officers and 35 non-commissioned officers, under Major Wagstaffe (South Persian Rifles) proceeded to Zinjan, 100 miles north-west of Kasvin; while Major Starnes, of the 2nd Canterbury Battalion, and with him 17 officers and 66 other ranks, including most of the New Zealanders, went to Bijar, which is on the more southern route and some 100 miles north-west of Hamadan.

With the assistance of a considerable body of loyal Russian troops still in Western Persia, General Dunsterville broke through to Enzeli. Shortly after this the Bolshevik leaders in Baku were deposed, and their successors invited Dunsterville to come to their aid. This was the opportunity for which he had been waiting, and on August 5th he embarked a mixed force consisting, in addition to a part of Dunsterforce, of a battalion of North Staffords, a detachment of the Hants Regiment, some field artillery, and two armoured cars, these reinforcements having been sent up from Mesopotamia. He did not remain long in occupation. The organization of the more or less friendly Russians and the 5,000 Armenian auxiliaries was from the first a hopeless task, for all idea of discipline had long since gone by the board; and, when the expected Turkish attack came on August 26th, the British troops amongst whom they had been sandwiched in the defensive lines were left in the lurch to fight a rearguard action until the very outskirts of Baku were reached. The enemy attack was renewed on September 14th, and the same treacherous weakness being displayed by the auxiliaries, General Dunsterville, realizing at last the impossibility of saving the city, gave orders for immediate embarkation. This was successfully accomplished, and, notwithstanding the presence in the harbour of the Caspian Fleet, once more under the control of the Bolsheviks, the transports got safely off to Enzeli. Next day the Turks entered Baku.

Some success had also attended the activities of that portion of the Turkish force moving south-east by the inland route. Major Wagstaffe and his detachment had pushed on towards Tabriz, and, making contact, drove in the enemy's advanced posts. The Turks had evidently been deceived as to the strength of the British here, for their threatened attack did not eventuate until early September, three months later. At the first shot the levies deserted, and the tiny British force had to fall back, but, contesting every yard of the way, they finally brought the enemy to a standstill near Zinjan.

Adventures of a different nature had fallen to the lot of Major Starnes and his party on the parallel route farther south. This way runs from Lake Van, skirts Lake Urumiah, and passes through Bijar to Hamadan. Having arrived at Bijar on June 18th, the detachment promptly set about training Persian levies, reconnoitring the country westwards, and establishing friendly relations with the Kurdish tribes in the neighbourhood. Owing to a bad season the district was in the throes of a famine, and, in order to mitigate the prevailing distress, relief works, notably the construction of an aerodrome and a motor road to Hamadan, were inaugurated, men, women and children being employed, and payment being made for the most part in the form of tickets for the soup-kitchen. Hemmed in along the western shores of Lake Urumiah were some 80,000 survivors of the Nestorians, or Christian Assyrians, a thriving people that at the beginning of the war had occupied the fertile lands between the two lakes. Though reduced by repeated massacres they had succeeded in holding their own here against the Turks; but now their ammunition was running short, and utter annihilation stared them in the face. On learning of their predicament the British authorities made arrangements to send up supplies under cover of a sortie by the Assyrians, and, on July 19th, six officers and fifteen non-commissioned officers of Major Starnes's detachment set off from Bijar with the ammunition, an escort of Hussars from Hamadan accompanying them. They were to be met half-way by a small column of mounted Assyrians, but after waiting at the rendezvous for some days without news of any movement they were unexpectedly joined by the bulk of the Assyrian army, numbering some 10,000, who had inflicted a somewhat severe blow upon the Turks. The engagement, however, had taken longer than was anticipated, and, in the absence of the fighting men, the remainder of the Nestorians became panic-stricken and began to rush southwards along the road on the heels of the army. Now the latter in their turn became infected, and there ensued a frightful and disastrous rout. Presently wounded women and children began to straggle in. This sight was too much for the Dunsters, and three officers and three sergeants, taking Lewis guns and a liberal supply of ammunition packed on baggage-mules, moved back along the human stream until they encountered the Turko-Kurdish brigands at their foul work of slaughter. Fighting, withdrawing, and fighting again, in a series of rearguard actions lasting all through a day and a night, these six brave fellows kept at bay a force of over 200 strong, until the arrival of a detachment of Hussars finally relieved the pressure. In this gallant action Captain K. G. Nicol, M.C., of the Wellington Regiment, lost his life.

About the middle of September, "Dunsterforce" ceased to exist. It had not accomplished all it had set out to do, but there is ample evidence that the influence of the dauntless little band was widely felt throughout the Middle East. The Mesopotamian Expeditionary Force, having at last driven the Turks from the south, now took over the work that had grown beyond the powers of Dunsterville and his handful of men. The enemy, though beaten in Mesopotamia, still had strong forces at Baku, and Tabriz, and they now prepared to attack Bijar with the aid of Kurdish tribes, thus threatening the main line of communications to Hamadan. Then came General Allenby's smashing drive through Palestine and the final discomfiture of the Turks. The detachments at Bijar and Zinjan were recalled, the 14th Division then in north Persia embarked at Enzeli for Baku, and the remaining Dunsters as released moved out by various routes to their home lands.

It is impossible to give in this brief sketch an adequate account of the varied duties performed by the representatives of the New Zealand Rifle Brigade while attached to Dunsterforce. The general nature of their task has been indicated, and this, as we have seen, was strangely different from that to which they had become accustomed in the trenches of Flanders. Two of our sergeants were with Major Starnes's detachment, where, in common with others, they were frequently detailed for post-duty, involving the establishment, at any distance up to sixty or even a hundred miles from the main position of a lonely post garrisoned by the one New Zealander and five or six unreliable native levies. Lieut. Scoular became chief Field Engineer for Hamadan Province, and he and Lieut. Rutherford, of 1st Canterbury, appointed to a similar position in Kasvin Province, carried out the greater part of the Royal Engineering work of Northern Persia. The former also has to his credit the construction of a British General Hospital consisting of eighteen buildings and fitted to accommodate 520 patients, the staff of 1,500 native workmen having been controlled by himself, Lieut. Wells of the Otago Mounteds, four non-commissioned officers, and two privates. Lieut. Kingscote distinguished himself as right-hand man to Major Saunders, of the 8th Sikhs, General Dunsterville's chief Intelligence Officer, and under these two the secret service was very highly developed. Through their hands by devious ways passed all correspondence to and from the Turkish and German delegations in Teheran, the headquarters of the rebel tribes, and Constantinople; they knew every enemy move and every enemy agent, native or European; and their skill was fully recognized by our opponents, one of whom wrote, in a letter itself intercepted, "The English hear even our whispers."

How fully General Dunsterville appreciated the work of those associated with him in this, one of the strangest and most romantic of missions, may be judged from the following passage taken from his farewell order of the day:—

"I am prouder of having had in my command these gallant officers and non-commissioned officers than of any other command I have held. Brought together from every corner of the Empire, all have vied with one another to show the absolute unity of our national aspirations. Their work varied from valuable administrative tasks to daring achievements on the battlefield, and all have striven to do their utmost, even in circumstances for which they were never prepared, and which they never would have chosen for themselves. They have had the privilege of showing the varied races in the lands through which they passed the pattern of the finest army of present times."

APPENDIX VI.

THE THIRD FIELD AMBULANCE.

Soon after the mobilization of the New Zealand Rifle Brigade, General Henderson, Director-General of Medical Services, decided to establish at Awapuni Racecourse, Palmerston North, the training depot for the New Zealand Medical Corps. Arrangements for this purpose were completed by the end of September, 1915, when two sections under Major J. Hardie Neil took up their quarters there. Drafts for New Zealand's two hospital ships, as well as further reinforcements of N.Z.M.C. personnel, subsequently came in, the strength in camp being thus brought up to nearly four hundred.

There now followed the organization, at this depot, of the No. 2 Field Ambulance, a unit whose subsequent activities were so closely linked up with those of the New Zealand Rifle Brigade that it was commonly, though unofficially, considered to be an integral part of that body. The 1st and 2nd Battalions of the Rifle Brigade had already moved up from Trentham to their camp at Rangiotu, and after the departure of those units for service overseas the same camp was occupied by the 3rd and 4th Battalions early in December. With these latter the No. 2 Field Ambulance embarked for active service two months later; and when, at the beginning of March of the following year, the troops from this Dominion were organized as the New Zealand Division and the Rifles became the 3rd Brigade, the associated medical unit had its designation similarly altered, being thereafter styled the No. 3, or in common practice, the 3rd, Field Ambulance.

At the Awapuni depot, the preparation of the men for their specialist work in the Medical Corps was accompanied by a thorough grounding in the elements of infantry training and general discipline in accordance with the scheme outlined by Lieut.-Col. Tate, of the Headquarters' instructional staff. The value of this general training, which was carried out to an extent hitherto unusual with medical personnel, was afterwards demonstrated in the unbroken morale and consistent efficiency of the unit throughout its service in the field. The medical training consisted of lectures, illustrated by lantern-work, together with practical demonstrations by the medical officers. Finally the unit was so thoroughly trained in the organization and routine of dressing stations that it was possible to select the most suitable personnel for the various departments and accustom them to their special duties before the departure of the unit from New Zealand. The original section which was organized at Awapuni for main dressing station work continued to act almost without change throughout the period of the Division's activities in France. The Ambulance had the inestimable benefit of the services of Major A. A. Martin, who trained the men at the Palmerston Public Hospital, and of Matron Kilgour, of the Old Men's Home at Awapuni, under whose careful tuition they became remarkably efficient in ward duties and nursing.

It was determined to secure for the unit as many musicians as possible, with the object not only of providing for the welfare of the sick who now came under its care, but also of contributing to the success of the troops at the front, the underlying idea being that healthy, elevating recreation for the men would be of more use from the moral and morale points of view than trite exhortations. Substantial help was received from the Palmerston North Patriotic Society in this connection as in others, and the orchestra subsequently formed, under Capt. D. Kenny, the nucleus of the New Zealand Divisional Pierrot Troupe known as the "Kiwis."

In addition to Major Martin, the section officers were Capt. W. G. Borrie, who eventually became the Divisional Gas Officer; Capt. McGregor Grant, an Auckland surgeon; Capt. T. E. Guthrie, from Feilding; and Lieut. E. M. Finlayson, who was Unit Quartermaster. Sergt.-Major R. Copeland and Staff-Sergt. D. H. Heron were the principal non-commissioned officers. The Camp Adjutant was Capt. P. Baldwin, an officer of outstanding ability and personality, whose name must be linked with the training of the New Zealand Medical Corps. The instruction of the unit was completed towards the end of January, 1916. Mr. J. A. Nash, M.P., Mayor of Palmerston North, by his consistent work and self-sacrifice for their comfort and welfare, laid every officer and man in the Medical Corps who went through the camp under a deep obligation; and the whole population of Palmerston North and Feilding showed so keen a solicitude for the welfare of the Ambulance that their kindly interest must have been an inspiration to the men throughout their subsequent work. Passing through Auckland to join the troopship, the personnel were billeted by the citizens of that city; and the Mayor, Mr. J. H. Gunson, acting on behalf of the Auckland Patriotic Association, further augmented the funds of the orchestra and made its permanency assured.

On February 4th the Ambulance, under Major (now Lieut.-Col.) J. Hardie Neil, who continued in its command until the Armistice, embarked on the transport "Navua" with "C" Company of the 4th Battalion. During the voyage the orchestra regularly entertained the troops, and their concert given to the people of Albany appeared to have been deemed an equivalent return for the great hospitality extended to the men of the troopship.

On arrival at Suez the Ambulance entrained for Moascar, on the outskirts of Ismailia, where another section, with Major A. S. Brewis as commanding officer, was drafted to it. It was now the middle of March, and the details in connection with the organization of the New Zealand Division, to which Col. C. M. Begg was Assistant Director of Medical Services, were already completed. The 3rd Field Ambulance, after a short period of intensive training, embarked with the Division for France during the first week in April.

The Ambulance served the New Zealand Rifle Brigade, which was established in a group of villages just west of the Forest of Nieppe. At Thiennes Major Martin set up our first dressing station in France. Thence the unit marched with the Brigade to Estaires, and shortly afterwards reached Armentieres, establishing its main dressing station in the Cercle St. Joseph in the Rue Denis Papin, just behind the church of Notre Dame. The advanced dressing station was in the brick-kiln at La Chapelle d'Armentieres, and here were received the casualties from the New Zealand right sector. The aggressive nature of the New Zealand Division's activities is shown by its 400 graves in the cemetery of La Cite Bon Jean. In July Capt. T. E. Guthrie was killed by a shell from Lille, which struck the 4th Battalion headquarters. This occurred shortly after the treachery of the infamous Nimot, who deserted to the enemy's lines from one of the New Zealand Regiments and probably gave such information as enabled the enemy to inflict numerous casualties. Incidentally, the dressing room of the station, which had been handed over to No. 1 Field Ambulance, was demolished by shell-fire during the same bombardment. At the end of July Major R. Neil Guthrie joined from England, and the unit proceeded to a rest-camp at Morbecque. Subsequently the rest-camp was removed to L'Estrade, between Steenwerck and Armentieres. An advanced dressing station under Major Guthrie was set up at Erquinghem, a spot that will be recalled by those acquainted with "The Three Musketeers." It received many Australian wounded during the attack on Fromelles, in which some six thousand casualties were sustained.

The duties of a Field Ambulance on service are many and varied. "C" Section at this period had charge of the Divisional Baths at the Pont de Nieppe Brewery, where hundreds of women were employed laundering and repairing the garments of the Corps in the area.

Early in August the Ambulance moved up through Nieppe to the dressing station at L'Ecole in La Rue de Messines, Armentieres. The activities of the Brigade in the sector were very marked, raiding and trench work causing constant casualties. The shattering effect on the nervous system caused by minenwerfer fire resulted in many serious cases of shell-shock.

In the middle of August the Ambulance entrained with the Division for the Somme, after having been relieved by the 1st/3rd Highland Field Ambulance, which had come direct from that region. After a period of training at Allery, a quiet village in a beautiful farming district where harvesting was nearing completion, the unit followed the New Zealand Rifle Brigade through the castle-crowned old-world town of Picquigny, and marched to a bivouac behind Albert, whence it moved to Fricourt. The New Zealand Division now took over a section of the battle-front, and the bearers of "A" and "C" Sections, under Major Martin, were detached to the No. 2 Field Ambulance, which was commanded by Lieut.-Col. D. N. W. Murray, and which was doing the bearer-work of the Division. The Headquarters of No. 3 Field Ambulance being in reserve, "C" Section tent subdivision, under Major Guthrie, was incorporated in the personnel of the Corps dressing station at Becordel.

On September 15th the Rifle Brigade passed through the 2nd Brigade, which had captured Switch Trench, and made the memorable attack down the slope of the ridge stretching between Delville Wood and High Wood, and forward to Flers. Here, on the exposed slope, which was under observation from rising ground on the right and from innumerable vantage points on the front, the Brigade fought its way to a position which should ensure the advance of the whole British line in this neighbourhod. Pride in the achievements of the Division was tempered by the knowledge of the commensurate loss sustained, and anxiety was much increased by the reports brought back to the A.D.M.S. that over 100 of the Rifle Brigade wounded were lying on our side of Flers, their evacuation being held up through the inability of the Ambulance bearers to make their way forward owing to the persistence of the heavy barrage which the enemy put down to cut off further reinforcements to the Brigade. On September 16th the A.D.M.S. instructed the officer commanding the Ambulance to explore the possibilities of evacuation by the line of the road that runs from Delville Wood to Flers. On arriving at the Wood in the late afternoon the O.C. found that Capt. A. M. Grant, acting on the orders of the D.A.D.M.S., Major A. Carberry, had taken up a volunteer party of stretcher-bearers from the Horse Transport and had made his way down the slope to the bank behind which the wounded were lying. The headquarters' staff of the Ambulance, and as many as were available of the "C" Section bearers who had been detailed to help the Division on our right, were collected, and at early dawn on the 17th this party, accompanied by a Ford car, went down the Delville Wood-Flers road. The roadside was littered with broken wagons, dead drivers and horses. On the right was a disabled tank, one of the first used in the war, and strewn around in clusters lay the dead of a West Surrey Battalion. These had come under machine-gun fire of such severity that whole platoons were lying in regular order in their tracks. On the left of the road, amongst the German dead, lay those of the New Zealand Rifle Brigade killed in the rush towards Flers. In the dug-outs which marked the Brown Line, halfway between Switch Trench and Flers, were many Germans whose death from Mills bombs thrown down must have been instantaneous. The country seemed to have been pulverized to a depth of from five to six feet by the hurricane bombardment, first by the British barrage, and subsequently by that of the Germans. Near a bank between the Brown Line and the west end of Flers lay about eighty severely wounded men. They had evidently been struck down while endeavouring to penetrate the barb-wire defences round the village. Their grey, shocked appearance, marked many of them for death. On a stretcher lay Capt. G. V. Bogle, of the 1st Battalion, a greatly esteemed Medical Officer whose death from shell-fire was a loss to the Division. Capt. P. B. Benham, Medical Officer of the 2nd Battalion, who had taken the place of Capt. Falconer Brown (wounded), with Capt. W. S. Robertson, the Bearer Officer of "C" Section, was here attending the wounded. It had been necessary to clear away a large number of German corpses in order to secure what little shelter was afforded by the bank.

The Ambulance headquarters' staff manned every stretcher possible and started a stream backwards. Here the track gave ample explanation of the difficulties with which the bearers had had to contend. It was strewn with livid, dew-soaked dead. In one place a wounded man, now dead, was lying on a stretcher. The rear bearer, with his stretcher-slings still on, had fallen forward on his knees and remained in that position beside him. Along the track the numerous dead bore testimony to the overwhelming nature of the barrage, as well as to the endurance of the men who had carried the stretchers. The bearers had to force their way back regardless of the artillery fire, for to take cover would generally have meant desertion of the patient. Here, amongst others, lay Corporal J. Bailey, the originator of the ambulance orchestra. He was one of the many men in the secondary service of the Division who insistently pleaded to be allowed to take some part either in the fighting or in assisting the fighting men.

Farther back lay the Switch Trench captured by 2nd Auckland and 2nd Otago. It presented an extraordinary spectacle. Having been a German front-line trench, it possessed many dug-outs, and had been well manned on the 15th. The bodies of a large number of Germans, some of whom were fair-haired and blue-eyed, were huddled on the remains of the fire-steps, while some lay half-covered by debris on the bottom of the trench which had been so severely battered by the fierce barrage put down. Those who had preferred the safety of the dug-outs had met swift death from Mills bombs, which had a deadly effect in the confined space of these "unterstanden." The dead in the trench were thicker near the traverses and machine-gun positions, and the majority seemed to have met their death by rifle-fire or shrapnel, although some, presenting no marks of violence, had evidently died from the concussion of the bursting shells. The deep lividity of the faces could not conceal in some the pure Saxon type.

We turn now to the sections detached for bearer-work with No. 2 Field Ambulance. On arrival at Thistle Alley, towards Bazentin-le-Grand, Major Martin was met at the bearer post, and instructions were given him to join headquarters at Green Dump on the right behind Delville Wood. Here a dressing station was set up in the dug-out that had been made by the New Zealand Pioneers. Heavy work was immediately entailed in dealing with casualties coming through from the right, as well as in succouring the sick, among whom were broken-down men from those English battalions, including a battalion of the King's Royal Rifles, that had been shattered in the attack. In the afternoon word came through that Major Martin had gone down to the group of wounded near Flers and had there been struck by a high explosive shell. His death occurred next day in Amiens Hospital, where the New Zealand No. 1 Stationary Hospital had been established under Lieut.-Col. D. J. McGavin. Major Martin's death was deemed a catastrophe to the Division. His standing as a surgeon and his genius as a writer were known throughout the Empire. In his innermost conversation he always expressed his conviction that the Rifle Brigade would attain a place of honour in the records of the Division. His constant wishes for its welfare, and his whole-hearted desire to help the New Zealand soldier on every occasion, manifested the spirit of service by which he was ever actuated.

During the period at Green Dump the work was incessant. Here Major H. M. Buchanan joined the unit and filled the vacancy caused by the death of Major Martin. The area around the station was frequently subjected to shell-fire, and this caused several casualties among the headquarters' staff. Of 90 available bearers, eight were killed and 46 wounded.

Towards the end of the Division's stay in the line the weather broke, and the mud made the work of the bearers extraordinarily difficult. Fortunately the trench dug by the Pioneers under Lieut.-Col. G. A. King, stretching from Switch Trench right forward to Flers, brought the work within physical compass. The dressing station at Green Dump evacuated the wounded by general service wagons, the stretchers being lashed to duck-boards placed upon the raves. They passed down the hill from Green Dump, skirted the Quarry, and climbed the slope to the church at Montauban, where the Ambulance cars were parked. These took the wounded to the Corps dressing station at Becordel by the densely-crowded road through Carnoy and Mametz.

It is distressing to record that in the first Somme battle 75 per cent. of cases of fractured thighs died. They were prepared for transport by means of Liston's splint, which consists of long laths of wood stretching from the arm-pit to the ankle and secured by bandages to the body and leg, but unfortunately this device failed to steady the fragments. Subsequently, in the battles of Messines and Bapaume, Thomas's splint, a light iron frame-work effecting separation of the broken ends and the immobilization of fragments, was used, and the rate of mortality was reduced to 20 per cent., and, in favourable conditions, to as low as 15 per cent. This diminution may, of course, have been partly due to improved surgical methods in the casualty clearing stations and hospitals; but one is compelled to assign to shock, from injury to the tissues and nerves by the movement of the broken ends during prolonged transport, the major portion of the blame for the previous wastage of life. The New Zealand Division suffered 8,700 casualties in the three weeks' battle against the enemy's prepared positions. The battalions were fighting for the first time under lifting barrages; the resulting obliteration of land-marks aggravated the usual confusion arising from the clash of battle, and the movements of the men were impeded in country pulverized by shell-fire and soddened by rain. Such conditions would try the morale of the stoutest of seasoned veterans.

From the Somme the Ambulance moved up with the Division to the area about Armentieres, where, for the time being, the trenches of the old sector were held by that composite British and Colonial formation known as "Franks' Force." The main dressing station was established in the Rue de Messines, Armentieres, the commanding officer being deputed to act as the Senior Medical Officer of the formation.

In December the Ambulance moved to Estaires, and was established in the Ecole Pensionnat de Notre Dame de Lourdes, a three-storeyed building round three sides of a quadrangle. Here, in earlier days, had been received the British wounded from Neuve Chapelle, and in the garden the sites of the hospital marquees could still be seen. In the town was a large brewery that had been converted into baths and laundry, to which some of our personnel were detached for duty. Near by was the bridge over the Lys by which the Germans had retreated when driven out in the early part of the war. They had placed French women and children on the bridge to deter the French from firing upon it, and finally blew it up. Bishop Cleary, of Auckland, was attached to the Division for a period after its return from the Somme, and was a frequent visitor to the Ambulance. The stories unfolded to him during his calls at some of the surrounding farms aroused his intense indignation, in particular that of a farmer who had hidden in his haystack, and upon being discovered by the Germans was incontinently shot, notwithstanding that he was unarmed, above military age, and in civilian clothes.

The headquarters' mess of the Ambulance was in the residence of a local wine merchant. During the German occupation in the first few months of the war the household had objected to the billeted officer stabling his horse in the kind of courtyard-vestibule of the house. His answer was prompt and characteristic. He opened the door leading from the vestibule to the drawing room and had his steed quartered in that apartment. Luckily the grand piano escaped destruction, and, providentially, according to madame, the only marked damage sustained was the abrasion of the corner of an inlaid ebony table.

In January, 1917, the Ambulance moved to Fort Rompu, a large brewery not far from Armentieres, to serve the northern part of the New Zealand sector. Here, after a short enemy bombardment in the depth of an exceptionally severe winter, one of the companies of the Rifle Brigade suffered a number of casualties from gas-poisoning owing to the freezing of the moisture from the breath as it passed through the thin rubber expiry valve of the box-respirators. The gas used was evidently phosgene. In the more serious cases the usual distressing symptoms were displayed,—cough, irritation, pain in the chest, and an increasing production of white frothy phlegm which eventually seemed to drown the patient.

In the spring the Ambulance moved to Nieppe, a village between Armentieres and Bailleul, and established an advanced dressing station at Underhill Farm on the rear slope of Hill 63, which overlooks Messines. Elaborate preparations were made to withstand heavy bombardment. Dug-outs lined with "elephant-iron" were driven into the hill, and the original farm buildings were buttressed with girders and topped with concrete slabs to act as shell bursters. Elaborate precautions were also taken to render the dressing rooms gas-proof, and these measures were necessary, for, as the day of battle approached, the area was frequently subjected to gas-shelling. A few yards behind was a New Zealand howitzer battery; another, belonging to an English unit, almost touched the left of our lines; while at intervals of about 100 yards back there was a succession of batteries of large-calibre guns. The activities of these guns provoked retaliation which seemed to be intensified at night. The burning of an ammunition dump in Ploegsteert Wood, just on the other side of the road on which the dressing station was situated, luridly illuminated the neighbourhood. Seas of gas frequently involved the whole area. The enemy, as was usual on such occasions, added to the turmoil with shrapnel and high explosive, and developed the habit of bracketing the road by which the cars left the dressing stations. Capt. J. McGhie, who took charge of the construction work, made use of 29,000 sandbags, and completed what must be deemed to have been an outstanding work of field engineering by the Medical Corps. The medical arrangements made by Col. McGavin, the A.D.M.S., were complete and ample in every detail, the alternative routes of evacuation in particular being well organized. In the meantime the consistent shelling of Hill 63, Ploegsteert Wood, Hyde Park Corner, and the surrounding area, brought an endless stream of cases, many with severe shell-wounds. The gas-shelling at night increased in severity, and the dressing room required constant guarding against the fumes.

This state of affairs was incessant up to the opening of the battle of Messines just after 3 a.m. on June 7th, when the dressing station threatened to collapse owing to the explosion of the mines under Messines Hill. This was followed instantly by the roar of guns of all calibres and of unlimited number firing apparently from every point of the compass. Conversation was impossible in the open, and indeed difficult even in the shelters. The various sounds of the different arms could not be distinguished in the shattering roar, which was overwhelming to the senses, rocked the earth, and stripped the roofs from the buildings. Within a few moments there was added a quick succession of eight-inch German naval shells, which, being directed at the batteries around the Ambulance, smashed into the surrounding forest, filling the air with branches of trees, masses of mud, and pieces of tiling. In a short time the yards of the dressing station were covered with clay, leaves, and broken tiles, until this material lay ankle deep. Fortunately after a few minutes the shelling of our immediate neighbourhood suddenly ceased. The continuous roar of the bursting barrage seemed to be lifting onward, and one became accustomed to the discharge of the guns near by.

Then cases began to come through. First came those who had been gassed whilst waiting in the assembly trenches, to be followed soon after by the wounded and prisoners of war from the battle. In order to effect evacuation, the drivers and car orderlies took spades and filled in the shell holes. Then they ran the gauntlet of the fire down the Petit Pont Road to the main dressing stations, fortunately taking no harm beyond damage to a car returning empty. Soon the dressing station was working at full pressure, but without a hitch. The majority of the bearers had been attached to No. 2 Field Ambulance, which was working the sector immediately in front of Messines, but no fewer than 1,167 casualties were dealt with by us between the 7th and the 12th, mainly during the first two days. On the 10th, heavy casualties came in from the Australian Division on the right of the New Zealand sector. Here Lieut.-Col. J. S. Purdy, late N.Z.M.C., who commanded a very fine Australian Ambulance, was in charge of the line work. Sick parades, as is usual after all big engagements, became heavy from all units in the neighbourhood. The constant shelling disinterred many corpses on the slopes of Hill 63 in front of the British howitzer battery, and another cemetery had to be opened in a more sheltered spot.

Prior to and during the battle of Messines, the area of Hill 63 and Ploegsteert Wood was rather insanitary owing to the number of troops in the neighbourhood and to the neglect of previous occupants. Private A. M. Douglas, of the Ambulance, was placed in charge of the whole locality, and so skilfully did he carry out the duty of cleansing and conserving it that he was specially mentioned in Sir Douglas Haig's Despatches. Throughout the unit's service in France Douglas supervized the erecting of its dressing stations, he being in charge of the constructional and sanitary squad. During the Passchendaele operation he acted as bearer, and on a recommendation by the commanding officer of another unit was awarded the Military Medal.

A week after the capture of Messines the unit, relieved by an Australian Field Ambulance, took over from Col. Maguire, of the 9th Australian Field Ambulance, a large dressing station at Pont d'Achelles. Here the Ambulance set up the main dressing station of the New Zealand Division, taking in the wounded from the operations in Ploegsteert Wood, which the Division occupied after the battle of Messines. The station consisted of large Nissen huts for the reception, dressing, feeding and evacuation of the wounded, with smaller huts and marquees for sick and gas cases. Capt. Robert Stout joined up with the unit at this time. The Ambulance was kept fully employed, though its work was carried out under such exceptionally favourable conditions as to permit the administering of the maximum amount of help and comfort to those engaged throughout a very trying period, during which Ploegsteert Wood was frequently saturated with gas. Pont d'Achelles dressing station, being situated upon the main road from Armentieres to Bailleul, had evidently been used as a locating point by enemy aeroplanes, the previous units having made no attempt to conceal lights; and what with exploding bombs, anti-aircraft shelling, and the rattle of innumerable Lewis guns, the area at night time was a veritable pandemonium. Fragments from missiles nightly rattled upon and often penetrated the roofs of our buildings. One of the few cases of an enemy soldier with a bayonet wound passed through this dressing station. It was that of a fair-haired German youth, by that time a corpse, with a bayonet-thrust through the chest from beneath the right armpit. From this station the unit evacuated 6,040 cases of sick and wounded, and served as many as 698 meals in one day. The clearing station which received our casualties was that of the Australians at Trois Arbres, and one may bear testimony to the professional skill and extreme kindness that marked the attention of the Australians to the wounded of the New Zealand Division.

Whilst at Pont d'Achelles the Ambulance had the melancholy duty of receiving and conveying to the grave the body of General Earl Johnston, who at that time had been Brigadier of the Rifle Brigade; and two days later General Young, his successor, was brought in, he having been shot transversely through the centre of the neck. The sniper's missile had traversed behind the gullet in front of the spine, and emerged behind the top of the shoulder. The General's ultimate recovery was as gratifying as it was miraculous.

The Division had only just gone into reserve at Doullieu, after its heavy labours in this region, when the Rifle Brigade was sent to the area north of Ypres for digging work in association with the French. No. 3 Field Ambulance detached a section to serve them. Subsequently the Ambulance had pleasant association with the Brigade at Vieux Berquin, and the personnel were stimulated by the splendid training and bearing of the Brigade Model Platoon, which later unfortunately suffered overwhelming casualties at Passchendaele.

For the Passchendaele operations the headquarters of the Ambulance formed a walking-wounded collecting post, practically an advanced dressing station, at Spree Farm, beyond Wieltje, and was there stationed when the Rifle Brigade was called upon to continue the New Zealand attack on October 12th. At Spree Farm, by the junction of the St. Jean road, terminated the planking on the road which led forward towards Passchendaele. Apart from an interrupted duck-board track leading towards Kansas House, half way to Brigade Headquarters at Korek, the country was a mass of mud beneath which firm ground could not be felt, and the shell-holes filled with water were so numerous as to allow of no direct track beyond a few yards. The conditions were so bad that the removal from the forward area of the casualties of the Division relieved by our own had not yet been completed, and the combined bearers of the New Zealand Division had to slave throughout the 11th at the task of bringing back British wounded who were still lying on the ground as a result of the previous week's fighting. Over one hundred of these were brought in, and their rescue exhausted the first flush of the bearers' energy. One case received at the station was that of a man who had been lying out for five days and nights unattended and without sustenance. He had a large gaping wound in the shoulder, and the work of the numerous flies in the vicinity showed itself in the horrid maggot-infested condition of his wound. His dry tongue and the back of his mouth required cleansing before stimulants could be given him. His condition was typical of that of the majority of the wounded.

Spree Farm consisted of a German pill-box almost submerged beneath earth and mud, and standing in a sea of shell-holes which had to be filled in in order to provide walking space of a few yards around. By means of tarpaulins a dressing shelter and a kitchen for food distribution were erected. The Ambulance Quartermaster, Capt. E. M. Finlayson, scoured the country for additional supplies, and the whole Division is indebted to him for that forethought and labour which enabled him to satisfy the wants of all persons requiring food on the way to and from the front line, and this without discrimination. Many of these extra rations were sent from the Rifle Brigade, who had a surplus owing to their heavy casualties. In all, over 1,800 extra twenty-four-hour rations were received and dealt out by the Ambulance between the 11th and the 14th of October.

On the morning of the 12th, anxiety for the Brigades in front, practically isolated owing to the conditions already detailed, was heightened by the feeble nature of the barrage put down for their protection; and soon the wounded began to come in, exhausted, covered with mud, and bringing disheartening reports which were later to be confirmed in a very distressing manner. The Medical Corps was hampered almost to impotence by the unavoidable slowness of evacuation. At least six men were required to a stretcher. The main road leading back was submerged, with the water up to the knee level. Many wounded lying around the pill-boxes perished either from exposure to the elements or from almost uninterrupted shell-fire. The only possible tracks were harried by the enemy's artillery, and it is more than probable that many men, whose bodies were found unburied months afterwards, had been drowned in the liquid mud, which in places acted like a quick-sand.

News received from the firing-line of the death of Lieut.-Col. Winter-Evans from hæmorrhage occasioned a sense of personal loss, for he had come with the Ambulance in the transport "Navua," and was a kindly friend.

Day and night the work of rescue continued, and every available man who could be sent forward as a bearer was pressed into this special service. Medical comforts, in the shape of spirits and other restoratives, were obtained by one means or another from all depots in the neighbourhood, and these, supplemented by the rum ration which, owing to the difficulty of carrying up supplies, had been cut off from the troops in the front line, were served in the form of hot drinks. The 12th, 13th and 14th passed, and still the work was unfinished. On the evening of the 14th fifty men from the Field Artillery reported at Spree Farm for bearer-duty. Accommodated with us for the night, they were sent forward next morning, and during the day they completed the clearing of the front line area. The unit thereupon handed over to No. 2 Field Ambulance, and moved out a few minutes before some high explosive from an enemy battery, which had frequently shelled the station, effected a direct hit on an ammunition dump a few yards behind. The Ambulance baggage awaiting removal suffered almost complete destruction.

The Brigade and Ambulance went into rest in the area near Boulogne. Up to this period battle casualties had changed the personnel of the Rifle Brigade twice over since its landing in France. After some time spent in refitting and training, the Ambulance moved up to l'Ecole Bien Faisance on the Menin Road, and about 1,000 yards in front of Ypres. Though a charity school, this building had been a palatial two-storey structure, with a tiled central pavilion and four wings, and had accommodated over 1,000 boys. Everything above ground had been reduced to little more than rubble, but the ample cellars beneath had been converted into dressing rooms and made use of by the various Ambulances that had previously served the sector. About a mile and a half along the Menin Road was Hooge, the principal feature of which was a great crater that had resulted from a mine exploded by the 5th Division when the first of Kitchener's Army went into the front line. Immediate preparations were made to serve the troops engaged in the attack on Polderhoek Chateau. Major Neil Guthrie was in charge of the bearer work at Clapham Junction, in front of Hooge, and it was mainly owing to his fine efforts and personal supervision that the wounded from this operation were so quickly brought to shelter from a heavily shelled area. The carry, across a broad plateau, was exceedingly long and exposed, and the N.C.O. in charge of the bearers, Staff-Sergt. Heron, gained a well-merited Military Medal.

During the month of December, when this area was ice-bound and frequently under snow, the centre of activity was Polygon Wood. Artillery fire had obliterated much of the Wood, and the country was everywhere pitted with shell-holes. The condition of the wounded from the front area round the Polygon Butte, a tunnelled mound just forward of the Wood, required the strictest attention. Their injuries were frequently attended by shock, which the intense cold served to aggravate. Six bearer posts were placed along the track from the Butte to the dressing station at l'Ecole, a distance of about four and a half miles. Primus stoves and hot water were always in readiness at every post. Fortunately the dressing room arrangements for the re-heating and general comfort of patients were very complete and effective.

After a stay with the Brigade in the area west of Ypres, the unit, towards the end of March, 1918, moved down to the Somme. This was the very anxious time when the Fifth Army had been driven back by overwhelming superiority of numbers after having been subjected to a deluge of gas. The tide of civilians and straggling military straining towards Amiens formed a distressing sight, and portended an irresistible advance against which the New Zealand Division, now thrown into the breach about Mailly Maillet, could only hope to form, as it were, a rock in a swirling stream.

The Ambulance bearer work devolved on the No. 1 Field Ambulance under Lieut.-Col. G. Craig. Our unit was in reserve at the start of the operation, but Col. McGavin, A.D.M.S. of the Division, received information that a railway line, with engines and carriages complete, had been abandoned by the French at Acheux, the nearest available point on a light-railway line. Accompanied by the O.C. Ambulance he went into the matter, and at once determined to set up a receiving post at the railway station. He authorized arrangements for an attempt to reinstate the running of trains as an extemporized Ambulance service, but the French employees, having in mind the numerous German balloons with full observation of the position, were unwilling to bring up the train. However, the Ambulance itself provided a qualified engineer and stokers, and in a few hours the train was ready. Its first freight comprised the wounded from the 2nd Auckland Battalion after their brilliant achievement about the Serre Road, as well as a large number of English wounded from the Aveluy Wood on our right. By an extraordinary coincidence, the first train, which, owing to confused conditions, had been sent away to the indefinite neighbourhood of Doullens, was enabled to unload its wounded into a casualty clearing station which was just opening at Gezaincourt, near that town. A walking-wounded post was established by the unit beside the main dressing station at Beaussart, in the rear of Mailly Maillet. By the 29th a complete system had been established for the removal of all wounded to the railway station with the minimum amount of inconvenience.

A few days after our arrival in this area, General Fulton, of the Rifle Brigade, was mortally wounded by a shell which demolished the cellar behind Colincamps in which his headquarters had been established. He will always be remembered in connection with the formation, the excellent discipline, and the fine achievements of the Brigade. Amongst those killed, and whose body the Ambulance conveyed to the cemetery at Doullens, was Major "Bob" Purdy, M.C., the Brigade Major. He was a clever, gallant and kindly young officer, the son of Lieut.-Col. Purdy, N.Z.M.C., who had borne the brunt of the earlier work of mobilizing the New Zealand Medical Corps.

On April 4th a wireless message emanating from Berlin appeared in the Continental Daily Mail, stating that the Germans had captured Colincamps. This was evidently an anticipatory notification of the driving back of the New Zealanders, for which preparations of such a nature had been made that success seemed assured. The attack on Colincamps was not made until the following day, and the anticipated capture failed to materialize. Early in the morning of the 5th a barrage commenced on our front line and worked backward, and this was of such intensity as profoundly to modify opinions regarding the unique severity of the British barrage at Messines. The depth of the tornado of shell-fire was so great that casualties came in not only from the forward area but also from about a mile behind Colincamps. The walking-wounded post had its remaining windows shattered, and the walls were so perforated by shrapnel fragments that it was necessary to make use of the cellars around. Fears for the safety of those in front were aggravated by the absence of reports, and by the commencement of a stream of wounded who came from the support area behind the front line. However, the Rifle Brigade met the oncoming waves of Germans, who, with full packs up, advanced in such formation as would be adopted by those who deemed all resistance in front completely shattered. Passchendaele was then well avenged. The slightly wounded amongst our men were so frequently possessed of binoculars and valuables that the reported slaughter of many German officers seemed to be amply confirmed.

The desperate results of the attempt of the 5th of April staggered the enemy in this sector, and, with the New Zealand Artillery now well established, both sides settled down for the time being to trench warfare, our leading troops occupying, for the most part, the old British front line as held before the advance of 1916. Owing to enemy shell-fire the dressing station was presently moved back to the next railway station, which was at Louvencourt. Here was met the Ambulance of the French 21st, the famous "Steel Division," which had been sent up to be in readiness to reinforce the New Zealanders' line. Judging by the paramount importance given to the matter in the Parisian daily papers, there can be no doubt that the French public realized that the New Zealand sector was truly a vital point. After a few days the French were apprised of the situation, and the "Steel Division" was sent elsewhere. The Ambulance had the very melancholy office of transferring in the train the bodies of Capt. A. M. Tolhurst and Padre A. Allan, both of the 4th Battalion of the Rifle Brigade, who had been killed in the aid post at the Sugar Factory in front of Mailly Maillet. Capt. Tolhurst, who had been detached from the Ambulance to the Battalion, was a man of high professional attainments, had a charming personality, and had won the admiration of both units; while the Revd. Allan's kindliness and self-sacrificing services were not unknown to the personnel of the Ambulance.

During this period the early spring weather was cold, the roads muddy, and only the fighting-kit was carried. This meant that the blankets and overcoats had been discarded, the waterproof sheet being the only source of protection and comfort. The Ambulance had to exercise much care and discretion in avoiding unwarranted evacuations from minor maladies, and at this very trying time, when the maintenance of man-power was of most vital importance, the New Zealand Division had the lowest sick-rate in the Army. The unit was very busy with its train, nevertheless, and also with the dressing station in the schoolhouse. It commandeered, as additional quarters for patients, the haylofts and outbuildings of seven farm-houses in the neighbourhood, as well as the entire accommodation of a large chateau. During the first few days of the stay in Louvencourt the Ambulance received a visit from the Senior Medical Officer of the Army, who questioned the advisability of retaining so many patients near the front line. The reply of the O.C. Ambulance was that six trains could be arranged for daily, that he knew the Division in front, and that he was sure of at least twenty-four hours' notice.

After being in rest at Authie, where the Ambulance was inspected by the Rt. Hon. W. F. Massey and Sir Joseph Ward, the Division once more manned the front line on the eastern slope of the plateau over which the Germans had hoped to advance to Doullens. The Ambulance, in its turn, took up front line work and established an advanced dressing station, with headquarters at Bayencourt and another station at Fonquevillers. As is usual, it was reinforced by bearers from other field ambulances. Major H. M. Goldstein, M.C., here joined the unit, and thereafter had charge of the dressing room up till the Armistice.

About the middle of July it was determined to drive the enemy from Fusilier Trench, on the edge of the plateau, east of Hebuterne, which overlooked the valley beyond. On the farther side of the valley was the ridge of Puisieux, which in its turn gave a commanding view over Bapaume and the surrounding country. The attack of the 1st and 4th Battalions of the Rifle Brigade was brilliantly successful, though it cost two officers and forty other ranks. On subsequent days 100 wounded passed through the Ambulance, most of the casualties having been caused by retaliatory shelling. Among them was the Brigadier, General A. E. Stewart, who had been wounded while inspecting the new line. General Stewart's enforced departure from the Brigade was deeply regretted. It is impossible to forget this gallant officer's action in halting his battalion on the way out from the line at Flers to help with the evacuation of the wounded. As shewing the definite nature of the observations carried out by the General Officers of the Division, it may be noted that the number of killed and wounded amongst these officers was proportionately higher than that in any other of the grades or ranks. The greater an officer's experience in war, the more considerate and kindly did he show himself towards the medical service. This may possibly have been the result of past personal experience, for every General Officer in the Infantry of the New Zealand Division was, at one time or other, a battle casualty. Fortunately the G.O.C., whose frequent visits to the front line were a source of anxiety to all concerned, escaped lightly, his most serious injury being a scalp-wound from a sniper's bullet.

The combat at the Fusilier Trench was the first blow of the series which sent the Germans back to the Hindenburg Line. Their retirement, though gradual at first, soon gained momentum, and became hurried when the British Army as a whole forced its way onward. At the head of the valley between Gommecourt and the Puisieux-Serre crest was Rossignol Wood, and here, immediately after the success nearer Hebuterne, a series of severe encounters took place. The enemy, fully recognizing the importance of keeping the New Zealanders away from Puisieux, was firmly entrenched, and many casualties were sustained by the Division. Fortunately the dressing posts and stations were well forward, with communications effectively organized for rapid evacuation. In the Wood, from which the enemy was eventually cleared, was a large dug-out that had been crushed in by one of our heavy shells. The practical Germans had simply closed it up with its contained dead, marking the place with the usual sign and inscription.

In the last week of August the Rifle Brigade, now under General Hart, carried Puisieux, established itself on the farther slope towards the Ancre, and overlooked the country about Bapaume. Summer was now well on, and, the roads being in good condition, the light Ambulance cars were brought into use, and the wounded from this fighting were thus able to receive what virtually was immediate attention.

In connection with the next advance, the capture of Bapaume was assigned to the New Zealand Division. For some reason the warning notice to the No. 3 Field Ambulance, which was then in the line, did not come to hand until the evening of the 23rd of August, though the battle was to take place on the following morning. The dressing stations in front of Gommecourt and Hebuterne were at once abandoned, the bearers and equipment hurried to Bucquoy, and a dressing station selected, perforce, in the dark. Although a ruin above, the building chosen proved to have ample white-washed cellars below. The A.D.M.S. had arranged with Col. Avery, A.Q.M.G., for 100 reserve infantry to be attached to the Ambulance as bearers, and these were reinforced by a number of bearers from the other Field Ambulances. Parties with wheeled stretchers were attached to each battalion of the attacking Brigade. Light cars with shell-dressings, stretchers, blankets and water were assembled under cover at Achiet-le-Petit. In front of this village was a collection of iron huts, and here, on the Grevillers Road, an advanced collecting station was set up for the transfer of cases to the larger Ambulance cars.

Soon after dawn the battle opened, and the wounded from the 2nd Auckland Battalion, who had advanced with scarcely any barrage, began to come in. The preliminary attack on Grevillers was successful; and subsequently the 1st Brigade, under General Melvill, whose staff work on the first day was described by the "Times" as magnificent, moved to the south of Bapaume. The bearers had a trying time keeping in touch with the battalions, as the Division on the right did not seem to be able to afford protection from flank fire. Certainly the number of dead found in the saps just west of the Bapaume-Albert railway, where Judson, V.C., gained his supreme honour, seemed almost too many to have been accounted for by frontal fire alone. The dressing station was pushed up to Achiet-le-Petit, and 500 casualties were passed through. Here three German medical officers presented themselves. One was the A.D.M.S. of a Naval Division; another, one of his staff; the third, Lieut. Schmelsing, of the 14th Bavarian Regiment. It transpired that this last was the medical officer who had been in charge of that cellar in Flers in which such ample personal correspondence, supplies, surgical instruments and medical comforts were found, these coming into Major Goldstein's possession at that time. Lieut. Schmelsing stated that the New Zealand attack on Flers was so unexpectedly successful that he had been unable to get back to his dug-out, and that the battalion to which he was attached became too disorganized to permit of any recovery. He added that during the past few months existence above ground in the front line area had been rendered practically impossible. Our 18-pounders harried their line day and night, and our 60-pounders and howitzers were altogether demoralizing, especially the former, which, he said, were positively nerve-racking. Our aeroplanes were the bane of their existence. On one occasion his unit decided to brave an open-air dinner, but an aeroplane bomb smashed the building beside the mess-room, and as he put it, "destroyed the cooks and the prepared food." His story was confirmed when towns which the enemy had held were reached, for aeroplane shelter notices had been posted everywhere. We had repeatedly observed, when doing bearer work, that many German prisoners came back with brand-new brassards, the badges of

A REGIMENTAL MEDICAL OFFICER,
stripped to the waist, attending to the wounded in a trench.

A FIELD AMBULANCE.

The Interior of a Dressing Station (1).

Flashlight Photo.

The Interior of a Dressing Station (2).

Flashlight Photo.

A STATIONARY HOSPITAL.

the medical service, upon their arm, and, moreover, that those brassards had the appearance of having recently been removed from packages. When the German medical officer was asked why the men donned them on the occasions when our troops were close up to them, he stated that everyone in the German army went through various courses of training, and that when a man had completed a course in first-aid he was entitled to wear a Red Cross brassard. Many of the Germans evidently treasured these as a safeguard to be used as a last resort. Experience throughout the whole stay of the Division in France and in every big operation does not permit one to say that the Germans ever intentionally fired on any dressing station or field ambulance; but there can be no doubt that men who must have fought in the front line, and who were reported as having surrendered from pill-boxes, wore these spotless brassards, and one is convinced that they made use of them to save their lives. Lieut. Schmelsing, while at our Ambulance, was pressed into the service of dressing the German wounded, of whom there was a large number, and his multitudinous details of treatment were, from the point of view of British practice, quite unusual, and might, indeed, have been superfluous.

The 1st and 2nd Brigades fought their way close up to the north-western outskirts of Bapaume, and the Rifle Brigade, crossing behind through Biefvillers, moved eastwards to relieve the 2nd and carry on the advance round the north of the city. The Ambulance placed posts in Biefvillers, in a factory on a road leading down to the Monument on the Bapaume–Arras Road. Here Major F. N. Johns, M.C., with four of his men, was killed near the 2nd Brigade headquarters. He was an officer who had been through every engagement from the first Somme battle, and was throughout a fearless bearer commander.

On August 26th the Rifle Brigade advanced and captured a section of the Bapaume–Beugnatre road, but, owing to the cover afforded by the railway material at the St. Aubin siding, and to the fact that the buildings of Bapaume provided secure nests for the enemy machine-gunners and snipers, little further progress was made till the evening, when the 2nd Battalion succeeded in establishing itself on the railway beyond St. Aubin. In this fighting the sons of two medical men were killed, Lieut. L. I. Manning, M.C., of Christchurch, and 2nd Lieut. P. G. Clark, of Auckland. The conflict was very severe and the casualties were heavy. The regimental aid post and the Ambulance advanced bearer post were established in the Quarry west of the Monument. Round about it were the bodies of many British soldiers who had been killed by machine-gun fire. The enemy evidently deemed it to be the location of a battalion headquarters, for it was soon enveloped in a tornado of bursting shells, and it was only when our heavy batteries engaged in a smashing battle with the German artillery that Capt. W. H. Davy, medical officer of the 2nd Battalion, could escape with the personnel. From the elevated position of Biefvillers, the Arras Road near by could be seen with shells from guns of all calibres bursting on it every few yards. The trees in front, momentarily silhouetted by the lurid glints from exploding shells, swayed and crashed, and the smoke columns merged above to form a pall that caught the rays of the setting run. From all points bearers could be seen making for the bearer post. Evacuation of the wounded was effected without interruption during the night, the cars being pushed up to the advanced posts, thus reducing the work of the bearers to short carries. The falling of a shell into the car post at Biefvillers resulted in the blowing off of the tops of two large vehicles, luckily empty at the time, and the only casualty caused by it was a Y.M.C.A. attendant, who lost a leg. The Y.M.C.A. organization during this Bapaume operation sent parties forward to advanced posts, from which they dealt out, without charge, comforts, food and drink to all men passing through. Let it here be said that those who contributed to the support of the Y.M.C.A. may rest assured that their gifts were expended in a manner which earned the praise of all who were personally acquainted with the activities of the organization at the front.

The Rifle Brigade having forced its way on to the Bapaume–Cambrai road, Bapaume fell into the hands of the New Zealanders, and a dressing station was established at Grevillers. It was considered advisable to avoid the schoolhouse where the Germans had had their main dressing station, as the cellar beneath had evidently been used at some time or other as their Corps telegraph station. German prisoners were employed to clean up the yard of the farm-house, from which had to be removed some dead Germans who, from all appearances, had been just emerging from a cellar when the 2nd Auckland men rushed the village.

The 1st Battalion of the Rifle Brigade attacked Fremicourt at the end of August, and at the same time the 2nd Auckland and 1st Wellington Battalions struggled for the possession of Bancourt. It was necessary to clear these places in order to complete the expulsion of the enemy from the Bapaume neighbourhood. The fighting at Fremicourt appeared to be very severe, judging by the roar of machine-gun fire and the large number of wounded prisoners that came through. The satisfaction felt by the prisoners at being safe was demonstrated in one case by the hysterical outbursts of a wounded

German, whose unstinted praise of his British brothers in general, and of the Ambulance in particular, came out in gasps between his gulpings of the food given him. In response to a request for a verse of the Hymn of Hate, he cried out in broken English, "No, no! No longer will I England Gott strafe! My hair is white and my eyes are blue. The English are Saxons, the Germans are Saxons, we are all brothers. Down with the capitalism and the industries!" Meanwhile Lieut.-Col. Austin, of the 1st Battalion, was brought in with a dangerous wound caused by a fragment of shell which had passed through his side. In the role of wounded men, he and Lieut.-Col. R. C. Allen, his successor, were previously well acquainted with Ambulances. Lieut.-Cols. Stephen Allen, of 2nd Auckland, and Beere, of the 4th Battalion Rifles, were also amongst the casualty cases received during the fighting about Bapaume, and a few days later Lieut.-Col. Bell, commanding the 3rd Battalion, was brought in with a severe wound.

. The 2nd Auckland and the 1st Wellington Battalions continued the engagement with the enemy about Bancourt. Fire from machine-guns, anti-tank rifles and field-guns at short range, particularly that from an exposed flank, inflicted serious casualties upon them. The passing back of the wounded was a perilous business, but, the roads being suitable, the light cars ran the gauntlet of the barrage and maintained an uninterrupted though precarious evacuation. The burial of 110 dead in the cemetery between Bancourt and Fremicourt attested to the severity of this conflict. Nearly all the remaining veterans of that fine fighting battalion, the 2nd Auckland, were killed or wounded. A station was established in an old field hospital close to the ruins of a sugar factory at the nearest point on the Cambrai Road. Here the bodies of some Germans, who had been caught by our barrage, lay amongst the huts. Little medical equipment was found, for, apparently, the Germans did not have their ambulances actively operating as near the front line as did the British.

The area on the east of Bapaume was at length cleared. The enemy was then swiftly driven to the outskirts of Havrincourt Wood, and General Young's 2nd Brigade pushed them farther east beyond Metz-en-Couture, where the Guards had met and driven back the Germans advancing after the Cambrai counter-attack. The dressing station in a German field hospital at Bertincourt, being rather far up and in the midst of our artillery, was moved back to Haplincourt. Here it experienced a severe aeroplane bombing, happily without casualties. The wounded, who, in their mental anxiety, always yearn for removal from the shelled area, suffered additional terrors that night.

The Rifle Brigade now took up the line again, and during the second week of September forced the enemy up the slopes of Trescault Ridge, along the top of which ran part of the outworks of the Hindenburg Line. The eastern portion of Havrincourt Wood was lined with our guns almost literally wheel to wheel. Our artillery was subjected to heavy gassing, practically the whole of one battery becoming casualties. The car post was at Mill Farm, on the southernmost portion of the Wood, and an advanced dressing station was established in the village of Neuville. Heavy rain came on at this time, accentuating the miseries and dangers of the wounded. Here the Ambulance received a typical stretcher-bearer affectionately known to the men of the 3rd Battalion as "Dad" Vernor. He had been dangerously wounded in the thigh by a ricochet shell. He felt that he was dying and asked how his pulse was, remarking that he knew one often judged a man's condition by it. In spite of the gum solution put into his veins he rapidly sank; but before he died he said that he had carried out many who were "for it," but they were, he averred, better men than he. He was typical of the regimental stretcher-bearers, those hardy men, usually volunteers, whose frightful mortality was the measure of the danger of their work, and who were universally classed with the bravest of the brave.

Passing through Metz to the forward bearer posts, the O.C. Ambulance, owing to some temporary artillery activity on the part of the enemy, deemed it advisable to draw the ambulance car under cover off the main road, whilst he himself retired into what apparently had been a village sick inspection room. There he found a German lying dead upon a stretcher. He had received a severe thigh wound, and had evidently been dead two or three days. In his hand he held tightly a copy of a German trench booklet, the title of which was "The Lying Press of Our Enemies."

The roar of artillery heralding the launching of the attack by the Rifle Brigade was very comforting, and the large number of new German graves that were subsequently found near Gouzeaucourt on the hill testified to its deadly effect. General Hart's headquarters were established in the small mausoleum at the shrine on the road leading from Metz-en-Couture through the neck of the Wood to Trescault, and, although much cramped, he forbore to make more room at the expense of the coffins. One is afraid that compunction of this kind would not have appealed to the Germans. In the sunken road running alongside the Shrine a bearer post was established. The accuracy of the gas and general shelling was extraordinary, and as the route lay through a fierce retaliatory barrage a number of the bearers were disabled. The prisoners were freely employed at the task of carrying back the wounded, but one unfortunate party of four Jager bearers were all killed by a shell which left the man on the stretcher untouched, and only slightly wounded on the heel the bearer in charge. The bearers were fearless and efficient veterans, and the award of the D.C.M. to our Sergt.-Major Roberts, M.M., was thoroughly merited. Particularly fine work was done here by Capt. P. G. McEvedy, one of the unit's medical officers attached to the 3rd Battalion of the Rifle Brigade, whose dressing station seemed to be in the vortex centre of the artillery "hate" put down to hamper the bringing up of reinforcements.

On the right, the 2nd Battalion of the Rifle Brigade, under Lieut.-Col. L. H. Jardine, was maintaining a characteristically tenacious grip on the edge of Gouzeaucourt Wood. His contra-regulation request for Ambulance bearers to assist his regimental aid-post staff was acceded to as a tribute to his judgment of an emergency situation. Prominent in this combat was Lieut. J. G. Holmes, who had joined the Brigade from the 3rd Field Ambulance, in which he had been from its inception an excellent sergeant-clerk. He had a lucky escape from a bullet which glanced off a safety-razor in his knapsack. At the same time another of the former N.C.O.'s, Lieut. E. Farnsworth, M.M., who had just joined the 3rd Battalion, was killed; and Lieut. J. N. R. Jones, late sergeant in the Ambulance, but now a 4th Battalion officer, was severely wounded. Yet another former Ambulance sergeant, Lieut. J. H. Straw, of the Otago Regiment, was killed in this area. This was only in keeping with the casualties sustained by the Division's promoted N.C.O.'s, who, as subalterns, were prominent in every fight.

A few days later the Division was withdrawn to rest near Bapaume, and thus closed one of the most brilliant phases of the war. On March 26th the Division had met the Germans advancing victoriously towards the coast, and had stemmed at Mailly Maillet the tide that was threatening to sever the British Army. After having successfully withstood the impetuous attack, the Division had established a firm line on the eastern edge of the Hebuterne Plateau; then, having shaken off the enemy's hold upon Fusilier Trench, it had driven him eastwards, and, gathering momentum in the severe conflict at Bapaume, had pursued and forced him back to entrench in the Hindenburg Line whence he had thrust his way in the March offensive. Twelve hundred New Zealand dead lay on the battlefields around Bapaume, and these, together with the 4,964 wounded, of whom one in eight would die, attested to the price the New Zealanders paid for the honour of having been, **as a senior English medical officer declared, "the spearhead of the Army."**

The 3rd Field Ambulance was in charge of the rest station during the operations leading to the Escaut at the beginning of October, but supplied the main dressing station in connection with the advance beyond that canal. It was here that Capt. P. A. Ardagh, M.C., an officer originally attached to the unit, gained the D.S.O.; while Capt. H. Paterson, another of its former officers, did some fine work with the 1st Battalion of the Rifle Brigade at Crevecoeur. At Solesmes the unit put up the main dressing station for the Division when in front of Le Quesnoy, and while here an opportunity was taken to record, by means of flashlight photography, the details of the working of a dressing station.

Elaborate precautions were taken to counteract the deadly shock produced by the action of cold upon wounded men. Teams of three were trained just as precisely as a gun-team, each man being allotted a particular task which he alone was permitted to perform. The senior soldier was the surgeon's immediate assistant. The second placed waterproofs and towels in the desired positions, and stood by to hold the bowls of lotion or the tins of dressings. The third cut off the soiled clothing and first field-dressing, held the limbs in position as directed by the surgeon, and, where necessary, also held an electric torch. The teams were under the control of a senior N.C.O., who directed the rendering of further assistance when required, called for the evacuating stretcher-staff waiting in readiness at the door to remove the cases dealt with, and gave the word for the bringing in of the next cases for treatment. In addition, there was a separate staff detailed to attend to the special heating arrangements and to the feeding of the patients. Each case, whilst being treated, was placed over a blanketed frame heated by oil stoves. Over 20,000 sick and wounded were taken through the Ambulance during its work in France, and definite organization such as that described was necessary in order to ensure efficient and expeditious treatment.

Through the station at Solesmes came the wounded of the New Zealand Rifle Brigade, which attacked and captured Le Quesnoy. The many expressions of gratitude to the men of the Brigade must indeed have been genuinely sincere, for the tales told by the inhabitants when the Ambulance established in Le Quesnoy itself the last main dressing station of the New Zealand Division during the fighting in Flanders, were borne out by the haggard appearance and pitiable physical condition of the children of the town. The dressing station was located in the general hospital buildings, the modern or military part of which had been used as a German hospital, and the civilian portion partly as a stable and partly as accommodation for the sick amongst the British prisoners of war. The deaths amongst these unfortunate men, hastened by ill-treatment, were so frequent that Sister St. Jean, one of the Sisters of Mercy who remained throughout the occupation by the Germans, declared that a day passing without one of them being carried out to the well-filled cemetery was exceptional.

The town-crier was sent round with an invitation to all willing to assist in the cleaning-up of the hospital, the Germans having left it in a very insanitary condition. German prisoners of war were secured from the Brigade and compelled to make amends for the gross delinquencies of their comrades. They were made to clear up also the beautiful little hospital chapel, one wall of which had been partially destroyed and the interior littered with wreckage and rubble. In response to the earlier invitation a small army of girls and young children appeared. Their rush-brooms and tongues flew in unison, and in a remarkably short space of time the place was made presentable. On the completion of their labours, these young volunteers were entertained at the Quartermaster's store to an "afternoon tea" of biscuits, cocoa and chocolates, luxuries to which they had been strangers for many months. Their rapturous singing of the Marseillaise, and their loud cries of "Long live the brave New Zealanders and the good chocolate!" came from full hearts; for many had obviously suffered from restricted nourishment and from those other measures of repression which the Germans so readily employed.

Beneath the hospital was a series of underground caves. Those nearest the outlet had been occupied by the Sisters and their staff, while those farther in had contained a number of extemporized beds. The latter, it transpired, had been made use of to conceal the refugees suspected and sought for by the Germans, but these, under cover of darkness, were passed by the devoted nurses into the Forest of Mormal, close by. Thence they proceeded towards the border, and, if fortune favoured them, finally reached safety in a friendly or a neutral country. Sister St. Jean organized the chain of deliverers, the last link of which was that lady of immortal memory, Nurse Edith Cavell.

APPENDIX VII.

"DIGGER" AND "DINK."

The origin of the sobriquet "Digger," as applied to the New Zealand and Australian soldier, is shrouded in mystery. It is known that the men of the Working Battalion, a temporary unit formed of drafts from the three Brigades, occasionally addressed one another as "Digger" when cable-burying in March, 1917, in preparation for the Messines battle. In our Brigade it became fairly common when we were engaged on similar work for the French Army on the northern part of the line in the following July; and, during the long month spent on duty of the same nature in the Ypres Salient just before Passchendaele, its use became fully established. It is probably safe to say that the Australians were the inventors of the term as a form of address or salutation.

Like many other slang expressions, the term "fair dinkum" is not easy of definition. In the same class as the school-boy declaration "honour bright," and the coarser vulgarism "my oath," it would seem to convey the idea that any statement with which it may be used is to be looked upon as absolutely reliable and true. Similarly, any person or thing declared to be "dinkum" is to be considered as possessing the qualities of genuineness and excellence in the highest degree.

The application of the term to the New Zealand Rifle Brigade as a nickname dates from the early days of 1916. On its return from Dabaa, the 2nd Battalion joined the veterans from the Dardanelles then concentrating at Moascar after the evacuation, the 1st Battalion being still at Mersa Matruh. The Riflemen, realizing that the honour and credit of the Brigade were in their keeping, relaxed nothing of their old smartness on parade, more particularly at guard-mounting, and were more punctilious than usual in regard to their soldierly conduct when off duty. The old ill-feeling, almost akin to animosity, was still in the air, and the general bearing of the Riflemen evoked considerable comment, mainly of a derisive nature. No distinguishing colour patch had yet been adopted outside the Rifle Brigade, except by the Samoan Relief Force, and the square "blaze" on the puggaree of the men of the 2nd

Battalion was thus all the more conspicuous. With the idea of conveying the impression that the Riflemen were inordinately proud of themselves, the term "The Square Dinkums" was, in derision, applied to the 2nd Battalion, and afterwards, when the other units arrived, to the whole Brigade.

This is the generally accepted opinion as to the origin of the nickname, but there are some who maintain that it came into vogue still earlier, and in this way: When the 1st Battalion's wounded from the Christmas Day fight at Mersa Matruh reached the hospital at Cairo, they were questioned by the Gallipoli patients regarding the details of the action. On learning of the comparatively small number of casualties, one of the veterans, accustomed to the horrors of a very different kind of warfare, exclaimed ironically, "It must have been a 'fair dinkum' fight!" The arrival of the 2nd Battalion soon afterwards was the signal for the modification of the epithet, by an easy process, into the nickname that ever after stuck so firmly.

We were a little sensitive about the nickname when first saddled with it, but in course of time came to look upon it as something to be proud of, realizing that it was used less and less as an expression of scorn till at last it became a term of genuine esteem. Shortened to "The Dinkums," and again to "The Dinks," it was an appellation fully recognized within and without the Brigade, becoming eventually almost official.

APPENDIX VIII.

CHEERFULNESS AT WARNETON.

Following is a copy of a letter, written to a brother officer by a platoon-commander in charge of one of the outposts in the Warneton Sector. It is a request for sundry supplies, and its frivolous tone is indicative of that cheerfulness which sustained our fellows in the midst of the most appalling conditions. The writer was killed by shell-fire some three hours after the despatch of the note.

"Hors d'Œuvre,
15/8/17

"Dear Woody,—

"This war is ——————*——! Tell Rogers.

REQUESTS.

"1. See that we get a feed toot sweet, and a good one, with rations dry and wet, lest we starve.

"2. Take heed that bombs be brought unto us to the tune of three boxes, lest Fritz decide to visit us and we have nought wherewithal to make him welcome. This applies to our brother in distress, Peter.*

"3. Also we have need of boards which be called duck, in numbers even up to two figures, which, being interpreted, is ten. Peter likewise hath great need.

"4. Cause an N.Z. mail to be brought to us, for we greatly love to hear tidings of the brethren of that land.

"5. An you see the Colonel, our Great Master, mention that we have Sweet Field Artillery in the way of wire. Peradventure he will cause some to be erected. Perchance, also, he will lust to send hommes to establish a straight and narrow path between us and you, that we may go in and out by day and hold sweet converse.

"6. An you have in possession the lights of Mr. Verey, in colours green and white, we should be delighted. We should take great pride in casting them into the heavens, and opine

---

*His trusty platoon-sergeant.

that our brother Fritz would also have great delight. We have none of these things save an empty pistol, a rocket which, on dit, bursts into twins red and white; but it is considerably damped by the dews of heaven, and we fear it may have unto itself lost its dash.

"7. That we might gaze on the celestial beauty of the city of Warneton, we crave a periscope. Peter hath one, and tells me much of the delights of the place which we would further learn of by the evidence of our own eyes.

"8. I would esteem it a great privilege to have speech with you after vespers or stand-down, if you would name the time and place, when I could come with a great big feller plenty hurry.

"Joy be unto you and peace; and may we also have sand-bags from you at an early date."

APPENDIX IX.

NOTES ON
MARLBOROUGH'S CAMPAIGNS, 1708-1710.
(From Nelson's History of the War, by John Buchan.)

Marlborough's campaigns in West Flanders covered much of the ground of the late war. The aim of the Allies in 1708 was to strike at France through the Artois, and for this purpose the control of the navigation of the Scheldt [Escaut] and Lys was essential. It was the object of Vendome's army, which marched north in the summer of 1708, to recapture Bruges and Ghent, which were the keys of the lower waterways. It succeeded in this task, but was decisively defeated by Marlborough on 11th July at Oudenarde on the Scheldt, after one of the most wonderful forced marches in history. Marlborough himself now desired to march straight into France, detaching troops to mask Lille, and co-operating with General Erle's projected descent upon Normandy—a proceeding which would have automatically led to the evacuation by the French of Ghent and Bruges. This bold stroke the caution of the Dutch deputies forbade, and the Allies sat down before the fortress of Lille, bringing their siege train by road from Brussels, since the Scheldt and the Lys were closed to them. Vendome and Berwick united their armies, and marched from Tournai to Lille, where, however, they did not dare to offer battle, and Marlborough was prevented by his Dutch colleagues from forcing it on them. The French now attempted to hold the line of the Scarpe and Scheldt to Ghent, and cut off all convoys from Brussels; but Marlborough held Ostend, and Webb's victory of Wynendale enabled the convoys to get through.

Lille, gallantly defended by old Marshal Boufflers, fell on 9th December, and Bruges and Ghent quickly followed. The way to Paris was now dangerously open, and Villars, who took command of the French armies when the campaign opened in the spring of 1709, resolved at all costs to cover Arras, which he rightly regarded as the gate of the capital. He drew up lines of entrenchments from the Scarpe to the Lys, passing through La Bassee. Marlborough, lying to the south of Lille, made apparent preparations for assault in force, and induced Villars to summon the garrison at Tournai to his aid. Meantime the duke had sent his artillery to Menin, and on the 26th of June marched swiftly eastward to Tournai, which fell to him on the 23rd of July. While the siege was going on, Marlborough led his main army back before the La Bassee lines. His object was to turn those lines by striking eastward, and entering France by way of the rivers Trouille and Sambre, and he wished to mislead Villars as to his purpose. On the last day of August, Orkney with twenty squadrons was sent to St. Ghislain to the west of Mons, and the Prince of Hesse-Cassel and Cadogan followed, in the midst of torrential rains. Villars, fearing for the fortress of Mons, hastened after them, and on 7th September had arrived before the stretch of forest which screens Mons on the west, and is pierced by two openings—at the village of Jemappes in the north and at Malplaquet in the south. Mons was by this time invested by the Allies, and to cover its siege Marlborough fought the Battle of Malplaquet on 11th September. In that battle—"one of the bloodiest," says Mr. Fortescue, "ever fought by mortal men" —the Allies had 20,000 casualties as against the French 12,000; and though it was a victory, and Mons fell a month later, the season was too far advanced, and the Allies had suffered too heavily, to allow of an invasion of France. But with Mons and Tournai in their hands, they controlled the Lys and Scheldt, and protected their conquests in Flanders.

In the campaign of 1710 Marlborough's thoughts again turned westward, and on 26th June he captured Douai. But he found Arras and the road to France protected by a vast line of trenches, which Villars had constructed to be, as he said, the "ne plus ultra of Marlborough." The duke had to content himself with taking Bethune, Aire, and St. Venant, which gave him the complete control of the Lys. He was in a difficult position for bold action, for his political enemies were lying in wait for the slightest hint of failure to work his ruin. During the winter the work of entrenching went on, and in the spring of 1711 the French lines ran from the coast, up the river Canche by Montreuil and Hesdin, down the Gy to Montenancourt, whence the flooded Scarpe carried them to Biache; thence by canal to the river Sensee; thence to Bouchain, on the Scheldt, and down that river to Valenciennes. The story of how Marlborough outwitted Villars and planted himself beyond the Scheldt at Oisy, between Villars and France, and within easy reach of Arras and Cambrai, deserves to be studied in detail, for it is one of the most wonderful in the whole history of tactics. Thereafter the jealousy and treachery of Marlborough's political enemies achieved their purpose, and the great duke's campaigns in Flanders were at an end.

Marlborough's objective was, of course, the opposite of that of the Allies in 1914. They were moving from the southwest, while he moved from the north-east, and the lines of Villars were meant to hinder attack from the east, whereas the Germans at La Bassee were entrenched against an attack from the south and west. But all the line of Northern France from the Scarpe to the Sambre was Villars' front of defence, as it was the German flank defence about 10th October, 1914, when the race to the sea was in progress. If the Allies had been able to push through the gap between Roulers and the Lys and turn the German right, they would have followed the identical strategy of the movement which led to Malplaquet, with this difference, that their object would have been not an invasion of Paris, but the turning of the flank of an entrenched invader.

APPENDIX X.

THE RIFLE BRIGADE.
(Prince Consort's Own).

(Adapted Extracts from "A Short History of the Rifle Brigade," by Captain H. G. Parkyn.*)

A new era in the history of the British Army began with the introduction of light infantry regiments and rifle corps. A new era—not only because they were a new branch, dressed, drilled and intended for an entirely different purpose from the rest of the Infantry, but also because the establishment of such bodies constituted the first actual departure from the theories and principles on which our soldiers had been trained for years, in fact the first cutting of Army "red tape."

In the early days of the Army, indeed down to a quite recent date, the only thing required of the British soldier was that he should be a sort of mechanical being, who would march in close formation or in line and keep step, and above all not think for himself. The idea of a regiment raised and trained in direct opposition to these lines, and in which the men were taught to think and act for themselves, was looked upon with horror and distrust by our military authorities, who were soon to have their pet ideas upset by the brilliant achievements of The Rifle Corps, as the Rifle Brigade was then styled, during the first few years of its career.

In 1755, during the war in North America, Great Britain was fighting against the French, who were aided by French Canadian backwoodsmen and Indians, all expert shots and born skirmishers, who inflicted heavy losses on our troops. It was then realized that our close formations were of no use against a well-armed and active enemy who refused to come to close quarters.

The first movement in the right direction was not a success, as it consisted in the formation of a light battalion by taking all the men of the grenadier companies of the different

*John Bale Sons and Danielsson, Ltd., London, 1917.

regiments then in America. The result of this was a collection of all the biggest men in the Army, the anger of whom was raised by the order to cut off the tails of their long coats as well as their much-prized pigtails. These men were, from their size and training, quite useless as light infantry, and they were soon returned to their ordinary duties.

Two years later we find that Wolfe selected all his best shots, employed them as skirmishers, and called them the light Infantry. So strong, however, was the feeling against the loose drill which was necessary for these troops, that soon afterwards the men were all returned to their ordinary regimental work, and for some years it was left to colonial and foreign corps in the British pay to fulfil the important duty of skirmishers.

In 1758, a Colonial corps, composed of loyal Canadians, and called Colonel Gage's Light Infantry, was raised. They were dressed in short brown jackets. At the close of the war they were disbanded; but the lesson of their use bore fruit, for in 1771 it was ordered that every Infantry Regiment should have a "Light Company" for the duties of skirmishing, etc. This company was to be composed of all the most active men and the best shots in the regiment, and was to be distinguished from the "Grenadier" and "Battalion" companies of the regiment by the wearing of green tufts or plumes in their shakos, short tails to their coats, and various other minor differences. On parade they always stood on the left of the regiment when in line. It was not till the outbreak of the American War of Independence that the real need was felt not only for Light Companies, but for whole regiments trained on these principles; and a force called the Legion, composed of both horse and foot, was raised in Canada. This was the first corps in the British pay to be dressed in green.

Several Light Infantry Regiments had been raised as far back as 1759, but on peace being signed they were disbanded, to be resuscitated and again disbanded, finally coming into a lasting existence in 1794. These are now represented by the 2nd Battalion Scottish Rifles and the 2nd Battalion Shropshire Light Infantry.

In 1777, Colonel Ferguson, who was the inventor of a capital breech-loading rifle, was given orders to form a Corps of Riflemen for service in America, the men being drafted from the regulars. With this Corps he did fine service, but was eventually surrounded by superior forces at King's Mountain, and he and many of his men slain.

In 1795, a suggestion was made by General Money that one-fifth of the whole of the British Infantry and half the Supplementary Militia should be made Rifles, but this was received with such great opposition that only two companies of one corps, the North Riding of York Militia, were put into green. Even then they were not trained as riflemen.

Later on, in the last days of 1797, a Special Act of Parliament authorized the addition of a Fifth Battalion to the 60th (or Royal American) Regiment (now the King's Royal Rifle Corps), in which Foreign troops might be enlisted "to serve in America." This battalion was dressed in green coats and blue trousers, and was formed in the West Indies, in 1798, out of foreign corps which had been in the British service for some years and a detachment from a foreign rifle corps from the Isle of Wight. Although the 60th, which at this time was a red-coated regiment armed with muskets, thus had one out of its five battalions dressed and trained as riflemen, the broad fact remains that this fifth battalion was composed of foreigners enlisted for service in America, and that there was still no regiment of British Riflemen in our Army. The unfortunate Expedition to the Helder in 1799, where the lack of riflemen was keenly felt, once again proved how urgent was the necessity for such a corps.

So it was that in January, 1800, in spite of much opposition, Colonel Coote Manningham was given permission to raise an "Experimental Corps of Riflemen." For this purpose fourteen different regiments were called upon to send drafts of thirty-two men each. The detachments assembled at Horsham in April, and shortly afterwards marched to a camp in Swinley Forest for training.

In addition to these drafts, volunteers for the Rifle Corps were called for from the Fencible Regiments, each man thus recruited receiving a bounty of ten guineas. In the "History of the Rifle Brigade," by Colonel Verner, it is stated that 396 men were thus obtained from Fencible Corps, and that out of this number no fewer than 230 were from Highland or Scottish Corps; thus originated the "Highland Company" that existed in the early days of the Regiment and during the Peninsular War.

The dress of the officers of The Rifle Corps in 1800 was almost identical with that of the Light Dragoon officer.

Coote Manningham was the first Colonel of the Rifle Corps, and is justly looked upon as the founder of the Rifle Brigade.

Colonel Manningham wrote his famous "Regulations for the Rifle Corps" in the year 1800. This book formed the basis of the system upon which all British Riflemen were organized and disciplined and taught their duties in camp, in quarters, and in the field. His name will endure for all time owing to the old Riflemen's song which has been sung in the Regiment from its early days:

> Oh, Colonel Coote Manningham, he was the Man,
> For he invented a Capital Plan.
> He raised a Corps of Rifle Men
> To Fight for England's Glory.
>
> He dressed them all in Jackets of Green
> And placed them where they could not be seen,
> And sent them in front, an invisible screen
> To Fight for England's Glory.
>
> Etc., etc.

The "Experimental Corps of Riflemen" was in action for the first time on August 25th, 1800, when a strong detachment under Lieutenant-Colonel Stewart fought against the Spaniards at Ferrol. When the officers of the Corps were subsequently gazetted, all their commissions bore this date. For these two reasons British Riflemen have ever since observed August 25th as the "Regimental Birthday."

Early in 1803 the Rifle Corps was directed to be styled the 95th Rifles. Lieutenant-Colonel Sydney Beckwith was now placed in command, and in the spring, Colonel Coote Manningham, in accordance with his own Standing Orders, gave a series of Lectures at Shorncliffe Camp to the Officers on the Duties of Riflemen and Light Infantry on Active Service. These were subsequently printed, and upon these, coupled with the "Regulations" already described, the 95th Rifles were trained. Later, a Camp of Exercise was formed at Shorncliffe under the personal direction of Sir John Moore, and here, together with the 43rd and 52nd Light Infantry (now 1st and 2nd Battalions, the Oxfordshire and Buckinghamshire Light Infantry) the Regiment was trained as a Brigade by the General under whom a few years later they were to gain such undying glory.

In 1805 a second, and four years later a third Battalion was raised at Canterbury, and so popular was the Regiment that in three days over 1,100 recruits were obtained for the Regiment from the Militia.

In 1816 the Regiment was taken out of the numbered Regiments of the Line and constituted a separate Regiment, styled the Rifle Brigade, the only instance in the history of the British Army where such a distinction has been conferred on a Regiment.

Two years later, on the death of Sir David Dundas, the Duke of Wellington was appointed Colonel-in-Chief of the Regiment, and at the State funeral of the Duke in 1852, the

2nd Battalion, which had been brought from Canterbury to London for the occasion, headed the procession from Chelsea Hospital to St. Paul's.

The Duke was succeeded as Colonel in Chief of the Regiment by His Royal Highness the Prince Consort.

During the Crimean War the Rifle Depot was formed at Winchester, where it has remained ever since, except when the old barracks were destroyed by fire in 1894 and the Depot was sent to Gosport as a temporary measure, returning to Winchester in 1904.

In 1857 a fourth Battalion was added to the Regiment.

1861 saw the death of His Royal Highness the Prince Consort, and in the following year, Queen Victoria, "desiring to perpetuate the remembrance of her beloved husband's connection with the Rifle Brigade," commanded that the words "The Prince Consort's Own" should be added to the title of the Regiment.

Field-Marshal H.R.H. Albert Edward, Prince of Wales, became Colonel-in-Chief in 1868.

In 1877 the helmet was introduced as a universal headdress for all infantry other than Highland and Fusilier regiments, but was not taken into wear by the Rifle Brigade until 1884. This head-dress was very unpopular in the Regiment, and after a few years was discarded for the Rifle cap.

In 1880 H.R.H. the Duke of Connaught was appointed Colonel-in-Chief, H.R.H. the Prince of Wales being transferred to the command of the three Regiments of Household Cavalry.

Upon the augmentation of the Army in 1914, the new "Service" Battalions of the Regiment were raised. Eight of these Battalions and the four Regular Battalions were actively engaged with the Expeditionary Force.

The original Badge of the Rifle Corps (1800–1803) was the Crown and Bugle Horn. This design, with the addition of the number "95" between the Bugle Horn strings, was its Badge when the title was changed from "The Rifle Corps" to that of the "95th, or Rifle Regiment," and in consequence it was under this Badge that the Regiment fought throughout the Peninsular War and at Waterloo.

When, in 1816, the Regiment was taken out of the numbered Regiments and was ordered to be styled "The Rifle Brigade," the numeral "95" was replaced by the letters R.B. This is the Badge as at present worn on the officers' buttons.

The same Badge, without the letters R.B. (which is practically identical with the original badge worn by the Rifle Corps) now forms the centre of the Regimental Badge of the

Regiment. It is also displayed on the boss of the full headdress (the Rifle cap) and is found on the Bandsman's music pouches.

Many fresh Battle Honours having been granted to the Regiment in connection with the Peninsular War, the need was felt for some means of displaying them, for, as is well known, the Rifle Brigade, unlike other regiments, has no colours on which the honours may be inscribed. This led to the evolution of the present badge, a Maltese Cross surrounded by a laurel-wreath and surmounted by a crown. In the centre of the cross is the old Bugle and Crown, encircled by a ring bearing the title of the Regiment. The major honours, Waterloo and Peninsula, are inscribed below the greater crown and at the base of the badge, the remainder on the arms of the cross and on the ribands entwined about the wreath. In the main, the badge appears to have been copied from the Cross of the Order of the Bath. This Order had been reconstructed into three branches in 1815, and the three Colonels of the Regiment at the time had had the Military Branch conferred upon them.

BATTLE HONOURS OF THE RIFLE BRIGADE UP TO THE OUTBREAK OF THE GREAT WAR.

Copenhagen, 1801; Montevideo, 1807; Roleia, 1808; Vimiera, 1808; Corunna, 1809; Busaco, 1810; Barrosa, 1811; Fuentes d'Onoro, 1811; Ciudad Rodrigo, 1812; Badajos, 1812; Salamanca, 1812; Vittoria, 1813; Pyrenees, 1813; Nivelle, 1813; Nive, 1813; Orthes, 1814; Toulouse, 1814; Peninsula; Waterloo, 1815; South Africa, 1846-47; South Africa, 1851-53; Alma, 1854; Inkerman, 1854; Sevastopol, 1854; Lucknow, 1857; Ashantee, 1873-74; Ali Musjid, 1878; Afghanistan, 1878-79; Burma, 1885-87; Khartoum, 1898; Defence of Ladysmith, 1899-1900; Relief of Ladysmith, 1900; South Africa, 1899-1902.

"What more can be said of you Riflemen than that wherever there has been fighting there you have been, and wherever you have been there you have distinguished yourselves?"—(H.R.H. the Duke of Clarence, 1828.)

APPENDIX XI.

DIARY OF THE WAR.
(From "The Times" of November 12, 1918.)

1914.

June 28.—Francis Ferdinand shot at Serajevo.
July 5.—Kaiser's War Council at Potsdam.
    23.—Austro-Hungarian Note to Serbia.
    28.—Austria declared war on Serbia.
    31.—State of war in Germany.
Aug. 1.—Germany declared war on Russia.
    2.—German ultimatum to Belgium.
    3.—Germany declared war on France.
    4.—Great Britain declared war on Germany.
    10.—France declared war on Austria.
    12.—Great Britain declared war on Austria.
    15.—Fall of Liege.
    16.—British Army landed in France.
    20.—Germans occupied Brussels.
    23.—Japan declared war on Germany.
    24.—Fall of Namur.
    25.—Sack of Louvain.
    26.—Battle of Tannenberg.
    28.—British Victory off Heligoland.
    29.—New Zealanders in Samoa.
Sept. 2.—Russians took Lemberg.
    3.—Paris Government at Bordeaux.
    5.—End of Retreat from Mons.
    6.—First Marne Battle begun.
    15.—First Aisne Battle begun.
    16.—Russians evacuated East Prussia.
    23.—First British Air Raid on Germany.
Oct. 9.—Fall of Antwerp.
    13.—Belgian Government at Havre.
    20.—First Battle of Ypres begun.
Nov. 1.—Naval Action off Coronel.
    5.—Great Britain declared war on Turkey.
    7.—Fall of Tsingtau.
    10.—Emden sunk.
    21.—British occupied Basra.

Dec. 2.—Austrians in Belgrade.
    8.—Naval Battle off the Falklands.
   14.—Serbians retook Belgrade.
   16.—Germans bombarded West Hartlepool.
   18.—Hussein Kamel, Sultan of Egypt.
   24.—First Air Raid on England.

1915.

Jan. 24.—Naval Battle off Dogger Bank.
Feb. 3.—Turks defeated on Suez Canal.
   18.—U-Boat "Blockade" of England.
   25.—Allied Fleet attacked Dardanelles.
Mar. 10.—British captured Neuve Chapelle.
   27.—Russians took Przemysl.
April 22.—Second Battle of Ypres begun.
   25.—Allied Landing in Gallipoli.
May 3.—Battle of the Dunajec.
   6.—Battle of Krithia, Gallipoli.
   7.—Lusitania torpedoed.
   8.—Germans occupied Libau.
   11.—German repulse at Ypres.
   12.—General Botha occupied Windhuk.
   16.—Russian Retreat to the San.
   23.—Italy declared war on Austria.
   25.—Coalition Cabinet formed.
June 2.—Italians crossed Isonzo.
   3.—Russians evacuated Przemysl.
   22.—Austro-Germans recaptured Lemberg.
July 2.—Pommern sunk in Baltic.
   9.—German South-West Africa conquered.
   24.—Nasiriyeh, on Euphrates, taken.
Aug. 4.—Fall of Warsaw.
   5.—Fall of Ivangorod.
   6.—New Landing at Suvla Bay.
   8.—General Birdwood's advance at Anzac.
   9.—British success near Hooge.
   15.—National Registration.
   17.—Fall of Kovno.
   18.—Russian victory in Riga Gulf.
   19.—Fall of Novo-Georgievsk.
   21.—Cotton declared contraband.
   25.—Fall of Brest-Litovsk.
Sept. 1.—General Alexeieff as Chief of Staff.
   2.—Fall of Grodno.
   5.—Tsar as Generalissimo.
   7.—Russian victory near Tarnopol.
   18.—Fall of Vilna.

Sept. 21.—Russian Retreat ended.
    25.—Battle of Loos and in Champagne.
    28.—Victory at Kut-el-Amara.
Oct. 4.—Russian Ultimatum to Bulgaria.
    5.—Allied Landing at Salonika.
    6.—Austro-German invasion of Serbia.
    9.—Belgrade occupied.
    14.—Bulgaria at war with Serbia.
    17.—Allied Note to Greece.
    19.—Lord Derby on the 46 Groups.
    22.—Bulgarians occupy Uskub.
    28.—M. Briand French Premier.
Nov. 5.—Fall of Nish.
    22.—Battle of Ctesiphon.
    29.—British withdrew from Ctesiphon.
Dec. 2.—Fall of Monastir.
    3.—General Townshend at Kut.
    9.—Allied Retreat in Macedonia.
    13.—Salonika lines fortified.
    15.—Sir D. Haig C.-in-C. in France.
    19.—Withdrawal from Gallipoli.
    25.—Turkish defeat at Kut.

1916.

Jan. 8.—Gallipoli evacuation complete.
    13.—Fall of Cettigne.
Feb. 9.—General Smuts appointed to East Africa.
    16.—Russians enter Erzerum.
    18.—German Kamerun conquered.
    21.—Battle of Verdun begun.
    24.—Germans took Fort Douaumont.
Mar. 16.—Admiral von Tirpitz dismissed.
April 9.—German assault at Verdun.
    17.—Russians entered Trebizond.
    24.—Rebellion in Ireland.
    29.—Fall of Kut-el-Amara.
May 24.—British Conscription Bill passed.
    31.—Battle of Jutland.
June 4.—General Brusiloff's offensive.
    5.—Lord Kitchener lost at sea.
    14.—Allied Economic Conference in Paris.
    21.—Mecca taken by Grand Sherif.
July 1.—Somme Battle begun.
    25.—Russians occupied Erzinjan.
Aug. 6.—Italian offensive on Isonzo.
    10.—Russians at Stanislau.
    27.—Rumania entered the war.

Aug. 29.—Hindenburg Chief of Staff.
Sept. 3.—Zeppelin destroyed at Cuffley.
    26.—British took Thiepval and Combles.
Oct. 10.—Allied Ultimatum to Greece.
Nov. 1.—Italian Adance on Carso.
    13.—British Victory on the Ancre.
    18.—Serbians and French took Monastir.
    29.—Grand Fleet under Sir D. Beatty.
Dec. 1.—Anti-Allied Riot in Athens.
    5.—Resignation of Mr. Asquith.
    6.—Germans entered Bukarest.
    7.—Mr. Lloyd George Prime Minister.
    12.—German "Peace Proposals."
    15.—French Victory at Verdun.
    20.—President Wilson's Peace Note.

1917.

Jan. 1.—Turkey denounced Berlin Treaty of 1878.
Feb. 1.—"Unrestricted" U-Boat War begun.
    3.—America broke with Germany.
    6.—British captured Grandcourt.
    24.—British took Kut-el-Amara.
Mar. 11.—British entered Baghdad.
    12.—Revolution in Russia.
    15.—Abdication of the Tsar.
    18.—British entered Peronne.
    21.—First British Imperial War Cabinet.
April 6.—America declared war on Germany.
    9.—Battle of Vimy Ridge begun.
May 4.—French took Craonne.
    14.—New Italian Offensive.
    15.—General Petain French C.-in-C.
June 7.—British Victory at Messines Ridge.
    12.—Abdication of King Constantine.
    26.—First American troops in France.
    27.—Mesopotamia Report issued.
    29.—General Allenby commander in Egypt.
July 1.—Last Russian offensive begun.
    14.—Bethmann-Hollweg dismissed.
    17.—British Royal House styled "Windsor."
    19.—Reichstag "Peace" Resolution.
    24.—Russian defeat in Galicia.
    31.—Great Allied attack around Ypres.
Aug. 29.—President Wilson's Note to the Pope.
Sept. 4.—Germans occupied Riga.
    15.—Russian Republic proclaimed.
    28.—British Victory at Ramadieh.

Oct. 9.—Allied attack in Flanders.
    24.—Italian defeat at Caporetto.
    29.—Fall of Udine.
    30.—Chancellor Michaelis dismissed.
    31.—British captured Beersheba.
Nov. 1.—German Retreat on Chemin des Dames.
    4.—British troops in Italy.
    6.—British stormed Passchendaele Ridge.
    7.—British captured Gaza.
    8.—Bolshevist coup d'etat in Russia.
    9.—Italian stand on the Piave.
    17.—British in Jaffa.
    18.—General Maude's death in Mesopotamia.
    20.—British Victory at Cambrai.
    30.—German reaction at Cambrai.
Dec. 6.—Armistice on Russian Front.
    9.—British captured Jerusalem.
    22.—Brest Conference opened.
    26.—Sir R. Wemyss First Sea Lord.

1918.

Jan. 5.—Mr. Lloyd George on War Aims.
    20.—"Breslau" sunk. "Goeben" damaged.
Feb. 1.—Germany recognized Ukraine.
    9.—First Brest Treaty Signed.
    16.—General Wilson Chief of Staff.
    18.—German invasion of Russia.
    21.—British capture Jericho.
    24.—Turks recovered Trebizond.
    25.—Germans at Reval.
Mar. 3.—Second Brest Treaty.
    7.—German peace with Finland.
    11.—Turks recovered Erzrum.
    13.—Germans at Odessa.
    14.—Brest Treaty ratified at Moscow.
    21.—German offensive in the West.
    24.—Bapaume and Peronne lost.
April 5.—Allied landing at Vladivostock.
    9.—New Military Service Bill.
    11.—Armentieres lost.
    13.—Turks occupied Batum.
    14.—General Foch, Allied Generalissimo.
    15.—Bailleul lost.
    18.—Lord Milner War Secretary.
    22.—Naval Raid on Zeebrugge and Ostend.
    26.—Kemmel Hill lost.
    27.—Turks occupied Kars.

April 30.—Germans at Viborg.
May 1.—Germans at Sebastopol.
9.—Second Raid on Ostend.
27.—Second German Offensive.
29.—Soissons lost. Rheims held.
31.—Germans reached Marne.
June 1.—Attacks towards Paris held.
9.—New German Assault.
15.—Austrian Offensive in Italy.
23.—Great Austrian Defeat.
July 2.—1,000,000 Americans shipped to France.
15.—Third German Offensive.
Second Marne Battle begun.
16.—Ex-Tsar shot at Ekaterinburg.
18.—General Foch's Counter-attack.
20.—Germans recrossed the Marne.
Aug. 2.—Soissons recovered.
8.—British attack at Amiens.
29.—Bapaume and Noyon regained.
Sept. 1.—Peronne recovered.
2.—Drocourt-Queant line breached.
12.—American attack at St. Mihiel.
15.—Austrian Peace Note.
17.—New Macedonian offensive.
19.—British advance in Palestine.
25.—Bulgaria proposed armistice.
27.—Hindenburg Line broken.
29.—Bulgaria surrendered.
30.—Fall of Damascus.
Chancellor Hertling resigns.
Oct. 1.—St. Quentin regained.
4.—Abdication of King Ferdinand.
9.—Cambrai regained.
10.—British took Le Cateau.
13.—French recovered Laon.
14.—British troops at Irtkutsk.
15.—British in Homs.
17.—Ostend, Lille, Douai, regained.
19.—Bruges reoccupied.
20.—Belgian Coast clear.
25.—Ludendorff resigned.
26.—Aleppo fell to the Allies.
27.—Austria sued for Peace.
28.—Italians crossed Piave.
29.—Serbians reached the Danube.
30.—Turkey granted Armistice.
Nov. 1.—Versailles Conference opened.

Nov. 2.—British at Valenciennes.
     3.—Austrian Surrender. Kiel Mutiny.
     4.—Versailles Armistice Agreement.
     5.—Full Powers for Marshal Foch.
         President Wilson's Last Note to Germany.
     6.—Americans reached Sedan.
     7.—Bavarian Republic Proclaimed.
     9.—Foch received German Envoys.
         Abdication of the Kaiser.
         Chancellor Prince Max resigned.
         Berlin Revolution.
    10.—Kaiser's flight to Holland.
         British at Mons.
    11.—Armistice Terms Accepted.

PEACE.

The Treaty of Peace between the Allies and Germany was signed at Versailles on June 28th, 1919.

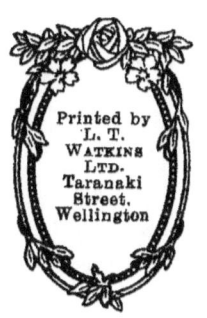

Printed by
L. T.
WATKINS
LTD.
Taranaki
Street,
Wellington

Map No. 1—NORTHERN EGYPT

For Enlargement of area within dotted lines see Map No. 2

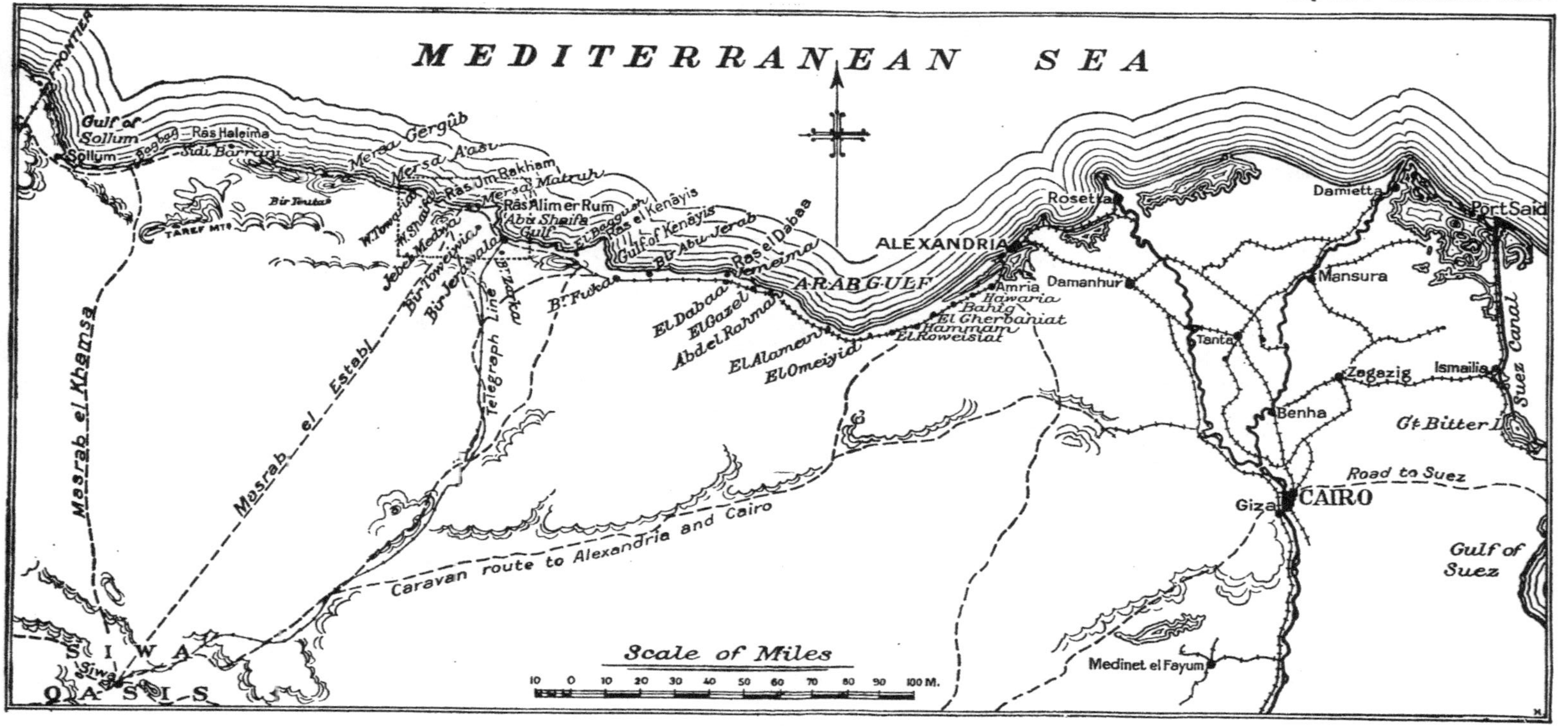

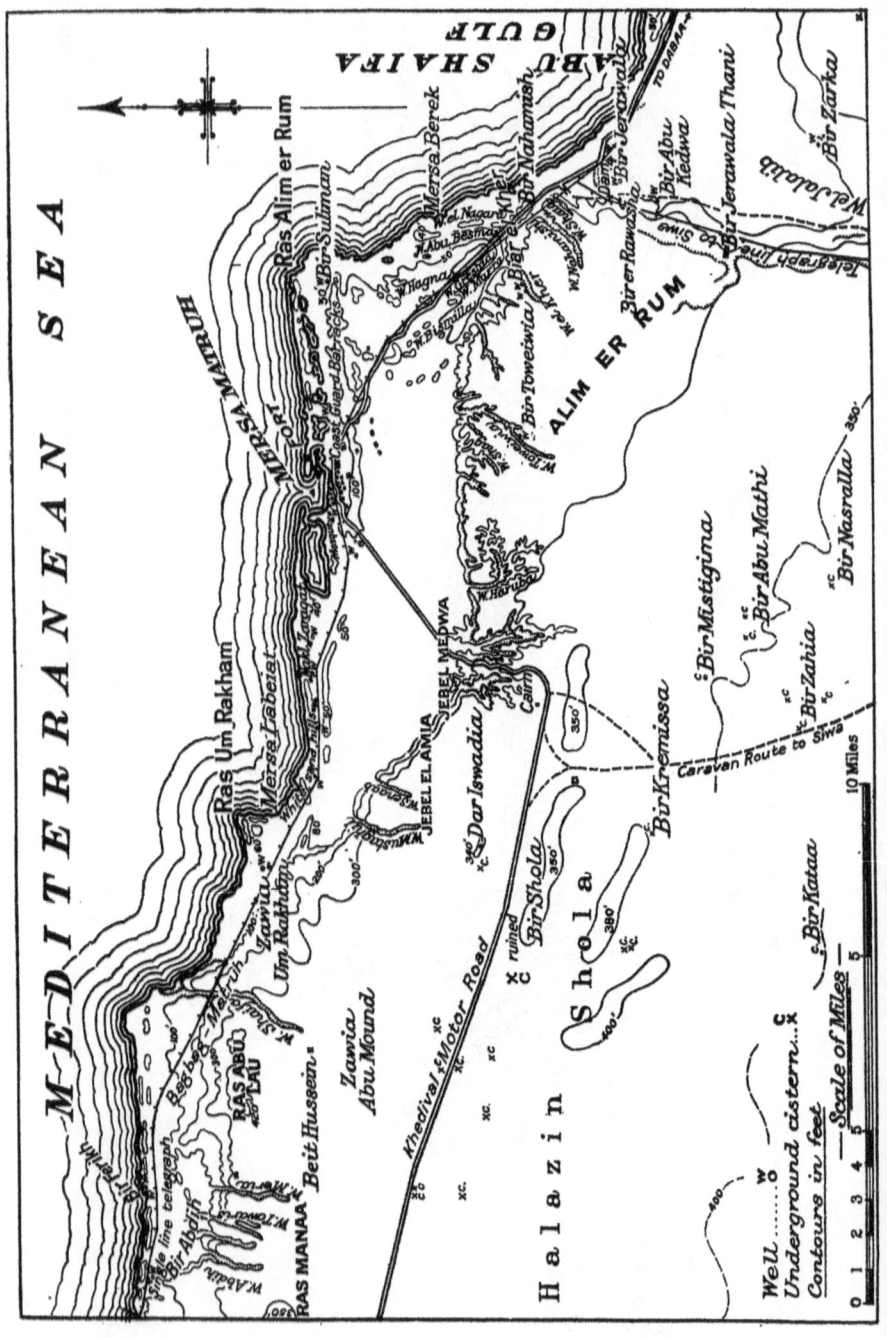

Map No. 2—MATRUH

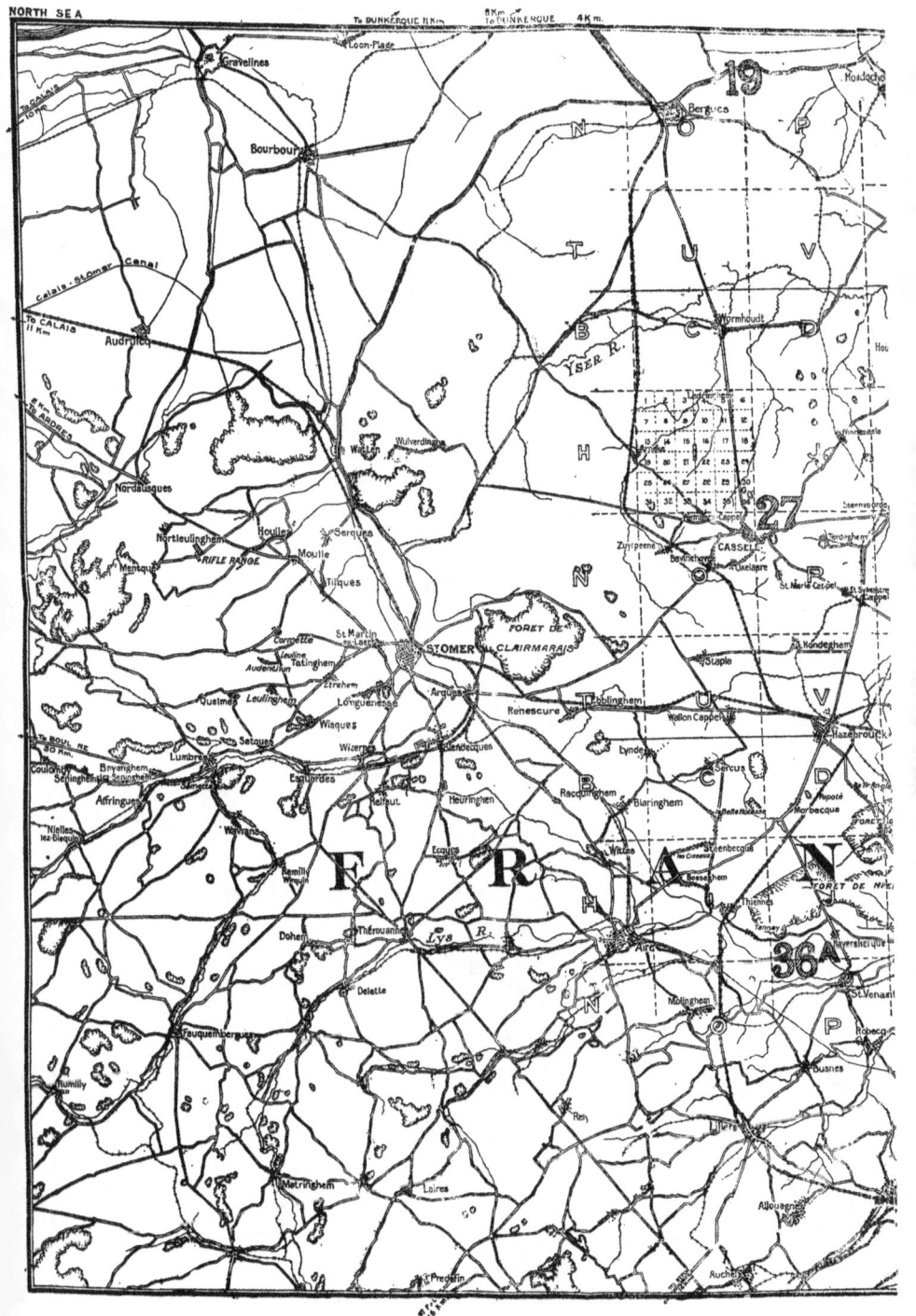

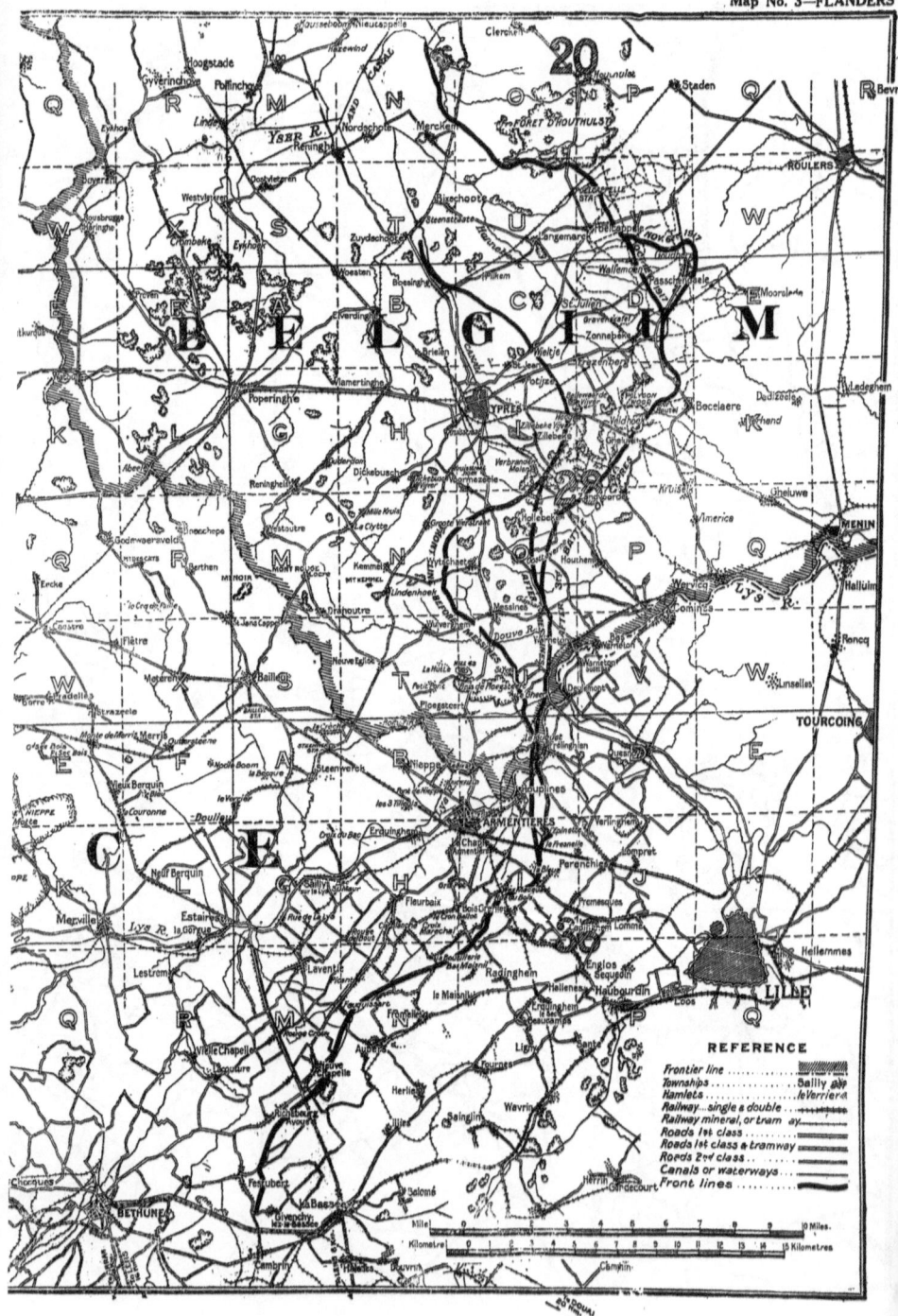

Map No. 3—FLANDERS

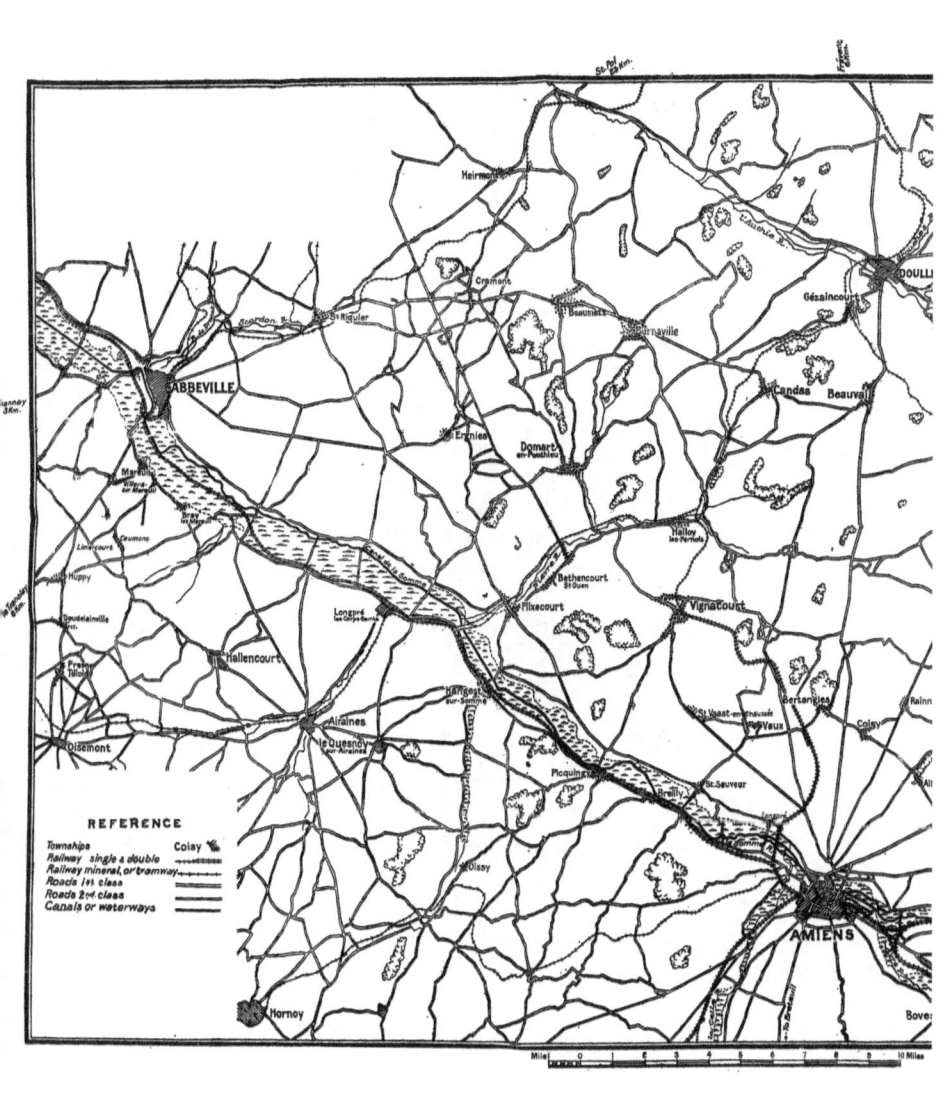

Map No. 4—THE SOMME

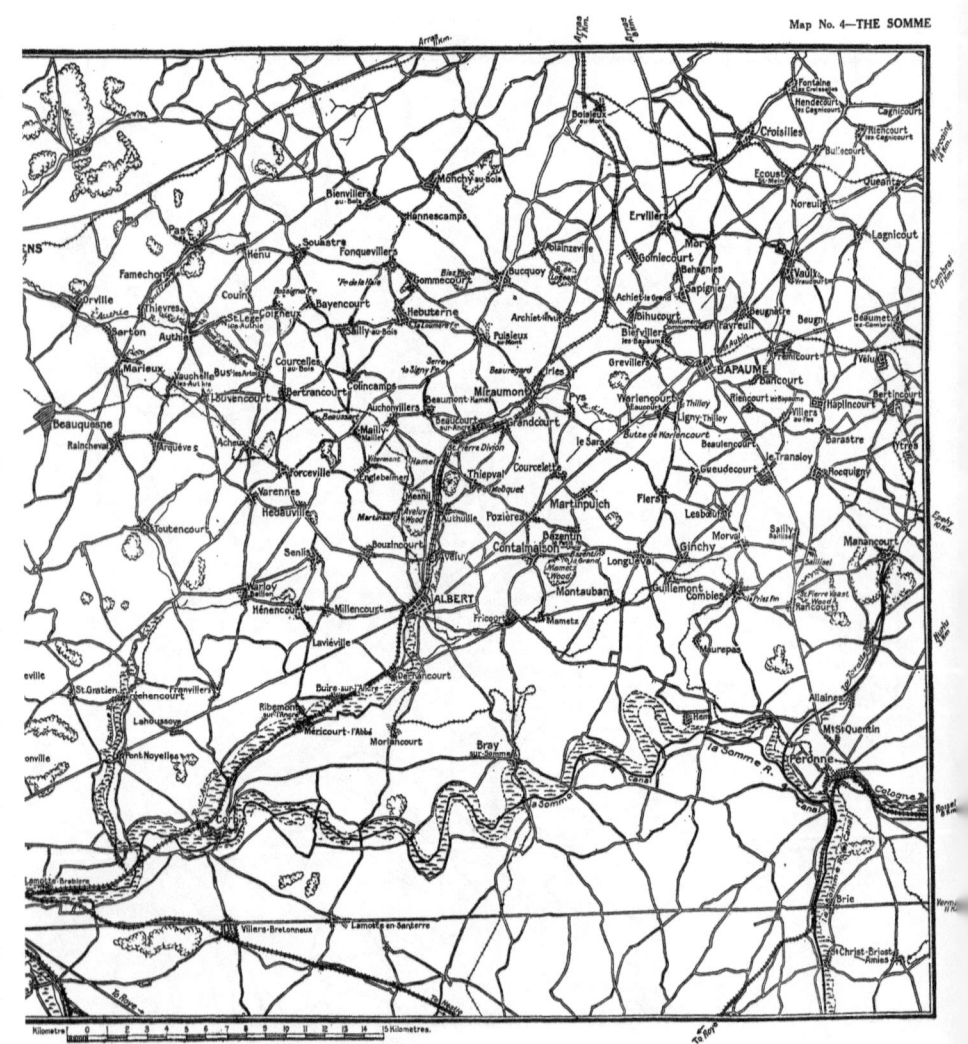

Map No. 5—FLERS

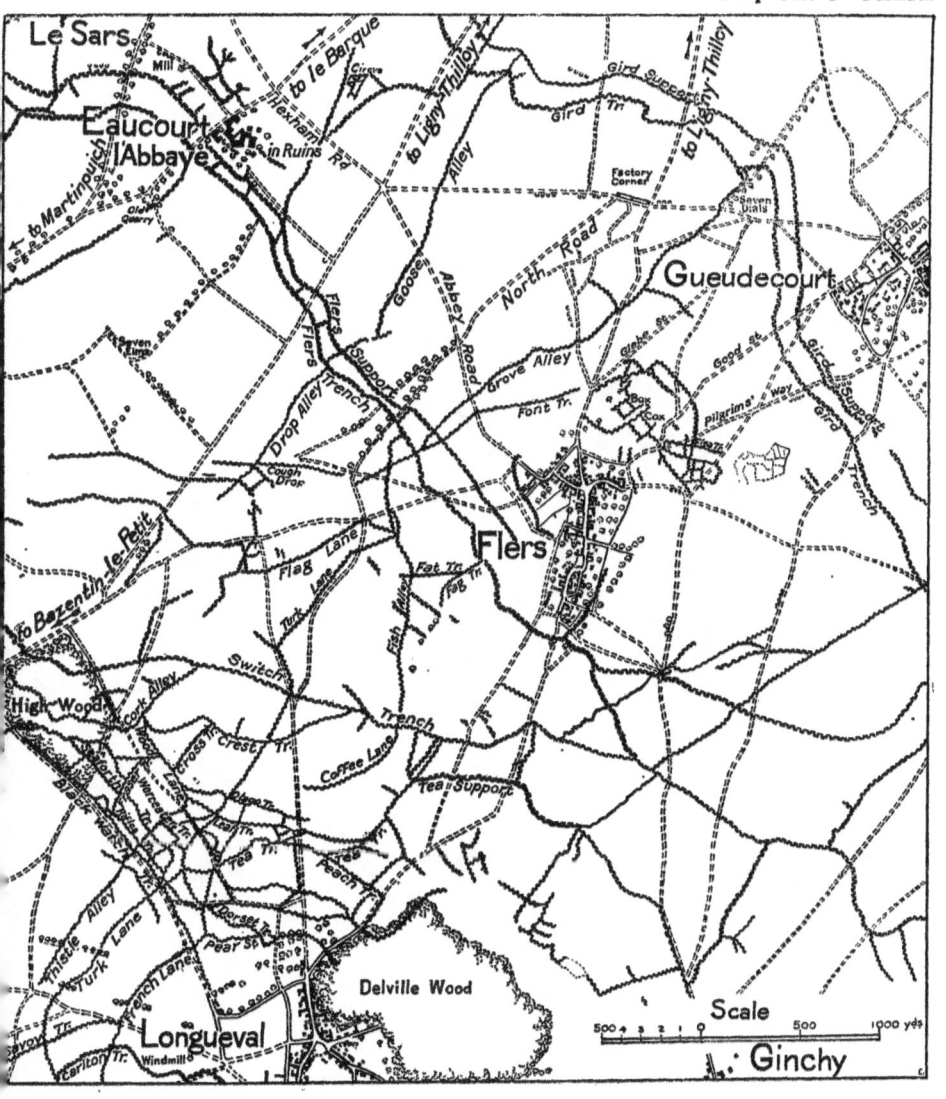

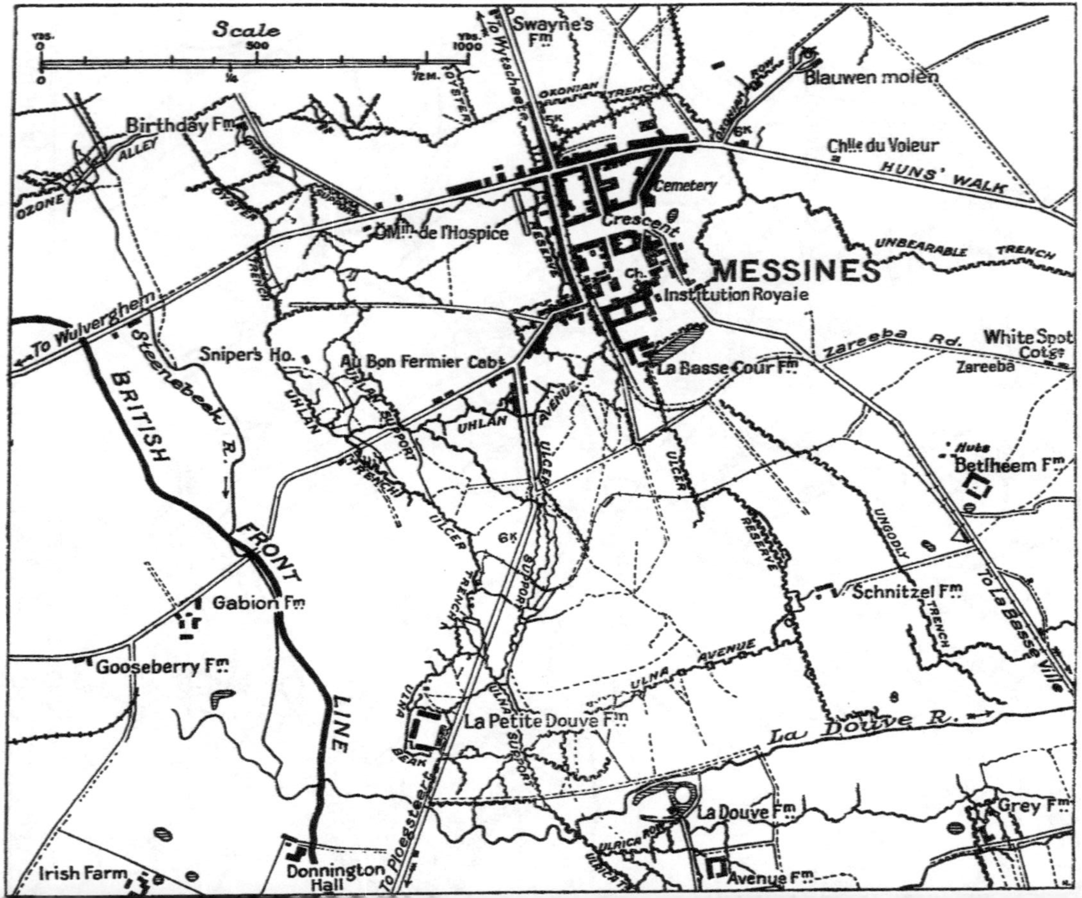
Scale
0
500
1000
¼
½ M.
To Wytschaete
Swayne's Fm
Blauwen molen
Birthday Fm
ALLEY
OZONE
OYSTER
OKONIAN
TRENCH
Chlle du Voleur
HUNS' WALK
Cemetery
Crescent
Ch.
MESSINES
Institution Royale
UNBEARABLE
TRENCH
Mn de l'Hospice
RESERVE
To Wulverghem
Steenebeek R.
Sniper's Ho.
Au Bon Fermier Cabt
La Basse Cour Fm
Zareeba Rd.
White Spot Cotge
Zareeba
UHLAN
SUPPORT
AVENUE
ULCER
Huts
Betlheem Fm
UNGODLY
RESERVE
BRITISH
FRONT
LINE
Gabion Fm
Gooseberry Fm
6K
Schnitzel Fm
TRENCH
To La Basse Ville
ULNA
AVENUE
La Petite Douve Fm
La Douve R.
BEAK
To Ploegsteert
La Douve Fm
Grey Fm
ULRICA
Irish Farm
Donnington Hall
Avenue Fm

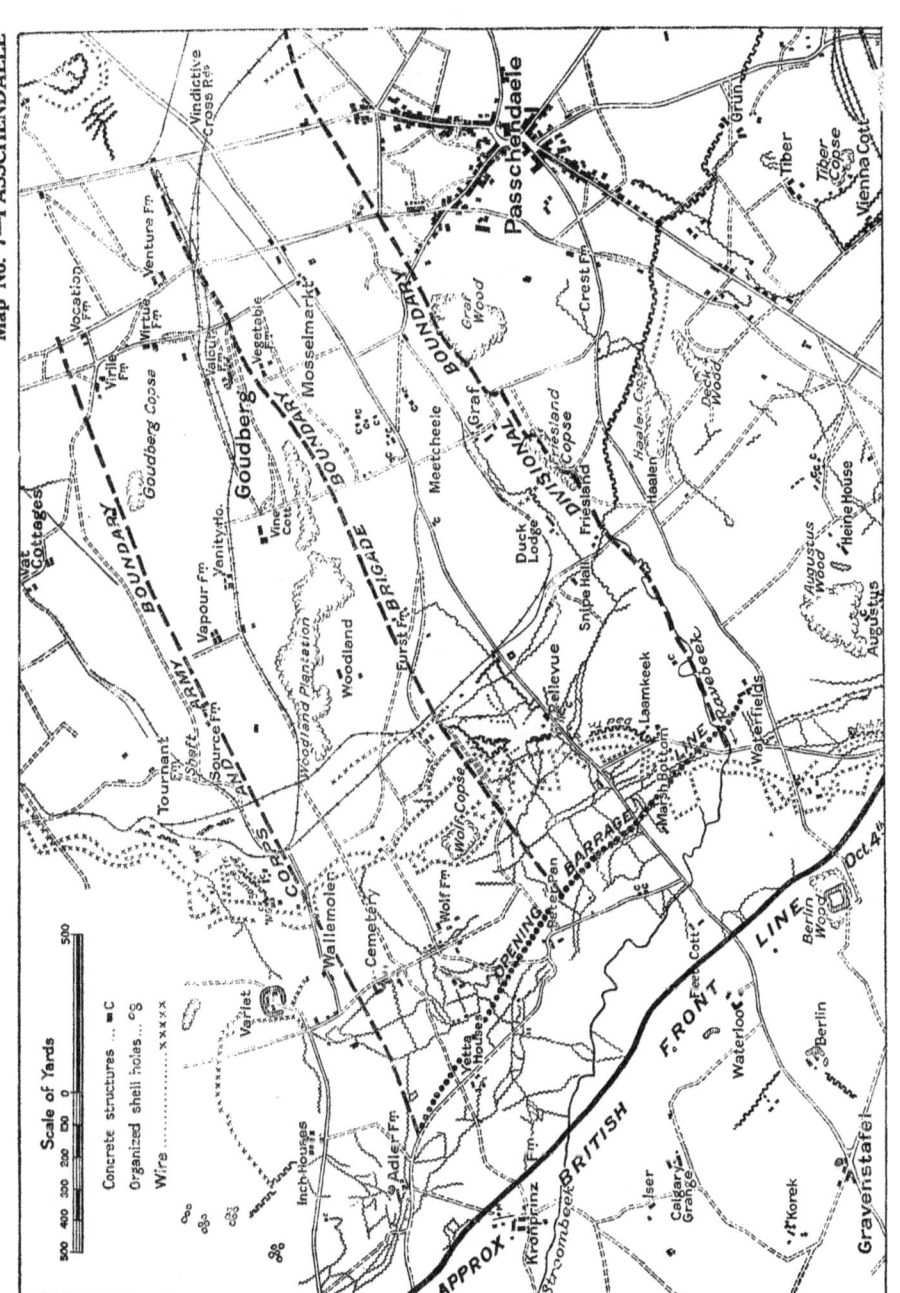

Map No. 7—PASSCHENDAELE

Map No. 8.—HEBUTERNE to PUISIEUX-AU-MONT

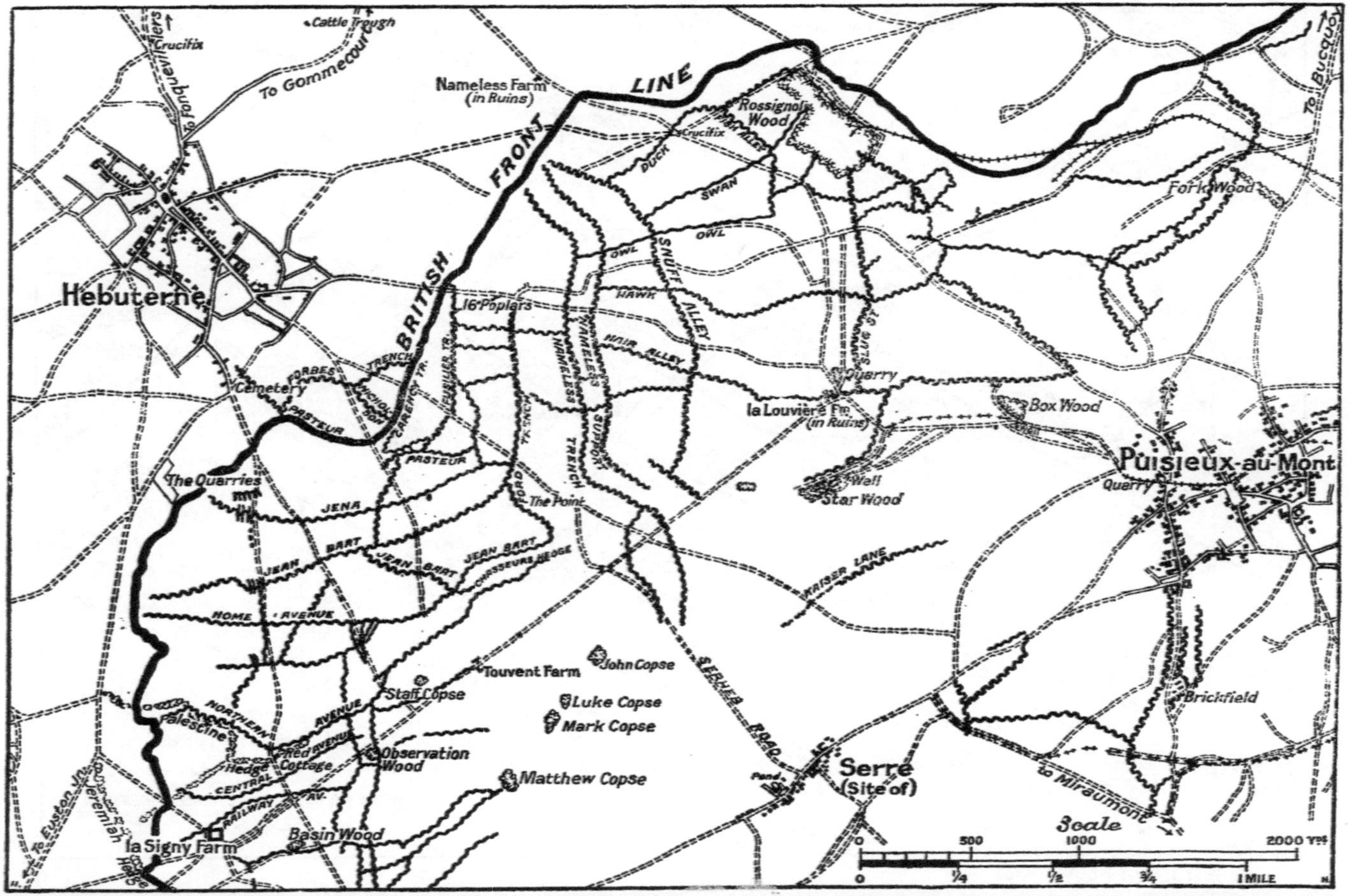

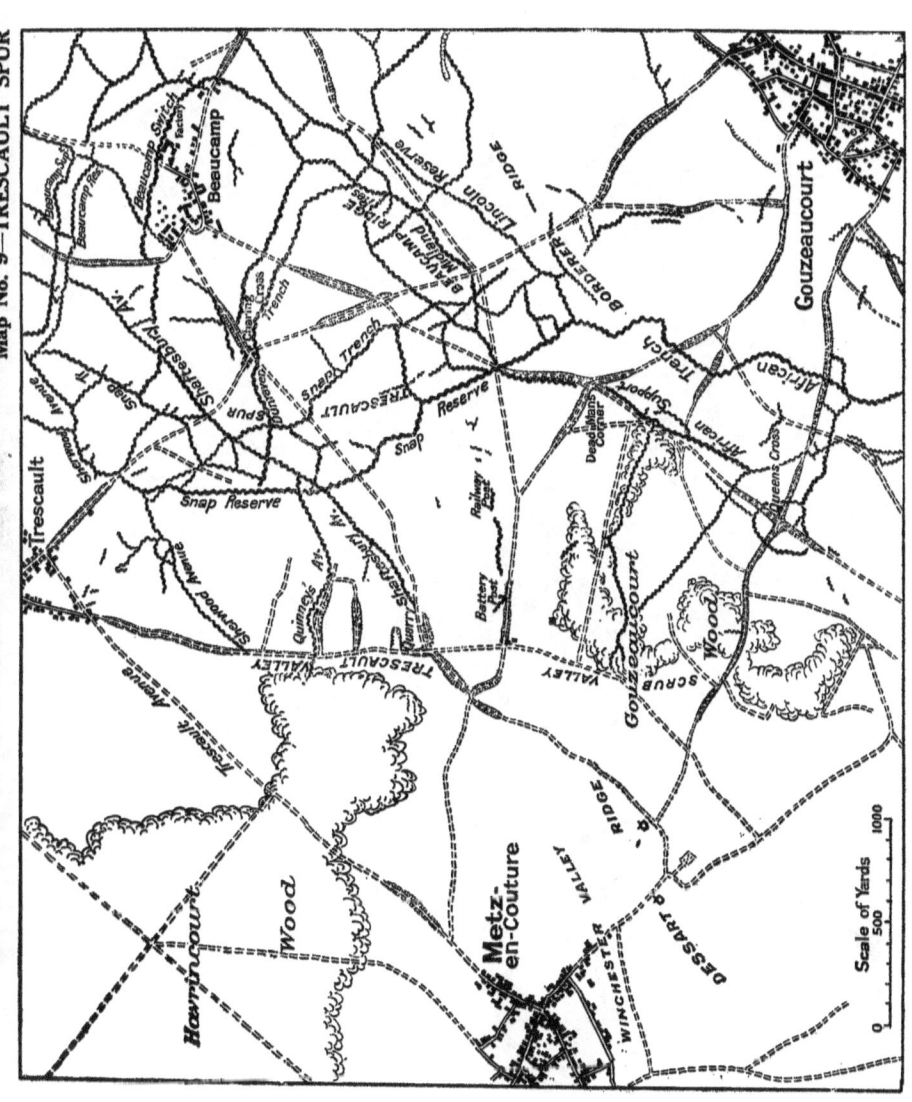

Map No. 9.—TRESCAULT SPUR

Map No. 10—LE QUESNOY

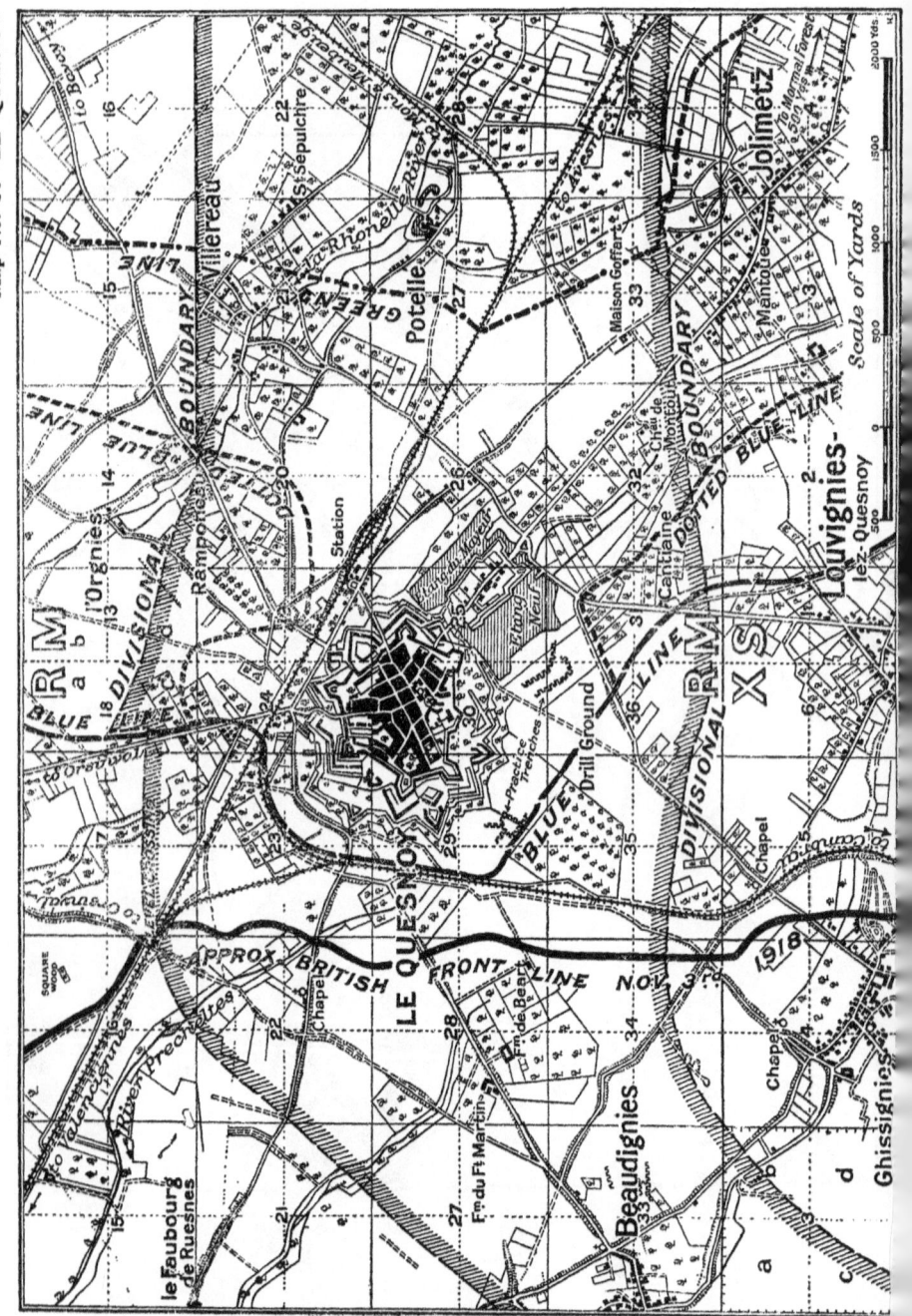

MAP SHOWING THE COUNTRY OVER WHICH THE NEW ZEALAND DIVISION FOUGHT IN THE ADVANCE TO VICTORY

HEBUTERNE TO LE QUESNOY, JULY 15 TO NOVEMBER 5, 1918

Captures: 9,000 prisoners, 145 guns, 3 tanks, 1,263 machine-guns

The shaded sections represent captures in which the Division did not participate.

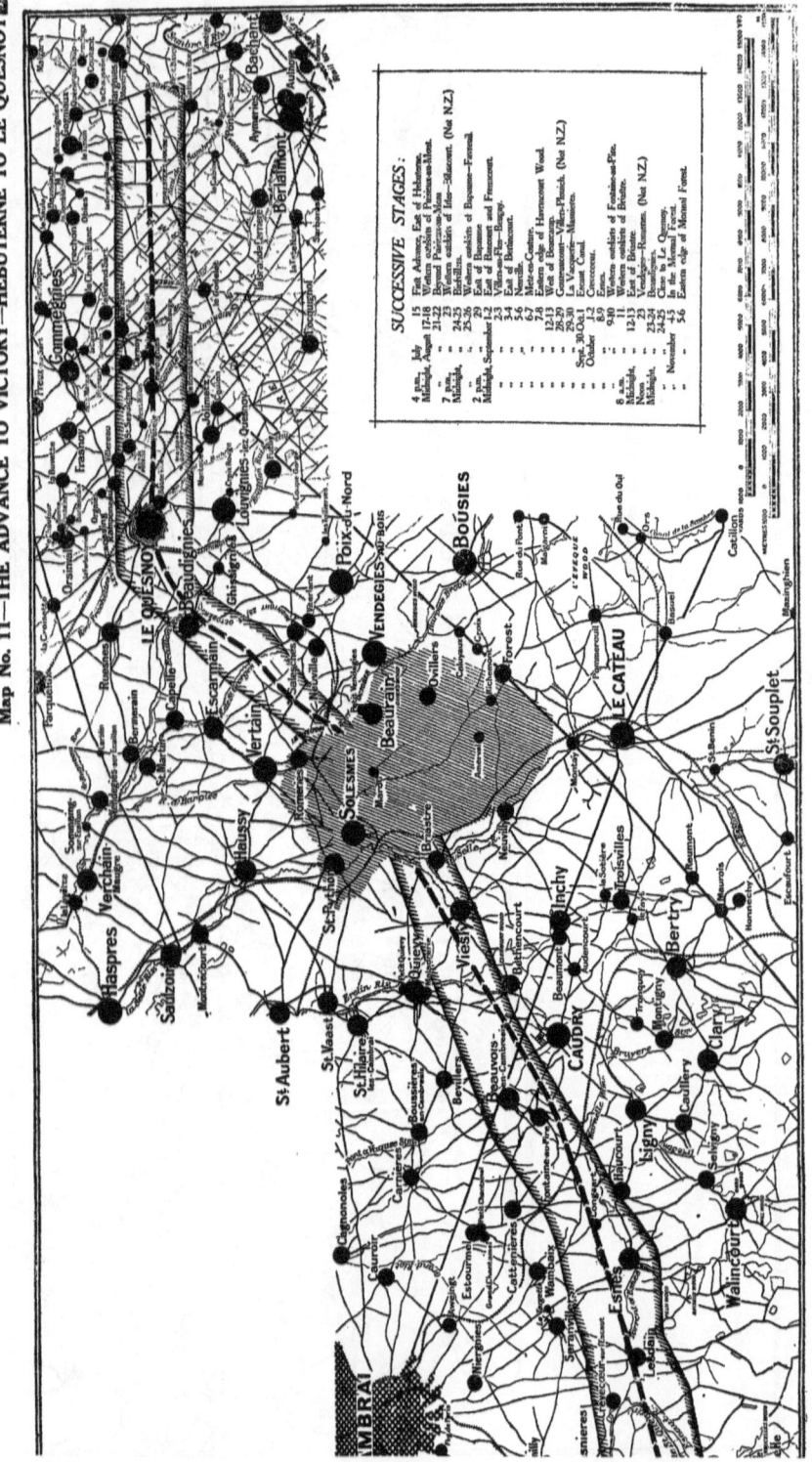

Map No. 11—THE ADVANCE TO VICTORY—HEBUTERNE TO LE QUESNOY

www.ingramcontent.com/pod-product-compliance
Lightning Source LLC
Chambersburg PA
CBHW021711300426
44114CB00009B/105